DISESTABLISHMENT AND RELIGIOUS DISSENT

Disestablishment and Religious Dissent

Church-State Relations in the New American States

1776–1833

Edited By

Carl H. Esbeck and Jonathan J. Den Hartog

UNIVERSITY OF MISSOURI PRESS

COLUMBIA

Publication of this volume has been supported with a gift from the
Kinder Institute on Constitutional Democracy

Library of Congress Cataloging-in-Publication Data

Names: Esbeck, Carl H., editor. | Den Hartog, Jonathan J., editor.
Title: Disestablishment and religious dissent : church-state relations in
    the new American states, 1776-1833 / edited by Carl H. Esbeck and
    Jonathan J. Den Hartog.
Description: Columbia : University of Missouri Press, 2019. | Series:
    Studies in constitutional democracy | Includes bibliographical
    references and index.
Identifiers: LCCN 2019023253 (print) | LCCN 2019023254 (ebook) | ISBN
    9780826221933 (hardcover) | ISBN 9780826274366 (ebook)
Subjects: LCSH: Church and state--United States--History--18th century.
Classification: LCC BR516 .D565 2019 (print) | LCC BR516 (ebook) | DDC
    322/.1097309033--dc23
LC record available at https://lccn.loc.gov/2019023253
LC ebook record available at https://lccn.loc.gov/2019023254

Typefaces: Minion

STUDIES IN CONSTITUTIONAL DEMOCRACY

Justin B. Dyer and Jeffrey L. Pasley, Series Editors

The Studies in Constitutional Democracy Series explores the origins and development of American constitutional and democratic traditions, as well as their applications and interpretations throughout the world. The often subtle interaction between constitutionalism's commitment to the rule of law and democracy's emphasis on the rule of the many lies at the heart of this enterprise. Bringing together insights from history and political theory, the series showcases interdisciplinary scholarship that traces constitutional and democratic themes in American politics, law, society, and culture, with an eye to both the practical and theoretical implications.

Previous Titles in Studies in Constitutional Democracy

Lloyd Gaines and the Fight to End Segregation
James W. Endersby and William T. Horner

Aristocracy in America: From the Sketch-Book of a German Nobleman
Francis J. Grund
Edited and with an Introduction by Armin Mattes

From Oligarchy to Republicanism: The Great Task of Reconstruction
Forrest A. Nabors

John Henry Wigmore and the Rules of Evidence: The Hidden Origins of Modern Law
Andrew Porwancher

Bureaucracy in America:
The Administrative State's Challenge to Constitutional Government
Joseph Postell

The Myth of Coequal Branches: Restoring the Constitution's Separation of Functions
David J. Siemers

The Panic of 1819: The First Great Depression
Andrew H. Browning

The Pursuit of Happiness in the Founding Era: An Intellectual History
Carli N. Conklin

The Federalist Frontier: Settler Politics in the Old Northwest, 1783–1840
Kristopher Maulden

CONTENTS

ACKNOWLEDGMENTS

As the editors, we would like to express our gratitude to the Kinder Institute on Constitutional Democracy at the University of Missouri for supporting this project and for bringing us together to work on it. We appreciate the encouragement provided by Justin Dyer and Jeffrey Pasley, director and associate director, respectively, of the Kinder Institute. We are particularly grateful for the work done by each of our chapter contributors. They each enthusiastically supported the larger project and energetically took to their state assignments. They did excellent research and presented their own conclusions clearly. For a large project, everyone responded well and met deadlines. Their dedication to the project helped it come together in a timely and effective fashion. We are grateful for the opportunities we have already had to share the fruits of this project. Abram Van Engen welcomed the participants to present as a panel series at the Religion and Politics in Early America Conference, held at Washington University in St. Louis, March 2018. Kevin den Dulk invited us to present the volume's methods and findings at the Henry Symposium on Religion and Public Life at Calvin College in April 2019. Further, we are thankful for the staff at the University of Missouri Press. Editor in chief Andrew Davidson has valued this project and carefully shepherded it to press. The production staff has done an outstanding job preparing the manuscript.

Finally, we would like to acknowledge Fr. Thomas Buckley, SJ, an outstanding scholar of church and state matters, especially in Virginia. Fr. Buckley had agreed to participate in this project before his passing in November 2017. *Requiescat in pace.*

Carl H. Esbeck: I would like to thank my deans of law, Gary Myers and Lyrissa Lidsky, for their encouragement over the span of this project, as well as travel funds to make presentations at conferences. The support of

the University of Missouri School of Law's librarians was unflagging, especially that of Randy Diamond, director, and Diane Collins, the force that
makes interlibrary loan still work in a digital age of information technology.
And, of course, down through the years my go-to research assistants fielded
countless e-mails to locate this 'n that and produce it yesterday: law students
Cailynn D. Hayter, Anna El-Zein, and Gavin K. Thomas.

Jonathan Den Hartog: I would like to start by thanking my undergrad-
uate professors for spurring my interest in American religion and politics.
John Willson, Mark Kalthoff, and David Stewart served as readers for an
undergraduate thesis on religious disestablishment in three American states.
It has been a unique opportunity to return to this subject twenty years later.
I appreciate having been able to work on this project at the University of
Northwestern–St. Paul, Minnesota. There, my history colleagues Matthew
Miller and Jonathan Loopstra were wonderful collaborators on all matters of
the life of the department. My dean, Jeremy Kolwinska, and Vice President
Janet Sommers encouraged my research and writing. An additional Faculty
Development Grant provided travel funds to share the research. I would also
like to thank the staff at the Berntsen Library for their research assistance.
This project has been helped along by student workers Nathan Runke, Me-
gan McCrary Rach, and Chatham Hedges. Benjamin Mueller deserves special recognition for jumping into the indexing project. I am also grateful for
the warm welcome I have received from my new colleagues in the History
Department at Samford University. Finally, a huge thank-you to my children
and my wife, Jacqueline, for listening to me talk about the project for hours,
from its conception to its completion.

Acknowledgments of Related Publications and Assistance

Carl H. Esbeck gratefully acknowledges that his chapter on Virginia is
adapted in part from "Protestant Dissent and the Virginia Disestablishment,
1776–1783," *Georgetown Journal of Law and Public Policy* 7, no. 1 (2009):
51–103.

Joel A. Nichols gratefully acknowledges that his chapter on Georgia is adapt-
ed in part from "Religious Liberty in the Thirteenth Colony: Church-State
Relations in Colonial and Early National Georgia," *New York University Law
Review* 80, no. 6 (2005): 1693–1772.

John Witte Jr. gratefully acknowledges that his chapter on Massachusetts is adapted in part from "A Most Mild and Equitable Establishment of Religion: John Adams and the Massachusetts Experiment," *Journal of Church and State* 41, no. 2 (1999): 213–52.

Michael S. Ariens thanks Scott A. Britton, executive director of the Castle in Marietta, Ohio, for generously sharing his archival work on the history of glebe lands in southeastern Ohio. He also thanks Valerie Sanchez for her assistance in the preparation of Chapter 13.

Evan Haefeli would like to thank the staff of the Historical Society of Delaware for their generous assistance.

James S. Kabala would like to thank Catherine and Stanley Kabala, C. Morgan Grefe, J. Stanley Lemons, John F. Quinn, and the staffs of the Rhode Island Historical Society, the Mary Elizabeth Robinson Research Center, the Newport Historical Society, the Rhode Island State Library, the Rhode Island State Law Library, the Rhode Island Judicial Records Center, and the John D. Rockefeller Jr. and John Hay Libraries of Brown University.

CONTRIBUTORS

Coeditors

Carl H. Esbeck (chapter 1, Introduction; chapter 8, Virginia) is the R. B. Price Professor Emeritus and Isabelle Wade & Paul C. Lyda Professor of Law Emeritus at the University of Missouri. He has published widely on the First Amendment and church-state relations, and his articles have appeared in *Emory Law Journal, William and Mary Law Review, Washington and Lee Law Review, Notre Dame University Law Review, Iowa Law Review, Utah Law Review, Journal of Law and Religion, Georgetown Journal of Law & Public Policy, Journal of Law and Politics* (UVA), *Journal of Church and State, Kentucky Law Journal, BYU Law Review, and Mississippi Law Journal*. Professor Esbeck has served as special counsel in the Office of Deputy Attorney General, U.S. Department of Justice. He received his JD from Cornell University School of Law.

Jonathan J. Den Hartog (chapter 1, Introduction) is professor of history at Samford University in Birmingham, Alabama, after serving for more than a decade at the University of Northwestern–St. Paul, Minnesota. He received his PhD in American history from the University of Notre Dame in 2006. Den Hartog's first book, *Patriotism and Piety: Federalist Politics and Religious Struggle in the New American Nation*, was published by the University of Virginia Press in 2015. He has published articles in *Early American Studies*, the *Journal of Church and State*, and the *Faulkner Law Review*, as well as essays in four edited volumes. His public writing has appeared in the *Wall Street Journal* and the *Philadelphia Inquirer*. He has held research fellowships at Princeton University, the American Antiquarian Society, and the Washington Library at Mount Vernon.

Contributors

Nathan A. Adams IV (chapter 20, Florida) is a partner with Holland & Knight LLP, in Tallahassee, practicing in complex commercial and appellate litigation. He holds his PhD from the University of Florida, JD from the University of Texas School of Law, and a BA from Wheaton College. Before joining Holland & Knight, Dr. Adams worked for the Florida Executive Office of the Governor, Florida Department of Education, and Christian Legal Society's Center for Law and Religious Freedom.

Michael S. Ariens (chapter 13, Ohio) is a professor of law and Englehardt Research Fellow at St. Mary's University School of Law in San Antonio, Texas. He teaches and writes in the fields of constitutional law, American legal history, and legal ethics. He is the author, with Robert A. Destro, of a casebook, *Religious Liberty in a Pluralistic Society*. He has written three other books, including the award-winning *Lone Star Law: A Legal History of Texas*, and more than three dozen law-review articles.

Marc M. Arkin (chapter 19, Maine) is a professor of law at Fordham University School of Law. Professor Arkin holds JD and PhD degrees from Yale University, the latter from the Department of Religious Studies, where she studied with Sydney E. Ahlstrom and Edmund S. Morgan. She has written extensively about religion and culture in the early Republic and the antebellum period, in publications including the *New England Quarterly*, *Journal of American History*, and *Journal of the Early Republic*. In addition, she has contributed widely to popular publications such as the *Wall Street Journal* and the *New Criterion* on subjects ranging from U.S. law to religion, English literature, and world history.

Shelby M. Balik (chapter 15, Vermont) is an associate professor of history at Metropolitan State University of Denver, specializing in early American history and American religious history. She holds degrees from Brown University, the University of Michigan, and the University of Wisconsin. She has published in the *Journal of Social History*, *New England Quarterly*, and *Journal of Church and State*, among others. She is the author of *Rally the Scattered Believers: Northern New England's Religious Geography* (2014) and is currently researching a book on the politics and practice of household religion in eighteenth-century North America.

Michael D. Breidenbach (chapter 16, Maryland) is assistant professor of History at Ave Maria University. He received his PhD from King's College, Cambridge University. He is coeditor of the *Cambridge Companion to the First Amendment and Religious Liberty*. His article "Conciliarism and the American Founding" was published in the *William and Mary Quarterly*. He has also published in *Perspectives on Political Science* and has held fellowships at Princeton, Oxford, and Cambridge.

Kyle T. Bulthuis (chapter 7, New York) is associate professor of history at Utah State University in Logan. He teaches courses in colonial and revolutionary America, history of American race and slavery, and American religion. His first book, *Four Steeples over the City Streets: Religion and Society in New York's Early Republic Congregations*, was published in 2014. That monograph examines the relationship between religious experience and social change in what became the nation's largest city. His current research examines the experiences of black writers, and their networks, in the eighteenth-century Atlantic world. Bulthuis earned his PhD in American history at the University of California–Davis.

Edward R. Crowther (chapter 11, Tennessee) is emeritus professor of history at Adams State University, where he taught for thirty years and served as department chair for twenty. He is the author of *Southern Evangelicals and the Coming of the Civil War* and coeditor of *Between Fetters and Freedom: African American Baptists since Emancipation*. His articles have appeared in the *Journal of Southern History*, *Journal of Negro History*, and many edited volumes, including *The Field of Honor*. Crowther earned his PhD at Auburn University.

John Fea (chapter 2, New Jersey) is professor of history at Messiah College in Mechanicsburg, Pennsylvania. He is the author or editor of six books, including *The Way of Improvement Leads Home: Philip Vickers Fithian and the Rural Enlightenment in Early America*; *Was America Founded as a Christian Nation: A Historical Introduction*; *Why Study History? Reflecting on the Importance of the Past*; and *The Bible Cause: A History of the American Bible Society*. He received his PhD from the State University of New York–Stony Brook.

Brian Franklin (chapter 18, New Hampshire) serves as the associate director of the Center for Presidential History and lecturer in the Department of History at Southern Methodist University in Dallas. Franklin's research interests revolve around American religious and political history in eighteenth- and nineteenth-century America. His current project, *America's Missions: The Home Missions Movement and the Early Republic*, explores Protestant home missions and their influence on political, regional, and denominational development in the early United States. At the Center for Presidential History, Franklin directs the Collective Memory Project, a filmed oral history program dedicated to expanding the archival record of the George W. Bush presidency. He earned his PhD in history from Texas A&M University.

Evan Haefeli (chapter 3, Delaware) is associate professor of history at Texas A&M University. He received his PhD from Princeton University. Previously he taught at Princeton, Tufts, and Columbia Universities and was a visiting fellow at the London School of Economics. He has held a variety of fellowships at archives and institutions around the United States. Dr. Haefeli's published work includes "Toleration and Empire: The Origins of American Religious Diversity," in *British North America in the Seventeenth and Eighteenth Centuries* (part of the Oxford History of the British Empire series); "The Problem with the History of Toleration," in the edited volume *Politics of Religious Freedom*; and *New Netherland and the Dutch Origins of American Religious Liberty* (2012).

Keith Harper (chapter 10, Kentucky) is senior professor of Baptist studies at Southeastern Baptist Theological Seminary in Wake Forest, North Carolina. He is the author of *The Quality of Mercy: Southern Baptists and Social Christianity, 1890–1920*, and the editor or coeditor of several volumes, including *Between Fetters and Freedom: African American Baptists since Emancipation*. Harper also edits the America's Baptists Series for the University of Tennessee Press. He earned his PhD from the University of Kentucky.

Robert J. Imholt (chapter 17, Connecticut) is professor emeritus of history at Albertus Magnus College in New Haven, Connecticut. Past president of the New England Historical Association, he has published numerous articles on Connecticut in the early Republic, most recently "Connecticut Confronts the Guillotine: The French Revolution and the Land of Steady Habits," *New England Quarterly* 90, no. 3 (2017): 385–417. His current project is a biographical study of Timothy Dwight, poet, preacher, and president of Yale from 1795 until his death in 1817. He received his PhD from the University of Kentucky.

James S. Kabala (chapter 4, Rhode Island) is adjunct professor of history at Rhode Island College and at the Community College of Rhode Island. He received his BA from Providence College and his PhD from Brown University. Kabala is the author of *Church-State Relations in the Early American Republic, 1787–1846.*

Justin Latterell (coauthor of chapter 21, Massachusetts) serves as research director for law, history, and Christianity at Emory University's Center for the Study of Law and Religion and as assistant professor in the practice of sociology of religion at the Candler School of Theology. He received his PhD from Emory University. Latterell's research focuses on the intersections of religion, law, and politics in nineteenth- and twentieth-century U.S. history.

David Little (chapter 5, Pennsylvania) is a fellow at the Berkley Center for Religion, Peace, and World Affairs at Georgetown University and is a retired professor emeritus of religion and international affairs at Harvard Divinity School. He received his doctorate from Harvard University.

Nicholas P. Miller (chapter 6, North Carolina) has a JD from Columbia University and a PhD in American religious history from the University of Notre Dame. He is a professor of church history at Andrews University, where he also directs the International Religious Liberty Institute. He has published more than forty articles and book chapters on issues of church, state, and religious history. Miller is also the author or editor of several books in the field, including *The Religious Roots of the First Amendment* (2012) and *500 Years of Protest and Liberty: From Martin Luther to Modern Civil Rights* (2017).

Joel A. Nichols (chapter 12, Georgia) is associate dean for academic affairs and professor of law at the University of St. Thomas School of Law in Minnesota as well as a senior fellow at the Emory University Center for the Study of Law and Religion. Nichols writes about the intersection of law and religion in family law, legal history, human rights, and the First Amendment. He coauthored *Religion and the American Constitutional Experiment*, 4th ed. (2016) (with John Witte Jr.). He received his JD and MDiv from Emory University.

Kevin Pybas (chapter 14, Louisiana and Missouri) is associate professor of political science at Missouri State University. His research and writing focus on issues of law and religion, particularly with respect to the U.S. Supreme Court's Religion Clauses. His work has appeared in *Justice System Journal* (coauthored), *Perspectives on Political Science, Valparaiso University Law Review, Cumberland Law Review, University of Detroit Mercy Law Review*, and *Texas Review of Law & Politics*. He received his PhD from the University of Georgia.

Miles Smith IV (chapter 9, South Carolina) is an independent scholar, most recently serving as assistant professor of history at Regent University. His research and teaching interests include the American South, the Atlantic world, and U.S. intellectual and religious history. He received his PhD from Texas Christian University.

John Witte Jr. (coauthor of chapter 21, Massachusetts) is the Robert W. Woodruff University Professor of Law, McDonald Distinguished Professor, and director of the Center for the Study of Law and Religion at Emory University. He has published more than two hundred articles and nearly thirty books, most recently *Church, State, and Family: Reconciling Traditional Teachings and Modern Liberties*, Cambridge Studies in Law and Christianity (2019). He received his JD from Harvard University Law School.

DISESTABLISHMENT AND RELIGIOUS DISSENT

CHAPTER ONE

INTRODUCTION
The Task, Methodology, and Findings

Carl H. Esbeck and Jonathan J. Den Hartog

On May 10, 1776, the Second Continental Congress sitting in Philadelphia agreed to a resolution urging each of the British colonies in North America "to adopt such government as shall . . . best conduce" in response to the impending crisis with Great Britain.[1] A preamble was added on May 15 that was further suggestive of a break with the mother country, and Congress then directed that the document be released to the public. The resolution of May 15 set in motion a round of constitution making in the Atlantic Seaboard colonies, several of which proceeded to declare themselves sovereign states and sever ties with the British Crown. In the remaining months of 1776, Virginia, New Jersey, Delaware, Pennsylvania, Maryland, and North Carolina adopted their first constitutions. Georgia, New York, and Vermont followed in 1777.[2] South Carolina adopted its second constitution in 1778, Massachusetts followed with its first in 1780, and New Hampshire ratified a second constitution in 1784.[3] Only Connecticut and Rhode Island failed to take this first republican step.[4]

These North American colonies, soon-to-be republics, meeting in representative conventions to debate and adopt state constitutions to govern themselves, were a novelty in government practice rooted in the consent of the governed. In laboring to agree on the terms of a written constitution, the delegates to the state conventions were forced to address collectively the issue of church-state relations and to do so far sooner than such questions would have otherwise come to a head.[5] Each colony had unique and differing traditions of church-state relations rooted in the colony's peoples, their countries of origin, church affiliations, and theological principles.[6] The state constitutional framers had to confront the issue of religion that some would have preferred to put off, at least until after the conclusion of military hostilities. Out of this unprecedented course of events, the newly emerging

3

republics took up the concerns of those who sought to disestablish religion where there was a state-established church or to lock in the current stage of what, over time, had evolved in the direction of no established church.

There was never a national disestablishment. Neither the federal government, instituted in 1789 in New York City, nor the Articles of Confederation, approved 1781 near the end of the revolutionary fighting, ever had anything resembling an established church. So there was nothing to dismantle. Rather, disestablishment was entirely a state-by-state affair. Establishment had been a matter reflecting colonial history, the European nations from which colonial subjects had emigrated, as well as each colony's unique religion, politics, and economy. Hence, the process of deregulating each of those establishments must be treated as discrete state-level stories. To regard disestablishment as a continental-wide movement, or as a development somehow channeled through the First Amendment, drafted in 1789 and added to the U.S. Constitution in 1791, is not merely to mislead. It is to falsify the historical experience.[7]

This volume is that state-by-state account of disestablishment in the original thirteen states, along with similar events in the soon-to-be-admitted states of Vermont, Kentucky, and Tennessee. Contributors to our chapters also discuss Ohio, the first state admitted from the Northwest Territory; the Catholic disestablishments in territorial Louisiana and Missouri, the first states admitted from the Louisiana Purchase; the unusual case of Maine, a state carved out of existing Massachusetts with its standing Congregational establishment; and Florida, which was wrestled from Catholic Spain under U.S. pressure. Each chapter begins with the colony's juridical ties to religion in its original charter and then walks forward through the events and people bearing on law, religion, and church relations, dwelling on revolutionary America, and then proceeding into the early American republic with the restructured church-state relations in that state.

What follows is a fascinating story in political and jurisprudential innovation that has no European parallel. Disestablishment in the several states is America's preeminent contribution to governmental theory. Yet this early state history has been far less explored in favor of a focus on the newly instituted federal government. The few attempts that have sought to give an account of this state-by-state development have come up short.[8] One approach has been to segment disestablishment into three phases: the mid-Atlantic colonies, the South, and finally Puritan New England, with Pennsylvania and Rhode Island cast as outliers to this three-pronged pattern. A second methodology has been to make a list of salient laws—say, a religious test for public office or the repeal of glebe lands (the rents from which supported the church)—and then tabulate those states that share in common the adopting or repealing of each such type of law. The first approach obscures and misleads by overgeneralization, as well as unnecessarily spends time explaining why this state or that state is an aberration to the three-prong typology. The second approach rips the adoption and repeal of laws out of their time frame, political context, and a law's actual application as opposed to the letter of a law perhaps rarely enforced. Both approaches try to anticipate what the contemporary reader wants to know and then supply it stripped of important local detail.

We present a more promising method, with chapters devoted to each colony-come-state. Our contributors—scholars of history, politics, and law—supply each state's story, unfolding it chronologically in its political and cultural milieu, accounting for all its complexity. Because the experience of lawmaking during the revolution and early republic was primarily at the state level—and this was decidedly so with regard to religion—the state-by-state perspective will prove to be most fruitful in providing historical detail.

What We Asked of Our Chapter Authors

The chapter authors were instructed to look for the cultural, political, biblical, and economic concerns bearing on their state's disestablishment. Why was disestablishment achieved in their state, and by what process was it accomplished? What people, groups, or immigrants populated the state, and how did that matter? How did the ideas of disestablishment play out "on the ground"? Did the practice of people's religion tell us how disestablishment was actually understood and new laws actually applied? What happened to those factions who unsuccessfully defended the establishment? Was there any consideration about how disestablishment would affect education? Relief to the poor and widows? Laws on public decorum, morals, blasphemy, or Sunday closing to retail commerce? Disestablishment was not just about changes in written law. Yet the written law did change. And those laws were unfailingly preserved, unlike other primary materials. Such laws provide, in brief and concrete form, what the leaders, or at least the majority thereof, were thinking about church-state relations in their state.

The editors found that what was most lacking in previous studies was the uncovering and organizing of primary materials (newspapers, pamphlets, sermons, private journals and letters, and judicial proceedings) that give evidence and color to the process of disestablishment in each state. We urged contributors to avoid conclusory statements. We requested that, to the extent possible, their declarative sentences be backed by reference to primary materials. Where such materials were not preserved, that also was to be noted. We hope that readers who are unable to devote their time to unearthing primary materials will rely on each chapter's reported evidence and then draw their own conclusions concerning what transpired in each state leading to disestablishment. The editors firmly instructed authors not to express their thoughts, if any, on history's application to issues that concern church-state relations in the twentieth and twenty-first centuries.

The reconsideration and repeal of state establishmentarian laws were almost always intertwined with the sponsorship of laws that bear on the protection of individual religious belief (often termed "the right of private judgment"). For example, a law barring clergy from holding public office imposed a cruel choice, implicating a cleric's personal religious liberty, but it also tells us something about how church-state relations were conceptualized. There is no neat way of differentiating between these two types of laws: those securing religious liberty of the individual and those deregulating the preferred institutional church. So the chapters on each state discuss developments in individual religious liberty as well, but with an eye to what those developments might tell us about the movement toward church disestablishment.

Although the path to disestablishment in each colony-come-state had features that were distinct to each state in both timing and substance, obviously there were some commonalities. For the guidance of our authors we provided a list of five recurring legal features that constituted a British-like establishment and thus likely targets of the push to disestablish.[9] It was also a matter of interest if some of these features did not occur in a given state. A commonality of all establishmentarian laws is they linked the state church or preferred religion to the regulating state. The list was not intended to be exhaustive, of course, and our authors were to report whatever they found.

1. Government financial support of the state church: assessments to pay ministers and rents from glebe lands.
2. Government control over the creeds, order of worship, polity, and clerical appointments of the state church. Licensure of state-tolerated dissenting (termed "nonconformist") clerics; licenses

tethered to a single meetinghouse, thereby preventing itinerant preaching by nonconformists.

3. Mandatory attendance at worship services in the state church, prohibitions on church services by others, and required licensure to open a meetinghouse for nonconformists.

4. Use of the state church to record births, marriages, and deaths; to perform all marriages and funerals; and to administer tax revenues for care of the poor and widowed. Today we regard these tasks as civil functions, but in the British-like establishments of the eighteenth century, these matters were within the jurisdiction of the church.

5. Religious tests. Public office and voting rights confined to members of the state church or a broader religious test to include nonconformists. Religious preferences for securing military commissions, government contracts, as well as admission to university and faculty appointments.

While not part of the foregoing working definition of an "establishment," there were three additional things for which our authors were to be on alert:

1. Although the editors regard the adoption of religious exemptions from public duties borne by others as a means of accommodating the religious exercise of dissenters or other minorities—as opposed to steps toward disestablishment—the chapter authors were told to look for religious exemptions from general laws, such as excusals from oath taking, hat removal in court, jury service, and the military draft.

2. Following disestablishment, some states imposed new disabilities on religious societies. This legislation was not part of the disestablishment process but a new phase. Examples are restrictions on the church polity permitted in order to incorporate a church under state law, with a bias toward lay governance, as well as statutory caps on church landholdings of more than a set acreage or on acquiring assets over a given value.[10] If these features appeared in a given state, authors were to report them and urged to uncover their purpose.

3. Following the Constitutional Convention of 1787 in Philadelphia, the several states were engaged in the ratification debate from

September 1787 through all of 1788. Additionally, following the First Federal Congress in New York City and its reporting out a Bill of Rights, state legislatures were engaged in the debate over ratification of these proposed amendments during the period October 1789 through all of 1790. Chapter authors were asked to report if either of these state-level contests had any bearing on their state's disestablishment.

Findings in the Face of Conventional Wisdom

The book's chapters make significant scholarly contributions by recounting in detail the process of disestablishment in each of the former colonies, as well as religion's legal place in the states of the new federal republic. Although we emphasize that each state disestablishment was unique, now that the editors have a full accounting from our chapter authors we are able to draw some commonality of principles at work across the states. In that spirit, we offer corrections to the past telling of the story.

The conventional wisdom in America is that disestablishment was a bold national experiment in religious freedom, one embodied in the First Amendment. While it is understood that the First Amendment (indeed, the entire Bill of Rights) bound only the new federal government, the popular claim is that the two Religion Clauses of the First Amendment soon set the model that eventually swept all of the states. The conventional telling, as well, is that Americans wanted religious freedom for their own sect but selfishly not for others. Yet pragmatism won out. All sects were a minority, it was observed, and thus people reluctantly came to understand that religious freedom had to be conceded to others if they wanted it for themselves. In this narrative, religious freedom is achieved not out of principle but out of practicality. These two claims are repeated as axioms in grade school social studies classrooms right on through textbooks for university undergraduates. The historical record is far more nuanced and complex. More important, the conventional axioms are false.

In the face of this standard narrative and based on the twenty chapters that follow, we report the following findings. Some findings are in the negative. That is, the nature of a given finding is what did not contribute, as opposed to what did contribute, to disestablishment in America's states. However, in a topic written on as much as church and state in the United States, the correcting of widely held misconceptions is just as salient as the identification of wholly new historical patterns and causes.

Finding 1. Neither the U.S. Constitution of 1787–88 nor the First Amendment of 1789–91 contributed to the disestablishment process in the original thirteen states. The same is true in the three admitted states that were never federal territories: Vermont, Kentucky, and Maine.[11] We see this in multiple ways:

1. No state modeled its constitution after the First Amendment, or even considered the amendment when making state religion law.[12]
2. Article VI (Clause 3) of the U.S. Constitution prohibits a religious test for federal office. The new states did not follow the federal lead. Indeed, most every state had a religious-test clause until well into the nineteenth century.
3. The oaths of office set forth in the U.S. Constitution permit an officer to either "swear or affirm" (see, for example, U.S. Constitution, Article I, Section 3 [Clause 6]), the latter being an option to accommodate Quakers and Anabaptists. Again, we found no evidence that this federal example influenced the law of any state. Some states did permit affirmations in lieu of oaths, but in doing so they were not influenced by the federal model.
4. No state's disestablishment was influenced by the state-level debate over ratification of the U.S. Constitution or, two years later, the state-level debate over the federal Bill of Rights.

The First Amendment did apply in U.S. territories, of course, and so it could have had a bearing on shaping the religion law in lands that were for a while federal territory, such as Tennessee, Ohio, Louisiana, Missouri, and Florida.[13] But it never happened. Our chapter authors found no reports of violations of the religious freedom protections in the First Amendment during the years when these states were federal territories.[14] Moreover, there is no record of the First Amendment being raised when these later-admitted states were being considered by the U.S. Congress for admission to the Union.

It was not until 1845 that the Religion Clauses of the First Amendment received even passing mention by the U.S. Supreme Court, and only then it was to acknowledge the truism that the First Amendment did not bind the states.[15] Indeed, from the outset the First Amendment had little impact even on religious freedom within the federal government. For example, there were nine U.S. Supreme Court cases involving church or religion issues before the

1845 High Court confirmed that the First Amendment bound only federal law.[16] None of these cases sought to apply the First Amendment to the issues in the case. There were ten more such cases before the first application by a member of the Court that assumed the Establishment and Free Exercise Clauses had something to say about federal law on matters of religion.[17]

Finding 2. Protecting the "right of private judgment" in individual religious observance and practice came easily to the new American states. However, voluntarism in the funding of ministers and churches—leading to the repeal of religious tax assessments and glebes—was slow and arduous work, spanning fifty years. The spirit of revolutionary liberty extended to liberty in individual religious belief or the "right of private judgment." Indeed, in a few states (New Jersey, Delaware, and Rhode Island), this personal religious liberty was a fact "on the ground" even before the American Revolution. When it came to financial support for the state church, however, disestablishment forces struggled against the axioms of the Old World—that a state secures unity by providing financial support for a religion that inculcates in its people the needed civic virtues. The advocates of financial voluntarism—that the churches are better off if they are alone supported by their followers—thus had a harder time with succeeding. Yet the dissenters persevered, and the growing numbers drawn to their denominations serve as vindication. They were convinced that past church dependence on state aid had led to religion's corruption where matters of religious doctrine and observance were bent to serve reasons of state. They believed religion's purity would follow a deregulated environment where each sect was entitled to wax or wane according to the zeal of its adherents and the appeal of its teachings. That said, an extension of the larger principle that underlay voluntarism in funding—that establishments corrupted religion and divided republics—would take decades to be worked out when it came to what this meant for public schooling,[18] as well as what it meant for a state's use of familiar Protestant symbols and a state's partaking in Protestant practices that had almost unthinkingly become part of the public civil religion.

Finding 3. Not only did each of the original and early admitted states have its own unique disestablishment, but it cannot be said that the disestablishment story in any one state was more important than that of others. This means we can find no warrant for the U.S. Supreme Court's step in *Everson v. Board of Education of Ewing Township* (1947),[19] and subsequent cases, that elevated the disestablishment in Virginia as the more impactful in schooling early Americans in disestablishment principles. Much the same is true for *Reynolds v. United States* (1879),[20] where the Supreme Court looked to disestablishment events in Virginia to construe the Free Exercise Clause of the First Amendment.[21]

Further, the more closely Virginia is studied, the more it appears that the Old Dominion was in certain respects an oddity among state disestablishments. For example, only Virginia totally prohibited churches from incorporating under state law, whereas all similarly situated voluntary organizations were permitted to enjoy the benefits and convenience of operating as a corporation. And of all the states, only Virginia compelled the formerly established church to return to the government the glebes and personal property vested while the church had been established.

Finding 4. A majority of the colonists who agitated for disestablishment were religious dissenters who, although in agreement concerning the general tenets of Protestant Christianity, still materially differed from the established Protestant church in their state. Their beliefs motivated them to seek freedom for reasons that are rooted in Christianity, as they understood the teachings of that faith. Christ's Kingdom is not of this world and rendering unto Caesar the things that are Caesar's were biblical passages strongly suggestive to these dissenters that state and church properly occupied different centers of authority under God.[22] They believed that religious freedom was a matter of individual religious conscience (termed "a right of private judgment") and that the Church, for reasons having to do with her role as understood biblically, was a body to be kept institutionally distinct from civil government and financially supported entirely by church members' tithes and offerings (termed financial "voluntarism"). That churches remain voluntaristic is essential to their health, it was believed, for too close an embrace by the state would only detract from and even corrupt the church.

These religious dissenters operated in an arena of increasing Protestant pluralism. While some states maintained a great deal of religious homogeneity, this began to break down into Protestant denominationalism through the eighteenth and into the early nineteenth centuries.[23] Some colonies—especially New Jersey, Delaware, and Rhode Island—were pluralist from their founding, whether by choice or accident. The Great Awakening of the 1740s was the first harbinger of emerging pluralism, as it increased the ranks of independent congregations in New England and introduced Baptists into the mid-Atlantic and South.[24] Migration from the British Isles and from colony to colony in the eighteenth century further increased the growth and splintering of religious denominations.[25] This reality would receive a new jolt in the early nineteenth century, with another round of revivals known as the Second Great Awakening, a movement that energized Methodists and Baptists, somewhat less so with Presbyterians, along with other formerly dissenting groups. The Second Great Awakening increased the ranks of fervent Christians that had no links to establishmentarian denominations. Many of these "enthusiastic" Christians explicitly preached individual liberty, political and otherwise; the institutional separation of church and state; voluntary associations as a primary means of social organization; and republicanism and local governance as the best forms of civil government.[26]

These origins work to depress claims that disestablishment was forged out of government indifference to religion, or even hostility to it. They also work to suppress the claim that disestablishment meant that religion was to have no role in shaping public affairs. Church and state could be separated, but religion and politics could not. Indeed, a majority believed religion (as they experienced it) was instrumental to the formation of virtue, and virtue was instrumental to the self-discipline of citizens thought necessary to sustain a republic.

Finding 5. Because establishments were complex and varied phenomena, so was the process of disestablishment. Disestablishment was a fifty-year project. In some states disestablishment has been portrayed as a singular or brief moment related to a single stroke of constitutional revision or new legislation. But many of our authors describe disestablishment in their states as a prolonged process—often a messy one shaped by local personalities. Moreover, because of the character of much religious practice and its establishment, the process varied down to the local level, and it happened unevenly across states. Thus, the chronological range of this volume indicates not only the varied experiences of the states, but that the process continued beyond the singular date often attributed to a given state's disestablishment.

Finding 6. Neither resistance to the Congregational (Puritan) establishment in New England nor the Church of England establishment in the southern colonies was a material cause of the War of Independence against Great Britain. This is in contrast to the French Revolution, which was intensely anticlerical and in significant part a revolt against the French Catholic Church for its ecclesiastical support of the oppressive French monarchy.

The Second Continental Congress failed even to mention opposition to religious establishments in its long list of Patriot grievances in the Declaration for Independence. The Quebec Act of 1774, which left in place the established Catholic Church in British Canada, was the only religious complaint recorded in the Declaration.[27] That Catholic establishment, however, was outside the borders of the rebellious colonies. Catholicism in Quebec was regarded by Patriots as an external threat, not a domestic establishment that would oppress them should they lose the War of Independence.[28]

Disestablishment was a powerful movement. But it was different from that other powerful movement of partially overlapping chronology, namely, the forces driving the American Revolution. Revolutionary fighting ended in 1781, and the war was concluded by treaty in 1783. In contrast, disestablishment was by no means a sudden, abrupt event occasioned by revolutionary events. The last traces of a full-on state church were not erased in New England until 1833—fifty years after the revolution ended. There was some overlap in the leading characters involved in both movements (for example, John Adams and Patrick Henry), but clarity only increases by keeping the two movements distinct.

We are not saying that religion had no role in the American Revolution. It did.[29] Our claim is narrower. We are saying that resistance to an established church in the original thirteen states had little role in the revolt against the British. Indeed, in New England the established church strongly supported the Patriot cause. In the South, many leading Patriots were members of the established Anglican church, starting with the commander in chief of the Continental Army, George Washington. The American Revolution was not anticlerical. Indeed, in New England the Congregational pastors were in the vanguard of the revolution.[30]

Religious dissenters did use their great numbers to withhold support for the revolution as leverage to expand religious freedom at the expense of the established Anglican church. This happened in Virginia and the Carolinas. That disagreement, however, was internal to the Patriot cause, not a grievance directed at the British Crown.

Admittedly, there was resistance by some Americans to the planting of a Church of England episcopate in the colonies, a step debated by the Anglican hierarchy in England as far back as 1741 but never taken. The installation of such a bishop would have increased the power of the Church of England in America—Anglicanism being an arm of Crown policy—and increased the authority of Anglican ecclesiastics at the expense of the Anglican laity.[31] Additionally, once the War of Independence was fully under way, there were times when Continental soldiers expressed their strong feelings against the British by defacing Church of England houses of worship, but that was anger toward those Americans thought to be in sympathy with the enemy rather than anger toward a religious establishment.

We acknowledge that in the years shortly before the revolution, British authorities in New York and the Carolinas sought to reinvigorate the Church of England as a means of taking a firmer hand in colonial political affairs. This attempt to use the Church of England as an agent to better implement British control was resisted by many colonists. Religious dissenters, in turn, sought to fend off Anglican church power as a matter of resistance to the political use of religion. This grievance, held by dissenters, contributed to revolutionary support in New York and the Carolinas. Unsurprisingly, British loyalists found succor in the colonial Anglican church, whereas Patriots naturally associated their Loyalist opponents with loyalty to Anglicanism. But this was revolutionary Americans opposing the politics of the Church of England, not opposition to establishmentarianism.

Finding 7. The contribution of anti-Catholicism to the process of disestablishment is overstated.[32] Being English, the British colonies in North America were anti-Catholic from the outset.[33] Although anti-Catholicism was a feature of the Protestant religious establishments in the British colonies and in the newly formed states, the movement toward disestablishment was not motivated by it.

What the state political leaders faced is well illustrated by the Carroll brothers and their political and religious place in Maryland. The Carrolls had different emphases than Catholics on the European Continent.[34] There were few Catholics in revolutionary America, and while a majority of America's Catholics lived in Maryland, even in Maryland Catholics were a minority.[35] Unlike dissenting Protestants, Catholics lacked a creedal tradition favoring religious tolerance.[36] They were pious and loyal to their faith, but conducted their observances privately, while just beginning to involve themselves in governmental affairs. Early support of the revolution by Maryland Catholics greatly helped to lead to a postwar thaw in hostile relations with Protestants.[37] Maryland's revolutionary constitution of 1776 had a religious test, but all Christians were preferred, thereby including Catholics in the polity.

In other states, some of what might appear to be anti-Catholicism was really disagreement between Catholic laity and Catholic priests. Influenced by the many Protestants around them, Catholic laity wanted more say in the operation of their parish churches, which under financial voluntarism they had built and paid for. Rather than resenting various state incorporation restrictions requiring that churches be overseen by an elected board of trustees, Catholic laity welcomed the laws. These state statutes, of course, were opposed by the magisterium because they were at odds with the episcopal polity of the Catholic Church. However, the Catholic laity were caught up in the liberty and republicanism afoot everywhere in the new nation.[38] It was not until the 1820s and thereafter that Roman Catholic immigration from Ireland and Germany began to generate a backlash and desire among nativists to counter Catholicism by making strict-separationist claims to chuch-state relations.[39] While we acknowledge that powerful anti-Catholic movements were just over the horizon and certainly regrettable, the state-by-state disestablishments were complete everywhere, or nearly so, before this resistance to Catholic immigration. Only after disestablishment was achieved was "strict separation of church and state" celebrated as a manifest good because it held down Catholicism as un-American.[40] And it can be admitted that after 1820, the increasing Catholic population helped Protestants to begin to realize the implications of disestablishment to their previous cultural dominance.[41]

In the period of this volume, anti-Catholicism was one of several motives for pressing Spain to yield Florida to the United States, expressed, for example, during the Patriots' War of 1810–11. But that was isolated to Florida. To its credit, the federal government took care to honor treaty provisions requiring respect for the land titles of the Catholic Church and religious orders in Florida, the Louisiana Purchase, and the American Southwest following the Mexican-American War.

Finding 8. States imposed regulatory disabilities on religious societies out of a populist desire to safeguard religious individuals from ecclesiastical authorities. This new phase of legislation was not part of the disestablishment project, which was a repealing of long-standing laws defining, regulating, and supporting the state church. Rather, having created a free market in religion, the aim was to safeguard the conscience of the individual religious consumer from overreach by church leaders.

The evidence in our chapters aligns with Philip Hamburger in recognizing that as first-generation Americans "idealized their individual independence, many of them came to worry that their new-found liberty was threatened not only by governmental power but also by religious authorities. They came to fear even the self-governing claims made by their own, disestablished, Protestant churches, but particularly those asserted by the Catholic Church."[42] This new phase was an egalitarian-prompted capping of church assets and restricting polity in order to protect the laity. The most constraining statutes were state incorporation acts that limited the corporate form to lay governance by a board of trustees. These laws affected Catholics more than Protestants because the former were hierarchical, whereas many Protestant churches were already of decentralized polity and lay controlled.

Sarah Barringer Gordon regards these new laws as part of the disestablishment project and so would stretch the process of disestablishment up to the start of the Civil War.[43] However, Hamburger is correct that this phase of state lawmaking was differently motivated. Disestablishment was out of fear for state entwinement with the church to the harm of genuine religion, whereas this new phase of state lawmaking was motivated by a fear of clerical power to the harm of the laity.[44]

These laws were especially liberating for lay American Catholics, taken as they were with newfound republican empowerment. They wanted greater say in the operation of their churches, which per voluntarism they were now paying for.[45] But Catholics were not alone. The frontier revivalists that arose out of the Second Great Awakening were, in their minds, up against an ecclesiastical monopoly of "respectable" clergy of the Protestant upper class. This attack on more settled, professionally trained clergy grew out of the leveling impulse that Nathan Hatch has labeled the "democratization of American Christianity." This populist surge of first-generation Americans in "common-man Christianity" sought these laws to unhorse the power centers of their perceived betters.[46]

Finding 9. Religious tests initially were narrow preferences in aid of the state church and thus encouraged conformity to it. In the first reforms, religious tests were broadened to embrace most or all Protestants and later all Christians. As things evolved still further, religious-test laws were repealed or their underlying purpose moved away from establishmentarianism. While many states repealed their religious tests entirely, those states retaining them refocused the test on an acknowledgment of God or theism. The latter, such as Maryland, did so believing that a government under a transcendent, superintending Being was necessary to sustain a republic.

Finding 10. The conventional view of Thomas Jefferson's broad influence on the disestablishment process in the states has little support in the evidence reported by our chapter authors. Even in Virginia, it was the writings and actions of James Madison, in both theory and practice, that played the leading and essential role in disestablishment. Jefferson's *A Bill for Establishing Religious Freedom* (first drafted in 1777, but not enacted until January 1786) was widely admired by free thinkers. But it was replicated only in Rhode Island,

and even there only after first excising the bill's phrases discounting theism.[47] The bill's impact was on extolling liberty of individual thought in religious questions ("a matter of private judgment"). But that proposition was widely held among Americans well before 1786 and in a few states before 1776. The bill's adoption in Virginia (thanks to astute legislative moves by Madison, including agreeing to tone down some of Jefferson's final draft) did not single-handedly disestablish the Anglican church. Moreover, the bill appears to be largely responsible for later discriminatory restraints imposed on all of Virginia's churches, not a cause for the expansion of religious freedom fully conceived. As historian Thomas Buckley observed, in antebellum Virginia the churches were less free than in any other state.[48] Thus, we note that Jefferson's popular reputation as America's foremost champion of religious freedom exceeds his state-level accomplishments, and it is in the states— not at the federal level—where disestablishment occurred. Conversely, it is James Madison who deserves a great deal of credit for his efforts in Virginia, along with being the essential man at the federal constitutional level when it comes to religious freedom.

Jefferson's significance should be revisited. During crucial events surrounding the federal Constitution and Bill of Rights, Jefferson was in France, and so, of course, he had little domestic impact in those years. We further bracket here whatever bearing Jefferson as President had on federal religious liberty.[49] Jefferson's main influence was on individual religious liberty, "a right of private judgment," not disestablishment. He was a primary inspiration leading to the formation of the Democratic-Republican Party, a party later known for its strong support for church-state separation. The latter, of course, aligns with the common understanding that Jefferson was both a religious skeptic and no admirer of Old World ecclesiastical power and clerical intrigues.

* * *

Finally, we offer two notes on presentation. As to organization, the state-by-state chapters that follow are arranged by date of each state's disestablishment. The date on which disestablishment occurred in a given state is often a matter of dispute, depending on how "establishment" is defined. In that event, the chapters are ordered according to the date that a given state repealed its ministerial assessment or religious tax (the state's embracing of financial voluntarism). The danger of this arrangement is that the more heated state contests come later and the easy cases come first. But, then, we anticipate many readers will skip around in the book, rather than reading the chapters in sequence.

Concerning style, when quoting historical documents, including state constitutions, we instructed our authors to retain the original spellings— however unconventional in the eye of the modern reader.

NOTES

1. Washington C. Ford, ed., *Journals of the Continental Congress, 1774–1789*, 4 vols. (Washington, DC: Government Printing Office, 1904–37), 4: 342.

2. Vermont was not one of the original thirteen states, nor was it represented at the Second Continental Congress. However, in other respects Vermont was acting in parallel with the thirteen colonies, although it did not ratify the Articles of Confederation. Vermont was admitted as the fourteenth state in 1791, the first state to be admitted to the Union by act of Congress.

3. Even prior to the resolution of May 15, New Hampshire and South Carolina had sought the advice of the Second Continental Congress with respect to self-governance. On November 3 and 4, 1775, Congress replied to these two colonies, recommending that they hold conventions and, if deemed warranted, to "establish a form of government." *Journals of the Continental Congress*, 3:319, 326–27. Subsequently, New Hampshire adopted a written constitution on January 5, 1776. *Constitution of New Hampshire*, reprinted in Francis Newton Thorpe, ed., *The Federal and State Constitutions, Colonial Charters, and Other Organic Laws of the States, Territories, and Colonies Now or Heretofore Forming the United States of America*, 7 vols. (Washington, DC: Government Printing Office, 1909), 4:2451. South Carolina likewise did so on March 26, 1776. *Constitution of South Carolina*, reprinted in Thorpe, *Federal and State Constitutions*, 6:3241. However, neither of these constitutions addressed religion or religious freedom.

4. Connecticut modified its colonial charter only as necessary to reflect that the state was no longer accountable to the British Crown. A new constitution was not adopted until 1818. Thorpe, *Federal and State Constitutions*, 1:529, 536. Rhode Island did not adopt a constitution until 1842, effective 1843. Thorpe, *Federal and State Constitutions*, 6:3222.

5. The process of constitution making was not, of course, always in lockstep with the process of disestablishment. While New Jersey and Delaware did codify their disestablishments in their first constitutions, Vermont's first constitution was 1777, but its disestablishment was 1807. Similarly, New Hampshire's first constitution was 1776, but its disestablishment was 1819.

6. See Jonathan J. Den Hartog, "Politics: Colonial Era," in *Encyclopedia of Religion in America* (Washington, DC: CQ Press, 2010), 3:1674–82.

7. We are not arguing that what constituted an establishment in the minds of Americans in the late eighteenth century has to be drawn exclusively from the process of disestablishment in the several states. Rather, our burden concerns the

emphasis on a few federal incidents when the only establishments in America were those in the several states, and consequently the mobilizations to disestablish and the forces behind these stories operated entirely at the state level.

8. A selected bibliography of state historical material appears just before the index, pages 425–26.

9. See Michael W. McConnell, "Establishment and Disestablishment at the Founding, Part I: Establishment of Religion," *William & Mary Law Review* 44, no. 5 (2003): 2105, 2131–81. McConnell formulated a six-part typology for the elements constituting an "establishment" similar to that in the text.

10. A helpful collection of these state laws appears in Sarah Barringer Gordon, "The First Disestablishment: Limits on Church Property and Power before the Civil War," *University of Pennsylvania Law Review* 162, no. 2 (2014): 307.

11. An interesting question, one somewhat the reverse of the finding in the text, is whether the state disestablishment experience from 1776 to 1789 influenced the debate in the First Federal Congress over what eventually became the Religion Clauses of the First Amendment, as well as the amendment's ratification in the states. Among other things, to answer that question one would have to consider the states' ratification of the 1787 U.S. Constitution. This is because the absence of a bill of rights in the 1787 draft figured heavily in the ratification contest. See Carl H. Esbeck, "Uses and Abuses of Textualism and Originalism in Establishment Clause Interpretation," *Utah Law Review* (2011): 489, 508–25.

12. The lack of modeling is also illustrated by the text of the Free Exercise Clause of the First Amendment. The federal free-exercise text reads as if absolute. Compare the federal right with the individual religious liberty safeguards in the constitutions of New Jersey, Maryland, North Carolina, Georgia, New York, Massachusetts, and New Hampshire, all of which have expressed conditions on religious liberty written into the text. Illustrative is New York Constitution's Article 38, which protects religious liberty but not if "to excuse acts of licentiousness, or [to] justify practices inconsistent with the peace or safely of this State."

13. States such as Ohio, Louisiana, and Florida were federal territories for about a decade before they were admitted as states. Tennessee was also a territory, but for a much shorter period. Ohio was the first state carved out of the Northwest Territory. Louisiana and Missouri were the first two states carved out of the Louisiana Purchase. As federal territories, these states were subject to direct regulation by Congress (see U.S. Constitution, Article IV, Section 3), which in turn was subject to the First Amendment. Thus, Congress could not have allowed a territory to have an established church nor have admitted a territory as a state if the state had sought to maintain an established church. To have done either would have been for "Congress to make a law respecting an establishment of religion," which Congress could not do. So unlike the original thirteen states, Vermont, Kentucky, and Maine, these later-admitted states were subject to the First Amendment when still territories.

14. We do have interesting religious liberty conflicts reported in territorial Louisiana and Florida, but the resolution of these disputes did not invoke the First Amendment. That the parties to a religious liberty conflict seemingly did not think to call on the First Amendment is itself testimony to its early lack of influence.

15. See *Permoli v. Municipality No. 1 of the City of New Orleans*, 44 U.S. (3 How.) 174 (1845).

16. The nine cases are as follows: *Terrett v. Taylor*, 13 U.S. (9 Cranch) 43 (1815) (dispute over glebe lands); *Town of Pawlet v. Clark*, 13 U.S. (9 Cranch) 292 (1815) (dispute over glebe lands); *Trustees of Philadelphia Baptist Ass'n v. Hart's Executors*, 17 U.S. (4 Wheat.) 1 (1819) (dispute over charitable bequest); *Trustees of Dartmouth College v. Woodward*, 17 U.S. (4 Wheat.) 518 (1819) (dispute over state attempt to alter charter of church-affiliated college); *Society for Propagation of the Gospel v. Town of New Haven*, 21 U.S. (8 Wheat.) 464 (1823) (dispute over treaty obligations and church property); *Mason v. Muncaster*, 22 U.S. (9 Wheat.) 445 (1824) (dispute over glebe lands); *Beatty v. Kurtz*, 27 U.S. (2 Pet.) 566 (1829) (dispute over church title to cemetery property); *Worcester v. Georgia*, 31 U.S. (6 Pet.) 515 (1832) (dispute with state over authority of federal agent to Indians); *Vidal v. Girard's Executors*, 43 U.S. (2 How.) 127 (1844) (dispute over validity of charitable bequest for antireligious purposes).

17. The dissenting opinion in *Ex Parte Garland*, 71 U.S. (5 Wall.) 333 (1867) (dissenting opinion), is the first mention in the U.S. Supreme Court that the First Amendment should guide the resolution of whether federal law preempted a state restraint on religion. The majority opinion appears at *Cummings v. Missouri*, 71 U.S. (5 Wall.) 277 (1867) (striking down the state law on other grounds).

18. See Steven K. Green, *The Bible, the School, and the Constitution: The Clash That Shaped Modern Church-State Doctrine* (New York: Oxford University Press, 2012).

19. *Everson v. Board of Education of Ewing Township*, 330 U.S. 1, 11–13 (1947).

20. *Reynolds v. United States*, 98 U.S. 145, 162–67 (1879). See Donald L. Drakeman, *Church, State, and Original Intent* (New York: Cambridge University Press, 2010), 2–4, 21–73. When construing the First Amendment in *Reynolds*, Drakeman points out that the Supreme Court quoted approvingly from the documents of Virginia and events surrounding the passage of Jefferson's *Act to Establish Religious Freedom*. The *Reynolds* Court attributed disestablishment to Jefferson and Madison, while ignoring the essential contributions by religious dissenters, as well as the contribution of several other states. In deciding *Everson*, Drakeman observes, the Court was again wide of the mark in using Virginia as the source for First Amendment interpretation of the Establishment Clause. Drakeman, *Church, State, and Original Intent*, 74–148.

21. The observation in the text that no one state's disestablishment story should have an outsize influence on the meaning of disestablishment is not a challenge to the "incorporation" of the Establishment Clause of the First Amendment through the Fourteenth Amendment in *Everson*, the first case to make the Establishment Clause applicable to the states. The Supreme Court's "incorporation" doctrine is about the meaning of the Fourteenth Amendment, not the First Amendment. Ratified in 1868, the Fourteenth Amendment was one of three Reconstruction-era amendments coming out of the Civil War. Its meaning and application have nothing to do with the period of interest here, 1776 to 1833, having to do with disestablishment in the states.

22. The phrase "my kingdom is not of this world" are the words of Jesus on trial before Pontius Pilate, the Roman governor in Palestine, as recorded in the Gospel according to John (18:36). The phrase "render unto Caesar" is the words of Jesus

appearing in all three of the synoptic gospels: Matthew 22:21, Mark 12:17, and Luke 20:25.

23. The implications of pluralism for American state disestablishments complement the account provided by Anthony Gill in *The Political Origins of Religious Liberty* (New York: Cambridge University Press, 2008), esp. 60–113.

24. Thomas S. Kidd, *The Great Awakening: The Roots of Evangelical Christianity in Colonial America* (New Haven, CT: Yale University Press, 2007); Douglas L. Winiarski, *Darkness Falls on the Land of Light: Experiencing Religious Awakenings in Eighteenth-Century New England* (Chapel Hill: University of North Carolina Press for the Omohundro Institute of Early American History and Culture, 2017).

25. S. Scott Rohrer, *Wandering Souls: Protestant Migrations in America, 1630–1865* (Chapel Hill: University of North Carolina Press, 2010).

26. The differing ways religious culture nurtured voluntarism are on display in Nathan O. Hatch, *The Democratization of American Christianity* (New Haven, CT: Yale University Press, 1989); and Jonathan J. Den Hartog, *Patriotism and Piety: Federalist Politics and Religious Struggle in the New American Nation* (Charlottesville: University of Virginia Press, 2015), 93–115, 201–6.

27. An oblique reference to the Quebec Act of 1774 is the only mention of a religious grievance in the Declaration of Independence ("For abolishing the free system of English laws in a neighboring province, establishing therein an arbitrary government . . . so as to render it at once an example and fit instrument for introducing the same absolute rule into these colonies:"). The complaint was that the British Crown had agreed to an arrangement that preserved the Catholic establishment in Quebec. This was said to threaten the security of the American colonies to the south because of the despotic tendency of Catholic governments. This was not, however, a grievance against the British Crown over an established church in the thirteen rebellious colonies.

28. Carl H. Esbeck, "Religion during the American Revolution and the Early Republic," in *Law and Religion: An Overview*, ed. Silvio Ferrari and Rinaldo Cristofori (Burlington, VT: Ashgate, 2013), 57, 60–70.

29. See Thomas S. Kidd, *God of Liberty: A Religious History of the American Revolution* (New York: Basic Books, 2010); James B. Bell, *A War of Religion: Dissenters, Anglicans, and the American Revolution* (New York: Palgrave Macmillan, 2008); James P. Byrd, *Sacred Scripture, Sacred War: The Bible and the American Revolution* (New York: Oxford University Press, 2013); and Daniel L. Dreisbach, *Reading the Bible with the Founding Fathers* (New York: Oxford University Press, 2016).

30. See Harry S. Stout, *The New England Soul: Preaching and Religious Culture in Colonial New England* (New York: Oxford University Press, 1986), 259–311; Spencer W. McBride, *Pulpit and Nation: Clergymen and the Politics of Revolutionary America* (Charlottesville, VA: University of Virginia Press, 2017); and Jay P. Dolan, *The American Catholic Experience: A History from Colonial Times to the Present* (Garden City, NY: Doubleday, 1985), 96–97.

31. An Anglican bishop was opposed in New England by the established Congregational Church. Obviously, a bishop on this side of the Atlantic would invigorate the Anglican church, a longtime competitor to the Congregationalists. In the South,

in the absence of a bishop the Anglican laity had long exercised significant control over the local parish Church of England. Many of the laity did not want to yield that power to a bishop in America. See Patricia U. Bonomi, *Under the Cope of Heaven: Religion, Society, and Politics in Colonial America* (New York: Oxford University Press, 1986), 199–209; and Kidd, *God of Liberty*, 57–74.

32. See, for example, Gerard V. Bradley, *Church-State Relationships in America* (New York: Greenwood Press, 1987), 124–25.

33. See Carla Gardina Pestana, *Protestant Empire: Religion and the Making of the British Atlantic World* (Philadelphia: University of Pennsylvania Press, 2009).

34. See Patrick W. Carey, *Catholics in America: A History* (Westport, CT: Praeger, 2004), 17–25; Dolan, *American Catholic Experience*, 90–97; Michael D. Breidenbach, "Conciliarism and the American Founding," *William and Mary Quarterly*, 3rd ser., 73, no. 3 (2016): 467–500; and Maura Jane Farrelly, *Papist Patriots: The Making of an American Catholic Identity* (New York: Oxford University Press, 2012).

35. Dolan, *American Catholic Experience*, 87, 111, 159–62.

36. Thomas J. Curry, *The First Freedoms: Church and State in America to the Passage of the First Amendment* (New York: Oxford University Press, 1986), 52–53.

37. Dolan, *American Catholic Experience*, 96–97, 102–03.

38. Robert F. McNamara, "Trusteeism in the Atlantic States, 1785–1863," *Catholic Historical Review* 30, no. 2 (1944): 139–40, 152–54; Dolan, *American Catholic Experience*, 101–24, 158–94.

39. See Philip Hamburger, *Separation of Church and State* (Cambridge, MA: Harvard University Press, 2002), 147–55, 189, 191–92, 201–19. Hamburger argues that anti-Catholic motivation in support of church-state separation did not appear in strength until the mid-nineteenth century.

40. Dolan, *American Catholic Experience*, 294–320.

41. Thomas J. Curry, *Farewell to Christendom: The Future of Church and State in America* (New York: Oxford University Press, 2001), 15–16.

42. Hamburger, *Separation of Church and State*, 192 (see also 189, 191–92). See also Philip Hamburger, *Liberal Suppression: Section 501(c)(3) and the Taxation of Speech* (Chicago: University of Chicago Press, 2018), 40–41, 47, 48–70.

43. Gordon, "First Disestablishment," 307.

44. This is not to deny Professor Gordon's basic point that these new state laws were inimical to what is today called church autonomy. Gordon, "First Disestablishment," 371–72. They were. More of interest here, these laws ran contrary to the disestablishment principle of voluntarism, that is, a deregulation of the state's ties to the church, thereby leaving a voluntary organization to wax or wane in accord with its own resources and merits. And while it took a generation or two, because of this inconsistency one would expect that the Gordon-type laws would be unevenly enforced and in time repealed. That is eventually what happened. Judges called on to enforce these laws knew that as civil officials they had no competence in theological disputes. Pressure also mounted from Catholics and hierarchical Protestants to defeat trusteeism and all of its offspring, thereby placing the matter of ecclesial polity under centralized church authority.

45. Dolan, *American Catholic Experience*, 101–24, 158–94. See generally Patrick W. Carey, *People, Priests, and Prelates: Ecclesiastical Democracy and the Tensions of Trusteeism* (Notre Dame, IN: University of Notre Dame Press, 1987).

46. Hatch, *Democratization of American Christianity*, 17–46.

47. Kentucky was carved out of western counties of Virginia, and thus the land was initially governed by Virginia law. However, upon becoming a state, Kentucky looked more to Pennsylvania than to Virginia in the formulation of its initial church-state laws.

48. Thomas E. Buckley, *Establishing Religious Freedom: Jefferson's Statute in Virginia* (Charlottesville: University of Virginia Press, 2014).

49. Hamburger, *Separation of Church and State*, 144–89. As president, Jefferson sought to exert influence on church-state relations in Connecticut, but the effort was unsuccessful. It was the ascendance of the Democratic-Republican Party that eventually brought on the disestablishment in Connecticut. There is, of course, the 1802 presidential letter to the Danbury Baptists, a letter having no contemporary impact on either state or federal disestablishment law, but outsize impact in the mid-twentieth century on the federal jurisprudence of the U.S. Supreme Court.

CHAPTER TWO

DISESTABLISHMENT IN NEW JERSEY

John Fea

ON JUNE 10, 1776, the New Jersey Provincial Congress convened in Burlington to guide the colony through the American Revolution. Some of New Jersey's most prominent patriots were present. Abraham Clark of Elizabeth-Town, Rev. John Witherspoon of Princeton, and John Hart of Hopewell would soon sign the Declaration of Independence. Rev. Jacob Green of Hanover used his pen and Presbyterian pulpit to promote independence. John Cleves Symmes of Sussex and Jonathan D. Sergeant of Newark would serve New Jersey in the Continental Congress. Philemon Dickinson would become a U.S. senator. Also present was William Patterson of Princeton, who would later sign the United States Constitution. On June 19, the Provincial Congress arrested royal governor William Franklin. Five days later the Congress commissioned a ten-man committee, led by Jacob Green, to draft a state constitution. As George Washington fortified Manhattan and watched the British navy arrive on Staten Island, Green and his team were putting the finishing touches on New Jersey's new government.[1]

All the members of the Provincial Congress were defenders of religious freedom and opposed to religious establishments. These beliefs were reflected in the Constitution they framed. Article XVIII stated:

> That no person shall ever within this colony be deprived of the inestimable privilege of worshipping Almighty God in a manner agreeable to the dictates of his own conscience; nor under any pretence whatsoever compelled to attend any place of worship, contrary to his own faith and judgment; nor shall any person within this colony ever be obliged to pay titles, taxes, or any other rates, for the purpose of building or repairing any church or churches, place or places of worship, or for the maintenance of any minister or ministry, contrary to what he believes to be right or has deliberately or voluntarily engaged to perform.

There could be no religious taxes to pay ministers or erect church buildings, doing away with the mainstays of state establishments.

While the Provincial Congress defended religious freedom for all the state's inhabitants, it reserved "civil rights" and office holding for Protestants. On the other hand, a preference for one religion over other was prohibited, so there could be no established church. Article XIX stated:

> That there shall be no establishment of any one religious sect in this province, in preference to another[,] and that no Protestant inhabitant of this Colony shall be denied the enjoyment of any civil right merely on account of his religious principles, but that all persons, professing belief in the faith of any Protestant sect, who shall demean themselves peaceably under the government as hereby established, shall be capable of being elected into any office of profit or trust, or being a member of either branch of legislature, and shall fully and freely enjoy every privilege and immunity enjoyed by others their fellow subject.[2]

Articles XVIII and XIX of the 1776 New Jersey Constitution do raise two central questions. First, why did the framers make such a strong statement defending religious liberty and rejecting religious establishment in Article XVIII and XIX? Second, why did they limit office holding and other civil rights to Protestants in Article XIX?

I.

Article XVIII defended liberty of conscience in matters of religion. A resident of the state was free to worship God in the way he or she saw fit. The reference to "Almighty God" does, however, seem to exclude all but monotheists. Church attendance was not required for anyone living in New Jersey, and a state church or religious establishment was prohibited. The incorporation of churches was never restricted in New Jersey, nor was a church's acquisition of real property.

Article XVIII would not have surprised any of the state's residents. From its birth in 1664, New Jersey championed religious freedom for its settlers. *The Concession and Agreement of the Lords Proprietors of the Province of New Caesarea, or New Jersey* (1665), a theory of government written by the colony's first proprietors, Sir George Carteret and Lord John Berkeley, included the following statement:

> That no person qualified as aforesaid within the said Province, at any time shall be any ways molested, punished, disquieted or called in question for any

difference in opinion or practice in matter of religious concernments, who do
not actually disturb the civil peace of the said Province; but that all and every
such person and persons may from time to time, and at all times, freely and
fully have and enjoy his and their judgments and consciences in matters of
religion throughout the said Province they behaving themselves peaceably and
quietly, and not using this liberty to licentiousness, nor to the civil injury or
outward disturbance of others; any law, statute or clause contained, or to be
contained, usuge or custom of this realm of England, to the contrary thereof in
any wise notwithstanding.[3]

East Jersey's commitment to religious freedom was closely linked to the
forging of a successful settlement. Carteret was involved in planning the
1664 naval expedition that removed the Dutch from power in the region.
James, the Duke of York, granted to him the colony's eastern tract as a reward for his loyalty. Carteret was a military man who was not known for
serious reflection on issues related to church and state. As he planned his
colony, he would have been aware that pockets of Dutch Calvinist settlers
lived in a cluster of small settlements bordering New York. The religious
liberty of the Dutch needed to be accommodated. Moreover, the promise of
religious freedom was an excellent means of attracting new settlers. This was
especially the case for the New England Puritans who settled in New Ark
(later "Newark"), Woodbridge, and Elizabethtown Tract; the Quakers who
helped to settle Shrewsbury; and the Baptists who settled Piscataway.[4]

After Carteret sold his interest in the colony in 1682, the East Jersey Proprietors, which were made up of almost entirely of Quakers (including future
Pennsylvania founder William Penn) chose Robert Barclay, a Scottish Quaker, as its absentee governor. A year later the East Jersey Proprietors drafted a
new government for the colony, *The Fundamental Constitution for the Province of East New Jersey in America* (1665). Article XVI of the *Fundamental
Constitution* upheld religious freedom for the colony's Christians:

All persons living in the Province who confess and acknowledge the one Almighty and Eternal God, and holds themselves obliged in conscience to live
peaceably and quietly in a civil society, shall in no way be molested or prejudged
for their religious perswasions and exercise in matters of faith and worship; nor
shall they be compelled to frequent and maintain any religious worship, place
or ministry whatsoever: Yet it is also hereby provided, that no man shall be
admitted a member of the great or common Council, or any other place of

publick trust, who shall not profaith in Christ Jesus, and solemnly declare that
he doth no ways hold himself obliged in conscience to endeavour alteration in
the government, or seeks the turning out of any in it or their ruin or prejudice,
either in person or estate, because they are in his opinion hereticks, or differ in
their judgment from him: Nor by this article is it intended, that any under the
notion of this liberty shall allow themselves to avow atheism, irreligiousness,
or to practice cursing, swearing, drunkenness, prophaness, whoring, adultery,
murdering or any kind of violence, or indulging themselves in stage plays,
masks, revells or such like abuses; for restraining such and preserving of the
people in deligence and in good order, the great Council is to make more particular laws, which are punctually to be put in execution.

By the end of the seventeenth century, East Jersey was religiously diverse.
Quakers, Scottish Presbyterians, New England Congregationalists, Dutch
Reformed, French Huguenot, and Regular (Calvinist) Baptists were all worshipping in the colony. East Jersey was also a colony filled with dissenters,
Protestants who did not conform to the Church of England. Many of these
dissenting Protestants descended from families that had fled persecution in
England. The colony's liberal views on religious freedom were enticing to
these Protestants. After East and West Jersey reunited in 1702 to become the
royal colony of New Jersey, Anglicans began to establish a presence as well.[5]

On March 18, 1674, Berkeley sold his share of the colony to two Quakers,
Edward Byllynge and John Fenwick. Both men attempted to found Quaker
settlements—Byllynge at Burlington and Fenwick at Salem. Eventually, Fenwick's colony was incorporated into the Byllynge settlement, and the colony
of West Jersey was founded. In 1677 West Jersey adopted the *Concessions
and Agreements of the Proprietors, Freeholders and Inhabitants of the Province
of West New Jersey* as its form of government. Article XIV of the 1677 *Concessions and Agreements* stated:

> That no men, nor number of men upon earth, hath power or authority to rule
> over men's consciences in religious matters, therefore it is consented, agreed
> and ordained, that no person or persons whatsoever within the said Province,
> at any time or times hereafter, shall be any ways upon any presence whatsoever,
> called in question, or in the least punished or hurt, either in person, estate, or
> privilege, for the sake of his opinion, judgement, faith or worship towards God
> in matters of religion. But that all and every such person, and persons may

from time to time, and at all times, freely and fully have, and enjoy his and their judgments, and the exercises of their consciences in matters of religious worship throughout all the said Province.[6]

West Jersey was neither as diverse at East Jersey nor as populated, but the Quaker commitment to religious freedom did attract a multitude of Protestant groups. The southern portion of the colony was dominated by Quaker meetings, with a few small enclaves of New England Congregationalists, New England Baptists, and Swedish Lutherans. The northern portion of the colony was slightly more diverse, due to Anglican and Presbyterians settlements in Hunterdon County.[7]

William Penn was part of the original proprietary group in West Jersey. Though the 1667 *Concessions and Agreements* was probably written by Byllynge, it is likely Penn contributed in some way. The same might be said for the 1665 *Fundamental Constitution of the Province of East Jersey*. Both documents reflect Penn's liberal views on religious freedom. If Penn did not directly contribute to the drafting of the 1667 *Concessions and Agreements* or 1665 *Fundamental Constitution*, his works on the relationship between religious liberty and civil society would have been known and available to those who did.[8]

Penn's social and political thought was forged out of his experience as a member of a persecuted English sect. He spent time in a British prison in the late 1660s on charges of anti-Trinitarianism and participation in Quaker meetings. During much of the next decade, his writings were dominated by the theme of religious toleration for Quakers and other dissenting Protestants. Penn challenged the English state-church tradition in several ways. His primary goal was to show that it was religious uniformity, not religious diversity, that contributed to social disorder. Penn blamed England's past problems on the refusal of the government to allow religious toleration. Indeed, he believed that religious toleration was the only way of promoting a peaceful and happy society. Religious establishments always engendered resistance, resulting in divisiveness, chaos, and disorder. People would be more devoted to a government that safeguarded individual liberties. When people worshipped freely, according to the dictates of conscience, they would be motivated to work harder and contribute to the economic well-being of the nation.[9]

It is difficult to trace the ideological origins of religious freedom in the 1776 New Jersey Constitution with certainty. The records of New Jersey's constitutional convention say little about religion and nothing about the discussions that led to Articles XVIII and XIX. It is likely that the framers did not deliberate much about the issue, since the articles codified the existing pattern of church-state relations in the colony for more than a century. We can, however, be safe in saying that New Jersey's revolutionary-era commitment to religious liberty was informed by a practical response to the Protestant diversity of the colony, an acceptance of Quaker thinking on the matter (even though there were few Quakers in the Provincial Congress), the significant number of Protestant dissenters in the colony, and the colony's long history of upholding religious liberty and rejecting religious establishments.

II.

Equally difficult to track is the decision in Article XIX to limit civil rights and office holding to Protestants. Again, the records of the constitutional convention are scant and do not mention any of the debate that led to Article XIX. The Protestant preference represents a break from the governing documents of colonial New Jersey. For example, *The Concession and Agreement of the Lord Proprietors of Nova Caesarea* (1664), the original plan of government written and endorsed by Lord John Berkeley and Sir George Carteret, did not mention any religious test for office. The 1677 West Jersey *Concessions and Agreements* required officeholders to uphold "Christian Belief," which was defined as anyone who could "Profess Faith in God the Father, and in Jesus Christ, his Eternal Son the true God, and in the Holy Spirit one God blessed evermore; and do acknowledge the Holy Scriptures of the Old and New Testament, to be given by Divine Inspiration."[10] Both Protestants and Catholics could fit comfortably within this definition.

The broad extensions of religious freedom in the 1677 *Concessions and Agreements* were a departure from Penn's view that religious freedom should be extended solely to Protestants.[11] Penn argued for religious liberty based on Protestant unity. Only by permitting freedom for all Protestants, he argued, could England present a unified front against the arbitrary and heretical encroachments of Roman Catholicism. Failure to do so would breed religious division among those of like-minded Reformation faith, opening the door for Catholics to conquer the nation. To sway skeptics who thought that the unity of different Protestant persuasions was not possible, Penn invoked the model of Holland. As a Protestant republic that afforded its people religious and civil liberties, Holland had been successful in keeping Catholicism from penetrating its ranks.[12] Penn called on Englishmen to lay aside their dogged commitment to creeds that led to "Animosities and Vexations about Matters of Religion" and to rally with the rest of their fellow Protestants around the common essentials of true Christian faith. The Protestant commitment to the authority of the Bible was one such rallying point. If all Protestants could agree on the "one Confession of Jesus" rather than man-made concessions" (Catholicism), Penn asserted, it "Twould be a Happy Day" followed by "Peace and Concord."[13]

It is unlikely, however, that the framers of the 1776 New Jersey Constitution drew heavily on William Penn's views when they limited civil rights and office holding to Protestants in Article XIX. Most of the members of the Provincial Congress were Calvinists—Dutch Reformed, Scots, Scots-Irish, New England Presbyterians, and Regular (Calvinist) Baptists. Of the ten delegates appointed by the Provincial Congress to draft the Constitution, seven were Presbyterian.[14] These Calvinists, like all Protestants in British North America, shared a view of church-state relations shaped by anti-Catholicism forged through a series of eighteenth-century colonial wars with the French (a Catholic establishment), an understanding of British identity shaped deeply by Protestant experience, and a belief that Protestant leaders were essential to founding a healthy republic. This is the likely origin of the Protestant test of Article XIX.

III.

Religious freedom in England was limited to Protestants. The 1689 Act of Toleration, which allowed certain religious groups that dissented from the Church of England to worship in peace, did not extend to Catholics. Freedom was a Protestant idea. During the Glorious Revolution (1688), the British removed the Catholic James II (he fled to France) and replaced him with William and Mary, Protestants whom they could trust to defend religious and civil liberty. Most British Protestants believed this bloodless revolution was a sign of God's providential endorsement of the Protestant faith and British exceptionalism. Moreover, in the period between 1689 and 1763, the British engaged in regular wars with Catholic France, culminating with the French and Indian War (1754–63). These military conflicts, which all had significant North American theaters, exacerbated British colonial fears of French political and religious tyranny. The British victory in the French and Indian War thus brought a spirit of British patriotism to the American colonies.[15] This sense of British nationalism focused on the glories of being part of a Great British Empire—the freest, economically strongest, and most

Protestant empire in the world. In New Jersey, the links between Protestantism and British liberty were evident in a 1698 East Jersey law that denied
religious liberty to "any of the Romish religion."[16]

In the years between the Treaty of Paris that settled the Seven Years' War
(1763) and the colonial break from England in 1776, the members of the
New Jersey Provincial Congress opposed what they believed to be Parliament's (and eventually King George III's) failure to uphold their political and
religious liberties. On the political front, New Jersey patriots reacted slowly
to the revolutionary sentiments of the people of Boston, Philadelphia, and
other British North American cities, but they eventually rallied behind the
movement to independence that reached its apex in July 1776.

Their fear of religious tyranny was not as strong as their political anxi-
eties, but New Jersey residents did worry that the Church of England, with
the support of Anglicans like their royal governor, William Franklin, would
organize a bishopric in the colonies.[17] In 1776, as many of these dissenters
gathered to draft a state constitution, including Article XVIII, the Church of
England was certainly on their minds. But at least Anglicans were Protestant. Most revolutionaries—in New Jersey and elsewhere—embraced some
degree of anti-Catholicism. Not only was Catholicism thought to be a false
system of religion, but throughout the eighteenth century it remained a
synonym for religious tyranny. Ironically, it was these long-standing British
anti-Catholic concerns that likely led the framers of the 1776 New Jersey
Constitution to limit civil rights and office holding to Protestants in Article
XIX. Catholics were incapable of exercising true liberty because their loyalty
was to the pope and not to the ideals of liberty on which the American republic was to be built.

In the minds of many New Jersey revolutionaries, Protestants also served
as a source of personal virtue and moral order. Though, as we have seen,
it was unlikely that many of the members of the Provincial Congress were
conversant with the writings of William Penn, their belief that Protestants
might contribute to social stability in the colony was similar to the ideas that
Quaker leaders had defended in the late seventeenth century. For example,
John Witherspoon, the President of the College of New Jersey at Princeton
and a member of the Provincial Congress, believed that morality and religion were necessary to secure God's continued blessing on the American
republics. He affirmed that the "best friend to American liberty" was the one
"who is most sincere and active in promoting true and undefiled religion."
For Witherspoon, Protestantism was the only true and undefiled religion.
Similarly, Jacob Green, the Presbyterian minister at Hanover and the chair

of the drafting committee for the 1776 Constitution, believed that Protestantism (particularly Calvinism) was vital to a properly ordered republic. The primary author of the Constitution, Jonathan Dickinson Sergeant, received drafting help from John Adams, a strong proponent of the idea that Christianity was essential to the moral order of a state.[18] The Calvinists in the Provincial Congress did not take New Jersey as far as some of its sister states in their religious requirements for office holding, but they certainly believed that Protestants were the only people suited to run the government of the new state they were just creating.[19]

IV.

The 1776 New Jersey Constitution remained the state's governing charter until 1844. From May 14 to June 29 of that year, a convention met at Trenton to write a second constitution. The document that emerged strengthened the office of the governor, added a bill of rights, and limited suffrage to white males. It also eliminated the Protestant qualification for office holding and other civil rights. Article I, Section 4, of the Bill of Rights stated: "There shall be no establishment of one religious sect in preference to another; no religious test shall be required as a qualification for any office or public trust; and no person shall be denied the enjoyment of any civil right merely on account of his religious principles."[20] The minutes of the 1844 constitutional convention are more extensive than those of the 1776 convention, but they still shed little light on the debate over removal of the Protestant test. At least one prominent New Jersey resident was not happy about the religious test in the original Constitution. In his introduction to *Proceedings of the New Jersey State Constitutional Convention of 1844*, historian John Bebout quotes a "Councilor Wright" who said in a speech supporting the new Constitution: "What more obnoxious provision could there be than that which establishes a restriction on religious liberty by providing that no man entertaining certain opinions shall hold an office." There is no evidence to suggest that adoption of Article 1, Section 4, met opposition.[21]

The timing of the repeal of the religious test is worth noting. The 1844 convention met in Trenton only days after the first of the Philadelphia "Bible riots." With a growing number of Catholic immigrants arriving to American shores, several cities experienced nativist violence against these newcomers. Between May 3 and May 10, two people were killed and several wounded before fighting was quelled by a combination of police, Pennsylvania militia, and federal troops. At stake was the role of Bible reading in public schools. Catholic leaders had protested the use of the Protestant King James Bible in

schools, preferring that their students read from the Catholic Douay trans-
lation. When Philadelphia Catholics suggested that Bible reading in schools
be suspended until their students could be accommodated, Protestant mobs
attacked several Catholic churches and residences in the Philadelphia district of Kensington.[22] Though the delegates to the New Jersey convention
discussed the "sectarian strife" taking place in nearby Philadelphia and other major U.S. cities during the debate over whether the new Constitution
should maintain a fund for education, there is little that connects the school-
funding question with the decision to drop the Protestant-only language of
the 1776 Constitution. What is certain is the decision of the delegates to rise
above the nativist spirit of the age and move to open government to officeholders of all religious faiths. By 1844 the last residual of establishment in
New Jersey was gone.

NOTES

1. Gerlach has suggested that Jonathan Dickinson Sergeant wrote a significant
portion of the New Jersey Constitution before the Provincial Congress appointed
an official drafting committee. Larry R. Gerlach, ed., *New Jersey in the American
Revolution, 1763–1783: A Documentary History* (Trenton: New Jersey Historical
Commission, 1975), 212. S. Scott Rohrer makes a similar argument for Sergeant's authorship in *Jacob Green's Revolution: Radical Religion and Reform in a Revolutionary
Age* (University Park: Pennsylvania State University Press, 2014), 157–59. Sergeant, a
lawyer educated at the College of New Jersey at Princeton, served in the New Jersey
Provincial Congress from 1774 to 1776 and the Second Continental Congress from
1776 to 1777 before moving to Pennsylvania. See "Jonathan Dickinson Sergeant" in
the Biographical Dictionary of the United States Congress, http://bioguide.congress.
gov/scripts/biodisplay.pl?index=S000247.

2. *Journal of the Votes and Proceedings of the Convention of New Jersey* (Burlington,
NJ: Isaac Collins, 1776), 84.

3. *The Concessions and Agreements of the Proprietors, Freeholders and Inhabitants
of the Province of West New Jersey, in America* (1677), in *The Colonial History of New
Jersey*, by Samuel Smith (Burlington, NJ: James Parker, 1765), 529.

4. John E. Pomfret, *Colonial New Jersey: A History* (New York: Charles Scribner's
Sons, 1973), 23–24.

5. Pomfret, *Colonial New Jersey*, 23–24. For an overview of early Protestant pluralism in colonial New Jersey, see Douglas G. Jacobsen, *An Unprov'd Experiment:
Religious Pluralism in Colonial New Jersey* (Brooklyn, NY: Carlson, 1991).

6. http://avalon.law.yale.edu/17th_century/nj05.asp. In 1681 the *Concessions and
Agreements* were replaced by *The Fundamental Agreements of the Freeholders, and*

Inhabitants of the Provinces of New Jersey. Article X stated, "That liberty of Conscience in matters of faith and Worship toward God shall be granted to all people within the Province aforesaid who shall live peaceably and quietly therein, and that none of the Free people of the said Province shall be rendered incapable of Office in respect of their faith and Worship." http://www.state.nj.us/njfacts/njdoc8a.htm.

7. Peter O. Wacker, *Land and People: A Cultural Geography of Preindustrial New Jersey* (New Brunswick, NJ: Rutgers University Press, 1975), 174–89. On the religious life of West Jersey, see John Fea, "Rural Religion: Protestant Community and the Moral Improvement of the South Jersey Countryside, 1676–1800" (PhD diss., State University of New York at Stony Brook, 1999).

8. On the development of West Jersey, see John E. Pomfret, *The Province of West Jersey, 1609–1702: A History of the Origins of an American Colony* (Princeton, NJ: Princeton University Press, 1956). On the *Concessions and Agreements*, see *The West Jersey Concessions and Agreements of 1676/77.*

9. William Penn, *One Project for the Good of England* (1679) in *The Select Works of William Penn in Three Volumes* (London: William Phillips and George Yard, 1825; reprint, New York: Kraus Reprint, 1971), 1:189–90; Penn, *The Great Case of Liberty of Conscience* (1670), in *William Penn on Religion and Ethics: The Emergence of Liberal Quakerism*, ed. Hugh S. Barbour (Lewiston, ME: Edward Mellen Press, 1991), 429, 430, 432; Mary Maples Dunn, *William Penn: Politics and Conscience* (Princeton, NJ: Princeton University Press, 1967), 63; J. William Frost, *A Perfect Freedom: Religious Liberty in Pennsylvania* (New York: Cambridge University Press, 1990).

10. "Acts and Proceedings of the Legislature of West Jersey, 1681–1701," in *The Grants, Concessions and Original Constitutions of the Province of New Jersey*, by Aaron Leaming and Jacob Spicer (Philadelphia: William Bradford, 1758), 549. This was a classic formulation of Quaker doctrine. See Thomas Evans, *An Exposition of the Faith of the Religious Society of Friends* (Manchester: William Irwin, 1867), 70.

11. In a 1659 work, *A Mite of Affection*, Byllynge upheld an expansive view of religious liberty that extended simply to "all persons . . . professing faith in Christ Jesus." The fact that he did not constrict religious liberty to Protestants suggests that he was probably the primary author of the West Jersey *Concessions and Agreements.* Byllynge, *A Mite of Affection* (1659), in *Early Quaker Writings, 1650–1700*, ed. Hugh Barbour and Arthur O. Roberts (Grand Rapids, MI: Eerdmans, 1973), 411. On the difference between Penn and Byllynge on this point, see Caroline Robbins, "Laws and Governments Proposed for West New Jersey and Pennsylvania, 1676–1683," *Pennsylvania Magazine of History and Biography* 105, no. 4 (1981): 387.

12. Penn, *One Project for the Good of England*, in *Select Works*, 192–94; Dunn, *William Penn*, 66–67.

13. Penn, *Address to Protestants*, in *William Penn on Religion and Ethics*, ed. Barbour, 457–58, 463.

14. The committee included Rev. Jacob Green (Presbyterian), Elijah Hughes (Baptist), John Symmes (Presbyterian), Samuel Dick (Presbyterian), Theophilus Elmer (Presbyterian), Lewis Ogden (Presbyterian), Jonathan Sergeant (Presbyterian), John Cooper (probably Quaker), Silas Condict (Presbyterian), and John Covenhoven

(Dutch Reformed). See *Journal of the Votes and Proceedings of Convention of New Jersey*, 35.

15. See, for example, Nathan O. Hatch, *The Sacred Cause of Liberty: Republican Thought and the Millennium in Revolutionary New England* (New Haven, CT: Yale University Press, 1977).

16. Cited in Oscar Reiss, *The Jews in Colonial America* (Jefferson, NC: McFarland, 2004), 35. It is unclear how long this law stayed on the books or how it was enforced.

17. Nelson R. Burr, *The Anglican Church in New Jersey* (Philadelphia: Church Historical Society, 1954), 335–72.

18. John Witherspoon, "Thanksgiving Sermon, 1782," quoted in *John Witherspoon and the Founding of the American Republic*, by Jeffry H. Morrison (Notre Dame, IN: University of Notre Dame Press, 2005), 29; Gideon Mailer, *John Witherspoon's American Revolution* (Chapel Hill: University of North Carolina Press, 2017), 407–8; Rohrer, *Jacob Green's Revolution*, 108; Robert L. Maddex, *State Constitutions of the United States*, 2nd ed. (Washington, DC: Congressional Quarterly, 2006), 271.

19. For example, the 1776 Pennsylvania Constitution required officeholders to "believe in one God, the creator and governor of the universe, the rewarder of the good and the punisher of the wicked" and "acknowledge the Scriptures of the Old and New Testaments. See "Constitution of Pennsylvania, September 28, 1776," http://avalon.law.yale.edu/18th_century/pa08.asp.

20. *Proceedings of the New Jersey State Constitutional Convention of 1844* (Trenton: New Jersey State House Commission, 1942), 614.

21. John Bebout, introduction to *Proceedings of the New Jersey State Constitutional Convention of 1844* (Trenton: New Jersey State House Commission, 1942), xliii.

22. On the Bible riots, see Amanda Beyer-Purvis, "The Philadelphia Bible Riots of 1844: Contest over the Rights of Citizens," *Pennsylvania History: A Journal of Mid-Atlantic Studies* 83, no. 3 (2016): 366–93.

CHAPTER THREE

DELAWARE
Religious Borderland

Evan Haefeli

D<small>ELAWARE'S</small> <small>CONSISTENT</small> <small>SUPPORT</small> for religious disestablishment is well known, but its origins and character are less so. Scholars assume Delaware's rejection of religious establishment was a legacy of its connection to Pennsylvania, which lasted from 1682 until 1776, when Delaware's first Constitution declared independence from the Penn family proprietorship as well as Britain. A second Constitution in 1792 maintained the earlier disestablishmentarian positions while also prohibiting clergy holding political office. These policies continued with slight modifications through the Constitution of 1831 into Delaware's current Constitution, the fourth, adopted in 1897.[1]

Despite superficial similarities to Pennsylvania, Delaware's relationship to religious pluralism was very different. In colonial Pennsylvania, the lack of an establishment strengthened Quaker hegemony. In Delaware disestablishment served to maintain a balance between several competing forms of Christianity. On the eve of the American Revolution, the colony included a slight Anglican majority, followed by a sizable Presbyterian community, a significant minority of Quakers, with much smaller numbers of Baptists and Lutherans, as well as a few Catholics. Many of these religious societies favored government support for religion, but none wanted a formal establishment that could privilege one group over the others. This logic continued to support disestablishment even as the revolution saw the denominational percentages change dramatically, with the growth of Baptists, the emergence of Methodism, and the decline of Anglicanism.

Delaware's stance on church-state relations reflects the confluence of a conservative but divided Protestant society of diverse national origin, one vulnerable to external influences from neighboring colonies or overseas. A reluctant supporter of the revolution, Delaware had a sizable Tory contingent, a number of whom became active loyalists. After the war, its conservatism, along with its weak position between larger states, combined to make Delaware the first state to ratify the U.S. Constitution, in December 1787. Small, poor, and rural, it remained a majority Federalist state until the end of the War of 1812, notwithstanding growing support for the party of Thomas Jefferson. These factors account for the moderate tone of its disestablishment, which supported moral legislation and insisted on the importance of public religious observance, even as it defended religious freedom.[2]

I.

Early Delaware was more of a borderland than a coherent society. Indeed, until it declared independence in 1776 as "the Delaware State," it was little more than the undigested consequence of five colonial enterprises stemming from three different countries. Originally part of the territory of the Lenape people (or Delaware Indians), in 1638 it was incorporated into a Swedish colony that claimed the Delaware Valley. In 1655 a Dutch conquest split New Sweden into two colonies divided by the Christina River in northern Delaware. To the north was New Netherland. The south became a colony of the City of Amsterdam: New Amstel. With the 1664 conquest by James, Duke of York, Delaware became part of New York. In 1682 the three counties that constituted Delaware (New Castle, Kent, and Sussex) were assigned to William Penn as an adjunct to his recent grant of Pennsylvania. Since few in the three counties were Quakers, they resisted their position as an appendage to Quaker-dominated Pennsylvania. The three counties gained legislative independence in 1704. Still, the "counties . . . upon Delaware" continued to share a proprietor and governor with Pennsylvania and, as their inhabitants acknowledged, interests in common with Pennsylvania, given how they were "Scituate by Nature." This geographic and political affinity was summarized by their common designation as Pennsylvania's "Lower Counties." Meanwhile, Maryland maintained territorial claims in Delaware until the Mason-Dixon Line fixed the border in the 1760s.[3]

The idea that Delawareans never had an established church is misleading. During the seventeenth century the colony was included in several different establishments. First was the Swedish Lutheran Church. Under the Dutch, the Reformed Church had pride of place. Between 1673 and 1682, New York's peculiar system of local multiestablishments gave both churches equal standing. On the other hand, New Amstel had been premised on religious disestablishment.[4]

Attachment to Pennsylvania thus represented a significant change in policy toward religion. William Penn's 1701 Charter of Liberties set the terms for coexistence until 1776, and its premises continued to shape Delaware's religious policy into the nineteenth century. The Charter affirmed freedom of conscience "as to their Religious Profession and Worship" and declared that no one "who shall confess and acknowledge One almighty God . . . and professes him or themselves obliged to live quietly under the Civil Government, shall be in any Case molested or prejudiced . . . because of their consciencious Persuasion or Practice." Nor would the inhabitants "be compelled to frequent or maintain any religious Worship, Place or Ministry, contrary to his or their Mind, or to do or suffer any other Act or Thing, contrary to their religious Persuasion." Meanwhile, public office "in any Capacity, both legislatively and executively," was open to "all Persons who . . . profess to believe in Jesus Christ, the Saviour of the World . . . notwithstanding their other Persuasions and Practices in Point of Conscience and Religion." The Quaker influence meant that the use of affirmations as well as oaths in court and other important political occasions, controversial in other parts of the British Empire, was common in Delaware. Although few of the original colonists had endorsed religious liberty on principle, by the eighteenth century they were familiar with the idea, as the local printing of John Locke's *Letter Concerning Toleration* in 1764 testifies.[5]

In the eighteenth century, the rise of slavery, together with growing immigration from Europe, Africa, and neighboring colonies, reconfigured Delaware's social and religious complexion. The descendants of the original Swedish and Dutch colonists became distinct minorities as English people (mostly migrants from neighboring colonies) became the majority. The Quaker minority (including, between about 1765 and 1800, a small, severe, splinter group known as Nicholites) mostly arrived from Pennsylvania. From Maryland came the Anglicans (the majority religion of the English) and a handful of Roman Catholics. From overseas came a sizable number of Irish, almost all of them Ulster Presbyterians, together with smaller numbers of Welsh, Huguenots, and Germans (who tended to be Baptist, Presbyterian, and Lutheran, respectively). The non-Christian community also changed as Native Americans moved out and African Americans (free and slave) moved in, making up about a fifth of the revolutionary-era population. Few of these African Americans were Christian before Methodists arrived in 1769 seeking converts. If they belonged to a church, it was usually Anglican. Finally, while an occasional Jewish individual resided in Delaware between 1671 and the 1850s, it was not until the 1870s that a community able to organize a congregation existed. In the meantime, Delaware's Christians professed the casual anti-Semitism common across the Anglo-American world.[6]

Disestablishment facilitated coexistence in this increasingly pluralistic environment, but few Delawareans objected in principal to the benefits of establishment. Instead, various colonial laws strengthened the position of "religious societies of Protestants within this government," as a 1744 Act characterized them. The act was designed to protect the property of religious societies, which before 1774 could be held only in the name of an individual. That had worked fine until the combined advent of the Great Awakening and the arrival of Jesuit missionaries from Maryland. Some of those property holders joined "other religious societies, of a different persuasion from the people by whome the said persons were at first intrusted," and tried to take the church property to their new church. The 1744 Act responded by allowing trustees to hold and manage the property on behalf of the church. The practice continued into the nineteenth century, along with ancillary legal privileges and tax exemptions. When glebes were later lost (as some were), it was due to mismanagement by trustees, not expropriation by the revolutionary government.[7]

Delaware's colonial laws supported Christian social and moral priorities. A Sabbatarian Act fought "to prevent the breach of the Lord's Day, commonly called Sunday," and no public business was carried out on Sundays. Another law defended "against drunkenness, and to prevent the grievous sins of prophane cursing, swearing and blasphemy." Several acts regulated sexuality, including one "against adultery and fornication," and another punishing "bestiality, incest and bigamy." Reinforcing the state's role in sanctioning proper sexual relationships, an "Act for preventing clandestine marriages" required weddings to be performed by a magistrate. Finally, the anti-Catholic culture of the British Empire was affirmed by requiring magistrates and voters to not only be Christian but also renounce papal authority and the doctrine of transubstantiation while affirming "that the invocation or adoration of the Virgin Mary, or any other saint, and the sacrifice of the Mass, as they are now used in the Church of Rome, are superstitions and idolatrous."[8]

This moral, Protestant, disestablishmentarian tradition rested on strong support from the laity. The legislation was drafted and enforced by local magistrates like Thomas Collins (1732–89), who also played a leading role in their congregations. An Anglican high sheriff of colonial Kent, Collins became a revolutionary militia commander, judge, and politician. An Episcopalian minister eulogized Collins for living "without pride" and dying "with composure and resignation, beloved, lamented and regretted by all honest men." While Collins had favored Anglicans when building his parish

church, his benevolence was ecumenical: "[T]he catholicism of his sentiments embraced all mankind in the affectionate circle of charity and frater-
nal regard. Though his salary as commander in chief, was not considerable,
yet he resigned the emoluments arising from marriage and tavern licenses
(being a part of that salary) . . . to the use of the state, to be applied to such
public and benevolent purposes as the legislature should think proper." Since
early Delaware's unhealthy environment and marginal situation meant that
clergy and ecclesiastical institutions were fairly thin on the ground, lay officials like Collins bore the primary responsibility for Delaware's religious
arrangements.[9]

II.

The American Revolution altered, but did not fundamentally change, this
soft establishment. Delaware's Constitution of 1776 guaranteed religious and
political rights to all Christians, but not all forms of Christianity benefited
equally. The revolutionary Constitution mandated that "no clergyman or
preacher of the gospel, of any denomination," could hold public office. In
the short term, ending the overt exclusion of Roman Catholics was the most
momentous change. Public office was restricted to those who "profess faith
in God the Father, and in Jesus Christ His only Son, and in the Holy Ghost,
one God, blessed for evermore" and "acknowledge the holy scriptures of the
Old and New Testaments to be given by divine inspiration." While a few
individuals entertained beliefs of a Unitarian or Deist bent, to be portrayed
as a Deist remained politically dangerous. In 1801 Federalist candidate Nathaniel Mitchell was denounced as anti-Methodist, "a professed Deist, an
open scoffer at, and riviler of the Christian religion." Alternative religions
would not begin to organize until 1815, when Swedenborgians established a
congregation in Wilmington.[10]

In an 1813 letter to John Adams explaining the course of the revolution
in Delaware, Thomas McKean, one of the state's prominent leaders, emphasized the role of religious and ethnic diversity from county to county. In
"Newcastle three fifths were at the time of the revolution Presbyterians, in
Kent, about five eighths Protestant Episcopalians, and in Sussex, two thirds
of the latter." Anglican ministers opposed independence, warning that it
"was a plan of the Presbyterians to get their religion established; that [the
revolutionary fervor] originated in New England, and was fostered by the
Presbyterians in every colony or province." In the end, "the most sensible of
the Episcopalians, [along with] the Baptists and Quakers, and the Presbyterians, with very few exceptions, prevailed against" the "majority" to support

independence. This move owed less to enthusiasm for the revolution than to a fear that "they would be overpowered, with the help of the other colonies, if they resisted."[11] Tepid patriots, indeed.

McKean understood the power of religious associations. His support for the revolutionary cause mirrored that of his fellow Presbyterians throughout the mid-Atlantic. Born and raised in Chester County, Pennsylvania, McKean's Presbyterian and Scotch-Irish connections had given him an entry into New Castle County, facilitating his successful legal and political career before the revolution. New Castle County's main port, the Town of New Castle, was the capital of the county, colony, and later state until 1777. The influence of its Presbyterian community dated back to its first Dutch Reformed colonists. In 1706 their descendants had joined the Philadelphia Presbytery, along with English and Scots-Reformed Protestants. In 1717 New Castle became the seat of its own presbytery, which covered Delaware and parts west. Over the next six decades, the number of Presbyterians increased dramatically with the immigration of thousands of people from Ulster.[12]

The seat of most of Delaware's early colonial history, New Castle County also had the most diverse population and developed economy. In 1689 Anglicans made New Castle their first parish in Delaware, with the help of clergy from Maryland. In turn, Jesuits from Maryland launched a mission to the county in the mid-eighteenth century and acquired a plantation in 1772 to support it. In the northern part of the county, Quakers from Pennsylvania prospered. They organized their first meeting of Friends at Newark around 1682. In the 1730s, Quakers developed mills along the Brandywine River, then established the town of Wilmington next to the small community descended from seventeenth-century Swedish Lutheran colonists. Later, a small iron industry attracted Welsh immigrants, mostly Baptists. Other Welsh people lived throughout the region and practiced as Quakers, Anglicans, and Presbyterians.[13]

The counties of Kent and Sussex, by contrast, were less diverse, more rural, more English, and more African American. Delaware's most famous revolutionary leader, Caesar Rodney, came from the Anglican gentry of this region. Here, the small to middling farms typical of the oldest corners of the state transitioned into larger plantations. Religiously, Anglican predominance was symbolized by the prominent location of an Anglican church at the center of each of the region's main towns: Dover, Lewes, and Georgetown. Presbyterians, Quakers, and Baptists existed as distinct minorities. After the British invasion of the Delaware Valley in 1777–78 rendered New Castle unsafe, Dover, county seat of Kent, became the state capital. The little port of Lewes governed Sussex, the most rural and Anglican part of the state, until 1791. When the county capital was moved inland to the new town of Georgetown, the Episcopalian church soon followed. Lewes's Presbyterians and Quakers did not.[14]

These southern counties became the seedbed for Methodism, whose explosive growth was one of many religious changes that followed the British army's withdrawal from Philadelphia in the spring of 1778. That June, in a newly radicalized political climate, the legislature passed an act requiring suspected loyalists to "solemnly swear (or affirm as the case may be)" their loyalty to the state's revolutionary government and yield "any allegiance or obedience to the King of Great Britain." Those who could not do so—mostly Anglicans and neutral Quakers—could neither vote, hold office, nor serve on a jury. The act was repealed in 1788, and former Loyalists did not regain full political rights until 1790.[15]

Methodist preachers helped fill the spiritual gap that opened after Anglican ministers, regarding the ban on praying for the king as persecution, shut down their worship services. Although Methodists were discouraged by their leaders from being politically active, they did not wholly abstain from politics. A number were Patriots. Their great leader, Francis Asbury, was not unsympathetic to the Patriot cause. One early Methodist convert, Richard Bassett of Kent, became a conservative revolutionary, then state assemblyman, delegate to the Federal constitutional convention, judge, U.S. senator, and governor of Delaware. Like most Delaware Methodists after the war, Bassett was a Federalist. Still, since Methodists were technically members of "societies" within the Church of England until they formed their own denomination in 1784, and since most of Delaware's militant Loyalists were Anglicans, Patriots viewed Methodists with suspicion. Asbury spent two years (February 1778–April 1780) laying low in Kent Country on the plantation of a Tory Methodist. It was there that he formulated the plan that made Methodism America's fastest-growing church. By the early nineteenth century, Methodism had become the largest single denomination of Delawareans, including among African Americans, whether free or slave. Some of these converts later became pioneers in forming separate African American Methodist churches.[16]

The alterations in the religious landscape made it harder than ever for a single denomination to dominate Delaware. Before the revolution, the Church of England had been strong enough to attract converts, especially from Presbyterianism. However, loyalty to the Crown and Methodism left it weakened at war's end. It rebounded slightly after the formation of the

Episcopal Church of America in 1789, but mainly because Swedish Lutherans, whose church was in decline, joined the Anglicans. Baptists, on the other hand, expanded, notwithstanding that their leading minister, Morgan Edwards, was the "only Baptist minister in America who was a Loyalist during the Revolution." Of Welsh origin, he had preached in Ireland, England, and Philadelphia before taking up his final post at the Welsh Baptist community near Newark. Edwards kept a low profile during the war but encouraged the work of missionaries in other states. In 1778 Baptists began to push their numbers to a peak reached in the 1790s. Meanwhile, Presbyterian and Quaker numbers held firm.[17]

III.

Against this backdrop of religious change, a conservative but enlightened set of Protestant interests informed Delaware's policies. For example, in June 1779 the general assembly made a point of repealing the Jacobean statute that had made witchcraft a crime since the early seventeenth century. Included within an "Act for the better proportioning the punishment to the crime of slave and horse-stealing, and conjuration," witchcraft was termed an "imposture" that imposed "on the folly and credulity of weak and ignorant people." In 1786 an "act for the suppression of idleness, vice, and immorality" fined those who organized and sold liquors to assemblies gathered "under the various pretences of horse-racing, foot-racing, cock-fighting, shooting matches." The following year, a new law allowed the trustees in charge of religious property to incorporate, as multiple petitions from "from sundry religious societies or congregations" had requested.[18]

These laws represented a fusion of mostly Presbyterian and Anglican interests, something epitomized by the career of the revolutionary leader George Read. The son of an Anglo-Irish immigrant who had become a planter in Maryland before moving to New Castle County, Read, like McKean, had been educated across the Pennsylvania border at Francis Alison's Presbyterian Academy in New London. Like McKean, Read then launched a successful legal and political career in New Castle, rising to become attorney general for the Lower Counties. When the revolution came, Read served as a delegate to the First and Second Continental Congresses, president of the convention that adopted Delaware's 1776 Constitution, a leading member of its assembly, a judge, a delegate to the 1787 Constitutional Convention in Philadelphia, and one of the state's first U.S. senators. Religiously, Read supported the Presbyterian Church even as he increasingly attended the

Anglican church. He married the daughter of New Castle's Anglican rector and was ultimately buried in its Episcopal churchyard in 1798.[19]

A political moderate like his more famous friend John Dickinson, Read favored some state support for Christianity. In 1786 he drew up a "plan for education" reminiscent of Patrick Henry's plan for Virginia to levy a general assessment to help maintain the pay of clergymen. The details of the failed plan do not survive, but Dickinson's thoughtful response does. It suggests both why it failed and the depth of elite interest in state support for religion. Dickinson noted that the plan "carries with it the idea of levying contributions *for the maintenance of ministers of the gospel* upon all persons but such as shall disclaim the general religion of the country." Dickinson, from a Quaker background, reminded Read of the "great numbers of Christians who regard the levying of such contributions to be utterly unjust and oppressive" and charged Read with acting "hastily, perhaps erroneously." At the same time, Dickinson agreed that "it is the duty of government . . . to promote and enforce the sublime and beneficial morality, as well as theology, of Christianity; and, considering them as connected with government, how can this be done better than by employing men of wisdom, piety, and learning to teach it?" Those teachers need to be "properly supported." Who better to do that than "the government that employs them? Let impositions be laid for this purpose. If any man conscientiously scruples their lawfulness, let him be permitted to appropriate his share to the use of the poor, or any other public services." Such a compromise, thought Dickinson, could allow government to "strenuously carry on the grand work of teaching virtue and religion, without offering the least violence to the conscience of any individual," a "sacred right" that governments neglected at their peril.[20]

The Quaker concerns raised by Dickinson could not be ignored, even though Quaker ambivalence about the revolution effectively kept them out of state politics until 1788. Their pacifist principles led them to stay neutral during the war, exposing them to persecution and crises of conscience over issues like accepting Continental currency. Still, they remained influential. For example, the wealthy Quaker landowner Warner Mifflin of Kent County was successfully advocating for the gradual abolition of slavery. So, when Quakers from Delaware, New Jersey, Pennsylvania, Maryland, and Virginia publicly addressed President George Washington on their hopes for both moral government and religious freedom in 1789, he listened. The Quakers urged Washington to "be an happy instrument . . . for the suppression of vice, infidelity and irreligion, and every species of oppression on the persons and consciences of men, so that righteousness and peace, which truly exalt a nation, may prevail throughout the land." At the same time, they reminded Washington that they considered "free toleration . . . in the public worship of the Almighty, agreeable to the dictates of their consciences," as "among the choicest of blessings," even when their consciences dictated that "we can take no part in carrying on war on any occasion, or under any power." The president agreed to accommodate the Quakers, but only as far "as a due regard to the protection and essential interests of the nation may justify and permit."[21]

The Quaker insistence on the necessity of both religion and religious toleration reflected the consensus of revolutionary Delaware. A 1786 plan for the Wilmington Academy (chartered by Thomas Penn in 1773) offers another articulation of these ecumenical priorities. The Wilmington Academy aimed "to promote the important cause of Religion, Morality and Literature." Consequently, it "strictly obliged" its teachers and students "to attend every Sunday at the places of public Worship to which they severally belong." Failure to do so would be punished "as severely" as absence "from academical duties."[22]

If anything, independence strengthened Delaware's support for institutionalized religion, evident in the growing support for clerical authority. The change was clearest in the revised marriage laws. Petitioners complained that "every common Magistrate learned or unlearn'd, religious or profane" was allowed "to buckle any sorts, in any Manner together." This practice was deemed "absurd in a Christian Country." Now that there were sufficient clergy available, it was fitting to restrict the authority to marry to "a minister or a religious society." The new act, passed in 1788, did not go so far, but it allowed religious leaders as well as magistrates to perform marriages. More complaints, spearheaded by an alliance of Presbyterian, Episcopalian, and Lutheran clergymen, led to a second act in 1790. It described "matrimony" as "an honorable institution of Almighty God, designed for the mutual convenience and happiness of mankind" and transferred the onus of responsibility for compliance with the law onto the would-be couples. They, not the clergymen, had to secure a license from the state and ensure that banns were published for two weeks before the wedding.[23]

With one important exception, the new state Constitution of 1792 continued support for institutional religion. Affirming that "Divine Good" gave to all "by nature, the rights of worshipping and serving their Creator according to the dictates of their consciences," the Constitution insisted, in Article I, Section 1, that, "it is the duty of all men frequently to assemble together for the public worship of the Author of the Universe; and piety and morality, on which the prosperity of communities depends, are thereby promoted." The Constitution also continued the colonial tradition of forbidding that anyone

> shall or ought to be compelled to attend any religious worship, to contribute to the erection or support of any place of worship, or to the maintenance of any ministry, against his own free will and consent; and no power shall or ought to be vested in or assumed by any magistrate, that shall in any case interfere with, or in any manner control the rights of conscience, in the free exercise of religious worship, nor a preference given by law to any religious societies, denominations, or modes of worship.

For a variety of reasons, however, including the anti-Trinitarian and anti-Calvinist leanings of some influential individual elites, this Constitution also rejected religious tests for office. The 1776 Constitution's requirement that officeholders recognize the Old and New Testaments as products of divine inspiration was omitted.[24]

In this light, continuing the ban on clergy serving in the legislature may have reflected a desire to preserve the tradition of magisterial influence over religious affairs. The prohibition was tested only once, when John Conklin Brush won election to the House of Representatives in 1800. Ordained a minister in the Dutch Reformed Church, Brush had been the pastor to two congregations in New York before accepting a call to Dover's Presbyterian congregation in 1796. However, between leaving his prior post and having his new appointment confirmed, Brush became a Unitarian and terminated his pastoral services to the Presbyterian Church. Uncertainties about exactly what had happened allowed his Federalist opponents to expel Brush from the legislature. After proving he was no longer serving in a "pastoral [role] or [performing] clerical functions," Brush was permitted to claim his seat.[25]

Keeping clergy out of government by no means made Delaware antireligious. In 1795 the legislature intervened on behalf of Christian priorities by replacing the colonial Sabbatarian law with a new "act more effectually to prevent the profanation of the Lord's day, commonly called Sunday." Claiming the colonial act's penalties "have been found insufficient to deter many persons from such immorality," the new legislation prescribed fines and even imprisonment for up to twenty-four hours for anyone who "shall do or perform any worldly employment, labour, or business whatsoever, upon the Lord's day." Evidently, legislators were unsettled by the uptick in commercial activity accompanying the region's economic development. They singled out any "carrier, pedlar, waggoner, or any driver of a travelling stage-waggon or coachee, carter, butcher, or drover, with his horse, pack, wagon" who "shall travel or drive upon the Lord's day." Their fine was twice that of other Sabbath breakers, including those caught "fishing, fowling, horse-racing, cockfighting or hunting of game." Moreover, they could "be stopped and detained . . . until the succeeding day" or imprisoned for up to two days.[26]

Nevertheless, a growing number of elites, like John Conklin Brush, Thomas Rodney (Caesar's younger brother), and Thomas's son Caesar Augustus Rodney, admired the Unitarian and philosophical stances on religion associated with Thomas Jefferson. Thomas Rodney had been a colonial judge and magistrate before becoming a revolutionary militia officer, politician, and Federal judge to Mississippi Territory (appointed by President Jefferson), where he ended his days in 1811. Before moving west, however, Rodney wrote of his belief that the American Revolution had "broken off all of those devious Tramels of Ignorance, prejudice and Superstition which have long depressed the Human Mind. Every door is now Open to the sons of genius and Science to enquire after Truth. Hence we may expect the darkening clouds of error will vanish fast before the light of reason; and that the period is fast arriving when the Truth will enlighten the whole world." His son had similar views. After graduating from the University of Pennsylvania in 1789, Caesar Augustus Rodney parlayed a law career into a leading role in the state's Democratic-Republican Party, rising to become a U.S. senator before President Jefferson appointed him attorney general in 1807 (he died in 1824 while serving as President Monroe's ambassador to Argentina). In 1801 Caesar Augustus Rodney described Jefferson's victory over the Federalists as replacing "a system of espionage & persecution" with "one of impartiality & equal justice; in the place of political proscription & intolerance, a manly liberality as to opinions & a due participation in office." He then professed, "I love moderation & every prudent conciliatory measure which can be adopted consistent with the principle."[27]

Religious reformers leavened but did not derail the largely conservative attitudes shaping nineteenth-century Delaware's religious policy. Regarding education, for example, the colonial system was largely preserved. Schools continued to be run by religious leaders or pious individuals, like the French Protestant immigrant Eleuthère Irénée du Pont, who established Delaware's first Sunday School in 1817. Accordingly, schools played their part in the religious competition that continued after disestablishment. For example, the Wilmington Academy, where a Lutheran pastor and Anglican minister worked together in harmony, was intended as an alternative to Wilmington's

Friends Academy, one of several Quaker academies in the state. Among the
Presbyterian academies, Francis Alison's school (where McKean and Read
had studied) was so important that it became the seed for the future University of Delaware. Moving from Pennsylvania to Newark in 1769, the school
received a charter from the proprietor, Thomas Penn, as the Academy of
Newark. This conservative (Old Side) Presbyterian institution offered an alternative to the evangelical Presbyterian College of New Jersey (Princeton).
In the 1830s, it became Newark College. Presbyterian influence over the
school remained until challenged in 1843. The legislature was unimpressed.
It determined "that religion was not a test for employment on the faculty
or for admission as a student . . . [but] that almost all colleges had religious
leadership of some sort." As ever, Delaware preferred to maintain a balance
between its different denominations rather than foment an open confrontation between the religious and secular spheres.[28]

IV.

Judged by the letter of its 1776 and 1792 Constitutions, Delaware appears
to belong with those states strongly opposed to religious establishment. On
closer inspection, it emerges as a largely rural and conservative society that
favored a soft Protestant establishment. Although a few individuals came
to favor the enlightened views of men like Thomas Jefferson, revolutionary
Delaware's disestablishment was not the fruit of a principle-driven movement. Instead, the state largely continued the colonial arrangement that had
so effectively balanced the religious diversity inherited from a complex history of multiple colonizations, conquests, and waves of immigration (forced
and free).

Delaware's support for radical disestablishment attitudes was superficial.
What this religiously diverse state objected to was not state support for religion so much as the privileging of one religious faction over the others.
Into the nineteenth century, the colonial Quaker legacy of a minimalist
religious establishment proved an effective means of appeasing the dominant Presbyterian and Anglican factions without disadvantaging the smaller
Protestant denominations or fully preventing the state from having a role in
religious life. Nevertheless, Delawareans repeatedly denied non-Christians
and even some Christians full religious freedom. At various points before,
during, or even after the revolution, Catholics, Quakers, Anglicans, Methodists, and Unitarians each suffered some religious burdens. Dominated
by a small circle of magistrates who were mostly affiliated with either the

Anglican or Presbyterian Church, Delaware was ever wary of the political and theological threat of dissent. Disestablishment in Delaware was not so much an ideal as an ongoing negotiated truce among religious groups in a provincial borderland.

NOTES

1. Winston L. Frost, "Colonial Delaware: An Exemplar of Early American Attitudes about Religion and Government," *Trinity Law Review* 9, no. 1 (1999): 1–31.

2. The best history of Delaware in the revolutionary and early national periods is John A. Munroe, *Federalist Delaware, 1775–1815* (New Brunswick, NJ: Rutgers University Press, 1954).

3. "To the Honourable William Keith, Esq.; with the royal approbation lieut. Governour of the counties of New-Castle, Kent and Sussex upon Delaware, and the province of Pennsylvania: The humble address of the said counties in General Assembly met at New-Castle the 13th day of June, anno, Domini, 1717," (Philadelphia?, 1717), 1, 3; John A. Munroe, *Colonial Delaware: A History* (Millwood, NY: KTO Press, 1978), chaps. 1–5. Among the issues pitting the two parts of Penn's proprietary against each other was military defense. Colony-wide militias were created for the duration of the Seven Years' War and the American Revolution, and a state militia established in 1793 by laws that did not make exceptions for Quakers or other conscientious objectors, only (in the case of the 1793 Act), several professions, among them "ministers of religion of every denomination, professors and teachers in colleges, academies, Latin schools, and schoolmasters." *Laws of the State of Delaware, from the fourteenth Day of October, One Thousand Seven Hundred, to the Eighteenth Day of August, One Thousand Seven Hundred and Ninety-Seven* 2 vols. (New Castle, 1797), 2 vols., 1:174–76, 349, 2:1134–47, quote on 1135.

4. Evan Haefeli, *New Netherland and the Dutch Origins of American Religious Liberty* (Philadelphia: University of Pennsylvania Press, 2012), esp. chap. 9; Haefeli, "The Pennsylvania Difference: Religious Diversity on the Delaware before 1683," *Early American Studies* 1, no. 1 (2003): 28–60; Haefeli, "Diversity on the Delaware from New Sweden to Pennsylvania: Connections and Contrasts," *De Haelve Maen* 85, no. 1 (2012): 13–16.

5. Francis Newton Thorpe, ed. *The Federal and State Constitutions, Colonial Charters, and other Organic Laws of the United States of America*, 7 vols. (Washington, DC: Government Printing Office, 1909), 1:558; John Locke, *Letter Concerning Toleration* (Wilmington, DE: James Adams, 1764). On affirmations, see *Laws of the State of Delaware, from the fourteenth Day of October, One Thousand Seven Hundred, to the Eighteenth Day of August, One Thousand Seven Hundred and Ninety-Seven*, 2 vols. (New Castle, 1797), 1:77, 149, 150, 155–56 and passim and 543 for a March 1775 "Act for the easing scrupulous consciences, in the mode of taking an oath" that allowed

people to not use the Bible while still swearing "by the ever living God, the searcher of all hearts."

6. Munroe, *Colonial Delaware*, chaps. 7–8; Patience Essah, *A House Divided: Slavery and Emancipation in Delaware, 1638–1865* (Charlottesville, VA: University Press of Virginia, 1996); Kenneth L. Carroll, "Joseph Nichols, of Delaware: An Eighteenth Century Religious Leader," *Delaware History* 7, no. 1 (1956): 37–48, points out that Nicholites were antislavery from the beginning and included a handful of black people as members. African American population figures in William Henry Williams, *Slavery and Freedom in Delaware, 1639–1865* (Wilmington, DE: SR Books, 1996), 16–17; M. David Geffen, "Delaware Jewry: The Formative Years, 1872–1889," *Delaware History* 16, no. 4 (1975): 269–74; Toni Young, *Becoming American, Remaining Jewish: The Story of Wilmington, Delaware's First Jewish Community, 1879–1924* (Newark: University of Delaware Press, 1999), chap. 1. For an anti-Semitic "Anecdote" about converting British Jews, see *Delaware Gazette*, September 5, 1789.

7. Gerard V. Bradley, *Church-State Relationships in America* (New York: Greenwood Press, 1987), 49–50; *Laws of the State of Delaware, from the fourteenth Day of October*, 1:271–74 and 516–22 for Anglican trustees being granted rights to land in New Castle and the trustees of Newark Academy the profit of rents on local market stalls, both in 1772. For Episcopalian trustee efforts to collect rents, see *Delaware Gazette*, March 19, 21, 28, and April 4, 1789. On Presbyterian glebes, see Rev. George Foot, *An Address embracing the early History of Delaware, and the settlement of its boundaries, and of the Drawyers Congregation, with all the churches since organized on its original Territory* (Philadelphia, 1842), 46, 49. For a Lutheran case, see Jeannette Eckman, *Crane Hook on the Delaware, 1667–1699: An Early Swedish Lutheran Church and Community* (Newark: Institute of Delaware History and Culture, 1958), 98–104. Rev. Paul J. Schierse, "Laws of the State of Delaware Affecting Church Property" (PhD diss., Catholic University of America, 1963), examines the Catholic experience.

8. *Laws of the State of Delaware, from the fourteenth Day of October*, 1:59, 105–09, 155–56, 173, 216, 225–26, 271–74.

9. *Delaware Gazette*, May 2, 1789. Gregory argues arrangements like Delaware's could be considered a kind of religious multiestablishment, given the support of pan-Protestant priorities. Jeremy Gregory, "'Establishment' and 'Dissent' in British North America," in *British North America in the Seventeenth and Eighteenth Centuries*, ed. Stephen Foster, supplemental volume, *Oxford History of the British Empire*, ed. William Roger Louis (Oxford: Oxford University Press, 2013), 136–69.

10. Anson Phelps Stokes, *Church and State in the United States* (New York: Harper, 1950), 1:436–37; Munroe, *Federalist Delaware*, 15–21, 170–71; *Mirror of the Times*, September 19, 26, 30, 1801. For the Swedenborgians, see Ophia D. Smith, "Daniel Lammot and His Role in the New Church in Delaware," *Delaware History* 8, no. 4 (1959): 321–42.

11. Thomas McKean to John Adams, November 15, 1813, in John Adams, *The Works of John Adams, Second President of the United States: With a Life of the Author, Notes and Illustrations*, 10 vols. (Boston, 1850–56), 10:81–82.

12. Gail Stuart Rowe, "Thomas McKean and the Coming of the Revolution," *Pennsylvania Magazine of History and Biography* 96, no. 1 (1972): 3–47; Joseph S. Tiedemann, "Presbyterianism and the American Revolution in the Middle Colonies," *Church History* 74, no. 2 (2005): 306–44.

13. Munroe, *Federalist Delaware*, 17–18, 21–24, 27–31, 47–52, 261; Liam Riordan, *Many Identities, One Nation: The Revolution and Its Legacy in the Mid-Atlantic* (Philadelphia: University of Pennsylvania Press, 2007), 16–23; Donn Devine, "Beginnings of the Catholic Church of Wilmington, Delaware," *Delaware History* 28, no. 4 (1999–2000): 323–41; Herbert Standing, "Quakers in Delaware in the Time of William Penn," *Delaware History* 20, no. 2 (1982): 123–47; Nelson R. Burr, "The Welsh Episcopalians of Colonial Pennsylvania and Delaware," *Historical Magazine of the Protestant Episcopal Church* 8, no. 2 (1939): 101–22.

14. Munroe, *Federalist Delaware*, 24–26, 93, 196–97. Caesar Rodney died in 1784. Jane Scott, *A Gentleman as Well as a Whig: Caesar Rodney and the American Revolution* (Newark: University of Delaware Press, 2000). On Presbyterians in Sussex, see Elbert Chance, "Matthew Wilson—Professor, Preacher, Patriot, Physician," *Delaware History* 10, no. 3 (1963): 271–84. A Presbyterian congregation was eventually established in Georgetown by the mid-nineteenth century.

15. *Laws of the State of Delaware, from the fourteenth Day of October,* 2:636–43, 968–69, quotes on 638; Munroe, *Federalist Delaware*, 43–58, 88.

16. Robert C. Monk, "Unity and Diversity among Eighteenth Century Colonial Anglicans and Methodists," *Historical Magazine of the Protestant Episcopal Church* 38, no. 1 (1969): 51–69, esp. 58–60; Dee Andrews, *The Methodists and Revolutionary America, 1760–1800: The Shaping of an Evangelical Culture* (Princeton, NJ: Princeton University Press, 2000), chap. 2, 103–4 for Bassett. Hancock notes most loyalists were Anglicans, while the "record of Presbyterian clergymen on behalf of the American cause is impressive." Harold B. Hancock, *The Loyalists of Revolutionary Delaware* (Newark: University of Delaware Press, 1977), 33, 90. On the growth of Delaware Methodism, see John Lednum, *A History of the Rise of Methodism in America: Containing Sketches of Methodist Itinerant Preachers, from 1736 to 1785* (Philadelphia, 1859), chaps. 7, 12, 31, 32, 34, 39, 44; and William Henry Williams, *The Garden of American Methodism: The Delmarva Peninsula, 1769–1820* (Wilmington, DE: Scholarly Resources, 1984), chaps. 2–3, esp. 46–56, 64–68, and 170–76 for their involvement in politics. On African American Methodism, see Williams, *Slavery and Freedom*, 120–29.

17. Waylen reported that Episcopal churches declined from forty before the revolution to about a dozen around 1840. Edward Waylen, *Ecclesiastical Reminiscences of the United States* (1846), 246–47; John Albin Stabb, "Why Did the Colonial Swedish Lutheran Congregations Become Episcopalian?," *Anglican and Episcopal History*, 61, no. 4 (1992): 419–31; Morgan Edwards, *Materials towards a History of Baptists in Delaware State*, ed. Horatio Gates Jones (Philadelphia, 1885), 46, 59–60; Carroll, "Joseph Nicholls," 48. For a family of Dutch and Presbyterian descent that became Anglican, see Bruce Bendler, "An English Tory and his Delaware Family: The Petersons of Delaware," *Delaware History* 31, no. 1 (2005), 31–51.

18. *Laws of the State of Delaware, from the fourteenth Day of October,* 2:667, 669, 866, 878. Delaware's temperance movement began in the 1780s and culminated in 1855 with a law prohibiting the sale of alcohol "except for mechanical, chemical, sacramental, or medicinal purposes" and punishing individuals arrested for intoxication with fines or imprisonment. It was repealed the following year. Charles H. Bohner, "Rum and Reform: Temperance in Delaware Politics," *Delaware History* 5, no. 4 (1953): 237–69, quote on 265.

19. William Thompson Read, *Life and Correspondence of George Read, a signer of the Declaration of Independence: With some notices of some of his contemporaries* (Philadelphia, 1870), 2–3, 20, 36, 40; John A. Munroe, "Read, George (1733–1798)," in *Oxford Dictionary of National Biography* (Oxford: Oxford University Press, 2004). So important was Read that he became the subject of Delaware's only real political pamphlet in these years, written by James Tilton, a disgruntled revolutionary veteran of Presbyterian background appalled by Read's conservative politics. See John A. Munroe, ed., *Timoleon's Biographical History of Dionysius, Tyrant of Delaware* (Newark: University of Delaware Press, 1958).

20. John Dickinson to George Read, April 28, 1786, in *Life and Correspondence of George Read,* 412–13; Benjamin H. Newcomb, "Dickinson, John (1732–1808)," in *Oxford Dictionary of National Biography*; Jane E. Calvert, *Quaker Constitutionalism and the Political Thought of John Dickinson* (New York: Cambridge University Press, 2009); Thomas J. Curry, *The First Freedoms: Church and State in America to the Passage of the First Amendment* (New York: Oxford University Press, 1986), 221. Curry notes that in "1787 the Delaware General Assembly declared . . . 'it their duty to countenance and encourage virtue and religion by every means in their power, and in the most expeditious manner'" (221).

21. Munroe, *Federalist Delaware,* 48–49; Gary B. Nash, *Warner Mifflin: Unflinching Quaker Abolitionist* (Philadelphia: University of Pennsylvania Press, 2017); *To the President of the United States: The Address of the Religious Society called Quakers, from their Yearly meeting for Pennsylvania, New-Jersey, Delaware, and the western parts of Virginia and Maryland* (Philadelphia, 1789) [1 page].

22. *Draught of a Plan of Education for the Wilmington Academy* (Wilmington, 1786), 1–2; E. Miriam Lewis, ed., "The Minutes of the Wilmington Academy, 1777–1802," *Delaware History* 3, no. 4 (1949): 181–226.

23. Petitions quoted in Munroe, *Federalist Delaware,* 153; *Laws of the State of Delaware, from the fourteenth Day of October,* 59, 972–77, 1127–28, quote on 972.

24. *Laws of the State of Delaware, published by Authority* (Wilmington, 1793), 3–4; Munroe, *Federalist Delaware,* 170–71. Rodney was an aspiring intellectual who drafted a "Philosopher's Creed" and a plan for a new kind of church. Neither Trinitarian nor Calvinist, it resembled High Church Anglicanism more than anything else. See Thomas Rodney, "The Philosopher's Creed," n.d., and "The Form of the Church," n.d. (1790s?), H. F. Brown Collection, Historical Society of Delaware, box 23, folder 25.

25. Thomas McKean, believing the version of this clause in the 1776 Constitution targeted Presbyterians, had unsuccessfully opposed it. Clarified in 1832 by the addition of "ordained" before "minister," the ban was not repealed until 1897. Only

Maryland and Tennessee held on to their ministerial ban longer. John A. Munroe, "A Parson in Politics: The Expulsion of John C. Brush from the Delaware General Assembly in 1801," in *The Philadelawareans, and Other Essays Relating to Delaware*, ed. John A. Munroe, 268–82 (Newark: University of Delaware Press, 2004).

26. *Laws of the State of Delaware, passed at a Session of the General Assembly, Which was begun and held at Dover, on Tuesday, the sixth day of January, and ended on Saturday, the seventh day of February, in the Year of Our Lord One thousand Seven hundred and Ninety-five* (Wilmington, 1795), 336–38; *Laws of the State of Delaware, from the fourteenth Day of October*, 216, 1209–11.

27. Julian P. Boyd et al., *The Papers of Thomas Jefferson*, 43 vols. (Princeton: Princeton University Press, 1950–), 17:547–51, 35:70, 36:218.

28. Newark College closed in 1859, then reopened after the Civil War as the land-grant College of Delaware, now the University of Delaware. John A. Munroe, "Church versus State: The Early Struggle for Control of Delaware College," in *Philadelawareans*, ed. Munroe, 233–44, quotes on 239; Beverly McAnear, "The Charter of the Academy of Newark," *Delaware History* 4, no. 2 (1950): 149–56; Raymond F. Betts, "Eleuthère Irénée du Pont and the Brandywine Sunday School," *Delaware History* 8, no. 4 (1959): 343–53. For early Delaware's education history more broadly, see Munroe, *Colonial Delaware*, 172–75; Munroe, *Federalist Delaware*, 171–77; and Walter A. Powell, *A History of Delaware* (Boston: Christopher, 1928), 383–412.

CHAPTER FOUR

CHURCH AND STATE IN RHODE ISLAND

James S. Kabala

T HE RELATIONSHIP BETWEEN church and state in colonial Rhode Island differed greatly from the close associations found in many of the British colonies in North America and especially in the other New England colonies. Roger Williams, the founder of Providence, was one of the first advocates for complete religious liberty for all.[1] The Charter granted to the colony of Rhode Island and Providence Plantations by Charles II in 1663 codified the beliefs of Williams and other early leaders such as John Clarke. The Charter declared its support for the desire of Rhode Islanders to "hold forth a livlie experiment, that a most flourishing civil state may stand and best bee maintained . . . with a full libertie in religious concernements." The Charter further stated "that noe person within the sayd colonye, at any time hereafter shall bee any wise molested, punished, disquieted, or called in question, for any differences in opinione in matters of religion . . . but that all and everye person and persons may, from tyme to tyme, and at all tymes hereafter, free-lye and fullye have and enjoy his and theire owne judgments and consciences, in matters of religious concernments."[2]

A less-noted fact about the Charter of 1663 is that the text still assumed that membership in the Church of England was the default position for all English subjects. The document was very much a charter of toleration rather than a charter of true religious liberty. The official reason given for the lively experiment was that "some of the people and inhabitants of the same colonie cannot, in theire private opinions, conforms [sic] to the publique exercise of religion, according to the litturgy, formes, and ceremonyes of the Church of England, or take or subscribe the oaths and articles made and established in that behalfe." The Charter further said that the "remote distances of those places" would allow the lively experiment to go forward without causing any "breach of the unitie and unifformitie established in this nation."[3]

I.

The founding promise of complete religious freedom was not always kept. A Jewish population was attracted to Newport by this guarantee but was often deprived of full legal equality. For example, in 1762 the prominent Jewish merchant Aaron Lopez of Newport, a native of Portugal, was denied the right to be naturalized as a citizen of Rhode Island. Lopez temporarily relocated to Massachusetts, and, despite the strong Congregational establishment and Puritan mores of that province, he was able to gain naturalized citizenship by invoking British law.[4] Some older sources claim that other Jewish residents of Newport, including Aaron Lopez's brother Moses, were able to obtain citizenship, but later research has denied the claim.[5] It appears that neither Moses Lopez nor any other person who professed the Jewish faith received Rhode Island citizenship in the colonial era. James Lucena, a man of Sephardic Jewish ethnicity, was naturalized in 1761, but, unlike the Lopezes, he did not profess the Jewish faith in his naturalization petition and agreed to take the oath of allegiance "upon the faith of a Christian."[6]

In 1790 George Washington visited Newport as president and received an address of welcome from the Jewish congregation there. Washington later wrote a reply, "The Letter to the Hebrew Congregation in Newport," that became one of the best-known documents on religious freedom in American history. Washington famously said that "toleration" had given way to respect for "inherent natural rights" and that "the Government of the United States . . . gives to bigotry no sanction, to persecution no assistance."[7] He was right to specify the federal government, for at the time Jews still did not have full legal rights in Rhode Island.

Catholics were an all but nonexistent group in colonial Rhode Island. Yet due to the pervasively anti-Catholic atmosphere of eighteenth-century British America, they also lost legal equality. This appears to have been originally done by subterfuge. A law forbidding Catholics to hold office was inserted into a 1719 digest of laws, although such a law had never been passed by the general assembly.[8] The law was, however, subsequently reaffirmed by the assembly in 1730, 1745, and 1767. The anti-Catholic test did not survive the American Revolution and was repealed in 1783.[9]

II.

Although the Rhode Island of the later colonial period had deviated from the ideal of perfect religious liberty by imposing these religious tests, it remained faithful to its principled rejection of an establishment of religion. After the revolution, Rhode Island committed itself again to complete religious liberty. In 1798 the general assembly ordered a revision of the law code and included a statute that provided broad protections for religious freedom. Most of the law was taken verbatim from the Virginia Statute for Religious Freedom written by Thomas Jefferson. (However, some of the stronger statements made by Jefferson, such as "our civil rights have no dependence on our religious opinions any more than our opinions in physics or geometry," were omitted or toned down.) The general assembly apparently preferred to link itself with broader currents in the United States rather than to solely emphasize Rhode Island's own long history of religious freedom. Near the end of the bill, however, the assembly included a paragraph that invoked the Charter of 1663 with the comment that "a principal object of our venerable ancestors, in their migration to this country, and settlement of this State, was, as they expressed it, *to hold forth a lively experiment, that a most flourishing civil State may stand, and best be maintained, with a full liberty in religious concernments.*"[10]

The 1783 law in favor of Catholics explicitly had repealed the earlier anti-Catholic tests, given Catholics the right to vote and hold office, and declared that Catholics would have "all the Rights and Privileges of the *Protestant* Citizens of this State."[11] In contrast, the 1798 law made no explicit mention of the Jewish population or any other specific religious group. Because of its guarantee that "opinions in matters of religion . . . shall in no wise diminish, enlarge or affect . . . civil capacities," this law has usually been regarded as the end of Jewish civil disabilities. But there is no clear indication in the historical record that Jewish residents of Rhode Island ever invoked the law to exercise the right to vote. They may have believed that the older anti-Jewish policy was still in place.[12]

This 1798 law (and a general bill of rights passed the same year) guaranteed religious freedom only by statute. Rhode Island still operated under the Charter of 1663 and would not adopt a constitution until 1843, after the events known as the Dorr Rebellion.[13] The new Constitution guaranteed religious freedom in a section that was an abridged version of the 1798 law— including both the language borrowed from Jefferson and the reference to the "lively experiment" of "our venerable ancestors."[14]

As noted above, between 1798 and 1843 it was still somewhat ambiguous whether Jews had full legal equality. It might have been a moot point, since the Jewish population of Rhode Island gradually left the state in the decades after the revolution. The War of Independence and the British occupation of Newport had done severe and lasting damage to the economy of that city. The Jewish merchants moved to other cities and states in search of new economic opportunities. By 1822 the entire Jewish population of Newport had departed.[15] Yet Rhode Island laws continued to take into account the existence or potential existence of a Jewish population. The law on marriage and divorce exempted Jews from the law on consanguineous marriages. Any marriage between Jews that conformed to Jewish law was permitted even if it was otherwise against Rhode Island law.[16] The main consequence was legalization of marriage between an uncle and a niece, which is permitted by the Torah and was then common among Sephardic Jews. Early-twentieth-century historian Benjamin Hartogensis noted that, while other Rhode Island laws to accommodate Jewish practices were by his time "paralleled in codes of other states," this explicit permission to Jews to contract an otherwise invalid marriage remained "unique."[17] The law on clandestine marriages similarly permitted any marriage that followed Quaker or Jewish ritual, even if the marriage did not otherwise conform to the law.[18]

Those who observed Saturday as the Sabbath (both Jews and Seventh-Day Christians) likewise received a partial exemption from laws that prohibited labor on Sunday. This exemption was narrow and continued to restrict several of the most common forms of economic activity. An exempted person still could not operate a store, load or unload a mercantile vessel, work as a blacksmith, or hunt or fish other than on his own property.[19] Farmers were the primary group to benefit from the exemption.

Rhode Island was also affected by the nationwide controversy of this era concerning whether Universalists (or others who did not believe in the possibility of eternal damnation) could be trusted to testify in a court of law. The 1827 case of *Wakefield v. Ross* was heard in a federal trial court in Rhode Island by Supreme Court justice Joseph Story.[20] In this property dispute, a father and son named Richardson were called as witnesses. After opposing counsel accused them of nonbelief in the afterlife, Story ruled that they were ineligible to testify. This decision provoked a strong negative reaction in Rhode Island. The legislature quickly passed a law that declared that "no man's opinions in religion, his belief or disbelief, can be legally inquired into, or be made a subject of investigation, with a view to his qualifications to hold office, or give testimony, by any man or men, acting judicially or legislatively."[21]

III.

All of the above topics connect with issues of religious liberty but less directly to issues of establishment. Since Rhode Island had never had an establishment, it never had a process of disestablishment. It did, however, have to consider questions relating to the status of church property. The Rhode Island General Assembly apparently did not consider the incorporation of religious societies to be a violation of the principles of Roger Williams or the separation of church and state. This was in sharp contrast to Jeffersonian Virginia, which prohibited church incorporations throughout the early republic and continued this ban until it was found unconstitutional by a court in the twenty-first century.[22]

Incorporation of churches and other religious institutions in Rhode Island had begun in the colonial period. Probably the most notable incorporation of this era was the charter granted to Rhode Island College (later Brown University) in 1764. The charter explicitly forbade a religious test for admission of students but required the board of trustees to have a Baptist majority and to include Quakers, Congregationalists, and Episcopalians.[23] In the colonial era, and even in the early republic before the *Dartmouth College* decision in 1819, collegiate charters created institutions that did not fit neatly into modern concepts of private and public.[24] Brown was not merely a private institution meant only for Baptists. It had a public mission to serve all the people of Rhode Island.

The charter exempted from taxation not only the college but also the president and members of the faculty. The reason given was to ensure that the college would have "the same privileges, dignities, and immunities enjoyed by the American colleges and European universities"—a notable contrast with the lack of interest in worldly acclaim or honors that Roger Williams would likely have had.[25]

Incorporation of churches and other acts for their support remained routine for the assembly throughout the early republic. In 1805, to take a typical year, the Rhode Island General Assembly incorporated the Pawtuxet Baptist Church and Society in Cranston, authorized a lottery for the Union Baptist Church in Johnston, and revised the charter of the First Congregational Church in Newport.[26] Rhode Island Baptist churches regularly sought and received acts of incorporation from the general assembly. Massachusetts Baptist churches were often reluctant to incorporate, but Rhode Islanders did not share this reluctance. The lack of an established church in Rhode Island perhaps had the paradoxical effect of making Rhode Island Baptists less nervous about the dangers of asking for an accommodation from the state. In 1811 the Warren Baptist Association, which was based in Rhode Island but also included adjacent portions of Massachusetts, responded to a query about incorporation from a church in Middleborough, Massachusetts. The association replied that "though the kingdom of Christ is not of this world, we see no reason why the disciples of Christ may not, like other men, have the benefit of civil law, either for the protection of property, or for the fulfillment of voluntary obligations."[27]

Forty years later, not much had changed. New churches continued to proliferate. Rhode Island still lacked a general incorporation law, so every act of incorporation had to be approved by the general assembly. In January 1845 alone, for example, the assembly passed laws of incorporation for four Baptist churches and two Congregational churches.[28]

Another example of state entanglement with religion during this period was the maintenance of the Jewish synagogue in Newport (today known as the Touro Synagogue). Abraham Touro, the son of Isaac Touro, the first leader of the synagogue, had settled in Boston after the Jewish community of Newport dispersed. He died in 1822 and left a will in which he bequeathed $10,000 to the Rhode Island legislature "for the purpose of supporting the Jewish Synagogue in that State, in Special Trust to be appropriated for that object." An additional $5,000 was left to the Newport Town Council to be used to maintain the street that ran by the synagogue and Jewish burial ground. The general assembly and the town council of Newport were given joint control over the management of the bequest.[29]

The Touro bequest is a major moment in the history of historic preservation in America—possibly the very first time that a monetary donation was made to preserve an abandoned building.[30] Yet it involved a structure that had been built for a religious purpose and might (as eventually did happen) be used for that purpose again. The Touro bequest created an intimate connection between a religious building and the governments of both town and state, yet the acceptance of the bequest seems to have been uncontroversial. The *Newport Mercury* merely reported that the June 1823 general assembly had passed a bill directing the general treasurer to receive the sum bequeathed by Touro and "invest the same in stock." It added that "[t]he repairs, &c. of the Synagogue, to be done under the direction of the Town-Council."[31] In 1827 the assembly required that the Newport Town Council maintain the fence that surrounded the Jewish burial ground in Newport and authorized the general treasurer, a civil officer, to withdraw money from the Touro Fund for necessary repairs.[32] This had not been an explicit part of the original Abraham Touro bequest, but would later be funded by a donation from his brother Judah Touro.[33]

IV.

The year 1827 also saw the start of a protracted debate over taxation of religious property. The 1798 revision of the law code included a tax law whose twenty-seventh and final section decreed that "all estates, real or personal, granted or appropriated to religious uses, or to the use of schools or seminaries of learning, within this State, be and the same are hereby exempted from taxation."[34] The reasons this three-decades-old law suddenly became controversial are unclear. Advocates on both sides spoke in circumlocutions and avoided direct attacks on or defenses of particular institutions. The allusions likely would have been clear to contemporaries but are not to a modern historian. Some documents indicate that the issue behind the controversy was the large amount of property accumulated by the churches of Newport, which advocates at the time claimed had collectively taken $1 million off the tax rolls, and by one unnamed church in particular.[35] The Newport town meeting in April 1829 endorsed repeal of the exemption "by a large majority," but the record is silent concerning the reason behind the vote.[36] Trinity Church, the Episcopal church in Newport, is the most likely candidate for the church in question. The congregation of Trinity Church had just voted to establish a permanent fund as an endowment and to pay for all future operations from the interest.[37]

Trinity Church also owned property acquired from a bequest left in 1740 by a customs collector named Nathaniel Kay. In 1796 Trinity Church leased this property to Richard Harrison in a 999-year lease. This is an indication that Trinity may have been the target of the campaign, since Benjamin Hazard, the primary advocate in the legislature for an end to the tax exemption, referred to such "estates leased (for 999 years generally)" in his report on the subject.[38] Yet Hazard himself was a member of Trinity Church, as was Henry Bull, another leading proponent of ending the tax exemption. More strangely still, Hazard had been retained by Trinity to lobby the legislature for the passage of the law permitting the creation of the permanent fund.[39]

On the very day that the legislature first considered an end to the tax exemption, it also passed a bill to establish the Trinity Church permanent fund, almost word for word as the church had proposed it.[40] Another anomaly is that Trinity Church does not seem to have been a particularly wealthy parish during this time. Church records from the period frequently note financial difficulties. The creation of a permanent fund had been done to safeguard precarious finances, not to store up immense wealth. Yet it is unlikely that any other church in Newport was wealthier, as the entire town was in a poor financial state throughout this period. The official history of Trinity Church calls this the era of "A Poor Parish in an Impoverished Town."[41]

There are hints of a different explanation. Harrison, the lessee of the church property, had not maintained it and had been accused by the vestry of having caused "waste and destruction."[42] Benjamin Hazard had been asked for legal advice as to how Harrison could be compelled to take better care of the property.[43] By 1827 the matter had been resolved, and Harrison had agreed to give the property back to the church. Though the particular dispute had become moot, it is still possible that the real goal of this campaign was to ensure that negligent lessees of church property could not avoid taxation. But it is difficult to find evidence for that theory in the record, and the original bill had a much broader scope and taxed even church buildings themselves.

In 1827 Benjamin Hazard, a prominent member of the general assembly who represented Newport from 1809 to 1840, chaired a committee whose report recommended an end to the tax exemption for church property. The Hazard report did not invoke the memory of Roger Williams or frame the issue as one of church-state separation. Hazard took note of the religious aspects of the Brown charter and noted that both Brown and the Friends' School in Providence (today Moses Brown School) had become substantial property holders. But Hazard's primary argument was that these corporations were private institutions that served "the local and partial objects" of only a portion of the community, whereas taxes were levied to serve the entire community. The problem with the tax exemptions for Trinity Church, Brown, and the Friends' School was less that they were religious institutions and more that Episcopalians, Baptists, and Quakers were minorities (in a state with no religious majority) and thus should have no right to withhold taxes from the common treasury.[44]

Hazard made special mention of the personal tax exemption for members of the Brown University faculty. This clause, he said, did "very little good to the institution itself at a very considerable expense or loss to the public."[45] Once again, his emphasis was less on the religious affiliation of the faculty and more on the harm done to the collective good for the benefit of a few private individuals.

Hazard made no mention of the bright-line distinction between private and public institutions that Chief Justice John Marshall had made in the *Dartmouth College* case of 1819. Rather, in some ways Hazard's argument reflected the newer view that a charter was a contract that created a private corporation rather than a public or quasi-public body. Yet he also seemed to believe, contrary to the ruling in *Dartmouth College*, that the legislature had the authority to unilaterally revoke the terms of a charter and did not have to consider it a contract whose obligations a state could not constitutionally impair.

Hazard also contrasted a church funded by regular contributions of members with one that was able to draw from a permanent fund (such as Trinity Church, although again the allusion was not explicit). The citizens who supported the former church were not exempt from taxes, yet the property of the latter church, which had no greater intrinsic value to the community, was exempt.[46]

The legislative committee chaired by Hazard recommended that the assembly repeal the twenty-seventh section "except so far as it exempts from taxes property appropriated to the support of Public Free Schools—and for the schooling of poor children." The committee also advocated a separate law "to limit the quantities of real estate, which may be held by corporations," including religious corporations.[47]

In the subsequent debate in the House, Lemuel Arnold of Providence criticized the proposal to end the tax exemption. He supported a limitation on corporate real estate holdings as a justifiable compromise, even though "in this state there could not be any reasonable grounds" to fear that religious corporations might become dangerously powerful. But he considered an end to the religious tax exemption to be equivalent to a tax increase, as well as inconsistent with "the true policy of every state to encourage rather than discourage these institutions." Arnold sought postponement of consideration of the bill and said that notice should be printed in Rhode Island newspapers to inform corporations that the bill was under consideration. Hazard disagreed in terms that again made a sharp distinction between private and public interests. The legislature had "a right to pass such laws as we see fit, of a public nature, without giving private individuals or corporations notice of our intentions." After further debate, the house did vote to postpone the bill to the October session but declined to post any notice in the newspapers.[48]

The debate continued in fits and starts over the next two years. Despite the implicit promise that there would be further discussion and perhaps a vote in October 1827, the matter was not formally raised again until June 1828. There was "a warm debate" in June, followed by the appointment of another study committee, and then "a very animated discussion" in January 1829.[49] The latter debate finally saw direct mention made of the *Dartmouth College* decision: "Much discussion arose on the unconstitutionality of the second section, which provides that all property shall be liable to taxation, any private or public act to the contrary notwithstanding."[50] These arguments were unsuccessful, and a bill to repeal the tax exemption for all churches and schools was approved in the house by a vote of thirty-five to twenty-three. The matter was considered sufficiently important that the *Newport Mercury* printed a roll call of how members had voted.[51]

Modern historian Patrick Conley has divided the thirty-one Rhode Island towns that existed in this era into three groups: expanding, static, and declining. These classifications are based on population growth (or lack thereof—the twelve towns classified as declining all decreased in population between 1790 and 1840) but also reflect the degree of economic activity in each town. The expanding towns were generally among the centers of the American Industrial Revolution. The declining towns were generally agricultural.[52] If these categories are applied to the vote on the bill to end tax exemptions, a suggestive pattern emerges. Representatives from expanding towns voted fourteen to four against the bill—almost two-thirds of the no votes came from these towns. Representatives from static towns voted thirteen to six in favor of the bill. Representatives from declining towns voted eighteen to three in favor.[53]

This pattern supports the hypothesis that the motivation behind the bill was a desire to increase the tax base of communities on the decline. Newport in particular, although it had modest population growth and was therefore classified as static by Conley, was an economically depressed town throughout the early nineteenth century. Representatives from a prosperous town, such as Providence, perhaps could better afford to keep religious property off the tax rolls.

A detailed and impassioned response against repeal of the religious property-tax exemption came from an anonymous pamphleteer who published *An Appeal to the Senate of Rhode-Island*. The pamphlet was addressed to the senate after the bill to end the exemptions had already passed the house. The author praised the "distinguished statesman and divine" Roger Williams and argued Williams opposed only "the tyranny which the civil power undertook to exercise over the conscience," not the positive encouragement of religion. However, the author seemed to be not completely in accord with Rhode Island traditions of church-state separation. He asserted (rather oddly, since his facts were outdated) that "[p]olitical wisdom has led many other states to tax property for the support of religious teachers, as well as for the support of public schools." He lamented that the Rhode Island House not only "would not do any thing themselves, by taxation, for literature and religion," but now would "throw obstacles in the way of others; to prevent others, who are willing, from giving their property to support the public good." He even dared to mock a sacred Rhode Island passage when he associated supporters of the tax bill with "an *experiment, in revolutionary France, where it was undertaken [to have a nation without religion], but how soon was anarchy the consequence!"[54] (It was commonplace in this period for opponents of church-state separation to mention the horrors of the French Revolution. It provided a useful counterpoint to separationists who were equally likely to cite the Spanish Inquisition or witch trials.)[55] Finally, the pamphleteer made arguments that were grounded in the law, rather than the emotional rhetoric that underlay most of the pamphlet. He noted that Brown University, the Friends' School, and the (completely secular) Blackstone Canal Company had been issued charters that exempted them from all taxation. The author did not specifically mention *Dartmouth College*, but he raised the possibility of costly litigation if these charter-based tax exemptions were not continued.[56]

The senate voted to postpone consideration of the bill, effectively killing it in its original form. A new version of the bill proposed in May 1829 was substantially modified. The earlier house bill would have ended the tax exemption for all church-owned property. The new bill maintained the exemption for "meeting-houses and the pews therein, colleges, academies and school-houses, with the land on which they stand, and burial grounds." The bill now targeted possession of surplus property and no longer aimed at core property used by churches and schools. It passed the house unanimously, but the senate again voted to postpone consideration.[57]

In June 1829, the senate and then the house passed another version of the bill that included an amendment "exempting . . . the property of such institutions as are exempted by their charters."[58] Apparently, the assembly had acceded to the *Dartmouth College* decree that a state-granted charter could not be modified—or at least they had realized that it was wise to avoid the possibility of a lawsuit.

V.

By the time Rhode Island approved its Constitution of 1843, its first, it was no longer the extreme outlier that it had been two centuries earlier. All other states had abolished their establishments, and many had abolished their religious tests for public office. The lively experiment of no establishment and complete religious liberty for all had been largely embraced by the nation as a whole. Yet in Rhode Island, as elsewhere in other states, the debate over where to draw the line between church and state continued for decades to come.

NOTES

1. Roger Williams founded Providence in 1636 after his forced expulsion from Massachusetts Bay and failure to obtain refuge in Plymouth Colony. Williams was a radical who broke with his fellow Puritans in his beliefs that the government had no authority to compel religious belief or enforce the first table of the Ten Commandments (those that relate to religious rather than moral duties) and that all men and women had the right of "soul liberty." The most recent full biography of Williams is John M. Barry, *Roger Williams and the Creation of the American Soul: Church, State, and the Birth of Liberty* (New York: Viking, 2012). A classic study is Edwin S. Gaustad, *Liberty of Conscience: Roger Williams in America* (Grand Rapids, MI: Wm. B. Eerdmans, 1991). The writings of Williams on religious liberty are collected in *On Religious Liberty: Selections from the Writings of Roger Williams*, ed. James Calvin Davis (Cambridge: Belknap Press of Harvard University Press, 2008).

2. Francis Newton Thorpe, ed., *The Federal and State Constitutions, Colonial Charters, and Other Organic Laws of the States, Territories, and Colonies Now or Heretofore Forming the United States of America* (Washington, DC: Government Printing Office, 1909), 6:3212–13.

3. Thorpe, *Federal and State Constitutions,* 6:3212.

4. Morris A. Gutstein, *The Story of the Jews of Newport* (New York: Bloch, 1936), 159–62; David C. Adelman, "Strangers: Civil Rights of Jews in the Colony of Rhode Island," *Rhode Island History* 13, no. 3 (1954): 72–76; Patrick T. Conley, *Democracy in Decline: Rhode Island's Constitutional Development, 1776–1841* (Providence: Rhode Island Historical Society, 1977), 34–35.

5. Gutstein, *Jews of Newport,* 158–59.

6. Adelman, "Strangers," 72.

7. "To the Hebrew Congregation in Newport, Rhode Island," August 18, 1790, in *The Papers of George Washington*, ed. Dorothy Twohig, Presidential Series, ed. Mark A. Mastromarino (Charlottesville: University Press of Virginia, 1996), 6:284–85.

8. The discovery of this apparent deception was first made by nineteenth-century historian Sidney Rider. Rider was a Rhode Islander and a prolific author who took a special interest in historical frauds and forgeries. See Sidney S. Rider, *An Inquiry Concerning the Origin of the Clause in the Laws of Rhode Island Disfranchising Roman Catholics* (Providence, 1889). The more recent historian Patrick Conley agrees with the analysis made by Rider. Conley, *Democracy in Decline,* 33–34.

9. *At the General Assembly of the Governor and Company of the State of Rhode-Island and Providence Plantations, Begun and Holden by Adjournment, at Providence, Within and for the State Aforesaid, on Monday, the Twenty-Fourth Day of February, A.D. 1783* (1783), 79. Some have seen this decrease in anti-Catholic attitudes as having begun with the friendly relations between Rhode Islanders and the six thousand French soldiers who were stationed in Newport in the later years of the revolution (after the British evacuation of the city in October 1779). John Quinn, "From Dangerous Threat to 'Illustrious Ally': Changing Perceptions of Catholics in Eighteenth-Century Newport," *Rhode Island History* 75, no. 2 (2017): 56–79. See also Rockwell Stensrud, *Newport: A Lively Experiment, 1639–1969* (Newport, RI: Redwood Library and Athenaeum, 2006), 225.

10. *The Public Laws of the State of Rhode-Island and Providence Plantations, As Revised by a Committee, and Finally Enacted by the Honourable General Assembly, at Their Session in January, 1798. To Which Are Prefixed the Charter, Declaration of Independence, Articles of Confederation, Constitution of the United States, and President Washington's Address of September, 1796* (Providence: Carter and Wilkinson, 1798), 81–84 (emphasis in the original).

11. *At the General Assembly* (February 1783), 79.

12. Holly Snyder, "A Sense of Place: Jews, Identity and Social Status in Colonial British America, 1654–1831" (PhD diss., Brandeis University, 2000), 434–35. Whether colonial Rhode Island Jews had possessed and exercised the right to vote had already become a matter of dispute just a few decades later. In 1817 Samuel Eddy of Providence wrote to John Boss of Newport to try to figure out whether Rhode Islanders "had been persecutors" of Jews and Catholics during the colonial era or had maintained their principles of complete religious liberty. Notes on the back of the letter, probably by Boss, contain the conflicting answers he received to his inquiries on the question, with one J. A. asserting that "Jews always voted" and former town clerk Thomas Tew thinking it likely that "they were not permitted to vote before the Revolution." Moses Lopez is also mentioned in the notes as someone who had regularly voted, but the notes seem to date this to the years after the revolution—"more than 20 years ago" before 1817. Samuel Eddy to John L. Boss Jr., April 21, 1817, Newport Historical Society.

13. Opposition to property requirements for the franchise led to an unauthorized new Constitution, the concurrent election of two governors under the competing documents, an uprising led by Thomas Wilson Dorr against the Charter government, and ultimately an entirely new Constitution that (although many times amended) is still the governing document of the state to this day. The authoritative recent account of the Dorr Rebellion is Erik J. Chaput, *The People's Martyr: Thomas Wilson Dorr and His 1842 Rhode Island Rebellion* (Lawrence: University Press of Kansas, 2013).

14. Rhode Island Constitution, Article I, Section 3.

15. Gutstein, *Jews of Newport*, 225; Stensrud, *Lively Experiment*, 237.

16. *Public Laws*, 481.

17. Benjamin H. Hartogensis, "Rhode Island and Consanguineous Jewish Marriages," *Publications of the American Jewish Historical Society*, no. 20 (1911): 139–40.

18. *Public Laws*, 486.

19. *Public Laws of the State of Rhode-Island and Providence Plantations, as Revised by a Committee, and Finally Enacted by the General Assembly, at Their Session in January, 1844. To Which Are Prefixed the Charter of Charles II, Declaration of Independence, Resolution of General Assembly to Support the Declaration of Independence, Articles of Confederation, Constitution of the United States, Proceedings of the Convention on the Adoption of the Constitution of the United States by Rhode-Island, and President Washington's Address of September, 1796, and Constitution of the State of Rhode-Island and Providence Plantations* (Providence: Knowles and Vose, 1845), 345–46.

20. In the first century of the Supreme Court's existence, the justices not only heard cases as a group in Washington but were also obliged to hear circuit cases as trial judges. The intermediate Federal courts of appeal were created only in 1891.

21. *Wakefield v. Ross*, 5 Mason 18 (1827); *At the General Assembly of the State of Rhode-Island and Providence Plantations, Begun and Holden, (By Adjournment,) at Providence, on the Second Monday in January, in the Year of Our Lord One Thousand and Twenty-Eight, and of Independence the Fifty-Second* (1828), 20. For a fuller account, see James S. Kabala, *Church-State Relations in the Early American Republic, 1787–1846* (London: Pickering and Chatto, 2013), 140–42. For broader context, see Kabala, *Church-State Relations*, 121–50; and Ronald P. Formisano and Stephen Pickering, "The Christian Debate and Witness Competency," *Journal of the Early Republic* 29, no. 2 (2009): 219–48.

22. "In Win for Rev. Falwell (and the ACLU), Judge Rules Va. Must Allow Churches to Incorporate," www.aclu.org/news/win-rev-falwell-and-aclu-judge-rules-va-must-allow-churches-incorporate.

23. These required denominational affiliations were not fully abolished until 1942. "The Charter of Brown University," https://www.brown.edu/about/administration/corporation/sites/brown.edu.about.administration.corporation/files/uploads/charter-of-brown-university.pdf.

24. See Mark Douglas McGarvie, *One Nation under Law* (DeKalb: Northern Illinois University Press, 2004), esp. chap. 7 (152–89).

25. In 1965 the university agreed that all faculty hired from that point onward would renounce the exemption as a condition of employment. "Tax Break Abandoned 30 Years Ago: Brown Asks Cities to Drop Mention of Personal Tax Exemption," http://www.brown.edu/Administration/News_Bureau/1987-95/94-146.html.

26. *At the General Assembly of the State of Rhode-Island and Providence Plantations, Begun and Holden at Newport Within and for Said State, on the First Wednesday of May, in the Year of Our Lord One Thousand Eight Hundred and Five, and in the Twenty-Ninth Year of Independence* (1805), 11; *At the General Assembly of the State of Rhode-Island and Providence Plantations, Begun and Holden by Adjournment at Newport, Within and for Said State, on the Second Monday of June, in the Year of Our Lord One Thousand Eight Hundred and Five, and in the Twenty-Ninth Year of Independence* (1805), 4, 7; *At the General Assembly of the State of Rhode-Island and Providence Plantations, Begun and Holden at South-Kingstown, Within and for Said State, on the Last Monday of October, in the Year of Our Lord One Thousand Eight Hundred and Five, and in the Thirtieth Year of Independence* (1805), 3.

27. *A Compendium of the Minutes of the Warren Baptist Association, from Its Formation, in 1767, to the Year 1825, Inclusive* (1825), 11.

28. *At the General Assembly of the State of Rhode Island and Providence Plantations, Begun and Holden by Adjournment, at Providence, Within and for Said State, on the First Monday of January, in the Year of Our Lord One Thousand Eight Hundred and Forty-Five, and of Independence the Sixty-Ninth* (1845), 13, 22, 24, 36, 63, 81.

29. The text of the will appears in Gutstein, *Jews of Newport*, 291–93.

30. Ellen Smith and Jonathan D. Sarna, "Introduction: The Jews of Rhode Island," in *The Jews of Rhode Island*, ed. George M. Goodwin and Ellen Smith (Waltham, MA: Brandeis University Press, 2004), 5.

31. *Newport Mercury*, June 21, 1823.

32. *At the General Assembly of the State of Rhode-Island and Providence Plantations, Begun and Holden at South-Kingstown, on the Last Monday of October, in the Year of Our Lord One Thousand Eight Hundred and Twenty-Seven, and of Independence the Fifty-Second* (1827), 38.

33. Gutstein, *Jews of Newport*, 243–44.

34. *Public Laws*, 419.

35. *An Appeal to the Senate of Rhode-Island* (Providence, 1829), 5–6.

36. *Newport Town Meeting Records, 1816–1831*, April 15, 1829, 401–2, manuscript from the Newport Historical Society. See also *Newport Mercury*, April 18, 1829.

37. John B. Hattendorf, *Semper Eadem: A History of Trinity Church in Newport, 1698–2000* (Newport, RI: Trinity Church, 2001), 171.

38. *Rhode-Island American and Providence Gazette*, July 3, 1827.

39. George Champlin Mason, *Annals of Trinity Church, Newport, Rhode Island, 1821–1892* (Newport, RI: V. Mott Francis, 1894), 22–23.

40. Compare the text in Mason, *Annals of Trinity Church*, 22, with the text in *At the General Assembly* (October 1827), 38. There are many changes in punctuation between the two, but except for one minor clause, the actual words are identical. See also *Rhode-Island American and Providence Gazette*, July 3, 1827.

41. Hattendorf, *Semper Eadem*, 165.

42. George Champlin Mason, *Annals of Trinity Church, Newport, Rhode Island, 1698–1821* (Newport, RI: George C. Mason, 1890), 317.

43. Mason, *Annals of Trinity Church*, 304.

44. Report printed in full in *Rhode-Island American and Providence Gazette*, July 3, 1827.

45. *Rhode-Island American and Providence Gazette*, July 3, 1827.

46. *Rhode-Island American and Providence Gazette*, July 3, 1827.

47. *Rhode-Island American and Providence Gazette*, July 3, 1827. The extant records unfortunately do not indicate the amount of the proposed limit or even whether the "quantities" would be defined in terms of a maximum acreage or a maximum monetary value.

48. *Rhode-Island American and Providence Gazette*, July 3, 1827. The newspaper recorded the brief debate between Arnold and Hazard and then noted that "[a]n interesting discussion ensued, which we have not room for in this paper."

49. *Newport Mercury*, June 28, 1828, and January 17, 1829.

50. *Providence Patriot*, January 17, 1829.

51. *Newport Mercury*, January 24, 1829. The *Mercury* gave the number of no votes as twenty-four but had mistakenly split a member named Bates Harris into two men named Bates and Harris. The *Providence Patriot* reported the result as thirty-five to twenty-eight but gave no roll call list. Perhaps the twenty-eight was a misprint derived from a written twenty-three. *Providence Patriot*, January 17, 1829.

52. Conley, *Democracy in Decline*, 150–61.

53. The list of members by towns is from *At the General Assembly of the State of Rhode-Island and Providence Plantations, Begun and Holden (by Adjournment) at Providence, on the second Monday in January, in the Year of Our Lord, One Thousand Eight Hundred and Twenty-Nine, and of Independence the Fifty-Third* (1829), 2. The roll call is in *Newport Mercury*, January 24, 1829. The representation of towns in the general assembly was still based on the rules set forth in the 1663 Charter, which resulted in malapportionment. The four oldest towns had four members or more each, and every other town had two. The expanding towns therefore had fewer seats than their share of the population would have dictated under a more equally apportioned system.

54. *An Appeal to the Senate*, 10, 5, 4 (emphasis in the original).

55. See Kabala, *Church-State Relations*, 46–48, 68–70.

56. *An Appeal to the Senate*, 9.

57. *Providence Patriot*, May 13, 1829; *Newport Mercury*, May 16, 1829. The newspapers seemed to have lost interest in the issue and no longer provided comprehensive coverage. The *Patriot* noted that the new bill was a "material modification" of the previous bill, but neither paper provided details about the purpose behind the change.

58. *Newport Mercury*, June 27, 1829. This also was laconically reported with no real detail as to the reasons for the change or to whether there was any opposition in either house. The final text of the law is in *At the General Assembly of the State of Rhode-Island and Providence Plantations, Begun and Holden (by Adjournment) at Newport, Within and for Said State, on the Fourth Monday of June, in the Year of Our Lord, One Thousand Eight Hundred and Twenty-Nine, and of Independence the Fifty-Third* (1829), 23–24.

CHAPTER FIVE

THE PENNSYLVANIA EXPERIMENT WITH FREEDOM OF CONSCIENCE AND CHURCH-STATE RELATIONS

David Little

BECAUSE PENNSYLVANIA NEVER instituted a conventional form of established religion, but instead had less regulation of religious belief and practice than every other colony except perhaps Rhode Island, its experience during the revolutionary and early national periods did not exhibit the same change and disruption in matters of church and state. Nevertheless, Pennsylvania was not without state efforts to regulate religion from the time of its founding in 1682 until 1776. Accordingly, the same social and political forces that affected relations between religion and state in the other colonies during and after the revolution had their decided, if unique, effects on Pennsylvania. While some effects were in the direction of greater religious freedom, some were not.

William Penn (1644–1718) converted to Quakerism in the 1660s, and thereafter was arrested, tried, and imprisoned in England for joining illegal Quaker meetings and for defying laws against publicly advocating prohibited beliefs. For Penn, the prevalent idea of state-enforced religion was an unthinkable violation of the very meaning of Christianity. His basic contention was that religious life is authentic only when allegiance to God is acknowledged on the basis of a conscientious commitment unsullied by the base distractions coercion engenders. Consequently, a well-ordered state gives wide latitude to the freedom of conscience, wherein every citizen enjoys the opportunity, unencumbered by the threat of legal punishment, to consent to what Penn called "the inner light" and to put those promptings into practice.

Penn's emphasis on the freedom of conscience was successfully extended to a wider range of religious believers than was true elsewhere. It led to an immigration policy that welcomed numerous Quakers, of course, but also made room for other unpopular minorities, like the Mennonites, Moravians, and some Jews, as well as larger, more mainstream groups, such as

Anglicans, Presbyterians, Baptists, as well as Lutherans and Reformed communities from Sweden and Germany.

Penn's respect for religious and ethnic diversity also included Native Americans who inhabited the region. Before leaving England and setting foot in his colony, which he acquired from Charles II as repayment for a debt owed his father, Penn made clear to commissioners who preceded him "to be careful not to offend" the Natives—"to court their good will, and let them know that the Christians had come to settle among them on terms of friendship."[1]

His solicitude toward them was to be a hallmark of his vision of Pennsylvania as a Peaceable Kingdom, made famous by the nineteenth-century painting of that name by Quaker artist, Edward Hicks, depicting animals and children lying down together in peace, with Penn and Native Americans amicably negotiating agreements in the background.

Another feature of Penn's Holy Experiment, as he called it, was the ideal of pacifism. That ideal colored in consequential ways the conduct of government right through the revolutionary period, where the call to arms against the English Crown represented a challenge to Quaker thinking. Though Quakers differed among themselves over the proper interpretation of "peace teaching," both at the beginnings of the movement in the 1650s in England and throughout the late seventeenth and eighteenth centuries in Pennsylvania, Penn's understanding would constitute a continuing influence. For him, Quakers were the advanced guard of the Kingdom of God, a reality already at work in the world, bringing about radically new forms of religious, social, and political life. This new world would come to depend less and less on rule by force. Voluntary compliance, based on love and mutual respect, would replace legal coercion in the state every bit as much as in the church.

For Penn, the Quaker meeting, allowing for maximum voluntary participation by members, was the perfect replica of civil government, one calling for the creation "of a weaponless state 'in accordance with the peace principles enunciated . . . in [the] sermon on the mount.'"[2] Government could function without force, "so long as God had full dominion over the spirits of the people—at least to the extent that those who were not subject to the truth themselves for love's sake submitted themselves willingly to the authority of their leaders."[3] The outlook reflected the optimism for human perfection that distinguished Penn and his fellow Quakers from the dour Calvinism of the New England Puritans,[4] and from the down-to-earth realism of many other colonists. The ideal of noncoercive government did encounter challenges in the real world of colonial politics, and it would become the subject of intense dispute and compromise among Quakers and fellow citizens. Still, the ideal stood as an enduring point of reference for the conduct of public affairs in Pennsylvania in a way that was unique in the American colonies. What is more, the ideal also produced a tendency among Quakers toward greater leniency, and even some reluctance, if not resistance, to enforcing the law.

Penn, along with much of the Quaker leadership that followed him, did not favor the complete separation of church and state or the untrammeled exercise of freedom of conscience. He developed what is best described as a theory of "soft establishment." The theory shared some features of estab-lished religion, insofar as it involved the coerced enforcement of certain laws regulating religious belief and practice and legal prescriptions taken to be expressions of key Quaker ideals. It was soft because of its broad in-clusiveness and because, as mentioned, it did not involve a legal union of government and a single church or denomination, mandating compulsory attendance and other preferences for church officials and the management of church property. In addition, it was soft because of the reluctance of Quakers toward using coercion to enforce the law. Finally, it was soft in that certain fundamental Quaker ideals did not find sufficient political support over the long term.

Penn's theory rested on the idea that Quakers, as the "only truly regenerate [people] of their time, if not since the Apostles," possessed the authority to form a uniquely legitimate government, one ruled "by the saints."[5] Because government and religion issue from the "same divine power," government may be described as "a part of religion itself, a thing sacred in its institution and end."[6] That meant that a proper government needed to be grounded in a "general religion," a "minimal set of religious beliefs." The set of beliefs would, of course, be broadly inclusive and make ample room for voluntary compliance and tolerance. It would not be parochial or demand allegiance to elaborate systems of dogma after the fashion of the established religions Penn rejected. But it would, nevertheless, impose some legal limits on reli-gious belief and practice and give specific legislative direction as inspired by Quaker ideals. Notably, the legislative prescriptions accorded with Quaker convictions concerning authentic religion.

In sum, though Penn and the Quaker leadership in Pennsylvania uni-formly rejected any "hard" form of religious establishment, a gentler version was not entirely missing from their thinking. "In Pennsylvania, there would be no [conventional] legal establishment, no tithes or forced maintenance of any minister. . . . [B]ut the Society of Friends would occupy a position comparable [in some unexpected ways] to that of the Church of England. Friends would determine the laws and government and the tone of the society. Others would be welcome, but they would have to be governed by Quaker principles."[7]

I.

Legislation Derived from Quaker Principles, 1682–1776
Legal Limits on Religious Belief and Practice

1. *Freedom of Conscience.* The Charter of Privileges of 1701, which would stand as the constitution of Pennsylvania until 1776, guaranteed that "no person or persons" living in the colony, who "confess and acknowledge one almighty God, the creator, upholder and ruler of the world, and profess him[,] . . . themselves [being] obliged to live quietly under the civil government[,] . . . shall be in any case molested or prejudiced in his or their person or estate because of his or their conscientious persuasion or practice or be compelled to frequent or maintain any religious worship place or ministry contrary to his or their mind." "Atheists were thus barred from the colony," as one scholar concludes.[8]

   Though Penn was critical of Catholicism because he believed it to inspire persecution, superstition, and popery, Pennsylvania authorities, under his influence, came to tolerate the right to worship of Roman Catholics.[9]

2. *Eligibility for Public Office.* The Charter of Privileges goes on to declare that "all persons who also profess to believe in Jesus Christ, the savior of the world, shall be capable, notwithstanding their other persuasions and practices in point of conscience and religion to serve this government in any capacity, both legislatively and executively." Perhaps because of the small number of Jews and other non-Christians in Pennsylvania, this law, and later versions of it, appears not to have been contested until after 1776.

   In 1696 a Frame of Government was adopted, limiting government service to Protestants. That restriction was briefly revoked in 1701. Under pressure from the British government to deny Roman Catholics the right to hold public office, however, the assembly passed a law in 1705 requiring officeholders to renounce Catholicism. The law held until the revolution.[10]

3. *Blasphemy, Defamation of Religion, and Profanity.* The *Act for Freedom of Conscience of 1682* states that "if any person shall abuse or deride any other for his or her different persuasion and practice in matters of religion, such person shall be looked on as a disturber of the peace and shall be punished accordingly." A later act passed by the assembly in 1700 ordains, "Whosoever shall willfully, premeditatedly and despitefully blaspheme, and speak loosely and profane Almighty God, Christ Jesus, the Holy Spirit of Truth, and is legally convicted thereof shall . . . pay . . . ten pounds." As to enforcing crimes of blasphemy or defamation, a permissive attitude prevailed until after the revolution. "In theory, but not in practice, God, Christ, and the Bible received legal protection from blasphemy, but not the ministers, sacraments, and most religious beliefs. Freethinking and scoffing at divine providence were not crimes."[11]

The same *Act of Conscience* declares "that whosoever shall swear in their common conversation by the name of God or Christ or Jesus, being legally convicted thereof, shall pay, for every such offense, five shillings or suffer five days imprisonment in the house of correction at hard labor to the behoof of the public and be fed with bread and water only during that time." The same punishment applies to "whoever shall speak loosely and profanely of almighty God, Christ Jesus, the Holy Spirit, or the scriptures of truth," as well as "to whosoever shall, in their conversation, at any time curse himself or any other."

The law was enforced, at least early on. Between 1684 and 1700, five convictions are recorded in Bucks County for swearing "by the name of God." The offenders received fines of five to ten shillings and/or five days imprisonment. One of the convicted was fined twenty-five shillings for having sworn "several oaths (4 at least) against God," and he "once cursed the Quakers."[12]

In comparison to New England, Pennsylvania's attempt to enforce laws against profanity "was brief and arguably faint. The data show that in the decade of 1701–1710 the prosecution of [profanity and other morals crimes] declined and thereafter disappeared." Although they remained on the books, blasphemy laws were less enforced than antiprofanity laws. One case was prosecuted in the early period and one other in the 1790s.[13]

4. *Sabbath Observance*. In the words, again, of the 1682 *Act of Conscience*: "[T]o the end that looseness, irreligion, and atheism may not creep in under pretense of conscience in this province, be it further enacted that . . . every first day of the week, called the Lord's day, people shall abstain from their usual common toil and labor that . . . they may the better dispose themselves to read the scriptures of truth at home or frequent such meetings of religious worship abroad as may best suit their respective persuasions."[14]

Quakers did not consider Sunday a holy day, though they wanted all labor on that day (except charitable work) to be prohibited. In other legislation, they outlawed frivolous sports and theater, all with the objective of having citizens "better dispose themselves" toward the cultivation of religious virtues. Most other denominations, like the Presbyterians, Baptists, and Lutherans, agreed with them. Anglicans largely agreed but would permit innocent recreations and sports, and the Crown, in reviewing Sunday laws in Pennsylvania, accepted the Anglican position. "Seventh-Day Baptists wanted a strict observance of Saturday and freedom to labor on Sunday, but their wishes were ignored." Moravians favored Saturday observance but compromised by recognizing both Saturday and Sunday.[15]

Key Subjects of Legislation

1. *Oaths*. Penn's instructions that "all evidence or engagements be without oaths," and instead be accompanied by a simple affirmation,[16] conformed to Quaker doctrine that oaths ought never be required in political or legal settings. Quakers took seriously the words of Jesus against swearing oaths and saw no reason individuals should not be held accountable for speaking truth by simple affirmation.

Early laws enshrined the right of Quakers to affirm, though they also accommodated the right of non-Quakers to take an oath.

In the early years, Quaker officials predominated in the courts and were reluctant to administer oaths when requested or even to remain on the bench while oaths were administered. This led to criticism by non-Quakers, especially Anglicans, who thought proceedings were biased against them. Absent the solemnizing act of oath taking, non-Quakers doubted justice could be done. They petitioned against the practice of affirmation as a way of weakening Quaker control over political and legal institutions. Thanks in part to the mediating influence of the British government, which had come to trust the loyalty of the Quakers, and to the diversity of appointments to the court owing to the influx of non-Quakers beginning in the first quarter of the eighteenth century, the dispute was resolved by making room for both oaths and affirmations.[17]

2. *Pacifism.* Apart from the treatment of Native Americans, with which the subject was deeply intertwined, the task of trying to implement the pacifist ideal, so urgent an ambition of Penn's vision, was the cause of political turmoil throughout the colony's first eighty years. Partly, it was a problem of the structure of government. Penn was ambivalent over the distribution and responsibilities of political authority. The 1681 Charter from Charles II granted proprietary control to Penn and his heirs over twenty-nine million acres, as well as strong executive authority over political affairs, including defense. Though committed in Quaker fashion to popular government, Penn enjoyed these prerogatives and would have enshrined them in the constitution. But he was rebuffed by the colonists and reluctantly agreed to a unicameral legislature—known as the assembly—with greatly expanded powers. The office of proprietor was much reduced, although the occupant, with all the financial benefits and political influence that went with it, retained authority over land transactions. He was also governor with veto power, held the ability to appoint a deputy in absentia, and was minister of defense. In addition, the British Crown continued to play an important role in Pennsylvania until the revolution, regularly exerting its Charter authority to review colonial laws and throw its weight behind the proprietor. That inclination would have importance in the debates over pacifism.

This arrangement resulted in an intense and enduring struggle between the assembly and the proprietor. Since Quakers dominated the assembly until the 1750s, and most of the governors, except for Penn, were either nominal Quakers or non-Quakers, the struggle between the executive and the legislature often turned into a contest over laws implementing pacifism. The reasons underlying the contest were complex. Calculations of financial and political advantage were seldom lost sight of, but the problem was also deeply philosophical. On one side, Quakers were not alone in supporting pacifism. They had their allies, like the Mennonites and Moravians, who were equally dedicated to renouncing force, along with other less principled citizens, who liked not having to pay taxes for defense.

At the same time, the opposition, made up of non-Quakers under the influence of Whig philosophy, believed self-defense to be the natural right of every human being and, consequently, to be the obligation of government to protect that right with force. In the name of conscience, Quakers should be exempt from military service, but not free from the duty to support a substitute or pay taxes for defense. Otherwise, pacifists would be free riders, reaping the benefits of defense of life and property, while not bearing the sacrifices. Moreover, nonpacifists reckoned it a bad bet that refraining from force would beget the same inclination in one's enemies. Above all, to disregard these fundamental convictions was as much a violation of conscience as suppressing the pacifist convictions of Quakers.

The controversy set in early. Despite Penn's commitment to founding a "weaponless state," he encountered obstacles already in the late 1680s when he admitted to a lack of order in the colony. Regenerate as much as unregenerate citizens, he conceded, needed restraint, a concession that led him to support a justice system backed by force. His reaction accounts in part for the relatively high number of prosecutions for violations of laws against profanity during the first three decades of Pennsylvania history, though it also depended on the uniformity of religious standards coincident with a homogeneous Quaker population.[18]

Penn's departure for England in 1701, subsequent infirmity in 1712, and death in 1718 may partly explain the decline of enforcement of such crimes in the early 1700s and after.[19] However, equally important were the results of a welcoming immigration policy, also traceable to the benevolent optimism of Quakers. It brought an ever-increasing influx of non-Quaker, non-English immigrants—Germans, Swedes, and especially Scots-Irish—that "diluted any consensus about proper behavior." "How hard could [Quakers] push their religious preferences on a hostile, politically potent population of non-Quakers," especially given their dedication to pacifism? In the face of growing diversity, Quakers often inclined because of their nonviolent predilections to favor conciliation in the resolution of differences to formal legal proceedings.[20]

A preference for conciliation was part of an antipathy toward the law reinforced by Quaker convictions. One was the deep-seated opposition to using force.[21] There was also the suspicion of political institutions born of a long-standing record of legal abuse inflicted on Quakers in England, as well as by select colonies in America.[22] A third reason was the belief, insisted on by Penn, that all worldly institutions, including governments, were undergoing radical transformation, superseding old forms of obedience to government. There were other causes, as well. The vast expanses of frontier territory were not readily subject to the administration of justice. Also, there was the hostile attitude toward government and a tolerance for lawbreaking among non-Quaker immigrants, especially the Scots-Irish, inspired by their own experience of political abuse back home and further encouraged by the absence of effective government at the frontiers, where they often settled.

Still, according to the "peace teaching," Pennsylvania should have been a place of tranquillity and good order. In the years leading up to the revolution, there was prosperity and the widespread guarantee of civil and political rights. However, there was nothing close to a Peaceable Kingdom. The incidence of violent crimes and other offenses was high relative to other colonies, especially after the 1730s, as Marietta and Rowe demonstrate.[23] "Peace teaching" also ran into difficulties on the question of military defense. The Crown temporarily revoked Penn's proprietorship in 1693, in part because of his failure to respond to demands for appropriations in support of England's military effort against France during King William's War (1688–97).

In 1701 the deputy governor, acting in Penn's absence and now eager to comply, took it upon himself to organize a militia in keeping with Charter powers. The Quaker-dominated assembly was relieved, since members were then not required to pass a militia bill and thereby compel all able-bodied citizens, including Quakers, to fight. While members would not prevent non-Quakers who desired to serve in the military from doing so, they could not in conscience force Quakers to serve.[24]

Between 1710 and 1739, spanning three decades of relative peace, the assembly utilized this compromise as the expedient for providing defense funds. So long as Quakers were not compelled to serve, assigning funds to the budget without specifying how the moneys might be used meant assembly members were not directly complicit in supporting military operations. Quakers also believed that lasting peace was a divine reward for practicing nonviolence and that faithful Christians might themselves abjure violence while still obeying divinely appointed magistrates who used the sword.

The compromise worked well until 1739 and the War of Jenkins' Ear (1739–48). The governor, appointed and egged on by Penn's sons, now proprietors by inheritance, was sympathetic to Britain's demand for colonial assistance against Spain and against Spanish and French pirates marauding the coastline. The governor called for the assembly to support raising a militia. He argued that trust in divine protection alone was unrealistic, that the assembly's support of force by police but not militia was inconsistent, and that as representatives of all citizens the assembly was obliged to provide for the colony's protection. If their principles prevented their paying for defense, were not those principles contrary to the very ends of government? "This question was asked with increasing frequency in the ensuing years, by Quakers and non-Quakers alike."[25]

The assembly weathered the storm by providing funds in its circuitous fashion and by attracting increased political support for its policies because of growing antagonism among citizens toward the financial appetites of the proprietors. Out of frustration, the governor called on Quakers to consider withdrawing from government, and he lobbied Parliament for help in bringing that about. The governor's appeals failed in the short term, but support began to gather strength in the 1740s and came to fruition in the '50s and '60s with the outbreak of the French and Indian War

(1754–63). Prior to that, there was unrest and sporadic violence on the frontiers, principally over land disputes with the Indians, many of whom, because of their grievances, were disposed to join forces with the French, who had territorial designs of their own.

With the drift toward warfare within the precincts of Pennsylvania itself, tensions regarding pacifist policies grew intense. There was a movement, going back to the early 1740s, consisting of Anglicans, German Lutherans and Reformed, and Scots-Irish Presbyterians, that criticized the Quaker government for its reticence concerning defense and called for strengthened efforts against the threat of Indian violence. It gained support in the late 1740s and '50s, fed by rumors of attacks against Philadelphia and other targets in the eastern colony, something unimaginable until that time. Naturally, war fever intensified demands on the assembly by a succession of governors for increased defense appropriations.

All this created a severe crisis in Quakerism and, consequently, the Pennsylvania government. By now, the assembly included a pro-proprietary party, diluting Quaker support in disputes over pacifism. Quakers entered the decade of the 1750s in full control of the assembly, but they "left it with their assembly majority forever broken," and with deep divisions among themselves about future Quaker involvement in politics.[26]

This did not mean Quaker political influence was gone forever. Quakers would continue to be elected to the assembly and to occupy positions of leadership until the 1770s for several reasons: their financial and social status,[27] the unpopularity of the proprietors, the widespread belief that Quakers best protected the people's interests, and the fractiousness of the opposition. But it did mean Quakers would never again be as unified as they had been in pursuing the ideals of the Holy Experiment, primarily because of disputes over pacifism.

The issue was joined in 1756. A group of Quaker assembly members, together with some pro-proprietor members, passed a bill to support a voluntary militia by means of new taxes, something that led to a declaration of war against the Indians and calling for a bounty on Indian scalps. A few Quaker members strongly dissented against the bill, and a petition submitted to the assembly signed by twenty-three Quakers strongly opposed paying taxes directly for military purposes.

Failing to distinguish between Quakers in support and those in dissent, opponents demanded, as a means for excluding all Quakers from government, that assembly members be required to take an oath of allegiance to the king and to provide aid for the military defense of the province, a demand opponents knew no conscientious Quaker could meet. In response, a significant number of Quaker members resigned from the assembly, enough to lose their majority. This dramatic act gave expression to a gathering spirit of reform within Quakerism for reaffirming the fundamental ideals of the movement, in particular devotion to nonviolence. It was born of the frustrations of trying to accommodate the insatiable appetite for war and of the unavoidable corollary that the outbreak of violence and disorder signaled God's displeasure with the degeneracy of the people. What was needed, above all, was for Quakers to return to the obligations of sainthood by withdrawing altogether from the thrall of earthly politics and the illusion that violence in any form could beget anything but more violence.

Giving up worldly power did not imply forsaking righteous living, since Quakers could display their beliefs through virtuous behavior outside government. They exemplified just that from the 1750s on by benevolent acts toward the victims of war; by persistent, if unsuccessful, attempts at peaceful reconciliation with the Indians; and by willingly bearing the "sufferings" inflicted upon them that resulted from those efforts. However, it did imply tolerating fellow Quakers who refused to follow their lead and who continued to think that God and Caesar could mix. Those who so behaved were eventually expelled from the Society of Friends. The rupture could not be healed; it would only grow worse before and after the revolution.

This situation represented a blow to the confident optimism so much a part of Penn's original vision. His belief that Quakers were the leading edge of a world-transforming movement, one that was in process of refashioning civic institutions, including government, was a crucial source of inspiration for the early colonists. Rude experience convinced Penn that the process would not come as easily as he thought. Provisional compromises had to be made between commitment to nonviolence and the responsibilities of government to enforce the law and protect the public. Though the compromises left Quaker consciences unsettled, most of the Quaker politicians who succeeded Penn went along with them for roughly two decades beyond his death.

After that, the conflicting ideas could no longer be held together. Quakers were now forced to stand up for true pacifism and completely turn their backs on politics or acquiesce to the imperatives of earthly government and become just another political party. One group of moderates, refusing to accept that stark choice, continued to try to make Quaker ideas politically relevant up to and beyond the revolution. They made a noble attempt to find peace with the Indians through nonviolent mediation and advocated nonviolent alternatives to war in the lead-up to the revolution. Though their efforts may have had some influence on the tone of American political life,[28] their policy recommendations were decisively rejected.

3. *Indian Relations.* Toward demonstrating his ambition to live peacefully with the Indians, Penn purchased land from them "fairly and openly," as ratified by numerous treaties, even though ownership of Pennsylvania had been granted to him as "the largest individual landlord in the British empire" without regard to Indian interests.[29] As an example of his solicitude, Penn and his successors undertook to establish safe havens for Indians willing and eager to establish peaceful relations with white settlers.

Penn and one of his sons took the trouble to learn the Native language, and the father was a frequent visitor in Indian communities, producing a bond of mutual affection and respect. One year after his death, his successors tried to extend his vision of a Peaceable Kingdom by working out an amicable agreement between warring Indian tribes.

Penn was particularly emphatic about applying the principle of equal protection of the law to whites and Indians alike. He left instructions that traders be licensed and trade carefully regulated so that Indians would not be defrauded and mistreated. Of special concern was the sale of alcohol, a substance as appealing as it was disruptive to Indian communities. In 1701 laws aimed at preventing abuses and ensuring Indians fair treatment were duly passed by the assembly, with similar laws passed in the decades leading up to the revolution.

One central objective of such laws, including laws against selling alcohol, was religious, and, accordingly, thoroughly consistent with Penn's original vision. Addiction to alcohol, like violations of other rules of virtuous living, impeded access to the Quaker lifestyle. Therefore, the laws, "along with kind and obliging treatment," might serve to induce Indians "to embrace the Christian religion." Law and missionary activity were deeply intertwined.[30]

For many reasons, however, Penn's Indian policy was doomed to failure from the start. One source of failure was the structure of government itself, giving so much power over land transactions and management to the proprietors. The problem started with William Penn himself but became acute in the hands of his heirs, especially John and Thomas Penn, whose passion for profits overrode all their father's ideals.

Penn's sons, from the 1720s on, resented assembly demands that they help pay for the gifts given to Indians in exchange for land purchased and for the treaties of friendship required to sustain the transactions. There were also cultural differences in the understanding of land ownership. Unlike the colonists, Indians believed land was held in trust to sustain life rather than to make profit.[31] More important, Penn's sons would go to any length to advance their fortune, including acts of fraud. In one instance, they conspired with the Iroquois Indians, dominant in the region, to disenfranchise the local Delawares and Shawnees, making them subservient to the Iroquois. Then the sons used that alliance to enforce "a crude forgery," known as the "Walking Purchase Hoax of 1737."[32] It resulted in the loss of 710,000 acres of local tribal lands,[33] based on a fifty-year-old "deed" produced by Penn's sons falsely alleging that their father had acquired a vast tract of Indian land whose full dimensions had yet to be established by walking them off in a day-and-a-half trek. Indian leaders were at first suspicious and then thoroughly outraged by the unscrupulous way in which the trek was carried out.

Though it was just one of a large number of injustices visited upon the local Indians by the proprietors, the Walking Purchase "remained a burning grievance." It "transformed the landscape"

west of the Delaware River, "doomed the region's native inhabitants," and became "the main catalyst for the Delawares eventually
going to war against Pennsylvania" in the 1750s and '60s.[34]

The other source of failure was a combustible combination of
factors: a massive influx of settlers giving Pennsylvania the third-
largest population among the colonies by 1755; the practical challenges of enforcing laws regarding property, trading, and other
matters affecting settlers and Indians on the frontier; a lenient and
sometimes reluctant attitude among Quakers toward law enforcement[35] and military defense on the frontier;[36] widespread anti-
Indian prejudice and abuse; defiance toward law enforcement;
and outright vigilantism on the part of many non-Quaker settlers,
especially the Scots-Irish, who on occasion publicly threatened "to
oppose every one of Pennsylvania's laws," and regularly sheltered
fellow settlers charged with violating those laws.[37]

The final defeat of the Indian policy was marked by armed attacks on settlements of Indians in Conestoga and Lancaster in late
1763 and the threat of an attack on a settlement near Philadelphia
in early 1764, all by a group of Scots-Irish frontiersmen known as
the Paxton Boys. They were part of the militia that had been bat-
tling Indians during the French and Indian War. Embittered and
frustrated by the losses and damage sustained, and by what they
believed to be government indifference to their plight, the Paxton
Boys developed intense animosity against all Indians and decided
to kill some twenty unarmed settlement residents. The attack on
Conestoga was especially notable, since William Penn himself had
established a treaty of peace with the Indians in that area.

The threatened attack near Philadelphia led to a standoff because nearby residents, including a large number of younger
Quakers, proved ready to provide an armed defense of the Indians, even though many German and Scots-Irish residents would
not resist the Paxtons out of loyalty to the frontiersmen. Instead
of carrying out their attack, the Paxton Boys presented a list of
grievances they demanded be addressed—among other things
banishing some Indians from the province and excluding all Indians from "inhabited" areas during times of war. As a result of
widespread support from non-Quakers, as well as weak law enforcement, the Paxton Boys were never brought to justice.

II.

Legislation Derived from Quaker Principles,
1776–1820 and Beyond
Legal Limits on Religious Belief and Practice

1. *Freedom of Conscience.* A new Constitution was enacted on September 28, 1776, by proclamation of a state constitutional convention. Promulgated in response to instructions by the Second Continental Congress and the Declaration of Independence to reject British rule, the Pennsylvania Constitution did not significantly alter the language of the 1701 Charter of Privileges with regard to freedom of conscience. Although broadly inclusive, the text retains the same limits as earlier. Citizens retain "a natural and unalienable right to worship Almighty God according to the dictates of their own consciences and understanding," and no one "who acknowledges the being of a God" may "be justly deprived or abridged of any civil right as a citizen." Atheists were still unprotected. That was reinforced by explicit references in the preamble to the "Author of existence" and the "great Governor of the Universe" whose "goodness was confessed" and "demonstrated" by allowing the people to form a new government and "reach hitherto undreamed of heights of happiness."

In one important respect, though, the 1776 Constitution and subsequent laws strongly committed to the revolution greatly narrowed the range of freedom of conscience by introducing burdens on the beliefs and practices of Quakers and their close religious allies, the Moravians and Mennonites. Members of these groups were of one mind in refusing to use force in opposing the British. The Constitution exempted "any man who is conscientiously scrupulous of bearing arms," just so long as "he will pay such equivalent." Even that provision was too high a bar for those who opposed the war on grounds of conscience. Quakers declared officially that they were neutral in the Revolutionary War. They "would not fight, would not make declarations of allegiance to anyone, would pay no taxes to governments of uncertain legitimacy, and would not vote." They would wait for God to favor one side or the other.[38]

Because the revolutionary government took neutrality for near treason, required military service or support for a substitute of all able-bodied citizens, and demanded loyalty oaths, Quakers, Moravians, and Mennonites suffered severe legal and extralegal penalties, including imprisonment, fines, destruction of property, and public humiliation.

2. *Eligibility for Public Office.* The 1776 Constitution liberalized opportunities for public service by dropping the restriction against Roman Catholics and by initially considering broadening the religious test to make eligible anyone who would simply affirm the existence of a God who punishes the wicked and rewards the good. That looser standard marked a sharp departure from the narrower test long established by the Charter of Privileges of 1701 that the government be conducted by Protestants. However, there was such a strong reaction to the looser standard by non-Quakers, now vastly outnumbering the Quakers, that the test was tightened. In addition to avowing a God who rewards and punishes, officeholders must also acknowledge "the Scriptures of the Old and New Testament to be given by Divine inspiration."

That test was challenged in 1783 by several Pennsylvania Jews as unfairly barring them from public office, as casting "a stigma on them and their religion," and as contradicting declarations of freedom of conscience elsewhere in the Constitution. Four years later, a Jewish leader requested that a convention, then considering a new constitution, eliminate all religious tests. That did not happen, but the Constitution of 1790 did modify the test by removing the reference to the Old and New Testaments, thereby making Jews eligible for public office. Though the new Constitution retained the connection between freedom of worship and service to "Almighty God," as well as the broad religious tests for public office, it departed from inherited practice by eliminating all references to divine authority in the preamble.

3. *Blasphemy, Defamation of Religion, and Profanity.* "The approach of the Revolution quickened the impulse of Pennsylvania's leaders for moral legislation."[39] That involved passing a

series of laws in the latter eighteenth and early nineteenth centuries intended to prohibit a wide array of acts regarded as a
threat to public virtue and good order. They included consum-
ing alcohol, gambling, cockfighting, horse racing, and staging
plays. This particularly included the use of profanity, the punishment of which exemplified the enduring religious tone of
Pennsylvania political culture during and after the revolution.
For example, the *Act for the Suppression of Vice and Immorality*,
adopted in 1779, imposed penalties of ten shillings or imprisonment at hard labor for up to five days "if any person of the age of
sixteen years or upwards" "shall profanely swear or curse by the
name of God, Christ, Jesus, or the Holy Ghost" within the hearing of any officer of the law, the testimony of one witness, or the
confession of the offending party.[40] A similar bill, also outlawing
profane swearing or cursing, was passed in 1794, entitled *An
Act for the Prevention of Vice and Immorality, and of Unlawful
Gaming, and To Restrain Disorderly Sports and Dissipation*.

Blasphemy continued to be a subject of both concern and dispute well into the nineteenth century. In 1818 one Robert Murphy
was convicted of blasphemy in the Mayor's Court in Philadelphia,[41] a case that generated protest by a local newspaper. The opposition gained momentum in the late 1820s, led by the newly
formed Working Men's Party that denounced all blasphemy laws,
religious tests for office, Sabbath laws, and prayer at public functions as violations of the separation of church and state.

The issue came to a head in *Updegraph v. Commonwealth*, a
case that reached the state supreme court in 1824. Abner Updegraph was a member of a debating society where he stated that the
Bible is full of fables and myths. He was convicted by a lower court
and fined ten shillings under the statute passed in 1700 outlawing utterances that do "blaspheme, and speak loosely and profane"
the members of the Holy Trinity or the scriptures. Justice Thomas
Duncan, writing for the court, reversed the decision against Updegraph on technical grounds, claiming that the lower court failed
to charge him with "profane" speech, as required under the statute.[42] However, Justice Duncan left no doubt that if he had been
so charged, Updegraph would have been found guilty, since the
major thrust of his opinion aims to uphold the 1700 law. Citing

William Penn, Duncan contended that "general Christianity is, and always has been, part of the common law of Pennsylvania." He continued, "While our own free constitution secures liberty of conscience and freedom of religious worship for all, it is not necessary to maintain that any man should have the right publicly to vilify the religion of his neighbors and of the country . . . licentiousness endangering the public peace, when tending to corrupt society, is considered as a breach of the peace, and punishable by indictment."[43]

4. *Sabbath Observance.* "Virtually no one opposed some kind of Sunday legislation in either the colonial or the early national period, and every state had some restrictions." In Pennsylvania, "where legislation was on the books and remained so throughout the nineteenth century," there was not much controversy.[44] There were some disputes over what sort of business might be undertaken on Sunday (whether buses could take people to church and whether churches might restrict street traffic in front of their buildings), but there was a general disposition, even on the part of nonreligious citizens, to support a day of rest for secular, if not religious, reasons.

Key Subjects of Legislation

1. *Oaths.* During the revolution, Quakers made it clear that they "would not make declarations of allegiance to anyone," an objection for which they paid dearly. No longer was it a matter of being accommodated for refusing to swear an oath. Quakers were free to affirm and not swear. The problem was what they were being asked to affirm. In 1777 the assembly enacted a law intended to weaken further Quaker political influence and to dilute their dissent.

The law required an oath or affirmation of all males over eighteen renouncing the king of Great Britain and pledging faithful adherence to the Commonwealth of Pennsylvania. Anyone refusing to comply was prohibited from "holding any office or place of trust" in the government, including "serving on juries, suing for any debts, electing or being elected, buying, selling or transferring any lands, tenements, or [items of inheritance]." Widespread non-compliance by Quakers, together with other forms of resistance to the revolutionary cause, resulted in seizure of property, the occupation of meetinghouses by the army, imprisonment, ridicule, and assault. Violators were also liable to pay taxes double the amount paid by those subscribing to the test. Convictions for violations of the test act declined sharply from 1779 to 1783, as the fighting subsided, and the act was repealed in 1787.[45]

2. *Pacifism.* After the crisis of 1756 over whether the assembly should openly and directly support war against the Indians, Pennsylvania Quakerism was never the same again. Of all Penn's original ideals, the principle of nonviolence was the most important, but also the most disruptive. Frustrating attempts to implement it with the realities of earthly government over a period of roughly eighty years was a principal cause of the decline of Quaker rule in the colony and of the abrupt and extensive reorientation of Quaker self-understanding in regard to the life and culture of Pennsylvania.

Widespread Quaker neutrality toward the revolution was largely the result of devotion to the "peace testimony"—the ideal of pacifism. But differences over adhering to that ideal also caused the fragmentation of Quakerism, as well as the loss of the ideal's political potency. Many Quakers were able to stand firm for their principles against the challenges of the revolution, and being steadfast meant cleansing their ranks of backsliders. By 1778, 418 members had been disowned for participating in the revolution, and by the end of the war the number was 908.[46]

While some in the Society of Friends later returned to the fold, many did not, but rather went on in 1781 to form their own society, known as the Free Quakers. Explicitly rejecting an absolute commitment to the principle of nonviolence, they embraced the Whig idea that the fundamental purpose of earthly government is to use force, where necessary, proportional, and probably effective, to protect against arbitrary violence. "When government is threatened by domestic treason or foreign invasion, every man is duty-bound to come to its defense, even to the extent of waging defensive war, which, although extreme, would still be justified."[47]

Notably, Free Quakers invoked another of William Penn's key ideals, freedom of conscience, in support of their position. They had, they said, "no new doctrine to teach, nor any design of promoting schisms in religion. We wish only to be freed from every species of ecclesiastical tyranny, and mean to pay due regard to the principles of our forefathers, and to their rules and regulations, *so far as they apply to our circumstances*, and hope, thereby, to preserve decency and secure equal liberty to all."[48] In the spirit of Penn, argued Free Quakers, orthodox Quakers ought to renounce "ecclesiastical tyranny" and respect their right of free conscience to apply principles to circumstances as they saw fit. Whether Penn would have concurred on the merits is surely debatable.

Except for a small number, orthodox Quakers after the revolution largely withdrew from politics, thereby reducing concern with Quaker dominance. Because fewer officeholders were Quakers, "the secular political power of the Quakers was no longer a public issue." It was thereby apparent "that for the most part the Friends desired to remain aloof from partisan involvement, maintaining their disengagement even in the face of attempts by both major parties to woo their allegiance." Before the start of the revolution, "a real cleavage existed within the Society on the issue of political behavior, but in the postwar period the situation was rather one of a small number of deviants from the norm upheld by a well-disciplined and homogeneous body."[49]

3. *Indian Relations.* In *Peaceable Kingdom Lost*,[50] historian Kevin Kenny concluded that the mass slaughter of the Conestoga Indians by the Paxton Boys in 1763 was decisive for both the past and the future understanding of Indian relations in Pennsylvania. Not only did the event mean that "what was left of the Peaceable Kingdom had broken down entirely," it also set the stage for what policies would prevail in the revolutionary period and beyond.

In regard to the treatment of Indians, Kenny declared that "the idea that the Paxton Boys were precursors of the republican revolution is brutally accurate." The revolution did not just destroy oligarchy and proprietary privilege, which it did; it also "doomed

the region's Indians." "During the pamphlet war of 1764 defenders of the Paxton Boys argued that killing Indians was a form of
loyal opposition to bad government. This idea reached fruition
during the American Revolution, when exterminating Indians
became an act of patriotism." He continued, "Although William
Penn's legacy ensured that relations with Indians were at first
more harmonious in Pennsylvania than in other colonies, the
eventual outcome was everywhere the same: expropriation, conquest, and extermination."[51]

III.

From the beginning, the Pennsylvania experiment with freedom of conscience and church-state relations was based on high hopes. William Penn
envisioned a radically new society guided by the principles of love and peace.
Governments would no longer need to rely on force, and different religions,
treated fairly, would come to honor one another, as would the wide variety of
ethnic groups welcomed into the colony. Everyone would live harmoniously
with Indians.

These hopes were partially, if imperfectly, realized throughout the colonial,
revolutionary, and early national periods. There was no established religion
in the conventional sense, and a wide array of religious groups, including
several unpopular minorities, were hospitably accommodated. There were
laws against blasphemy, profanity, and violating the Sabbath, but they were
erratically enforced. The principle of pacifism influenced policy up until the
1750s by inhibiting full support for military defense, and some Quakers continued to treat Indians with justice and equity.

Penn's Holy Experiment, however, by no means worked out as planned.
Religious and ethnic strife were never absent, lawlessness was at times widespread, and vigilantism left a distressing mark on Pennsylvania history.
Above all, the ideal of pacifism proved hard to apply as a principle of government, and efforts to try eventually undermined support for Quaker rule.

The other problems were the structure of government and ambivalent
Quaker attitudes toward governance and law enforcement. The substantial
economic and political power invested in the office of proprietor created
severe tension with the assembly and was the cause of much political mal-
practice, particularly as regards the expropriation of Indian land. Quaker
reluctance toward extending government and enforcing the law, especially
when combined with similar, if differently motivated, propensities on the

part of many immigrants who settled the frontier, greatly reduced chances for realizing Penn's vision of a Peaceable Kingdom.

NOTES

1. George Arthur Cribbs, *The Frontier Policy of Pennsylvania* (Pittsburgh, 1919), 5.

2. H. J. Cadbury, "Penn as Pacifist," in *Pacifism in the United States: From the Colonial Era to the First World War*, ed. Peter Brock (Princeton, NJ: Princeton University Press, 1968), 83.

3. Based on a letter from William Penn to English Quakers (1684), summarized in Melvin B. Endy Jr., *William Penn and Early Quakerism* (Princeton, NJ: Princeton University Press, 1973), 354.

4. Jane E. Calvert, *Quaker Constitutionalism and the Political Thought of John Dickinson* (New York: Cambridge University Press, 2009), 29.

5. Endy, *William Penn*, 320.

6. Penn, "Good Advice," cited in *William Penn*, by Endy, 328.

7. J. William Frost, *A Perfect Freedom: Religious Liberty in Pennsylvania* (New York: Cambridge University Press, 1990), 18.

8. Sally Schwartz, *"A Mixed Multitude": The Struggle for Toleration in Colonial Pennsylvania* (New York: New York University Press, 1987), 31.

9. Frost, *Perfect Freedom*, 12.

10. Frost, *Perfect Freedom*, 21.

11. Frost, *Perfect Freedom*, 45.

12. Records of Quarter Sessions and Common Pleas of Bucks County, 1684–1700 (Meadville, PA: Tribune, 1943).

13. Jack D. Marietta and G. S. Rowe, *Troubled Experiment: Crime and Justice in Pennsylvania, 1682–1800* (Philadelphia: University of Pennsylvania Press, 2006), 41–42.

14. See James Mitchell and Henry Flanders, *Statutes at Large of Pennsylvania* (Harrisburg, PA: State of Pennsylvania, 1896), 2:175–77, for similar acts passed in the early 1700s.

15. Frost, *Perfect Freedom*, 69.

16. Frost, *Perfect Freedom*, 69–70.

17. See Frost, *Perfect Freedom*, 23–24; and Schwartz, *"Mixed Multitude,"* 43–46.

18. Marietta and Rowe, *Troubled Experiment*, 45, 50.

19. Still, ambivalence toward law enforcement, evident in the 1680s and '90s, apparently continued through the early decades of the eighteenth century. Calvert acknowledges that since the Quaker theory of punishment was aimed at restoration and rehabilitation, it was "more lenient" than was the case in the other colonies. At the same time, she speaks of the *Act for the Advancement of Justice of 1718* as adding twelve new capital crimes and harsher punishments for other offenses, probably

because of fear the Crown might again revoke the Charter, as it had done for two years in 1692 (*Quaker Constitutionalism*, 149–50).

20. Marietta and Rowe, *Troubled Experiment*, 43.

21. Marietta and Rowe, *Troubled Experiment*, 132.

22. Marietta and Rowe, *Troubled Experiment*, 134.

23. Marietta and Rowe, *Troubled Experiment*, 134.

24. Richard Bauman, *For the Reputation of Truth: Politics, Religion, and Conflict among the Pennsylvania Quakers, 1750–1800* (Baltimore: Johns Hopkins University Press, 1971), 5.

25. Bauman, *Reputation of Truth*, 6.

26. Bauman, *Reputation of Truth*, 6.

27. See Richard Alan Ryerson, "Portrait of a Colonial Oligarchy: The Quaker Elite in the Pennsylvania Assembly, 1729–1776," in *Power and Status: Office holding in Colonial America*, ed. Bruce C. Daniels (Middletown, CT: Wesleyan University Press, 1986), 106–35.

28. In *Quaker Constitutionalism*, Calvert argues that certain Quaker ideals, as advanced particularly by "quasi-Quakers" like John Dickinson, did have an important influence on American constitutional thinking.

29. Kevin Kenny, *Peaceable Kingdom Lost: The Paxton Boys and the Destruction of William Penn's Holy Experiment* (New York: Oxford University Press, 2009), 2.

30. Citations in Calvert, *Quaker Constitutionalism*, 150–51.

31. Kenny, *Peaceable Kingdom Lost*, 2.

32. Ray Thompson, *The Walking Purchase Hoax of 1737* (Fort Washington, PA: Bicentennial Press, 1973), 37.

33. See Kenny, *Peaceable Kingdom Lost*, 45–49, for a good summary.

34. Kenny, *Peaceable Kingdom Lost*, 49.

35. Marietta and Rowe, *Troubled Experiment*, 158–65.

36. How much effect Quaker pacifism had on the failure to provide adequate defense of the frontier is a disputed point. Cribbs contends that "before 1755 the pressure of danger was never sufficiently great to overcome the religious prejudices of the Quakers against the establishment of a militia" (*Frontier Policy of Pennsylvania*, 62). He suggests that Quaker assembly members went along with the militia policies of the governors as long as service was purely voluntary, but then notes that the militia law passed by the assembly in 1755 "was wholly inadequate" (64), precisely because it lacked enforceable discipline. Kenny claims that "Quaker pacifism was not a principal obstacle" to providing a militia (*Peaceable Kingdom Lost*, 74). However, he concedes that the group of soldiers assembled in 1755 as the result of the militia bill was "a ramshackle and loosely disciplined outfit" and not a serious fighting force. Kenny also states that "the creation of the official militia" at the time "marked a decisive break in the history of Quaker Pennsylvania" by provoking "a bitter dispute within the Society of Friends about the legacy of William Penn and his holy experiment" (79). It is hard not to conclude that up until that time, Quaker assembly members were at most halfhearted about supporting a militia, that such reticence was a serious obstacle to adequate defense, and that this was the case because the legacy of pacifism was such a central part of the colony's ideals from the beginning.

37. Cribbs, *Frontier Policy*, 165, 13.

38. Frost, *Perfect Freedom*, 66.

39. Frost, *Perfect Freedom*, 71.

40. Section II, Statutes of Pennsylvania, Mitchell and Flanders, 9:1776–79.

41. Mentioned in Frost, *Perfect Freedom*, 95 (though I have been unable to find additional details on the case).

42. *Updegraph v. Commonwealth*, 11 Serg. & Rawle. (26 Pa.) 394 (1834). See Thomas Sergeant and William Rawle, *Reports of Cases Adjudged in the Supreme Court of Pennsylvania* (Philadelphia: Kay & Brother, 1871).

43. Michael S. Ariens and Robert A. Destro, *Religious Liberty in a Pluralistic Society* (Durham, NC: Carolina Academic Press, 1996), 115–17.

44. Frost, *Perfect Freedom*, 134–35. See p. 142 for a discussion of scattered opposition to Sabbath laws in early Pennsylvania history.

45. Cited in Arthur J. Mekeel, *The Relation of the Quakers to the American Revolution* (Washington, DC: University Press of America, 1979), 166, 189, 200.

46. Bauman, *Reputation of Truth*, 165.

47. Bauman, *Reputation of Truth*, 167.

48. Bauman, *Reputation of Truth*, 167 (emphasis added).

49. Bauman, *Reputation of Truth*, 179.

50. Bauman, *Reputation of Truth*, 179.

51. Kenny, *Peaceable Kingdom Lost*, 231.

CHAPTER SIX

NORTH CAROLINA
Early Toleration and Disestablishment

Nicholas P. Miller

NORTH CAROLINA WAS one of the earliest British colonies in North America with a robust religious toleration. Indeed, the closest North Carolina came to having an operating Church of England establishment was a century after its initial founding in 1663. It was a belated push in the 1760s and '70s by the British Crown to reassert control over its colony by invigorating an anemic Anglican establishment that triggered a backlash in the form of a comprehensive disestablishment in North Carolina's Constitution of 1776.

Dissenting religious groups in colonial Carolina labored under a variety of statutory disabilities for several decades, but often the laws were not enforced. Dissenting clergy had their authority to perform marriages denied and their ability to establish and operate schools restricted. But these limits were on paper, and the enforcement seems to have been episodic and in many instances the law was never implemented.[1]

Disestablishment, when it came to North Carolina in 1776, brushed aside an establishment that existed mostly on paper and codified what had been occurring on the ground for some time: a practical toleration of a variety of Protestant churches and denominations. The power of North Carolina's story lies in its lack of drama and ordinariness to us today. But its occurrence was not experienced as ordinary in its own time. It built on colonial precedents and demonstrated religious freedom put into action.

I.

The history of the colony of Carolina (divided in 1720s into North Carolina and South Carolina) originated by a grant of land in 1663 from Charles II to eight British noblemen, known as the Lords Proprietor. The grant was given in return for the Proprietors' support in restoring the king to the British throne. The Lords Proprietor included Edward Hyde, First Earl of Clarendon, who was Lord Chancellor of England for nearly ten years; George Monck, First Duke of Albemarle, a military leader who had charge of the admiralty; and William Craven, First Earl of Craven, who held various court offices.[2]

The best known of the Lords Proprietor was Anthony Ashley Cooper, First Earl of Shaftesbury, a capable politician, military leader, and religio-political philosopher.[3] Cooper played the leading role among the Lords Proprietor organizing the Carolina colony and writing its colonial constitution. Cooper had the assistance of his secretary, political philosopher and essayist John Locke. The *Fundamental Constitutions of Carolina* was highly tolerant of religious diversity and practice. The Anglican church was situated as the established church, an arm of the Crown and supported by it. However, other religious bodies were acknowledged and protected by law, so long as they comprised seven or more people who believed in a God that was to be worshipped, which could serve as a basis to swear or affirm the truth of legal declarations.[4]

The provisions regarding religion in the 1669 *Fundamental Constitutions of Carolina* run from Section 95 to 109. Select provisions include:

> 95th. No man shall be permitted to be a freeman of Carolina, or to have any estate or habitation within it, that doth not acknowledge a God, and that God is publicly and solemnly to be worshipped.
>
> 96th. As the country comes to be sufficiently planted, and distributed in fit divisions, it shall belong to the Parliament to take care for the building of churches and the public maintenance of divines, to be employed in the exercise of religion, according to the Church of England; . . . it alone shall be allowed to receive public maintenance by grant of parliament.
>
> . . .
>
> 100th. In the terms of communion of every church or profession, these following shall be three, with out which no agreement or assembly of men upon pretence of religion, shall be accounted a church or profession within these rules.
>
> 1st. That there is a God.
>
> II. That God is publickly to be worshipped.
>
> III. That it is lawful and the duty of every man being thereunto called by those that govern, to bear witness to truth . . .
>
> . . .
>
> 109th. No person whatsoever shall disturb, molest, or persecute another, for his speculative opinions in religion, or his way of worship.[5]

The foregoing sections encompassed a broad toleration for its time. Inhabitants could embrace not just dissenting Protestantism but also Roman Catholicism, Judaism, and paganism, as well as Native American spiritualism. Some scholars have attributed this remarkable sweep of toleration to the involvement of John Locke. As secretary to the lead Proprietor, Anthony Ashley Cooper, Locke was doubtlessly involved with the drafting of the constitution. Though the centrality and impact of his hand in producing the document is contested, it is generally acknowledged that Locke's contribution was more than that of a clerical secretary.[6] But it was not just Locke among the organizers of Carolina that had convictions favoring religious toleration. The lives of Cooper and Edward Hyde had been touched by dissenting Protestants committed to respecting religious conscious. Moreover, Locke had his limitations. For example, the religious politics of Great Britain found Locke unwilling to tolerate Catholics, which the Carolina colonial constitution did do.

Anthony Ashley Cooper famously authored a lengthy pamphlet against a proposed Test Act to be enforced against Catholics and Protestant dissenters alike. Entitled *Letter from a Person of Quality*, the pamphlet opposed both royal and episcopal absolutism, and especially opposed combining the two. Christ is head of the church, Cooper argued, whose kingdom is not of this world.[7] For the civil power to decide who is in charge of the church, wrote Cooper, what its doctrines should be, and how God is to be worship usurped that intrinsic distinction between church and government. Further, to insist that the established religion can never be altered ignored the fact that all creedal documents of the Church of England, including the Thirty-Nine Articles, the Book of Common Prayer, and the Catechism, contained items that were argued over and opposed by well-known Protestant teachers and leaders. Who could resolve such differences except each church deciding for itself?[8]

The problem of interpretation and creedal authority was a well-known issue in dissenting Protestant circles, including those frequented by other Proprietors. Edward Hyde, known for his attempts to extend toleration to additional groups of dissenters, was a prominent member of the Great Tew Circle. This was a group of progressive thinkers and intellectuals who gathered regularly at a country house in Great Tew, Oxfordshire, and were known for their views on the importance of religious toleration.[9] The central figure in the Great Tew Circle was William Chillingworth, who authored the influential work *The Religion of Protestants a Safe Way to Salvation*. The essay argues for the sole authority of the Bible in spiritual questions and the right of individual believers to interpret Scripture according to their personal judgment and conscience.[10]

Still other Proprietors had shown an interest in and supported dissenters. George Carteret and John Berkeley combined their efforts in founding the colony of New Jersey. They jointly drafted *The Concession and Agreement of the Lords Proprietors of the Province of New Caesarea, or New Jersey* (1665), a document that provided broad freedom of religion in that colony. Sir John Colleton wrote in 1663 that those persons planning to settle in Carolina "expect liberty of conscience and without that will not go." Elsewhere, in promotional material for the colony, the Proprietors promised that they would "grant, in as ample manner as the undertakers shall desire, freedom and liberty of conscience in all religious or spiritual things." In 1667 the Lords Proprietor instructed the first governor of Carolina that he should see to it that "all . . . persons may . . . at all times freely and fully have and enjoy their judgments and conscience in matter of religion."[11]

This stream of biblically conservative dissenting Protestantism had been known to exist for some time on the margins of seventeenth-century English society. But it is lesser known that it had a real and lasting impact in the distant Carolina colony. This commitment by the colony's founders led to a weak Church of England establishment that had little support in the hearts of the settlers or even much of a physical presence by way of church structures.

II.

Carolina was not settled by a vibrantly religious people. Foremost it was planned and settled by the Lords Proprietor with commercial objectives. The religiosity of first residents could be perfunctory, with religious involvement secondary to carving out a living on the colonial frontier.[12] That said, remarks like that by William Byrd II, an eminent Virginian political leader and Anglican who visited in 1728, overstate the matter when he wrote, "I believe this is the only metropolis in the Christian or Manhometan world where there is neither church, Chappel, Mosque, Synagogue, or any other place of Public Worship of any Sect or Religion whatsoever."[13] Another scholar writes that in 1700, while there were five thousand whites, "plus Negroes and Indians," there were "no clergyman or regular forms of public worship."[14] Yet in Carolina's first two decades, various nonconformist and dissenter groups had become quite active in the colony.

The earliest settlers to the area known as Carolina had trickled down in the 1650s from Virginia into northeastern Carolina, just north of the

Albermarle Sound.[15] They were mostly nominal Anglicans and had no minister or church building among them. When first in receipt of their grant, the Lords Proprietor did not intend to implement the Anglican establishment called for by the 1669 *Fundamental Constitutions of Carolina*. Indeed, in that same year they passed an act "permitting civil marriages, for [there was a] lack of clergy to perform the ceremony."[16] This was a simpler and less expensive solution than actually making Anglican priests available to the colonists, and it was consistent with the views of the Proprietors about the dangers of an established episcopacy.

The first religious leaders to work consistently in Carolina were Quaker missionaries. They began to arrive in the 1670s and, noting the general ir-religion of the inhabitants, began a robust effort.[17] From a combination of conversions and continued influx from the north, Quakers became the dominant religious group by the 1690s. Indeed, the Quaker influence was such that one of their number, John Archdale, served as proprietary governor in the 1690s.[18] Archdale's governorship marked the height of Quaker influence. In 1696 the assembly passed a bill guaranteeing "all Christians (Papists only excepted) . . . full liberty of conscience."[19]

At the turn of the century, new dissenting groups began to make their presence known. Before 1710 a number of Presbyterians had become resident in the colony. They rapidly became the second most numerous religious group, behind the Quakers but more numerous than Anglicans.[20] Presbyterians eventually replaced the Quakers in political influence. They became the main group sparring with the Anglican establishment and arguing against restrictions in the legal code imposed on behalf of the establishment.[21]

Also by 1700, "no Episcopal ministers had come to the colony; no parishes had been laid off, no churches had been built, no tithes had been levied; absolutely nothing was done by the Established Church for the spiritual advancement of North Carolina."[22] Additionally, the influence of the Lords Proprietor began to wane. Organized religion was not the only area of colonial administration that the Lords Proprietor had been neglecting, or so many colonists thought. There had been a general failure to provide security and military support, especially in the southeastern part of the colony.

The Carolina Assembly, realizing that the Proprietors would probably never act on the matter of establishment, took matters into their own hands. In 1701 the assembly passed a *Vestry Act* that authorized the purchase of parish land to serve as glebes, the building of Anglican churches, and the financial support of its ministers. That same year, the metes and bounds of five parishes were laid out, vestries named, and instructions given to levy a tax of five shillings from each colonist to pay the Anglican clergy, put up church buildings, and purchase glebe lands. The salary of these ministers was fixed at thirty pounds yearly. Upon being notified, the Lords Proprietor annulled the *Vestry Act*, ostensibly because they viewed the proposed salary of the ministers as being inadequate.[23] The official reason was likely to hide the people's general opposition to the Anglican establishment.

Some Carolinian leaders resolved to ignore the annulment of the Vestry Act of 1701. They proceeded to erect a number of church buildings, to which the governor provided funding. Two years later, in 1703, the assembly passed a *Religious Test Act* requiring all of its delegates to take communion according to Anglican rites. The act barred most dissenters, including Quakers, from holding political office. Three years later, Queen Anne in council disallowed the *Test Act*. In 1711 the assembly acquiesced and proceeded to adopt the laws of England regarding establishment, including the laws' protection of dissenters. This act allowed dissenters to hold office if they affirmed the Holy Trinity and the Thirty-Nine Articles of the Church of England, with exceptions for the form of church polity, baptism of infants, and permitting Quakers to affirm rather than swear support for the Crown.[24] The 1711 Act, making applicable in the colony the *Toleration Act of 1689*, effectively excluded only Unitarians and Roman Catholics, neither of whom had meaningful numbers in the colony.[25]

In 1715 the assembly passed a new Vestry Act, replacing the annulled 1703 version. This 1715 Act created nine parishes, raised the salary of Anglican rectors from thirty to fifty pounds a year, and gave instructions to levy a tax on each colonist to put up Anglican church buildings and purchase glebe lands.[26]

In 1719 the colonists to the south became sufficiently frustrated with the lack of protection from the Spanish in Florida and the French and Indians to the west, such that they formed a breakaway government. These southern inhabitants then invited Great Britain to directly govern the southeastern portion of the colony. The Crown did so, forming the separate colony of South Carolina in 1720. Proprietary rule continued in the North until 1729, when the *Fundamental Constitutions* was revoked and the Crown assumed royal control.[27]

By 1720, when the Crown separated South Carolina from North Carolina, Presbyterian and Quaker dissenters in the North had spread geographically and gained sufficient numbers that even a royal government highly motivated to create a robust Anglican establishment would have had difficulty. The ranks of the dissenters soon swelled by the arrival of Baptists. In 1727 the first Baptist church in Camden County was founded in the northern colony. Like the Quakers, the Baptists came down from Virginia and farther north. They were initially General Baptists, a type advocating for the right of personal judgment in religious matters and a church supported entirely by the voluntary contributions of members. Over the next few decades, "the Baptists were the most active and successful group of dissenters in the province."[28]

From 1730 to 1773, the royal government of North Carolina enforced the *Schism Act*, thus undermining the Toleration Act. The *Schism Act* excluded dissenters from virtually all offices of power or profit, even barring them from holding positions in schools and academies. In response, the Baptists were persistently nettlesome to the Anglican establishment. As a consequence, Baptists were the only dissenters actively persecuted in the colony, even being sentenced to jail. For example, in 1741 Baptists in New Bern petitioned authorities for permission to build a church, at the same period of time that Anglicans were raising funds for a chapel. The petition was denied, and the judge threw several Baptists in jail when they refused to cease efforts at putting up a meetinghouse.[29]

III.

Between 1729 and 1765, efforts by the Crown were made to enhance support for the Anglican church, but they produced meager results. Even after the arrival of the royal governor in 1730, who had instructions to secure the Anglican establishment, it took a decade for the apathetic assembly to move to revitalize the parishes. In 1741 the assembly passed another *Vestry Act*. In an effort to generate local enthusiasm by allowing greater local control, the act allowed the colonists to choose their own vestrymen rather than have them appointed by the assembly.[30] It did not work well. Due to religious demographics, high numbers of dissenters were elected to vestry boards. These dissenters would then take no action as a board, or they would attempt to provoke the Anglican minister to leave town. One clergyman reported that the majority of vestrymen in Wilmington were "professed dissenters" who did their best to get him to leave.[31]

This pattern of dissenter resistance was quite effective. Between 1700 and 1730, there were "never more than two [Anglican clergy] in the colony, and at times none." Between when the royal governor took over in 1730 and the *Vestry Act of 1741*, the highest number of established clergy was three. Yielding greater local control seems to have further harmed the establishment. Between 1741 and 1760, there is evidence only of one or two Anglican clergy, and for significant periods none at all, along with a scarcity of church buildings.[32] In 1754 the assembly tried to revise the 1741 *Vestry Act*, but the attempt was nullified by the British Crown.

It was not until the 1760s when the British Crown took a truly ambitious interest in building up the Anglican church. The Crown moved to implement a more centralized and robust establishment than either the dissenters or the Anglicans desired. The assembly passed a series of Vestry Acts between 1760 and 1764 that were unacceptable either to local royal authorities or to the Crown. It was not until 1764–65 that Vestry and Clergy Acts received the support of both local authorities and the Crown.

With these two acts, North Carolina, as one historian put it, "now had as strong a legal establishment as any other [American] colony," at least on paper.[33] But reality continued to lag behind the law. There were only five or six ministers for twenty-nine vestries and fewer than five Anglican church buildings in all of North Carolina, along with some small chapels.[34] This compares with approximately thirty ordained ministers working for Baptist congregations alone. The paucity of Anglican clergy is illustrated by the fact that when Governor Dobbs died in 1765, he had to be buried without benefit of clergy, there being no Anglican minister in southern Brunswick County, where he was interred.[35]

Ironically, the robust nature of the *Vestry and Clergy Acts of 1764 and 1765* proved to be the beginning of the end for the legal establishment. The legislation threatened to put meaningful civil enforcement behind what had been an impotent establishment, and this roused dissenters of every denomination into open and active resistance.[36] In the words of historian Gary Freeze:

> Establishment, politically a dead letter, needed only to be blotted from the law books. The church establishment seems to have had so few friends that, in changing government it was hardly noticed . . . . Anglican interests, which had sought autonomy for years, had little to lose in the disestablishment of a nearly defunct church. Dissenters, particularly Baptists, had much to gain, for their doctrines would enjoy legal and social acceptance. Thus, the conservative Anglicans could easily give in to any dissenter position, obtaining support for patriot government in return.[37]

A long-standing point of contention was the authority of dissenting clergy to perform marriages. The *Vestry Act of 1741* said that only Anglican clergy or civil magistrates could perform marriages, but this largely had been ignored. Following the *1765 Clergy Act*, however, the assembly declared that any clergy in violation of the marriage restriction would be fined fifty pounds. An allowance was made for Presbyterians, who could seek a license to perform marriages and transfer the fee paid by the couple over to an Anglican minister. But the arrangement annoyed Presbyterians who went uncompensated, not to mention the other dissenters for whom no allowance was made.[38]

The marriage issue, as well as new efforts to enforce religious taxes imposed by the *1764 Vestry Act*, served to unite the Quakers, Baptists, and Presbyterians in a campaign to overturn the establishment. They began a decade-long effort to stack vestry boards with dissenters, violate the marriage restriction, evade the religious tax, and otherwise disrupt the royal efforts to maintain the Anglican establishment. One tactic was to elect dissenters as vestrymen, then the elected candidate would refuse to take the prescribed oath, automatically disqualifying himself and preventing a vestry from forming. Those refusing to take the oath would incur a fine, but the community of dissenters created a fund to pay the fines. As one historian described it: "From 1765 until 1776 there were almost constant evasions or criticisms of either the vestry acts or the governor's interpretation of them. When enforced against the will of the people, these acts were part of the bitter fruits of an established church."[39]

Attempts by William Tryon, the royal governor, to strengthen the establishment only served to reinforce the resistance. The Presbyterians and Baptists formed a bloc opposed to the royal governor's work to invigorate the establishment. Seeking religious liberty, they were potential patriots, but only if their disaffection with the Anglican church was assuaged by ending the establishment. Concerning the actions of Governor Tryon to divide the dissenters, one historian writes: "[I]n differentiating between the two [churches] he produced two reactions—one of political cohesion among Presbyterians which enable them to write the actual disestablishment laws, and one of resentment toward the Crown which fostered a spirit of democracy among the Baptists. These factors, born in a tradition of local autonomy, fueled with the enthusiasm of the Great Awakening, and nurtured by the political controversies leading to the Revolution assured the end of establishment." The need to unite the dissenters behind the state's revolutionary leadership, and in turn the leaders being asked to give up an establishment that had always been marginal, made for an easy agreement.[40]

IV.

A state constitutional convention was called to meet in Halifax, North Carolina, in 1776. The delegates, assembled in "Congress," met from November 12 until reporting out a Constitution on December 18. The records of the constitutional convention contain no accounts of discussions or debates surrounding these provisions. Nor are there any extant newspapers during the period of the Constitution's passage. But the provisions themselves clearly dispelled the shadow of an Anglican establishment and left only a theoretical multiestablishment—albeit decidedly Protestant—in its place. It certainly meant that nobody could be forced to either attend church or worship services or to pay money to support any religious minister, church, or denomination. All persons were free to choose, support, and exercise the religion of their choice. But the prohibition against government support or promotion of religion was not seen as inconsistent with the law's alignment with an orthodox Protestant understanding of public virtue and private morality.

The 1776 Constitution included several provisions dealing with religion and religious freedom. It began with a Declaration of Rights that provided in Article XIX: "That all men have a natural and unalienable right to worship Almighty God according to the dictates of their own consciences." The Declaration's protection of religious conscience was stated specificity in the body of the Constitution, which contained three distinct provisions regarding religion. Article XXXI declared: "[T]hat no clergyman, or preacher of the gospels of any denomination, shall be capable of being a member of either the Senate, House of Commons, or Council of State, while he continues in the exercise of the pastoral function."[41] This prohibition against clergy serving in public office had deep roots in English common law, where clergy were excluded from the House of Commons, as they were considered already represented in the House of Lords. The motive behind the exclusion was not anticlericalism, for at least one clergyman was a member of the convention that wrote the Constitution. The restraint was apparently borrowed from the Delaware Constitution, which had passed shortly before.[42]

Article XXXII provided that only orthodox Protestants could hold public office: That no person, who shall deny the being of God or the truth of the Protestant religion, or the divine authority either of the Old or New Testaments, or who shall hold religious principles incompatible with the freedom and safety of the State, shall be capable of holding any office or place of trust or profit in the civil department within this State."[43] The Constitution concluded its treatment of religion with a thoroughgoing antiestablishment clause in Article XXXIV:

That there shall be no establishment of any one religious church or denomination in this State, in preference to any other; neither shall any person, on any pretense whatsoever, be compelled to attend any place of worship contrary to his own faith or judgment, nor be obliged to pay, for the purchase of any glebe, or the building of any house of worship, or for the maintenance of any minister or ministry, contrary to what he believes right, or has voluntarily and personally engaged to perform; but all persons shall be at liberty to exercise their own mode of worship:—*Provided*, That nothing herein contained shall be construed to exempt preachers of treasonable or seditious discourses, from legal trial and punishment.[44]

The disestablishment of the Anglican church came with one meaningful concession to the Anglicans. In legislation passed at the same time as the Constitution, it was provided that church property, including "all Glebes, Lands and Tenements," which had been "purchased, given or devised" for the support of any church [which would be Anglican in North Carolina], would "remain forever to the Use and Occupancy" of the church to which it had been given, purchased, or devised. Thus, Anglican church lands and properties would not be stripped from them upon the Constitution becoming effective.[45]

V.

When North Carolina delegates met in July and August 1788 to consider whether to ratify the United States Constitution proposed by the 1787 Philadelphia Convention, the delegates chose to withhold approval until a bill of rights was added. Of particular concern to the state convention was the lack of protection for religious freedom. There was extended discussion concerning the Religion Test Clause in Article VI, Clause [3] of the federal Constitution, some fearing that this would allow Jews, pagans, and atheists to hold federal office. Others responded that test clauses had been the basis of persecution in the past and that adopting such provisions would not keep unscrupulous persons out of government, as such would be willing to swear falsely to such tests. In defense of the Philadelphia draft, several argued that the federal government had been delegated no power over the subject of religion and thus could not infringe on religious liberty. But others thought the right of religious exercise so precious that they wanted an expressed guarantee of it.[46]

North Carolina's ratification convention had not assembled until July 21, 1788. In early August, the convention voted not to ratify.[47] Thus, North

Carolina joined Rhode Island as the only holdouts. There was lively debate in North Carolina concerning religious freedom and the federal Constitution. The discussion began with Henry Abbot stating that the people harbored a fear for religious conscience under the new system and that by the treaty power, the central government might "make a treaty engaging with foreign powers to adopt the Roman Catholic religion in the United States." He went on to claim, "Many wish to know what religion shall be established. I believe a majority of the community are Presbyterians. I am, for my part, against any exclusive establishment; but if there were any, I would prefer the Episcopal." Turning his attention to the Religious Test Clause, Abbot said that some worried "if there be no religious test required, pagans, deists, and Mahometans might obtain offices among us, and that the senators and representatives might all be pagans."[48]

A leading Federalist in the state, James Iredell, responded to these fears by first extolling the spirit of toleration in the American states and pointing out that the Religious Test Clause was to restrict Congress (not empower it), and thus it promoted religious liberty.[49] Addressing frontally the matter of congressional power over establishment, Iredell responded with the longest dissertation at any ratification convention on the matter of establishing religion:

> They certainly have no authority to interfere in the establishment of any religion whatsoever; and I am astonished that any gentleman should conceive they have. Is there any power given to Congress in matters of religion? Can they pass a single act to impair our religious liberties? If they could, it would be a just cause of alarm. If they could, sir, no man would have more horror against it than myself. Happily, no sect here is superior to another. As long as this is the case, we shall be free from those persecutions and distractions with which other countries have been torn. If any future Congress should pass an act concerning the religion of the country, it would be an act which they are not authorized to pass, by the Constitution, and which the people would not obey. Every one would ask, "Who authorized the government to pass such an act? It is not warranted by the Constitution, and is barefaced usurpation." The power to make treaties can never be supposed to include a right to establish a foreign religion among ourselves, though it might authorize a toleration of others.
>
> . . . It would be happy for mankind if religion was permitted to take its own course, and maintain itself by the excellence of its own doctrines. The divine Author of our religion never wished for its support by worldly authority. Has he

not said that the gates of hell shall not prevail against it? It made much greater
progress for itself, than when supported by the greatest authority upon earth.[50]

Iredell envisioned a central government that was barred from more than just
the establishment of a national church. Rather, the prohibition goes to any
interference in matters of religion. Organized religion was to be left to wax
or wane on the merits of its own doctrines.

The Reverend David Caldwell, a Presbyterian minister, rose to express
dismay that the Religious Test Clause could be understood as "an invitation
for Jews and pagans of every kind to come among us." A leading Antifederalist, Samuel Spencer, took Caldwell's remarks to be proposing an exclusive
establishment by way of a religious test. He went on to argue that religious
tests not only had been instruments of religious persecution, but had also
kept virtuous men from office while acting as no impediment to those of low
principles. Spencer then extolled the Test Clause because "it leaves religion
on the solid foundation of its own inherent validity, without any connection
with temporal authority; and no kind of oppression can take place." William
Lenoir raised the lack of express limits on congressional power, fearing the
absence of any restraint "against infringement on the rights of conscience.
Ecclesiastical courts may be established, which will be destructive to our citizens. They may make any establishment they think proper."[51] Lenoir's long
of list of possible civil-liberty abuses, including those as to religion, drew a
rebuke from Richard Dobbs Spaight. Spaight had been one of North Carolina's delegates to the Constitutional Convention in Philadelphia. On the
matter of religion, he said:

> I thought what had been said [by James Iredell] would fully satisfy that gentle-
> men and every other. No power is given to the general government to interfere
> with it at all. Any act of Congress on this subject would be a usurpation.
>
> No sect is preferred to another. Every man has a right to worship the Su-
> preme Being in the manner he thinks proper. No test is required. . . . A test
> would enable the prevailing sect to persecute the rest. . . . He says that Con-
> gress may establish ecclesiastical courts. I do not know what part of the Consti-
> tution warrants that assertion. It is impossible. No such power is given them.[52]

Spaight was thus in agreement with Iredell's understanding of the principles.
With these exchanges, there was more discussion about religious establishment in North Carolina than at any other state convention.

Although the vote for ratification failed, North Carolina did propose a host of amendments. Twenty amendments were to constitute a Declaration of Rights, and twenty-six additional amendments sought to alter the particular frame of the new federal government.[53] North Carolina's proposed amendment with respect to religious freedom was nearly identical to that of Virginia.[54] This is puzzling. The Virginia language, and now that recommended by North Carolina, prohibited only the establishment of one religion over others—leaving open the implied possibility of equal congressional support for all religions.

However, in the debate set out above, most delegates—especially the remarks of the Federalist James Iredell and the Antifederalist Samuel Spencer, as well as Richard Dobbs Spaight, a delegate to the Philadelphia Convention—were in agreement that religious freedom was best secured when religion was left on its own to flourish or decline on the basis of its merit and the zeal of its adherents. Accordingly, the thrust of the debate was to oppose nonpreferential state support because government involvement in religion had led only to corruption of the church and religious persecution.

In November 1789, a second North Carolina convention was held to consider the matter of ratification. At this point, eleven other states had ratified the federal Constitution, and the pressure was great on North Carolina to do the same. The delegates did so, but with a ratification message that again attached a copy of a Declaration of Rights and additional proposed amendments to the US Constitution.[55]

VI.

Despite powerful arguments by North Carolinians for religious freedom and no religious preferences at the state ratification convention, North Carolina's own Constitution still contained a religious test for public office. This issue is more complex than it appears on the surface. There is a lack of evidence that the religious test was ever enforced. William Gaston, a prominent Catholic lawyer, was active in North Carolina politics and held a variety of state and federal offices between 1800 and 1843, including that of state senator and state representative, during which he also served as Speaker of the House. Gaston also served as a justice of the state supreme court for nearly the last decade of his life.[56] Apparently, Gaston's Catholicism was never raised to challenge his holding these offices.

Gaston eventually played a central role in ending the Protestant test for office. In 1835 he delivered a two-day speech as a delegate to the state constitutional convention. Gaston argued for the ending entirely any religious test for public office. He was unsuccessful in this larger effort but was able to have the word *Christian* substituted for the word *Protestant* in Article 32, thus ending the barrier to Catholics. It was not until the Constitutions of 1868 and 1876 that the language was further amended to allow any believer in God to hold public office, thereby opening the door to Jews, Muslims, and theists generally, but continuing to exclude atheists.[57]

VII.

The North Carolina experience with disestablishment has its origins in a liberal toleration that found currency in well-placed nobles persuaded by the practical and biblical arguments for charity in religious concerns. It originated in the dissenting margins of British society, but the idea spread to influential parts of English nobility. It was from this broader movement that matters were put into practice in a distant and sparsely populated Carolina. And from there the cause of religious liberty was taken up by dissenting churchmen throughout North Carolina, little resisted by an Anglican establishment that existed more on paper than in practice.

Once the seeds of freedom were planted, it was ordinary plain-folk dissenters who resisted any meaningful establishment from being revived when the Crown took an interest in doing so, and this set the stage for the establishment's inevitable legal demise in the Constitution of 1776. The North Carolina experience shows the impact of British openness to toleration and the Protestant dissenter support that took advantage of that opportunity to make it a reality.

NOTES

1. See Gary Freeze, "Like a House Built upon Sand: The Anglican Church and Establishment in North Carolina, 1765–1776," *Historical Magazine of the Protestant Episcopal Church* 48, no. 4 (1979): 416–18.

2. Paul Seaward, "Hyde, Edward (1609–1674)," in *Oxford Dictionary of National Biography* (Oxford: Oxford University Press, 2004), 29:132–34; Ronald Hutton, "Monck, George, First Duke of Albemarle (1608–1670)," in *Oxford Dictionary of National Biography*, 38:587–90; R. Malcolm Smuts, "Craven, William, Earl of Craven (bap. 1608, d. 1697)," in *Oxford Dictionary of National Biography*, 14:65–67.

3. Tim Harris, "Cooper, Anthony Ashley," in *Oxford Dictionary of National Biography*, 13:205–11.

4. Lords Proprietor, "The Fundamental Constitutions of Carolina," March 1, 1669, in *Colonial and State Records of North Carolina*, 25:133–34 (Goldsboro, NC: Nash Brothers, 1906).

5. Lords Proprietor, "The Fundamental Constitutions of Carolina," 25:133–35.

6. David Armitage, "John Locke, Carolina, and the *Two Treatises of Government*," *Political Theory* 32, no. 5 (2004): 605.

7. Cooper's argument paraphrases from the New Testament, as his readers would have recognized. See Ephesians 5:23 and John 18:36.

8. Anthony Ashley Cooper, *A Letter from a Person of Quality to His Friend in the Country* (1675), https://en.wikisource.org/wiki/A_Letter_from_a_Person_of_Quality_to_His_Friend_in_the_Country.

9. Seaward, "*Hyde, Edward (1609–1674)*," 29:121, 132–33.

10. Warren Chernaik, "*Chillingworth, William (1602–1644)*," in *Oxford Dictionary of National Biography*, 11:456–59.

11. Stephen Beauregard Weeks, *The Religious Development in the Province of North Carolina* (Baltimore: Johns Hopkins University Press, 1892), 14–16; "The Concessions and Agreements of the Proprietors, Freeholders and Inhabitants of the Province of West New-Jersey, in America" (1677), in *The Colonial History of New Jersey*, by Samuel Smith (Burlington, NJ: James Parker, 1765), 529. See also the discussion of The Concession and Agreement in chapter 2, "Disestablishment in New Jersey."

12. See Freeze, "House Built upon Sand," 414.

13. William Byrd II, *The History of the Dividing Line Between Virginia and North Carolina: Run in the Year 1728; The Westover Manuscripts* (Petersburg, VA: Edmund and Julian Ruffin, 1841), 29.

14. Sarah McCulloh Lemmon, "The Genesis of the Protestant Episcopal Diocese of North Carolina, 1701–1823," *The North Carolina Historical Review* 28, no. 4 (1951): 437 n.78.

15. Spencer Ervin, "The Anglican Church in North Carolina," *Historical Magazine of the Protestant Episcopal Church* 25, no. 2 (1956): 103.

16. Lemmon, "Protestant Episcopal Diocese of North Carolina," 426.

17. Weeks, *Religious Development*, 22–27; Grant Wacker, "A Tar Heel Perspective on *The Third Disestablishment*," *Journal for the Scientific Study of Religion* 30, no. 4 (1991): 522.

18. Freeze, "House Built upon Sand," 414.

19. Thomas J. Curry, *The First Freedoms: Church and State in America to the Passage of the First Amendment* (New York: Oxford University Press, 1986), 56.

20. Lemmon, "Protestant Episcopal Diocese of North Carolina," 437.

21. Freeze, "House Built upon Sand," 414–15.

22. Weeks, *Religious Development*, 32. See also Stephen Beauregard Weeks, *Church and State in North Carolina* (Baltimore: Johns Hopkins University Press, 1892), 7.

23. Lemmon, "Protestant Episcopal Diocese of North Carolina," 427.

24. Weeks, *Church and State in North Carolina*, 9–10.

25. Lemmon, "Protestant Episcopal Diocese of North Carolina," 427–28.

26. "Act of the North Carolina General Assembly concerning establishment of churches," North Carolina General Assembly, 1715, *Colonial and State Records of North Carolina*, 2:207–13.

27. Ervin, "Anglican Church," 103.

28. Freeze, "House Built upon Sand," 419–20.

29. Freeze, "House Built upon Sand," 421.

30. Paul Conkin, "The Church Establishment in North Carolina, 1765–1776," *North Carolina Historical Review* 32, no. 1 (1955): 2.

31. As early as 1714, there was a vestry board of "two Anabaptists, three vehement Scotch Presbyterians, and one man descended from Quakers . . . never baptized." Ervin, "Anglican Church," 141.

32. Ervin, "Anglican Church," 142–49.

33. Conkin, "Church Establishment," 5.

34. Sources differ on whether five or six clergymen were in the colony when the 1765 Clergy Act was passed. Gary Freeze reports five, and Paul Conkin reports six. Compare Freeze, "House Built upon Sand," 409–10; and Conkin, "Church Establishment," 5. Further, while Conkin claims around ten Anglican churches, with some smaller chapels, Spencer Ervin reports with greater specificity around five churches, one in "good repair, two others wanting considerable repairs, and two under construction." See Ervin, "Anglican Church," 142.

35. Freeze, "House Built upon Sand," 419.

36. Freeze, "House Built upon Sand," 419, 423, 428–31.

37. Freeze, "House Built upon Sand," 428 (internal quotation marks omitted).

38. Conkin, "Church Establishment," 18.

39. Conkin, "Church Establishment," 17, 16.

40. Freeze, "House Built upon Sand," 412–13, 419, 423, 431 (quote), 428, 430–31.

41. Constitution of North Carolina, December 18, 1776, *The Proceedings and Debates of the Convention of North Carolina, called to amend the Constitution of the State, which assembled at Raleigh, June 4, 1835. To which are subjoined the Convention act and the Amendments to the Constitution together with the votes of the People* (Raleigh: Joseph Gales and Son, 1836), 409, 424.

42. Frederic S. Le Clercq, "Disqualification of Clergy for Civil Office," *Memphis State University Law Review* 7, no. 4 (1977): 582–83. The clergy disqualification was enforced on at least three separate occasions between 1800 and 1820.

43. Le Clercq, "Disqualification of Clergy," 582–83.

44. Le Clercq, "Disqualification of Clergy," 582–83.

45. *Ordinances of Convention, 1776—North Carolina. Provincial Congress, November 22, 1776–December 23, 1776* (Goldsboro, NC: Nash Brothers, 1904), 23:986–87.

46. *Proceedings and Debates of the Convention of North-Carolina, Convened at Hillsborough, on Monday the 21st Day of July, 1788, for the Purpose of Deliberating and Determining on the Constitution Recommended by the General Convention at Philadelphia, the 17th Day of September, 1787* (Edenton, NC: Hodge & Wills, 1789), 225–27, 220, 235.

47. Richard Beeman, *Plain, Honest Men: The Making of the American Constitution* (New York: Random House, 2009), 404. See also Jonathan Elliot, ed., *The Debates in the Several State Conventions on the Adoption of the Federal Constitution*, 2nd ed. (1836; reprint, Buffalo, NY: William S. Hein, 1996), 2:331 (giving the date as August 1, 1788).

48. Elliot, *Debates*, 4:192 (emphasis omitted).

49. Elliot, *Debates*, 4:193. See also Elliot, *Debates*, 4:196–98 (additional comments by James Iredell on the Test Clause).

50. Elliot, *Debates*, 4:194. The "greatest authority" referred to was the Roman Empire. See also Elliot, *Debates*, 4:198–99 (comments by Governor Samuel Johnston on how America's many sects were an assurance against a religious establishment).

51. Elliot, *Debates*, 4:199, 200, 203.

52. Elliot, *Debates*, 4:208. Richard Dobbs Spaight's argument relies on the point that when a power is not expressly delegated it is thereby denied.

53. Beeman, *Plain, Honest Men*, 405.

54. Elliot, *Debates*, 4:244. The amendment read: "That religion, or the duty which we owe to our Creator, and the manner of discharging it, can be directed only by reason and conviction, not by force or violence: and therefore all men have an equal, natural, and unalienable right to the free exercise of religion, according to the dictates of conscience; and that no particular religious sect or society ought to be favored or established by law in preference to others." There were minor changes in punctuation from the Virginia version. See also Neil H. Cogan, ed., *The Complete Bill of Rights: The Drafts, Debates, Sources, and Origins* (New York: Oxford University Press, 1997), 12.

55. Elliot, *Debates*, 1:333. Just two months before this ratification in North Carolina, the First Federal Congress, in September 1789, had reported out twelve proposed amendments to the US Constitution. Ten of the twelve that were eventually ratified by three-quarters of the states later took on the appellation "Bill of Rights."

56. Charles H. Bowman Jr., "William Joseph Gaston, 19 Sept. 1778–23 Jan. 1844," in *Dictionary of North Carolina Biography*, ed. William S. Powell (Chapel Hill: University of North Carolina Press, 2004), https://docsouth.unc.edu/browse/bios/pn0000574_bio.html.

57. John V. Orth, "Constitution, State," in *Encyclopedia of North Carolina*, ed. William S. Powell (Chapel Hill: University of North Carolina Press, 2006), https://www.ncpedia.org/government/nc-constitution-history.

CHAPTER SEVEN

RELIGIOUS DISESTABLISHMENT IN THE STATE OF NEW YORK

Kyle T. Bulthuis

THE ROOTS OF religious establishment in New York started with the Dutch colony of New Netherland. Founded as a fur trade outpost for the Dutch West India Company, the colony had settlements at Fort Orange up the Hudson River and on Manhattan and Long Islands. The colony remained under Dutch rule until 1664, when the English forced the Dutch to surrender in the Second Anglo-Dutch War. The Dutch briefly retook the colony in 1674, but lost it again never to regain control, and Dutch New Netherland became English New York.

Scholars have traditionally asserted that religious establishment was nominal in Dutch New Netherland. This narrative argues that company directors, aiming for profit rather than purity, and hoping to encourage immigration, promoted a tolerant stance toward inhabitants' religious practice. Calvinist patriots such as colony director Pieter Stuyvesant fumed alongside isolated and ignored Dutch Reformed ministers, but such outnumbered voices were forced to accommodate a range of believers, including Jewish refugees who arrived from Brazil in 1654.[1] The most recent and in-depth studies, however, suggest that New Netherland contained an intentional and comparatively strong religious establishment. While the colony hosted an environment of religious pluralism in practice, the fact of legal religious establishment was clear and provided a base for what would become an Anglican establishment in New York.[2]

I.

Religious establishment in New Netherland centered on a state church, dedicated to the Reformed branch of Protestant Christianity. Its ministers were state employees, and government officials supported the church. These connections could be close-knit. Manhattan's first minister, the Reverend Jonas

Michaelius, worked with a consistory, or governing council, composed of the colony's director, Peter Minuit, and Minuit's brother-in-law and chief storekeeper, Jan Huyghens. Michaelius noted that ideally, civil and religious offices should be kept separate but saw himself as fully qualified to provide "good advice" to the civil ruling body. Later relationships, including that among minister Everardus Bogardus and colony directors Wouter van Twiller and Willem Kieft, were riddled with conflict. However, the theory of church-state cooperation was a firm part of the colony's structure. Indeed, the final director of the colony, Pieter Stuyvesant, like Minuit, served on the consistory and actively promoted the Reformed Church's interests in the colony.[3]

The Reformed Church alone held the right to worship publicly and to administer the sacraments of baptism and the Lord's Supper. However, as the colony's public church, it had a duty to serve all subjects, even those who did not subscribe to its order of worship or theology. Because the United Provinces were a decentralized republic and because of uniquely Dutch ideas about liberty and toleration, the administration of the state church had unique characteristics. On a colony level, the West India Company and its directors oversaw all civil governance of New Netherland, so corporate interests merged with political ones. Religiously, the *classis* of Amsterdam administered the church in New Netherland, so Amsterdam's unique pluralistic composition affected enforcement on the ground. Decentralized enforcement remained a hallmark of the colony. When the Dutch Reformed Synod (ruling council) told each minister to "keep himself within the limits of his calling" and not practice medicine, as apparently some were doing, it required local churches and *classes* to enforce the directive on a case-by-case basis.[4]

New Netherland was initially unique in North America in that while Dutch officials insisted on an orthodox religious establishment, the Dutch also embraced an individual's right to liberty of conscience on a private level. Having suffered under the Spanish Inquisition, Dutch sensibilities insisted that individuals should never be persecuted for their beliefs alone, or for their religious affiliation as such. This position led to the practice of connivance. As explained by historian Evan Haefeli, connivance entailed a conscious willingness on the part of authorities to look away from religious practices by minorities, so long as those practices did not demand public recognition or full and explicit acceptance. Over time in the Netherlands, some groups gained full and public worship rights, especially if those groups were ethnic outsiders (and thus holding a sort of diplomatic recognition of their separate status) or if they wielded enough demographic and economic power that persecution would be imprudent.[5]

Compared to elsewhere in the Dutch imperial world, where authorities dealt with Catholics, Jews, Hindus, Buddhists, Muslims, and practitioners of traditional Chinese religions, New Netherland was a homogeneous backwater. In New Netherland, the greatest competition came from Lutherans. Sometimes English radicals in New Netherland caused problems and split from their Reformed communities, with whom the Dutch generally had good relations. But in most cases, New Netherland's religious establishment did not grant liberties to any groups beyond informal concessions.[6]

The longest-standing religious conflict in New Netherland lay with Lutherans of Dutch and German extraction. Repeatedly, the Lutheran community attempted to gain greater public recognition in the colony, and repeatedly they were denied. Ironically, such rejection came because both groups were quite similar in form and makeup. However, this closeness meant that the Reformed Church, as a public church, had to accommodate such residents. In 1658 the company directors informed Stuyvesant that ministers should use less exclusive wording when administering the sacrament of baptism, so that Lutheran parents had no grounds to object.[7]

One striking example of toleration, oft cited by historians, is the 1654 arrival of Jews from Brazil, where the Dutch had recently been defeated by the Portuguese. Company director Pieter Stuyvesant wished to bar the Jews' arrival, but their status as Portuguese merchants granted them some diplomatic rights of residence. True to Dutch methods, however, the group did not acquire any formal statutory religious rights, and the exigencies of life in New Netherland eventually led most of them to depart, rendering the issue moot. By the time of the English conquest, there were probably no Jews left in New Netherland, and thus no problems to mediate.[8]

More vexing were the more aggressive English religious radicals. Dutch officials (and English-speaking officials in English towns under Dutch rule) repeatedly punished Quakers for their refusal to remain silent or private in their preaching. The Flushing Remonstrance of 1658 reflected the attempt of one English community to demand greater religious toleration, such as existed in the nearby colony of Rhode Island. While the Remonstrance gained fame in the twentieth century as a harbinger of modern toleration, Dutch officials ultimately rejected those demands and continued with the practice of official establishment and unofficial connivance for outsiders, as the circumstances warranted.[9]

The Dutch insistence on formal religious establishment was so strong that, having lost the colony in 1664, upon taking it back briefly in 1674, officials reinstated full religious establishment for the Reformed Church, with no concessions for "any other Sects." The reconquest of New Netherland was brief, however, and the English retook it that year. Ultimately, the Dutch model of full religious establishment combined with full liberty of conscience provided ideal types or extremes with which subsequent English attempts to establish the Anglican church had to contend.[10]

II.

It was the English, not the Dutch, who offered a less restrictive form of establishment. Much of this impulse came from a reaction to the English Civil War and Cromwellian Protectorate, which had only ended with the Restoration of Charles II as monarch in 1660. Recently returned to power, the Royalists were eager to reverse the excesses of the Calvinists and dissenters who had overthrown Charles I. In England this entailed a strong reassertion of the Anglican establishment and restrictions placed on dissenting clergy. In the colonies, however, and especially in New York, there appeared to be a desire to avoid thorny religious questions and consequently to promote a comparatively weak Anglican church.[11]

The Duke's Laws governed the colony from the takeover from the Dutch in 1664 until the Glorious Revolution. Deputy governor Richard Nicolls, acting under the authority of James, Duke of York and brother of the king, proclaimed the laws by royal authority. Notwithstanding these antidemocratic origins, the laws reflected an unusual degree of religious freedom.[12]

The Duke's Laws decentralized the implementation of religious establishment. Each parish was to build a church and pay a minister's salary. The parish would then elect eight overseers, from which two would be chosen as church wardens. The law did not specify the religion, noting, however, that ministers had to be ordained from "some Protestant bishop" or had ministered in "his Majesties dominions or the Dominions of any foreign Prince of the Reformed Religion." Few churches were built in colonial New York under these laws. The practice of religion lagged the prescription.[13]

The Duke's Laws enforced a general morality, providing fines and jailing for offenses ranging from swearing and Sabbath breaking to drunkenness and adultery. They evinced a peculiarly Royalist tinge, requiring prayers for the king, Duke of York, and royal family, while requiring a fast day for the regicide of Charles I and a thanksgiving day for the Restoration of the monarchy, as well as the typical English celebration of the November 5 anniversary of deliverance from the Catholic Gunpowder Plot. Buried in the list of requirements was that no congregation should be disturbed in any religious meetings, nor any individual "molested fined or Imprisoned for differing in Judgment in matters of Religion who Profess Christianity." All Christians, it seems, had gained religious freedom at least in private.[14]

In October 1683, New York's legislature passed an act affirming religious liberty of conscience for all Christians, within the compilation "Dongan Laws," so named for Governor Thomas Dongan, the second Earl of Limerick and a practicing Catholic. This proclamation affirmed the principle of freedom of conscience in the colony, making explicit what Dutch practice (and the Duke's Laws) only implied. The act stated:

> Noe person or persons which professe ffaith in God by Jesus Christ Shall at any time be any ways molested punished disquieted or called in Question for any Difference in opinion or Matter of Religious Concernment, who doe not actually disturb the Civill peace of the province, But that all and Every such person or persons may from time to time and at all times freely have and fully enjoy his or their Judgments or Consciencyes in matters of Religion throughout all the province.

However, this full-on affirmation of religious liberty was vetoed by Charles II in March 1684, leaving the question of religious liberty ambiguous. The following year Charles's brother, James II, a practicing Catholic, would ascend to the throne. As Duke of York, James had named Dongan to his office and likely supported the increase in rights of conscience for all Christians—particularly Catholics.[15]

While the law ostensibly promoted the Church of England, in New York the reality was that there were few Anglicans, and no Anglican churches were built in this era. Further, a wide diversity of religions (including the lack of religion) had developed. Governor Dongan cataloged the religions in New York City, counting, "First a chaplain belonging to the Fort of the Church of England; secondly a Dutch Calvinist, thirdly a French Calvinist, fourthly a Dutch Lutheran—Here bee not many of the Church of England; few Roman Catholicks; abundance of Quakers preachers.... Women especially; Singing Quakers, Ranting Quakers; Sabbatarians; Antisabbatarians; Some Anabaptists; some Independents; some Jews; in short, of all sorts of opinions there are some, and the most part are of none at all."[16] The religious composition of New York suggested that any establishment favoring the small and inconspicuous Anglican church might only decline. Through many twists and turns, however, it strengthened.

The Glorious Revolution in England occasioned Leisler's Rebellion in New York. Just as Parliament ousted the Catholic James II from the Crown, militia captain Jacob Leisler attempted to enforce a pure vision of Calvinism in the colony of New York. Leisler's allies were Dutch families of the middling and poorer sort. His piety and politics broke up privileged monopolies and tweaked financially leading families in the process. Leisler, already unpopular with colonial elites, alienated his supporters in an attempt to invade Catholic Canada, which entailed increased taxes to pay for the military venture. Further, he misjudged his support from England, in which the new monarchs, William and Mary, promoted a Protestant religion but frowned on the revolutionary implications of Leisler's seizure of power. Consequently, upon the arrival of a new governor in 1691, Leisler was condemned and executed. For decades afterward, political divisions rent along pro- and anti-Leislerian lines. To combat such tensions, New York's English leaders wanted to promote a religious uniformity built around the Anglican church and thereby neutralize dissident voices. Because it was so clearly partisan in its connections to financial and government elites, Anglicanism also attracted controversy and opposition.[17]

Religious establishment in New York took hold after the Glorious Revolution with the support of Royal governors intent on strengthening their control. Proestablishment forces held influential positions but were never close to a majority of the population, or even of the propertied classes. One observer dryly noted that at the time of establishment the Church of England in New York could barely claim ten members who were not government officials.[18] Accordingly, an aggressive minority with connections to the mother country was attempting to create a fully ordered, hierarchical, and government-supported church without extensive precedent or material resources.

Governor Benjamin Fletcher pushed through the legislature an attempt at a more explicit establishment with the Ministry Act of 1693. The establishment encompassed only a portion of the colony. Four of the ten counties (New York, Westchester, Richmond, and Queens) were to raise taxes for the support of "a good sufficient Protestant ministry." As with the Duke's Laws, Anglicans were not directly specified as the beneficiaries of the law. Rather, in parish elections, freeholders would select ten vestrymen and two church

wardens, the whole of which called a minister and the latter of which distributed taxes as the minister's salary.[19]

The location of the counties with an Anglican establishment huddled
around the center of English power in New York City. New York County,
where the city lay, had an Anglican establishment, as did the adjoining counties of Westchester (the Bronx), Richmond (Staten Island), and Queens. As
a site of extensive Dutch settlements, King's County (Brooklyn) did not have
an establishment, nor did Suffolk (eastern Long Island) or the Hudson River
counties upstate—Albany, Dutchess, Orange, and Ulster. Indeed, the Ministry Act nominally reduced the scope of religious establishment from the
Duke's Laws. Following the act, however, were repeated attempts by the governors to enforce it with a specifically Anglican vision.

The unusual nature of having an establishment in some counties but
not others likely lay in a power-sharing model with the Dutch Reformed
Church. Governor Fletcher granted the Dutch Church, alone among all
non-Anglican churches, the ability to incorporate. While Dutch Reformed
Churches were not formally established in the upstate and rural Long Island
counties, where they faced little to no Anglican opposition, they operated as
a de facto coestablished church. Indeed, Dutch Reformed clergy often sided
with Anglican clergy in political battles throughout the eighteenth century.
Anglicans returned the favor by supporting the Dutch ministers and churches, often unofficially, with cash payments or grants of land.[20]

The greatest beneficiary of the establishment was on Manhattan Island,
where elites erected a building in 1697, what would become Trinity Church.
After repeated clashes with the colonial assembly, Governor Fletcher issued
Trinity Church a corporate charter that affirmed that the 1693 Ministry Act
was specifically intended to support the Anglican church. Further, the charter established a vestry for Trinity Church within the city vestry—that is,
the city vestry, which included dissenting and nonreligious members, was
required to turn over finances and all other decision making to a vestry composed wholly of Anglicans from Trinity. As he was leaving office, Fletcher
granted Trinity Church a sizable parcel of land or glebe for its future support consisting of most of the west side of Manhattan Island. These valuable
holdings would prove a continuing source of Trinity's influence and power.[21]

A further aid to the establishment arrived with the Society for the Propagation of the Gospel, a missionary organization formed in London in 1701.
The SPG evangelized for the Church of England by placing missionaries in
all areas of the British Empire. While these missionaries were ostensibly

placed to convert Indians and African slaves, often their focus was as much to Anglicize European immigrants and to sway Anglo Protestants to full identification and membership with the Anglican church. Evangelical ministers noted as much, complaining that SPG missionaries generally arrived in an area ready to poach from other Protestant groups rather than head to the unchurched frontier. In New York, this meant SPG ministers were often posted in established parishes.[22]

While the establishment privileged Anglican bodies over other religious groups, legislation expressly forbade Catholic practice in the colony. In 1700 the legislature passed an act barring Jesuits and other Catholic priests from practicing their vocation. Citing attempts to create Indian insurrection, the law gave Catholic clergy just under three months to leave the colony or suffer life imprisonment (with the death penalty for escape). To aid in enforcement, any layperson who harbored a priest would stand for three days on a pillory and be fined the magisterial sum of 200 pounds, half of which would go to the person reporting the sympathizer.[23]

Enforcement of the Anglican establishment at the turn of the eighteenth century moved in fits and starts, ebbing under Tory governors Benjamin Fletcher and Edward Hyde, the Viscount Cornbury, and waning with their Whig replacements, such as Richard Coote, the first Earl of Bellomont. Fletcher and Cornbury advanced the position that the 1693 Ministry Act specifically and exclusively established the Anglican church. Laws that specified, then erased, the Anglican church as the explicit object of the Ministry Act passed and were repealed within years of each other. After the first decades of the eighteenth century, tensions cooled, but the establishment-dissenter rift remained a regular feature of colonial politics.[24]

Conflicts over religious establishment burned hottest under the governorship of Lord Cornbury. Political invective of the era has resonated down through the years and rendered Cornbury a villain in many historical interpretations. He was, certainly, pro-Anglican. Cornbury explained to SPG authorities that he hoped to make all churches Anglican over time, mostly by recommending Anglicans to replace departing or deceased ministers at dissenting churches. As governor Cornbury presumably claimed such a prerogative, implying no church existed completely separate from the political matrix of the Crown.[25]

Governor Cornbury expected dissenting ministers to show him proper respect and claimed the right to monitor their movements. The governor invited to dinner two Presbyterian ministers, Francis McKemie, formerly of Virginia, and John Hampton of Maryland, in part to inquire as to their plans in New York. When they concealed from the governor their plans to preach at multiple locations, Cornbury had McKemie arrested and tried for unlawful preaching. The exchange between the two is a telling indication of the issues of the day: McKemie pressed his rights as a queen's subject to full freedom of conscience, a right he noted the queen granted to all nonpapists. Cornbury retorted that McKemie might well be a papist, since he had not fully submitted to the governor's examination as the law required. McKemie's acquittal in a jury trial suggests that many New Yorkers did not align with the governor's position.[26]

An even more striking conflict lay in the parish of Jamaica in the county of Queens, where the establishment funded a Presbyterian minister, John Hubbard. The county's Anglican minority, however, organized a soft coup in 1703, in which they occupied the church before Hubbard could take residence. Hubbard proceeded to preach outside, and a number of congregants left the building to join him, pulling out seats as they went. The contending groups came to blows over the right to inhabit the church building, and legal battles over who was the established church body in the county lasted for decades.[27]

III.

After Cornbury's departure in 1708, religious conflicts cooled at least until midcentury. For the rest of the eighteenth century, the number of Anglican churches increased steadily, and sometimes dramatically, in New York. From a colony with no Anglican churches for decades after the English takeover, the practice of official sanction and support eventually made something out of nothing from the top down. Culturally, the Church of England offered laity pretensions to power. Immigrants and subjects of the second or third generation from Dutch, German, or French background entered the church, many drawn by its promise of Anglicization.[28]

Outside of the four southern counties with establishments, the Dutch Reformed Church faced internal division over its status within the establishment. A more hierarchically inclined, elite, and rationalist faction, generally those who had joined English elites in condemning Leisler, supported continued affiliation with the Anglican church. Led by ministers such as Henricus Boel and later John Ritzema, its power was based in New York City. A more populist, decentralized, and heartfelt revival-based faction connected with fellow Calvinists among the English Presbyterians. This latter group took part in the revivals of the Great Awakening in the 1740s and favored greater local control over their church. In so doing, they not only renounced rule from Amsterdam but also spurned affiliation with the Anglican church and the benefits of establishment. For these revivalists-dissenters, the vitality of heartfelt religion and the independence of local rule outweighed the privileges of shared authority. Their center of power lay in the Hudson River valley and gained support from the great revivalist minister Theodorus Frelinghuysen and his sons. This faction's defection to the dissenters over the course of the eighteenth century tended to politically isolate royalist Anglicans.[29]

While Anglicanism in New York colony enjoyed increased numbers and cultural prestige, a coalescing opposition questioned its status as the favored established church. Two controversies illustrate the growing unrest with both the ideal and the practice of religious establishment. In the 1750s, controversy broke out over the religious affiliation of the new King's College in New York City. The following decade, a pamphlet war erupted in the American colonies, with New York at the center, over a proposal to establish an Anglican bishopric in America.

In 1751 the proposed creation of King's College in New York City caused controversy when the initial boosters, seeking support from Trinity Church and the colonial government, proposed that the college train Church of England ministers and offer an explicitly Anglican curriculum. In return, Trinity offered a portion of its land. Proponents of the plan, almost exclusively Anglican clergy and government officials, claimed they wanted for their church only the same opportunity dissenters had, to raise a school to aid them in their mission.[30]

Opposition to an Anglican connection to the college attracted a range of rising colonial elites. Such men moved in eclectic literary circles, Anglicans and dissenters mingling with rationalist skeptics, and all alongside individuals who would fall on opposite sides of the Whig-Tory debate over the revolution. Three Presbyterians wrote a series of essays in the journal *The Independent Reflector*, designed to convince the public that the college should remain nonsectarian. All three held differing political views. William Livingston, later governor of New Jersey, was the most prominent, a true Whig, and would become a signer of the Declaration of Independence. A second, John Morin Scott, took part in New York's revolutionary adoption of a constitution during the war. But the third, William Smith, would become an outspoken Loyalist during the revolution. Thus, opposition to the college's Anglican establishment did not necessarily align with one's support of the Crown or for some laity even their Anglican status.[31]

The eventual resolution of the King's College conflict illustrates the balance of power: a prodissenting majority resisted a small but well-placed proestablishment elite that eventually prevailed. The rank and file of all non-Anglican denominations, as well as rationalists and deists within and without all denominations, united against the establishment. Dutch Reformed elites were wooed by the promise of a professorship for one of their ministers, and clergy of other denominations were similarly enticed by spots on the college board of directors. Repeatedly, New York's Anglican governor James DeLancey attempted to fund the college. He had the support of his council, but the dissenter-dominated general assembly refused to release funds. Not until the threat of a French invasion in 1756, and a financial kickback in the form of support for the new jail, did the college receive funding, but with half the total appropriation going to unrelated projects. Further, Anglican authorities at the college had to agree to educate students in a general Christian morality.[32]

Anglican clergy had won a training ground for ministers at King's College, albeit more modestly than initially sought. They next turned to enabling their ministers to be ordained this side of the Atlantic through the formation of an American bishopric. Recognizing that matters of ecclesiastical hierarchy rubbed many Americans the wrong way, Anglican clergy attempted to convince their superiors in London to take action without publicity or fanfare. However, the case for an American bishop was politically insurmountable, with most clergy and authorities in Britain seeing the issue as inexpedient, given the minority of Anglicans in the North American colonies, the even smaller minority who ardently desired a bishop, and the high political cost to forcing the issue in Parliament past Whig majorities. Nevertheless, a core of High Church clergy in the colonies continued to pen essays promoting the idea.[33]

In the instance of both the college and the bishop, antiestablishment voices rallied against what they deemed to be further encroachment by the Anglican establishment, real or fancied. They included pietists and revivalists (or "evangelicals") of all denominations, alongside rationalists and political radicals who were suspicious of all religion. Even the Dutch, who had nominally benefited from continued establishment, divided over these two issues, with larger numbers valuing their connections with fellow pietistic or Calvinist Protestants over whatever benefits they received from government sanction.

The core of support for Anglican establishment, in contrast, was more narrowly based after the 1750s, centering on New York's royally appointed governors and high officials, and especially the Anglican clergy. While many Anglican laity at midcentury held rationalist or heterodox views on religious matters, the orthodox faction of the clergy held a firm proestablishmentarian stance. This faction possessed a number of characteristics that contributed to its uncompromisingly prochurch position. For one, most of these priests were funded by the Society for the Propagation of the Gospel, based out of London. Of the 309 missionaries that the SPG employed on the British mainland in the eighteenth century, 58 were based in New York, the largest number for any single colony. When one adds the 44 based in New York's sister colony of New Jersey, one-third of all Anglican missionaries worked in a concentrated area. Therefore, their pay, professional networks, and institutional loyalty traced back to Britain, not New York.[34]

Most of New York's clergy were not native to the state, with many having New England origins. Several were not raised Anglican, instead converting to the church from more Calvinist-inclined denominations. The most significant of these represented (to New Englanders) a scandalous defection from Congregationalism: Samuel Johnson. An early convert to Anglicanism at Yale College, Johnson taught and thereby influenced a number of his students toward the Church of England, including Samuel Seabury, both father (1706–64) and son (1729–96); Isaac Browne; and Thomas Bradbury Chandler. With the zeal of the converted and little vested interest in local traditions or locally claimed rights, these men promoted a strong transatlantic connection with the Church of England over an affinity with local clergy.[35]

The issues of King's College and an American bishop might be seen as forerunners to the revolution, at least in creating factions that showed why the establishment crumbled upon the outbreak of the conflict. The core of clerics and transatlantic elites were too few and too dependent on England when faced with a united front of popular voices, including lay Anglicans who did not believe the episcopal structure of the church was doctrinal or otherwise essential to its success. While most scholars are rightfully cautious in attempting to trace connections between earlier conflicts and the push for independence, or between religious affiliation and later political affiliation during the revolution, it appears that Anglican priests' loyalty and royal governors' pro-Anglicanism proved to be a central cause in the disestablishment of religion in the state of New York.

Anglican ministers, the strongest proestablishment voices in the colony, were nearly universally Loyalist. A number were vocally and vociferously so. This was true of Samuel Seabury, who published pamphlets denouncing Patriot aims in New York, as well as Samuel Auchmuty and Charles Inglis, successive rectors of Trinity Church in New York City. Seabury and Inglis became bishops of the Protestant Episcopal Church in North America after the revolution, Seabury in Connecticut and Inglis in British Nova Scotia.[36]

Although the law concerning establishment was facially neutral in regard to the specific church to be funded, this group had consistently (and with royal support successfully) applied the Ministry Act to benefit the Anglican church. Groups outside that circle found few privileges granted to them. In the late 1760s, as High Church hopes for a bishop in America faded, outside the four southern counties where there was no establishment, non-Anglicans petitioned to have their churches incorporated. In the counties where there was an establishment, they sought to relieve their members from taxation for church support. Such petitions were repeatedly approved by legislative majorities but vetoed by the governor's council.[37]

IV.

New York's history up to this point suggests that religious establishment had generally been maintained as a top-down affair, with only nominal support from below. While the Anglican church did grow, the local populace never fully embraced and funded it. Thus, Anglican leaders in New York still tied to England, and explicitly Loyalist, caused the establishment to appear directly associated with a political position. In New York, accordingly, proindependence meant an explicit tearing down of the pro-British church.

The convention that met to frame a revolutionary constitution for New York assembled from July 1776 to April 1777. A drafting committee reported out a document more conservative and less radical than many other states. New York contained a number of prominent individuals, especially merchants, whose cautious stance rendered them ambivalent toward the revolution far longer than their peers in other states. For example, New York granted the governor extensive executive power and retained a property requirement for the right to vote.

Just under half of the appointees to the convention were Anglican Whigs. Most were conservative in politics, favoring social hierarchy and property rights and later affiliated with the Federalist Party. John Jay, Robert R. Livingston, and Gouverneur Morris were among the more prominent among them, individuals who gained influence nationally as well. One later addition to this group, James Duane, even began the conflict as a Loyalist. While significant, this group was slightly outnumbered on the committee

by non-Anglicans, one of whom, John Morin Scott, had authored antiestablishment essays against King's College in the 1750s. That the Anglican Whigs
were slightly outnumbered by dissenting opponents, coupled with the strong
Loyalist stance of the colony's clergy, likely influenced these Anglican elites
to refrain from keeping the establishment of religion.[38]

Shortly after the Second Continental Congress declared independence,
New York's provincial convention took the remarkable step of asking the
Continental Congress to intervene in a religious matter, namely, authorizing
deletion from the Book of Common Prayer "all such prayers as interfere with
the interest of the American cause." The convention ruefully noted that "it
is a subject we are afraid to meddle with," suggesting that Loyalists had with
some success convinced American Anglicans that the revolutionary cause
was opposed to their church. No record appears that the Congress dealt with
New York's request.[39]

The dispute over the prayer book was certainly one that could come to
blows. At the time of the request, Anglican priests, Loyalists to a man, refused to withhold or alter prayers for the king in their liturgy. The exchange
between Charles Inglis and envoys of General George Washington, when the
latter occupied New York City, reveals a tense dynamic. When the general's
representatives requested the prayers be removed before he attend services,
Inglis's response argued in the name of clerical independence and religious
liberty that the general's staff had no authority to make such a request. Inglis
did offer that it was in Washington's power as current civil leader to close the
church if he deemed it necessary. Washington demurred. Inglis himself later
closed the church, in part to avoid vandalism by Patriots. Turnabout was
fair play, however: when the British army forced Washington to retreat and
then occupied New York City in August 1776, they reopened the Anglican
churches that had faithfully retained the prayers for the king. Under British
occupation, officers ordered the closure of all other churches and forced on
some the further indignity of serving as hospitals for the wounded.[40]

It appears the tiff over the prayer book did not influence wavering Anglicans on either side: both attracted their share of adherents. However, the
clergy's continued insistence on fidelity to liturgical forms that supported the
British sovereign did push Whiggish Anglicans to support disestablishment
of their church once independence was achieved.

Unlike New England to the east or the Anglican-established states in the
South, neither of which initially disestablish their churches, New York clearly and decisively did so in its revolutionary Constitution. The convention

was divided along religious lines, with wealthier and more conservative pro-property Anglicans aligned against less elite and generally Presbyterian and Dutch Reformed opponents. Anglican clerical Loyalism steeled even conservative Anglicans against any thought of keeping a state church. Indeed, the language of the Constitution linked religious favoritism with the despised royal prerogative. What became Article 35 of the Constitution, in a Rules of Decision Clause, explicitly preserved as the law of New York the English common law, British statuary law of a general nature, and the acts of the New York Legislature through 1775, with the exception of those laws "as may be construed to establish or maintain any particular denomination of Christians or their ministers, or concern the allegiance heretofore yielded to, and the supremacy, sovereignty, government, or prerogatives claimed or exercised by, the King of Great Britain and his predecessors, over the colony of New York and its inhabitants." In adopting this exception, the Constitution explicitly repealed the *Ministry Act of 1693*, thereby legally disestablishing the Anglican church. Like the *Ministry Act*, however, the Constitution did not mention the Church of England by name.[41]

Article 38 explicitly championed freedom of conscience and free exercise of religion. It cited a desire to defend against both civil and spiritual tyranny, and linked the "bigotry and ambition of weak and wicked priests [to] princes." Of course, such freedoms were not absolute. The constitutional convention limited religious practice by banning "acts of licentiousness" or practices "inconsistent with the peace or safety of this State." The wording was vague as to make consistent enforcement difficult in a legal sense, but the phrasing emerged only after extended debate over whether all religious groups, even non-Protestants, might appropriately practice their religion in the state.[42]

Led by John Jay, a significant minority of delegates spearheaded multiple attempts to limit Roman Catholic rights to unhindered religious practice. Jay's first proposed amendment allowed the legislature to determine if, and withhold toleration from, any group that held principles "inconsistent with the safety of civil society." Participants debated the phrase with little progress, so Jay withdrew this proposal and offered a more direct amendment. In this revision, Jay explicitly called for Roman Catholics to be barred from owning landed property or enjoying civil rights unless they swore before the state supreme court "that no pope, priest, or foreign authority on earth, hath power to absolve the subjects of this State from their allegiance to the same." A following clause delved into theological content, requiring that Catholics further "renounce and believe to be false and wicked, the dangerous and damnable doctrine, that the pope, or any other earthly authority, have power to absolve men from sins, described in and prohibited by the Holy Gospel of Jesus Christ, and particularly, that no pope, priest or foreign authority on earth, hath power to absolve them from the obligation of this oath." While the language of this proposed amendment suggests a Protestant assault on Catholic doctrines of justification, the debate that followed suggests that the main thrust of the proviso was to ensure Catholics did not lie when taking their oath or claim permission from their pontiff in so doing.[43]

The convention minutes record that "long debates arose thereon." Unlike Jay's first proposal, this language came to a vote, with the numerically larger counties of Albany, Dutchess, and New York voting it down over support from the upstate and frontier Orange, Tryon, and Ulster Counties. Jay was outvoted in his own county of New York and abstained from the final count. The following day, more wrangling over the wording of Article 35 ultimately led to acceptance of the text as adopted, which condemned any group that used religion to support licentious acts or that might endanger peace or safety within the state.[44]

This debate concerning Catholic free exercise of religion in New York State has been attributed to various causes. Charles Lincoln, whose magisterial early study evaluated the evolution of New York's constitutional history, noted that since 1691, royal instructions to governors had excluded Catholics from toleration, and therefore Jay's proposed amendments merely continued the colonial-era pattern. In contrast, Patricia U. Bonomi, perhaps the greatest recent authority on New York's eighteenth-century history, judged that Jay, of Huguenot heritage, retained an anti-Catholic bias stemming from his ancestors' persecution at Roman Catholic hands.[45]

The rationale behind Jay's amendments might be more immediate and less deep rooted than either of these suggestions. At the time of the debate in March 1777, New York City was in British hands, and the entire state was vulnerable to invasion by British forces through Canada. Such a campaign, which remained a threat until Burgoyne's defeat at Saratoga in the fall of 1777, would effectively cut off the state from New England and likely destroy Patriot resistance in the north. But fear of a Canadian invasion often held Catholic undertones for Anglo subjects, given French presence in the region for nearly two centuries. The Quebec Act of 1774, which extended French local law and Catholic establishment into territories to the northwest also claimed by American colonies, had been vigorously denounced by Patriots. Thus, Jay's amendments may reflect a fear of renewed Catholic martial presence that was strong in the year 1777. The smaller upstate counties that supported Jay, whose large dissenting populations might be inclined toward anti-Catholicism, were also exposed and vulnerable to British attack, linking temporal fears with spiritual.[46]

John Jay also carried a concern of Catholic insurgence into the debate over the issue of naturalization, which became Article 42 of the Constitution. Jay's proposed addition to that article required that prospective New York citizens renounce allegiance "to all and every foreign king, prince, potentate, and state, in all matters ecclesiastical as well as civil." This alteration carried with less debate than the issue of oaths. That this amendment carried with less debate suggests, again, that the issue of immediate concern was that of military invasion rather than anti-Catholicism. As with the previous amendment concerning oaths, the less populous upstate counties of Ulster, Orange, and Tryon served as the main support for this amendment, but this vote received greater support from the New York City delegation, thereby carrying the issue.[47]

Two other articles touched on the redefinition of the relationship between church and state in New York. Article 39 barred ministers of any denomination from holding public office, including in the military. Article 39 recited the desire of the law to keep ministers from being "diverted from their great duties" in service of God. This provision was passed with no debate and would remain in the revised 1822 Constitution and not be removed until 1846. Article 36 reaffirmed that all royal land grants made before October 14, 1775, would remain valid. This applied directly to the King's Farm, granted to Trinity Church in the 1690s. In those valuable land grants to the churches and in this article, the last great battle over disestablishment continued well into the nineteenth century.[48]

V.

When the Revolutionary War formally ended in 1783 and the British army left New York, the state legislature reaffirmed religious disestablishment in a series of acts. The first laws did so by explicitly meddling in church affairs. When Trinity Church's rector, Charles Inglis, decamped with British forces, the vestry nominated as his successor another Tory, Benjamin Moore. Many vestry members had comfortably lived in New York City during the British occupation, presumably holding Loyalist views similar to their clergy. Citing the discontent of exiled and silenced Patriot members of the church, who presumably could not attend church or speak freely while the British occupied New York, the general assembly affirmed that all individuals who attended Trinity Church or took the sacrament there at least once a year were rightful members of said church. The legislature appointed a new vestry, suggesting that the names the assembly forwarded had a general approbation among church members. After naming this new vestry, the legislature reaffirmed in a lengthy discourse its continued desire to allow for the free practice of religion in the state. The legislature went on to disavow all laws connected to the establishment, dating from the Ministry Act of 1693, in the four southern counties.[49]

Having stepped up on questions of internal church governance at the request of Episcopalian Whigs, the general assembly then receded. This new vestry quickly took steps to stamp Trinity Church as a pro-Patriot institution. Filled with prorevolutionary men who up to this time had taken little interest in church governance, the vestry replaced Benjamin Moore with Samuel Provoost, the one Anglican priest in New York who held Whiggish views during the revolution.[50]

Three days later, the general assembly passed an act repealing the establishment in the four southern colonies. The act may have been a form of legal housekeeping, since the Constitution seven years earlier and the legislation three days prior had already denounced establishment. Nevertheless, this act explicitly repealed not just the *1693 Ministry Act* but also eleven succeeding laws to the act that revised or clarified the initial establishment, ranging in time from the anti-Catholic statement in 1700 to another iteration of ministerial support in 1775. Other legislation concerning the collection of sales taxes for the support of religion, and the citywide election of the vestry as provided for in the initial establishment, were similarly repealed. This act seemed to bring the whole concept of religious establishment to an end in New York.[51]

Opponents of what was formerly the Church of England in New York attempted several more moves to reiterate the principle of disestablishment. In the fall of 1784, a half year after the aforementioned acts seemed to close the book on establishment in New York, a committee raised the issue of the large real estate holdings (or glebes) that the Anglican church had controlled for nearly a century. Noting that the Constitution did allow the legislature to make adjustments and amendments to the preexisting common law and statutes, a committee was formed to examine the status of the land grants to Trinity Church from the previous century.[52]

The committee traced the tortuous legal path that the land grants to Trinity took over the course of the eighteenth century. The committee argued that large grants of land offered by the governor did not generally, from their inception, outlast the governor's own term in office and were to be used at the pleasure of the governor, and ultimately at the pleasure of the king, who appointed the governor. In the case of Trinity Church, the King's Farm grant had been given in 1698, withdrawn in 1702, reaffirmed in 1705, and again broken in 1708. While the opposition to Trinity's holdings had lessened once Cornbury left office, the committee argued that these transactions demonstrated that the King's Farm was not a grant outright to Trinity Church but a gift of temporary use of the land still held by the king. As such, the revolution broke the king's hold on the property, which would thus revert to the state of New York. Following the committee's report, the legislature voted to take steps to remedy the situation, presumably by seizing the property then controlled by Trinity.[53]

Trinity Church, now headed by Patriots, resisted this taking of their property. Conservative Whigs such as John Jay and Alexander Hamilton feared attacks on property rights in general. Jay briefly served as churchwarden at this period, a position he eschewed both before and after the 1780s; Hamilton's law practice represented the church as a client. The church vestry and its new rector, Samuel Provoost, drew up petitions addressed to the general assembly. The church retreated from claiming rights under canon law and instead focused on natural law and the basic inviolability of property rights. Their petition to the senate argued that "this mode of enquiry into the right of property is not warranted by the spirit of our happy Constitution," presumably referring to general principles of the revolution that gave rise to the state Constitution. Further, the petitions argued that legislative seizures "tend to sap that grand bulwark of private right, the trial by Jury, which it is declared shall remain inviolate forever."[54]

Whether convinced by the argument, or persuaded through backroom channels, the legislature did not again approach the taking of Trinity property on behalf of the state. Subsequent petitions on behalf of descendants of the individuals who had held title to the lands before the Fletcher-Cornbury land grants to the church were dismissed by the courts, with the latest of them filed in the 1840s.[55]

In this final battle, an element of religious establishment lingered in New York. An earlier benefit of establishment—Anglican church landholdings entwined in property rights—persisted, even as all other benefits of religious establishment disappeared. The legal protection of private property in the early Republic was nearly absolute. The value of such property held by formerly established churches was considerable. Thus, a disproportionate influence as a result of this wealth remained with the Protestant Episcopal Church—and in particular Trinity Church—in New York City, even as all other preferences associated with that church had been abrogated. The influence lasted throughout the nineteenth century and indeed is with us to this day.

NOTES

1. Works that emphasize Dutch tolerance include Jay Gitlin, "Empires of Trade, Hinterlands of Settlement," in *The Oxford History of the American West*, ed. Clyde A. Milner II, Carol A. O'Connor, and Martha A. Sandweiss (New York: Oxford University Press, 1994); Benjamin Schmidt, "The Dutch Atlantic: From Provincialism to Globalism," in *Atlantic History: A Critical Appraisal*, ed. Jack P. Greene and Philip D. Morgan (New York: Oxford University Press, 2009); and Daniel K. Richter, *Before the Revolution: America's Ancient Pasts* (Cambridge, MA: Harvard University Press, 2011).

2. The most recent is Evan Haefeli, *New Netherland and the Dutch Origins of American Religious Liberty* (Philadelphia: University of Pennsylvania Press, 2012).

3. "Rev. Jonas Michaelius, First Minister of Manhattan, New Netherland, to Rev. Adrian Smoutius, one of the Ministers of the Collegiate Churches of Amsterdam, August 11, 1628," in *Ecclesiastical Records of the State of New York*, ed. Hugh Hastings (Albany, NY: James B. Lyon, 1901), 1:48–68, esp. 52–53, 55.

4. "Preachers Exercising the Practice of Medicine," 1633, in *Ecclesiastical Records*, ed. Hastings, 1:85.

5. On connivance, see Haefeli, *Dutch Origins*, 54–81.

6. On Dutch responses around the globe to religious pluralism, see Haefeli, *Dutch Origins*, 98–104, 129–33, 219.

7. "Letter from the Directors to Stuyvesant, 20 May 1658," in *Ecclesiastical Records*, ed. Hastings, 1:423.

8. Haefeli, *Dutch Origins*, 116–23.

9. On the Flushing Remonstrance, see Haefeli, *Dutch Origins*, 156–85.

10. On the brief reestablishment of the Dutch Reformed Church in New Netherland, see *The Colonial Laws of New York from the Year 1664 to the Revolution, including the Charters to the Duke of York, the Commissions and Instructions to Colonial Governors, the Duke's Laws, the Laws of the Dongan and Leisler Assemblies, the Charters of Albany and New York and the Acts of the Colonial Legislatures from 1691 to 1775 Inclusive* (Albany, NY: James B. Lyon, 1894), 1:102.

11. On the vision and actions of Restoration government leaders, see Richter, *Before the Revolution*, 241–64.

12. *Colonial Laws of New York*, 1:6.

13. *Colonial Laws of New York*, 1:24–25.

14. *Colonial Laws of New York*, 1:25–26, 32.

15. *Colonial Laws of New York*, 1:111, 115.

16. Dongan is quoted in Gabriel Poillon Disosway, *The Earliest Churches of New York and Its Vicinity* (New York: J. G. Gregory, 1865), 95.

17. For more on Leisler's Rebellion, see Richter, *Before the Revolution*, 310–13; and Randall Balmer, *A Perfect Babel of Confusion: Dutch Religion and English Culture in the Middle Colonies* (New York: Oxford University Press, 1989), 28–50. Balmer later demonstrates how divides over Leisler continued to influence New York religion and politics well into the next century.

18. Elizabeth Mensch, "Religion, Revival, and the Ruling Class: A Critical History of Trinity Church," *Buffalo Law Review* 35, no. 3 (1987): 445.

19. "An Act for Settling a Ministry & Raising a Maintenance for them in the City of New York County of Richmond Westchester and Queens County," 1693, in *Colonial Laws of New York*, 328–31.

20. Mensch, "Religion, Revival, and the Ruling Class," 447–48.

21. Mensch, "Religion, Revival, and the Ruling Class," 445–46.

22. On the SPG, see Frank J. Klingberg, *Anglican Humanitarianism in Colonial New York* (Philadelphia: Church Historical Society, 1940).

23. "An Act against Jesuits and Popish Preists [*sic*]," passed August 9, 1700, in *Laws of the Colony of New York from the Year 1664 to the Revolution* (Albany, NY: James B. Lyon, 1894), 1:428–30.

24. Mensch, "Religion, Revival, and the Ruling Class," 443–56.

25. Mensch, "Religion, Revival, and the Ruling Class," esp. 449–52, is critical of Cornbury. A Cornbury rehabilitation appears in Patricia U. Bonomi, *The Lord Cornbury Scandal: The Politics of Reputation in British America* (Chapel Hill: University of North Carolina Press, 1998). Charges of corruption and venality have been overshadowed by more sensational attacks on him as a sexual fetishist and cross-dresser.

26. Lord Cornbury to Lords of Trade, October 14, 1706, in *Documents Relative to the Colonial History of the State of New-York: Procured in Holland, England, and France* (Albany, NY: Weed, Parsons, 1853), 4:1186–87.

27. Bonomi, *Lord Cornbury Scandal*, 71; Richard W. Pointer, *Protestant Pluralism and the New York Experience: A Study of Eighteenth-Century Religious Diversity* (Bloomington: Indiana University Press, 1988), 36, 69.

28. Church buildings followed, rather than preceded, the law, as Anglican structures went up in the four established counties after passage of the Ministry Act. See Jon Butler, *Awash in a Sea of Faith: Christianizing the American People* (Cambridge, MA: Harvard University Press, 1990), 107, 113–14.

29. On this internal division, see Mensch, "Religion, Revival, and the Ruling Class," 447–48, 460–63; Pointer, *Protestant Pluralism*, 16–17; and Balmer, *Perfect Babel of Confusion*, 51–71

30. For an overall analysis of the King's College debate, see Donald F. M. Gerardi, "The King's College Controversy, 1753–1756, and Ideological Roots of Toryism in New York," *Perspectives in American History* 11 (1977–78): 145–96.

31. Milton Klein, introduction to *The Independent Reflector, or Weekly Essays on Sundry Important Subjects More Particularly Adapted to the Province of New-York*, by William Livingston et al. (Cambridge, MA: Harvard University Press, 1963), 18.

32. Gerardi, "King's College Controversy," 188–93.

33. On the American bishopric controversy, see Patricia U. Bonomi, *Under the Cope of Heaven: Religion, Society, and Politics in Colonial America* (New York: Oxford University Press, 1986), 199–209.

34. William Webb Kemp, *The Support of Schools in Colonial New York by the Society for the Propagation of the Gospel in Foreign Parts* (New York City: Columbia University Teachers College, 1913), 32. Adding in the 47 missionaries stationed in Pennsylvania and Delaware, almost half of all SPG appointees were sent to the middle colonies, compared to 107 in the southern colonies and 84 in New England.

35. Gerardi, "King's College Controversy," 156–59. See also Daniel J. Hulsebosch, "Imperia in Imperio: The Multiple Constitutions of Empire in New York, 1750–1777," *Law and History Review* 16, no. 2 (1998): 319–79.

36. Cho-Chien Feng, "Order and Peace: Samuel Seabury's Concept of Liberty" (master's thesis, Utah State University, 2012); Ruma Chopra, *Unnatural Rebellion: Loyalists in New York City during the Revolution* (Charlottesville: University of Virginia Press, 2011), 33–34.

37. "Journal of the Council, New York, May 1769" and "Proposed Act to Exempt Protestants from Compulsory Church Rates, Defeated," in *Ecclesiastical Records, State of New York*, ed. Hugh Hastings (Albany, NY: J. B. Lyon, 1905), 6:4149, 4178.

38. Within this group of Anglicans, rationalistically inclined individuals like Gouverneur Morris were temperamentally and ideologically opposed to any form of religious establishment. See, for example, Richard Brookhiser, *Gentleman Revolutionary: Gouverneur Morris, the Rake Who Wrote the Constitution* (New York: Free Press, 2004), 24, 33. For the composition of the framing committee, see Charles Z. Lincoln, *Constitutional History of New York, from the beginning of the colonial period to the year 1905, showing the origin, development, and judicial construction of the constitution*, vol. 1, *1609–1822* (Rochester, NY: Lawyers Co-operative, 1905), 491–92. The daily minutes of convention proceedings also provide a good look at the individuals involved. See *Journals of the Provincial Congress, Provincial Convention, Committee of Safety and Council of Safety of the State of New York*, 2 vols. (Albany, NY: Thurlow Weed, 1842), vol. 1.

39. *Journals of the Provincial Congress*, 1:520–21.

40. Charles Inglis, "State of the Anglo-American Church," October 31, 1776, in *Ecclesiastical Records, State of New York*, ed. Hastings, 6:4292, 4294.

41. The 1777 Constitution is reprinted in Lincoln, *Constitutional History of New York*, vol. 1; this article, 183–84.

42. Lincoln, *Constitutional History of New York*, 1:185–86.

43. *Journals of the Provincial Congress*, 1:844. On Jay's position here, see Jonathan Den Hartog, "John Jay and Religious Liberty," *Faulkner University Law Review* 7, no. 1 (2015): 63–78.

44. *Journals of the Provincial Congress*, 1:844–45.

45. Lincoln, *Constitutional History of New York*, 1:542; Patricia U. Bonomi, "John Jay, Religion, and the State," *New York History* 81, no. 1 (2000): 13, 15–16.

46. On the religious dimensions of the Quebec Act, which blended concerns for political rights, military security, and Catholic establishment, see Joseph J. Casino, "Anti-Popery in Colonial Pennsylvania," *Pennsylvania Magazine of History and Biography* 105, no. 3 (1981): 279–309. An older account can be found in Charles H. Metzger, *The Quebec Act: A Primary Cause of the American Revolution* (New York: United States Catholic Historical Society, 1936).

47. Because the federal Constitution addressed naturalization, this state article became null upon the U.S. Constitution's ratification in 1788. *Journals of the Provincial Congress*, 1:846, 860.

48. Lincoln, *Constitutional History of New York*, 1:184–86.

49. "Chap. 33, An Act for making such alterations in the charter of the corporation of Trinity Church, as to render it more conformable to the constitution of the state," passed April 17, 1784, in *Laws of the State of New York Passed at the Sessions of the Legislature Held in the Years 1777 to 1801* (Albany, NY: Weed, Parsons, 1886–87), 1:646–49.

50. For background, see Mensch, "Religion, Revival, and the Ruling Class," 477–79.

51. "Chap. 38, An Act to repeal an act intitled an act for settling a ministry and raising a maintenance for them in the city of New York county of Richmond West Chester and Queens county and also the several other acts therein mentioned," passed April 20, 1784, in *Laws of the State of New York*, 1:661–62.

52. Matthew Adgate, who authorized the commission, and Peter Yates, who headed it, were among the politicians who opposed the Schuyler faction's aristocratic or hierarchical tendencies. Their opponents tended to see them as dangerous "levelers" who evinced little respect for property rights. See Alexander Hamilton to Robert R. Livingston, April 25, 1785, in *Papers of Alexander Hamilton*, ed. Harold C. Syrett, vol. 3, *1782–1786* (New York: Columbia University Press, 1962), 608–9. Interestingly, Adgate had supported Jay's attempts to limit Catholic rights at the state convention.

53. "Resolution and Report of the House of Assembly on Title to King's Farm," appendix 7 in Morgan Dix, *A History of the Parish of Trinity Church in the City of New York*, pt. 2 (New York: G. P. Putnam's Sons, 1901), 285–93.

54. The petitions are reprinted in Dix, *History of the Parish of Trinity Church*, 2:87–91.

55. Dix, *History of the Parish of Trinity Church*, 93–101. See also Morgan Dix, *History of the Parish of Trinity Church in the City of New York*, pt. 4 (New York: G. P. Putnam, 1906), 315–17, for mention of one lawsuit that carried into the 1840s.

CHAPTER EIGHT

DISESTABLISHMENT IN VIRGINIA, 1776–1802

Carl H. Esbeck

The disestablishment story in the Commonwealth of Virginia is the one on which more has been written than any of the other British colonies in North America, and consequently it is a history on which interested persons have already developed well-formed opinions. It is also the history that has had the most impact on present-day America, largely because of a reliance placed on Virginia's disestablishment account as rendered by the Supreme Court of the United States.[1] However, as Donald Drakeman suggests and this volume confirms, Virginia's path to disestablishment was not a blueprint for the deregulation of the state church in the other original thirteen colonies. Thus, it would be a misstep to uncritically equate the Old Dominion's path to disestablishment in 1784–86 with the meaning and scope of the Establishment and Free Exercise Clauses in the First Amendment that was added to the federal Constitution in late 1791.[2] Moreover, as Thomas E. Buckley's close examination of the evidence concludes, Virginia's reputation as the champion of an uncompromising and enlightened church-state separation does not correspond to the facts. Rather, as soon as the revolutionary afterglow had passed, antebellum Virginia found the state reasserting control over the churches. Virginia legislation "obstructed [churches'] efforts and ability to raise funds, construct buildings, establish institutions, maintain works of charity, educate their clergy and adherents, and carry out missionary activities."[3] In the name of strict separation, lawmakers hobbled churches by denying them the ability to incorporate under the state's general incorporation act, by limiting the acreage that could be acquired for erecting houses of worship and to otherwise acquire assets, and by reaffirming the state's colonial-era prohibition on clergy holding public office. It took the upheaval of the Civil War to temper this asymmetrical notion of separationism with a rule of equal treatment, thereby cleansing the Old Dominion's legal regime of discrimination against religious societies.

I.

Virginia's revolutionary convention first met in Williamsburg on May 6, 1776. On May 15, the convention—soon the general assembly—appointed a drafting committee. As was the pattern of the day, Virginia planned to begin its constitution with a declaration of rights. The responsibility for drafting this important exposition fell to George Mason IV, a prominent planter, life-long member of the Church of England, and vestryman at Truro Parish in Fairfax.[4]

Mason's first draft of the declaration was not so much original as it was a compilation of the principles and theories that were increasingly read and debated in revolutionary America. Certain articles correspond to the English Bill of Rights adopted by Parliament in 1689. After stylistic amendments, Mason's article on religion passed out of committee on May 27 and read as follows:

> That religion, or the duty which we owe to our CREATOR, and the manner of discharging it, can be directed only by reason and conviction, not by force or violence; and therefore that all men should enjoy the fullest toleration in the exercise of religion, according to the dictates of conscience, unpunished and unrestrained by the magistrate, unless, under colour of religion, any man disturb the peace, the happiness, or safety of society. And that it is the mutual duty of all to practice Christian forbearance, love and charity, towards each other.

The draft was forwarded to the general assembly sitting as a committee of the whole. It was during the ensuing floor debate that monumental changes took place.

James Madison Jr., a freshman in the assembly and as yet untested in politics, was troubled by what he perceived to be unintended consequences of the committee's language. Madison objected to the term "toleration" and to the qualifications on religious liberty, beginning with his belief that the "unless" clause had dangerous implications. It was his view that toleration belonged to a system where there was an established church, and liberty of worship for dissenters was permitted only as a matter of sovereign grace and not as an unalienable right. Of course, Virginia had an established church, and thus the committee's draft made sense. For Madison, however, a civil state had no jurisdiction in matters of organized religion, and thus Virginia should do away with its establishment. Additionally, Madison feared that an easy overriding of religious liberty was invited by the "unless" clause, which was made more probable by a magistrate's natural bias for public order.[5]

Notwithstanding his junior status, Madison prepared an ambitious proposal, and apparently persuaded Patrick Henry to offer it on the floor.[6] Henry was thought to be sympathetic to religious dissenters because he had defended them in the famous Parsons' Cause,[7] and Henry had many dissenters in his district. The proposal is revealing of Madison's far-reaching thinking on church-state relations. Madison's amendment read:

> That Religion or the duty we owe to our Creator, and the manner of discharging it, being under the direction of reason and conviction only, not of violence or compulsion, all men are equally entitled to the full and free exercise of it accord'g to the dictates of Conscience; and therefore that no man or class of men ought, on account of religion to be invested with peculiar emoluments or privileges; nor subjected to any penalties or disabilities[,] unless[,] under &c.[8]

The change from "toleration" to "free exercise" is apparently the first occasion in America that this now famous First Amendment phrase was used. Moreover, the proposal took "magistrate" out of the role as decision maker when it came to overriding the right to free exercise. Madison's proposed text "no man or class of men ought, on account of religion to be invested with peculiar emoluments or privileges," drew strong opposition because it might be understood to disestablish the Church of England. For example, if no "class of men" could be vested with emoluments on account of religion, then Anglican clergy could not be specially supported by tax assessments.

To the popular mind, Mason's use of "toleration" was progressive because it was seen through the lens of John Locke's *Letter Concerning Toleration*.[9] To suggest that "toleration" was actually repressive, and to attack the established church in the same paragraph, was more than the delegates to the Virginia General Assembly were prepared to accept. The proposal was going nowhere.

In a demonstration of his now famous political skills, Madison accepted that the way forward was blocked and immediately set to work on a new approach. Madison convinced Edmund Pendleton—or perhaps Patrick Henry—to sponsor a second amendment that preserved the "free exercise" phrase but abandoned the more controversial disestablishment passage.[10] Pendleton, an opponent of any attempt to disestablish the Church of England, may have been convinced to sponsor such an amendment simply to rid the assembly of Madison's dangerous first proposal. The amendment read:

> That religion, or the duty which we owe to our CREATOR, and the manner of discharging it, can be directed only by reason and conviction, not by force or violence; and therefore, that all men are equally entitled to enjoy the free exercise of religion, according to the dictates of conscience, unpunished and unrestrained by the magistrate, Unless the preservation of equal liberty and the existence of the State are manifestly endangered; And that it is the mutual duty of all to practice Christian forbearance, love, and charity towards each other.

Once on the floor, the new trimmed-down proposal was attributed to Patrick Henry by Edmund Randolph. Randolph was likely mistaken about the amendment's sponsorship, but he later remembered that in floor debate Henry was asked "whether it was designed as a prelude to an attack on the established church, and he declaimed such an object."[11] The question was asked because some delegates to the assembly resisted even this new proposal insofar as the "equally . . . free exercise" text could be read to imply equality not with respect to individuals, but among all religions. The latter would disestablish the Church of England.

Madison was later successful in limiting the role of the magistrate to overriding the right to free exercise only when "the existence of the State [is] manifestly endangered." This change accorded with the Lockean principle of noninterference with religious liberty except to preserve civil peace. The right of religious conscience that remains is not absolute, but constrained as springing from a religion of reason and conviction, and thus the exercise of the right carries with it a mutual duty among citizens of forbearance and charity. Rights are thus understood as freely exercised in the context of a citizen's concomitant responsibility to the community; that is, rights are not divorced from one's civic duties. Once again, the text on the role of the magistrate was eliminated.

The article, as amended, passed the general assembly on June 12, 1776, as part of a larger Declaration of Rights. The final, and now familiar, language of Article 16 provides:

> That Religion, or the duty which we owe to our CREATOR, and the manner of discharging it, can be directed only by reason and conviction, not by force or violence; and therefore all men are equally entitled to the free exercise of

religion, according to the dictates of conscience; and that it is the mutual duty of all to practise Christian forbearance, love, and charity, towards each other.

Article 16 remains largely unchanged in the Constitution of Virginia to this day.[12]

In the foregoing debate, we see a telling bifurcation of the protection of personal religious conscience (also called "private judgment"), on the one hand, and religious disestablishment, on the other. A state can guarantee the free exercise of religion in the sense of an absence of state coercion while maintaining an established church. The same bifurcation appears in John Locke's extension of toleration to dissenting Protestants, while retaining an established English church. Patrick Henry, as a proponent of a tolerant establishment, was regarded as a progressive advocate of personal religious conscience. Non-Anglicans were free of state compulsion with respect to what they believed and observed about God, yet there was a Church of England by law established. This was not seen as contradictory.

For James Madison, Article 16 was a halfway measure. The article protected private judgment in one's religious observance but continued to permit civil government to assume authority over matters of church administration and order of worship. Whereas Henry and many others supported an individual's liberty from coercion with respect to religiously informed conscience, in 1776 Madison stood virtually alone in Virginia's assembly in support of anything resembling disestablishment of the Church of England. But, as so often happens, change was accelerated by war.

II.

With the revolutionary fighting now in its second year and independence having been declared in July 1776, the Virginia General Assembly met under its new Constitution in October 1776. In place of the House of Burgesses, there was a House of Delegates, and in place of the Council, there was a Senate. The governor was no longer appointed by the king but elected by the people to a one-year term.

Given the ongoing fighting with Great Britain, a surprising amount of legislative time was spent debating church establishment. The adoption of Article 16 unleashed a number of petitions signed by religious dissenters calling for the repeal of colonial statutes requiring the licensure of dissenting clergy, requiring the approval of meetinghouses for worship by nonconformists, restricting dissenting clergy from performing marriages, and restricting the incorporation of churches and other religious societies. Article 16 having granted an individual right to religious exercise, petitions from dissenters urged that the assembly "go on to complete what is so nobly begun" by proceeding to "pull down all Church Establishments [and] abolish every Tax upon Conscience and private judgment" in religious matters.[13]

The defenders of the Church of England urged the necessity of government support for religion, which they argued was instrumental to building civic unity and inculcating public virtue. Dissenters sought to place all churches on an equal footing and to repeal any requirement that citizens contribute to the monetary support of their own or the established church. For example, a petition sent from the Presbytery of Hanover and presented to the general assembly in October 1776 stated its argument as follows: that up until now Presbyterians had submitted to the laws, albeit discriminatory; that they had paid religious assessments to the support of the established clergy, even in counties where Episcopalians were but a small part of the population; that the taxes were in violation of their natural rights, and in consequence a restraint on free inquiry and private judgment; that because of the need for unity of every denomination behind the war effort, every religious bondage should be lifted; that any government with the authority to establish Christianity thereby has the authority to establish the tenets of Mohammed; that no civil magistrate can sanction a religious preference without claiming to be infallible in biblical matters, a claim harking back to the Roman church; that religious discrimination holds back population growth and thereby retards progress in the arts, sciences, and manufacturing; that the Gospel is in no need of government aid, for Christ declared that his kingdom is not of this world and not dependent on state power;[14] that in the days of the apostles, the church flourished in greatest purity when it was promoted on its religious merit and not its utility in building civic unity; that religion is not the proper object of civil government; that there should be equality before the law with respect to all denominations; and that religious taxes should be repealed, leaving support of any church a voluntary matter, thereby leaving every religion to stand or fall according to its own merit.[15]

A Committee for Religion was quickly formed in the House of Delegates to respond to the petitions, but the committee was divided. In early November 1776, the issue of disestablishment was removed from committee and taken up by the house sitting as a committee of the whole. After vigorous debate, a series of resolves were adopted. One resolution was to repeal those statutes that criminalized heretical opinion, required attendance at worship services, and dictated approved modes of worship. Another resolution would do away with religious taxes on dissenters. The collective impact of the resolutions was to place "all religious groups on a purely voluntary basis with respect to financial support, while vesting in the established church all the property and goods it possessed at the time."[16]

A second house committee was formed to draft a bill that would respond to these resolutions. The composition of this new committee was such that the dissenters lost influence and the momentum for disestablishment subsided. In late November 1776, a compromise was reached and a modest bill reported out by the committee. By early December 1776, with only minor amendments, the scaled-down bill passed both the house and the senate. The bill did away with colonial-era statutes still on the books requiring church attendance and exempted dissenters from the tax in support of the Anglican church, while leaving untouched other laws that maintained the establishment. Finally, even Anglican laity were also freed, at least temporarily, from paying the tax to support their church.

The status of the resulting establishment was ambiguous. For a time, no citizen was taxed to support the Anglican church, nor were dissenters forced to support their own church. Going forward then, in matters of monetary support "[r]eligion in Virginia had become voluntary, and a man could . . . contribute as much or as little [money] as he thought fit to whatever church or minister pleased him." In matters of religious observance, a person could believe as he wished and "also worship when and as he chose, within certain limits; for the Assembly maintained a measure of control over the external operations of the [dissenting] churches." For example, the legislature did not repeal the state's authority to approve meetinghouses and license dissenting preachers. But the ongoing war, as well as popular sentiment, precluded enforcement of these licensure laws, and they effectively lapsed.

It was also during these debates in the fall of 1776 that the propriety of a general assessment or earmarked tax in support of all Christian clergy was first raised. A novel proposition in America, a general assessment essentially would create a "multiple establishment" of Christian churches. Each citizen would pay a special tax and designate the church to receive it. With an eye to Article 16 of the Declaration of Rights, this was said by proponents to effect a fulfillment of "the duty we owe to our Creator," while not coercing behavior contrary to conscience because of the freedom to choose the church where one's tax money went in support. The scaled-down bill of December 1776 expressly reserved for future consideration such a general assessment law.[17] The Anglican church, however, retained its hold on the glebe lands, as well as all real estate with church buildings and chapels presently in its possession.

The bill of December 1776 suspended all religious assessments on Anglicans until the end of the next legislative session. The general assembly extended this suspension in May 1777, again in May 1778, and again in October 1778. The resulting lack of new tax revenues put the finances of the Anglican vestries into a state of disarray, and the salaries of Anglican clergy frequently went unpaid. But the war itself demanded money, and the loyalty of dissenters was not to be alienated by the renewing of a religious tax earmarked for the support of the Anglican establishment—even a tax that dissenters did not themselves pay.[18]

All during this period from late 1776 through 1778, dissenters continued to petition the general assembly against establishment and other religious regulation, such as restrictions on performing marriages. For example, a 1778 petition from the Presbytery of Hanover argued against the religious assessment along the following lines: that religious conscience is unalienable, beyond the jurisdiction of the state; that the proper objects of civil government are limited and do not extend to organized religion; that the church is Christ's, and He will adequately support her to final consummation; that to take government support would be an injury to the Presbyterian Church; that a minister financially supported becomes a hireling, thus subject to the paymaster's control with respect to who can preach, what he can preach, and where he can preach; that any government with authority to establish one sect has authority to establish any sect; and that a general assessment would subvert religious liberty.[19]

During the May–June session of the 1779 general assembly, several bills concerning the matter of church-state relations came up for consideration. As part of a larger package of law reform first commissioned in the fall of 1776, Thomas Jefferson unveiled his *Bill for Establishing Religious Freedom*, which was later assigned number 82. Bill No. 82 was debated but put over until the fall 1779 session but then not considered in the fall. The politics had turned against it.

The idea of a general assessment in aid of all Christian churches was actively revisited in the spring of 1779, but a divided legislature meant that the general assessment issue also was put over until the fall. The assembly again met in October 1779 and revisited the matter of a general assessment, as well as the ability under the law to incorporate a church or other religious society. By then the sentiment "in the press and [evident in] the religious petitions clearly showed that the weight of public opinion favored some form of governmental involvement in religious matters."

Any general assessment bill would need to define those Christian churches that would be eligible for tax moneys—those outside the definition being excluded. Accordingly, it was proposed that a qualifying church must conform to certain Articles of Faith, including that "there is one Eternal god and a future State of Rewards and Punishments, . . . the Christian Religion is the true Religion, [and] . . . the Holy Scriptures of the old and new Testament are of divine inspiration, and are the only rule of Faith." These Articles of Faith were borrowed from the South Carolina Constitution. The legislature was not about to fund the heterodox, let alone any non-Christian, religion.

The general assessment bill was vigorously debated but did not pass. George Mason then presented a more modest bill that would permanently repeal the authority of the Church of England to collect a religious tax from its members. This bill passed on December 13, 1779. Passage meant it was no longer necessary for the general assembly to periodically adopt measures to continue the suspension of the religious tax for those still holding membership in the Anglican church. The matter of glebes and church buildings in the possession of the Anglicans went unsettled.

It is tempting to look back at the events of 1776–79 with respect to church-state relations and pronounce an end to the establishment of the Church of England. A more cautious view is that while the Virginia General Assembly remained divided on the big issue, it could agree on pragmatic, short-term goals. The repeal of the religious tax for dissenters and of the tax suspension for Anglicans was welcomed in newly independent Virginia. Moreover, this fledging state was at war with the world's most powerful empire. Anglican clergy were sometimes Tory in their sympathies, and money collected for their salaries could be used elsewhere to equip and pay the Continental army. This is not to say that the Anglican clergy were left destitute. Retention of the glebe lands ensured that at least the well-endowed parishes could generate income for their ministers. As the fighting continued, Virginia repealed the statutes on religious assessments for the duration of the war while retaining the authority to revisit the matters of a general assessment and Anglican property holdings at a later date.

As the revolutionary fighting moved into Virginia during 1780–81, the legislature put aside many issues and was occupied with the commonwealth's survival. Nevertheless, the struggle between dissenters and establishmentarians continued. Issues such as barring preaching by all "nonjuror" Anglican ministers (that is, preachers who failed to take an oath of allegiance to Virginia) is exemplary of where energies were expended when there was any time to devote to religious questions. A Baptist petition of October 16, 1780, had two complaints. First, the Baptists were excluded from serving on the local Anglican vestry. This was a problem because taxes to care for the poor were administered by the vestry. Second, Baptist ministers were not permitted to perform marriages. Thus, a Baptist couple had to see the Anglican minister to lawfully marry. The second complaint was promptly corrected by legislation.

III.

In September 1783, the Treaty of Paris removed the distraction of the war, although most fighting had stopped with the surrender of Cornwallis at Yorktown in October 1781. The vast majority of the Anglican clergy had retired, died, fled to Canada, or returned to England.[20] The churches and chapels belonging to the Church of England in Virginia were in disrepair, owing at least in part to vandalism and other mischief by the Continental army. As soldiers returned home from their duties and the states' war debts demanded that the economy begin generating needed public funds, the Virginia legislature turned to the familiar vehicle of religion to unify and motivate the population.

In this immediate postwar period, Patrick Henry was the most popular politician in Virginia. Even detractors such as Jefferson acknowledged Henry's essential leadership in the cause for independence when the advisability of the initial break with England was much in doubt. As Henry returned to the House of Delegates, he was also coming off a successful performance as a three-term wartime governor.

Although progressive in his desire to safeguard individual religious conscience, Patrick Henry renewed consideration of a General Assessment Bill in November 1783. The idea was to create an establishment of multiple churches by adopting an earmarked tax where the payer could designate the amount to the church of his or her choice. Mistakes learned during consideration of the 1779 assessment bill were not repeated. Specifically, there was no codifying of articles of the Christian faith to limit the funds to churches regarded as orthodox. Initial debate by the general assembly in late 1783 settled little; no actual bill was drafted, and the matter was put over for consideration in the spring of 1784.

Relying on centuries of Western tradition, Henry and his supporters hoped to use the pulpit to encourage public order and stimulate economic productivity. Soldiers needed to transition back to being peaceful and productive citizens. Civic republicans reasoned thusly: a republican state required public virtue, virtue was largely derived from religion, and thus the state had an interest in aiding the churches in their task of religious training.

Obstructing Henry's way were two equally determined groups. On the one hand, James Madison championed the cause of the Enlightenment rationalists. On the other stood Protestant dissenters who believed that the government's involvement in religion was an encroachment on the authority of Christ over His church. These two parties, although ideologically distinct, formed a tacit alliance for the purpose of defeating the general assessment and toppling the remaining vestiges of the established church in Virginia.[21] The rationalists provided the political savvy and legislative know-how. The dissenters provided the petitions to the legislature, election-day votes, and other popular support necessary to keep the rationalists in office and advance the agenda in the legislature. Neither camp acted out of the same motive; both shared the same immediate objective. Neither would likely have succeeded without the other.

The general assessment idea had been debated in Virginia going back to the fall of 1776, and by the time the war ended the assessment had substantial support, due in part to dire social conditions. A petition from Warwick County, dated May 15, 1784, requested an assessment to revive the withering establishment. Days later petitions were prepared by the Hanover Presbyterians and the Virginia Baptists opposing an assessment. On May 27, the house committee to which the petitions had been assigned found the Warwick County petition persuasive and prepared to take favorable action. In June 1784, petitions arrived from the newly named Protestant Episcopal Church (successor to the Church of England in America) and from residents of Powhatan County supporting a general assessment. With backing from a handful of counties and solid control of the assembly, the advocates of an assessment were confident of success.[22]

On June 3, 1784, a petition was drafted by the Protestant Episcopal Church requesting a bill incorporating the Protestant Episcopal Church in Virginia. This petition was significant in two respects. First, it requested that the responsibility for tax-supported poor relief be taken away from the vestries. Vestry oversight of this charitable activity allowed dissenting sects to vote in vestry elections to have a say in the distribution of benefits. That enfranchisement resulted in non-Anglicans having a say in Episcopal governance. The petition also requested that the Episcopal hierarchy be granted the power to determine its own doctrine and internal church regulation, a seeming admission that the general assembly presently held that authority. Ultimately, the request to incorporate, although itself controversial at the time, proved to be less of a concern than the question of who governed the internal operations of the church. In a letter to James Madison, dated June 21, 1784, John Blair Smith stated the Presbyterian position on the Incorporation Act. "Smith . . . protested against the act granting the Anglican clergy the privilege of making the canons and regulations of their church as an assertion of the Assembly's right to legislate concerning religion."[23] As events unfolded, the Incorporation Bill served as a companion to the Assessment Bill. This linkage would prove to be a tactical mistake for the proassessment forces.

Meanwhile, the opponents of the general assessment were preparing for what seemed its inevitable passage. On October 27, 1784, the Presbyterian clergy met at Hanover to formulate a petition. Their petition attempted to limit the damage of an assessment by proposing more acceptable terms. The petition adopted the thinking of an assessment bill, but took pains to characterize an assessment as the church supporting and preserving the social bonds needed to sustain a representative government. James Madison's disgust with this position is apparent in his expostulation that the Presbyterians were "as ready to set up an establishment which is to take them in [as beneficiaries of the tax], as they were to put down that which shut them out."[24] Presbyterian laity also expressed alarm at this apparent reversal.[25] Viewed in context, the petition of October 1784 offered a compromise in the face of what was thought to be the inevitable adoption of a general assessment, rather than a statement of Presbyterian principle. As Eckenrode explains, "[T]he [Hanover] Presbytery never advanced beyond the position of accepting what was almost looked upon as a *fait accompli.*"

On November 11, 1784, the two champions, Henry and Madison, debated the proposed general assessment. Madison's first point was that religion was not within the "purview" of civil authority. His second point was to rephrase the issue as not whether religion was necessary to support a republic (he believed it was), but whether an establishment of religion is necessary for religion to flourish (and thereby be of support to society and government). Madison cited evidence of government's historical tendency to corrupt any religion it supports. Point three argued that an establishment would make Virginia inhospitable to dissenters, causing reduced immigration into the state as well as causing people to leave due to religious oppression. Madison's fourth point demonstrated that the social decay the assessment was intended to cure could in fact be remedied by social activity and personal example. His fifth point addressed the practical problems of a multiple establishment, most significantly the difficulty of adjudicating religious questions in a court of law. Such questions were inevitable if only orthodox Christian churches were to be eligible to receive tax payments. It is clear from Madison's outline that his aim was to protect and liberate religion, not to control or curtail it, as well as to avoid the inevitable civic division that follows when government involves itself in specifically religious doctrine and observance.[26]

Despite Madison's efforts, the house sitting as a committee of the whole reported out a resolution on November 11, 1784, stating that the people "ought to pay a moderate tax or contribution annually for the support of the Christian religion, or of some Christian church, denomination, or communion of Christians, or of some form of Christian worship." After the resolution was amended on the house floor, a committee was appointed, chaired by Henry, to reduce the resolution to a draft bill.[27]

On November 17, 1784, with plans for the Assessment Bill moving steadily through the legislative process, Patrick Henry left his seat in the general assembly to again assume the post as governor of Virginia. The responsibilities of that office allowed Henry to leave the capital at Richmond and return to his home and family. These events, perhaps more than any other, provided James Madison and the dissenter opponents of the assessment the opportunity to stop its momentum. Had Henry remained in the legislature, his reputation and influence would have likely ensured passage of the bill.

Popular opposition to the assessment was arriving regularly in the form of petitions. On November 18, 1784, John Blair Smith and John Todd, both Presbyterian lobbyists, presented a paper that sought to avoid any misunderstanding concerning the Presbyterian position as a result of the October 27, 1784, petition. That same November day, a petition arrived from Rockingham County opposing an assessment. Petitions favoring an assessment continued to arrive as well. On November 20, supporting petitions arrived from Lunenburg, Mecklenburg, and Amelia Counties. On December 1, supporting petitions from Dinwiddie and Surry Counties were delivered. Also on December 1, a petition from Rockbridge County opposing assessment was delivered.[28]

With success still probable, on December 3, 1784, Francis Corbin reported a bill to the entire assembly. At last put into written form, the printed bill was entitled A Bill Establishing a Provision for Teachers of the Christian Religion. The bill's supporters had astutely refrained from putting the assessment idea into written form for as long as possible in order to present less of a target. At this point, however, a written bill could be delayed no longer. The preamble of the bill began, "[w]hereas the general diffusion of Christian knowledge hath a natural tendency to correct the morals of men," and went on to state that the desired diffusion was not possible without teachers of the Gospel (that is, clergy or ministers). The bill did away with distinctions among Christians with respect to eligibility, giving each taxpayer the ability to divert the tax to aid the minister or church of his or her choice.[29] Accordingly, Catholics as well as all Protestants could benefit, but not Jews or any other non-Christians—albeit they were still subject to the tax. There was a brief movement to make all religions eligible to participate by substituting the word "religious" for "Christian," but that was soon reversed.[30] Unlike the draft bill back in 1779, this bill did not attempt to define Christian orthodoxy with articles of faith and then limit payments to churches who met the articles. Therefore, the civil resolution of certain religious questions was avoided. Because Quakers and Mennonites had no formal clergy to receive the tax funds and in some cases no church building, designations to these denominations were to be paid into their "general fund."

To deflect another objection that arose during floor debate, supporters inserted a default clause for those taxpayers who made no designation concerning where their payments should go. Any such amounts were to be deposited into the "Public Treasury" and held for the support of schools within the relevant county "for the encouragement of seminaries of learning within the Countries whence such sums arise." "Seminaries" meant schools of general education. While taxpayers could not direct their support to a non-Christian house of worship or religious leader, this default did give them the option of supporting schools. There were no public schools in Virginia at the time; there were, of course, private schools generally affiliated with a church. Accordingly, the character of these "seminaries of learning," whether they would be private or public, and whether secular or religious, necessarily awaited future refinement. The assembly would have to decide where to appropriate from this fund, and in what amount, these undesignated moneys collected in the "Public Treasury."

On November 14, 1784, Madison thought the bill would pass. It was given a second reading on December 3, and was then referred to the house sitting as a committee of the whole. With Henry now absent from the assembly, Madison sensed an opportunity for delay. Eckenrode traces Madison's thoughts from November 14 forward:

> "I think the bottom will be enlarged," he wrote, "and that a trial will be made of the practicability of the project." But on November 27, he wrote as follows: "You will have heard of the vote in favor of the Gen[eral] Assess[ment]. The bill is not yet brought in & I question whether it will, or if so whether it will

pass." A few days later, on December 4, his opinion was still stronger. "The bill for the Religious Ass[essment] was reported yesterday and will be taken up in a Com[mittee] of the whole next week. Its friends are much disheartened at the loss of Mr. Henry. Its fate is I think very uncertain."[31]

Meanwhile, the Incorporation Bill designed to grant a corporate charter to the Protestant Episcopal Church was debated by the entire house from December 18 to 21. The Incorporation Bill passed on December 22, by a vote of forty-seven to thirty-eight. Madison voted in favor of incorporation, a strategy that he explained as follows: "The necessity of some sort of incorporation for the purpose of holding & managing the property of the church could not well be denied, nor a more harmless modification of it now obtained. A negative of the bill, too, would have doubled the eagerness and the pretexts for a much greater evil, a general Assessment, which, there is good ground to believe, was parried by this partial gratification of its warmest votaries."[32]

The *Incorporation Act* became law upon the governor's signature, but remained controversial with dissenters, especially the Baptists. In the short term, the passage of the *Incorporation Act* caused Presbyterians to fear a resurgent Episcopal Church. This too added urgency to the Presbyterian opposition to the assessment bill.

Immediately after passage of the Incorporation Bill, the Assessment Bill was brought before the assembly. On December 23, 1784, the bill was debated and amended that day and the next and was then engrossed by a vote of forty-four to forty-two. The bill was to be read the third and final time on Christmas Eve, but a motion was made to defer the final reading until the beginning of the next legislative session, which would not start until November 1785. The motion passed by a vote of forty-five to thirty-eight. The next vote of the assembly ordered the printing and public distribution of the engrossed Assessment Bill to provide the people with an opportunity to express their opinions on the subject.[33]

IV.

On April 22, 1785, George Nicholas wrote a letter to James Madison, urging him to draw up a petition opposing the Assessment Bill. George Mason reached out to encourage Madison as well.[34] These appeals resulted in Madison's composition of June 1785 addressed *To the Honorable the General Assembly of the Commonwealth of Virginia A Memorial and Remonstrance*.[35] In

July 1785, Nicholas circulated Madison's *Memorial and Remonstrance* in the middle and western counties, where the proportion of dissenters was high and sentiment was generally against the assessment. Mason remained active, distributing the *Memorial* in Virginia's northern neck and also sending it to influential citizens seeking their backing.[36]

In a preamble, followed by fifteen numbered paragraphs, Madison built on a social-contract framework. Madison writes from the perspective of a Christian, but without any air of superiority or conversionary purpose. Madison's argument is presented in the form of a memorial (that is, a list of reasons) and a remonstrance (a protest). Following the preamble where signatories declare they "remonstrate against the said Bill," Madison begins each paragraph of his list of reasons with "Because." Some of the numbered paragraphs have multiple points. Stripped of its Madisonian rhetoric as well as repetition, summaries of his numbered paragraphs follow. The most fundamental, and the most in need of some additional context, are the summaries of Madison's paragraphs 1, 2, 5, 6, 7, and 8.

Summary of Paragraph 1: Religion is "the duty which we owe to our Creator and the manner of discharging it." It "can be directed only by reason and conviction, not by force."[37] Each man has a right to determine his own religion. This is a right as against other men, but as to God it is a duty. That is why it is unalienable. A duty to God precedes in both time and degree man's obligations undertaken when entering into the social contract. Because man's determination of his religion was never contracted away, indeed is a duty to God and thus not capable of being contracted away, government has no cognizance over religion.

Commentary: While the *Memorial and Remonstrance* is highly praised and much analyzed by writers, modern assumptions might obscure the logic of Madison's argument. A common mistake is the assumption that religious convictions are mere preferences in the nature of a "liberty" within the categories of life, liberty, and property. From Locke's *Letter Concerning Toleration*, religious convictions are a duty owed to God, not a personal preference.[38] If religiously informed conscience is unalienable (cannot be contracted away when making one's social contract), then necessarily the government is limited. This puts religion outside the jurisdiction of government. But it must be asked just how Madison in the *Memorial* parses the meaning of "religion" beyond its being a duty to God. Certainly, "religion" includes explicitly religious beliefs and observances, such as prayer, liturgy, Sabbath rest, a belief in the existence of heaven and hell—what he calls questions of "religious truth" in paragraph 5 of the *Memorial*. But if a government has no cognizance over "religion," then religion in that meaning could not possibly include the many ill behaviors of our common life to which most religions bring to bear their moral teachings, such as on stealing, lying, neglect of one's children, and murder.[39] So one must elsewhere attribute to Madison some further refinement of the meaning of "religion" that distinguishes between explicitly religious matters (for example, religious doctrine) as opposed to religious teachings that speak to moral issues of proper, even compelling, interest to our common life and hence to civil government.

Summary of Paragraph 2: If religion (as defined in paragraph 1) is exempt from the cognizance of government (as argued in paragraph 1), still less can religion be subject to the legislature. The legislature is but a department of the government. If the government has no jurisdiction over religion, then the same is necessarily true of the legislature. Not only is separation of powers among government's three departments essential to limiting government, but the departments must not "overleap the great Barrier" that limits all government.

Commentary: The limit on government's cognizance as noted in paragraph 1 is here called "the great Barrier." Neither one department nor the entire government has the authority to leap this barrier. There is a center of authority that exists apart from the government, an authority over religious matters. As with paragraph 1, Madison leaves us wanting to know more about the proper location of this "great Barrier" between government and those aspects of religion outside the reach of government.

Summary of Paragraph 5: A civil magistrate is not competent to judge religious truth. For government to employ religion "as an engine of civil policy" is an "unhallowed perversion" of the Christian Gospel.

Commentary: There are two points here. First, by establishing a religion the government is necessarily saying that that religion is true and other religions are false. But civil rulers through the ages have reached contradictory conclusions on correct doctrine, thereby refuting the claim that government can accurately determine religious truth. Second, to be used as a tool to accomplish the political goals of the civil state is, for Christians, to exploit and debase the faith. The negative view of the Roman Catholic Church begins to emerge in this paragraph, and later in paragraphs 6, 7, and 8.

Summary of Paragraph 6: Christianity does not need the support of government. Indeed, the Scriptures expressly teach against a dependence on worldly powers. Christianity flourished when government opposed it. Government support weakens the confidence of Christians in their own religion, and it raises suspicions by skeptics about Christians who apparently think so little of their religion that it needs propping up by the government.

Commentary: This is a normative claim about what Christianity teaches. It is being made by one presenting as a Christian. The Protestant dissenters argued that the church should not depend on government. However, that claim went against the teaching of other churches in that day, such as Catholic, Orthodox, and the Church of England.

Summary of Paragraph 7: From the Roman Empire's establishment of Christianity in the fourth century, the church was corrupted: in the clergy, pride and indolence; in the laity, ignorance and servility; and in both, superstition, bigotry, and persecution. Worthy of admiration is the primitive church before its establishment. A return to voluntary support of the church is predicted by some clerics to cause its downfall. Discount this prediction, given the self-interest of these clerics in continued establishment.

Summary of Paragraph 8: Government has no need of an establishment. What has been the consequence? Sometimes churches have dominated government and brought about spiritual tyranny. Sometimes governments have used establishments to reinforce political tyranny. A just government, however, will safeguard equal religious freedom and will neither invade any sect nor permit one sect to invade another.

There were at least thirteen copies of the *Memorial* filed with the general assembly, and 1,552 signatures appeared thereon. In all this flurry of activity, Madison successfully worked to keep his authorship anonymous. Indeed, it was not until 1826 that Madison publicly acknowledged that he had written the petition. The *Memorial*'s distribution in the summer and fall of 1785 was only one of a flood of antiassessment petitions. The most popular petition was from an evangelical point of view. It was submitted in twenty copies and had a total of 4,899 signatures—three times the number for Madison's *Memorial*.[40] The petitions especially attracted the signatures of the dissenting faiths. Eckenrode writes, "More important probably than the efforts even of Madison and Nicholas and their friends was the decision of the evangelical churches to oppose the assessment."[41]

V.

On August 13, 1785, the Baptists were drawing up a petition in Powhatan County, while the Presbyterians were doing the same in Hanover. On September 7, the Baptist General Association met at Orange and adopted a remonstrance. Pittsylvania County drafted an antiassessment petition dated November 7; Montgomery County's petition was dated November 15. On November 29, Botetourt County drew up a petition concerned that a general assessment would indiscriminately support the Christian heterodox along with the orthodox. Even the generally apolitical Quakers submitted a petition opposing an assessment. Eckenrode summarizes:

> The most popular argument in all these papers was the assertion, repeated in different terms in [Madison's] Remonstrance and in the Presbyterian and Baptist memorials, that Christianity [during its first three centuries] had grown and prospered in spite of the opposition of the State. A score of petitions declared that "certain it is that the Blessed author of the Christian Religion, not only maintained and supported his gospel in the world for several Hundred Years, without the aid of Civil Power but against all the Powers of the Earth, the Excellent Purity of its Precepts and the unblamable behavior of its Ministers made its way thro all opposition. Nor was it the Better for the church when Constantine the great, first Established Christianity by human Laws[;] true there was rest from Persecution, but how soon was the Church Over run with Error and Immorality."[42]

The exact proportion of the population for and against an assessment for religion is difficult to calculate. Eckenrode reports that the number of signatures on the antiassessment petitions was at least 10,000, and may have been more. He estimates that opponents outnumbered backers of the bill eight to one.[43] Supporters of the general assessment did not entirely disappear. But the proassessment forces were not equal to their opponents in energy and organization, producing the impression that an overwhelming majority of the people in Virginia were opposed.

While the many petitions signed by Presbyterians, Baptists, and other dissenters had more signatures and provided the show of force necessary to defeat Henry's Bill, Madison's *Memorial* has proven the more timeless American document on the subject of religious freedom. The other petitions were more openly religious, indeed Protestant. This is why they had more immediate appeal to the people than did Madison's *Memorial*. History may not have judged rightly, for a singular focus on the *Memorial* leaves a serious misimpression. Clearly, it was the combination of Madison's legislative acumen and the large-scale opposition by dissenters that set the assessment proponents on the defensive. Neither member of the alliance would have succeeded without the other; while they shared the same immediate goal, their long-range hopes were different.

Although factors such as the economic burden any tax would place on a largely impoverished postwar population contributed to the defeat of the Assessment Bill, it was the volume of disestablishment petitions awaiting the assembly that sealed its fate. When the delegates reconvened in October 1785, the bill died quietly.

William Rives in his biography of James Madison writes: "When the Assembly met in October [1785], the table of the House of Delegates almost sank under the weight of the accumulated copies of the memorials sent forward from the different counties, each with its long and dense columns of subscribers. The fate of the assessment was sealed. The manifestation of the public judgment was too unequivocal and overwhelming to leave the faintest hope to the friends of the measure."[44] There is no mention of the bill in the official journal in the fall of 1785, and no final reading on the house floor was ever held. It simply disappeared, never to be taken up again.

VI.

The Presbyterians and Baptists in Virginia, as well James Madison, made arguments in their petitions that can be usefully broken down into the categories of historical, theological/religious, and governmental/prudential. Clustering the arguments in this way sheds new light on the case for disestablishment in Virginia, as well as reveals the substantial overlap of Madison's *Memorial* with the dissenters' petitions.

Historical Arguments in the Petitions

1. In the first three centuries, the church grew rapidly and Christianity spread widely. This occurred despite the disapproval of and at times persecution by imperial Rome. It was during this time of the primitive church that Christianity flourished in its greatest purity.[45] It was the establishment of Christianity in the fourth century that caused the church to be corrupted by too close a proximity to government and its power.
2. What have been the fruits of establishment? "More or less in all places, pride and indolence in the Clergy, ignorance and servility

in the laity, in both, superstition, bigotry and persecution."[46] So not only was the church harmed, but it also did harm to others.

3. A return to the energetic and uncorrupted church of the first three centuries would entail having support for the clergy "depend[]on the voluntary rewards of their flocks."[47]

4. "[I]n many instances" the established church, in order to hold on to its privileges, helped to prop up a government with its "thrones of political tyranny." Never has an established church "been seen [as] the guardians of the liberties of the people."[48] Rather, establishment has alienated from Christianity those who yearn for greater liberty.

5. The medieval church was at times so powerful as to "erect a spiritual tyranny" by way of co-opting civil government.[49]

6. Civil magistrates are not competent to judge religious truth. Down through the ages, civil rulers have repeatedly contradicted one another in their resolution of central religious teachings. This proves false any claim that civil authorities can reliably judge religious truth.[50]

7. Religious inequality by the government differs only in degree from the Inquisition.[51]

8. Dialogue and negotiation to resolve disputes over religious doctrine can be slow and frustrating. To put an end to such squabbling so that there might be unity within the state, civil authorities in the past sought to impose creedal agreement by civil law. On other occasions, church authorities have invited civil authorities to intervene in religious disputes and impose a doctrinal settlement. This proved unwise. "Torrents of blood have been spilt in the old world, by vain attempts of the secular arm, to extinguish Religious discord, by proscribing all difference in Religious opinion."[52] Experience has shown that it is not for government to attempt to resolve religious doctrinal disputes. "The American Theatre has exhibited proofs that equal and compleat liberty, if it does not wholly eradicate [disharmony among churches], sufficiently destroys its malignant influence on the health and prosperity of the State." Since 1776, Virginia had also enjoyed the salutary effects of withdrawing state jurisdiction over such doctrinal disputes, but the old "animosities and jealousies" among the churches would be reintroduced should Henry's Assessment Bill be enacted.[53]

Religious Arguments in the Petitions

1. Authority over religiously informed conscience is vested in each individual, and it is a duty to God. People thus have two loyalties: God and state. Conscience or one's duty to God supersedes any duty to the state. Government is thereby limited by individual conscience.[54]

2. "Render therefore to Caesar the things that are Caesar's, and to God the things that are God's" (Mark 12:17).[55] From this passage and others, a dual-authority pattern developed between state and church (God's earthly surrogate). When the church is truly independent, it will criticize public officials, when warranted, and act as a check on injustice. Government is thereby limited by the church.

3. These two limits on government have worked in the West to help check the authoritarian pretensions of the state.

4. Christianity does not need the support of civil government.[56] Christ said that his kingdom is not of this world, thus renouncing dependence on worldly powers.[57]

5. Dependence on government weakens the faith of Christians, for they see their church propped up by the state. And such dependence by the church incurs the contempt of non-Christians.[58]

6. While civil society and our communal life together are important, ultimately the central purpose of Christianity is not to shape domestic policy or to preserve the unity of the state.[59]

7. Authentic religion will command respect and can stand on its own merit. It appeals to people who will in turn support the faith, not out of compulsion but willingly.[60]

8. For clergy to take the state's general assessment will harm their church.[61] The state's assessment may be used to control the church.[62]

9. Civil government inevitably will attempt to use the church as an "engine of Social Policy" to accomplish its political ends. Should the church become a tool of the state, for Christians this would be an "unhallowed perversion of the means of salvation."[63]

10. An established church makes evangelism harder. Juridically compelled support generates resentment toward the established church and thereby Christianity.[64]

Governmental/Prudential Arguments in the Petitions

1. To permit the state to establish a church necessarily yields to the government the authority to determine religious truth. To concede that the state has cognizance over such matters is to necessarily concede it has authority to establish a different Christian church or to even establish a non-Christian faith.[65]

2. In reason and fairness, all religions should be equal before the law. Each man leaves the state of nature and enters into the social contract on the same level as all others. Yet an establishment privileges one religion over others.[66] Moreover, the accommodation in the Assessment Bill for Quakers and Mennonites (their designated assessments are paid into their general church funds, because they have no formal clergy) is an illustration of unequal treatment.[67]

3. Discrimination on account of religion will be resented, the resentment being directed at the state and at the established church. This divides the body politic. Seditious thoughts come in response to such religious oppression.[68]

4. In a free society, the enforcement of laws requires broad public support. Religious discrimination generates animosity against the government and thereby undermines support for the rule of law.[69]

5. Discrimination on account of religion discourages immigration, and it causes current residents to leave the state. This loss of population is bad for the practical arts and thus harms the economy.[70]

6. Because of the Revolutionary War and the need to unify Americans, all religious oppression should stop.[71]

VII.

The victors in the assessment battle wasted no time. The Revised Code, first proposed to the House of Delegates back in June 1779, still had among its many provisions awaiting consideration Thomas Jefferson's *A Bill for Establishing Religious Freedom*, assigned No. 82.[72] In late 1785, Jefferson was serving as the U.S. minister in Paris. Once again Madison was the essential man.

On December 14, 1785, Bill No. 82 was plucked at Madison's initiative from the stack of bills awaiting attention in the winding-down session. The next day, the committee reported Bill No. 82 to the house but with an amendment that undermined its force. The house considered the amendment on December 16 and rejected it by a vote of thirty-eight to sixty-six. This decisive margin signaled the impotence of the establishmentarians in the aftermath of defeat of the Assessment Bill. After a third reading and the defeat of a motion to postpone a vote until the following session, on December 17 Bill No. 82 passed the House by a vote of seventy-four to twenty. A battle of amendments ensued between the house and the more conservative senate, resulting in a conference between the two chambers. With adjournment impending, Madison reluctantly agreed to some amendments.[73] The amendments rejected Jefferson's extremes. For example, Jefferson's attribution of religion to reason alone (as opposed to reason and revelation, as Christian orthodoxy would have it) was excised from the long preamble. Final passage of *A Bill Establishing Religious Freedom*, as amended, came on January 16, 1786.

Following a long preamble, the substantive provisions of Bill No. 82 are quite short. The most quoted section of the preamble is openly theistic. Jefferson wrote, for example, that civil restraints on religion "are a departure from the plan of the holy author of our religion, who being lord both of body and mind, yet chose not to propagate it by coercions on either, as was in his Almighty power to do." The operative substance of the bill provides as follows:

> Be it enacted by the General Assembly that no man shall be compelled to frequent or support any religious worship, place, or ministry whatsoever, nor shall be enforced, restrained, molested, or burthened in his body or goods, nor shall otherwise suffer, on account of his religious opinions or belief; but that all men shall be free to profess, and by argument to maintain, their opinions in matters of religion, and that the same shall in no wise diminish, enlarge, or affect their civil capacities.[74]

By its terms, the statute protects freedom of belief and speech in religious matters and provides that there are to be no civil disabilities or tests on account of religion. These freedoms were likely already safeguarded by Article 16 of the Declaration of Rights. New in Bill No. 82 was the affirmative declaration that financial support for religion is to be voluntary ("no man shall be compelled to . . . support any religious worship, place, or ministry"), albeit that had been the actual state of affairs in Virginia since 1776. Nevertheless, the codification of voluntarism gave statutory confirmation to wartime accommodations and was a cause for celebration by both Protestant dissenters and Enlightenment rationalists. Surprisingly, the bill did not expressly disestablish the Anglican church (or its successor, the Protestant Episcopal Church).[75] The church could, under the letter of Bill No. 82, continue to enjoy the preferential treatment of the state, just not its financial support. Something more like the reverse of such preferential treatment is what actually occurred, however, with the state further wounding the Episcopalians.

VIII.

The dissenters, energized by their victory, were not finished in setting things right, at least as they saw the right. The *Incorporation Act* that had passed the general assembly on December 22, 1784, allowing the formation in Virginia of the Protestant Episcopal Church, the postrevolutionary successor to the Church of England, was next up. The act was objectionable to dissenters in two respects. First, it did not simply incorporate the Episcopal Church, but gave the state general assembly authority to make certain decisions ecclesiastical in nature. Such a delegation of authority over internal church affairs is odd to us today. But to these Anglicans, members of Virginia's successor to the Church of England, it was commonplace to have the civil government making decisions concerning the inner workings of the church. Second, the *Incorporation Act* had settled legal title to the glebe lands in the Protestant Episcopal Church.

In August 1786, the Baptist General Committee petitioned the general assembly to have the eighteen-month-old *Incorporation Act* repealed. The Baptists began by reminding the assembly of the role of Baptists in fighting the late War of Independence, stimulated as they were by a liberal state Constitution "free in religious concerns" and promising "equal Liberty of conscience, and equal claim of property." Citing Sections 4 and 16 of the Virginia Declaration of Rights, as well as the new *Establishment of Religious Freedom Act* of the previous January, the petition asked how it was that those rights are not violated by private legislation that dictates "the character of [Episcopal Church] members, modulate[s] the forms of her government, & appoint[s] the Time and place of her meeting." This makes no sense, insisted the Baptists, if the new legal standard is one of disestablishment: "If the members of the Protestant Episcopal Church prefer Episcopacy to any other form of Government, they have an undoubted Right as free Citizens of the State to enjoy It; But to call in the aid of Legislature to Establish it, threatens the freedom of Religious Liberty in its Consequences." This was not just contrary to the highest civil law of the state, but to Baptists it was unbiblical: "New Testament Churches, we humbly conceive, are, or should be, established by the Legislature of Heaven, and not earthly power; by the Law of God and not the Law of the State; by the acts of the Apostles, and not by the Acts of an Assembly. The Incorporating act then, in the first place appears to cast great contempt upon the divine Author of our Religion, whose King-dom is not of the world."[76]

The general assembly convened in mid-October 1786, and by the end of that month the issue was joined. The committee for religion received memo-rials for and against repeal of the *Incorporation Act*, of which it is estimat-ed about five thousand signatures urged repeal. The petition from Orange County was typical. The attack was twofold: first, the *Incorporation Act* was "unprecedented in the New Testament and unwarrantable by the Bill of Rights," and, second, the grant of the glebe lands to the Episcopal Church was unfair because the property belonged to everyone. Virginia was the suc-cessor government to the former British colony, the memorial reasoned, and thus the property should revert to the state to the benefit of all citizens. "Let all Religious Societies stand on the same Level," argued the petition from the County of King George, and then the "jealousies will leave [our state] and Harmony abound." The Hanover memorial was practical in wondering just how the Episcopal Church "might advance in dignity and influence, when aided by large sums of money" that all other churches would have had to have acquired by voluntary donations from members. The petition from Au-gusta regretted the state's intimate involvement in the polity of one church, where the offending legislation "establishes an immediate[,] a dangerous and unwarrantable connection between the Legislature and that Church. By that Act the Assembly must be considered as the Head of that church and pecu-liarly interested in its welfare: for from the Assembly it receives its authority to Act."[77]

The defenders of the Protestant Episcopal Church did not stand silent for an undoing of the *Incorporation Act*. Their petitions were also numer-ous, especially from the tidewater and south-side areas, with estimates of twenty-five hundred names. There must be security in title to real estate, they maintained, and the glebes had by tradition and custom been held for the benefit of the English church. And as to the loss of harmony between religious groups, it was those who were trying to undo the settled past who were acting out of a "spirit of persecution" and thereby disturbing the peace. Those of the vestry in Fredericksville noted the poor financial condition of their Episcopal parish, begging that the incorporation be kept or the church's survival was in doubt.[78]

The House of Delegates sat as a committee of the whole, receiving peti-tions on November 2 and December 5. Following the second meeting, reso-lutions were reported: that a general incorporation law ought to be adopted, permitting religious societies of all types to incorporate for the purposes of holding title to land and otherwise; that existing incorporation laws ought to be repealed if they prohibited religious societies from forming internal regulations for their own governance; and the *Incorporation Act* of the Episcopal Church ought to be repealed. However, only the third of these threefold resolutions was pursued, and that only by half. On January 6, 1787, the house repealed that part of the *Incorporation Act* whereby the general assembly made ecclesiastical decisions on behalf of the Episcopal Church. However, the bill was silent concerning the fate of the glebes. The senate agreed with the house on January 8.[79]

James Madison did vote in favor of repeal of the *Incorporation Act*, but he was not an instigator behind its development. It was the religious dissenters who spearheaded the attack. A February 15, 1787, letter from Madison to Thomas Jefferson records Madison's bystander status.[80] He further notes without judgment that the dissenters tried but failed to reverse the matter of title to the glebes.

IX.

The business of Virginia's disestablishment was set aside for just a bit, as another matter vied for the available energy devoted to the making of a republic. The draft of a proposed United States Constitution, worked out in Philadelphia from May to September 1787, came before the Virginia state convention on the question of ratification. The Virginia convention got under way on June 2, 1788. Virginia was the most wealthy and most populous state, so its participation seemed essential to the success of the proposed central government. The opposition to ratification of the proposed Constitution had able leaders such as Patrick Henry, Richard Henry Lee, and George Mason. Mason had been one of Virginia's delegates to the Constitutional Convention in Philadelphia and had famously refused to sign when other delegates summarily dismissed consideration of a bill of rights.[81] Edmund Randolph, the governor of Virginia, was also a Philadelphia Convention delegate who refused to sign. However, through the quiet work of George Washington and James Madison, Randolph changed his mind, and by the time the state convention began he announced his newfound support for the Constitution.[82]

Like Antifederalists generally, Patrick Henry opposed ratification because the proposed Constitution took too much power away from the states. The issue of religious freedom came up only occasionally, and each time in reply to rather vague claims by Henry that the 1787 Constitution put civil liberties at risk, including the right of conscience, while possibly empowering

Congress to establish a national religion. Randolph was first to respond to Henry's claims that the congressional powers enumerated in Article I of the Constitution endangered a litany of rights, including religious freedom. Randolph said, "I inform those who are of this opinion, that no power is given expressly to Congress over religion." He went on to observe that the Religious Test Clause in Article VI "puts all sects on the same footing" and that the multiplicity of religious groups in the United States was a safeguard in "that [the many sects] will prevent the establishment of any one sect, in prejudice to the rest."[83]

James Madison likewise challenged Henry's insistence that a bill of rights was required to protect civil liberties, including religious freedom. Madison belittled the efficacy of a bill of rights to successfully protect religious freedom when a popular majority of the people was pressuring a legislature to favor one sect. Like Randolph, Madison said safety was to be found where there was a multiplicity of sects, each checking the ambitious plans of the others, as was the case in the vast United States. In the midst of this "rival sects" theory, Madison said that he was pleased to note that in Virginia, "a majority of the people are decidedly against any exclusive establishment." Then, in an oft-quoted passage, Madison said with apparent reference to the proposed federal Constitution, "[t]here is not a shadow of right in the general government to intermeddle with religion. Its least interference with it would be a most flagrant usurpation."[84] The Madisonian passage is singled out today because it conforms to a broad reading of the "no cognizance over religion" principle in Madison's 1785 *Memorial and Remonstrance.* No bill of rights was needed, argued Madison. He appealed to the delegates to trust him on this, for he was well known in Virginia as a champion of religious freedom. Zachariah Johnson, a Federalist, extolled the Religious Test Clause as a protection of religious conscience and also relied on the "rival sects" theory as sufficient assurance against a federal religious establishment.

Patrick Henry managed to partly undermine the argument that "all that is not delegated is denied" relied on by the Federalists. He pointed out that the Constitution did expressly declare certain rights, like habeas corpus. For example, Article I, Section 9, expressly denied certain powers to the federal government. Why were some rights necessary to declare, he asked sensibly, if all power not delegated was denied?[85] Thus, the "limited, delegated power" argument did not entirely ring true with the text.

On June 25, 1788, Virginia ratified the Constitution by the narrow margin of eighty-nine to seventy-nine. However, in order to secure ratification, the Federalists in Virginia, like those in Massachusetts and South Carolina before them, had agreed to have Congress consider a list of amendments recommended by the convention.[86] A motion by Patrick Henry had forty amendments, but the first twenty substantially paraphrase Virginia's Declaration of Rights. The proposed amendment numbered twentieth addressed religious freedom:

> That religion, or the duty which we owe to our Creator, and the manner of discharging it, can be directed only by reason and conviction, not by force or violence; and therefore all men have an equal, natural, and unalienable right to the free exercise of religion, according to the dictates of conscience, and that no particular religious sect or society ought to be favored or established, by law, in preference to others.[87]

The phrasing here was a combination of Article 16 of Virginia's Declaration of Rights as adopted in 1776, with language tacked on at the end requiring that no one religion be preferred over others. The latter language of nonpreferentialism, likely the work of Patrick Henry,[88] added a puzzling no-establishment feature to the rights-based terms in Virginia's Declaration of Rights. Did the text presume that the federal government—absent adoption of the Virginia amendment—had the power to affirmatively support religion so long as all religions were supported without preference? Certainly, Madison strongly opposed multiestablishment of religion, for that was the object of his contest with Henry just three years before. Multiestablishments would also violate Madison's promise to the Virginia Baptists. But surely Henry as well did not intend that adoption of this nonpreferential language was an indirect way of vesting Congress with the power to support all religions just so long as it did so without preferring some religions over others. With every fiber of his being, Henry stood for Congress having less power, not more.[89] Yet words are stubborn things. The text of the Virginia amendment is nonpreferentialist, and that wording could later cause trouble in the forthcoming debates over a federal bill of rights.

New Hampshire ratified the Constitution on June 21, 1788, becoming the ninth state to do so, with Virginia ratifying a few days later on June 25. Nine was the number needed for adoption. Accordingly, by its own terms the new Constitution led to the holding of federal elections in the fall of 1788. The First Federal Congress assembled and organized itself in New York City in February and March 1789. James Madison, a member of the House of Representatives from Virginia, first introduced a set of proposed amendments to the Constitution on May 4, 1789. On August 24 the House sent over to the Senate several articles of amendment. The Senate acted with dispatch, reporting back to the House on September 9. The House acceded to most of the Senate's alterations but on September 21 rejected those pertaining to religious freedom and requested a conference. Following the conference, where there was compromise on both sides, a joint report was issued to both houses on September 24. Favorable action was taken thereon by both chambers approving the conference committee's work, whereupon, on September 29, 1789, twelve Articles of Amendment were submitted by Congress to the states for ratification, with the Third Article being the only one to address religious freedom. Proposed Articles Third through Twelfth were in the nature of rights that acted as restraints on federal powers and later took on the appellation "Bill of Rights."[90]

Virginia ratified the first of the proposed amendments (concerning the size of the U.S. House) on November 3, 1791, and President Washington reported that partial ratification to Congress on November 14, 1791. When Virginia ratified the balance of the amendments on December 15, 1791, President Washington forwarded the full ratification message to the House and Senate on December 30, 1791.

In Virginia the ratification of the federal amendments took more than two years. It is the only state where some official record exists of a debate concerning the religion clauses. The record is complex and must be situated in the larger context of the Antifederalist struggle. Antifederalists aspired to have a second constitutional convention to secure amendments to the 1787 Constitution that would trim back the powers of the federal government with respect to direct taxation and the regulation of commerce.

In late September 1789, Virginia's two U.S. senators, Richard Henry Lee and William Grayson, wrote the governor and legislature, stating their disappointment with the twelve submitted Articles of Amendment. The letters complained that Virginia's proposed amendments had not been adopted by Congress, that the power of the central government remained unchecked, and that civil liberties were endangered by the central federal power. However, neither the Third Article nor religious freedom generally was explicitly mentioned.

The Virginia House, a majority of which were Federalists, quickly approved all the amendments on December 24, 1789. Dividing by a vote of eight to seven, the state senate held up ratification for almost two years, ostensibly because of objections to Articles Third, Eighth, Eleventh, and Twelfth.[91] Eight Antifederalist senators claimed that the proposed Third

Article did not protect the right of conscience or prohibit certain features commonly associated with an established church.[92] However, the real reason behind their opposition was that they hoped to defeat the amendments. If the Articles of Amendment failed ratification, then possibly an opportunity would open for another round of federal amendments more to their liking. James Madison counseled patience, thinking the public would tire of the delay tactics. His confidence was rewarded when the Virginia Senate ratified the amendments on December 15, 1791.

On March 1, 1792, Secretary of State Thomas Jefferson notified the states that Articles of Amendment Third through Twelfth had been successfully ratified, thus implying the First and Second Articles had failed. A stylist renumbered proposed Articles Third through Twelfth as successful amendments First through Tenth, and in time the ten amendments were called the Bill of Rights.

X.

In returning to the matter of confiscation of the glebes still held for the benefit of the Anglican church, Virginia's disestablishment entered its final stage. While just a few states (Vermont and New York) contemplated taking glebe lands from the formerly established church, only Virginia went so far as to do so.

The general assembly's bill of January 8, 1787, had repealed the act incorporating the Protestant Episcopal Church, but was silent on the matter of glebes held by Anglican ministers for the benefit of the church. The matter of title to the land was ambiguous, but there was no doubt that the Anglican ministers were in possession and had been in possession from the beginning.

Virginia Presbyterians were first to advance the claim that the income-producing property of the formerly established church was there to benefit all churches or perhaps all of the state's people. The basic conservatism of the Presbyterians, however, caused them to soon lose interest. Not so with the Baptist General Committee, which took the view that the glebes and other property should revert to the state for the enjoyment of all. The Episcopalian rejoinder was to rely on legal title to the property, which by custom had always vested with the Anglican minister for the benefit of the parish. A Presbyterian petition seeking confiscation was lodged with the assembly in 1787, as were Baptist petitions in 1789, 1790, 1791, 1792, 1794, and 1795. All were handily defeated by Episcopalian strength in the House of Delegates. Appeals by former dissenters that separation of church and state must be honored were skillfully turned by Anglican sympathizers into the suggestion that confiscation would have the state interfering with the internal workings of the church.[93]

As the dreary contest dragged on into the assembly's 1796 term, the Baptist assault on the glebes was nearing a tipping point. Sensing the danger, the Episcopal Church again pressed the argument that the contest was not a matter of religious freedom but one of title to property, a matter to be decided by the principle of repose. The Baptists countered that with the end of the state church, the investiture of the glebes shifted title to now lie with the people's representative—here, the successor to the British Crown being Virginia. To soften the blow, however, Baptists proposed a compromise: the glebes were to be sold, with proceeds held in trust for the education of poor children, provided, however, that existing Anglican ministers in possession were entitled to hold for life and only then would the land be sold. In 1796 things came to a draw, and the bill was tabled.

The indefatigable Baptists came back in 1797 and 1798. The Episcopalians, increasingly vulnerable given the rise of the Democratic-Republican Party, proposed that the general assembly frame the issue as one for resolution by the state courts. Such a bill was put to a vote in early 1798 and defeated. The Baptists returned with their proposed compromise late that year. In early 1799, Episcopalian efforts to shift the matter to the courts were again defeated. The Baptists then succeeded in having the assembly pass a bill on January 24, 1799, declaring that title to the glebes vested in the state. However, the recipient of the proceeds of the anticipated sale was left open. The following year, and again in 1801, saw Baptist petitions to have the state sell the land and bestow the proceeds on schools and academies or given over to the use by all churches.

The matter was finally resolved in late January 1802 by passage of an act directing county overseers of the poor to sell the glebes or do so once the incumbent Anglican minister should die. The money from the sale was "for the benefit of the poor or for any other object which a majority of voters in each county might decide." There was an Episcopal attempt to overturn the act in the state courts, but the appellate judges narrowly affirmed the legislation.[94]

In this fifteen-year contest, the Baptists were tenacious in fighting for what they saw as righting every last wrong of establishmentarianism, even at the cost to the security of property titles. Anglicans were at first resentful, but later philosophical. Their gifted leader, Bishop William Meade, later wrote that although the taking was unlawful, it eventually proved a blessing. Now supported by donations that were voluntary, Bishop Meade observed that the Episcopal Church had become more evangelical, and the laity had increased in membership and devotion. The fate of the proceeds from sale of the glebes was less of a blessing, for half the money was wasted through county mismanagement. Nonetheless, the other half was properly directed, with some going to build poorhouses and some to improve county roads and bridges.[95]

XI.

Not only did the repeal of January 8, 1787, unseat the Protestant Episcopal Church from its corporate status, but it also had Virginians believing that Jefferson's *A Bill for Establishing Religious Freedom* enacted January 16, 1786, required a radical separation where church and state were to minimize their interactions. The immediate application of such a rule was that no church could acquire corporate status under state law.[96] That, of course, made little sense once states adopted general incorporation acts and the convenience of the corporate form for management became widespread. The advantages of corporate status include limited liability, existence in perpetuity, and the ease of acquiring, holding, and conveying title to property. For two centuries, no church, religious charity, or school could secure corporate status in Virginia, even when every other sort of entity could.[97] The damage inflicted had real-world consequence. For example, Virginia law would not allow a church to receive a testamentary bequest because it was not incorporated.[98] The extreme separationism of Virginia's interpretation of Jefferson's Bill was eventually found at odds with the Free Exercise Clause of the First Amendment—but not until the early twenty-first century.[99]

The discrimination did not stop with churches blocked from incorporating. Under a fear that churches might amass wealth and thereby become too powerful (something that did happen in England before the Reformation), in 1842 Virginia limited church ownership of land to two acres in town and thirty acres in the countryside, as well as capped the total assets that could be held or possessed by a church.[100] This overt discrimination was prejudicial, as Thomas Buckley summarizes: "In the name of strict separation, Virginia's government withheld those neutral aids the churches needed to function as independent, autonomous entities in society." What was behind these laws? Legislatures adopted them out of their constituents' fear of control by ecclesiastical authorities and as a check on rising Catholicism.[101] Buckley's indictment is shocking: "Ironically, in light of the common perception that Jefferson's statute guaranteed 'Full religious freedom and separation of church and state,' churches and religious groups were less free in the Old Dominion than anywhere else in the Union."[102]

In yet another discriminatory provision, Virginia's revolutionary Constitution of 1776 prohibited clergy from holding public office. This law, however, is of a different character. The restraint has ancient English and colonial origins and was first initiated as a support to the established Church of England.[103] In being a member of the established clergy, an Anglican minister already held a government office. So it made little sense that he should hold a second office, the duties of a minister being sufficiently demanding.[104] Seven of the other original and newly admitted states had a restriction about clergy holding office like Virginia's. The law's source in English law explains why each state with a clergy restriction once had an Anglican establishment, as opposed to a Puritan establishment. That said, in 1827 Virginia's restriction on clergy holding public office was thoroughly revisited with an eye to repeal or retention. The law was retained, and the reason was anticlericalism. It was not until shortly after the Civil War, in its constitutional convention of 1867–68, that Virginia did away with this clergy restraint.[105]

This legislation hostile to churches is at odds with Virginia's reputation as America's heralded leader in religious freedom. It is also enigmatic. The early dissenters successfully sought separation of church and state because it was good for religion and good for the government. But a decade after the defeat of Patrick Henry's assessment bill, Virginia was adopting laws that were disabling to churches. These handicapping laws were passed because religious individuals feared not just excesses in the government's authority but also in ecclesiastical authority.[106] Parallel to these developments, but flowing in the opposite direction, the state was also enacting legislation supportive of Protestant morality: Sabbath-day closing laws, as well as limitations on alcohol, dueling, gambling, and crude amusements.[107]

XII.

The immediate and primary consequence of Virginia's disestablishment story, 1776–1802, was that henceforth funding for religion was entirely voluntary, and thereby financial aid to religion was only to the extent of each religion's merit as perceived by those who found refreshment in it. This created a free market, so to speak, in religion. One would expect that disestablishment would soon be followed by a growth spurt in popular religion. And that is exactly what happened, as historian Mark Noll writes: "Between 1790 and 1860, the United States population increased eight-fold; the number of Baptist churches increased fourteen-fold; the number of Methodist churches twenty-eight fold, and the number of Disciples or Restorationist churches cannot be figured as a percentage, since there were none of these churches in 1790 and more than two thousand in 1860." This expansion of voluntarist, modestly sectarian, and democratic forms of Christianity constituted a second founding of American religion.[108]

In Virginia the explosion in the revivalist religion of the former dissenters was no different from that recorded by Noll for the nation as a whole. As James Madison, now in retirement, was pleased to observe in Virginia thirty-seven years after the defeat of Patrick Henry's assessment bill:

> The examples of the Colonies, now States, which rejected religious establishments altogether, proved that all sects might be safely and advantageously put on a footing of equal and entire freedom. . . . [I]t is impossible to deny that [in Virginia] religion prevails with more zeal and a more exemplary priesthood than it ever did when established and patronised by public authority. We are teaching the world that great truth that governments do better without kings and nobles than with them. The merit will be doubled by the other lesson: that Religion flourishes in greater purity without than with the aid of Government.[109]

Virginia's essential man for religious freedom, James Madison, here appeals to sister states to complete the great work of liberating both conscience and church. In 1822 the only state with an old-time establishment still awaiting revision and purification was the Standing Order in Massachusetts. Clearly, however, Virginia's Madison had no business pointing with disapproval at the Bay State, for within Virginia's own borders the great task of policing the line between church and state, with the aim of keeping each within the domain suitable to its nature, was in no way finished.

NOTES

1. See *Everson v. Bd. of Educ. of Ewing Twp.*, 330 U.S. 1, 11–13 (1947) (Supreme Court looked principally to the disestablishment process in Virginia to interpret the Establishment Clause of the First Amendment); and *Reynolds v. United States*, 98 U.S. 145, 162–67 (1879) (Supreme Court looked to disestablishment events in Virginia in construing the Free Exercise Clause of the First Amendment).

2. Donald L. Drakeman, *Church, State, and Original Intent* (New York: Cambridge University Press, 2010), 2–4, 21–73. When construing the First Amendment in *Reynolds*, Drakeman points out that the Supreme Court quoted approvingly from the documents of Virginia and events surrounding the passage of Jefferson's Act to

Establish Religious Freedom. The *Reynolds* Court attributed disestablishment to Jefferson and Madison, while ignoring the essential contributions by religious dissenters, as well as the contributions of several other states. In deciding *Everson*, the Court was again wide of the mark in using Virginia as the primary source for First Amendment interpretation of the Establishment Clause. Drakeman, *Church, State, and Original Intent*, 74–148.

3. Thomas E. Buckley, *Establishing Religious Freedom: Jefferson's Statute in Virginia* (Charlottesville: University of Virginia Press, 2013), 255–57.

4. Daniel L. Dreisbach, "George Mason's Pursuit of Religious Liberty in Revolutionary Virginia," *Virginia Magazine of History and Biography* 108, no. 1 (2000): 5–16.

5. See Charles F. James, *Documentary History of the Struggle for Religious Liberty in Virginia* (Lynchburg, VA: J. P. Bell, 1900), 63–65.

6. See Thomas E. Buckley, *Church and State in Revolutionary Virginia, 1776–1787* (Charlottesville: University Press of Virginia, 1977), 18–19.

7. H. J. Eckenrode, *Separation of Church and State in Virginia: A Study in the Development of the Revolution* (1910; reprint, New York: Da Capo Press, 1971), 20–30, 43–44.

8. Dreisbach, "George Mason's Pursuit," 13–18. By "&c" Madison evidently meant for his amendment to continue on from this point with the text of the committee's draft beginning with the words "unless, under." Accordingly, the balance of Madison's amendment would read "colour of religion, any man disturb the peace, the happiness, or safety of society. And that it is the mutual duty of all to practice Christian forbearance, love and charity, towards each other." Dreisbach, "George Mason's Pursuit," 14n31.

9. John Locke, *Epistola de Tolerantia: A Letter on Toleration* (1689), ed. Raymond Klibansky (Oxford: Clarendon Press, 1968).

10. William Lee Miller, *The First Liberty: America's Foundation in Religious Freedom*, expanded and updated ed. (Washington, DC: Georgetown University Press, 2003), 7, 18.

11. James, *Documentary History*, 64, quoting Edmund Randolph, "History of Virginia," in *Virginia Historical Society Documents*, ed. Arthur Schaffer (Charlottesville: University Press of Virginia, 1970), 9:347.

12. See Virginia Constitution, Article I, Section 16 (1971).

13. Dreisbach, "George Mason's Pursuit," 19–27; James, *Documentary History*, 68–80, 95–100, 112–21, 187, 219–27.

14. This is a paraphrase of Jesus's words when on trial before Pontius Pilate, the Roman governor in Palestine, as recorded in the Gospel of John. See John 18:36.

15. James, *Documentary History*, 222–25.

16. Buckley, *Revolutionary Virginia*, 21–66, 185–86.

17. See Miller, *First Liberty*, 11–12 (setting forth the text of the assembly's resolution postponing the general assessment question).

18. Eckenrode, *Separation of Church and State*, 55, 64–65.

19. Robert Baird, *Religion in the United States of America* (1844) (New York: Arno Press, 1969), 230–38. The 1778 petition is reproduced on 236–38.

20. Buckley, *Revolutionary Virginia*, 43, 66, 80–88, 95–96, 99–109, 188–89.

21. Historian Sidney Mead describes the ultimately victorious alliance between the rationalistic statesmen and the dissenters, the latter he terms "pietists." Sidney E. Mead, *The Lively Experiment: The Shaping of Christianity in America* (New York: Harper & Row, 1963), 42–43, 62. See also Miller, *First Liberty*, 29–32, 37–41, 47–48.

22. Buckley, *Revolutionary Virginia*, 80–81.

23. Eckenrode, *Separation of Church and State*, 81–102.

24. Thomas Cary Johnson, *Virginia Presbyterianism and Religious Liberty in Colonial and Revolutionary Times* (Richmond, VA: Presbyterian Committee of Publication, 1907), 106.

25. James, *Documentary History*, 126–39, 189–90.

26. Eckenrode, *Separation of Church and State*, 85n355; Buckley, *Revolutionary Virginia*, 99–100.

27. James, *Documentary History*, 126; Buckley, *Revolutionary Virginia*, 105, 107–8.

28. Eckenrode, *Separation of Church and State*, 94–99.

29. The tax receipts could be used for Christian clergy or church buildings ("shall be by the . . . religious society, appropriated to a provision for a Minister or Teacher of the Gospel of their denomination, or the providing [of] places of divine worship, and to none other use whatsoever"). Accordingly, the assessment moneys were not limited to paying the salaries of clergy. James, *Documentary History*, 129–30.

30. Dreisbach, "George Mason's Pursuit," 33. The assessment bill being debated intentionally excluded non-Christians.

31. Eckenrode, *Separation of Church and State*, 99–100 (internal quotations are from Madison's private letters).

32. Eckenrode, *Separation of Church and State*, 99–100 (quoting from a private letter of Madison).

33. See John T. Noonan Jr., *The Lustre of Our Country: The American Experience of Religious Freedom* (Berkeley: University of California Press, 1998), 61–64, 72–74 (reproducing Madison's notes from the debate).

34. Eckenrode, *Separation of Church and State*, 104–12.

35. William T. Hutchinson and William M. E. Rachal et al., eds., *The Papers of James Madison* (Chicago: University of Chicago Press, 1973), 8:298–304.

36. Dreisbach, "George Mason's Pursuit," 34. Among others, Mason sought the support of George Washington. In his reply, Washington was ambivalent. He wrote that while he was not "alarmed" by the Assessment Bill so long as it provided "proper relief" to non-Christians, he went on to say that the bill "could die an easy death," which would "be productive of more quiet to the State." Should it pass, the assessment would "rankle, & convulse the State" for some time to come. Letter from George Washington to George Mason, October 3, 1785, https://teachingamericanhistory.org/library/document/letter-to-george-mason/.

37. Madison put in quotation marks the definition of "religion," indicating he was referencing another source. The source was Article 16 of the Virginia Declaration of Rights.

38. Locke, *Epistola de Tolerantia*, 52–55.

39. The Hanover Presbytery Petition of October 24, 1776, is more forthcoming with respect to the jurisdictional divide between church and state. Just before the definition of "religion," the petition states: "[T]he only proper objects of civil government are the happiness and protection of men in the present state of existence; the security of the life, liberty, and property of the citizens; and to restrain the vicious and encourage the virtuous by wholesome laws, equally extending to every individual." James, *Documentary History*, 224. The quoted passage is, in part, a paraphrase of Romans 13:3–4 and 1 Peter 2:13–16.

40. See Miller, *First Liberty*, 38.

41. Eckenrode, *Separation of Church and State*, 106.

42. Eckenrode, *Separation of Church and State*, 110.

43. See Noonan, *Lustre of Our Country*, 74 (reporting 10,929 antiassessment signatures).

44. William G. Rives, *The History of the Life and Times of James Madison* (Boston: Little, Brown, 1859–68), 1:632.

45. Hanover Presbytery Petition of October 24, 1776, *in* James, *Documentary History*, 234 ("[W]e are persuaded that, if mankind were left in the quiet possession of their inalienable religious privileges, Christianity, as in the days of the apostles, would continue to prevail and flourish in the greatest purity, by its own native excellencies, and under the all-disposing providence of God").

46. Madison, *Memorial*, paragraph 7.

47. Madison, *Memorial*, paragraph 7.

48. Madison, *Memorial*, paragraph 8.

49. Madison, *Memorial*, paragraph 8.

50. Madison, *Memorial*, paragraph 5; James, *Documentary History*, 223 (Hanover Presbytery Petition of October 24, 1776).

51. Madison, *Memorial*, paragraph 9.

52. Madison, *Memorial*, paragraph 11.

53. Madison, *Memorial*, paragraph 11.

54. Madison, *Memorial*, paragraphs 1–2; Hanover Presbytery Petition of 1778, in Baird, *Religion in the United States of America*, 237 ("to judge for ourselves, and to engage in the exercise of religion agreeably to the dictates of our own consciences, is an inalienable right, which upon the principles on which the gospel was first propagated, and the reformation from Popery carried on, can never be transferred to another").

55. The same passage appears in all three of the synoptic Gospels. See Matthew 22:21 and Luke 20:25.

56. See Madison, *Memorial*, paragraph 6. See also Hanover Presbytery Petition of October 24, 1776, in James, *Documentary History*, 224 ("Neither can it be made to appear that the gospel needs any such civil aid. We rather conceive that, when our blessed Saviour declares his kingdom is not of this world, he renounces all dependence upon state power; and as his weapons are spiritual, and were only designed to have influence on the judgment and heart of man, we are persuaded that, if mankind were left in the quiet possession of their inalienable religious privileges, Christianity, as in the days of the apostles, would continue to prevail").

57. See Hanover Presbytery Petition of October 24, 1776, in James, *Documentary History*, 224. This is a reference to Jesus's reply to a question asked by Pontius Pilate, the Roman governor of Palestine, recorded in John 18:36.

58. See Madison, *Memorial*, paragraph 6.

59. The dissenting Presbyterians were certain in their minds that they should not confuse the proper role of the church with the proper role of government. See Hanover Presbytery Petition of October 24, 1776, in James, *Documentary History*, 224 ("We would also humbly represent, that the only proper objects of civil government are the happiness and protection of men in the present state of existence; the security of the life, liberty, and property of the citizens; and to restrain the vicious and encourage the virtuous by wholesome laws, equally extending to every individual. But that the duty which we owe to our Creator, and the manner of discharging it, can only be directed by reason and conviction, and is no where cognizable but at the tribunal of the universal Judge"). The passage on the role of government is a paraphrase from Romans 13:3–4 and 1 Peter 2:13–16.

60. See Madison, *Memorial*, paragraph 6. See also Hanover Presbytery Petition of October 24, 1776, in James, *Documentary History*, 224–25 ("that all, of every religious sect, may be protected in the full exercise of their mutual modes of worship; exempted from all taxes for the support of any church whatsoever, further than what may be agreeable to their own private choice, or voluntary obligation. This being done, all partial and invidious distinctions will be abolished, to the great honour and interest of the state; and every one be left to stand or fall according to his merit").

61. See Hanover Presbytery Petition of 1778, in Baird, *Religion in the United States of America*, 237 ("In the fixed belief of this principle, that the kingdom of Christ and the concerns of religion are beyond the limits of civil control, we should act a dishonest, inconsistent part, were we to receive any emoluments from human establishments for the support of the gospel").

62. See Hanover Presbytery Petition of 1778, in Baird, *Religion in the United States of America*, 237 ("[I]f the legislature has any rightful authority over the ministers of the gospel in the exercise of their sacred office, and if it is their duty to levy a maintenance for them as such, then it will follow that they may revive an old establishment in its former extent, or ordain a new one for any sect that they may think proper; they are invested with a power not only to determine, but it is incumbent on them to declare who shall preach, what they shall preach, to whom, when, and in what places they shall preach; or to impose any regulations and restrictions upon religious societies that they may judge expedient").

63. See Madison, *Memorial*, paragraph 5. This is a remarkable statement, for Madison is close to calling the general assessment blasphemous.

64. See Madison, *Memorial*, paragraph 12. Just under the surface of many of these theological arguments is a negative opinion of the role played by the Roman Catholic Church.

65. See Madison, *Memorial*, paragraph 3. See also James, *Documentary History*, 223 (Hanover Presbytery Petition of October 24, 1776).

66. See James, *Documentary History*, 223–24 (Hanover Presbytery Petition of October 24, 1776).

67. See Madison, *Memorial*, paragraph 4.

68. See Madison, *Memorial*, paragraphs 6, 7, 13; James, *Documentary History*, 223 (Hanover Presbytery Petition of October 24, 1776).

69. See Madison, *Memorial*, paragraphs 13–14.

70. See Madison, *Memorial*, paragraphs 9–10. See also James, *Documentary History*, 223–24 (Hanover Presbytery Petition of October 24, 1776).

71. See James, *Documentary History*, 223 (Hanover Presbytery Petition of October 24, 1776).

72. Eckenrode, *Separation of Church and State*, 110–14. Jefferson's first draft of the bill dates back to 1777. Miller, *First Liberty*, 49. Jefferson's June 1779 version, as then introduced into the Virginia General Assembly and numbered 82, is reproduced in Miller, *First Liberty*, 256–57.

73. Miller, *First Liberty*, 40–41; see also 255–56 (reproducing Bill No. 82 with italics to indicate cuts and additions to Jefferson's original draft). See also 48–65 (parsing Bill No. 82, before it was amended, in terms celebratory of Jefferson).

74. Miller, *First Liberty*, 62, 358.

75. Dreisbach, "George Mason's Pursuit," 39.

76. See Eckenrode, *Separation of Church and State*, 118–28; Buckley, *Jefferson's Statute*, 82–85.

77. Eckenrode, *Separation of Church and State*, 118–28.

78. Eckenrode, *Separation of Church and State*.

79. Eckenrode, *Separation of Church and State*.

80. Letter from James Madison to Thomas Jefferson (February 15, 1787), in *Letters and Other Writings of James Madison, Fourth President of the United States* (Philadelphia: J. B. Lippincott, 1865), 1:272, 273–76.

81. Jonathan Elliot, ed., *The Debates in the Several State Conventions on the Adoption of the Federal Constitution*, 2nd ed. (1836; reprint, Buffalo: William S. Hein, 1996), 1:494–96.

82. Richard Beeman, *Plain, Honest Men: The Making of the American Constitution* (New York: Random House, 2009), 370–73, 396–400.

83. Elliot, *Debates*, 3:204, 330, 593, 645–59. Randolph spoke prudently here when he said that no power was "expressly" given over religion. He wisely left open the likelihood that general legislation on nonreligious subjects within Congress's enumerated powers might well have an effect on religious conscience. For example, a familiar quandary at the time was the matter of the military draft, clearly within congressional war powers, and whether and how the draft should accommodate religious pacifists.

84. Elliot, *Debates*, 3:330. The absoluteness of Madison's remark contrasts with Randolph's more prudent claim that the Constitution delegated no *express* power to touch on religion or religious freedom. Elliot, *Debates*, 3:204.

85. Vincent Phillip Muñoz, "The Original Meaning of the Establishment Clause and the Impossibility of Its Incorporation," *University of Pennsylvania Journal of Constitutional Law* 8 (2006): 585, 622.

86. Madison famously received Baptist backing for the ratification of the Constitution by promising the Reverend John Leland a Bill of Rights that protected religious freedom. Steven Waldman, *Founding Faith: Providence, Politics, and the Birth of Religious Freedom in America* (New York: Random House, 2008), 136–37.

87. Neil H. Cogan, ed., *The Complete Bill of Rights: The Drafts, Debates, Sources, and Origins* (New York: Oxford University Press, 1997), 13.

88. Irving Brant, *James Madison: Father of the Constitution, 1787–1800* (Indianapolis: Bobbs-Merrill, 1950), 269.

89. See Leonard W. Levy, *The Establishment Clause: Religion and the First Amendment*, 2nd ed. (Chapel Hill: University of North Carolina Press, 1994), 93, 107–11, 1176–77, 1184–91, 1201–02.

90. See Carl H. Esbeck, "Uses and Abuses of Textualism and Originalism in Establishment Clause Interpretation," *Utah Law Review* (2011): 489, 511, 527–67.

91. Bernard Schwartz, *The Roots of the Bill of Rights* (New York: Chelsea House, 1980), 5:1185, 1191–93.

92. *Senate Journal*, 14th sess., at 62–63 (Va. 1789).

93. Eckenrode, *Separation of Church and State*, 130–51; Buckley, *Jefferson's Statute*, 93–110.

94. Later still, Episcopalians who would not let go of the matter of the glebes brought suit in federal court. Being populated with Federalist judges, it was thought this venue would be friendlier to the cause. Federal court jurisdiction was obtained by the suit being instituted in the name of an Episcopal church in Alexandria, Virginia, then part of the District of Columbia. The claim was that the 1802 legislation was in violation of the Virginia Constitution. In time the case reached the U.S. Supreme Court, and in an opinion by Justice Joseph Story the ruling went in favor of the church. See *Terrett v. Taylor*, 13 U.S. (9 Cranch) 43 (1815). The litigation history is told in Michael W. McConnell, "The Supreme Court's Earliest Church-State Cases: Windows on Religious-Cultural-Political Conflict in the Early Republic," *Tulsa Law Review* 37 (2001): 7, 8–18. However, given that the case turned on a matter of state law, officials in Virginia ignored the ruling's prospective application, which the state was within its authority to do. Questions of state law are ultimately decided by the appellate courts of each state, not federal judges.

95. Eckenrode, *Separation of Church and State*, 152–55; Buckley, *Jefferson's Statute*, 114, 151–55; Rhys Isaac, "'The Rage of Malice of the Old Serpent Devil': The Dissenters and the Making and Remaking of the Virginia Statute for Religious Freedom," in *The Virginia Statute for Religious Freedom: Its Evolution and Consequences in American History*, ed. Merrill D. Peterson and Robert C. Vaughan (New York: Cambridge University Press, 1988), 139, 156–61.

96. Buckley, *Jefferson's Statute*, 128–41, 169–71, 255–56. See also *Trustees of the General Assembly of the Presbyterian Church in the United States v. Guthrie*, 86 Va. 125, 10 S.E. 318, 322 (1889), where Virginia's highest court attributes the state's strict separationism to the general assembly's act of January 24, 1799.

97. Only Virginia denied to churches the ability to form corporations. Virginia did so because of the belief that incorporation breached the wall of separation between

church and state. This is a mistake. It is common for legislation to give permission to those in the private sector to take some action. When a private entity acts pursuant to such a law, the entity's actions are not attributable to the state. *Flagg Brothers v. Brooks*, 436 U.S. 149 (1978). Without state action, there can be no establishment.

98. See, for example, *Trustees of Philadelphia Baptist Ass'n v. Hart's Executors*, 17 U.S. (4 Wheat.) 1 (1819), where a bequest to an association of Baptist clergy and laymen was held ineffective because under Virginia law, an unincorporated society was incapable of taking under a will. See also *Guthrie*, 10 S.E. at 322 (explaining legal background to and motive behind this Virginia rule).

99. See *Falwell v. Miller*, 203 F. Supp.2d 624 (W.D. Va. 2002), where in a lawsuit brought by the Reverend Jerry Falwell Sr., he successfully challenged, on federal constitutional grounds, Article 4, Section 14(20), of the Virginia Constitution, forbidding incorporation of a church or denomination. Section 14(20) was traced by the court to Jefferson's *A Bill for Establishing Religious Freedom*. 203 F. Supp.2d at 630.

100. Buckley, *Jefferson's Statute*, 255–56; *Guthrie*, 10 S.E. at 320, 322. In 2002 the Office of State Attorney General announced that it would no longer enforce the asset-limitation law because it was unconstitutional.

101. Philip Hamburger, *Separation of Church and State* (Cambridge, MA: Harvard University Press, 2002), 189, 191–92.

102. Buckley, *Jefferson's Statute*, 255–56.

103. William M. Hogue, "The Civil Disability of Ministers of Religion in State Constitutions," *Journal of Church and State* 36, no. 2 (1994): 329.

104. Not content with Virginia's revolutionary Constitution, in 1783 Thomas Jefferson drafted proposed revisions that he intended to promote. His draft retained the existing clergy disqualification. Jefferson sent the draft to James Madison for comment. Madison objected to the disqualification as not only not required by the principle of disestablishment but as denying a basic civil right merely because of one's vocation. In time, Jefferson agreed. Frederic S. Le Clercq, "Disqualification of Clergy for Civil Office," *Memphis State University Law Review* 7, no. 4 (1977): 555, 577–79; Buckley, *Jefferson's Statute*, 171–75.

105. In one respect, however, all of the other original states were discriminatory where Virginia was not, namely, Virginia's Constitution never had a religious test for citizenship or public office.

106. Hamburger, *Separation of Church and State*, 189, 191–92. As Americans "idealized their individual independence, many of them came to worry that their liberty was threatened not only by governmental power but also by assertions of religious authority. They came to fear even the claims made by their own, disestablished, Protestant churches, but particularly those asserted by the Catholic Church" (192).

107. See Buckley, *Jefferson's Statute*, 159–63, 176–86.

108. Mark Noll, "America's Two Foundings," *First Things* (December 2007): 29, 33.

109. Letter from James Madison to Edward Livingston, July 10, 1822, in *Letters and Other Writings of James Madison*, 3:273, 275–76.

CHAPTER NINE

SOUTH CAROLINA

Miles Smith IV

In the humid and hot August of 1769, William Henry Drayton wrote to a friend and political colleague, complaining about the increasingly sensational tone political radicals in the colony took toward the royal government in London. Opposition to the Townshend Acts especially annoyed Drayton. Two years earlier, Parliament had passed legislation sponsored by Chancellor of the Exchequer Charles Townshend. The measures raised duties on glass, lead, paint, paper, and most famously tea, enraging colonists along the thousand-mile stretch of North America's Atlantic Coast. The measures perturbed Drayton, but like most of the wealthy planters of South Carolina's Lowcountry, he remained firm in his loyalty to the British sovereign and to parliamentary government. Planters in South Carolina's coastal region, or Lowcountry, held prosperous indigo and rice plantations. Fueled by a constant infusion of bound human labor, Drayton and his peers enjoyed affluence unparalleled in British North America. The radicals in South Carolina hailed from the colony's backcountry, most recently immigrated from southeastern Pennsylvania and Virginia. They practiced the Presbyterianism of their Scots-Irish brethren in the British Isles and appeared thoroughly dangerous to landed Anglican magnates like Drayton. The conflict over British duties caused Drayton to evoke religious imagery to describe the conflict. He accused the parliamentary opposition of claiming to be a patriot and "friend to liberty" who "scruples not, like Cromwell, who was the patriot of his day, to break through and overthrow her fundamental laws, while he declared he would support and defend them all." Cromwell, Drayton warned, claimed to be a champion against royal tyranny but eventually enslaved his fellow subjects.[1]

Drayton's invocation of Cromwell proved prescient. Within a decade, revolutionaries overthrew first king and then church in South Carolina. The inauguration of republican government seemed probable when South

Carolinians wrote a constitution for the newly independent state. The Anglican establishment, however, proved more enduring. The state's Constitution of late March 1776, retained the Anglican church's privileged place. The 1778 Constitution widened the privilege to include recognized Protestant groups. By 1790 additional provisions began to eliminate privileges of churches altogether. Yet while Jeffersonian Republicans often lauded disestablishment, the attempts to remove and reduce the civil and social status of the Anglican church in South Carolina never enjoyed anything approaching unanimous support among the political class, nor did disestablishment fully remove Anglicanism from power. Property requirements, social status, and the sociointellectual constructions needed to affirm slavery all combined to diminish the political and social consequences of disestablishment. Although Anglicanism lost de jure privileges, Anglicans retained de facto preeminence in the state.

The process of South Carolina's disestablishment lacked the domestic fervor of the dissenter groups in Virginia. The state government declared that "free exercise and enjoyment of religious profession and worship, without discrimination or preference, shall forever hereafter be allowed within this State to all mankind." The only caveat the South Carolina General Assembly noted was "that the liberty of conscience thereby declared shall not be so construed as to excuse acts of licentiousness, or justify practices inconsistent with the peace or safety of this State." Religion remained an officially noted and important part of civil society. "The rights, privileges, immunities, and estates of both civil and religious societies and of corporate bodies," the general assembly declared in the Constitution of 1790, "shall remain as if the constitution of this State had not been altered or amended." In a final measure, they banned ordained ministers from serving as governor or in the South Carolina Senate or House of Representatives. Even so, the Anglican church remained powerful well into the nineteenth century.[2]

The greatest institutional reason for Anglicanism's continued influence in South Carolina was the Anglican church's ownership of glebes and other property obtained at the beginning of the eighteenth century. The *Church Act of 1706* specified that local communities—parishes, in the language of the era—might choose commissioners to select and oversee the glebes of churches built and those under construction. The commissioners had the power

> to take up by grant from the lords proprietors, or purchase the same from them, or any other person, and have, take and receive so much land, as they

shall think necessary for the several sites of the said several Churches, and the
Cemeteries or Church-Yards, for the burial of Christian people there, in the
several places above mentioned, and shall also direct and appoint the building
of the said several Churches not already built, according to such dimensions,
and of such materials, as they shall think fitting, and also the pulpit, desk and
pews in the said several Churches, and also the enclosing the several Cemeteries or Church-yards.

The commissioners were not members of the colonial government. The glebes were not held as state property. Rather, the churches were administered
and their lands received by vestries of private citizens. Disestablishment did
not change the glebes being administered and incorporated by vestries elected by local parishes. The parish of St. John's Berkley is representative of how
glebes were constituted in the colonial period. In 1706 the colony passed an
act incorporating the parish. A minister arrived in 1707. In 1710 the colony
granted money for the construction of the parish building, and in 1712 the
parish purchased land from one of the colony's proprietors, Sir John Colleton, for the parish's glebe.[3]

Glebes remained a constant source of power and stability for the Anglican
church of South Carolina. At no time during the colonial era, the revolution,
or the early national era did the Anglican church or its Episcopal successor
face a challenge to the ability to incorporate or hold property in its own
right. The property accrued to the glebes turned out to be lucrative. Anglican
ministers, called rectors, had and enjoyed, "to them and their successors, all
such negroes and their increase as have been already purchased, given and
allotted, or that shall be hereafter purchased, given and allotted to any of
the several parishes" founded by the colony's royal charter. The rectors also
gained "all such cattle and their increase, as hath been already purchased,
given and allotted, or shall be hereafter purchased, given and allotted to any
of the several parishes." Agricultural property and slaves guaranteed generational wealth for South Carolina's Anglican churches.[4]

The *Church Act of 1706* also established Anglican ministers and their
parishes as functionaries and sites of significant government activity and
function. Article XV allowed for state-chartered and -sanctioned charitable
associations to be housed on church property. The church in Charleston,
for instance, housed the provincial library. Article XIV placed the burden
of tax collection on the commissioners of various parishes and transformed
church vestries into civil officers who sometimes seized and sold property
from delinquent taxpayers. Article XXXIII mandated that the registration

"of all births, christenings, marriages and burials in each respective parish" be recorded at the church. Article XXVI mandated that all marriages be solemnized by a minister in the Church of England, and recorded in a Table of Marriages, held at each parish. South Carolina outlawed civil marriage. "No justice or magistrate, being a layman, shall presume to join any persons in marriage, under the penalty of one hundred pounds currant money of this Province, to be recovered and disposed of as hereafter in this Act is directed." Churches recorded births, marriages, deaths, taxes, and property deeds. Until 1712 the ability of dissenters in South Carolina to own property was ambiguous, but an amendment to the *Church Act* clarified that the "charity and the Christian Religion which we profess, obliges us to wish well to the souls of all men, and that religion may not be made a pretense, to alter any man's property and right." Although dissenters might hold property, the civil and religious limitations placed on dissenters meant that Anglicans enjoyed social privileges that allowed them to form the colony's elite and allowed their church to secure a firm place in South Carolina society.[5]

During the revolutionary and early national periods, South Carolinians reexamined and amended their religion's association with the state but did not make changes that radically affected religion's place in South Carolina's civil and social orders. Most of the church's political detractors chose to fight the church's privilege, not its power. Because disestablishment focused on the privileges of the Anglican church, its local governmental functions were never seriously debated. Nor did disestablishment target the massive and lucrative glebes retained by the church. It remained safely incorporated throughout the eighteenth century and was not altered by independence of the United States or three successive state constitutions. Thus, South Carolina's Anglican church retained a remarkable amount of economic and social influence well into the nineteenth century.

From the outset of intransigence toward the colonial government, South Carolina Whigs saw the Church of England's institutional presence in the colony as a dangerous auxiliary of royal oppression. The rabble-rousing Sons of Liberty, headed by merchant and planter Christopher Gadsden, especially disliked the Anglican establishment, largely because of the bureaucratic sway it gave the royal governors. When the admittedly radical Gadsden won election to the colonial assembly from St. Paul's Parish, Governor Thomas Boone used a procedural technicality involving church wardens to keep the patriot leader from taking his seat. The church wardens who certified the election had not yet been sworn in when Gadsden won election. The South Carolina assembly pressured the governor to no avail. Boone refused to seat Gadsden and prorogued the assembly, citing Gadsden's collective and "late contumacy."[6]

South Carolina elites' loyalty to the Crown stemmed from the king's maintenance of the social foundations on which rested time-honored ideals of English liberty. Protestantism and parliamentary government were the twin pillars of the Glorious Revolution. The Quebec Act of 1774, which allowed Roman Catholicism to continue its privileged status in Canada, appeared to abrogate both. "These acts, sunk deep into the minds of the people," lamented South Carolina memoirist and future governor John Drayton. The people of South Carolina "saw the Crown now made despotic, and the Romish Church established in a part of North America. Men openly said, George III, had broken his coronation oath; as well as the solemn contract, under which, he received his title to the Crown." Carolinians, noted Drayton, believed that "the Revolution of 1688, was effected, upon a principle of rescuing the English Dominions from the errors, and tyranny, of the Romish Church." A British king, sworn to protect Carolinians from a Catholicism perceived as tyranny, appeared to welcome it in one of his American dominions.[7]

Anglicanism represented a bulwark against Roman Catholicism, but dissenter groups saw the Church of England as a threat. The legacy of South Carolina's colonial governors convinced dissenting groups such as Baptists, Presbyterians, Quakers, and later Methodists that religious laws were oppressive and untrustworthy. Governor Francis Nicholson, a High Church Anglican soldier appointed as governor in 1721, reinstituted religious order in the colony. He believed dissenting groups were dangerous and seditious. He told a friend that he thought it a "no very difficult thing to prove that all dissenters here, in New England, and other His Majesty's colonies and provinces are of commonwealth principles both in church and in state and would be independent to the crown of Britain" if independence lay within their power. Nicholson enjoyed a good relationship with South Carolina's merchant- and planter-dominated colonial assembly, except for his reforms designed to remove dissenter influences. Nicholson insisted that members of the assembly take their oaths on the Bible. Several dissenters refused, and the governor refused to seat them. The assembly urged him to reconsider, and he agreed to seat them if they simply affirmed their allegiance to the Crown and agreed to do their duties. He also attempted to keep dissenters from performing marriages, but the assembly again overrode him. Nicholson's administration might not have clamped down on dissenter practices, but he strengthened the Anglican establishment in South Carolina by appointing rectors to isolated parishes and increasing their salaries.[8]

Baptists, numerically the most significant group of dissenters, remained apart from Anglicans socially and politically during the revolutionary and early national periods of South Carolina's history. The patriot fervor propelling Baptists to arms often included a powerful hatred of the Anglican church, which many Baptists believed stifled freedom of conscience and authentic religion. Presbyterians in the backcountry shared the Baptists' disdain for Anglicans. George Whitefield's crusade through the southern colonies in 1740 prompted Anglican clergymen to pursue their own evangelistic missions in the colonial interior. British-born Charles Woodmason, a cultured and educated Anglican rector from Charleston, traveled into the backcountry in the fall of 1766, seeking to convert Scots-Irish settlers to the Church of England. He failed, less because of his inability to articulate theological truths and more because religion operated as a powerful part of backcountry culture. Woodmason's journal recorded his harsh reception among Presbyterians in no uncertain terms.[9]

In 1770, only a few years after Woodmason's failed journey and at the height of the ferment over the Boston Massacre, the South Carolina General Assembly still went about its business. The combination of an increasingly diverse religious population in the Lowcountry and anti-British sentiment, the Townshend Acts, and the Stamp Act triggered a backlash against Britain. Loyal families like the Bulls, Gadsdens, Rutledges, and Wraggs—all Anglicans—for the first time questioned allegiance to the Crown. Yet during the tumult, the colony's leadership continued to support the Anglican church almost automatically. One example was the chartering of a new parish. The assembly gave the vestry and rector of St. Philip's the "power and authority . . . to lay out a piece or parcel of the said Glebe Land, not exceeding four acres in quantity, bounding to the south on Wentworth-street, and to the eastward on St. Philip's-street." The property was expensive and among the best land still available that close to the city. The assembly spared no expense and funded not only a new sanctuary but also "a new Parsonage-House and proper out-houses." They included money for "the laying out of a garden, orchard, and Pasturage for the habitation, use and occupation of the said Rector or Minister of the said Parish of St. Philip for the time being." Whether the assemblymen gave the money for spiritual, political, or social necessity, or mere duty, mattered little. The appropriations passed easily. South

Carolina's churches, like the newly created parish springing from St. Philip's, enjoyed durable support from the assembly and much of the population. The Anglican establishment was not powerless, and it retained power well into the revolution.[10]

A multiplying population of dissenter groups remained the most substantive threat to the Anglican establishment. South Carolina's planter-dominated assembly, however, feared a British plot to establish Roman Catholicism more than they feared the influx of Baptists (and later Methodists) into the colony. In August 1774, William Henry Drayton wrote to the First Continental Congress, complaining of a plan to "establish the Romish religion, in a very considerable part of the British Empire." Interestingly, Drayton tied his fear of Catholic influence to complaints about quartering British soldiers in homes. Drayton and most colonial subjects retained a provincial and overwhelmingly British Protestant conception of civil society. Irish soldiery or other functionaries from the diverse empire might bring unwelcome Roman Catholic or even non-Christian influences into the colonies. British soldiers, even in the best circumstances, seemed irreligious barbarians to Drayton. "The service of Almighty God in the colonies" was "greatly hindered" because Carolinians worried that if they went to church, soldiers would "rifle their houses in their absence."[11]

The decision to include dissenters in political affairs stemmed from wartime expediency. Presbyterians, especially in the South, volunteered for the patriot cause in droves. Eager to keep their support, Lowcountry planters began to include Presbyterians in revolutionary councils. In 1775 the colony's rebellious assembly dispatched William Henry Drayton and Rev. William Tennent, a Presbyterian minister, into the backcountry as propaganda ministers. Charged with explaining the assembly's disagreements with the Crown, they understood that they had to convince the Presbyterians that the assembly was in the right against Britain and that the Anglican-dominated assembly was friend and not foe. Tennent's inclusion proved a masterstroke. Whereas Woodmason brought his Anglican prejudices to dealings with Presbyterians, Drayton brought coreligionists to effectively "go into the interior parts of this Colony, at the public expense." He and Tennent explained "to the people at large, the nature of the unhappy public disputes between Great Britain and the American Colonies" and endeavored "to settle all political disputes between the people; to quiet their minds; and to force the necessity of a general union, in order to preserve themselves and their children from slavery."[12]

Drayton and Tennent's journey proved moderately successful. Tennent especially invoked religion to inspire his hearers to not just religious piety but also patriotic fervor and action. On the morning of August 13, 1775, Tennent preached a sermon to a mixed religious group at the Rocky Creek Presbyterian Meeting House. He breached long-maintained Calvinist restrictions on nonreligious pursuits on Sundays and proceeded to preach another sermon, this one on the need to resist the British menace. Drayton noted in his diary that after the sermon, he made "an apology for the necessity of treating on the subject of my mission on the Lord's day" and proceeded to give his speech declaring the righteousness of the patriot cause. "The heat almost melted me; but [I] had the pleasure to see all the people eagerly sign the Association fully convinced of the necessity of it."[13]

The success Tennent encountered may have been due to the presence of a local notable, Colonel Richard Richardson, at the Rocky Creek Meeting House. Local planters and militia officers supported Drayton and Tennent, adding a degree of respectability before suspicious local farmers. Richardson later became one of the state's more successful commanders in the Revolutionary War. In other locales, the lack of a unifying local figure like Richardson to legitimize the patriots' message often left Upcountry communities divided and deeply suspicious of Lowcountry patriots. Drayton, a Baptist layman, and the Presbyterian Tennent both hailed from the Lowcountry, and no matter their religion, many upstate South Carolinians hated anything that came out of the Lowcountry. Tennent understood that even his Presbyterianism might smack of Lowcountry aristocracy, so he requested that a Charleston Baptist, Oliver Hart, visit the region. Even Hart managed only middling success with the backcountry farmers.[14]

Dissenters fought bravely throughout the Revolutionary War. Even in its opening days, Presbyterians, Baptists, and the few Congregationalists actively aided the patriot cause. Debates over the nature of an independent South Carolina included the status of religion. William Tennent's revolutionary credentials and his position in the general assembly gave him status to not just celebrate the detachment of the state from Britain's religious hierarchy but champion a throwing off of the Anglican establishment. Anglicanism lost its political power when the colonies declared their independence in the summer of 1776, and the dissenting churches immediately lost the stigma laid on them by the British government. Presbyterian and Reformed churches quickly organized themselves. The visible manifestation of rising

Presbyterianism remained a secondary consideration of competing dissenters, such as Baptists and Congregationalists, whose primary object was to
loosen Anglicanism's hold in the new state.[15]

II.

South Carolina's Constitution of March 26, 1776, addressed the new political
milieu but made no mention of the former colony's religious laws. The preamble, however, indicted Britain for using Catholics in Quebec as a potential
weapon against the other North American colonies. In Quebec, declared the
South Carolinians, "the Roman Catholic religion (although before tolerated and freely exercised there) and an absolute government are established."
Since that province's boundaries "extended through a vast tract of country so
as to border on the free Protestant English settlements," Carolina Protestants
warned that the British prepared to use "a whole people differing in religious
principles from the neighboring colonies, and subject to arbitrary power, as
fit instruments to overawe and subdue the colonies." For South Carolinians,
American independence never meant the creation of a religiously plural or
even necessarily a disestablished order, although the latter eventually proved
more amenable than the former. Independence preserved Protestantism,
and among South Carolina's officialdom that meant the Anglican religion
along with a few officially tolerated Presbyterian churches.[16]

The 1776 Constitution operated as the declaration of a separated polity,
but its writers meant for it to be temporary. During the summer of 1776,
South Carolina's gathered assemblymen debated the state's religious situation as they observed the fast-developing conflict with London. The most
intense critics of disestablishment were the most devout Anglicans, who
viewed the maintenance of Anglican orthodoxy as a function of the state.
But they no longer constituted a majority of South Carolina's population,
and many dissenters balked at pursuing separation from Great Britain while
they still lacked representation or toleration in their own colony. Practical-
minded Anglican aristocrats committed to separation from Great Britain
recognized that in order to keep the revolution conservative and subdue dissenter intransigence, some concessions to Baptists, and Presbyterians especially, had to be made.

Charles Cotesworth Pinckney, scion of an important Lowcountry family, enthusiastically supported disestablishment. He argued that it was right
in principle, and it served the exigencies of the War of Independence by

incentivizing the patriot cause among dissenters who might otherwise refrain from fighting. Pinckney's sponsorship of disestablishment made that
same step more respectable among Charleston and Lowcountry Anglicans.
By the time South Carolina wrote a second Constitution in 1778, all Protestant bodies enjoyed equal standing before the law.[17]

Observers during the debates and subsequent historians credit Reverend
William Tennent with swaying the general assembly to disestablish the Anglican Church and implement a general Protestant establishment. Tennent
used the reception of a petition for disestablishment to address the assembly
in Charleston on January 11, 1777, in a speech marked for its scope and
influence on disestablishment. Tennent told his Anglican colleagues he bore
them no ill will and respected their faith. He dissented from the Church of
England, "it is true; but, I trust, it is upon the most liberal grounds: when I
oppose the establishment, I do not mean to oppose the church itself." Tennent's disestablishmentarian principles stemmed from his love of "free and
equal rights of mankind," and thus no preference of one denomination of
Christians over another. His argument for opposing "the religious establishment of any one denomination of Christians" in South Carolina originated
in his belief that establishments were "an infringement of religious liberty"
that inappropriately interfered with the right of private judgment. Establishments amounted to "nothing less than the legislature's taking the consciences of men into their own hands, and taxing them at discretion."[18]

The Constitution of March 19, 1778, loosened the Anglican hold on the
colony. It declared that "all persons and religious societies who acknowledge
that there is one God, and a future state of rewards and punishments, and
that God is publicly to be worshiped, shall be freely tolerated." The document
announced that the "Christian Protestant religion shall be deemed, and is
hereby constituted and declared to be, the established religion of this State."
Every denomination of "Christian Protestants" who conducted themselves
"peaceably and faithfully" were to enjoy "equal religious and civil privileges."
In order to receive incorporation from the now state of South Carolina, religious bodies needed to agree to and subscribe to the "following five articles,
without which no agreement or union of men upon presence of religion
shall entitle them to be incorporated and esteemed as a church of the established religion." The Constitution also left religiosity and state function
conjoined. The state provided in its fundamental law that "God is publicly
to be worshiped" and that "the Christian religion is the true religion." It also
established Protestantism explicitly by declaring that the "holy scriptures of

the Old and New Testaments are of divine inspiration, and are the rule of faith and practice."[19]

Religion's place in society remained expansive. The 1778 Constitution stipulated that elections to the general assembly "shall be conducted as near as may be agreeable to the directions of the present or any future election act or acts," which meant retaining Anglican parishes as the primary electoral district. Anglican structure for electoral administration continued in South Carolina after independence. South Carolina also continued a religious test to hold office, attached to steep property qualifications, virtually guaranteeing continued Anglican and Lowcountry aristocrat preeminence in affairs of state. Law enforcement officers, typically a local sheriff, enforced property qualifications and rent agreements and arbitrated land disputes. Similar property qualifications along with religious tests together ensured that most sheriffs were Anglicans. The statute read:

> The qualification of electors shall be that every free white man, and no other person, who acknowledges the being of a God, and believes in a future state of rewards and punishments, and who has attained to the age of one and twenty years, and hath been a resident and an inhabitant in this State for the space of one whole year before the day appointed for the election he offers to give his vote at, and hath a freehold at least of fifty acres of land, or a town lot, and hath been legally seized and possessed of the same at least six months previous to such election, or hath paid a tax the preceding year, or was taxable the present year, at least six months previous to the said election, in a sum equal to the tax on fifty acres of land, to the support of this government, shall be deemed a person qualified to vote for, and shall be capable of electing, a representative or representatives to serve as a member or members in the senate and house of representatives, for the parish or district where he actually is a resident, or in any other parish or district in this State where he hath the like freehold. Electors shall take an oath or affirmation of qualification, if required by the returning officer.[20]

Despite allowing considerable latitude in matters of religion, the general assembly inserted a provision prohibiting clergy from holding public office. The Constitution asserted that ministers of the Gospel were "by their profession dedicated to the service of God and the cure of souls, and ought not to be diverted from the great duties of their function." Article XX in the 1778 Constitution stated that "no minister of the gospel *or* public preacher of any religious persuasion"—a specification meant to include the sometimes-irregular nature of Baptist ordination—"while he continues in the exercise of his pastoral function, and for two years after, shall be eligible either as Governor, Lieutenant Governor, a member of the Senate, House of Representatives, or Privy Council in this state." One observer believed that the clergy-disqualification clause "got a place in the constitution chiefly to exclude one parson," William Tennent, "who opposed with great eloquence & finally with success the attempts that were made to establish hierarchy & fix the episcopalians as the only Legal & Supreme Church in this country." No other reason for the qualification was noted, and it seems likely this was a passing slight by devotees of the Anglican church not powerful enough to force their will on dissenting populations but not so powerless as to be taken lightly in society.[21]

The 1778 Constitution removed Anglicanism from its high perch, but by no means did it entirely disestablish Anglicanism. Anglican prevalence in public functionaries continued. However, all Protestant churches enjoyed the same legal privileges held by their Anglican brethren. The Constitution created what historian Jonathan Den Hartog called a multiple establishment. While allowing Baptists, Presbyterians, and later Methodists to join the ranks of respectable Protestantism, Roman Catholics were barred from holding office. "No person shall be eligible to sit in the house of representatives unless he be of the Protestant religion, and hath been a resident in this State for three years previous to his election." Further, it retained strict conditions for those desiring to hold public office: "The qualification of the elected, if residents in the parish or district for which they shall be returned, shall be the same as mentioned in the election act, and construed to mean clear of debt. But no non-resident shall be eligible to a seat in the house of representatives unless he is owner of a settled estate and freehold in his own right of the value of three thousand and five hundred pounds currency at least, clear of debt, in the parish or district for which he is elected." The provisions created a situation where the wealthiest planters enjoyed more geographic leeway on where they might run for office. The Constitution also practically guaranteed that Anglicans and a few Presbyterians would govern South Carolina. Even a generation later, two-thirds of the planter class in the state affiliated with the Church of England's successor, the Protestant Episcopal Church. Fifteen percent attended Presbyterian services. Elite slaveholders, and therefore elite political figures, continued to identify with Anglicanism.[22]

The Constitution said that "no person shall, by law, be obliged to pay towards the maintenance and support of a religious worship that he does not

freely join in, or has not voluntarily engaged to support." Seemingly conflicting, it also declared that the "churches, chapels, parsonages, glebes, and all
other property now belonging to any societies of the Church of England, or
any other religious societies, shall remain and be secured to them forever."
No matter how much social change the creation of a Protestant multiestablishment might mean for South Carolina, the Anglican churches retained a
wealth advantage through the retention of glebe lands.

Most important for the physical estate of the Anglican church was the
Constitution of 1778's guarantee of the colonial framework of incorporation
and glebes. Article XXXVIII stipulated:

> That all denominations of Christian Protestants in this State, demeaning them-
> selves peaceably and faithfully, shall enjoy equal religious and civil privileges.
> To accomplish this desirable purpose without injury to the religious property
> of those societies of Christians which are by law already incorporated for the
> purpose of religious worship, and to put it fully into the power of every oth-
> er society of Christian Protestants, either already formed or hereafter to be
> formed, to obtain the like incorporation, it is hereby constituted, appointed,
> and declared that the respective societies of the Church of England that are
> already formed in this State for the purpose of religious worship shall still con-
> tinue incorporate and hold the religious property now in their possession.

When "fifteen or more male persons, not under twenty-one years of age, professing the Christian Protestant religion, and agreeing to unite themselves in
a society for the purposes of religious worship," they constituted a church
and were "esteemed and regarded in law as of the established religion of the
State, and on a petition to the legislature shall be entitled to be incorporated
and to enjoy equal privileges." This provision moderated disestablishment
and meant that Anglicans retained the glebes, the right of incorporation, and
property vested during the colonial era.

The example of something as simple as church bells illustrated the tenacity
with which Anglicans guarded church property. During the American Revolution, a Royal Artillery major took down the bells of St. Michael's Church
"under pretense of being a military perquisite belonging to the Command-
ing Officer of Artillery." The infuriated vestry applied to the British commander, General Leslie, "to have them restored, as they had been bought
by subscription, and private property was secured by the capitulation."
The church eventually recovered the bells after a tortuous odyssey involving the bells traveling to Britain and back. But South Carolina's Anglicans

kept their bells, and disestablishmentarians in the general assembly did not have the support or will to try to remove Anglicanism's privileged position regarding property.[23]

The removal of the Church of England's political and social—but not property—privileges allowed a significant amount of religious freedom where previously little existed. The Revolutionary War, however, more than juridical disestablishment, modified South Carolina's religious reality. The war created large-scale disruptions of religious life. The conflict in South Carolina became a civil war, and military, political, and social considerations subordinated religion and suppressed public religiosity. People stopped attending divine services, and religious observance waned. Religious schools closed temporarily, or permanently, depending on the scale of local devastation. Most worrisome, as historian Erskine Clark notes, an "aggressive cult of reason grew in popularity and prestige—encouraged both by the spreading influence of enlightenment ideas and by the disorders of the times."[24]

Enlightenment ideas like Deism certainly emerged as a matter of public discussion during the American Revolution, but at no time did Deism represent anything but a small minority of Christians in South Carolina. The great purveyors of Deism, pamphleteer Thomas Paine and Virginia's Thomas Jefferson, never influenced the masses in South Carolina. Their politics, however, allowed for religious groups previously seen as outside the pale of respectability to gain a social, political, and religious foothold. Anglicans like Christopher Gadsden bragged of buying the first copy of Paine's *Common Sense* in South Carolina, and they used these polemical tracts to exhort "the absolute independence of America!"[25]

The Revolutionary War allowed various denominations to gain a foothold among South Carolina's military families. Baptists entered broader South Carolina society by serving the war effort as soldiers. The most notable Baptist in the fifty years after independence, the young minister Richard Furman, exemplified the integration of Protestant groups and proved among the more prominent beneficiaries of disestablishment. Furman came of age in South Carolina's backcountry in the 1760s and '70s in a society still officially Anglican. His New York–born parents held no generational affection for South Carolina's coastal grandees or their church. Furman called himself a Whig, as did many patriots, and believed that religious freedom came from God. Patriots, and especially Baptists, saw the English church as an enemy to liberty, or at least a stooge of Parliament and king. In 1787 Richard Furman accepted the call to the pastorate of Charleston's Baptist Church

and propelled South Carolina's Baptists into more political and social prominence than they held before the revolution.[26]

Even Furman, however, increased Baptists' status only to a modest degree.[27] South Carolina's culture and politics reflected the continued domination of Anglicans. Oliver Hart of Charleston's Baptist congregation and
Elhanan Winchester of Welsh Neck wrote to Henry Laurens—the devout
vice president of South Carolina—in the spring of 1776 regarding a vision
of the future. They hoped "to see hunted liberty on the throne, and flourish more than ever under the administration of such worthy patriots." Their
vision was that "the time is come, in which our rulers may be men fearing
God, and hating covetousness, a terror to evil-doers, and a praise to them
that do well." Baptists' numbers increased, as did their presence in the councils of state. But the state's high culture and politics remained in Anglican
control. Oliver Hart railed against the "merry gentry" of "wicked and sinful
Charleston," with their "frolicking . . . dancing, filthiness, foolish talking,
jesting and suchlike." Still, Charleston remained South Carolina's intellectual, political, and religious center until the Civil War. Anglicans continued to
dominate high office. Thirty-nine men served as South Carolina's executive
between the revolution and the beginning of the Civil War. More than half
held membership in the Protestant Episcopal Church. Nine worshipped as
Presbyterians, the only other Protestant church legally tolerated during the
colonial era. Only two governors were Baptists.[28]

III.

The debates over the place of religion in the Articles of Confederation solicited passing but not particularly dynamic interest from South Carolinians in
the Confederation Congress in the years between the revolution and ratification of the U.S. Constitution. The Anglican establishment relied on the power of Lowcountry gentry to fight for its preservation. The latitudinarianism
of the Anglican church in the eighteenth century created a class of regular
churchgoers who balked at the perceived secularization of the Virginians
and who tried to find a middle way between total disestablishment and the
colonial establishment. Success eluded them, as Antifederalist and dissenters
forced the hand of the South Carolina General Assembly, resulting in the
promulgation of the Constitution of 1790.

Even as the United States Constitution was debated during the Philadelphia Convention of 1787, Charles Pinckney attempted to find a middle way
on religion that pleased Anti-federalists while simultaneously preserving

religion's place in the nationalized political sphere. In May 1787, Pinckney proposed that the United States Congress be prohibited from passing any law on the subject of religion whatsoever. Pinckney understood the importance to the new United States of preventing "religious tests as qualifications to offices of trust or emolument." Such a prohibition proved "essential in free governments." The world, he argued, expected religious freedom from a beacon of liberty like the United States in "an age so liberal and enlightened as the present." Pinckney's argument lay less on a desire to secularize the new American regime and more in a desire to expand religious liberty to previously proscribed groups. The clearest example of this South Carolina middle way on religion in the new American regime centered on Article VI of the U.S. Constitution. The article asserted that state and federal officeholders would take an oath to the Constitution. Pinckney proposed that the phrase adding the stipulation that "no religious test shall ever be required as a qualification to any office or public trust under the authority of the United States." Quakers believed that swearing an oath was biblically prohibited. Pinckney undoubtedly knew of the concern. The Constitutional Convention adopted his suggestion. This was seen by a few as secularizing the federal regime, but Pinckney desired to prepare a way for previously unfranchised groups to participate in federal office.[29]

Some Presbyterians, surprisingly—who earlier led the charge toward disestablishment in South Carolina—found the federal Constitution's quietude on matters of religion concerning. Patrick Calhoun, a Scots-Irish Presbyterian and planter from upstate, warned that the new fundamental law for the Union allowed far too much latitude in matters of religion. Other South Carolinians were not so sure. Arthur Simkins, a well-regarded judge and early devotee of the patriot cause, asked the general assembly to request more information regarding potential federal prerogatives to interfere in matters of religion. Simkins requested a response from Charles C. Pinckney. Congress, Pinckney explained, had no power over religion in the states. The answer mollified Simkins for the moment, and he announced himself satisfied with Pinkney's response. Still, Simkins questioned the prudence of ratification—one of only three members of the assembly to do so. One of the others who likewise voted against ratification questioned the Constitution's lack of provision for religion.[30]

Influenced by the debate over the federal Constitution, South Carolina ratified a new Constitution on June 3, 1790. The Constitution lasted seven decades and governed the state until the Civil War began in 1861. The convention that promulgated the new fundamental law reflected the new religious order. Richard Furman, the noted Baptist minister, opened the state convention with a prayer and sermon. The convention officially recorded its thanks and commended Furman for his "able" and "well-chosen" address. But true to earlier form, an Anglican also spoke to the assembled delegates. Debate at the convention was minimal. As Jonathan Den Hartog notes, disestablishment in Federalist-era South Carolina occurred without acrimony or opposition. The document itself solidified the character of the disestablishment in South Carolina. It managed to say even less about religion than the 1778 Constitution. But its quietude spoke volumes. All religious qualifications for holding state office or serving in the general assembly that were in the 1778 Constitution were removed. The only mention of religion was the guarantee of religious freedom and a provision protecting religious incorporation and property holding. Article VIII, Section 1, declared that "free exercise and enjoyment of religious profession and worship, without discrimination or preference, shall forever hereafter be allowed within this State to all mankind." The only caveat was "that the liberty of conscience thereby declared shall not be so construed as to excuse acts of licentiousness, or justify practices inconsistent with the peace or safety of this State." The state's legal and legislative apparatus would decide what was licentious and inconsistent with the peace and safety of the state. Judges and legislators often remained Anglican, largely because Section 2 of Article VIII stated that "the rights, privileges, immunities, and estates of both civil and religious societies, and of corporate bodies, shall remain as if the constitution of this State had not been altered or amended." South Carolina protected the right of incorporation for all churches, but Anglican ownership of glebes and other property, as well as political control, meant their church retained economic and social power to a greater degree than other religious groups.[31]

Anglicans in South Carolina recognized that disestablishment preserved the social and economic place of their church, and in some ways even enhanced their status. In 1790 South Carolina clergymen quoted with approval a British bishop who argued that "to the Prince or to the Law we acknowledge ourselves indebted for all our secular possessions—for the rank and dignity annexed to the Superior Order of the Clergy—for our secular authority— for the jurisdiction of our Courts," and for all other civil effects that follow "the exercise of our spiritual authority." But the same bishop also argued that secular rights and honors, with which the church is adorned by the "Civil Magistrate, are quite distinct from the spiritual commission which we bear

for the administration of our Lord's proper kingdom. They have no necessary connection with it: They stand merely on the ground of human law."[32]

During the federal and state debates over religion in the new American
political order, South Carolina Federalists, many Lowcountry Anglican
grandees, held up the federal Constitution and South Carolina's 1790 Constitution as the best way to deal with potential disagreements over religion.
Such support did not necessarily mean that Anglican Federalists sought total
disestablishment. More likely, it was an attempt to take potentially controversial institutions like the church out of the hands of Anti-federalist parti-
sans. Charles Pinckney, no partisan of the federal Constitution, nonetheless
celebrated the document. His cousin, Charles Cotesworth Pinckney, understood the powerful social link between religion and politics, and most Lowcountry aristocrats feared Antifederalist attempts to use the lower classes
to hold Charleston's patricians politically hostage to increased democratization. Anglican churches remained the province, however, of elite property holders, and the South Carolina Constitution's property requirements
for office holding guaranteed a continual hold on power for elites. Church,
property, and power remained wedded in practice, although not in law.[33]

Convinced establishmentarians and religious dissenters existed in South
Carolina's politics, but they both accepted that the 1790 Constitution left
the state to deal with religion at the local level. Jonathan Den Hartog, in his
study of Federalism and religion, notes that the major religious groups in
South Carolina accepted the arrangement created by the new order and that
subsequently "the formal power of a state church was never debated during
the party struggles of the 1790s through 1810s." Den Hartog rightly argues
that most South Carolina politicians accepted religion's explicit place in civil
society, as well as its residual place in the state's political order. Most South
Carolinians to some degree remained establishmentarian, but in the new
context of that term. In South Carolina, that context "meant not supporting
an official denominational establishment but rather nurturing" a benevolent
regime that undergirded society's established moral order.

With good cause, historians typically look to slavery to provide the answer
to how South Carolina achieved substantive agreement on the boundaries of
church-state relations. The state's delegation to the Philadelphia Constitutional Convention all represented elite slaveholding interests. Pierce Butler,
Charles Pinckney, Charles Cotesworth Pinckney, and their powerful leader, John Rutledge, were related to one another, and all held membership in
Anglican churches. It was in the best interest of the Anglican elites to bring

dissenting groups into the fold as quickly as possible. Disestablishment might weaken the Anglican church institutionally, but it strengthened Anglican sociocultural dispositions in the long term.[34]

IV.

Over a period of fifteen years, South Carolinians wrote disestablishment into their laws, but not into their cultural, political, or social practice. Despite a substantive change in the state's constitutional regime, many of the functions of the state church remained unaltered. By retaining property and social position first accrued during the era of colonial establishment, the Church of England and its Episcopal successor continued these civil-law functions throughout the early republic. All births, marriages, and deaths continued to be registered at local parishes until the late 1850s, when the state began to reform the parish system and create counties. The Episcopal Church's role in local government would not officially end until Reconstruction gave South Carolina yet another Constitution in 1868.[35]

NOTES

1. Aaron Palmer, *A Rule of Law: Elite Political Authority and the Coming of the Revolution in the South Carolina Lowcountry, 1763–1776* (Leiden and Boston: Brill, 2014), 241; Arthur M. Schlesinger, *The Colonial Merchants and the American Revolution, 1763–1776* (New York: Columbia University Press, 1918), 203.

2. The Constitution of South Carolina, 1790, Article VIII, Section 2, in *The Federal and State Constitutions: Colonial Charters, and Other Organic Laws of the United States*, ed. Benjamin Perley Poore (Washington, DC: Government Printing Office, 1878), 2:1633.

3. Frederick Dalcho, *An Historical Account of the Protestant Episcopal Church in South Carolina* (Charleston: Archibald E Miller, 1820), 3.

4. Church Act of 1706, in *The Statutes at Large of South Carolina*, ed. Thomas Cooper (Columbia, SC: A. S. Johnston, 1837), 2:282–94; Dalcho, *Protestant Episcopal Church in South Carolina*, 440.

5. Church Act of 1706, in *Statutes at Large of South Carolina*, ed. Cooper, 2:282–94; Dalcho, *Protestant Episcopal Church in South Carolina*, 94.

6. Henry Flanders, *The Lives and Times of the Chief Justices of the Supreme Court of the United States* (Philadelphia: J. B. Lippincott, 1858), 1:453.

7. John Drayton, *Memoirs of the American Revolution: From Its Commencement to the Year 1776* (Charleston: A. E. Miller, 1821), 1:136.

8. M. Eugene Sirmans, *Colonial South Carolina: A Political History, 1663–1763* (Chapel Hill: University of North Carolina Press, 1966), 163–64.

9. Richard J. Hooker, ed., *The Carolina Backcountry on the Eve of the Revolution: The Journal and Other Writings of Charles Woodmason, Anglican Itinerant* (Chapel Hill: University of North Carolina Press, 1953), 46.

10. Edward McCrady, *The History of South Carolina under the Royal Government, 1719–1776* (New York: Macmillan, 1899), 557; Dalcho, *Protestant Episcopal Church in South Carolina*, 461.

11. William Henry Drayton, "A Letter from Freeman of South-Carolina, to the Deputies of North America," in *Documentary History of the American Revolution, 1764–1776*, ed. R. W. Gibbes (New York: D. Appleton, 1855), 11.

12. *Collections of the South Carolina Historical Society* (Charleston: South Carolina Historical Society, 1858), 2:58.

13. Gibbes, *Documentary History*, 228.

14. Jon Butler, *Awash in a Sea of Faith: Christianizing the American People* (Cambridge, MA: Harvard University Press, 1990), 205–7; Gibbes, *Documentary History*, 228.

15. James Underwood and William Burke, *The Dawn of Religious Freedom in South Carolina* (Columbia: University of South Carolina Press, 2006).

16. Preamble, South Carolina Constitution of 1776, in *The Statutes at Large of South Carolina: Acts, records, and documents of a Constitutional Character*, ed. Thomas Cooper (Columbia, SC: S. C. Johnston, 1836), 128–37.

17. Marvin R. Zahniser, *Charles Cotesworth Pinckney: Founding Father* (Chapel Hill: University of North Carolina Press, 1967), 51.

18. "Mr. Tennent's Speech on the Dissenting Petition," in *The History of the Independent or Congregational Church in Charleston, South Carolina*, by David Ramsay (Philadelphia: J. Maxwell, 1815), 54–71.

19. Constitution of 1778, Article XXXVIII, in *The Statutes at Large of South Carolina: Acts, records, and documents of a Constitutional Character*, ed. Cooper, 144.

20. Benjamin James, *A Digest of the laws of South-Carolina: containing the public statute law of the State, Down to the Year 1822* (Columbia: Telescope Press, 1822), 343.

21. Constitution of 1778, Article XX; "Diary of Timothy Ford," *South Carolina History and Genealogy Magazine* 13 (1912): 197.

22. Constitution of 1778, Article XIII, in *Federal and State Constitutions*, ed. Poore, 2:1623; Jonathan J. Den Hartog, *Patriotism and Piety: Federalist Politics and Religious Struggle in the New American Nation* (Charlottesville: University of Virginia Press, 2015), 142; William K. Scarborough, *Masters of the Big House: Elite Slaveholders of the Mid-Nineteenth-Century South* (Baton Rouge: Louisiana State University Press, 2003), 53–54.

23. Dalcho, *Protestant Episcopal Church in South Carolina*, 188; Constitution of 1778, Article XXXVIII, in *The Statutes at Large of South Carolina: Acts, records, and documents of a Constitutional Character*, ed. Cooper, 1:137–46.

24. Erskine Clarke, *Our Southern Zion: A History of Calvinism in the South Carolina Low Country, 1690–1990* (Tuscaloosa: University of Alabama Press, 1996), 106.

25. Moncure Daniel Conway, *The Life of Thomas Paine: With a History of His Literary, Political, and Religious Career in America, France, and England* I (New York and London: G. P. Putnam and Sons, 1908), 78; Thomas Paine, *Common Sense* (1776; reprint, New York: Peter Eckler, 1922), 46.

26. H. A. Tupper, ed., *Two Centuries of the First Baptist Church of South Carolina, 1683–1883* (Baltimore: R. H. Woodward, 1889), 145.

27. Charles G. Sommers, ed., *The Memoir of Rev. John Stanford* (New York: Stanford and Sword, 1844), 405–6.

28. Durward T. Stokes, "The Baptist and Methodist Clergy in South Carolina and the American Revolution," *South Carolina Historical Magazine* 73, no. 2 (1972): 87–96; Alexander Gregg, *History of the Old Cheraws* (Columbia, SC: State, 1905), 260–63; "Diary of Rev. Oliver Hart from A.D. 1740 to A.D. 1780," quoted in *Yearbook: 1896, City of Charleston, South Carolina* (Charleston: Walker, Evans, Cogswell, 1896), 393–99; Walter B. Edgar, *The South Carolina Encyclopedia Guide to the Governors of South Carolina* (Columbia: University of South Carolina Press, 2012).

29. Frank Moore, ed., *American Eloquence: A Collection of Speeches and Addresses by the Most Eminent Orators of America* (New York: D. Appleton, 1872), 1:369; Thomas H. Calvert, *The Federal Statutes Annotated* (Northport, NY: Edward Thompson, 1905), 8:242–46.

30. *The Debates in the Several State Conventions on the Adoption of the Federal Constitution* (Philadelphia: J. B. Lippincott, 1888), 4:312; *Debates Which Arose in the House of Representatives of South Carolina* (Charleston, SC: A. E. Miller, 1831), 42; Pauline Maier, *Ratification: The People Debate the Constitution, 1787–1788* (London and New York: Simon and Schuster, 2010), 249.

31. Francis M. Hutson, ed., *Journal of the Constitutional Convention of South Carolina, May 10, 1790–June 3, 1790* (Columbia, SC: State Commercial Printing, 1946), 16; Den Hartog, *Patriotism and Piety*, 142.

32. Dalcho, *Protestant Episcopal Church in South Carolina*, 418.

33. Zahniser, *Charles Cotesworth Pinckney*, 75; Marty D. Matthews, *Forgotten Founder: The Life and Times of Charles Pinckney* (Columbia: University of South Carolina Press, 2004), 68.

34. Den Hartog, *Patriotism and Piety*, 142; Richard Beeman, *Plain, Honest Men: The Making of the American Constitution* (New York: Random House, 2009), 59; David Waldstreicher, *Slavery's Constitution: From Revolution to Ratification* (New York: Hill and Wang, 2009), 53.

35. Ruth S. Green, Charles H. Lesser, and Charles R. Lesser, "South Carolina Marriage Records," *South Carolina Historical Magazine* 79 (1978): 155–62.

CHAPTER TEN

DISESTABLISHMENT IN KENTUCKY

Keith Harper

On june 1, 1792, the Commonwealth of Kentucky entered the Union as its fifteenth state. Article XII, Section 3, of the state's Constitution stipulated: "That all men have a natural and indefeasible right to worship Almighty God according to the dictates of their own consciences; that no man can of right be compelled to attend, erect, or support any place of worship, or to maintain any ministry against his consent; that no human authority can, in any case whatever, control or interfere with the rights of conscience; and that no preference shall ever be given by law to any religious societies or modes of worship." Section 4 stipulated, "That the civil rights, privileges, or capacities of any citizen shall in no wise be diminished or enlarged on account of his religion."[1] With the foregoing sections, Kentuckians articulated their understanding of religious liberty and church-state relations.

At first glance, religious freedom in Kentucky might appear to have been a straightforward proposition. Most of Kentucky's earliest and most powerful settlers came from Virginia, where religious dissenters had successfully allied themselves with powerful advocates such as James Madison Jr.[2] As far as politics was concerned, dissenters claimed only a minimal role or no role in the political process prior to the American Revolution. Yet many of them had supported independence, and they continued to believe in its ideals. Their postwar struggles focused on creating their own distinct place in the political world, and powerful forces were not especially inclined to accept them simply because they wanted in the game. Moreover, for many dissenters, the stiffest opposition to real political equality came from within their own ranks.

I.

Given that the Commonwealth of Kentucky was formed from western land once claimed by Virginia, one might assume that Kentuckians would follow

Virginia's Constitution of 1776. Ultimately, however, they chose Pennsylvania's Constitution of 1790 as their model. According to legal historian Robert M. Ireland, "A full 75 of the 107 sections of the constitution were taken, verbatim or substantially, from the Pennsylvania charter, including 27 of 28 sections of the Bill of Rights." Ireland further observes, "Indeed, Kentucky's commitment to . . . [church-state] separation exceeded that of older states such as Pennsylvania, whose early constitutions required legislators to pledge by oath their belief in the existence of a divine being and a future state of rewards and punishments. Kentucky not only did not require such an oath, it forbade clergy from serving in the legislature or as governor."[3] By using the Pennsylvania Constitution as their model, Kentuckians produced one of the most democratic constitutions in the early republic. But by far, slavery proved to be the most contentious issue in framing the Constitution. Many of Kentucky's earliest ministers furnished spirited opposition to human bondage.[4]

In December 1776, the region of Virginia beyond the Appalachian Mountains was designated by the Virginia General Assembly as Kentucky County. In June 1780, Kentucky County was divided into Fayette, Jefferson, and Lincoln Counties. As Kentucky inched closer to forming its own state, entering the Union and drafting a constitution became leading topics of conversation. In August 1791, the Elkhorn Association, the first Baptist association west of the Appalachian Mountains, appointed three of its affiliated ministers, James Garrard, Augustin Eastin, and Ambrose Dudley, to draft a memorial "to take up the subject of religious liberty and perpetual slavery in the formation of the constitution in this district." The memorial was adopted. The association met four months later, in December 1791, this time noting without further explanation, "Resolved that this association disapprove of the memorial which the last Association agreed to send to the convention on the subject of Religious liberty and the abolition of slavery."[5] The August memorial has not been preserved, but one can infer what happened over the ensuing four months: the Baptists divided over the question of emancipation.[6]

The Elkhorn Association was not conflicted over the issue of religious freedom. Baptist ministers saw themselves as ardent Democratic-Republicans, and they gloried in their liberty.[7] The question was precisely how they would exercise that freedom. For many, Kentucky offered the opportunity to achieve wealth and power. Ministers from all denominations understood this well, but it is significant that the Elkhorn Association coupled religious freedom and slavery. Slavery emerged as the more dominant issue, for it in turn shaped religious liberty in Kentucky's earliest days.

Between 1784 and 1792, Kentuckians convened ten conventions to determine their future status. Virginia clamed title to the land, but protecting and supplying settlers was difficult. As settlers moved westward, it became increasingly important to determine the region's status. Some pushed for independence. Most, however, wanted to either remain a part of Virginia or separate with the intention of entering the Union. Separation and entering the Union emerged as the most popular choice, especially when one considers that Virginia's Constitution of 1776 allowed for Kentucky's separation. Thus, the "Ten Conventions" met to discuss all viable options and ultimately to hammer out the details of Kentucky's separation from Virginia. The "Tenth Convention" met in April 1792 and ratified the commonwealth's first constitution, thereby allowing Kentucky to enter the Union as the fifteenth state on June 1, 1792.

When the Constitutional Convention met in April 1792, seven of the convention's forty-two delegates were clergy.[8] Unlike the original colonies, where religious establishment had been the norm, Kentucky had the opportunity to create a new order, one that reflected God-ordained rights without religious establishment. David Rice was one of the delegates. He saw emancipation as the government's first priority, and he spoke forcefully for emancipation of slaves. As Kentucky's leading Presbyterian minister, "Father Rice," as he was affectionately known, penned a document titled *Slavery Inconsistent with Justice and Good Policy*. Rice argued that slavery was an evil that should be eradicated. Rather than merely proof-texting from the Bible, Rice based his arguments on natural law and reason, as well as Scripture. He defined slavery as a legal status whereby "a human creature [is] made by law the property of another creature, and reduced by mere power to an absolute unconditional subjection to his will." Notwithstanding this definition in the law of property, Rice maintained, "As creatures of God we are, with respect to liberty, all equal."[9]

Before coming to Kentucky, Rice served churches in Virginia, where he observed many injustices perpetrated against African Americans. He hoped that Kentucky would not create a similar situation. His observations led him to declare that slavery was based on unjust law, which, inevitably, led to unjust policy. Slaves produced wealth and ease for others while receiving nothing for their labor. Rice argued that there was no divine right to this exploitation, and he admonished fellow delegates that in drafting Kentucky's constitution, they were responsible to God for creating a just state:

> Human legislatures should remember, that they act in subordination to the great Ruler of the universe, have no right to take the government out of his hand, nor to enact laws contrary to his; that if they should presume to attempt it, they cannot make that right, which he has made wrong; they cannot dissolve the allegiance of his subjects, and transfer it to themselves, and thereby free the people from their obligations to obey the laws of nature. The people should know, that legislatures have not this power; and that a thousand laws can never make that innocent, which the divine law has made criminal; or give them a right to that, which the divine law forbids them to claim.[10]

Rice worried that "national vices" would meet with "national calamities," and he encouraged his fellow Kentuckians to "endeavor so to act, as to secure the approbation and smiles of heaven."[11]

Notwithstanding the specter of a "national calamity," other Kentuckians were not interested in Rice's arguments. They found their spokesperson in George Nicholas, one of two lawyer-delegates at the 1792 convention. According to historian Lowell Harrison, inexperience among delegates could have been "disastrous" had it not been for Nicholas. As a seasoned, respected lawyer, Nicholas understood the law at both the state and the federal levels. Harrison says:

> "Old Nick" was familiar with the Pennsylvania constitution of 1776 which, written by the likes of Kentucky's partisans, had been the most radical of democratic constitution of the Revolutionary era. In 1790 another convention had rewritten the 1776 document along more conservative lines, and Nicholas was determined to keep Kentucky from undergoing the Quaker state's experience. . . . Nicholas went to the Tenth Convention armed with that determination, his skill as a debater, his reputation as being the best lawyer in Kentucky and well formulated ideas on what form the constitution should take.[12]

Nicholas pointed out to the assembly of delegates that slavery was already entrenched in Kentucky. Emancipationists were either altruistic or simply jealous of wealthy people. Either way, it really did not matter. He claimed that Kentucky needed slavery if it hoped to attract wealth.[13] North Carolina had ceded to the federal government its claim to the Tennessee Territory on December 22, 1789, and two things were certain: a new state, Tennessee, would soon petition for statehood, and it would enter the Union as a slave state. Should Kentucky opt for emancipation, it would discourage slaveholders from moving to the state. It might also pressure slaveholders who were present in Kentucky into leaving. Tennessee was nearby and would look attractive. It was a forceful argument, as many settlers were relocating to the area for economic reasons.[14] Nicholas made no effort to counter Rice's natural-law and scriptural arguments; he simply ignored them. Kentucky boasted great economic potential, and Nicholas needed no scriptural underpinnings to legitimize prosperity's claim on human nature.

As the delegates were putting the finishing touches on the proposed constitution, slavery was the only measure brought to a vote. Rice resigned as a delegate in protest of emancipation's anticipated defeat. It lost by a tally of sixteen to twenty-six.[15] The proslavery forces had won a victory, but emancipationists and their cadre of outspoken ministers counted for a sizable minority. Nicholas later briefed James Madison on the proceedings, wherein he described the emancipationists as "clamorous on that subject, as well in the convention as out if it."[16]

II.

Kentucky's Constitution of 1792 stated that certain provisions might need to be revisited. Following Nicholas's lead, everyone agreed to allow for at least seven years before any reconsideration.[17] By 1799 Kentuckians did in fact revisit the document. Kentucky's emancipationists continued to oppose slavery, but they were fighting a losing battle. By 1800 the state's population had expanded to 220,955, with 40,343 slaves.[18] As we have seen, Kentucky's 1792 Constitution recognized no established church, and citizens were free to worship God according to the dictates of their consciences. Nevertheless, everything about the 1792 Constitution would be open for discussion in 1799, including religious freedom.

David Barrow, a respected Baptist minister, had fought in the revolution and suffered religious persecution in Virginia. He moved to Kentucky in 1798 and settled near Winchester, just ahead of the second Constitutional Convention. Barrow explained his reasons for leaving Virginia in a letter to friends. The letter outlined his religious convictions in fifteen points and his political convictions in twenty-six points. Six of the latter are relevant here:

3. I believe that Government is an evil, as it cannot be supported without making considerable sacrifices of natural liberty; but,

in our present state of depravity, it is to be preferred to a state
of nature.

4. That Government, is a civil compact, of a people emerging from a
state of nature, contrived by themselves for their own severity, and
is subject to the controul, and liable to alteration, when thought
proper by a majority of such community. . . .

13. That all religious tests, and ecclesiastical establishments, are oppressive, and infringe on the rights of conscience.

14. That civil rulers have nothing more to do with religion, in their
public capacities, than private men; save only, that they should
protect its professors in the uninterrupted enjoyment of it, with
life, property, and character, in common with other good citizens.

15. That no man, or set of men, in a community, are entitled to exclusive privileges.

. . .

25. That no community can long enjoy tranquility, but by strict adherence to virtue, and frequent recourse to fundamental principles.[19]

Barrow's observations that governments are evil and that laws were subject to revision likely struck a chord with those who had been persecuted
in Virginia for their faith. But as the convention's delegates looked to revise
their first Constitution, other issues demanded attention.

While ministers had offered stiff opposition to slavery in 1792, they would
not have that opportunity in 1799. Only two ministers served as delegates to
the 1799 convention, and by the end of the proceedings the delegates would
adopt a measure prohibiting clergy from serving as governor.[20] There is no
direct evidence that clergy were systematically excluded from the proceedings. Rather, other delegates were simply chosen in their place. Emancipationists fought valiantly for their cause, but too many settlers saw Kentucky's
future primarily in economic terms. Many had moved to Kentucky with
slaves or expected to purchase them once they arrived.[21]

The Constitution of 1799 reaffirmed Kentucky's commitment to slavery
and private property. Delegates made minor modifications to the foundations of religious freedom. Whereas Article XII, Section 3, of the Constitution of 1792 said that "no man *can of right* be compelled to attend, erect, or
support any place of worship," the Constitution of 1799 said "no man *shall be*
compelled to attend, erect, or support any place of worship." Further, Article
XII, Section 3, of the Constitution of 1792 said "that no human authority

can, in any case whatever, control or interfere with the rights of conscience; that no preference shall ever be given by law to any religious societies or modes of worship," whereas the Constitution of 1799 said "that no human authority *ought*, in any case whatever, to control or interfere with the rights of conscience."[22] These alterations were of style rather than substance.

The Constitution of 1799, however, adopted more targeted measures in separating church and state, especially with respect to elected representation. The Constitution of 1792 said, "no minister of religious societies, member of Congress, except attorneys at law, justices of the peace, militia officers, and coroners, shall be a member of either House during his continuance to act as a minister, in congress, or in office." Whereas, the Constitution of 1799 said, "No person, while he continues to exercise the functions of a clergyman, priest, or teacher of any religious persuasion, society or sect, or whilst he holds or exercises any office of profit under this Commonwealth, shall be eligible to the General Assembly, except Attorneys at law, justices of the peace, and militia officers."[23] Article III, Section 6, of the 1799 Constitution reflected the most dramatic change in thinking between the two Constitutions: "No member of Congress, or person holding any office under the United States, *nor minister of any religious society*, shall be eligible to the office of Governor."[24]

For Kentuckians, the separation of church and state was of interest but not the defining question. The main issue was how a religiously free people might exercise their freedom in the public sphere, especially when it came to slavery and finding a public voice on the matter. The Constitution guaranteed free speech, but taking a stand on moral issues invited opposition, even censure, not from the state but from those of like-minded faith.[25] Many clergy who had fought for American independence hoping to gain religious freedom now found themselves disabled from holding public office.

III.

Kentuckians worried that church people, especially ministers, would interfere with the politics of the state. Whereas some saw slavery as an evil that had to be eliminated, many more did not agree, and for them the subject was not open to discussion. In 1805 the Elkhorn Association determined that it was "improper for ministers[,] Churches or Associations to meddle with emancipation from Slavery or any other political Subject and as such we advise ministers & Churches to have nothing to do therewith in their religious Capacities."[26] The association's minutes do not say as much, but it appears most believed that the issue had been settled in the debates at the Constitutional Convention, and the association intended its statement to silence further clamor over emancipation.

At least, that is the way the North District Association of Baptists took it. As an association of like-minded Baptists, the North District noted Elkhorn's pronouncement and embraced it for their own. David Barrow was an outspoken emancipationist and one of Kentucky's leading Baptist ministers. Barrow served a church in Mount Sterling that was affiliated with the North District Association. When he expressed his opposition to human bondage, the North District Association not only expelled his church from the association's fellowship but also tried to get Barrow removed as pastor of his church. Soon, emancipationists throughout the commonwealth faced ostracism in their local churches and in their church associations. With no other place to turn for church-related fellowship, Barrow and fellow minister Carter Tarrant organized the Baptized Licking Locust Association, Friends to Humanity, a new association repudiating slavery.[27] Barrow published a lengthy treatise titled *Involuntary, Unmerited, Perpetual, Absolute, Hereditary Slavery, Examined; on the Principles of Nature, Reason, Justice, Policy, and Scripture.* Barrow had heard all the proslavery arguments, but he believed that slavery was contrary to all that was holy. He noted the irony in a people who demanded their personal liberty but did not extend that liberty to African slaves.

As a Revolutionary War veteran, Barrow came to see freedom for all people regardless of race as a feature of genuine republicanism. He reminded his generation that they had fought against British tyranny. "Now, if *liberty* be such an inestimable blessing and the *birth right* of all *mankind,*" Barrow intoned, "can that be honest policy especially in America, which withholds the blessing from one million of our fellow creatures!"[28] He slammed "high toned republicans" for lofty, one-sided rhetoric that did not extend to all men equally. The Elkhorn Association had deemed it improper to "meddle with emancipation," words that bewildered Barrow. "The above advice," he observed, "seems to hold out the doctrine of passive obedience and nonresistance; and looks like the ecclesiastical, playing into the hand of civil power: —and is as much as to say, if the legislature passes a wicked law, we will tamely and silently submit to, and recommend it."[29] Preachers might be free to preach what they liked, but they ran the risk of alienating their fellow ministers. As Barrow saw it, such peer pressure to conform to a standard that violated one's conscience amounted to swapping one form of tyranny for another.

Kentucky's earliest religious leaders and laity closed ranks against emancipation and made an example of David Barrow and others like him.[30] White
men, both secular and clergy, forged a relationship between church and
state that allowed for maximum economic development. Churches could
"speak into" the public arena and share political power because power rested
squarely in the hands of elite white men. This environment allowed for the
emergence of an honor culture that permeated southern states throughout
the nineteenth century. Honor shaped the cultural sphere, while slavery supported the economic and political machinery.[31]

If some feared that reform-minded ministers might "meddle" in state political affairs like emancipation, others feared that ministers might become too
comfortable working alongside the state. Elijah Craig, numbered among the
early ministers to come to Kentucky, was also one of Kentucky's most radical
figures. As one of Virginia's persecuted ministers, Craig longed for religious
freedom. But in an odd twist on religious freedom, Craig worried that his fellow ministers were too comfortable under Kentucky's 1799 Constitution and
that they were becoming entangled in governmental matters: "The treatment
I met with under the old government, and men in some degree of a similar
disposition not in power, rivetted in me the firm disposition of a republican,
in things civil and religious, which has remained invariable, and has kept my
eyes open in some degree to both the liberties of the church and state; and
with pain of mind from time to time have beheld the church in the scriptures
called the spouse of Christ, oppressed by men professing their business was
to comfort and support her." Religious freedom created unexpected opportunities, but Craig saw them as potential dangers for the church. "I suppose,
[he intoned,] it to be this root of evil which induces ministers to debase their
sacred office, received from Jesus Christ, so far as to choose to be state officers,
to join the people together in matrimony, which ought to be performed by the
civil magistrate, both which (marriages and funerals) I suppose, the minister
has no scripture authority for meddling in, and is a real deprecation of his
ministerial character in the eyes of deserving me, and [it helps] to make deists."[32] In Craig's opinion, even ministers officiating at weddings and funerals
served as an opening to unhealthy relations between church and state. Ultimately, he believed it was a sign that the world would soon come to an end.[33]

IV.

Kentucky has a legacy of separating church and state that runs throughout its history. Yet slavery raised the more serious issue in Kentucky's early
history and overshadowed the former. That caused church-state relations

in the commonwealth to remain subdued in the early nineteenth century. Kentucky did, however, stand at the forefront of articulating—if not always upholding—religious freedom.

NOTES

1. Kentucky State Constitution, 1792, Article 12, Sections 3–4. Officially, Kentucky is a commonwealth along with Pennsylvania, Virginia, and Massachusetts.

2. Lance Banning, *The Sacred Fire of Liberty: James Madison and the Founding of the Federal Republic* (Ithaca, NY: Cornell University Press, 1995), 81–97, 270–97, 308–9.

3. Robert M. Ireland, *The Kentucky State Constitution*, Oxford Commentaries on the State Constitutions of the United States (Oxford: Oxford University Press, 2011), 5. See also John D. Barnhart, "Frontiersmen and Planters in the Formation of Kentucky," *Journal of Southern History* 7, no. 1 (1941): 19–36.

4. For a brief summary, see Lowell H. Harrison, *Kentucky's Road to Statehood* (Lexington: University Press of Kentucky, 1992). Harrison maintains that while the Pennsylvania Constitution of 1790 served as a model for how Kentuckians would frame their constitution, they actually used Pennsylvania's 1776 Constitution as a guide for things to avoid (116).

5. Minutes of the Elkhorn Association, August and December 1791.

6. For persecution of ministers, see Lewis Peyton Little, *Imprisoned and Religious Liberty in Virginia, a Narrative Drawn Largely from the Official Records of Virginia Counties, Unpublished Manuscripts and Other Original Sources* (Lynchburg, VA: J. Bell, 1938). The Elkhorn Association corresponded with other Baptists in Virginia. On August 8, 1789, John Leland proposed the following resolution: "Resolved: That slavery is a violent deprivation of the rights of nature and inconsistent with a republican government, and therefore recommend it to our brethren to make use of every of every legal measure to extirpate this horrid evil from the land; and pray Almighty God that our honorable Legislature may have it in their power to proclaim a great Jubilee, consistent with the principles of good policy." See Robert Baylor Semple, *History of the Baptists in Virginia* (Lafayette, TN: Church History Research and Archives, 1976; reprinted from revised edition, 1894), 105.

7. See Nathan O. Hatch, *The Democratization of American Christianity* (New Haven, CT: Yale University Press, 1989).

8. The ministers serving as delegates to the convention were John Bailey, George Smith, James Garrard (Baptist), James Crawford, Benedict Swope, David Rice (Presbyterian), and Charles Kavanaugh (Methodist).

9. Rev. David Rice, *Slavery Inconsistent with Justice and Good Policy* (Philadelphia: M. Gurney, 1792), 3, 4.

10. Rice, *Slavery Inconsistent with Justice and Good Policy*, 14.

11. Rice, *Slavery Inconsistent with Justice and Good Policy*, 24.

12. Harrison, *Kentucky's Road*, 104. As for Harrison's observation that Nicholas wanted to avoid the "Quaker state's experience," he means Pennsylvania had ratified a radically democratic Constitution in 1776 only to modify it significantly in 1790. He anticipated a certain amount of adjustment to Kentucky's first Constitution would be necessary, even desirable, but he wanted to avoid offering sweeping liberties only to curb them.

13. In 1790 Kentucky claimed a total population of 73,677, of whom 12,430 were slaves, or 17 percent.

14. See Elizabeth Fortson Arroyo, "Poor Whites, Slaves, and Free Blacks in Tennessee, 1796–1861," in *Tennessee History: The Land, the People, and the Culture*, ed. Carroll Van West (Knoxville: University of Tennessee Press, 1998), 101–12.

15. Harrison, *Kentucky's Road*, 104–14.

16. Nicholas to Madison, May 2, 1792, as quoted in Patricia Watlington, *The Partisan Spirit: Kentucky Politics, 1779–1792* (New York: Atheneum, 1972), 220. It is not exactly clear why Nicholas wrote to Madison regarding Kentucky's Constitution. According to Lowell Harrison, Madison enjoyed great popularity among Kentuckians, and while there were no official requests for his aid in framing Kentucky's constitution, several private citizens sought his unofficial aid. Nicholas emerged as a strong voice in the proceedings, and it is possible, perhaps likely, that he informed Madison of the convention's result out of personal friendship. See Harrison, *Kentucky's Road*, 94–114.

17. Joan Wells Coward, *Kentucky in the New Republic: The Process of Constitution Making* (Lexington: University Press of Kentucky, 1979), 45–46.

18. Charles B. Heinemann and Gaius Marcus Brumbaugh, *"First Census" of Kentucky, 1790* (Washington, DC: G. M. Brumbaugh, 1940). See also G. Glenn Clift, *"Second Census" of Kentucky, 1800* (Frankfort, KY: G. Glenn Clift, 1954; reprint, Baltimore: Genealogical Publishing, 1976).

19. David Barrow, "Circular Letter of 1798," printed in *William and Mary Quarterly* 20, no. 3 (1963): 444–49.

20. See Kentucky Constitution, 1799. The measure apparently passed without dissent.

21. Coward, *Kentucky in the New Republic*, 62. As Coward puts it, "demographic trends and agricultural patterns combined to make their efforts increasingly difficult" (62).

22. Compare Article 12, Section 3, of the Constitution of 1792 with Article 10, Section 3, of the Constitution of 1799. Emphasis added.

23. Compare Article 1, Section 26, of the Constitution of 1792 with Article 2, Section 26, of the Constitution of 1799.

24. See Article 3, Section 6, of the Constitution of 1799.

25. For free speech, see Kentucky State Constitution, 1972, Article XII, Section 7; and Kentucky State Constitution, 1799, Article X, Section 7.

26. Minutes of the Elkhorn Association, 1805. At the same meeting, the Glen's Creek Church queried, "Is it right for Baptists to join in & assemble at barbecues on the 4th of July." The association answered simply, "No."

27. David Barrow, *Involuntary, Unmerited, Perpetual, Absolute, Hereditary, Slavery, Examined; on the Principles of Nature, Reason, Justice, Policy, and Scripture* (Lexington, KY: printer illegible, 1808). See also J. H. Spencer, *A History of Kentucky Baptists from 1769 to 1885*, revised and corrected by Mrs. Burrilla B. Spencer (Cincinnati: J. R. Baumes), 192–97; and Frank M. Masters, *A History of Kentucky Baptists*, Publication no. 5 (Louisville: Kentucky Baptist Historical Society, 1953), 167–69. Much like Barrow, Carter Tarrant had moved to Kentucky from Virginia.

28. Barrow, *Involuntary, Unmerited*, 18.

29. Barrow, *Involuntary, Unmerited*, 24. Ultimately, Barrow concluded that only "a strange kind of Christian" would argue for divine right of slavery when the historical record demonstrated its cruelty (32–33). See also Monica Najar, "'Meddling with Emancipation': Baptists, Authority, and the Rift over Slavery in the Upper South," *Journal of the Early Republic* 25, no. 2 (2005): 157–86.

30. For the complex interplay between religion and politics in the late colonial/early national periods, see Charles F. Irons, *The Origins of Proslavery Christianity: White and Black Evangelicals in Colonial and Antebellum Virginia* (Chapel Hill: University of North Carolina Press, 2008).

31. On honor culture, see Bertram Wyatt-Brown, *Southern Honor: Ethics and Behavior in the Old South* (Oxford: Oxford University Press, 1982); and Robert Elder, *The Sacred Mirror: Evangelicalism, Honor, and Identity in the Deep South* (Chapel Hill: University of North Carolina Press, 2016).

32. Elijah Craig, *A Few Remarks on the Errors that are Maintained in the Christian Churches of the Present Day; and also, on the Movements of Divine Providence Respecting Them*, (Lexington, KY: printed by James H. Stewart, 1801), 2, 15. Legally speaking, Kentucky law allowed clergy to perform marriages and conduct funerals. Craig's views were in the minority among Kentucky ministers.

33. Craig, *A Few Remarks*. A close reading of *A Few Remarks* indicates that Craig's real complaint centered on ministers receiving financial compensation for their services.

CHAPTER ELEVEN

DISESTABLISHMENT IN TENNESSEE

Edward R. Crowther

Methodist bishop francis Asbury had spent the early winter months of 1797 traveling and preaching in the Carolinas, before he turned west through the "rocks, hills, and mountains" separating North Carolina from its former western territory, now the nascent state of Tennessee. After a rugged journey "under Providence," Asbury preached on March 26 at a quarterly meeting of Methodists near the first white settlements in eastern Tennessee. Exhorting from Isaiah 1:9, "Except the Lord of hosts had left unto us a very small remnant, we should have been as Sodom, and we should have been like unto Gomorrah." However, Asbury faced a residuum of the dissenter culture that characterized the colonial backcountry of Virginia and the Carolinas before its vanguard migrated into Tennessee. He speculated that most migrants had come west to find land but ventured that some of these settlers might "lose their souls."[1] Asbury's pastoral concern underestimated the efforts by Tennesseans in securing a central place for religion in their new state. More than he knew, Asbury's visit was to a displaced people who had left a land of privileged religion and eagerly embraced democracy and liberty of conscience in the aftermath of the American War of Independence.

The terrain Asbury trekked was both a geographic and a cultural wilderness where revolutionary-era beliefs about civil and ecclesiastical polity evolved. As settlers drove out Native peoples, they installed a constitutional order reflecting the concerns and experiences of the early national period in the new West. These settlers both reflected and shaped a consensus of the frontier, over against past struggles with an Anglican establishment. They were a republic of commoners consisting, according to John Wigger, of "churches unaided and not coerced by government intervention, operating outside the control of social elites." Hailing mostly from Virginia, North Carolina, and Pennsylvania, early Tennesseans drew on a dissenter tradition, one hostile to religious establishment, especially its connection to the Virginia "tidewater gentry," but sympathetic to a social-leveling, evangelical religion. These pioneers engaged in ongoing negotiations over religion's proper place in promoting good government and a virtuous society. Their efforts to define the relationship between private faith and public duty in democratic governance generated an "intense religious contest" among competing visions of church and state. The stillborn constitution of the State of Franklin (1784–88) and the Tennessee Constitution of 1796 provide a lens on disestablishment, as settlers, many of whom came of age under religious establishment, created new political structures in a new western state.[2]

I.

The Franklin and 1796 Constitutions followed yet earlier efforts to craft a series of short-lived local constitutional arrangements to bring a measure of governmental structure to these fledgling settlements. The Watauga Association (1772) and Washington Association (1776) attempted to establish self-government in eastern Tennessee. The Cumberland Association (1780) sought to impose similar order around the wilderness outpost at Nashville. These precedents reflected ambivalent and sometimes contentious relations with the territory's initial overseer, North Carolina. These three failed attempts at state building found clergy as prominent among the early settlers, including Baptist and Presbyterian preachers. Moreover, the texts of the Franklin and 1796 Constitutions demonstrate the importance of church-state relations, and the roles of religion and ministers in government, to early Tennesseans.[3]

The constitution of the State of Franklin was born of the desire of Tennesseans to frame a government independent of North Carolina. In April 1784, North Carolina offered to cede to Congress its claim to western territory that ran to the Mississippi River, as an offset to its war debts. The offer was good for only two years. Congress was reluctant to accept the responsibility of governing the area, which included protecting the westward frontiersmen. Dissatisfied with North Carolina's administration and meager protection, local leaders called for the formation of a separate and secure state. On August 23, 1784, delegates of several counties in eastern Tennessee met in Jonesborough. There they declared the lands to be independent of North Carolina and chose the name of Franklin. In December 1784, delegates were called to a constitutional convention with the eventual aim to petition Congress for admission as a state. Franklin's leaders first adopted for their own the Constitution of North Carolina to serve as a provisional constitution. A committee chaired by Samuel Houston, a minister, began work to compose a permanent constitution. In November 1785, the entire convention considered the work of the Houston Committee.

The draft constitution proposed by the Houston Committee mixed provisions from North Carolina's 1776 Constitution with features of the more radical Pennsylvania Constitution of 1776, including the latter's unicameral legislature, as well as some miscellaneous "collected pieces" from other state constitutions and legislative sources. It copied its religious liberty clause directly from North Carolina's Bill of Rights. Section 3 of the draft was prescriptive, specifying that legislators had to believe in the Trinity, divine inspiration of the Scriptures, and heaven and hell. It proscribed those who were immoral, lewd, or given to drunkenness from holding public office. Section 24 of the draft enshrined religious liberty, affirming the rights of individuals to practice religion freely and to prevent "the civil power usurping spiritual supremacy" through religious establishment. Believers could join whatever society or fellowship they chose, hire and support clergy through private collective means, and organize churches that could hold and convey property. It further enjoined the "civil authority" from making "any law, act, or resolve respecting religion" and confined legislating to "matters purely civil." The scant documentary record only hints at why the Houston draft did not garner convention support. Section 3 prescribing specific doctrinal beliefs for officeholders and a unicameral legislature provoked "controversy and angry debate." Tennesseans struggled with whether and to what degree they should dictate doctrinal beliefs for officeholders.[4]

Eventually, the delegates rejected the whole of the Houston Committee's proposal and simply adopted for its own the North Carolina Constitution of 1776. There were five provisions directly relating to church-state relations. Article 19 of the Declaration of Rights was the first of these, safeguarding individual religious liberty. It guaranteed men the right to worship "according to the dictates of their own conscience."[5]

Section 31 of the constitutional framework barred clergymen who were actively "in the services of the pastoral function" from serving in the legislature. The record is silent on the purpose of this disability. However, given the major role ministers played in governmental affairs, anticlericalism was not the likely motive.[6] Section 32 was a religious test for public office. It provided: "No person who shall deny the being of God, or the truth of the Protestant religion, or the divine authority of either the Old or New Testaments, or who shall hold religious principles incompatible with the freedom and safety of the State, shall be capable of holding any office, or place of trust or profit, in the civil department, within this State."[7]

Section 34 forbade the state from establishing a sect, favoring one sect over another, compelling attendance at worship services, providing governmental financial support for ministers, erecting houses of worship, or keeping people from doing so voluntarily. The section went on to protect the "free exercise" of religious worship. As to the latter, however, police power trumped liberty, as ministers faced punishment for proclaiming "treasonable or seditious doctrines."[8]

Section 41 created common schools to be operated by each county. This development had about it an element of disestablishment. For education to become a state-funded and -regulated enterprise, it thereby was no longer a matter of ecclesiastical jurisdiction.[9]

The leaders of the State of Franklin hoped to obtain statehood, but the vote in 1785 by Congress was in the negative. The two-year offer by North Carolina soon expired. It was not until 1790 that North Carolina ceded its western lands to the central government as an offset for assuming its war debt, and Tennessee became a federal territory.

II.

Governance was by *The Territory of the United States South of the Rivers of Ohio* ("Southwest Ordinance") enacted by Congress in 1790.[10] The ordinance extended the same terms of the Northwest Ordinance of 1787,[11] except for permitting slavery. A brief document, it created a government whose "inhabitants . . . shall enjoy all the privileges, benefits and advantages, set forth" in the Northwest Ordinance and subjected Tennessee to the same governance and requirements for statehood. The ordinance declared that "no person, demeaning himself in a peaceable and orderly manner, shall ever be molested on account of his mode of worship or religious sentiments, in the said territory." Records indicate no legal actions or controversies arising under this provision.[12]

The Southwest Ordinance required a minimum of sixty thousand settlers before submission of a petition for statehood. In the fall of 1793, Tennessee passed that threshold. Territorial governor William Blount called for a convention to draft a constitution and begin the statehood process.[13]

Voters selected representatives from each of the eleven territorial counties. The lone territorial newspaper, the widely read *Knoxville Gazette*, chronicled the topics that engaged Tennessee settlers. The *Gazette*'s editor and publisher, George Roulstone, was well connected, and his newspaper shaped and reflected many of the concerns in the region. Roulstone's readers could follow the French Revolution and imbibe Thomas Paine's *Rights of Man* from excerpts that appeared regularly. Subscribers could learn of the latest land sales; review the new Kentucky Constitution of 1792, including its religious liberty clauses; and revisit past struggles with North Carolina over its mismanagement of Tennessee.

The *Gazette* covered a bitter doctrinal fracas in the Abington Presbytery, involving a dispute between the Reverend Hezekiah Balch and his fellow Presbyterian ministers over the latter's attempts to prohibit Presbyterian laity from hearing sermons of preachers from other denominations. Balch termed such a restriction "an arbitrary exercise of tyrannical power." Eventually, Balch apologized to his fellow ministers, and the rift in the Presbytery appeared to heal. But this peace did not come about before prompting one letter writer to note that religious fanaticism was an ever-present threat in an erstwhile "age of reason and liberality." A belief in God and the Golden Rule provided a path to a better future, opined the letter's author, not closed-minded dogmatism.

Such denominational disputes and debates over religious doctrine occurred alongside the tasks of governance. Even here, Tennesseans engaged indirectly with questions of church and state. Territorial sheriffs and their deputies, for example, were to "swear (or affirm)" that they would do their duty, without also being required to invoke divine assistance in that task.[14]

III.

Against this backdrop of political and religious culture, fifty-five delegates gathered on January 11, 1796, to draft the first state constitution. A committee, chaired by James Houston, a Revolutionary War veteran and cousin of the Reverend Samuel Houston, did the actual writing in just over three weeks. Convention delegates then debated the document for three days, producing a final version the following week. Most of the Constitution dealt with representation in the legislature and the powers of government officials. However, four articles reflected the ongoing sentiments concerning the role of religion in government.[15]

Article XI, Section 3, carried forward a practice and belief about religious establishment, largely combining Article 19 and Clause 34 of the Constitution of North Carolina and the later part of the draft constitution of the

State of Franklin. Headed "Freedom of Worship," it addressed both personal liberty and establishmentarian issues. The clause declared: "[T]hat all men have a natural and indefeasible right to worship Almighty God according to the dictates of their own conscience; that no man can of right be compelled to attend, erect, or support any place of worship, or to maintain any minister against his consent; that no human authority can, in any case whatever, control or interfere with the rights of conscience; and that no preference shall ever be given, by law, to any religious establishment or mode of worship."[16] These several clauses represent a consensus about the meaning of religious freedom in an era of disestablishment. They were approved without debate.

Article VII, as originally drafted, provided for a militia, including the election of its officers. On February 5, 1796, William Fort, a delegate from Tennessee County, moved to add Section 7, "The legislature shall pass laws exempting citizens belonging to any sect or denomination of religion, the tenets of which are known to be opposed to the bearing of arms, from attending private or general musters." This conscientious-objection measure passed without need for a roll-call vote. Given the ongoing and violent struggle with Native Americans and the need to police the growing system of plantation slavery, its passage without recorded controversy indicates a strong commitment to protecting religious observance. Pacifism received double protection, as Article VIII, Section 2, provided: "No man belonging to any sect or denomination of religion, the tenets of which are known to be opposed to the bearing of arms, shall be liable to be fined for non attendance [*sic*] at general or private musters." A subsequent motion to strike this exemption failed, thirty-nine to sixteen. Quakers had resided in Tennessee since 1787, but the record is silent whether accommodating them is what motivated the delegates.[17]

On February 2, the delegates considered an amendment: "No person who publicly denies the being of a God, and future rewards and punishments, or the divine authority of the old and new testament, shall hold any office in the civil department in this state." On reconsideration, the phrase referring to the Old and New Testaments failed by a single vote, twenty-seven to twenty-six. The remainder of the amendment was adopted and became Section 2 of Article VIII.[18] A second amendment to Article VIII involved the holding of public office by ministers. As originally submitted to the convention, ministers were not eligible to hold "any civil or military office or place of trust within this state," lest they be deterred from their spiritual duties.

On reconsideration, this clause was narrowed to barring clergy from serving only in the legislature. The prohibition reflected long-standing concern about combining certain vocations and office holding, much as where the constitution for the State of Franklin would have barred clergy, barristers, and physicians from seeking election to office.[19]

The convention approved without debate Article IX, Section 2: "No atheist shall hold a civil office. No person who denies the being of God, or a future state of rewards and punishments, shall hold any office in the civil department of this state." This section remained part of the Constitution until modern times. The clause operated like a religious test for public office. At one point, it justified striking atheists from serving as courtroom witnesses. Like many unenforceable provisions in state statutes and constitutions, the provision remains in Tennessee's organic laws, emblematic of a time when general Christianity was widely assumed. The generation that had chafed under religious establishment now saw itself making a distinction between requiring one to worship contrary to the dictates of conscience and prescribing necessary qualifications for republican governance. For them, delineating certain generally held religious beliefs as a requisite for office holding was akin to specifying age and residency requirements.[20]

Article XI, Section 4, read, "That no political or religious test, other than an oath to support the Constitution of the United States and of this State, shall ever be required as a qualification to any office or public trust under this state." But other sections in the Constitution, such as Article IX, along with long practice, such as the precise phrasing of the prescribed oaths of office, indicate that the scope of these clauses was unclear.[21] Indeed, actual practice by Tennessee's government in its earliest days suggests an assumed Protestant culture rather than forensic consistency. For example, while oaths of office prior to statehood included the phrase "so help me God," that feature was absent in the 1796 Constitution. The Constitution required "each member of the senate and house of representatives . . . take an oath or affirmation of fidelity to this state."[22] Yet when Tennessee's legislature convened in March 1796, it appointed a senate committee to prepare an oath of office for the elected Governor. The oath read: "I A. B. do solemnly swear, that I will support the constitution of the United States.—So help me God." When the house met in its initial session in late March 1796, members took the prescribed oath mandated by the Constitution but added a clause to it, that each member would "solemnly swear (or affirm, as the case may be) that I will support the constitution of the state of Tennessee." Apparently, the authors of the oaths believed that incidental aids to religion—invoking God—did not constitute an establishment of religion.[23]

IV.

Tennessee was admitted as the sixteenth state of the Union by act of Congress on June 1, 1796.[24] The third state to enter the Union after ratification of the U.S. Constitution, Tennessee's disestablishment differs from eleven of the original thirteen states because it was never a British colony with an established religion. Yet Tennessee reflects some of the patterns of the eleven. There was a disestablishment ethos that pushed to free religious societies from the corrupting hand of government. Because Tennesseans valued religion, they struggled to find the proper place for it in their new state. Heirs to the struggle against established religion in the original states, they sought to promote religious freedom, especially the right to worship as one chose and freedom from supporting a religion not of one's choosing. At the same time, religious expression found a place in the exercise of public duties. The Reverend Samuel Carrick, a Presbyterian minister from Knoxville, was invited to offer a prayer and a sermon at the convention that drafted the Tennessee Constitution. Moreover, lawmakers required many officials taking their oaths of office to swear "so help me, God," notwithstanding a rubric of disestablishment.[25] In a frontier society that valued religious liberty, Tennesseans did not find generalized Protestant utterances in governmental ceremony to violate church-state separation.

Tennessee's disestablishment reflected its own unique history. It experienced a contentious relationship with North Carolina, both reflecting and rebelling against its mother state's cultural and political dominance. The state was also settled by people from the backcountries of the Carolinas and Virginia, as well as religiously tolerant Pennsylvania, and in this respect Tennesseans acquired a highly individualistic notion of religion and religious liberty, even as they reserved a place for civil religion in the public operations of state government.

NOTES

1. Francis Asbury, *The Journal of the Rev. Francis Asbury, Bishop of the Methodist Episcopal Church, from August 7, 1771, to December 7, 1815* (New York: N. Bangs and T. Mason, 1821), 286.

2. John Wigger, *Francis Asbury and the Methodists* (New York: Oxford University Press, 2009), 13; Jonathan J. Den Hartog, *Patriotism and Piety: Federalist Politics and Religious Struggles in the New American Nation* (Charlottesville: University of Virginia Press, 2015), 201.

3. J. G. M. Ramsey, *The Annals of Tennessee to The End of the Eighteenth Century* (Charleston, SC: John Russell, 1853), 106, 134, 184; Wilma Dykeman, *Tennessee: A Bicentennial History* (New York: W. W. Norton, 1975), 61; John D. Barnhart, "The Tennessee Constitution of 1796: A Product of the Old West," *Journal of Southern History* 9, no. 4 (1943): 536; Lewis Laska, *The Tennessee State Constitution* (New York: Oxford University Press, 2011), 3–4; Gerard V. Bradley, *Church-State Relationships in America* (New York: Greenwood Press, 1987), 33.

4. Ramsey, *Annals*, 286, 292, 296, 326; Francis A. Ramsey, "The Provisional Constitution of Frankland," *American Historical Magazine* 1, no. 1 (1896): 54–55; Barnhart, "Tennessee Constitution," 538; Edwin R. Keedy, "The Constitutions of the State of Franklin, the Indian Stream Republic, and the State of Deseret," *University of Pennsylvania Law Review* 101, no. 4 (1953): 516–17. On the radical nature of the Pennsylvania Constitution, see Gary B. Nash, "Philadelphia's Radical Caucus that Propelled Pennsylvania to Independence and Democracy," in *Revolutionary Founders: Rebels, Radicals and Reformers in the Making of the Nation*, ed. Alfred F. Young, Gary B. Nash, and Ray Raphael, 67–86 (New York: Vintage Books, 2012).

5. Samuel Cole Williams, *History of the Lost State of Franklin* (New York: Press of the Pioneers, 1933), 339–47; *Constitution of North Carolina, December 18, 1776*, www.nhinet.org/ccs/docs/nc-1776.htm. Section 44 incorporated the Declaration of Rights and gave its words juridical authority.

6. Williams, *Lost State of Franklin*, 339–47; *Constitution of North Carolina*.

7. Williams, *Lost State of Franklin*, 339–47; Barnhart, "Tennessee Constitution," 538.

8. Williams, *Lost State of Franklin*, 339–47.

9. Williams, *Lost State of Franklin*, 339–47.

10. An Act for the Government of the Territory of the United States, South of the River Ohio, 1st Cong., chap. 14 (2nd sess., 1790).

11. The Northwest Ordinance was first enacted by the Continental Congress in 1787. Once the new nation was formed, the ordinance was reenacted by Congress without change. See An Act to Provide for the Government of the Territory North-West of the River Ohio, 1st Cong., chap. 8 (1st sess., 1789).

12. Dykeman, *Tennessee*, 70; Michael Toomey, "'Doing Justice to Suitors': The Role of County Courts in the Southwest Territory," *Journal of East Tennessee History* 62 (1990): 33–53.

13. *Knoxville Gazette*, November 23, 1793, 1; December 4, 1795, 2.

14. *Knoxville Gazette*, December 17, 1791, 1; February 11, 1792, 3; July 28, 1792, 1; August 25, 1792, 1; September 26, 1794, 3; July 31, 1795, 4 (quote on 2); August 1, 1796, 4; December 12, 1796, 1; May 8, 1797, 1 (quote on 1, 2]; Samuel C. Williams, "George Roulstone: Father of the Tennessee Press," *East Tennessee Historical Society Publications* 17 (1945): 51–60; Ramsey, *Annals*, 650, 652–53.

Edward R. Crowther

15. Barnhart, "Tennessee Constitution," 539, 544–45.

16. Laska, *Tennessee State Constitution*, 39.

17. *Journal of the Proceedings of the Convention Began and Held at Knoxville, January 11, 1796* (Knoxville: George Roulstone, 1796), 29, 18.

18. *Journal of the Proceedings*, 23–24; Sanford, *Constitutional Convention*, 33.

19. Laska, *Tennessee State Constitution*, 143; *McDaniel v. Paty*, 435 U.S. 618 (1978) (plurality opinion), overturning this provision in the Tennessee Constitution as violating religious liberty protected by the First Amendment.

20. Laska, *Tennessee State Constitution*, 144; Burdett A. Rich, ed., *The Lawyer's Reports Annotated: Book XLI, 1898* (Rochester, NY: Lawyers Co-operative, 1915), 565; Vincent Phillip Muñoz, "Church and State in the Founding-Era State Constitutions," *American Political Thought* 4, no. 1 (2015): 31. See John Fea, *Was America Founded as a Christian Nation? A Historical Introduction* (Louisville, KY: Westminster John Knox Press, 2011), 4–21.

21. Laska, *Tennessee State Constitution*, 144; Burdett A. Rich, ed., *The Lawyer's Reports Annotated: Book XLI, 1898* (Rochester, NY: Lawyers Co-operative, 1915), 565; Vincent Phillip Muñoz, "Church and State in the Founding-Era State Constitutions," *American Political Thought* 4, no. 1 (2015): 31. See John Fea, *Was America Founded as a Christian Nation? A Historical Introduction* (Louisville, KY: Westminster John Knox Press, 2011), 4–21.

22. *Journal of the Proceedings*, 18.

23. *Journal of the Senate of the State of Tennessee* (Knoxville: Roulstone, 1796), 8; *Journal of the House of Representatives of the State of Tennessee* (Knoxville: Roulstone, 1796), 3.

24. An Act for the Admission of the State of Tennessee into the Union, 4th Cong., chap. 47 (1st Sess. 1796).

25. *Journal of the Proceedings*, 4.

CHAPTER TWELVE

GEORGIA
The Thirteenth Colony

Joel A. Nichols

From its founding in 1732, Georgia was a place of both religious tolerance and religious pluralism. Early Georgians valued liberty of conscience
and free exercise of religion, direct but nonpreferential governmental support for religion, and nondiscrimination based on religion.[1] These multiple
principles of religious liberty found in the colonial Charter stemmed from
the necessity of recognizing divergent religious beliefs and religious faiths.[2]
A mixture of religious adherents was welcomed, and the various faiths were
not asked to conform to or support the Church of England. This pluralism
served as an ameliorating feature helping to render "reality milder than the
law" with respect to church-state relations.[3] There was a gradual movement
toward recognizing the value of disestablishment, and even when in 1758
the Church of England became the official church in the colony, the establishment was, in practice, a weak (or "soft") establishment with limited real
ecclesiastical presence.

I.

Georgia's religious pluralism was so accepted that it was seen as unremarkable at the time, and relations between religious groups were relatively
harmonious. Aside from the prohibition against Catholics, it appears that
itinerant preachers were welcome in Georgia, especially after the revolution
and especially in the frontier regions. During the period of establishment
in the colonial period, 1758–76, dissenters still played a prominent role in
civic life.[4]

  At Georgia's founding, the trustees of the colonial corporation decided
against establishing an official church, but they sent an Anglican minister
with the first group of colonists in November 1732, who was the first in a line
of rapid turnover.[5] Parishes struggled to attract ministers, both before and

after the 1758 establishment of the Church of England. Further, the numerical strength of the Anglican church remained surprisingly low throughout the entire eighteenth century.[6] For example, in 1748 there were 388 dissenters and only 63 Anglicans in Savannah, with as few as 200 practicing Anglicans in the whole of Georgia by the end of the proprietary period.[7] That number seems implausibly low, but there are no other reliable estimates. What does seem sure is that the Church of England was not the strong force that established churches were in South Carolina and Virginia. By the turn of the century, the now Protestant Episcopal Church had gone from the preferred religion of the colonial founders to the legally established religion to merely one of many diverse religious groups.

There was surprising variation in religious groups in Georgia. Jews were present from the inception of the colony, such that one-fourth or one-fifth of Savannah's citizens were Jewish at the end of the first year. The Jewish community continued throughout the period up to the revolution, with Georgia granting the congregation a charter of incorporation and land for a new synagogue.[8]

Two groups of Lutherans settled in Georgia, known commonly as "Salzburgers" (so named because they generally emigrated from Salzburg in modern Austria) and "Moravians." The trustees convinced the pietistic and persecuted Salzburgers to immigrate by stressing free exercise of religion and offering to fund their migration.[9] The Salzburgers settled in their own community (Ebenezer) and continued to increase, reaching as many as 1,200 by the early 1770s.[10] In 1735 two groups of Moravians arrived and stayed in Savannah (instead of proceeding to possess their land grant).[11] Numbering no more than 30, the pacifist Moravians' tenure was very short. Because of their conscientious objection to military service, Moravians ceased coming to Georgia, and those already in Georgia eventually moved to Pennsylvania.[12]

Scottish Presbyterians began arriving in early 1736, coming more for land than to escape religious persecution. By 1755 Savannah's Presbyterian population founded the Independent Presbyterian Church, with John J. Zubly serving as minister to patrons inside and outside of Savannah.[13] Other Presbyterians from the older North American colonies settled in the frontier regions of Georgia and petitioned the legislature for land grants, although they did not form any churches that we know of. These Presbyterians also petitioned the governor and council in 1765 to grant fifty thousand acres for immigrants from Ireland. Settlers that arrived as late as 1769 were granted land and funds by the Governor's Council, with grants limited to Protestants.[14]

Congregationalists arrived in 1752, coming to Georgia because of the availability of land, and were soon joined by others from New England.[15] By 1771 their geographic area boasted about 350 white inhabitants and 1,500 slaves, and they controlled about one-third of Georgia's wealth.[16] After some hardship, the Congregational Church reconstituted itself and became strong enough to incorporate under the 1789 incorporation law.[17]

There was a halting Quaker presence in Georgia. While Quaker settlers were explicitly contemplated by the 1732 Charter, no families arrived until 1767, when a group from Pennsylvania was given land grants. After the revolution, these Quakers eventually migrated to Ohio due to internal strife and opposition to slavery.[18]

By the turn of the century Baptists gained large numbers of adherents through revivalism. Sustained growth and the presence of a Baptist church did not take hold until the early years of the revolutionary period.[19] By 1793, however, Baptists were the most numerous denomination in the state, and they grew in influence as well as numbers.[20] There were also Black Baptist churches in Georgia, including the largest Baptist church after the War of Independence at Savannah, which climbed to around 700 members by 1800.[21]

Methodism was slower to come to Georgia than to other parts of the United States.[22] The first Methodist societies were not present until the mid-1780s, when there were only 70 members in the state. In just a few years, Methodism grew to more than 1,100 members, with rapid expansion during the 1790s and beyond.[23]

Catholics were always few in number, and their exclusion had both religious and political motives. Both the initial Charter and the continuing use of oaths were largely effective against Catholicism, as the largest number reported in Georgia over the first twenty years was 4, in 1747.[24] The trustees tried to prevent Catholics from obtaining land and canceled grants when the grantees were found to be Catholic, and they prevented any Catholics from acquiring land through will, deed, or trust.[25] Catholics continued to struggle for legal equality after the revolution, and little is known about their actual numbers.[26]

The relative equality of the Protestant dissenting groups alongside the then established Anglican church at the time of revolution can be seen in the 1773 report by Zubly: "[I]n the present house of Representatives, a third or upwards are dissenters, & most of the churchmen of moderate principles." With such political clout in the hands of dissenters, we may believe Zubly when he reports that "[t]here has been little or no altercation between the church & dissenters."[27]

II.

After years of urging by South Carolinians, Great Britain relented in deciding to establish a series of settlements to the south of South Carolina for protection against the Spanish and Native Americans in Florida. The initial impetus for settling Georgia in the late 1720s was to provide a haven for debtors languishing in English jails. By the time of the Crown's grant of a Charter in 1732, the underlying goals for the colony had expanded to include "all unfortunates," and colonial Georgia quickly became a haven for European groups that had been persecuted because of religion.[28] This religious pluralism was due to explicit guarantees of religious liberty in Georgia's initial Charter.[29]

King George II issued a Charter to the corporate trustees of the colony of Georgia on June 9, 1732. The Charter makes explicit the "liberty of conscience" for *all* persons, including Catholics, but "free exercise" of religion is granted to all persons *except* Catholics. There is no establishment of the Church of England in the Charter. Indeed, the Charter makes no mention of the need to spread Christianity through evangelism (which was standard in previous American colonial charters). The only invocation of the divine is a statement that the success of the colony will depend upon the blessing of God. There is an implicit acknowledgment of the religious pluralism that would soon exist in the colony through an allowance for the possibility of affirmation, in lieu of oath swearing, for the "persons commonly called quakers." There is no conscientious objection clause, since one of the founding purposes was to provide a defensive buffer for South Carolina against the Spanish and others. Finally, the text of the Charter is only the starting point for religious liberty in Georgia, for it provides that the corporation behind the venture should make laws "fit and necessary for and concerning the government of the said colony, and not repugnant to the laws and statutes of England."[30]

During this proprietary period, the government provided direct support to religion in several ways. The salaries for Anglican ministers initially came primarily from the Society for the Propagation of the Gospel in Foreign Parts (SPG), whereas the corporate trustees set aside glebe lands and provided indentured servants to work those lands, from which the proceeds would go to support the church and the ministry. While these glebes were not specifically designated for the Church of England, they were so used in fact.[31]

Aside from the glebes and moneys from the SPG, Anglican ministers were paid out of a general grant by Parliament, from donations by individuals designated to Georgia for "religious uses," and by a twenty-pound stipend the

British government made payable to every Anglican minister who went to the colonies.[32] The trustees took additional actions to support religion in the colony: providing clothing and supplies for the traveling evangelist George Whitefield, funding the construction of parsonages and churches, and arranging for a catechist in Savannah to educate the children in religious matters.[33]

When the SPG discontinued paying the salary of the rector of Christ Church parish in Savannah in 1771, Parliament provided seventy pounds to the rector each year, as well as providing funds for two schoolmasters.[34] Additionally, the Georgia Legislature provided money for ministers through a tax on liquor, applied to liquor purchases by Anglicans and dissenters alike.[35]

Direct governmental support for religion was strikingly not limited to the Church of England. The Salzburgers petitioned the trustees for a grant of glebe land in the 1740s, receiving five hundred acres, and other direct support for their church: paint and oil for constructing churches; an altar cloth, vestments, a chalice, and other articles for use in services; and money to help build houses for their ministers.[36]

In 1741 the trustees directed that marriages should be performed according to the canons of the Church of England. However, the Salzburgers were exempt from this requirement, provided their clergy obtained licenses from a magistrate. Salzburger ministers were not allowed to marry Englishmen without permission from civil officials, unless there was no English minister available. In the royal period, the governors were given power to grant marriage licenses and charged with ensuring that marriages conformed to rites of the Church of England, securing a colonial law to that effect, if possible. However, such a law was never passed in Georgia.[37]

Education in Georgia was somewhat haphazard and occurred under the auspices of the government, the churches, and sometimes a combination of the two.[38] For example, the Anglican church maintained a direct role in the education of children in Savannah, even though the schools were officially run by the civil government. The Salzburgers provided education for the young of their community, with religion playing a role in curriculum and instruction.[39] An attempt was made by the touring evangelist George White-field to create a college for further education. This never came to fruition because various patrons added conditions to funding, including one by the archbishop of Canterbury that the college always be led by a member of the Church of England and the liturgy used at the college would always be Anglican.[40] These conditions conflicted with Whitefield's vision that the college would rest upon "a broad bottom, and no other."[41] While Whitefield did not give up on his plans, he died before any alternate could be secured.[42]

III.

In 1752, due to financial pressures, the trustees surrendered their interests to George II, and the royal period began.[43] This era also marked a movement toward greater favoritism of the Church of England by the Crown and its colonial supporters. It was not until October 1754 when the president of the corporation received the royal decree to turn over power to the governor and his council. The transfer of power little touched matters of religion. Not all appointed council members were required to be Anglicans.[44] All those appointed took oaths and met religious tests, including allegiance to the king and rejection of transubstantiation, the latter excluding Catholics from office.[45] However, there is some evidence that the insistence upon oath taking was not strictly enforced, for by 1773 as many as one-third of the assembly were dissenters and there is no record of any dissenters being excluded.[46] The assembly and council did try to liberalize their policies on oaths in 1756, but that attempt was overturned by the Privy Council in 1759 because dissenters in England did not enjoy a similar exemption.[47] The governor and council continued the practices of the trustees and were generous with dissenters—especially regarding land grants for church construction and glebes.[48]

The formal establishment of the Anglican church in Georgia was a three-year process. In 1755 a bill to establish the Church of England was passed by the assembly, but failed to pass the council (a body appointed by the king that included one dissenter and one dissenter sympathizer).[49] Two years later, the assembly proposed a similar bill, and again the council did not approve it.[50] The assembly tried again the following year and succeeded in overcoming the opposition of two prominent dissenting groups: the Salzburgers and a Congregationalist community. The latter had urged the assembly to remember that the colony was founded as "an Asylum for all sorts of Protestants to enjoy full Liberty of Conscience Prefferable [*sic*] to any other American Colonies."[51]

When this third bill went to the council—which was composed entirely of Anglicans, except for two dissenters—it stalled until the bill was amended in a way that omitted the words "Church of England" and substituted the phrase "to establish the Worship of God in the Province of Georgia."[52] Because some on the council feared this phrasing would establish religion too broadly, the assembly met in conference with the council to create a compromise. The final bill functionally established the Church of England, but omitted any express mention of the Church of England, as established, or mentioning Anglicanism as the "official religion of the colony." It mentioned the phrase "Church of England" only in the title and preamble.[53] This third bill passed within fourteen days of its introduction.[54]

The 1758 act divided Georgia geographically into eight parishes.[55] The ministers/rectors were authorized to sue and be sued in the church's name, were endowed with the cure of all souls in their parish, and were given possession of all the Anglican church property in the parish—including houses of worship, cemeteries, glebe lands, and any other church realty. The law also established a system for election of church wardens and vestrymen, charged with caring for and governing the churches. All freeholders or taxpayers in a parish were entitled to vote, and the only requirement for serving as a vestryman or church warden was to be an inhabitant of the parish (and a freeholder, in the case of church wardens).[56]

The rector, wardens, and vestrymen were empowered to raise money in their parishes by taxes "on the estate, real and personal," of all people within the parish. These tax revenues not only covered church expenses but were also for the general well-being of the community. Ministers and rectors were forbidden from exercising "any ecclesiastical law or jurisdiction whatsoever." This was an important jurisdictional separation for non-Anglicans, who feared the power of canon or ecclesiastical courts common in England.[57] Part of the general tax revenue of Georgians also went to support Anglican ministers. Ironically, most of the ministerial salary paid by the colonists came not from the 1758 act but from taxes on alcohol.[58] The lack of a religious test for vestrymen and church wardens was a clear victory for dissenters. Historical records, though scarce, indicate that at least some non-Anglicans were elected as vestryman and church wardens.[59]

The royal instructions to the governor of Georgia provide additional insight into the control over religion in this period. Governors were instructed to ensure that God was worshipped in accordance with the rites of the Church of England and that ministers were assigned, churches were built, and glebes maintained. The governor was to grant licenses to perform marriages and probate wills, and he was required to see that vice was punished. The governor was given the authority to appoint an Anglican minister to a benefice when a parish became vacant.[60] In practice, however, the appointment of ministers was largely done by a vestry's appeal to the SPG in England.[61]

Immediately after the passage of the 1758 act, the Georgia Assembly passed a bill empowering constables to enforce the peace on Sundays in Savannah. Ministers of the Church of England and many others were exempt from being selected as a constable, which was akin to jury duty.[62] If a person was not exempt and failed to serve as constable when selected, he was required to pay ten pounds sterling to the parish.

If a man did serve as a constable in Savannah (and only Savannah, it appears), he was to "attend, aid, and assist the church wardens" in preventing "tumults from Negroes and other disorderly people." Even more striking is the language requiring constables to "take up and apprehend all such persons who shall be found loitering or walking about the streets and compel them to go to *some place* of divine worship."[63] This directive to compel attendance at a church service, and not specifically at the Anglican service, underscores the strength of competing religious groups—at least Protestant groups—even after establishment.

Four years later, in 1762, the Georgia Legislature outlawed the sale of most goods and services on "the Lord's Day." Church wardens and constables of each parish were authorized to roam the streets twice each Sunday, during worship time, to ensure compliance.[64] There are no records that indicate that a fine was ever imposed, evidencing a general solicitude for religion and Sabbath quietude rather than support specifically for the Church of England.

While the establishment of the Anglican church was not particularly onerous for dissenters, disputes did occasionally arise. The most prominent clash regarding religious liberty in royal Georgia centered on whether dissenters would have to pay fees to the Anglican rector and sexton when they used the services of the church in burying their dead.[65]

Reverend Samuel Frink was a convert to Anglicanism who had grown up the son of a Congregational minister in New England. Seeking to increase his income, Frink took the side of the Church of England, as the established church, and sought to incorporate privileges he deemed appropriate to that status. His theory was that any fees paid for the utilization of religious services at the Anglican church should be paid to the Church of England and its minister—none other than himself. The assembly had designated an appropriate schedule of fees for the performance of certain tasks, including bell ringing and grave digging, by the Anglican sexton at funerals and burials. Frink sought to enforce payment of the fees even when the Anglican sexton did not perform the duties, bringing a lawsuit in 1769 against a leading Presbyterian, Reverend John J. Zubly, who had arranged a funeral for a pauper.[66] At a trial in the Court of Conscience, the jury brought in a verdict in favor of Frink. The judge quickly affirmed the decision, claiming that the sexton had a right to fees for burials anywhere in the parish, and thus dissenters had no right to a bell of their own.[67]

The judgment infuriated the editor of the *Georgia Gazette*. Reporting the case in editorial fashion, the newspaper decried the ruling as biased against dissenters and counter to the "FREE exercise" of religion guaranteed by "the charter of this province."[68] Zubly, too, was outraged by the decision. Publishing letters addressed to Frink, Zubly protested the injustice of paying fees to a sexton and rector for work that they never performed.[69] Zubly's primary concern was the precedential value of the case—that it might to be used to assess fees against dissenters all across Georgia.[70] Provincial legislators introduced bills to address the matter, but the bickering over bells and cemeteries was interrupted before final action was taken. Rather, the interests of the colony were consumed by the deteriorating relations with England. The controversy sufficiently subsided that Zubly could later write, "We now bury in the same Ground unmolested, & pay no fees except to the sexton, which I have consented to pay whenever his attendance should be required, & not otherwise."[71]

Another dispute between Anglicans and dissenters centered on licenses to perform marriages. Governor Ellis (1758–60) had altered marriage licenses upon request to authorize dissenters (instead of an Anglican rector) to perform weddings. Governor Wright (1760–76), however, would not grant this courtesy, apparently thinking it not within his power. Reverend Frink therefore allowed Reverend Zubly to perform ceremonies on licenses made out to Frink, but Zubly declined any fee payment from the betrothed couple. Frink soon tired of endorsing licenses to Zubly with no benefit, save Frink's ability to boast that he was the only licensed minister in the parish. So Frink changed the relationship such that Zubly was to charge a fee and give half of the money to Frink. This provoked Zubly to cease seeking endorsements from Frink. Zubly stubbornly continued to perform marriage ceremonies even though he lacked government sanction.[72] Meanwhile, the Lutheran Salzburger ministers at Ebenezer continued to perform marriages between couples of their own flock in accord with their rites and could perform marriages among non-Salzburgers in accord with the rites the Anglican church.[73]

Thus, as the revolution approached, there was increased debate and irritants among religious groups about the proper role of government in religion, especially resentment concerning preferences vested in the established religion. The revolution cut short this discussion. Yet it would take several years of evolving legal formulations for Georgia to work out a more nuanced and evenhanded position on these matters.

IV.

Revolutionary feelings took hold only slowly in Georgia. In 1774 Georgia sent no delegates to the First Continental Congress, notably irritating the other colonies.[74] The following year, Georgia did send five delegates to the Second Continental Congress. Only a few months later, in February 1776, the colonists conclusively wrested control of the government from the royal governor, James Wright, who had been under house arrest.[75] A state Provincial Assembly met and promulgated a short document on April 15, 1776,[76] which was the "first written fundamental document ever made by Georgians." It was not so much a constitution as a "short text of eight rules and regulations," designed to be temporary and contingent upon developments in the Second Continental Congress and the exigencies of the time.[77] The document made no mention of religion, but merely set down rules for keeping the peace until such time as a fuller form of governance could be constructed.

Upon official receipt of the Declaration of Independence on August 10, 1776, Archibald Bulloch, then president and commander in chief of Georgia, convened the Provincial Assembly to read the document, begin securing delegates, and calling a constitutional convention. The convention met in Savannah from October 1, 1776, to February 5, 1777, and resulted in the adoption of the Constitution of the State of Georgia.[78] The bulk of the 1777 Constitution addressed structural governmental concerns, resulting in the formation of legislative and executive branches, the latter consisting of both a council and a weak governor. It addressed religion in Article 56: "All persons whatever shall have the free exercise of their religion; provided it be not repugnant to the peace and safety of the State; and shall not, unless by consent, support any teacher or teachers except those of their own profession."[79]

This provision echoed some of the more tolerant sentiments of the 1732 Charter. It apparently subsumed liberty of conscience in the text "free exercise of their religion." It also began to disestablish religion—although there was neither a formal statement of disestablishment of the Church of England nor a measurable level of religious agitation or malcontent expressed at the Georgia convention. Government financial support for religion persisted, but persons were not forced to contribute money to the religion of others. The 1777 Constitution did retain the "peace and safety of the State" proviso, which could result in government control over religious practices that were harmful to others.[80]

While Catholics and non-Christians were guaranteed free exercise of religion, they were excluded from serving as representatives in the assembly.

Only persons "of the Protestant religion" were eligible to serve in that capacity.[81] This policy actually was an advance for the period—especially when coupled with the lack of a religious test for voters.[82] The other explicit mention of religion in the Constitution was the exclusion of clergy of all denominations from holding a seat in the legislature.[83] Such an exclusion was common in state constitutions for many years.[84]

There is no mention of "God" or "Almighty" anywhere in the 1777 Constitution—not even in the preamble. This omission stands in contrast to a number of other state constitutions at the time. Nor is there any mention of religion in the provision for education, which simply reads: "Schools shall be erected in each county, and supported at the general expense of the State, as the legislature shall hereafter point out."[85] Finally, the 1777 Constitution made some allowance for Quakers and Anabaptists, whose beliefs did not allow them to swear oaths.[86] Such individuals were allowed to affirm, instead of swear, in denoting their allegiance to Georgia.[87] However, the document did not make such an allowance for persons being sworn into state offices.[88]

The 1777 Constitution, similar to its progeny, made no mention of conscientious objection for pacifism—despite the fact that a town of Quakers had settled in Wrightsborough. Rather than a right to conscientious objection from military service, Georgia—like other states and even the federal government—chose to deal with the matter by legislative discretion rather than by constitutional right. In 1778 Georgia excused persons from military service for reasons of conscience, but it imposed double taxation for exercising such a choice.[89] The exemption was discontinued in 1792 for three years and then reinstated. During this three-year interim, Quakers were allowed to pay an additional 25 percent tax for conscientious objection. From 1784 to 1792, clergy were unconditionally exempt.[90]

One other feature of the Constitution touches on religion—that of the renaming of parishes. Newly designated "counties," the geographic areas received nonreligious appellations in place of their old titles, which had been based upon saints and tied to the 1758 establishment of the Church of England.[91]

The 1777 Constitution left open the possibility of a state tax to support religion of each person's "own [religious] profession." In 1782 an attempt at such a statute was introduced in the assembly that provided for the establishment of churches and schools. Nothing came of this. Two years later, another attempt was made to pass a bill to promote religion and piety by

granting certain rights and material aid to religious societies and school-
houses.[92] In 1785, however, a funding measure found success. The Georgia
Legislature passed a bill allowing tax moneys to be used in each county "[f]
or the regular establishment and support of the public duties of Religion."[93]
The statute proclaimed that the "regular establishment and support [of the
Christian religion] is among the most important objects of Legislature [sic]
determination."[94]

The Georgia Baptist Association sent a lengthy Remonstrance (probably
authored by Silas Mercer) to the legislature, decrying the 1785 bill and pro-
testing the intervention of the government in religious affairs: "[R]eligion
does not need such carnal weapons as acts of assembly and civil sanctions,
nor can they be applied to it without destroying it." The Baptist Association
was also worried that passage of one such law might lead to others of an even
more intrusive nature—including laws that would lead "to the establishment
of a particular denomination in preference and at the expense of the rest."
The state's role was, rather than passing laws supporting religion, to support
morality generally and to ensure that "all are left free to worship God according to the dictates of their own consciences, unbribed and unmolested."[95]

The 1785 act guaranteed "all the different sects and denominations of the
Christian religion . . . free and equal liberty and Toleration in the exercise of
their [r]eligion," and confirmed all the "usages[,] rights, [i]mmunities and
privileges . . . usually . . . held or enjoyed" by religious societies.[96] Each county with at least thirty heads of families was to select a minister of a church of
its choosing to whom state tax dollars would flow. The tax rate was set at four
pence on every hundred pounds' valuation of the property owned by church
members. Upon receipt of the tax revenue, the sum would be paid from the
state treasury directly to the minister. When the population grew sufficient
to warrant another church, at least twenty heads of families could petition to
be recognized as a separate church and its minister receive a proportionate
share of tax dollars.

The only evidence of implementation of the 1785 act is an advertisement
in the *Georgia Gazette* on January 26, 1786. The advertisement urged all
Episcopalians in Chatham County to register with their church wardens so
that their numbers might be determined for submitting an application of the
tax moneys from the treasury.[97] There is no other known implementation,
and the law was subsequently superseded by an article concerning religious
freedom in the 1798 Constitution.[98]

V.

Following ratification of the United States Constitution in late 1788, Georgians revisited their state Constitution. The legislature appointed three individuals from each county, and this assembly drafted a proposed constitution from November 4 through 24, 1788. Copies were circulated throughout the state.[99] The people then elected delegates who convened to consider the document. The delegates made so many alterations as to necessitate a second convention. So in April 1789 a second constitutional convention met and completed the document. It was ratified on May 6, 1789.[100] Unfortunately, there are no extant records or journals of the two conventions.[101]

The 1789 Constitution provided for a bicameral legislature and a stronger executive. The major clause on religion was shortened to read: "All persons shall have the free exercise of religion, without being obliged to contribute to the support of any religious profession but their own." The "peace and safety" provision was happily dropped, possibly due in part to James Madison's prominent fight in Virginia to remove similar language from the Virginia Declaration of Rights. There was no clause on the disestablishment of religion, and citizens were presumably still subject to being compelled to support their own religion should the 1785 act be enforced.

Other changes regarding church-state relations found their way into the 1789 Constitution in more subtle ways. The requirement of professing the Protestant faith as a prerequisite for public office dropped out, but the exclusion of clergy "of any denomination" from membership in the general assembly was retained. As a further acknowledgment of the religious pluralism in the state, the opportunity to affirm rather than swear to the oath of office was extended to members of the state senate and house of representatives as well as to the governor. Although the foregoing concession was primarily an accommodation to the Quakers, the right of conscientious objection from military service was still omitted. Another notable omission was the removal of any mention of education in the Constitution, whether public or private schools. Finally, the 1789 Constitution still did not mention God or "the Almighty" in its preamble or in its text. The latter continued to run counter to many other states.[102]

A nonreligious issue of great importance in the 1789 Constitution was the provision for a convention to revise the document just five years later.[103] So in 1795 (a year late), delegates met and made several amendments to the Constitution that entered into force without popular ratification. But no mention was made of religious issues. The delegates further provided for a constitutional convention to be held just three years later.[104]

The *Journal* from this 1795 convention shows that a delegate moved that "Rev. Mr. Mercer be requested to offer up a Prayer to the Supreme Being." Mercer complied.[105] This is potentially important because sources indicate this was probably Silas Mercer, a Baptist preacher present at both the 1795 and the 1798 constitutional conventions. Sources conflict on the number of Baptists at these two conventions. Their influence on the issue of disestablishment is not certain but likely material.[106] Other than the one statement about prayer, the 1795 *Journal* has no discussion of religion.

The 1798 constitutional convention met amid increasing tensions over fair representation between the growing upcountry settlers and the long-standing inhabitants of the coastal cities. The new Constitution retained the formal structure of the old, but allowed for more flexibility in designating new counties and more allowance for representation to meet the crisis over voter apportionment. Delegates provided enough changes that the document is considered a new constitution instead of merely amendments to the earlier one, as first contemplated. The 1798 Constitution proved stable enough to last Georgia until the eve of the Civil War.

The *Journal* of the 1798 convention reveals only hints at the mind-set of the delegates, and external historical sources are not illuminating regarding the rationale for the presence or absence of various provisions. The first mention of religion is on the opening day. The delegates resolved that "the Convention will attend divine service tomorrow [Wednesday, May 9, 1798] at 11 o'clock, in conformity to the proclamation of the President of the United States."[107] This was in response to President Adams's call for a day of fasting and prayer over the threat of war with France.

With the 1789 Constitution (as amended in 1795) serving as a template, sections were read aloud and then agreed upon or amended by delegates present. The 1798 Constitution lengthened the religion clause, providing for a fuller range of religious liberty and disestablishment. Article IV, Section 10, provided:

> No person within this State shall, upon any pretence, be deprived of the inestimable privilege of worshipping God in a manner agreeable to his own conscience, nor be compelled to attend any place of worship contrary to his own faith and judgment; nor shall he ever be obliged to pay tithes, taxes, or any other rate, for the building or repairing any place of worship, or for the maintenance of any minister or ministry, contrary to what he believes to be right,

or hath voluntarily engaged to do. No one religious society shall ever be established in this State, in preference to another; nor shall any person be denied the enjoyment of any civil right merely on account of his religious principles.[108]

The drafters chose to elaborate in some detail their intentions regarding religion, rather than invoking the commonly used terms of art such as "free exercise" and "liberty of conscience." Thus, an individual's freedom to worship, and to worship according to his or her conscience, was made sacrosanct. No compulsion in matters of religion was secured. Disestablishment took the form of a guarantee that an individual was not required to pay monetary support for a place of worship, minister, or ministry contrary to an individual's beliefs. The principle of nonpreferential treatment of religions was constitutionalized. This, however, left open the possibility of nonpreferential government aid to religion in general. All religious tests were ended.

The 1798 *Journal of the Convention* sheds little light on this expanded section. The previous religion clause was read (by an unnamed person), and then "it was moved to amend the same by Mr. [Jesse] Mercer [a Baptist minister and Silas's son], as follows. . . . On the question thereupon, it was agreed to."[109] Although the 1798 *Journal* gives no additional information to indicate authorship of the religion clause, it has long been speculated that Silas Mercer, the prominent Baptist minister previously mentioned, was behind it.[110] There is no textual support for this other than the single statement from the 1798 *Journal* quoted above and that the completed clause moved Georgia closer to Baptist understanding of the relationship between church and state. It appears that seven or more Baptists, including Mercer, attended the convention, which would have meant that seven of sixty-eight delegates were Baptists.[111] The measurable Baptist presence lends to the plausibility of Baptist influence on the religious freedom section.

The 1798 Constitution contained additional provisions touching on religion. First, the option of affirmation instead of oath swearing was retained for the offices of governor, senator, and representative.[112] Second, the ban on clergy holding seats in the legislature was discontinued.[113] Finally, the 1798 Constitution retained some notable omissions from its predecessors: no mention of education (let alone private religious education), no reference to God or a deity in the preamble or elsewhere, and no mention of conscientious objection to military service.

With the adoption of the 1798 Constitution, Georgia set in place the elements of modern religious freedom: free exercise was guaranteed to all, the state was to have no single established church and no preference among religions, clergy were not excluded from public or political life, oaths or affirmations were allowed for discharging public duties or holding public office, there were no religious tests, and no one could be forced to support a minister or church unless they agreed to its tenets.

VI.

Religious pluralism was the norm in colonial Georgia as dissenters and persecuted groups came to the new colony, often lured by the promise of land and tranquillity to worship in accord with conscience. As evidenced by its policies regarding glebes and education, the proprietary colonial government did not show significant favoritism among religious groups—at least for those Protestant faiths with sufficient adherents. Even when the royal government established the Church of England in 1758, the actual relationship between religion and the Crown did not change markedly. Georgia's Anglican establishment was a "soft" establishment, as the laws relating to establishment were weakly enforced and were, in practice, more for the maintenance of the welfare of the poor and needy than for the promulgation of the Christian Gospel. Because religion and morality were seen as important in civil society, the authorities were willing to foster and aid religion whenever possible. This continued even after the revolution, with the passage of a rather striking 1785 act that provided for direct governmental support of religion through collection and redistribution of tax dollars. While there is little record of enforcement of the 1785 act, its text was not limited to the Protestant Episcopal Church. Apparently never implemented generally, the statute was repealed by the 1798 Constitution.

Georgia was explicitly founded as a Protestant Christian colony, but its founders and Charter alike readily accorded all its new inhabitants a good measure of religious freedom. Liberty of conscience was promised to all, and free exercise to all except Catholics and non-Christians. These seminal principles seem to have held sway throughout eighteenth-century Georgia, and citizens were free to observe their own religious beliefs and practices relatively unmolested—even after an established church was instituted. The principles of liberty of conscience and free exercise later evolved into the modern disestablishment formulations put forth by dissenters as the fledgling state progressed through three constitutions.

Viewed collectively, the record indicates that most early Georgians thought there should be close cooperation between church and state, with no clear preference for only one Protestant denomination. Early Georgia was a place

with respect for religion and religious differences; a place that experiment-
ed with a "soft" Church of England establishment, only to move away from
the idea after less than twenty years; and a place that believed government
had a direct role to play in fostering religion and morality generally. With
the adoption of the 1798 Constitution, the state took a material step toward
embracing the view of Baptists and other Protestant dissenters, whereby the
support of each church was entirely voluntary for those who adhered to its
doctrines and engaged with its practices.

NOTES

1. Allen D. Candler, ed., *The Colonial Records of the State of Georgia* (Atlanta:
Franklin-Turner, 1907), 13:257–58.

2. John Witte Jr. and Joel A. Nichols, *Religion and the American Constitutional
Experiment*, 4th ed. (New York: Oxford University Press, 2016), 41–48, 108–10.

3. Hugh Trevor-Roper, "Toleration and Religion after 1688," in *From Persecution
to Toleration: The Glorious Revolution and Religion in England*, ed. Ole Peter Grell,
Jonathan I. Israel, and Nicholas Tyacke (New York: Oxford University Press, 1991),
389, 400.

4. Rev. John J. Zubly, letter, Savannah, GA, July 11, 1773, *Proceedings of the Massachusetts Historical Society* 8 (1865): 216.

5. Henry Thompson Malone, *The Episcopal Church in Georgia, 1733–1957* (Atlanta: Protestant Episcopal Church in the Diocese of Atlanta, 1960), 5–6, 24–42; Ju-
nius J. Martin, "Georgia's First Minister: The Reverend Dr. Henry Herbert," *Georgia
Historical Quarterly* 66, no. 2 (1982): 113–18. See, for example, William R. Cannon,
"John Wesley's Years in Georgia," *Methodist History* 1 (1963): 1.

6. Reba Carolyn Strickland, *Religion and the State in Georgia in the Eighteenth
Century* (New York: Columbia University, 1939), 15–34, 52–53.

7. Malone, *Episcopal Church in Georgia*, 25; Edwin Scott Gaustad, *Historical Atlas
of Religion in America* (New York: Harper & Row, 1962), 8.

8. See generally Saul Jacob Rubin, *Third to None: The Saga of Savannah Jewry,
1733–1983* (Savannah: S. J. Rubin, 1983); B. H. Levy, "The Early History of Georgia's
Jews," in *Forty Years of Diversity: Essays on Colonial Georgia*, ed. Harvey H. Jackson
and Phinizy Spalding (Athens: University of Georgia Press, 1984), 163; and Edmund
S. Morgan, *Roger Williams: The Church and the State* (New York: W. W. Norton,
1967), 51.

9. George Fenwick Jones, *The Salzburger Saga: Religious Exiles and Other Germans
along the Savannah* (Athens: University of Georgia Press, 1984), 4, 9.

10. Harold E. Davis, *The Fledgling Province: Social and Cultural Life in Colonial
Georgia, 1733–1776* (Chapel Hill: University of North Carolina Press, 1976), 16–
17; George Fenwick Jones, *The Georgia Dutch: From the Rhine and Danube to the*

Savannah, 1733–1783 (Athens: University of Georgia Press, 1992), 38–39, 48; *Colonial Records of Georgia,* 5:674.

11. Wallace Elden Miller, "Relations of Church and State in Georgia, 1732–1776" (PhD diss., Northwestern University, 1937), 184–88; *Colonial Records of Georgia,* 2:81, 29:143. See also Jones, *Georgia Dutch,* 49–51; and Miller, "Relations," 188–90.

12. Strickland, *Religion and the State in Georgia,* 76–78; Davis, *Fledgling Province,* 18; Jones, *Georgia Dutch,* 52–53. On the Moravians leaving Georgia, see *Colonial Records of Georgia,* 21:364–65, 404–5, 503–5, 4:22–23.

13. Miller, "Relations," 194–95; Orville A. Park, "The Georgia Scotch-Irish," *Georgia Historical Quarterly* 12, no. 2 (1928): 115; Ernest Trice Thompson, *Presbyterians in the South* (Richmond, VA: John Knox Press, 1963), 37.

14. Strickland, *Religion and the State in Georgia,* 117–18.

15. Allen P. Tankersley, "Midway District: A Study of Puritanism in Colonial Georgia," *Georgia Historical Quarterly* 32, no. 3 (1948): 149; Strickland, *Religion and the State in Georgia,* 115–16.

16. Davis, *Fledgling Province,* 22, 201.

17. James Stacy, *History and Published Records of the Midway Congregational Church: Liberty County, Georgia* (Spartanburg, SC: Reprint, 1979), 45; Horatio Marbury and William H. Crawford, eds., *Digest of the Laws of the State of Georgia* (Savannah: Seymour Woohopter & Stebbins, 1802), 144–45.

18. Alex M. Hitz, *The Wrightsborough Quaker Town and Township in Georgia* (Bulletin of Friends Historical Association) (1957): 10–12, reprinted in Robert Scott Davis Jr., ed., *Quaker Records in Georgia: Wrightsborough, 1772–1793* [Friendsborough, 1776–77] (Augusta, GA: Augusta Genealogical Society, 1986): 2–4.

19. J. H. Campbell, *Georgia Baptists: Historical and Biographical* (Macon: J. W. Burke, 1874), 1–2; Jesse Mercer, *History of the Georgia Baptist Association* (Washington, GA: Georgia Baptist Association, 1979), 13–18. See also Robert G. Gardner et al., *A History of the Georgia Baptist Association, 1784–1984* (Atlanta: Georgia Baptist Historical Society, 1988), 12.

20. Gardner, *History of Georgia Baptist Association,* 41.

21. Ronald W. Long, "Religious Revivalism in the Carolinas and Georgia from 1740–1805" (PhD diss., University of Georgia, 1968), 117; Gardner, *History of Georgia Baptist Association,* 17.

22. Frederick E. Maser and Howard T. Maag, eds., *The Journal of Joseph Pilmore, Methodist Itinerant, for the Years August 1, 1769 to January 2, 1774* (Philadelphia: Message, 1969), 180–81. See also Warren Thomas Smith, *Preludes: Georgia, Methodism, The American Revolution* (Athens: Methodist Administrative Services, 1976), 18; and Alfred Mann Pierce, *A History of Methodism in Georgia, February 5, 1736–June 24, 1955* (Atlanta: North Georgia Conference Historical Society, 1956), 27.

23. Maser and Maag, *Journal of Joseph Pilmore,* 37–38; George G. Smith, *The History of Georgia Methodism from 1786 to 1866* (Atlanta: A. B. Caldwell, 1913), 26–29; Pierce, *History of Methodism in Georgia,* 34–38, 56–57, 59; Warren Thomas Smith, *Preludes,* 22–27.

24. Strickland, *Religion and the State in Georgia,* 43.

25. *Colonial Record of Georgia*, 1:319, 550, 2:230, 271; Strickland, *Religion and the State in Georgia*, 81.

26. Correspondence of Henry Laurens, of South Carolina, microformed on "Materials for History Printed from Original Manuscripts," 39–45 (Frank Moore ed., 1861); Georgia Constitution of 1777, Article VI (1785), reprinted in Francis Newton Thorpe, *Federal and State Constitutions, Colonial Charters, and Other Organic Laws of the States, Territories, and Colonies Now or Heretofore Forming the United States of America* 2 (1909): 773.

27. Zubly, letter, Savannah, July 11, 1773, 216.

28. E. Merton Coulter, *Georgia: A Short History* (Chapel Hill: University of North Carolina Press, 1960), 16; E. Merton Coulter and Albert B. Saye, eds., *A List of the Early Settlers of Georgia* (Athens: University of Georgia Press, 1949); Davis, *Fledgling Province*, 31–32; Strickland, *Religion and the State in Georgia*, 115; *Colonial Records of Georgia*, 38:120; *Collections of the Georgia Historical Society* 3 (1873): 167.

29. *Charter of Georgia* (1732), reprinted in Thorpe, *Colonial Charters*, 773.

30. Thorpe, *Colonial Charters*, 765, 772–74.

31. Thorpe, *Colonial Charters*, 45–54; Strickland, *Religion and the State in Georgia*, 47–48, 53; *Colonial Records of Georgia*, 2:148–49, 200–202, 509–10.

32. *Colonial Records of Georgia*, 3; Strickland, *Religion and the State in Georgia*, 45, 51.

33. *Colonial Records of Georgia*, 19:394–96, 29:200, 31:25, 27, 3:51, 135, 141, 165.

34. *Colonial Records of Georgia*, 34:124, 161–62, 218.

35. Strickland, *Religion and the State in Georgia*, 112–13; *Colonial Records of Georgia*, 28:24, 26.

36. Compare Strickland, *Religion and the State in Georgia*, 70–71, 76, with *Colonial Records of Georgia*, 26:164, 6:255; Davis, *Fledgling Province*, 207–12; *Colonial Records of Georgia*, 2:379, 481, 507, 22:299.

37. Strickland, *Religion and the State in Georgia*, 69, 123. See also *Colonial Records of Georgia*, 34:296.

38. Strickland, *Religion and the State in Georgia*, 92–99, 176–79.

39. Davis, *Fledgling Province*, 236, 239–40; *Colonial Records of Georgia*, 34:69–70, 298–99, 483; Henry Melchior Muhlenberg, *The Journals of Henry Melchior Muhlenberg*, ed. Theodore G. Tappert and John W. Doberstein (Camden, ME: Picton Press, 1945), 669.

40. See George Whitefield, *The Works of the Reverend George Whitefield* (London: Edward & Charles Dilly, 1771), 3:475–79; Peter Y. Choi, *George Whitefield: Evangelist for God and Empire* (Grand Rapids, MI: Eerdman's, 2018), 194–232.

41. Whitefield, *Works of Whitefield*, 3:481–82.

42. Long, "Religious Revivalism," 206–7; *Georgia Gazette*, January 31, 1770.

43. *Colonial Records of Georgia*, 2:523–25.

44. W. Keith Kavenaugh, ed., "Transfer of the Government of Georgia from a President and Assistants to a Royal Governor and Council, October 13, 1754," *Foundations of Colonial America: A Documentary History* (New York: Chelsea House, 1973), 3:1835–36, 1839. See also *Colonial Records of Georgia*, 7:183.

45. Kavenaugh, "Transfer of the Government," 1838. See, for example, *Colonial Records of Georgia*, 34:66, 295.

46. "Estate of Lucretia Triboudite, Feb. 27, 1770," in *Inventories of Estates*, book F, reel 40/33, 448–50 (Georgia Department of Archives and History); Zubly, letter, Savannah, July 11, 1773, 214, 216; *Colonial Records of Georgia*, 7:12–13, 15, 335–36.

47. *Colonial Records of Georgia*, 18:158–59, 16:111, 126; William L. Grant and James Munro, eds., *Acts of the Privy Council of England, Colonial Series* (London: HMSO, 1908–12), 4:407–8.

48. *Colonial Records of Georgia*, 7:183, 293, 388, 588, 749, 8:111; Strickland, *Religion and the State in Georgia*, 124.

49. *Colonial Records of Georgia*, 13:66. See also 16:55, 62, 65.

50. *Colonial Records of Georgia*, 13:156–57, 159, 16:180–81.

51. "Unsigned Letter in Favor of Ottolenghe, Without Date, Read in Committee (Jan. 15, 1759)," *SPG Archives*, series C, AM.8, #1 (Misc. Docs. Ga., 1758–84), microformed on "Society for the Propagation of the Gospel in Foreign Parts, American Material in the Archives of the United Society for the Propagation of the Gospel" (Micro Methods, 1964), at reel C2, 2; *Colonial Records of Georgia*, 13:257–58.

52. "Ottolenghe Letter," January 15, 1759.

53. "Ottolenghe Letter," January 15, 1759, 4–5. The *Colonial Records* say that the assembly portion of the conference committee consisted of six members and not three (contrary to the report of Ottolenghe's letter). *Colonial Records of Georgia*, 13:294, 16:287.

54. *Colonial Records of Georgia*, 13:248, 260–61, 265–66, 270, 274, 277–78, 291–95, 298, 305, 16:266–68, 272–73, 277–79, 282–84, 287–88, 297; "Ottolenghe Letter," January 15, 1759.

55. *Colonial Records of Georgia*, 18:690.

56. Kavenaugh, "Transfer of the Government," 3:2309, 2311.

57. Kavenaugh, "Transfer of the Government," 3:2312, 2314.

58. Strickland, *Religion and the State in Georgia*, 112–13.

59. *Georgia Gazette*, July 12, 1769 (listing John Rae as vestryman); Muhlenberg, *Journals of Muhlenberg*, 625, 630, 644.

60. See *Colonial Records of Georgia*, 34:3ff (1754), 245ff (1758), 390ff (1761), 424ff (1761).

61. Davis, *Fledgling Province*, 204.

62. See act of March 27, 1759, *Foundations of Colonial America*, 3:2062–66.

63. *Foundations of Colonial America*, 3:2065 (Section XI) (emphasis added).

64. The law further stated that violators must be prosecuted within ten days after committing the offense and that a person was entitled to treble damages if he was prosecuted and acquitted. Act of March 4, 1762, *Foundations of Colonial America: A Documentary History*, 3:2314–17 (Section II).

65. To some extent, though, the disagreements were mostly a personal squabble between the two leading ministers of Savannah. For more on Zubly, see Joel A. Nichols, "A Man True to His Principles: John Joachim Zubly and Calvinism," *Journal of Church & State* 43, no. 2 (2001): 297.

66. Frink also brought a lawsuit against the captain of a ship for having his Presbyterian mate buried in Savannah according to the same protocol. Davis, *Fledgling Province*, 204, 224–25.

67. Davis, *Fledgling Province*, 226; *Georgia Gazette*, May 10, 1769.

68. *Georgia Gazette*, May 10, 1769. This was a historical error by the editor, as the provincial charter had been superseded by royal charter and only liberty of conscience was protected—not free exercise.

69. Randall M. Miller, ed., *"A Warm & Zealous Spirit": John J. Zubly and the American Revolution, a Selection of His Writings* (Macon, GA: Mercer University Press, 1982), 86–88.

70. Indeed, Frink proceeded with at least one other suit against a recently widowed female dissenter. Miller, *"Warm & Zealous Spirit,"* 90. There are no historical records indicating a court appearance on the matter.

71. Zubly, letter, Savannah, July 11, 1773, 217.

72. Zubly, letter, Savannah, July 11, 1773, 218.

73. Strickland, *Religion and the State in Georgia*, 123.

74. Franklin Bowditch Dexter, ed., *The Literary Diary of Ezra Stiles, D.D., L.L.D. President of Yale College* (New York: Charles Scribner's Sons, 1901), 544–46.

75. Coulter, *Georgia: A Short History*, 118–26.

76. This document is reproduced in Allen D. Candler, ed., *The Revolutionary Records of the State of Georgia* (Atlanta: Franklin-Turner, 1908), 1:274–77.

77. Coulter, *Georgia: A Short History*, 129.

78. Cynthia E. Browne, *State Constitutional Conventions from Independence to the Completion of the Present Union, 1776–1959, a Bibliography* (Westport, CT: Greenwood Press, 1973), 8:43.

79. Georgia Constitution of 1777, Article LVI, reprinted in Thorpe, *Colonial Charters*, 784.

80. Georgia Constitution of 1777, Article LVI, reprinted in Thorpe, *Colonial Charters*, 784.

81. Georgia Constitution of 1777, Article VI (1785), reprinted in Thorpe, *Colonial Charters*, 779.

82. Georgia Constitution of 1777, Article IX.

83. Georgia Constitution of 1777, Article LXII.

84. See, for example, Anson Phelps Stokes, *Church and State in the United States* (New York: Harper, 1950), 1:622–28.

85. Georgia Constitution of 1777, Article LIV, reprinted in Thorpe, *Colonial Charters*, 784.

86. Georgia Constitution of 1777, Article XIV ("Every person entitled to vote shall take the following oath or affirmation, if required, viz . . .").

87. Georgia Constitution of 1777, Article XIV.

88. Georgia Constitution of 1777, Article XXIV.

89. *Colonial Records of Georgia*, 19:96.

90. Marbury, *Georgia Digest* 356, 359–60.

91. Georgia Constitution of 1777, Article IV, reprinted in Thorpe, *Colonial Charters*.

92. Candler, *Revolutionary Records*, 141, 465; *Journal of the General Assembly, House* (January 21, 1784–August 15, 1786), 9, 11, 19, 53–54.

93. *Colonial Records of Georgia*, 19:395–98; *Journal of the General Assembly, House* (January 21, 1784–August 15, 1786), 161, 167, 227, 233, 248, 266.

94. *Colonial Records of Georgia*, 19:395.

95. Samuel Boykin, *History of the Baptist Denomination in Georgia* (Atlanta: Jas P. Harrison, 1881), 1:262, 263.

96. *Colonial Records of Georgia*, 19:397–98.

97. *Georgia Gazette*, January 26, 1786.

98. Georgia Constitution of 1798, Article IV, Section 10, reprinted in Thorpe, *Colonial Charters*, 791.

99. Walter McElreath, *A Treatise on the Constitution of Georgia* (Atlanta: Harrison, 1912), 86–87.

100. John N. Shaeffer, "Georgia's 1789 Constitution: Was It Adopted in Defiance of the Constitutional Amending Process?," *Georgia Historical Quarterly* 61, no. 4 (1977): 339; Coulter, *Georgia: A Short History*, 173; Fletcher M. Green, *Constitutional Development in the South Atlantic States, 1776–1860: A Study in the Evolution of Democracy* (Getzville, NY: William S. Hein, 2015), 127–28.

101. Browne, *State Constitutional Convention*, 43; Green, *South Atlantic States*, 127–28.

102. Georgia Constitution of 1789, Article I, Sections 1, 3, 7, 18; Article II; Article IV, Section 5, reprinted in Thorpe, *Colonial Charters*, 785.

103. Georgia Constitution of 1789, Article IV, Section 8.

104. See generally *Journal of the Convention of the State of Georgia, Convened at Louisville, on Monday, May 3d, 1795, for the Purpose of Taking into Consideration, the Alterations Necessary to be Made in the Existing Constitution of this State. To Which Are Added, Their Amendments to the Constitution* (Augusta: A. M'Millan, 1795) (hereafter cited as *1795 Journal*). The amendments are reprinted in Thorpe, *Colonial Charters*, 790, and they touch on such matters as length of service for a senator, method of gubernatorial election, date of meeting of the assembly, reapportionment of representation in the lower house, and place of the capital of the state (moved to Louisville).

105. *1795 Journal*, 4.

106. *1795 Journal*, 3–4. Silas Mercer's son Jesse Mercer was also a Baptist minister reputedly at this convention, though his name does not appear in the *Journal*. A "James Mercer" is mentioned in the *Journal*, but the relation of these men is unclear. See *1795 Journal*, 4. James Mercer may have been Jesse Mercer's uncle, though about his same age. See C. D. Mallary, *Memoirs of Elder Jesse Mercer* (New York: John Gray 1844), 18. Another source proclaims that three Baptist ministers (Silas Mercer, Benjamin Davis, and Thomas Polhill) were present at this 1795 convention. Boykin, *Baptist Denomination in Georgia*, 1:263.

107. *Journal of the Convention of the State of Georgia* (Louisville 1798), 2 (hereafter cited as *1798 Journal*).

108. Georgia Constitution of 1798, Article IV, Section 10.

109. *1798 Journal,* 21.

110. William Bacon Stevens, *A History of Georgia, from Its First Discovery by Europeans to the Adoption of the Present Constitution MDCCXCVII* (Philadelphia: E. H. Butler, 1859), 2:501. Stevens asserted that section of Constitution "securing religious liberty of conscience, in matters of religion, was written by the Rev. Jesse Mercer." See also *1798 Journal,* 28.

111. Boykin, *Baptist Denomination in Georgia,* 263; Spencer B. King Jr., *Baptist Leaders in Early Georgia Politics, 5 Viewpoints: Georgia Baptist History* 45 (1976). This would have meant that Baptists constituted 10 percent of the convention, or four times the percentage of Baptists in the overall state population at the time.

112. Georgia Constitution of 1798, Article I, Section 18–19; Article II, Section V.

113. When the section that excluded ministers of all denominations from the legislature came up for discussion, it was initially retained with no discussion in the journal. However, the following day, "Mr. [James] Simms" from Columbia County proposed to amend the exclusion by including practicing attorneys in the exclusion; the amendment passed. *1798 Journal,* 12. No further move was made on the offending section until the following day, when the convention struck the entire section from the constitution. *1798 Journal,* 16.

CHAPTER THIRTEEN

CHURCH AND STATE IN OHIO, 1785–1833

Michael S. Ariens

In late 1831, Alexis de Tocqueville traveled to Cincinnati, Ohio, and spoke with a number of lawyers and other leading citizens of the Queen City. Tocqueville spent a significant amount of time with a recent arrival, the Massachusetts-born lawyer Timothy Walker. Among the subjects of their conversations was the role of religion in Ohio, and by extension, the western region of the United States.[1] Tocqueville asked Walker whether religious ideas were "less powerful" than in the other parts of the Union. Walker thought there were many more open unbelievers and many more believers among ordinary persons in Ohio than elsewhere in America. Walker noted that religious believers found less religious instruction available to them, as "many of the settlements have neither church nor regular worship."[2] Itinerant ministers took on as much of the work done in other regions by paid, settled ministers as they could, though Walker concluded such ministers were of lesser quality than those in New England.[3]

From this conversation and many others, Tocqueville concluded "mores to be one of the great general causes responsible for the maintenance of a democratic republic in the United States." And religion, "though it did not give [Americans] the taste for liberty, it singularly facilitates their use thereof." Tocqueville believed that religion promoted virtue among citizens, and virtue was crucial to the maintenance of a republic. In asking whether a republic should thereby directly finance religion or if doing so only corrupted genuine religion, he found that a majority of Americans aligned behind the second proposition. Indeed, Tocqueville's inquiries of priests and other clergy led him to conclude that "the main reason for the quiet sway of religion over their country was the complete separation of church and state."[4]

I.

The disagreement over the necessity of direct government financing of religion dramatically played out in the formation and governance of the territory and later state of Ohio. After the 1783 Treaty of Paris was signed with Great Britain, the Confederation Congress sought to settle the numerous and various claims to the Northwest Territory.[5] Although the British ceded any claims to the Northwest Territory in the treaty, others made their own. The treaty ignored any possible claims of the various tribes of Native Americans. The indigenous tribes, in turn, believed the former belligerents lacked the authority to decide who controlled this land.[6] These claims were only slowly and partially resolved by the end of the eighteenth century, even though the Confederation Congress spoke in terms of the purchase of Indian lands in the Northwest Territory before settlement.[7] In addition to Native Americans, significant areas of what became the state of Ohio were claimed by Connecticut and Virginia, as well as by Massachusetts.[8] The Confederation Congress settled the claims of Virginia in 1784 and Connecticut in 1786, and in time Massachusetts also gave way.

On March 1, 1784, the day Virginia ceded its claim to Ohio land, Thomas Jefferson presented a report to the Confederation Congress outlining an approach to organizing this territory.[9] On April 23, 1784, Jefferson's initial plan or report was amended slightly and then adopted by the Confederation Congress.[10] It did not speak of religion.

A second bill more fully organizing the land of the Northwest Territory was offered to Congress by Jefferson in May 1784. Soon thereafter, Jefferson left the United States to serve as a diplomat in Europe.[11] His second bill was again presented to the Confederation Congress in March 1785, eventually becoming known as the Land Ordinance of 1785. The committee to which Jefferson's second bill was referred made amendments and reported back to Congress. The amended bill was largely the work of Rufus King of Massachusetts and William Grayson of Virginia.[12] On April 23, 1785, Congress began its review of the amended version. The bill included a provision reserving a section of land in each township "for the support of religion," the profits from which were to be applied "according to the will of the majority of male residents of full age."[13] This provision was an approximation of the Massachusetts system, in which a religious denomination (ordinarily Congregational) was established by a majority vote in a smaller geographic area called a parish. Each parish included glebe lands, publicly owned land the revenues from which were used by the government to support religion. Government support of religion in Massachusetts included paying the salary of the settled minister of the parish. Paying the minister's salary would also have occurred if Congress had adopted King and Grayson's bill.

The provision reserving a section of land to support religion was challenged in late April 1785. A motion was made by Charles Pinckney of South Carolina to amend the ordinance by deleting the phrase "for the support of religion" and replacing it with "for religious and charitable uses." This broadened the scope of the government's authority and diluted the concentration on religion. Rhode Island delegate William Ellery moved to amend Pinckney's amendment "by striking out the words 'religious and,' so that it read 'for charitable uses,'"[14] thus narrowing the government's reach and eliminating religion as an object of direct aid. Ellery's amendment failed.[15]

Ellery immediately made a second and similar motion. He proposed eliminating the entire paragraph reserving a section of each township for the support of religion.[16] The question to the body was oddly phrased: "shall the words moved to be struck out of the amendment, stand?" To vote "yes" was to keep the paragraph permitting aid to religion.

Delegates in the Confederation Congress voted by state. If a state was represented by just one voting delegate, its vote, though cast, did not count. Further, an evenly divided state's vote also did not count. For the question to be won, that is, for the paragraph reserving a section for the support of religion to remain in the bill, an absolute majority of seven states was required to vote in favor. New Jersey had no delegates present and thus no vote. Three other states had just one voting delegate. Two states were divided, which meant all of the remaining seven had to agree that the language reserving a section for the support of religion should remain in the bill. Two were opposed. Thus, the paragraph requiring the government of the territory to support religion was struck, even though just six of the twenty-three delegates voting supported the Ellery amendment.[17]

Congress adopted the Land Ordinance on May 20, 1785. The only reference to religion to survive debate is the reservation of lands adjoining several towns "for the sole use of the Christian Indians, who were formerly settled there, or the remains of that society."[18] Adoption of the "no-aid" position pleased James Madison. He wrote in late May to fellow Virginian James Monroe, one of the delegates who voted to delete the paragraph reserving lands for the support of religion: "It gives me much pleasure that, in the Latter Congress had expunged a clause contained in the first for setting apart a district of land in each Township for supporting the Religion of the majority of inhabitants. How a regulation . . . smelling so strongly of an antiquated Bigotry, could have received the countenance of a Committee is truly [a] matter of astonishment."[19] Madison then referenced the ongoing controversy over the pending Virginia bill taxing its citizens to pay teachers (that is, clergy) of the Christian religion. His successful *Memorial and Remonstrance* against that bill was anonymously published three weeks after he wrote Monroe.

The Land Ordinance of 1785 provided a start in encouraging the settlement of the Northwest Territory. But the Confederation Congress needed to adopt a framework of government for this vast land, which was eventually carved into the states of Michigan, Indiana, Illinois, Wisconsin, and northeastern Minnesota, in addition to Ohio. That framework is found in the Northwest Ordinance of 1787.

The Confederation Congress meeting in New York City adopted the Northwest Ordinance on July 13, 1787, as the delegates of the Constitutional Convention met in Philadelphia.[20] The adoption at that particular moment was related to the need of the debt-ridden confederated states to sell land to pay debts, including moneys owed veterans of the Continental Army.[21] The final push for adoption of the ordinance came from a Massachusetts-based venture called the Ohio Company.

The Ohio Company was formed in early 1786.[22] Two Revolutionary War officers, Rufus Putnam and Benjamin Tupper, soon joined by Manasseh Cutler, created the Ohio Company to purchase land to sell to veterans and others.[23] All three were important figures in the venture's success, but Cutler's work was crucial to the Ohio Company's initial progress in the Confederation Congress.

Cutler was neither a soldier nor an entrepreneur but a minister. He served as a Congregational minister in Hamilton (formerly Ipswich Hamlet), Massachusetts, for more than fifty years. He was also a substantial investor in the Ohio Company. In March 1787, Cutler, Putnam, and a Revolutionary War general, Samuel Parsons, were appointed company directors.[24] Parsons was sent in May 1787 to New York to request Congress to sell Northwest Territory land to the Ohio Company.[25] His effort failed. So too did the proposed ordinance. Cutler soon supplanted Parsons as the Ohio Company's representative. On July 6, 1787, Cutler presented his petition that Congress allow the treasury to contract with the company.[26] Cutler's petition was sent to committee, apparently the same committee that could not reach agreement with Parsons.[27] The committee almost immediately acted on Cutler's petition. Massachusetts congressional delegate Nathan Dane, a lawyer and a member of the committee preparing the bill, initially sent a copy of the draft to Cutler, who suggested several amendments, which may have been incorporated into the committee's final version.[28]

On July 10, 1787, Cutler met with the Committee on Western Lands. This committee later recommended the Board of Treasury of the Congress begin negotiations with the Ohio Company. One condition imposed by Cutler was that Section No. 29 (of thirty-six equal-size sections in every six-square-mile township) be "given perpetually for the purposes of religion."[29] This reprised the system of glebes for land purchased by the Ohio Company, an approach earlier rejected in the 1785 Land Ordinance. The next morning, July 11, Congress read the Northwest Ordinance for the first time. A second reading was the next day, July 12, and the third reading and adoption followed on July 13.[30]

Cutler had left for Philadelphia on July 11 and returned to New York on July 18. He was apparently unaware that Congress had adopted the ordinance during his absence. Cutler received a copy of the adopted bill on July 19. About the version approved by Congress, Cutler wrote, "It is in a degree new modeled. The amendments I proposed have all been made except one, and that is better qualified."[31] Congress permitted the Board of Treasury to negotiate with the Ohio Company, and on October 27, 1787, after hard bargaining by Cutler, a contract was signed for the sale of land in what became southeastern Ohio.[32]

The Northwest Ordinance of 1787 contains three references to religion. The initial part of the Ordinance had fourteen sections creating a government. Section 13 offers a justification for the territorial government's existence: "And for extending the fundamental principles of civil and religious liberty, which form the basis whereon these republics, their laws and constitutions, are erected; to fix and establish those principles as the basis of all laws, constitutions, and governments, which forever hereafter shall be formed in the said territory."[33]

The fourteen sections framing the territorial government are followed by six articles. Article I guarantees to the residents religious liberty: "No person, demeaning himself in a peaceable and orderly manner, shall ever be molested on account of his mode of worship, or religious sentiments, in the said territory."[34]

The third and most-quoted provision of the Northwest Ordinance concerning religion is Article III. It was the subject of considerable debate in the Confederation Congress and was twice amended between the first reading on July 11 and adoption on July 13. As presented by the committee to Congress,

Article III begins, "Institutions for the promotion of religion and morality, schools and the means of education shall forever be encouraged, and all persons while young shall be taught some useful Occupation." During the July 12 debate, Congress amended this provision in Article III to read, "Religion, morality, schools and the means of education shall forever be encouraged." In the course of the final debate on July 13, Article III was again amended. As adopted by Congress, it declared: "Religion, Morality and knowledge being necessary to good government and the happiness of mankind, Schools and the means of education shall forever be encouraged."[35] The provision makes encouraging schools and other means of education a duty of the government. Religion as well as morality and knowledge are acknowledged to be foundations of good government and happiness of the people. It did not, however, require local citizens to pay taxes for the support of religion or ministers of religion. It did not require the territorial governments to reserve sections of land for the financial support of religion.

The inclusion of Article III in the Northwest Ordinance is also a halfway proposition in light of its predecessor, the 1785 Land Ordinance. The 1787 Ordinance declares that religion and morality are necessary to good government; the 1785 ordinance had no such language. As amended between July 11 and July 13, the reshaping of Article III demonstrates divergent views in the Confederation Congress concerning government support for religion. The adopted text explicitly ties religion and morality to good government but stops there. Most Americans, in thinking about government, agreed on this point. More specific interpretations that would have government directly supporting religion were avoided, as they led to disagreement and dissension. Still, later in life Manasseh Cutler claimed credit for the language linking religion, morality, and knowledge to republican government. In doing so, "he was acting for associates, friends and neighbors who would not embark in the enterprise unless these principles were unalterably fixed."[36]

II.

Although the Ordinance did not require reservation of land for the support of religion, the October 27, 1787, contract with the Ohio Company did.[37] The contract for purchase of the land between the Confederation Congress and John Cleves Symmes (called the Symmes Purchase or the Miami Purchase) in southwestern Ohio, in which Cincinnati is located, also reserved Section 29 land for the support of religion.[38] No other sales contract for the purchase from the federal government includes this reservation, including the contract with the Connecticut Congregationalists who purchased the Western

Reserve in northeastern Ohio.[39] In the land purchased by the Ohio Company and in the later purchase by Symmes, the reservation of what Ohio called ministerial lands or Section 29 lands remained in existence in some respects for more than a century and a half.[40]

Although the Confederation Congress agreed to sell 1.5 million acres to the Ohio Company, the company eventually purchased 750,000 acres of land (later totaling 918,883 acres), in what is called the First Purchase.[41] Each six-square-mile township was divided into thirty-six equal sections, and Section 29 land was reserved for support of religion. Section 16 land was reserved for support of schools.[42] Well before the time President George Washington issued a patent for the sale of this land in 1792, the First Congress had readopted the Northwest Ordinance.[43] A Second Purchase of 214,285 acres was issued by Washington on the same day in 1792.[44] Symmes requested 1 million acres. In 1794, when Washington signed the patent, the Symmes entity received only 248,250 acres.[45]

Together the Ohio Company and Symmes Purchases constituted slightly more than 4 percent of Ohio. The contracts reserving ministerial lands for the support of religion would have a greater impact than the sale of these relatively modest parcels suggest.

Ohio's census population in 1800 was about 45,000. The territorial governor was a Federalist, Arthur St. Clair,[46] as had been the situation since the government was formed in 1787. In the 1800 presidential election, Democratic-Republican Thomas Jefferson defeated incumbent Federalist John Adams.[47] Jefferson's victory energized the Democratic-Republican Party in Ohio. A year after his inauguration, Jefferson signed an Enabling Act inviting Ohioans to organize and become the seventeenth state.[48]

In October 1802, voters elected "26 Republicans, 7 Federalists and 2 doubtful" as delegates to the Ohio Constitutional Convention.[49] Ten were originally from Virginia, seven from Pennsylvania, and five from Maryland. "[O]nly a handful were from New England," one of whom was Judge Ephraim Cutler, Manassah's son. Five delegates were "prominent church leaders,"[50] and many were lawyers. The delegates completed their work in less than a month. A journal was kept and some votes were recorded, but no record of debates exists.[51]

The Ohio Constitution of 1802 reflects some of the ideas found in state constitutions of the late 1770s, particularly with regard to the diminution of executive power and increase in legislative power. It is also reminiscent of those constitutions in the manner in which it privileges religion. The final form of the Ohio Constitution also suggests the division of the delegates. For example, slavery was constitutionally prohibited, but this was a difficult and contentious issue for the delegates. This was so even though Jefferson's plan for the Northwest Territory was to outlaw slavery. The settling of Ohio by emigrants from New England and Pennsylvania as well as Virginia and other southern states may have fueled some of the controversies.

Two provisions concerning religion are found in the 1802 Constitution. Both are in Article VIII, which consists of twenty-eight rights. No votes are recorded on either provision. Ephraim Cutler wrote in his journal that the convention delegates "appeared to look to me . . . to fill up the balance of the eighth article; and I prepared and introduced all that part which relates to slavery, religion, and schools or education."[52] The first provision on religion is Article VIII, Section 3:

> That all men have a natural and indefeasible right to worship Almighty God according to the dictates of their conscience; that no human authority can, in any case whatever, control or interfere with the rights of conscience; that no man shall be compelled to attend, erect, or support any place of worship, or to maintain any ministry, against his consent; and that no preference shall ever be given by law to any religious society or mode of worship; and no religious test shall be required as a qualification to any office of trust or profit. But religion, morality, and knowledge being essentially necessary to the good government and the happiness of mankind, schools, and the means of instruction shall forever be encouraged by legislative provision, not inconsistent with the rights of conscience.[53]

The first four clauses of Section 3 repeat nearly verbatim language found in the 1790 Pennsylvania Constitution,[54] the 1792 Kentucky Constitution,[55] and the 1796 Tennessee Constitution,[56] transposing only the second and third clauses. This is not surprising, given that Ohio bordered two of these states and all three states had promulgated recent constitutions. The Ohio delegates included unchanged (or modestly altered) a number of other provisions of the bill of rights from the three states.[57]

Section 3 emphasizes individual conscience, using the word in each of the first two clauses of the section and noting the requirement in the third clause of a person's "consent" to attend or support any place of worship. In the fifth clause, Ohio joined Kentucky, Tennessee, and the federal Constitution in banning a religious test for any office of trust or profit.[58] This "no religious test" provision was not, however, the majority view at the time. Pennsylvania had modified but not abolished its religious test in its 1790 Constitution,[59] and Massachusetts required officeholders to possess a belief in Christianity and "a firm persuasion of its truth."[60]

The fourth clause, again identical to the Pennsylvania, Kentucky, and Tennessee Constitutions, imposes a restraint on government preferences with regard to religion. Ohio declared that "no preference shall ever be given by law to any religious society or mode of worship." This constraint was originally from colonial New England–based Congregationalists, who feared the government's imposition of "modes of worship" and "articles of faith." Congregationalist ministers believed that, if the Church of England was allowed to impose articles of faith and "particular modes of worship," it would be a type of established church that ought to be forbidden.[61]

The second sentence in Section 3 largely quotes Article III of the Northwest Ordinance. The difference is one of emphasis. The sentence in Section 3 assumes schools serve as the primary channel linking virtuous citizens and good government. Religion, morality, and knowledge are "essentially necessary" to republican government. To prevent decay and corruption, schools would inculcate that virtue essentially necessary for maintaining good government. The closing words of Section 3 caution both the schools and the legislature to be mindful of the essential roles of "religion, morality, and knowledge," but not so as to transgress individual conscience.

The second provision on religion in the Ohio Constitution of 1802 is found in Article VIII, Section 26. It declares: "The laws shall be passed by the legislature which shall secure to each and every denomination of religious societies in each surveyed township, which now is or may hereafter be formed in the State, and equal participation, according to their number of adherents, of the profits arising from the land granted by Congress for the support of religion, agreeably to the ordinance or act of Congress making the appropriation."[62] Section 26 is unique in state constitutions, yet it has rarely been discussed.[63] The section does not disestablish but directly connects religion and the state. Section 26 applies only to the land contracts Congress made with the Ohio Company and with Symmes. It assumes the existence of denominations made up of religious societies, that is, local churches, as well as the possible formation of new denominations. It disburses any profits from the Section 26 lands by proportional membership in each of the churches in the township.

The first settlers on Ohio Company land were from New England. They began arriving in the spring of 1788 and founded Marietta, Ohio's first postordinance settlement. The Ohio Company intended "from the first to establish churches and schools in the new settlement."[64] By that summer,

Marietta residents heard Calvinist preachers Daniel Breck and, in his only visit to Ohio, Manasseh Cutler.[65] Within a year of Marietta's settlement, Cutler wrote a letter introducing a Calvinist minister to its residents.[66] That preacher, Daniel Story, soon arrived.[67] In 1796 Marietta's First Congregational Church was founded, and Story was ordained as its minister in 1798.[68]

III.

Ohio's duty in Article VIII, Section 3, to protect liberty of religious conscience did not give persons license to behave as they desired. For example, the Ohio Legislature in 1805 banned work and play on Sunday, as well as actions that would "interrupt, molest or disturb, any religious society or any member thereof, when meeting or met together for the purpose of worship." The law also criminalized the utterance of someone fourteen or older who "shall profanely curse, damn or swear, by the name of God, Jesus Christ or the Holy Ghost."[69] For over thirty years, the Ohio General Assembly regularly readopted the crime of blasphemy.[70] The Sunday closing law was amended a decade later by exempting those "who conscientiously do observe the seventh day of the week as the Sabbath."[71]

Sunday closing laws were common in the states in the early nineteenth century.[72] So too were laws making crimes of blasphemy and profanity.[73] What was uncommon were the efforts by the Ohio Legislature to manage the system of government-funded religion in the lands settled through the Ohio Company and Symmes Purchases. Even before statehood, the legislature adopted laws providing for the public support of religion in those lands. That continued during much of the first third of the nineteenth century.

The Ohio territorial legislature first met in September 1799. Less than two months later, it adopted a law allowing Marietta freeholders to lay a tax for the support of religion on those occupying Section 26 land.[74] It did so because settlers had unknowingly built part of Marietta on Section 26 land.[75] In its second session in November 1800, the legislature created a Board of Trustees to manage ministerial lands in Washington County, in which Marietta was located.[76] The board, whose members included Ephraim Cutler, was given the authority to lease the land and to use the revenues to support religion. The act required that three-quarters of the income be paid to the "teachers of piety, religion, and morality" of the subsequently formed religious societies and one-quarter reserved for building "houses of worship."[77]

The Board of Trustees immediately began surveying the land and setting rents.[78] Spurred by the legislation, in early March 1801 the First Religious Society (that is, church) in Marietta was formally organized. The First

Religious Society was the successor of the First Congregational Church of Marietta. Article 3 of the society's bylaws declared it "shall determine, by a majority vote, what public teacher or teachers of Piety, Religion, and Morality they will employ." The voters unsurprisingly chose Daniel Story, the ordained Congregational minister of the First Religious Society. Story's election as the "public Teacher [that is, clergy] of Piety, Religion, and Morality" was reaffirmed at the next annual election of the First Religious Society in April 1802.[79]

The delegates to the Ohio Constitutional Convention met in Chillicothe in November 1802. By then a system of township-based government support in Ohio Company land for teachers of the piety, morality, and religion (that is, clergy) was enshrined in territorial law. If Ephraim Cutler's declaration in his journal that he filled up the constitutional provisions concerning "slavery, religion, and schools or education" is true, it makes clear that Article VIII, Section 26 was intended in part to recognize a system already in place, one with which Cutler was intimately involved.

By the spring 1803 annual meeting of the Marietta Society, a division between Congregationalists and Presbyterians led the latter to request the Society equally support two teachers, Story and Presbyterian Stephen Linsley.[80] It did so. The following year, dissatisfied Presbyterians formally left the First Religious Society to form the Second Religious Society. Section 26 of the Ohio Constitution required the income from the rents on ministerial lands be divided proportionally between the two churches, which the trustees did.

Historian Scott Britton has examined the public records of early Marietta. He found that ministerial land revenues totaling $550 were apportioned to five religious societies in 1807.[81] The First Religious Society sent to the "trustees for Leasing Lands granted for Religious purposes, etc.," a signed list of "Subscribers residing in Marietta and in Township #2, of the 8th Range, [who] do hearby [sic] Certify that we belong to the first religious Society in Said town of Marietta."[82] Twenty-eight men signed the list, which was inaccurately recorded as totaling twenty-six. As found by Britton, the record of 1807 revenue distributions shows amounts given by the trustees to the First, Second, Fourth, Union, and Religious Meeting House Societies. All of these religious organizations were either Congregational or Presbyterian. The Second, Fourth, and Union Societies were all formed between 1804 and 1806. The records also indicate that, despite the longer existence of the First Religious Society of Marietta, its membership was such that its proportionate funding in 1807 was less than that received by all but one other society.[83] Yet only the First survived; the other four societies receiving funds in 1807 all dissolved no later than 1818. Pursuant to the command of Section 26, they "received dividends from the Ministerial Fund until [they dissolved]."[84]

Two other religious groups existed in Marietta in the early nineteenth century. One was the Halcyon Church, led by Abel M. Sargent.[85] Sargent apparently did not request moneys from the ministerial land revenues. In addition, Methodists organized a preaching circuit and first visited Marietta in 1804.[86] Neither the itinerant Methodist preachers nor laity embracing Methodism appear to have requested funding from the ministerial lands. The settled, community-based system of distributing land rents in early Ohio history ill-fitted the idealistic and emotive nature of the Second Great Awakening. This system was also ill-adapted to the proliferation of Protestant denominations, of differing views regarding the relationship of church and state, and any rapid shifts in membership.

Peter Cartwright, a twenty-one-year-old Methodist deacon, was assigned to the Marietta circuit in 1807. The circuit was an area of about "three hundred miles round."[87] Cartwright states in his autobiography that he met Sargent in Marietta. Sargent claimed to speak with angels, saw visions, and "proclaimed himself the millennial messenger." Cartwright alleged the "Presbyterian and Congregational ministers were afraid of him."[88] He was given use of the Congregational Academy to preach and "gave battle to the Halcyons." After his success against Sargent, Deacon Cartwright wrote that he had been "treated with great respect by the Congregational minister and his people," but was asked to preach in its academy no more. Cartwright requested one final opportunity and, when given it, attacked Calvinism. The result was some new followers of Methodism and, according to Cartwright, "a name among the living."[89]

Early Ohio legislatures regularly adopted laws on the leasing of school and ministerial lands, collection of rents, and disbursement of revenues.[90] Meeting in 1805, the legislature adopted a law requiring the formation in Washington County of a corporate entity to oversee the leasing of ministerial lands.[91] If a disagreement arose concerning disbursement of ministerial land moneys, the act permitted the aggrieved to appeal to the court of common pleas, which made a final determination and distributed the funds.[92] The law implies a proliferation of religious organizations in early Ohio and an interest in resolving such issues at the level of a local court of general jurisdiction. The same legislature gave the trustees of school lands in the Symmes Purchase the duty of administering the leases of Section 29 lands, which the trustees were required to let at the same price as the school land.[93] In 1806 the Ohio Legislature clarified the law regarding the peculiarity of the Ohio Company and Symmes lands and installed in statutory law what had been understood in light of contract, custom, and a few modest acts of the legislature. The law explicitly condoned the leasing of ministerial lands, the income of which was used for the support of religion in both the Ohio Company and the Symmes land.[94]

On February 4, 1807, the Ohio Legislature adopted a bill authorizing the First Religious Society of Marietta to incorporate.[95] This allowed the church to sue and be sued, to buy or sell property, to enter into contracts, and to exist in perpetuity. Section 3 of the act declared the society was lawfully permitted to take the "proportion of rents arising from any lands given or granted by the United States for religious purposes," as long as the annual income did "not exceed the sum of three thousand dollars." Another legislative condition was that the revenue be held in trust "for the purpose of defraying the expenses incident to their religious worship, to the support of schools[,] and affording such relief to the poor as their funds may from time to time allow, and for no other purpose."[96] The distribution of $550 in 1807 was significantly less than the $3,000 statutory limit.

The system of support of religion through land rents continued, but its efficacy soon dissipated. The general assembly adopted an act making it possible for leaseholders of ministerial and school lands to surrender their leases or, if they so choose, to renew "on the same conditions."[97] The duration of the leases was often ninety-nine years, with static lease amounts. With inflation, of course, the real value of the rents received decreased. In the event of deflation, the person renting the land could return it without penalty.

The legislature offered incentives to reduce dependence by religious organizations on land rents. In December 1824, the Ohio Legislature granted religious societies title to all lands "not exceeding twenty acres" that had been previously held in trust for religious societies, as long as that land had a "meeting house, burying ground or residence for their preacher."[98] In addition, the government moved away from an overbearing regulation of religious societies by granting them authority to elect trustees in a manner they desired. When incorporating the First Religious Society of Marietta, the legislature had required the dating of voting (the first Monday of every April), the number of trustees (at least three and no more than seven), and the composition of corporate officers (such as treasurer), by a majority vote of members.

In a private act by the 1837 Ohio Legislature, the First Religious Society's corporate charter was amended. The act set the rule of voting membership and authorized the Society to assess "an annual tax on the pews in the meeting-house," as long as that tax was not less than one dollar and no more than three dollars per year.[99] Eventually, this funding by ministerial lands, part of the "relic of the old parish system of New England," was "superseded by the legal incorporation of the church itself."[100]

Just four years prior, in 1833, Congress had adopted a law authorizing Ohio to sell "all or any part of the lands heretofore reserved and appropriated by Congress for the support of religion with the Ohio Company's and John Cleeves [*sic*] Symmes purchases."[101] The statute contained a proviso that any money obtained from these sales was to be placed "in some productive fund; the proceeds of which shall be for ever annually applied, under the direction of said legislature, for the support of religion within the several townships for which said lands were originally reserved and set apart, and for no other use or purpose whatsoever." Thus, Ohio continued to have a duty to support religion in a small part of the state, using money obtained from the sale of the Section 26 lands. It does not appear that anyone challenged this system on Establishment Clause grounds.

This proviso requiring income from the invested proceeds of the sales of ministerial lands be used for religious purposes may have been the catalyst for an important provision in Ohio's 1851 Constitution. Though the 1851 Constitution eliminated Section 26, Ohio continued to recognize a duty to support religion. New Article VI, Section 1, required that the principal from the sale or other disposition of school or ministerial lands be "entrusted to this state for educational or religious purposes" and that "the income arising therefrom, shall be faithfully applied to the specific objects of the original grants, or appropriations."[102] Thus, consistent with Congress's 1833 mandate, income from the sale of ministerial lands was to support religion, and the principal was to be indefinitely maintained. This remained Ohio law until 1968, when voters amended Article VI, Section 1.

The 1968 constitutional amendment permitted the Ohio Legislature to use or dispose of the principal for the support of education and religion.[103] The amendment corresponded by half with a 1968 act of Congress that declared that the "proceeds from the sale of such lands [shall be used] for educational purposes."[104] Accordingly, Ohio was no longer permitted to use proceeds from the sale of ministerial lands for the support of religion.

Article I, Section 7, the religious liberty provision in Ohio's 1851 Constitution and still in effect, is remarkably similar to its predecessor, Article VIII, Section 2. Section 7 was expanded to make nonbelievers competent witnesses, though this did not "dispense with oaths and affirmations." Section 7 also included an amended version of the original statement on the relation of religion, morality, and government: "Religion, morality, and knowledge, however, being essential to good government, it shall be the duty of the general assembly to pass suitable laws to protect every religious denomination in the peaceable enjoyment of its own mode of public worship, and to encourage schools and the means of instruction."[105] This updated proclamation again indicated the instrumental value of religion and morality in fostering republican government, as well as the state's continued belief in the importance of education. It newly acknowledged the state's duty to protect "every religious denomination" to hold worship services in peace.

IV.

Ohio presents a unique challenge to historians assessing the history of law and religion in America. Two areas of the state were organized around the proposition that republican government needed a religious and moral people to succeed, and to ensure such success a state had a duty to financially support religion, including the salaries of public teachers (that is, clergy) of the Christian religion. For more than a century and a half after Massachusetts became the last state to abolish such a system of established religion, the rents from government lands in the Ohio Company and Symmes Purchases were applied to the support of select Protestant churches.

NOTES

1. George Wilson Pierson, *Tocqueville in America* (1938; reprint, Baltimore: Johns Hopkins University Press, 1996), 563–64. On Walker, see Walter Theodore Hitchcock, *Timothy Walker, Antebellum Lawyer* (New York: Garland, 1990); and Alonzo H. Tuttle, "Walker, Timothy," in *Dictionary of American Biography* (New York: Scribner's Sons, 1958), 19:363 (hereinafter cited as *DAB*).

2. Pierson, *Tocqueville in America*, 564. On the religiousness of those in the French settlement in territorial Ohio, see R. Douglas Hurt, *The Ohio Frontier: Crucible of the Old Northwest, 1720–1830* (Bloomington: Indiana University Press, 1996), 195: "Instead of learning Catholicism, the settlers practiced 'infidelity, deism and other such abominations.'"

3. Pierson, *Tocqueville in America*, 564.

4. Alexis de Tocqueville, *Democracy in America*, ed. J. P. Mayer, trans. George Lawrence (New York: Doubleday, 1969), 287, 292, 295.

5. The Paris Peace Treaty of September 30, 1783, Article II, Avalon, Yale Law School, http://avalon.law.yale.edu/18th_century/paris.asp.

6. George W. Knepper, *The Official Ohio Lands Book* (Columbus: Auditor of State of Ohio, 2002), 4–5.

7. The treaty signed by the nascent United States with several Ohio Indian tribes at Fort McIntosh in 1785 was considered "a valid treaty" by the United States. The Shawnee and other tribes "refused to abide by a treaty negotiated under duress by minor tribal chiefs who lacked authority to speak for their people and for other tribes." Knepper, *Ohio Lands*, 4–5. The initial paragraph of the resolution of Congress declared that after the states ceded their claims to the Northwest Territory, "whensoever the same shall have been purchased from the Indian inhabitants," sale and settlement of those lands would begin. *March 1, 1784, Resolution on Western Territory Government*, in *Journals of the Continental Congress, 1774–1789*, ed. Worthington C. Ford et al. (Washington, DC, 1904–37), 26:118 (hereinafter cited as *JCC*).

8. Knepper, *Ohio Lands*, 7.

9. See George Knight, *History and Management of Land Grants for Education in the North West Territory* (New York: G. P. Putnam's Sons, 1885), 9. Other states eventually ceded their claims. Knepper, *Ohio Lands*, 7.

10. *JCC*, 26:275–79.

11. Jefferson was named Minister Plenipotentiary on May 7, 1784, and left for Europe on July 5. See Dumas Malone, *Jefferson the Virginian*, vol. 1 of *Jefferson and His Time* (Boston: Little, Brown, 1948), 419, 422. On the history of the Land Ordinance of 1785, see Knight, *History and Management*, 11–15; and Ronald A. Smith, "Freedom of Religion and the Land Ordinance of 1785," *Journal of Church & State* 24, no. 3 (1982): 589.

12. On Rufus King, see Claude M. Fuess, "King, Rufus," *DAB*, 10:398; on William Grayson, see Frank Edward Ross, "Grayson, William," *DAB*, 7:525.

13. *JCC*, 28:255, 293. The amended bill provided that one section be reserved for public schooling and that the section immediately northward of the school section be reserved for the support of religion. The profits from both sections were to be distributed based on majority vote. The reservation of a section for public schooling was adopted.

14. *JCC*, 293. Ellery was a Congregationalist, and his view of church and state was contrary to most Congregationalists then. He never explained his reasoning for his amendments, but it is possible that his understanding of the separatist views of Baptists in Rhode Island influenced his opinions. See Jared Sparks, *Lives of William Pinkney, William Ellery, and Cotton Mather* (Boston: Hilliard, Gray, 1836), 122–28.

15. *JCC*, 28:294.

16. The text Ellery moved to strike was "and the section immediately adjoining the same to the northward, for the support of religion, the profits arising therefrom in both instances, to be applied for ever according to the will of the majority of male residents of full age within the same." *JCC*, 28:294.

17. The Confederation Congress's procedure required the motion to be framed, "And on the question, shall the former part [reserving a section for the support of religion] stand?" The votes of Connecticut, South Carolina, and Georgia did not count because only one delegate from each state voted. See Articles of Confederation of 1781, Article V, "No state shall be represented in Congress by less than two, nor more than seven members," Philip B. Kurland and Ralph Lerner, eds., *The Founders' Constitution* (Chicago: University of Chicago Press, 1987; Indianapolis: Liberty

Fund, n.d.), 1:23. When the vote took place in May 1785, Maryland and Virginia, each with three, were the only states with more than two delegates present to vote.

18. *JCC*, 28:375, 381. The land was reserved to Moravian Christian Indians in compensation for the massacre of nearly one hundred Christian Indians on March 8, 1782, which explains the textual reference to providing for the "remains of the society." Knepper, *Ohio Lands*, 48–49.

19. Madison to James Monroe, May 29, 1785, in *The Writings of James Madison*, ed. Gaillard Hunt (New York: G. P. Putnam's Sons, 1902), 2:145.

20. "Adopted," *JCC*, 32:343; Northwest Ordinance of 1787, in *The Founders' Constitution*, ed. Kurland and Lerner, 1:27. For more detail, see Carl H. Esbeck, "Religion during the American Revolution and the Early Republic," in *Law and Religion: An Overview*, ed. Silvio Ferrari and Rinaldo Cristofori (London: Routledge, 2013), 1:73–74.

21. Congress offered land to officers and soldiers as partial compensation in 1776 (*JCC*, 5:763) and failed to pay its soldiers during the war's final stages. See Charles Rappleye, *Robert Morris: Financier of the American Revolution* (New York: Simon & Schuster, 2010), 351–77, noting the crisis regarding the inability to pay Continental army soldiers and the fear of insurrection in March 1783. "Sell land," Knight, *History and Management*, 10, 14, 16.

22. Caleb Atwater, "Art. II—Transactions of the Historical and Philosophical Society of Ohio," *North American Review* 53, no. 113 (1841): 323–25; William Parker Cutler and Julia Perkins Cutler, eds., *Life, Journals and Correspondence of Rev. Manasseh Cutler, LL.D.* (Cincinnati: Robert Clarke, 1888), 1:179.

23. On Cutler, see Claude M. Fuess, "Cutler, Manasseh," *DAB*, 5:12; and the Rev. C. E. Dickinson, "Rev. Manasseh Cutler," in *Papers of the Ohio Church History Society*, ed. Delavan L. Leonard8 (Oberlin: Ohio Church History Society, 1895), 6:7; and Cutler and Cutler, *Life*. On Putnam, see Beverley W. Bond Jr., "Putnam, Rufus," *DAB*, 15:284; on Tupper, see Randolph C. Townes, "Tupper, Benjamin," *DAB*, 18:52.

24. Cutler and Cutler, *Life*, 1:192.

25. Jay A. Barrett, *Evolution of the Ordinance of 1787* (New York: G. P. Putnam's Sons, 1891), 46.

26. Cutler and Cutler, *Life*, 1:228.

27. Two of the committee's members, James Madison and Rufus King, were absent, as both were then serving as delegates of the Constitutional Convention in Philadelphia.

28. On Dane, see H. W. Howard Knott, "Dane, Nathan," *DAB*, 5:63; and Charles Warren, *History of the Harvard Law School* (New York: Lewis, 1908), 1:413–32; "member," Barrett, *Evolution*, 48; Cutler and Cutler, *Life*, 1:243. See also William Frederick Poole, "Dr. Cutler and the Ordinance of 1787," *North American Review* 122, no. 251 (1876): 262, which claims Cutler was responsible for the provisions outlawing slavery and promoting religion and education; this article is reprinted as William Frederick Poole, *The Ordinance of 1787 and Dr. Manasseh Cutler as an Agent in Its Formation* (Cambridge: Welch, Bigelow, 1876); whether Poole's claims are accurate is unknown. McCullough credits Cutler with both the promotion of education and the banishment of slavery in the Ordinance. See David McCullough,

The Pioneers: The Heroic Story of the Settlers Who Brought the American Ideal West (New York: Simon & Schuster, 2019), 29–30.

29. *JCC,* 32:312.

30. Cutler and Cutler, *Life,* 1:242; *JCC,* 32:313. See also Beverley W. Bond Jr., *The Foundations of Ohio* (Columbus: Ohio State Archeological and Historical Society, 1941), 270, concluding Cutler left for Philadelphia because "he was not altogether pleased with these terms."

31. Cutler and Cutler, *Life,* 1:292. The exception added to the ordinance was the ban against continental taxation without representation. Cutler and Cutler, *Life,* 1:292.

32. "Allowed," *JCC,* 33:427–29; the general terms of the contract are found in *JCC,* 33:399–401. On Cutler's shrewd negotiating, including his original negotiating stance, see Bond, *The Foundations of Ohio,* 270–71; the contract is reprinted in *Records of the Original Proceedings of the Ohio Company,* Ohio Company Series (Marietta: Marietta Historical Commission, 1917), 1:29–37.

33. Northwest Ordinance, Article 13, Kurland and Lerner, *The Founders' Constitution,* 1:28.

34. Northwest Ordinance, Article 13, Kurland and Lerner, *The Founders' Constitution,* 1:28. Article I uses the verb "molested," which is also found in Article II of the Massachusetts Constitution. See Massachusetts Constitution, Article II, Kurland and Lerner, *The Founders' Constitution,* 1:11. "Molest" is not used in any other state constitution at that time. Early dictionaries defined "molest" as "To disturb; to trouble; to vex." Samuel Johnson, *A Dictionary of the English Language* (London: W. Strahan, 1755; New York: AMS Press, 1967). It is also defined as "to trouble; to disturb; to render uneasy." Noah Webster, *A Dictionary of the American Language* (New York: S. Converse, 1828).

35. *JCC,* 32:318, 340.

36. Cutler and Cutler, *Life,* 1:344. McCullough ignores this declaration, instead concluding that the Northwest Ordinance was intended to provide "absolute freedom of religion." McCullough, *Pioneers,* 12. McCullough does not mention the existence of Section 29 lands reserved for religious purposes.

37. *Records of the Original Proceedings of the Ohio Company,* 1:32–33. The same provision is found in the contract with John Cleves Symmes, Knight, *History and Management,* 18.

38. Symmes's father was a minister who left New York for New Jersey after a theological dispute in the flush of the Great Awakening. Betty Kamuf, "The Life of John Cleves Symmes," Cincinnati.com: The Enquirer, July 20, 2016, www.cincinnati.com. Symmes was largely raised in New Jersey, which had no history of reserving land for the support of religion. Other than mimicking the contract of the Ohio Company, why Symmes included a Section 29 reservation for the support of religion is unknown.

39. See Beverley W. Bond Jr., *The Civilization of the Old Northwest* (New York: Macmillan, 1934), 14, noting that the Connecticut Congregationalists "brought with them the usual support for public education and religion, although, strange

to say, there were no public reserves for these purposes in the original plans of settlement."

40. See "An act to amend the Act of February 1, 1826," Public Law 90-304, 82 Stat. 120, 120–21 (1968), § 2, May 13, 1968, amending Act of February 2, 1833 (4 Stat. 138), "that the Legislature of the State of Ohio may sell all or any part of the lands heretofore reserved and appropriated by Congress for the support of religion with the Ohio Company and John Cleves Symmes' purchase in the State of Ohio and may use the proceeds from the sale of such lands for educational purposes, as the Legislature of the State of Ohio in its discretion shall deem appropriate."

41. Knepper, *Ohio Lands*, 27–28.

42. Sections 8, 11, and 26 were reserved for later sale by Congress.

43. The Northwest Ordinance was readopted, without change, relatively early in the first session of the First Federal Congress. See Act to Provide for the Government of the Territory Northwest of the River Ohio, 1 Stat. 50 (Aug. 7, 1789).

44. A third area of land, consisting of one hundred thousand acres and known as the Donation Tract, was at the northern edge of the Ohio Company land and was intended to serve as a buffer between white settlers and Native American tribes. As suggested by its name, any white male who would settle there was given, without charge, a one-hundred-acre plot. This land was not subject to a Section 29 reserve. Knepper, *Ohio Lands*, 30. See also Lessee of Coombs and Ewing v. Lane, 4 Ohio St. 112 (Ohio 1854), which discusses the history of the Donation Tract lands, including Congress's effort in 1818 to sell public land subject to the exception of school (but not religion) lands.

45. Knepper, *Ohio Lands*, 31.

46. On St. Clair, see Randolph C. Townes, "St. Clair, Arthur," in *DAB* 16:293.

47. See Edward J. Larson, *A Magnificent Catastrophe: The Tumultuous Election of 1800, America's First Presidential Campaign* (New York: Free Press, 2007); and John Ferling, *Adams v. Jefferson: The Tumultuous Election of 1800* (New York: Oxford University Press, 2004).

48. The Enabling Act for Ohio of April 30, 1802, in *The Federal and State Constitutions, Colonial Charters, and other Organic Laws of the United States*, ed. Benjamin Perley Poore (Washington, DC: Government Printing Office, 1877), 2:1453.

49. Alfred Byron Sears, *Thomas Worthington: Father of Ohio Statehood* (Columbus: Ohio State University Press, 1958), 94, quoting Thomas Worthington's diary, October 31, 1802.

50. "Delegates," in *The Ohio State Constitution*, by Steven H. Steinglass and Gino J. Scarselli (New York: Oxford University Press, 2011), 14–15. On Ephraim Cutler, see Sears, *Thomas Worthington*, 102–6; and more fully in Julia Perkins Cutler, ed., *Life and Times of Ephraim Cutler, Prepared from His Journals and Correspondence* (Cincinnati: Robert Clarke, 1890); "leaders," Randolph Chandler Downes, *Frontier Ohio, 1788–1803*, Ohio Historical Collection (Columbus: Ohio State Archaeological and Historical Society, 1935), 99.

51. "First Constitutional Convention Convened November 1, 1802," *Ohio Archaeological & Historical Society* (Columbus: Fred J. Heer, 1897), 5:80.

52. Cutler, *Life and Times*, 77.

53. Poore, *Federal and State*, 2:1461–62.

54. Pennsylvania Constitution of 1790, Article IX, Section 3, in *Federal and State*, ed. Poore, 2:1554.

55. Kentucky Constitution of 1792, Article XII, [Section 3], in *Federal and State*, ed. Poore, 1:654. This is repeated verbatim in the 1799 Kentucky Constitution. See Kentucky Constitution of 1799, Article X, Section 3, in *Federal and State*, ed. Poore, 1:666.

56. Tennessee Constitution of 1796, Article XI, Section 3, in *Federal and State*, ed. Poore, 2:1673–74.

57. See Pennsylvania Constitution of 1790, Article IX, Section 7, in *Federal and State*, ed. Poore, 2:1554; Kentucky Constitution of 1792, Article XII, [Section 7], in *Federal and State*, ed. Poore, 1:654–55; Tennessee Constitution of 1796, Article XI, Section 19, in *Federal and State*, ed. Poore, 2:1674; and Ohio Constitution of 1802, Article VIII, Section 6, in *Federal and State*, ed. Poore, 2:1462, all ensuring that "the printing-presses shall be open and free to every citizen."

58. Kentucky Constitution of 1792, Article VII, in *Federal and State*, ed. Poore, 1:653; Tennessee Constitution. of 1796, Article XI, Section 4, in *Federal and State*, ed. Poore, 2:1462; U.S. Constitution, Article VI, Section 3, clause 2.

59. Pennsylvania's 1776 Constitution required legislators to believe in "God, the creator, and the governor of the universe" and in the "divine inspiration of the Old and New Testaments." Pennsylvania Constitution of 1776, *Plan and Frame of Government*, Section 10, in Poore, *Federal and State*, 2:1543. Its 1790 Constitution allowed any person "who acknowledges the being of a God and a future state of rewards and punishments" to hold public office, Pennsylvania Constitution of 1790, Article IX, Section 4, in *Federal and State*, ed. 2:1554.

60. Massachusetts Constitution of 1780, chap. 6, Article I, in *The Founders' Constitution*, ed. Kurland and Lerner, 1:21.

61. Thomas J. Curry, *The First Freedoms: Church and State in America to the Passage of the First Amendment* (New York: Oxford University Press, 1986), 116, 117.

62. Poore, *Federal and State*, 2:1463.

63. It is noted in Anson Phelps Stokes, *Church and State in the United States* (New York: Harper & Brothers, 1950), 1:481.

64. Cornelius E. Dickinson, "History of Congregationalism in Ohio before 1852," *Papers of the Ohio Church History Society* (Oberlin: Ohio Church Society, 1896), 7:34; Anselm T. Nye, "The Marietta Conference," *Papers of the Ohio Church History Society* (Oberlin: Ohio Church Society, 1892), 3:100–101. On Marietta's settlement, see Bond, *The Foundations of Ohio*, 279–90.

65. Dickinson, "History of Congregationalism," 7:35; Cutler and Cutler, *Life*, 1:344–45, 413–19; Bond, *The Foundations of Ohio*, 285.

66. Cutler and Cutler, *Life*, 1:435 (printing letter to Putnam introducing Daniel Story, a "Preacher"). On Story, see William Warren Sweet, *Religion on the American Frontier* (1931; reprint, New York: Henry Holt, 1964), 3:71. Story was the uncle of Supreme Court justice Joseph Story, who wrote in support of the idea that, as

properly understood, Christianity was a part of the common law. See Michael S. Ariens and Robert A. Destro, *Religious Liberty in a Pluralistic Society*, 2nd ed. (Durham, NC: Carolina Academic Press, 2002), 142; and Joseph Story's opinion in *Vidal v. Girard's Executors*, 2 How. (43 U.S.) 127 (1844).

67. Dickinson, "History of Congregationalism," 7:35; Cutler and Cutler, *Life*, 1:435 (reprinting Cutler's letter introducing Story to Putnam). On Story's work, see Dickinson, "Rev. Manasseh Cutler," 6:83–86; and Nye, "Marietta Conference," 3:101–3.

68. C. E. Dickinson, "A History of the First Religious Society in Marietta," in *Papers of the Ohio Church History Society*, ed. Frank Hugh Foster, 1:78 (Oberlin: Ohio Church Society, 1890); Sweet, *Religion on Frontier*, 3:20.

69. Chap. XLIII, February 14, 1805, Third Ohio General Assembly, 1st sess., Acts of the State of Ohio (Chillicothe: N. Willis, 1805), 3:218, Sections 1, 2; see also chap. LV, February 9, 1809, "An act for the prevention of certain immoral practices," Seventh General Assembly, 1st sess., *Acts of the State of Ohio* (Chillicothe: J. S. Collins, 1809), 7:215, repealing and replacing earlier act. The same statute is printed as chap. CXXI, February 9, 1809, Eighth General Assembly, *Acts of the State of Ohio* (Chillicothe: J. S. Collins, 1809), 8:563. It appears that this latter listing is incorrect.

70. See "An act to amend the act entitled 'An act for the prevention of certain immoral practices,'" passed February 17, 1831, March 26, 1841, Thirty-Ninth General Assembly, *Acts of a General Nature of the State of Ohio* (Columbus: Samuel Medary, 1841), 39:33.

71. Chap. XLIII, February 8, 1815, 1st sess., Thirteenth Ohio General Assembly, *Acts of the State of Ohio* (Chillicothe: Nashee & Denny, 1814), 13:147, 148, Section 1.

72. See Ariens and Destro, *Religious Liberty*, 124–31.

73. See Ariens and Destro, *Religious Liberty*, 113–20, which discusses cases assessing blasphemy laws in the antebellum United States. See generally Leonard W. Levy, *Blasphemy: Verbal Offense Against the Sacred, from Moses to Salman Rushdie* (New York: Alfred A. Knopf, 1993).

74. Chap. XLII, December 19, 1799, 1st sess., First Ohio Territorial Legislature, *Laws of the Territory of the United States, North-West of the River Ohio* (Cincinnati: Carpenter & Findlay, 1800), 1:232.

75. The Seventh General Assembly remedied this difficulty in part by limiting the amount of rent a resident of Marietta paid. It created a maximum amount of nine dollars per acre paid to the Trustees for rent of Section 29 land. The law also gave lessees the right to lease that land for ninety-nine years, renewable forever. See chap. XXXV, February 20, 1809, "An Act supplementary to an act for leasing sections Nos. sixteen and twenty-nine, in fractional township, within the Ohio Company purchase," Seventh General Assembly, 1st sess., *Acts of the State of Ohio* (Chillicothe: J. S. Collins, 1809), 7:165.

76. Chap. III, 2nd sess., First Ohio Territorial Legislature, November 27, 1800 (Chillicothe: Winship & Willis, 1801), 8.

77. Section 12, Chap. III, 2nd sess., First Ohio Territorial Legislature, November 27, 1800, 15.

78. Cutler, *Life and Times*, 44–47.

79. Dickinson, "History of the First Religious Society," 1:80–81, 82.
80. Dickinson, "History of the First Religious Society," 1:83.
81. Scott Britton unpublished presentation (copy on file with author). My thanks to Mr. Britton for his archival research.
82. Washington County Archival Records, copied and reprinted by Scott A. Britton (copy on file with author).
83. The records are reprinted in Britton's presentations.
84. Dickinson, "History of the First Religious Society," 1:83–84. Dickinson indicates the Second Religious Society received ministerial land revenues until 1816. Britton slightly disagrees. He notes Section 29 revenues were received by the Second Religious Society until it dissolved in 1818. Britton states the Religious Meeting House Society, some of whose members had employed the Rev. Mr. Stephen Linsley, minister of the Second Religious Society, was dissolved in 1816. The First Religious Society claims it is the oldest Congregational church in the West.
85. W. P. Strickland, ed., *Autobiography of Peter Cartwright, The Backwoods Preacher* (New York: Carlton & Porter, 1857), 98, discussing Sargent's background as a Universalist minister and that Sargent "assumed the name of Halcyon Church, and proclaimed himself the millennial messenger"; Fawn M. Brodie, *No One Knows My History: The Life of Joseph Smith, the Mormon Prophet* (1945; reprint, New York: Alfred A. Knopf, 1957), 98, noting that Sargent "suffered eclipse in Marietta" when a convert, following Sargent's assertion that the sufficiently holy did not need food to survive, fasted for nine days and died.
86. Sweet, *Religion on Frontier*, 4:56 (noting creation of Muskingum Circuit).
87. Strickland, *Autobiography of Cartwright*, 98. On Cartwright, see Ernest Sutherland Bates, "Cartwright, Peter," in *DAB*, 3:546.
88. Strickland, *Autobiography of Cartwright*, 99. Cartwright does not name the ministers but is clearly referring to Story and Linsley.
89. Strickland, *Autobiography of Cartwright*, 100–101, 102.
90. In addition to those acts discussed in the text, see chap. XIX, Section 9, April 15, 1803, First Ohio General Assembly, *Acts of the State of Ohio* (Chillicothe: N. Willis, 1803), 1:61, 65, which required the lease terms on Section 29 of Symmes's land to be same as for Section 16 school land.
91. Chap. XXXV, February 21, 1805, Third Ohio General Assembly, *Acts of the State of Ohio* (Chillicothe: N. Willis, 1805), 3:200. This act was amended in 1810 to reduce the number of trustees from nine to three. See chap. XXXV, February 14, 1810, "An act, to amend the act entitled, An act authorizing the leasing of certain lands in the county of Washington, granted for religious purposes," Eighth General Assembly, *Acts of the State of Ohio* (Chillicothe: J. S. Collins, 1810), 8:115.
92. See chap. XXXV, February 21, 1805, Third Ohio General Assembly, *Acts of the State of Ohio* (Chillicothe: N. Willis, 1805), 3:205–6 (Section 12). The court of common pleas consisted of either three or four judges who sat together in deciding cases. See Ohio Constitution of 1802, Article III, Section 3, in *Federal and State*, ed. Poore, 2:1458. Britton notes one such lawsuit in 1818.

93. Chap. XII, April 15, 1803, "An Act, to provide for the leasing of certain lands therein named," Third Ohio General Assembly, *Acts of the State of Ohio* (Chillicothe: N. Willis, 1805), 3:325 (Section 9).

94. "An act, for leasing section number twenty-nine, granted for religious purposes," January 22, 1806, Fourth Ohio General Assembly, *Acts of the State of Ohio* (Chillicothe: T. G. Bradford and J. S. Collins, n.d.), 4:33.

95. Chap. XLIX, February 4, 1807, Fifth Ohio General Assembly, *Acts of the State of Ohio* (Chillicothe: Joseph S. Collins, 1807), 5:122. McCullough notes the church building, "an almost exact duplicate of the Hollis Street Congregational church in Boston" (*Pioneers*, 173), was completed in 1808, one of two churches built beginning in 1807.

96. Chap. XLIX, February 4, 1807, Fifth Ohio General Assembly, *Acts of the State of Ohio*, 5:123.

97. "An Act to authorize the trustees of section twenty nine in Columbia, Township, Hamilton county, to grant leases in certain cases therein named," December 31, 1832, 1st sess., Thirty-Second, General Assembly, *Acts of a Local Nature* (Columbus: David Smith, 1832), 31:14.

98. "An act securing to religious societies a perpetuity of title to lands and tenements, conveyed in trust for meeting houses, burying grounds or residence for preachers," January 3, 1825, Twenty-Third Ohio General Assembly, *Acts of a General Nature* (Columbus: P. H. Olmsted, 1825), 23:9.

99. "An Act to amend 'An act to incorporate the First Religious Society in Marietta,'" March 3, 1837, Thirty-Fifty General Assembly, *Acts of a Local Nature* (Columbus: James B. Gardiner, 1837), 35:128, 129.

100. Dickinson, "History of the First Religious Society," 1:95.

101. Act of February 20, 1833, chap. 42, 4 Stat. 618–19.

102. Ohio Constitution of 1851, Article VI, Section 1, in *Federal and State*, ed. Poore, 2:1472–73.

103. Article VI, Section 1 (amended July 1, 1968), Ohio Constitution, Ohio Legislature, www.legislature.ohio.gov/laws/ohio-constitution/section?const=6.01.

104. Public Law 90-304, 82 Stat. 120, May 13, 1968.

105. Poore, *Federal and State*, 2:1465–66. The preamble also referred to God: "We, the people of the State of Ohio, grateful to Almighty God for our freedom, to secure its blessing and promote our common welfare, do establish the Constitution" (1465).

CHAPTER FOURTEEN

DISESTABLISHMENT
IN THE LOUISIANA AND MISSOURI TERRITORIES

Kevin Pybas

WHEN THE UNITED States acquired the Louisiana Territory in 1803, Roman Catholicism had been the established religion for more than one hundred years. The establishment can be traced to April 9, 1682, and the conclusion of a successful expedition by Robert Cavelier, Sieur de la Salle, to find the mouth of the Mississippi River. La Salle claimed the river and the land over which its tributaries flowed for, and named it Louisiana after, the French monarch, King Louis XIV. In memorializing the claim, La Salle wrote that "as eldest son of the Church[,]" the king's "principal care" for the region was "to establish the Christian religion."[1]

The establishment was maintained through both French and Spanish rule. As defeat by the British in the French and Indian War became all but certain, France secretly ceded the territory to Spain in 1762, as both powers sought to counter British expansionism in North America. Spain initially hoped to forge a connection between the territory and its empire in Mexico to the southwest. However, the expense of doing so and the distance from Mexico proved to be formidable obstacles. Further lessening Spain's interest in the territory was the financial strain it experienced in the 1790s upon being drawn into, and suffering defeat in, the French Revolutionary Wars and the fact that in 1795 it entered into the Treaty of San Lorenzo, also known as Pickney's Treaty, with the United States, whereby it relinquished its claim to parts of present-day Alabama and Mississippi. In 1800 Spain retroceded the territory to France, now under the leadership of Napoleon Bonaparte. Bonaparte's interest in the territory was connected to French efforts to preserve control of Saint Domingue (Haiti), an important source of revenue for France over which it was slowly losing control.[2]

In early 1803, Bonaparte's interest in the territory waned as French rule over Saint Domingue was slipping away. Moreover, as war with Britain loomed, Bonaparte feared he could lose the Louisiana Territory to the British. After brief negotiations with American representatives, France agreed to sell the Louisiana Territory for $15 million. The treaty of sale was finalized on April 30, 1803, and ratified by the U.S. Senate on October 20, 1803. Although the Spanish retrocession occurred in the fall of 1800, by agreement Spain continued to govern it until November 30, 1803, when France assumed control in order to facilitate the formal transfer to the United Sates. This occurred on December 20, 1803, in New Orleans, the largest city in the territory and, since shortly after its founding in 1718, the seat of French and Spanish territorial authority.[3]

The New Orleans ceremony transferred the entire territory, but because of the vastness of the territory, a second ceremony was held in St. Louis, the location from which Upper Louisiana had been governed. The transfer was to have taken place on March 9, 1804, outside Government House, the headquarters of the Spanish lieutenant governor. Captain Amos Stoddard, the head of the United States Army in Upper Louisiana, was the American official charged with accepting the transfer from France. No French officials were on hand, but Stoddard had been authorized by the French to receive on France's behalf the transfer from Spain, which was accomplished on March 9. The population of St. Louis was around 1,000 and overwhelmingly French, and a significant portion of them turned out for the event. When the Spanish flag was lowered and the French flag raised, the crowd became very emotional and asked Stoddard to allow the Tricolor to fly one night. Stoddard, knowing that while St. Louisans were now U.S. citizens but their loyalty had yet to be won, wisely allowed the Tricolor to fly overnight. The next day, the Tricolor was lowered and the Stars and Stripes raised to the salute of guns and the cheers of American soldiers.[4]

As it happened, Meriwether Lewis and William Clark were in the area, making final preparations for their now legendary exploration of the Upper Louisiana Territory and the Pacific Northwest and were invited to attend the transfer ceremony. Lewis, in fact, was asked to and signed the formal transfer papers as an official witness for the United States. Their journey up the Missouri River got under way on May 14. Two days later, their party stopped for several days in St. Charles, a village of about 450 French inhabitants founded in 1769. Before departing, about 20 of the party asked to attend a final Mass, and all were entertained by local French families. Lewis and Clark recorded in their respective journals that the inhabitants were welcoming, convivial with one another, poor, and ill-housed; disparaged the vocation of farming; and were overly influenced by the local Catholic priest.[5]

I.

Because of financial difficulties caused by ongoing wars, from 1712 to 1720 France granted a series of private investors and companies the right to explore and settle Louisiana. The early mind-set of the establishment was perhaps best expressed in a 1717 royal decree granting management of the territory to the Company of the West. The relevant part reads:

> Since in the settling of the lands granted to the Company by these present letters, We look particularly to the glory of God, in procuring the salvation of the settlers, the Indians, the Savages, and the Negroes, whom we wished to be instructed in the true Religion, the said Company will be obliged to build at its expense the churches of the place of its plantations, as well as support the number of the approved churchmen that will be needed, whether in the office of pastor or some other as will be proper, there to preach the Holy Gospel, conduct divine service, and administer the Sacraments.

According to Mary Veronica Miceli, O.P., this clause marks the formal beginning "of an organized effort to establish the Church in Louisiana." Be that as it may, the Catholic Church was never well organized in the territory. No doubt the fact that the colony was so vast—ranging from the Mississippi River to the Rocky Mountains and from the Gulf Coast to Canada—and so sparsely populated helps explain this. Figures are hard to come by, but in 1795 the population of Lower Louisiana was roughly 36,000, including an indeterminate number of free blacks and nearly 20,000 slaves. Upper Louisiana was even more thinly populated. For example, a 1766 census indicates that the population of St. Louis, founded in 1764, was 332, of which 75 were slaves, and that St. Genevieve, which is two or more decades older than St. Louis, had a population of 547, including 228 slaves. Correspondingly, there were never many priests in the territory. In 1803, when control of the territory was formally transferred to the United States, there were only 26 priests in all of the colony, which was divided into twenty-one parishes. Within a decade, moreover, the number of priests had dwindled to 12, owing to the death of some and others leaving for Spain or Spanish-controlled territory so as to continue in the pay of the Spanish government.[6]

Further contributing to the ecclesiastical disorganization of the territory was that the church's affairs were managed from afar for most of the period of the establishment. According to Charles Edward O'Neill, S.J., "the planting of the Church is not complete until a resident bishop's see is established." Yet no diocese was established in the territory until 1793. In the ecclesiology of the church, upon La Salle claiming the territory for France, the French Crown made Louisiana Colony part of the Diocese of Quebec. After France ceded Louisiana to Spain in 1762, King Charles III of Spain, in 1771, placed Louisiana under the authority of the Diocese of Santiago de Cuba. Sixteen years later, Santiago became an archdiocese, at which time Louisiana became part of the Diocese of Havana. In 1793, pursuant to the direction of King Charles IV, the Diocese of Louisiana and the Floridas was formed, with New Orleans as the see city. The following year, Charles IV named Luis Peñalver y Cárdenas of Cuba the first bishop of the newly created diocese. He formally assumed his duties in New Orleans in July 1795 but left in 1801 upon being named archbishop of Guatemala. On July 20, 1801, Charles IV named Francisco Porro y Reinado to succeed Peñalver in New Orleans. However, after Reinado was formally consecrated a bishop in Rome but before he sailed for Louisiana, church authorities learned that Spain had retroceded the territory to France. He thus never took up the bishopric. Accordingly, throughout the 121-year rule of France and Spain, the church in Louisiana had a resident bishop for only 6 years.[7]

Well organized or not, attributes of the Catholic Church establishment included the French and Spanish Crowns paying priests' salaries and building churches. At the time of the transfer of the territory to the United States, priests were receiving up to forty dollars per month from the king of Spain. When Spain took over the colony in the 1760s, public officials were required to take an oath swearing "before God, on the Holy Cross and the Evangelists, to maintain and defend the mystery of the Immaculate Conception of Our Lady the Virgin Mary, and the royal jurisdiction [of Spain]." The establishment was also reflected in civil law. For example, the 1724 Royal Edict Regarding Slaves (the Black Code) required slave owners to, among other things, ensure their slaves received instruction in Catholicism and were baptized. Owing to religious indifference and a lack of priests, however, this requirement went unenforced.[8]

Spain officially assumed authority over the territory in 1766 with the arrival of its first territorial governor, Antonio de Ulloa. In 1772 Luis de Unzaga, the third Spanish governor, prepared a report for the bishop of Havana entitled "Religious Conditions in Louisiana." Unzaga intended the report to give a picture of religious life in the territory. Among other things, the report suggests the king of France had been lax in promoting Catholicism. He had "left the province in complete and absolute liberty. . . . The whole object of the government was to settle and develop [the territory]. . . . So long as a settler was active, diligent, and laborious, he was inconvenienced by no [religious demands]. Religious opinions were tolerated in order that disputes on such topics might not embarrass the development and progress of the settlement of the country." So appalled by the low state of faith and morals in the territory was Alejandro O'Reilly, the second Spanish governor, that when he took office in 1769 he announced punishments for individuals lacking in religious observance. The penalty for blasphemy against both Jesus and the Virgin Mary, for example, was to have one's tongue cut out and his property seized. A decree similar to the one issued by the king of France obligating slave owners to instruct their slaves in Catholicism was issued in 1789. James M. Woods notes, however, that there were still too few clergy to enforce such regulations, and because of the paucity of priests, "slave owners were often as ignorant of Catholicism as the slaves."[9]

Yet another feature of the establishment, first expressed in the 1717 royal decree noted above, was that the colony was open only to Catholic immigrants. Similarly, the Black Code regarded non-Catholic religious assemblies as "illicit and seditious councils" and prohibited them. While authorities in France may have wished to exclude from the colony all but Catholics, in Louisiana itself the policy was largely ignored. O'Neill estimates that in 1720s, when the code was issued, there were about twenty-three hundred people of European descent in the colony—about fifteen hundred civilians and eight hundred soldiers—of which about 10 percent were Protestant.[10]

The policy of excluding non-Catholics from the territory continued under Spanish rule, as did the practice of not enforcing it. Louis Houck notes that from about 1770 on, there was a steady trickle of Americans (Protestants) settling in present-day Missouri. To encourage this emigration by the hardworking Americans, who typically cleared land and began farms that in turn expanded the economy, Spanish law was modified in the late 1780s to officially allow Protestants to settle in the territory. They were even offered free land as an enticement, with the requirement, of which there was no enforcement, that their children be raised Catholic. Spanish officials sought population growth as a means to expand the economy and to check any British Canadian ambitions for the vast territory.[11]

Non-Catholic religious assemblies remained illegal, however, but the prohibition was not strictly enforced. One Methodist minister from Illinois, then part of the U.S. Northwest Territory, crossed the Mississippi every month during this period to conduct religious services for Protestants, all with the tacit approval of Spanish authorities. However, during this period in Lower Louisiana, a Baptist leader was arrested for conducting public worship services. After being threatened with banishment to Mexico to work in Spain's silver mines, the Baptist halted his open disobedience.[12]

II.

When the territory was formally transferred to the United States, the Catholic establishment quietly ended. The Spanish Crown ceased paying priests' salaries, and Spanish laws promoting the establishment became inoperative. Although the Catholic establishment passed uneventfully from the scene, adjusting to the new church-state framework of the Protestant nation to which the people of the territory, overwhelming French and Catholic, now belonged was not without some difficulty—for both Catholics and American civil authorities.

On March 26, 1804, President Jefferson signed into law the *Governance Act* for the Louisiana Territory, of which he, secretly, was the author. When news of the Louisiana Purchase reached America, Jefferson was heavily criticized for the acquisition, especially by Federalist Party politicians, on the grounds that the president lacked constitutional authority for the action and that he was a hypocrite betraying his professed commitments to limited government. Jefferson himself was initially doubtful of his constitutional authority, as evidenced by the fact that he drafted a constitutional amendment that would have made "Louisiana as ceded by France to the US [*sic*]" a part of the United States. However, by the fall of 1803, he became persuaded that the purchase was constitutional and, perhaps not coincidentally, saw that he had sufficient support in the Senate to gain ratification of the purchase treaty, so he dropped the idea. Worried about the difficulty of incorporating Louisiana Territory into the Union, Jefferson did not want its political organization left to Congress. Yet, stung by criticism of the purchase, he did not want it known that he had authored the *Governance Act*, which if known would have likely provoked further criticism. Jefferson thus relied on his close ally Senator John Breckenridge of Kentucky to introduce and shepherd the bill through the Senate, which he succeeded in doing without significant changes to Jefferson's draft. "In communicating [the plan of government] to you[,]" Jefferson wrote to Breckenridge, "I must do it in confidence that you will never let another person know that I have put pen to paper on the subject . . . because you know with what bloody teeth & fangs the federalists [*sic*] will attack any sentiment or principle known to come from me."[13]

The *Act* divided Louisiana into Orleans Territory, largely encompassing what would become the State of Louisiana, and the District of Louisiana, consisting of the rest of the territory. It empowered the president to appoint a territorial governor and thirteen-person legislative council to govern Orleans Territory and placed the District of Louisiana under the authority of the governor and officials of Indiana Territory. The governor of Orleans Territory was subject to confirmation by the U.S. Senate, but Jefferson had full authority in the appointment of the legislative council. The *Act* also guaranteed religious liberty to the people of both Orleans Territory and the District of Louisiana. Section 4 of the *Act*, on the power of the legislative council of Orleans Territory, states that "no law shall be valid which . . . shall lay any person under restraint, burthen, or disability, on account of his religious opinions, professions or worship; in all which he shall be free to maintain his own, and not burthened for those of another." Section 12 of the *Act* speaks to the powers the governor and judges of Indiana Territory had in the District of Louisiana and is substantively identical to Section 4, though it omits the word "burthen" and uses "profession" instead of "professions."[14]

When word reached Orleans Territory and the District of Louisiana about the substance of the *Act*, protest ensued in both regions. The people of both registered their complaints in lengthy memorials, written in New Orleans and St. Louis, which were received by Congress on December 31, 1804, and January 4, 1805, respectively. Both memorials objected to the Governance Act on multiple, though not identical, grounds. Broadly, both argued that the *Act* violated the equality principle of the Declaration of Independence and the Treaty of Cession itself, specifically Article III, which states that the "inhabitants of the ceded territory shall be incorporated in the Union of the United States and admitted as soon as possible according to the principles of the federal Constitution to the enjoyment of all these rights, advantages and immunities of citizens of the United States, and in the mean time they shall be maintained and protected in the free enjoyment of their liberty, property, and the Religion which they profess." Because the people of Orleans Territory and Louisiana District had no say in selecting the governing officials or in the laws they would live under, they argued that the *Act* denied them "rights, advantages, and immunities" of American citizenship due them under Article III. As the remonstrance from Orleans Territory put it, "[w]ithout any vote in the selection of our Legislature, without any check on our Executive, without any one incident of self-government, what valuable 'privilege' of citizenship is allowed us, what 'right' do we enjoy, of what 'immunity' can we boast, except, indeed, the degrading exemption from the cares of legislation, and the burden of public affairs?" Their complaint, in short, was that the U.S. government was treating them as subjects rather than citizens, thereby threatening their rights, especially property rights, in both slaves and land, vested under French and Spanish rule.[15] The *Territorial Act*, lacking self-determination for the new citizens of the territory, was thought flawed. Yet Jefferson was never criticized for this deficiency because his authorship was never disclosed.

Contributing to the unease over property rights was that the *Act* voided Spanish land grants made after October 1, 1800, the date of the Treaty of San Ildefonso, whereby Spain retroceded the territory to France unless, with several caveats, the grants were finalized prior to December 20, 1803, the date the United States formally took possession of the territory, and it prohibited the slave trade in Orleans Territory but generally allowed slave owners who were U.S. citizens moving into the territory to bring their slaves with them, yet was silent as to the status of slavery in the District of Louisiana. Notably, neither remonstrance raised issues of religious liberty. Perhaps they enjoyed broad religious freedom and the explicit protection of religious liberty in the act explains this. Or perhaps religion was less important to the men involved in producing the memorials than land and slaves.[16]

Among those in New Orleans anxious about their property rights were the Ursuline nuns, whose convent was established in New Orleans in 1727. Along with the convent, the nuns operated a school for young women and girls of all races, free and enslaved, an orphanage and a hospital. Additionally, by 1803 the Ursulines held title to about one thousand acres of land they leased to area planters that generated revenue for the convent. The "Remonstrance of the People of Louisiana" was addressed to Congress, but the mother superior of the convent, Therese de St. Xavier Farjon, appealed to President Jefferson in a letter dated June 13, 1804, asking him to communicate a supportive message to Congress. The nuns believe, she wrote, that "the treaty of Cession, and the sence [sic] of Justice which marks the character of the United States, would have secured to them the property they now possess," the original title of which would have been received from France, without cost, as the state church. But because their property was a "sacred deposit" entrusted to them, "they would fail in a duty they deem essential were they to ommit requesting" that Congress explicitly "confirm[]" the security of their property. This request, the mother superior added, was not born of a desire for "personal gratification or private agrandisement," but because the Ursulines were "bound by a solemn obligation to employ their revenue in charitable uses, & their time in the education of youth," it is for "the Public which they plead—it is the cause of the Orphan, of the helpless child of want, of the many who may be snatched from the paths of vice &

infamy" to "be trained up in the habits of virtue & religion to be happy and useful,—of society which will be spared the burthen of the indigent & the depredations of vice—of their country itself which cannot but acquire honor in fostering & protecting such beneficent purposes."[17]

Jefferson replied to the mother superior just one month later, on July 13, 1804, writing:

> I have received, holy sisters, the letter you have written me wherein you express anxiety for the property vested in your institution by the former governments of Louisiana. the [sic] principles of the constitution and government of the United states [sic] are a sure guarantee to you that it will be preserved to you sacred and inviolate, and that your institution will be permitted to govern itself according to it's [sic] own voluntary rules, without interference from the civil authority. whatever [sic] diversity of shade may appear in the religious opinions of our fellow citizens, the charitable objects of your institution cannot be indifferent to any; and it's [sic] furtherance of the wholesome purposes of society, by training up it's [sic] younger members in the way they should go, cannot fail to ensure it the patronage of the government it is under. be [sic] assured it will meet all the protection which my office can give it. I salute you, holy sisters, with friendship & respect.

Whereas the mother superior spoke of property rights, Jefferson's reply is more encompassing, affirming to the convent a broad right of self-governance and religious liberty.[18]

The broad nature of Jefferson's reply leads one to speculate that perhaps he used the opportunity of the nun's letter to calm fears about an incident that occurred sometime in the spring of 1804—the precise date is unknown—in a remote parish about 140 miles west of New Orleans. According to a letter dated May 29, 1804, from W. C. C. Claiborne, the governor of Orleans Territory, to James Madison, Jefferson's secretary of state, the civil commandant of the District of Attakapas, had "a few Sundays Since" shuttered the doors of the parish church in response to a conflict between two priests concerning who was the rightful leader of the congregation. In Claiborne's telling,

> the rival Priests appeared at the Church attended by their different partisans who were numerous and very much inflamed. Lieutenant Hopkins, the Civil Commandant of the District, apprehending that the public peace was endangered, took upon himself to Shut the Doors of the church and deny entrance to either party, until the matter was reported to me, and my instruction received.

This expedient preserved the public peace and was[,] I learn[ed,] very pleasing
to all parties. I have referred the affair to Revd. Mr. Welsh [*sic*], the Head of the
Catholic Church in Louisiana.

While Governor Claiborne was satisfied with the handling of the dispute,
Jefferson was not. Madison apparently passed on Claiborne's letter to Jefferson, for in a July 5, 1804, letter to Madison, Jefferson wrote that "it was an
error in our officer to shut the doors of the church, and in the Governor to
refer it to the Roman catholic head. The priests must settle their differences
in their own way, provided they commit no breach of the peace. If they break
the peace they should be arrested. On our principles all church-discipline is
voluntary; and never to be enforced by the public authority."[19]

There is no record indicating the Ursulines knew of the commandant's
intervention in the parish dispute, nor is it referenced in the "Remonstrance
of the People of Louisiana." But given that Claiborne reported the episode
to Reverend Walsh in New Orleans, it is conceivable that other Catholics in
New Orleans learned of it. In any event, Jefferson was aware of what happened in Attakapas, and only eight days before his letter to the mother superior had written to Madison that the commandant and Claiborne had erred.
So perhaps the Attakapas matter was on Jefferson's mind when he responded
to the Ursulines, prompting him to assure them not only of their property
rights but also of their right of self-governance "without interference from
the civil authority."

Claiborne confronted another conflict among Catholic priests about fourteen months after reporting the Attakapas incident to Madison. Although he
was not asked to intervene, his response was in line with Jefferson's earlier
guidance. On July 11, 1805, Father Walsh, the acting vicar general to whom
Claiborne had reported the Attakapas episode, wrote to Claiborne to apprise
him of developments in the schism that had developed in the Church of
St. Louis (now St. Louis Cathedral) in New Orleans. According to Walsh,
a "Refractory Monk, supported in his Apostacy by the fanaticism of a mis-
guided populace," was promoting "views equally dangerous to religion and
to Civil order." Walsh had sought to remove the priest from the pastorate of
the church in March 1805, but the priest, supported by the congregation,
defied Walsh's authority. Walsh asked Claiborne for no assistance, but said
that it was his "duty as an Ecclesiastic, and as a faithful Citizen," to inform
Claiborne that he suspected that the renegade priest, a Spaniard, was trying
to recruit Spanish priests from Havana to bolster him in his conflict with
Walsh (who was from Ireland).[20]

Claiborne's response the next day was two-edged. First, perhaps chastened by Jefferson's response to the Attakapas incident, he declared that church matters were not the business of civil authorities, "unless indeed the public peace should be broken or menaced, and then it becomes their duty to act." Walsh had written that the priest also threatened civic peace, so Claiborne asked for the name of the priest (his name was Père Antoine) and the names of his close supporters.[21]

By the fall of 1806, Claiborne had come to believe that Antoine was sowing dissension in New Orleans against the U.S. government. In an October 8, 1806, letter to Henry Dearborn, Jefferson's secretary of war, Claiborne wrote, "We have a Spanish Priest here who is a very dangerous Man; he rebelled against the superiors of his own Church, & even (I am persuaded) rebel [sic] against the Government whenever a fit occasion may serve. . . . This seditious Priest, is a Father Antoine . . . ; he is by some Citizens esteemed an accomplished hypocrite, has great influence with the People of Colour, and report says, embraces every opportunity to render them discontented under the American Government." Claiborne concluded his report by assuring Dearborn that "I shall watch [Antoine's] movements, and as the safety of the Country is paramount to every consideration, if his conduct should continue exceptionable, I shall send him off."[22]

Claiborne apparently thought he should do more than simply observe. Two days later, on October 10, 1806, in another letter to Dearborn, Claiborne reported that that morning he, the mayor of New Orleans, and a member of the territorial legislative council had, at Claiborne's request, met with Antoine, at which time "the Priest declared his innocence, and avowed his determination to support the Government, and to promote good order." Even so, Claiborne added that "he nevertheless thought it proper to administer to [Antoine] the oath of allegiance." Although Antoine continued in defiance of Walsh, Claiborne's intervention was aimed not at settling the ecclesiological dispute but toward ensuing Antoine's loyalty to the U.S. government.[23]

Because of the Catholic Church's requirement that separate political sovereignties require separate ecclesiastical jurisdictions, upon the transfer of the territory to the United States, the Diocese of Louisiana and the Floridas was divided. The Florida portion, still under the control of Spain, reverted back to the authority of Havana. The Diocese of Louisiana was placed under the authority of Bishop John Carroll of the Diocese of Baltimore, at the time the only diocese and bishop in the United States. When Father Walsh, the most senior Catholic in Orleans Territory, died on August 22, 1806, it fell to Carroll to appoint his replacement. Carroll was an American born in Maryland in 1735, educated in Catholic institutions in Europe, and the brother of Daniel Carroll, a signatory of the Articles of Confederation and the U.S. Constitution. Carroll was considering a French-born priest to replace Walsh but, sensitive to the difficulty the United States faced in integrating the French Catholic inhabitants of the Louisiana Territory into the Union, worried that Jefferson would object to a Frenchman filling such an important position.[24]

Carroll wrote to Madison on November 17, 1806, explaining that the difficulties presented by Père Antoine, the insubordinate priest, and the "disorders, wch. have grown up during the relaxed states of civil & ecclesiastical authority" called for particular skills and qualities of which few available priests in the United States had, asking:

> If a native of this Country, or one, who is not a Frenchman, tho well acquainted with the language, cannot be procured, would it be satisfactory to the Executive of the U.S. to recommend a native of France, who has long resided amongst us, and is desirous of continuing under this government? In the mean time [*sic*], as the only Clergyman in Louisiana, in any degree qualified to act with vigor & intelligence in restoring order in the Cat. Ch. is a French emigrant priest, far from any attachment to the present system of his country, may be be [*sic*] appointed to act as my Vicar, without the disapprobation of our Executive? I have many reasons to believe, that this person rejoices sincerely in the cessation of that Country to the U.S.

Madison replied to Carroll on November 20, 1806, by means of two letters, one an official reply and the other a private letter.[25]

In the official letter, Madison did not address the question Carroll had raised, stating that because the matter "is entirely ecclesiastical it is deemed most congenial with the scrupulous policy of the Constitution in guarding against a political interference with religious affairs, to decline the explanations which you have thought might enable you to accommodate the better, the execution of your trust, to the public advantage." Although Madison declined to answer directly, he left no doubt as to Jefferson's hopes, adding that the president has "perfect confidence in the purity of your views, and in the patriotism which will guide you, in the selection of ecclesiastical individuals, to such as combine with their professional merits, a due attachment to the independence, the Constitution and the prosperity of the United States." In the private letter, Madison referenced the official letter and notes that "the reason for declining" Carroll's inquiry "does not however forbid my saying in a private letter" that "no objection can lie against the use you propose to make of [the French-born priest]: and that in general it affords satisfaction to find you, as might well be presumed, so fully in disposition to admit into the stations for which you are to provide as little of alienage of any sort as will consist with the essential attention and duties of them." Carroll did not respond directly to Madison's letters, but his nephew Daniel Brent worked in the State Department under Madison. In a March 3, 1807, letter to Brent, the bishop conveyed assurance that if any priest under his "authority should ever betray dispositions, or countenance measures unfriendly to the Sovereignty of the United States; or if ever he should hold correspondence of a suspicious nature with a foreign nation, he shall be deprived of any commission from me and of the care of souls."[26]

III.

While there were strains between Catholic officials and civil authorities in Orleans Territory in the early years of American rule, nothing comparable arose in Louisiana District to the north. As of 1804, there were six parishes in Louisiana District, but not all had a resident priest. When Spain ceased paying priests' salaries, only one resident priest remained in the district, and the church fell into further decline. On March 3, 1805, Louisiana District was designated low-level territorial status with a residential governor and ruling council consisting of the governor and three judges. It was renamed the Territory of Louisiana, with St. Louis as the capital. Further adjustments to the territorial status were made on June 4, 1812, chief of which was the creation of a territorial elected house of representatives that shared legislative power with the governor and an appointed legislative council. To avoid confusion, the Territory of Louisiana was renamed Missouri Territory because Orleans Territory had recently become the State of Louisiana. That church-state relations were unremarkable in this region was likely because the Catholic Church was even more poorly organized there than in Orleans Territory, thereby giving little occasion for friction.[27]

The fortunes of the church began to turn in 1818 when Bishop William Louis Du Bourg took up residency in St. Louis. From 1812 to 1815, Du Bourg had been a senior administrator in New Orleans. While in Europe in 1815 recruiting priests for the diocese, Du Bourg was nominated and consecrated bishop of Louisiana, the first bishop of the diocese since the region became part of the United States. He returned to America in September 1817 but did not arrive in St. Louis until January 5, 1818. He lived in St. Louis for five and a half years, reconstituting the church in Missouri Territory on a new, solid trajectory. He then took up residence in New Orleans.[28]

IV.

On April 30, 1812—the ninth anniversary of the Louisiana Purchase— Orleans Territory became the State of Louisiana, the first state to enter the Union from the Louisiana Purchase. Its Constitution was written in New Orleans over a three-month period, from November 1811 to January 1812. Religion is addressed three times in the Constitution, but it does not explicitly protect religious liberty or prohibit the establishment of religion. Article II, Section 22, makes men who "exercise the functions of a Clergyman, Priest or Teacher of any religious persuasion, society or sect" ineligible for "the general assembly, or to any office of profit or trust" in the state. Article III, Section 6, is similar in that it makes any "minister of any religious society" ineligible for the office of governor. Article III, Section 22, exempts from the militia "those who belong to religious societies, whose tenets forbid them to carry arms" but requires them to "pay an equivalent for personal service."[29]

The absence of explicit religious freedom protection in the 1812 Constitution was addressed by the Louisiana Supreme Court in 1844 in the case of *The Wardens of the Church of St. Louis of New Orleans v. Antoine Blanc, Bishop of New Orleans*. The case involved the ongoing schism in the Church of St. Louis of New Orleans that began in 1805 when a priest, backed by the congregation, defied the bishop's attempt to transfer the priest. The facts of the case are lengthy, but the essence of the conflict was whether primary ecclesiastical authority over the parish belonged to the wardens (lay leaders) or the bishop. The Diocese of Louisiana was divided in 1826 into the Dioceses of New Orleans and St. Louis. Antoine Blanc became bishop of the Diocese of New Orleans in 1835 and began to resist the wardens in ways previous bishops had not, which ultimately led to the warden's lawsuit against Bishop Blanc for his purported interference in the affairs of the parish.[30]

The Louisiana Supreme Court rejected the wardens' claims against the bishop, holding that the reason the 1812 Constitution contained no explicit protection for religious freedom "was because it was thought unnecessary." This was because, the court reasoned, the protection for religious freedom in the Northwest Ordinance of 1787, which had been made applicable to Orleans Territory in the 1805 amendments to the 1804 *Governance Act*, carried into statehood. The first article of the Northwest Ordinance provides that "[n]o person, demeaning himself in a peaceable and orderly manner,

shall ever be molested on account of his mode of worship or religious sentiments, in the said territory." Reading this in conjunction with the preamble
to the ordinance, which states that the articles form a "compact between the
original States and the people and States in the said territory and forever
remain unalterable, unless by common consent," the state court concluded
that no alteration had been consented to, so religious freedom was protected
in Louisiana, even though the 1812 Constitution was silent on the matter.
The terms of the first article of the ordinance were interpreted to prevent a
state court from resolving a dispute concerning the internal governance of
the Catholic Church.[31]

V.

The religious liberty guarantee for the people of the District of Louisiana
in the 1804 *Governance Act*, noted above, was restated in virtually identical
terms in both the 1805 and the 1812 acts changing the territorial status and
name of the region. Missouri became the first state carved out of the Missouri Territory and was formally admitted to the Union in 1821. Its first Constitution was drafted in June and July 1820 in St. Louis. Like the three territorial
laws, it too contained a strong statement on religious liberty, declaring in
Article XIII, Section 4, that "all men have a natural and indefeasible right to
worship Almighty God according to the dictates of their own consciences;
that no man can be compelled to erect, support, or attend any place of worship, or to maintain any minister of the gospel, or teacher of religion; that no
human authority can control or interfere with the rights of conscience; that
no person can ever be hurt, molested, or restrained in his religious profession or sentiments, if he do not disturb others in their religious worship."[32]

Section 5 of the same article states that one's "religious opinions" did not
disqualify a person from public office. It indicated that the state would have
no established church, declaring that "no preference can ever be given by law
to any sect or mode of worship; and that no religious corporation can ever be
established." But Section 5 did not apply to active members of the clergy, as
Article III, Section 13, declared that "[n]o person while he continues to exercise the functions of a bishop, priest, clergyman, or teacher of any religious
persuasion, denomination, society, or sect, whatsoever, shall be eligible to
either house of the general assembly; nor shall be appointed to any office
of profit within the state, the office of justice of the peace excepted." Finally, Article XIII, Section 18, exempted from militia service those "religiously
scrupulous of bearing arms" but who nevertheless "may be compelled to pay
an equivalent for military service in such manner as shall be prescribed by

law" and declares that "no priest, preacher of the gospel, or teacher of any religious persuasion or sect, regularly ordained as such, be subject to militia duty, or compelled to bear arms." Though beyond the period of consideration of this study, the case of *State v. Ambs*, an 1854 decision of the Missouri Supreme Court, is the first published judicial interpretation of any of the above-noted clauses of the 1821 Missouri Constitution. The high court rejected a tavern owner's challenge to an 1835 Sunday-closing law that was said to violate Sections 4 and 5 of Article III.[33]

For President Jefferson, the challenge of integrating Louisiana Territory into the United States was akin to "incorporating [a] foreign nation[] into our union." The difficulties were numerous, but the end of the Catholic establishment was not one of them. Nor did the end of Spain's financial support lead to the ruin of Catholicism in Missouri and Louisiana. After an initial period of malaise, the fortunes of the church in both Missouri and Louisiana began to turn following the arrival of Bishop Du Bourg in 1818. The Catholic turnaround lends credence to Alexis de Tocqueville's argument, less than two decades later, that separating church and state in America benefited Catholicism by freeing priests from political concerns, thereby allowing them to focus on promoting Catholic beliefs.[34]

NOTES

1. Charles Edward O'Neill, *Church and State in French Colonial Louisiana: Policy and Politics to 1732* (New Haven, CT: Yale University Press, 1966), 12 (quoting and translating *Procès-Verbal*, April 9, 1682, a report prepared by La Salle).

2. Alfred E. Lemmon, "Spanish Louisiana: In the Service of God and His Most Catholic Majesty," in *Cross, Crozier, and Crucible: A Volume Celebrating the Bicentennial of a Catholic Diocese in Louisiana*, ed. Glenn R. Conrad (Lafayette, LA: Archdiocese of New Orleans in cooperation with the Center for Louisiana Studies, 1993), 16; Arthur P. Whitaker, "The Retrocession of Louisiana in Spanish Policy," *American Historical Review* 39, no. 3 (1934): 454–56.

3. William Foley, *A History of Missouri*, vol. 1, *1673–1820* (Columbia: University of Missouri Press, 1971), 70–71; Jon Kukla, *A Wilderness So Immense: The Louisiana Purchase and the Destiny of America* (New York: Alfred A. Knopf, 2003), 213–14, 254–58. The agreement between the United States and France comprised three separate documents, all of which were signed May 2, 1803, but which had been finalized April 30, 1803, the date that in America came to be most closely associated with the purchase. One document is the Treaty of Cession itself, while the others contain the specific terms of sale and address diplomatic relations between the two

countries. Peter J. Kastor, ed., *The Louisiana Purchase: Emergence of an American Nation* (Washington, DC: CQ Press, 2002), 142.

4. Stephen E. Ambrose, *Undaunted Courage* (New York: Simon & Schuster, 1996), 129–30; Duane G. Meyer, *The Heritage of Missouri*, 3rd ed. (St. Louis: River City, 1982), 106.

5. William E. Foley, *The Genesis of Missouri* (Columbia: University of Missouri Press, 1989), 139–40; Ambrose, *Undaunted Courage*, 138.

6. O'Neill, *Church and State*, 84–111, quote on 111 (citing "Lettres patentes en forme d'Edit portant l'établissement d'une Compagnie de Commerce, sous le nom de Compagnie d'Occident," Aug. 1717, printed Archives du Ministère des Affaires Etrangères [Paris], Mémoires et Documents, p. 18); Mary Veronica Miceli, O.P., "The Christianization of French Colonial Louisiana: A General View of Church and State in the Context of Eighteenth Century French Colonization and a Theory of Mission," *Southern Studies* 21, no. 4 (1982): 388; James M. Woods, *A History of the Catholic Church in the American South* (Gainesville: University Press of Florida, 2011), 192; Carl J. Ekberg and Sharon K. Person, *St. Louis Rising* (Urbana: University of Illinois Press, 2015), 228; Reverend Canon Thomas Hassett to Bishop John Carroll, December 23, 1803, in *The Life and Times of John Carroll*, by Peter Guilday (1922; reprint, Westminster, MD: Newman Press, 1954), 704–5; Annabelle M. Melville, "John Carroll and Louisiana, 1803–1805," *Catholic Historical Review* 64, no. 3 (1978): 435.

7. O'Neill, "A Bishop for Louisiana," in *Cross, Crozier, and Crucible*, 96–105.

8. Reverend Canon Thomas Hassett letter to Bishop Carroll, December 23, 1803, in *Life and Times of John Carroll*, by Guilday, 704–5; Roger Baudier, *The Catholic Church in Louisiana* (New Orleans: n.p., 1939), 179; Carl A. Brasseaux, "The Administration of Slave Regulations in French Louisiana, 1724–1766," *Louisiana History* 21, no. 2 (1980): 141–42, 148 (citing Black Code or Royal Edict Regarding Slaves, March 1724, Paris, Archives Nationales, Archives des Colonies, Series A [*Edits du Roi*], vol. 22, folios 119ff).

9. Louis Houck, *The Spanish Regime in Missouri: A Collection of Papers and Documents Relating to Upper Louisiana Principally within the Present Limits of Missouri during the Dominion of Spain* (Chicago: R. R. Donnelly & Sons, 1909), 1:114; Baudier, *Catholic Church in Louisiana*, 180 (no citation to original source), 206; Woods, *History of the Catholic Church*, 193.

10. O'Neill, *Church and State*, 113 (without a citation to the edict), 269–71 (quoting Archives de Colonies [Paris], B 43, 388–89), 281, 269 (citing Archives de Colonies [Paris], B 43, 388–89).

11. Louis Houck, *A History of Missouri* (Chicago: R. R. Donnelly & Sons, 1908), 2:73–74, 115; Gilbert C. Din, "The Immigration Policy of Governor Esteban Miró in Spanish Louisiana," *Southwestern Historical Quarterly* 73 no. 2 (1969): 155–75; Foley, *A History of Missouri*, 55.

12. Meyer, *The Heritage of Missouri*, 101–5; Christine Alice Croxall, "Holy Waters: Religious Contests and Commitments in the Mississippi River Valley, 1780–1830" (PhD diss., University of Delaware, 2016), 34–35.

13. James E. Scanlon, "A Sudden Conceit: Jefferson and the Louisiana Government Bill of 1804," *Louisiana History: The Journal of the Louisiana Historical Society* 9, no. 2 (1968): 139–62; Kastor, *Louisiana Purchase*, 190, 193; Thomas Jefferson to John Breckenridge, November 24, 1803, in *The Works of Thomas Jefferson*, ed. Paul Leicester Ford, 12 vols. (New York: G. P. Putnam's Sons, 1905), 10:51–52.

14. "An Act erecting Louisiana into two territories, and providing for the temporary government thereof," March 26, 1804, in *Organic Acts for the Territories of United States* (Washington, DC: Government Printing Office, 1900), 17, 18, 22.

15. Treaty between the United States of America and the French Republic, in *Louisiana Purchase*, ed. Kastor, 143; "Remonstrance of the People of Louisiana against the Political System Adopted by Congress for Them," in *American State Papers: Documents, Legislative, and Executive, of the Congress of the United States* (Washington, DC: Gales and Seaton, 1834), 1:396–400, 398. "The remonstrance and petition of the representatives elected by the freemen of their respective districts in the District of Louisiana" (401–4).

16. "An Act erecting Louisiana into two territories," 23–24. The U.S. government's efforts to sort out land titles in Missouri and Louisiana cannot be told here, but it was a process that took decades and multiple acts of Congress to complete. However, it does not appear that the U.S. government ever challenged title to lands belonging to Catholic churches or the Ursuline convent. Overviews of the complexity and process of reconciling land titles in Missouri and Louisiana are Lemont K. Richardson's three-part "Private Land Claims in Missouri," *Missouri Historical Review*, 56, nos. 2–4 (1956); and Harry L. Coles Jr., "The Confirmation of Foreign Land Titles in Louisiana," *Louisiana Historical Quarterly* 38, no. 4 (1955).

17. Henry Churchill Semple, S.J., *The Ursulines in New Orleans, 1727–1925* (New York: P. J. Kennedy & Sons, 1925), xi; *An Account of Louisiana; Being an Abstract of Documents, in the Offices of the Department of State, and the Treasury* (Philadelphia: William Duane, 1803), 34; Sr. Therese de St. Xavier Farjon to Thomas Jefferson, June 13, 1804, in *The Thomas Jefferson Papers, Series 1: General Correspondence, 1651–1827*, Library of Congress Manuscript Division, www.loc.gov/item/mtjbib013530/.

18. Thomas Jefferson to Sr. Therese de St. Xavier Farjon, July 13, 1804, in *Thomas Jefferson Papers*, www.loc.gov/item/mtjbib013625/.

19. W. C. C. Claiborne to James Madison, May 29, 1804, in *Official Letter Books of W. C. C. Claiborne, 1801–1816*, ed. Dunbar Rowland, 6 vols. (Jackson, MS: State Department of Archives and History, 1917), 2:170–71; Jefferson to Madison, July 5, 1804, in *The Republic of Letters: The Correspondence between Thomas Jefferson and James Madison, 1776–1826*, ed. James Morton Smith, 3 vols. (New York: W. W. Norton, 1995), 2:1328.

20. Patrick Walsh to Claiborne, July 11, 1805, in *Letter Books*, 3:121.

21. Claiborne to Walsh, July 12, 1805, in *Letter Books*, 3:123.

22. Claiborne to Henry Dearborn, October 8, 1806, *Letter Books*, 4:25.

23. Claiborne to Dearborn, October 10, 1806, *Letter Books*, 4:28.

24. Melville, "John Carroll and Louisiana," 411–12. On Carroll's commitment to republicanism, see Michael D. Breidenbach, "Conciliarism and the American Founding," *William and Mary Quarterly*, 3rd ser., 73, no. 3 (2016): 467–500.

25. Carroll to Madison, November 17, 1806, in *The John Carroll Papers*, ed. Thomas O'Brien Hanley, S.J., 3 vols. (Notre Dame, IN: University of Notre Dame Press, 1976), 2:535. Patrick Carey notes that the vicar general appointed by Carroll to restore order in New Orleans did not succeed because the laity rejected his authority because they had no role in his selection. Patrick W. Carey, *People, Priests, and Prelates: Ecclesiastical Democracy and the Tensions of Trusteeism* (Notre Dame, IN: University of Notre Dame Press, 1987), 242–43.

26. Madison to Carroll, November 20, 1806, in *John Carroll*, ed. Guilday, 708–9; Carroll to Daniel Brent, March 3, 1807, in *Carroll Papers*, 3:11.

27. *Guide to St. Louis Catholic Archdiocesan Parish Records*, rev. ed. (St. Louis: St. Louis County Library, 2015), 327; Croxall, "Holy Waters," 46; Foley, *A History of Missouri*, 184; "An Act further providing for the government of the district of Louisiana," March 3, 1805, in *Organic Acts*, 28; "An Act providing for the government of the territory of Missouri," June 4, 1812, in *Organic Acts*, 35–36.

28. O'Neill, "A Bishop for Louisiana," 106; Annabelle M. Melville, *Louis William DuBourg*, 2 vols. (Chicago: Loyola University Press, 1986), 1:337, 428, 2:689.

29. Louisiana Constitution or Form of Government for the State of Louisiana, in *Constitutions of the State of Louisiana*, ed. Benjamin Wall Dart (Indianapolis: Bobbs-Merrill, 1932), 499.

30. *The Wardens of the Church of St. Louis of New Orleans v. Antoine Blanc, Bishop of New Orleans*, in *Reports of Cases Argued and Determined in the Supreme Court of Louisiana* (1844), 13:55–60, 91.

31. *Wardens of the Church of St. Louis*, 87–88. "An Ordinance for the Government of the Territory of the United States North-West of the River Ohio," in *Organic Acts*, 5; "An Act Further Providing for the Government of the Territory of Orleans," in *Organic Acts*, 26.

32. Missouri Constitution of 1820, in *Missouri's Struggle for Statehood, 1804–1821*, by Floyd Calvin Shoemaker (Jefferson City, MO: Hugh Stephens, 1916), 347.

33. Shoemaker, *Missouri's Struggle for Statehood*, 348, 332, 349–50; *State v. Ambs*, 20 Mo. 214 (1854).

34. Thomas Jefferson to John C. Breckinridge, August 1, 1803, National Archives, https://founders.archives.gov/documents/Jefferson/01-41-02-0139; Alexis de Tocqueville, *Democracy in America*, trans. and ed., Harvey C. Mansfield and Delba Winthrop (1835; reprint, Chicago: University of Chicago Press, 2000), 275.

CHAPTER FIFTEEN

IN THE INTERESTS OF TRUE RELIGION
Disestablishment in Vermont

Shelby M. Balik

W HEN VERMONT BECAME the first New England state to end religious tax-ation in 1807, many fretted that it was standing on the precipice of spiritual ruin. Those who supported the move, wrote Congregationalist missionary Aaron Cleveland, were "infidels, Baptists, and nothingists" who aspired to "outlaw all religion." If they pursued their secular aims, no law protecting religious worship or public morality would be safe from repeal. "Even the observance of the Christian Sabbath stands on slippery ground," Cleveland fretted, "as it respects the Legislature of Vermont."[1] For many—particularly Congregationalists—publicly funded worship was the bedrock of a broader system that safeguarded a moral and ordered society. With religious taxa-tion came membership in a spiritual community (even for those who had not joined a church in full communion), along with the privileges and ob-ligations that membership entailed. Among the most important privileges was access to regular worship and the spiritual and moral edification that communal observance fostered. Among the important obligations was sub-mission to the community's moral standards, which in turn ensured public peace and virtue. Without public support for worship, would the finely bal-anced system of personal privileges and public obligations fall apart? Would the state simply become indifferent to religion, or even turn openly hostile? And if the state should abandon its guardianship of religious authority, what would be the fate of morality and order?

The answer, which few could have predicted at the time, was that Vermont would do nothing of the sort. Although the state ended compulsory religious taxation, it did not sever ties with churches or religion more broadly. Rath-er, Vermont retained old laws and enacted new ones that not only provid-ed support for worship, but actively promoted religious institutions. While Vermont showed no de jure preference for Congregationalism, it continued to privilege de facto the town-church model of religious organization and unified community that was inextricably associated with the establishment.

The Revolutionary War and its rhetoric of liberty stirred debate over the proper scope of religious toleration. Americans grappled with the implications of disestablishment in the nascent republic, where many thought that churches alone were able to compel moral behavior.[2] As the story is usually told, revolutionary principles won out and disestablishment proceeded apace. Studies of church and state in revolutionary America posit disestablishment either as the end of a long struggle for religious liberty or as the beginning of a new era of freedom of conscience. Either way, as Nathan Hatch put it, the language of establishment or dissent became "anachronistic" in the United States after 1800.[3] The exception was New England, where debates over church-state ties raged through the early nineteenth century. There, many continued to argue that ending state support for churches would result in a religious free-for-all, or—worse—secularization. But here too, the revolutionary rhetoric of liberty and equality discredited any system that required individuals to finance churches that contradicted their own beliefs, and so disestablishment prevailed in the end.

Or did it? Vermont's example shows that the story is more complicated than widely believed. Even as state lawmakers celebrated religious liberty, they hesitated to sever church-state ties outright. There was no decisive moment of disestablishment. Rather, disestablishment progressed in a contested struggle that took decades. Adoption of statutes ending religious taxation convinced citizens that they had achieved religious liberty, but inequalities persisted. Instead of cutting ties between church and state, Vermont merely shifted them as the relationship between religious and civil institutions assumed new forms.

I.

Vermont was admitted to the Union on March 14, 1791, as the fourteenth state and the first New England state beside Rhode Island to reject a constitutional religious establishment. That Vermont's Constitution failed to explicitly link church and state did not mean such a relationship did not exist. Indeed, an establishment persisted for thirty years after the territory first organized in 1777. Establishment in Vermont, as in most of New England, rested upon the long-standing Puritan assumption that neighbors should pray together. Its organizing basis, before and after disestablishment, was the parish system. The system designated two types of religious entities: territorial parishes (the original town churches, which included everyone in the town by default) and poll parishes (which separated from the town and included only members who joined). Territorial parishes existed as geographic and spatial units. The law defined such a parish by the land it occupied. Poll parishes existed only as legal entities, without inherent claims to property or people. State laws and the Constitution granted territorial parishes legal privileges that poll parishes did not enjoy, including the rights to ministerial land and meetinghouses.

Although Vermont's establishment resembled that of other New England states, its political heritage was different.[4] As elsewhere in New England, Vermont supported the ideal of a covenanted community by requiring each town to supply its own minister and support public worship.[5] Dissenters could gather in poll parishes or seek exemption from ministerial taxes, but they relied on the goodwill of town leaders, who might or might not enforce the law and respect exemptions. Vermont was more socially and religiously diverse than its neighbors, however, and this diversity challenged the town-church ideal. Settlement in Vermont started in the mid-eighteenth century as migrants arrived from southern New England, New York, and elsewhere. They included the prosperous holders of the Wentworth grants in the Connecticut Valley, along with those of humbler origins who arrived after the American Revolution seeking to escape poverty and debt. Congregationalists were (and, through the early nineteenth century, remained) the most populous denomination, but they had a late start. Bennington organized the first town church in 1763, and the pace of church building picked up slowly thereafter.[6] The Regular Baptists started just as slowly but eventually became Vermont's fastest-growing denomination.[7] Soon, Methodists, Universalists, and Freewill Baptists also found footholds in Vermont.[8] By the 1810s, these denominations had joined the Regular Baptists as Vermont's leading dissenters.

The resulting religious landscape resembled less a neat division of town parishes than a jumble of congregations, upstart sects, and the unchurched. Nathan Perkins observed during a 1789 missionary tour that many of the settlements he encountered were full of "a miserable set of inhabitants—no religion, Rhode Island haters of religion—baptists, quakers, and some presbyterians." He estimated that "about 1/2 would be glad to support public worship and the gospel ministry," but that "the rest would choose to have no Sabbath—no ministers—no religion—no heaven—no hell—no morality."[9] As a Congregationalist missionary, Perkins might, out of prejudice, have lumped too many dissenters with the unchurched, but there was no mistaking that Vermont lacked a churchgoing culture. By 1791 only about one-fourth of Vermont towns had organized churches.[10] This deficiency resulted less from spiritual apathy than from towns lacking enough people of any single denomination to support a church. Nonetheless, the scarcity of churches gave pious Vermonters cause for concern.

Through early constitutions and statutes, Vermont's lawmakers sought to give churches a secure foundation by promoting public piety along with religious liberty. Accordingly, they framed establishment in flexible and ambiguous terms. Each of Vermont's early constitutions (successively ratified in 1777, 1787, and 1793) included a provision in the Declaration of Rights that protected freedom of conscience. These articles identified the "natural and unalienable right" to worship according to one's faith and freed citizens from compulsion to "attend any religious worship, or erect or support any place of worship, or maintain any minister" not of their own persuasion. The constitutions further protected Protestants—and after 1787 all persons—from violations of their civil rights due to religious belief and practice. The 1787 version, however, retained a Protestant test for members of the state legislature. The Constitution of 1793 eliminated all religious tests.[11]

Since the constitutions were silent on the overlapping questions of parish formation and religious taxation, legislators sought to clarify these matters through a series of Parish and Ministry Acts. In 1783, declaring that Christian worship and education were "of the greatest Importance to the Community at large, as well as to Individuals," the general assembly laid out how towns would form new parishes, build meetinghouses, hire preachers, and collect religious taxes, as well as how dissenters could obtain exemption from parish taxes. The Ministry Act required that two-thirds of voters in each town agree on a place of worship and a minister. Dissenters could obtain exemptions with certificates signed by church officials representing their congregations. This requirement reflected a suspicion that some might "pretend to differ from the Majority with a Design only to escape Taxation." By default, each adult was assumed to be "of Opinion with the major part of the Inhabitants within such Town or Parish where he[,] she or they shall dwell" until producing a certificate.[12] Even with these provisions, however, many towns were so divided in their beliefs that they had trouble garnering the two-thirds majority needed to form churches and settle ministers.

Vermont's Parish and Ministry Acts comprised the most liberal religious establishment in New England at the time. Unlike elsewhere, its statutes did not endorse specific dissenting groups as legitimate denominations, nor did it specifically favor Congregationalism.[13] By emphasizing consensus over orthodoxy, the state preserved a general Protestant establishment in which the bonds of the community church took precedence over its members' personal beliefs. But the very concept of the community church was rooted specifically in Congregational doctrines and practices, and Vermont's efforts to support worship through law proved incompatible with its complex religious landscape. At issue was not simply church gathering (which dissenters could do), but which churches were eligible to receive town funding. In the Ministry Acts of the 1780s, lawmakers underscored the importance of the town church in terms of its role in the larger community, and they legislated with the tradition of the New England parish in mind. The town, according to law and custom, remained the default unit of both civic and religious life.

By privileging the town church, Vermont's establishment helped Congregationalists and hindered dissenters. Dissenters complained bitterly about the certificate law, which required a signature by a verified leader of a dissenting church. In a state with few organized churches, such evidence was difficult to obtain and easy to challenge. In Weathersfield the Baptists failed to file their certificates in time to obtain exemption from taxes. After the tax collector seized their property in 1787 to cover the delinquency, Baptists petitioned the state general assembly, all to no avail.[14] The same year, sixty-five inhabitants of Chester petitioned the assembly for relief from a tax to fund a meetinghouse "for a Different denomination of Christians" (in other words, for the Congregationalists). The Congregationalist majority challenged the petitioners' status as Baptists (and legal dissenters), arguing that "there is but Six Baptists Male Persons in the town of Chester that have made So much Profession of the Baptist Religion as to be Baptised, and one of them is Their Preacher, Who is Ordained at Large and is not Obliged to Stay in Chester only During his Pleasure." As to the remaining Baptists, the Congregationalists guessed the petitioners "will be Put to their Trumps to find them."[15] The petitioners and the Congregationalists were using two different standards of membership to argue their cases: the Baptists argued that churchgoers who affiliated with their denomination should receive exemptions, but the Congregationalists accepted only the exemptions of professed and converted Baptists. This time the Baptists got their way: the assembly exempted them from the meetinghouse tax. Clearly, though, the certificate exemptions were not functioning as lawmakers had intended.

Dissenters increasingly argued that the Vermont establishment—which allowed for majority rule in the towns and the certificate system—did not comport with the constitutional principle of religious liberty. In an election sermon before the general assembly in 1792, Baptist preacher Caleb Blood warned against "religious establishment by law, which never fail[s] of pernicious consequences to both church and state." Legal compulsion to support churches, he argued, "fills the mind with prejudice for both the doctrine and the preacher, and of course does hurt to the cause of religion."[16] Two years later, about two hundred Vermonters petitioned for the repeal of the 1787 Ministry Act.[17] Citing the third article of Vermont's Declaration of Rights, dissenters pointed out that "civil Authority have no Right to intermeddle with ecclesiastical affairs." Dissenters claimed the Ministry Act not only violated individual liberties, but also was "detrimental to the interests of true Religion" because the act "has a tendency to increase the number of hypocrites and infidels," create "prejudices *among* different sects," and disturb "the peace of neighbors." Religion could prevail only when "the Church is in no sence dependent on the civil Power for its support." Calling the act the "bane of peace [and] the hinge of Contention," the dissenters urged its repeal.[18]

They did not immediately achieve their goal, but lawmakers did take steps to bring the act in line with the Constitution. In 1797 the general assembly broadened the guidelines for founding religious societies and parishes, as well as building meetinghouses. Although it still required a two-thirds majority to form a town church, any group could found a religious society and contract with ministers, build meetinghouses, and raise funds. The *1797 Act for the Support of the Gospel* also liberalized the certificate laws by providing that any minister, deacon, or elder of the "sect or denomination" to which the dissenter belonged could sign a certificate, without regard to whether the dissenter was a converted church member. Further, anyone who moved into a town or parish had one year to file a certificate.[19] The Ministry Act still assumed that those who failed to do so favored the town majority and would be liable for town religious taxes, but now dissenters bore less of a burden.

Even so, critics argued that the law did not go far enough to ensure religious liberty. The Council of Censors, an elective body that assessed the constitutionality of the government's actions and proposed constitutional amendments, proclaimed that the *Ministry Act* was "repugnant to the Constitution" and ought to be repealed.[20] The council argued that, despite protections for dissenters, the 1797 act "expressly binds the citizens of this state, indiscriminately, to erect and support places of public worship, and to maintain ministers . . . provided they are so unfortunate as to be in the minority of any town . . . and who are not at the time of taking the vote, possessed of a certain prescribed certificate." That exemptions for dissenters existed was beside the point. Rather, "in no case have [a] civil power any constitutional right to interfere in religious concerns."[21] In claiming such authority in the Ministry Act, the legislature overreached.

Over the next several years, the general assembly relaxed restrictions on dissenters. Still, the political momentum favored ending any certificate law, however liberal. In 1807 the assembly proclaimed that "in the interest of "promot[ing] harmony and good order in Civil Society," the Ministry Act "ought to be repealed." With that, lawmakers removed the last provision for publicly funded religion in Vermont.[22] Congregationalist observers outside the state predicted that a wave of religious anarchy and moral depravity would follow. A writer in the *Dartmouth (NH) Observer* warned that disestablishment would lead to "the eradication of every moral, virtuous, and religious principle from the human heart." A Connecticut pastor worried that "we have almost ceased to be a Christian nation." There was little outcry in Vermont, however. Although missionary Aaron Cleveland feared that the repeal of the 1807 act would "occasion the dismissal of many Ministers" in the short term, he also predicted that "those who are hereafter settled, will be settled on more permanent ground." A few years later, Baptist historian David Benedict wrote that none of Vermont's Congregationalist ministers had lost his pulpit due to disestablishment.[23] In Vermont the severing of ties between church and state—weak to begin with—appeared to have been a smooth transition.

II.

After ending religious taxation, Vermont witnessed neither the dawn of religious liberty nor a slide into godlessness. Rather, the state continued to encourage worship and buttress religious institutions, often through similar means as before. Vermont endorsed the churches' roles as guardians of morality by empowering them to enforce Sabbath worship and moral norms such as temperance. The state went further, using the law to promote a particular kind of religious community: a stable congregation built around a partnership between a town and its settled minister. It did so by securing the town church's access to the two resources most important to its survival: property and people. Town churches claimed land, funds, and members by default. Dissenting churches were left with their followers and perhaps some church property, but they did not enjoy an automatic right to public land or buildings, nor could they automatically claim members or their money. Even as Vermont removed the legal backing for religious taxes, it continued to use the law to support the parish system, which privileged territorial parishes over poll parishes, and thereby Congregationalists over dissenters. By tying some religious communities (and not others) to land and other assets, the law placed these parishes on unequal footing.

As territorial parishes, town churches continued to claim the land their religious communities occupied. Vermont, like other New England states, had long favored these parishes by granting plots of public land, which, according to town charters, were reserved for each town's first settled minister. These provisions assumed that only one minister would serve each town at a time and that the established church would settle a minister before any of the town's dissenters did. But the ministerial plots did not always work as intended. Moreover, the laws that protected these plots sometimes grew out of step with the changing realities in religious life, which featured not united churches but religiously fragmented populations and empty pulpits.

As these incongruities became apparent, Vermonters grappled with how to handle ministerial plots that seemed to have outlasted their purpose. In 1798 the legislature allowed towns without settled ministers to divide the lease income from ministerial plots to benefit all the churches in a town. As soon as one church settled a minister, however, the plot would revert to him. Further, though these new laws supported dividing ministerial plots to aid multiple ministers, the wording to permit such action was often so vague and contradictory that the towns lacked guidance on how to allocate land. Conflicts over land rights soon erupted. A plot of as many as three hundred acres could be a great boon to a church that would otherwise have to provide a parsonage by its own means, so many congregations raced to settle clergy before their neighbors did. Such "scrambling for the Right" to the ministerial plot, complained Vermonters, produced a decidedly un-Christian climate.[24] Even as towns wrestled over the rights to ministerial plots, the question of who could claim these resources might become moot. Plots stood empty as churches and societies in divided towns failed to settle clergy. Other towns tried to liquidate the ministerial plots so they could divide the proceeds among their churches, but ambiguous laws clouded title to the lands, discouraging potential buyers. In 1813 the selectmen of Ripton, Vermont, complained that the laws governing the use and distribution of ministerial plots were obsolete. Not only did the town charters fail to account for the "great increase of religious sects" and the "liberal views" about religion that had become the norm, but they also contradicted the 1807 Ministry Act that abolished government taxes for religion. "How a Minister can be settled in any town under the present existing laws," the selectmen wondered, "your petitioners are unable to perceive."[25] Even when a town's citizens tried to abandon the older strictures of establishment, the law got in their way.

A town's changing religious makeup might ignite new conflicts over long-decided agreements as to how to divide religious assets. In Craftsbury, Vermont, where the religious society had once been multidenominational, Congregationalists gained a majority and took control of the meetinghouse. But then the Baptist membership surged, and by 1810 they comprised about half the town's churchgoers. That year they petitioned to use the meeting-house half the time, proportionate to the taxes they paid to build and maintain the structure.[26] In a contentious town meeting, the Congregationalists prevailed by two votes and so retained control. A Baptist partisan immortalized this "late unjust event" in a satirical poem, portraying the Congregationalists as conspiratorial villains who gathered in a "secret conclave" to "rule and reign o'er rights divine." The poet saw the Congregationalist victory as a cabal of political and religious power—made more shocking because the vote took place three years *after* Vermont had disestablished religion. Writing from what he imagined to be the Standing Order's perspective, the poet predicted a grim future for dissenters:

> All, that against *our Church* rebel,
> By Inquisition, we'll compell
> To own, by force, our potent sway,
> And all our covenants obey. . . .
> All sects obey our will, divine,
> And Church and State, in one combine,
> To make us *great*, our power enhance
> And us to rank supreme advance. . . .
> Now, Democratic rights must fall,
> And Church and State be all in all.[27]

Using the rhetoric of tyranny and liberty, this Baptist suggested that disestablishment had done little to sever church from state.

To resolve such conflicts over religious resources, in 1814 the Vermont Legislature guaranteed corporate status—including the right to acquire and manage property—for any organized religious society.[28] But even this measure did not resolve all property disputes. Several dissenting churches petitioned the legislature for special resolves to help them acquire or protect church property. Usually, the general assembly granted such requests.

But when the Baptist church in Brandon petitioned for a law to protect the property of *unincorporated* churches, the legislature balked.[29] Baptists resisted incorporation because the resulting regulations violated their belief concerning the separation of church and state. Incorporated societies, for example, were expected to command financial support from their members, but doing so infringed upon the Baptists' insistence on voluntary contributions. When unincorporated Baptist societies sought limited legal protection, they failed to secure it. Only churches that organized according to the state corporation law could protect their property. Those that did not, even for doctrinal reasons, were denied equal status.

Just as Vermonters struggled to fairly allocate property in a parish, they also had to negotiate over members. Membership—how churchgoers identified themselves and churches identified their followers—lay at the heart of the town-church establishment, and now it surfaced as a problem that post-establishment law sought to solve. The state did not manage church membership, which was usually determined by a valid conversion experience or otherwise assessed by the church. Parish membership was a more bureaucratic matter, and that was the type of membership subject to law. And now the problem of membership raised new questions. Would parishioners remain members of their town parishes until they indicated otherwise? Many towns and churches assumed they would. Prior to prohibiting religious taxes, Vermont assumed that the town was the default religious community for all residents. Only those who furnished evidence to the contrary could direct their taxes to another parish. The Parish Acts charged towns with hiring ministers and building meetinghouses, even if parishioners represented different faiths.[30] As poll parishes broke from territorial parishes, towns tried to sort out who belonged where. Inevitably, ill-defined procedures for incorporation set poll parishes at a further disadvantage, which ignited a firestorm over rules that determined how to allocate dissenters' taxes and define poll parishes' rights and responsibilities.

State law continued after 1807 to treat territorial and poll parishes differently. Territorial parishes held an advantage in claiming members and securing assets, because even after banning religious taxes, Vermont allowed establishment-era ministerial contracts pledging town support to remain in effect. As a result, people found themselves liable to support churches they did not attend. The problem especially affected those who had not formally withdrawn from territorial parishes, simply because members of poll parishes always joined by choice rather than by default. Moreover, the first section of the *1797 Act for the Support of the Gospel*, which authorized towns, parishes, and religious societies to enter into contracts and raise taxes to support churches, remained in effect.[31] Anyone who paid religious taxes prior to 1807 would, barring a formal separation from a town, parish, or religious society, continue to do so. Further, because Vermont considered taxpayers to be part of their town parishes unless they filed certificates to indicate otherwise, some people continued to fund churches whose doctrines conflicted with their own. Accordingly, even though Vermont no longer allowed towns to levy religious taxes, it still supported a system of religious funding that harked back to the town-church tradition.

Town churches expected parishioners' support. The Middlebury Congregational Church repeatedly confronted members who were delinquent in paying taxes. In 1815 the church charged Levi Hooker with failing to pay his ministerial tax. A few years later, the church challenged Bela Sawyer's certificate (filed with the town clerk) that claimed he no longer owed taxes because he no longer believed in Congregationalist doctrine. A similar conflict arose in 1829 when the church complained that Jonathan Sawyer filed a certificate with the town that "prevents his supporting the gospel in common with his brethren."[32] In all of these cases, the church challenged current and former members for nonpayment of taxes even when they had filed certificates to withdraw. More to the point, by the time these members filed those certificates, they had spent months or years after disestablishment paying taxes to support a church they did not attend or with which they did not agree. Even after 1807, such arrangements were still the norm, and the town clerk—who had the final say on acceptance of certificates—remained the arbiter of church funding.

Despite the acceptance of disestablishment, publicly supported religion survived in new ways. Vermont determined how parishes should raise funds, and those parishes asserted the authority to define church membership. In doing so, the state involved itself in the internal matters of religious polity and the laity's means of identifying with the church. Even though parishes now raised their own funds, they determined each member's financial obligation in much the same way as before, by property assessment. The assessments were mandated by law. Most religious societies even continued to call these assessments "taxes," despite the fact that religious—not civil—institutions now collected them. Regardless of the state's guarantee that no one would pay taxes to support a minister of a different religion, the law still determined how individuals withdrew from parishes. Sometimes the criteria for membership placed people in parishes without their consent. Because state and local authorities continued to set these criteria, people did not have the unconditional right to define church membership for themselves. In this sense, the old system persisted with slight modifications. The law supported a partnership between churches and towns that privileged territorial parishes and their ministers. By granting those ministers public funding and property, Vermont favored the Congregationalist assumption that a minister served all the people in the town, converted and unconverted alike.

III.

If we define disestablishment as the cessation of mandatory ministerial taxes, it is easy to pinpoint 1807 as the moment of separation between church and state. But if we define disestablishment more broadly, by looking at how Vermont connected churches and ministers to property and parishioners, the process becomes more difficult to untangle. Although Vermonters embraced religious liberty and did not allow the state to openly endorse any particular denomination, they did not fully break the ties between church and state. The end of ministerial taxation in 1807 left in its wake ambiguous laws and knotty questions about the relationships among citizens, churches, and governments. New laws transferred responsibility for religious fundraising from town to parish, but the state continued to define parishes and grant their corporate powers to manage membership and property.

By classifying different kinds of parishes—and assigning them different privileges to claim public lands and town funds—Vermont created a hierarchy of wealth, privilege, and authority among territorial and poll parishes. The town church's legal privilege meant that a modified establishment persisted—one that came to embody a more complicated dynamic between religious and civil authorities. So indelible was the town church's imprint on Vermont's religious character by the early nineteenth century that the state could not shake free of its strictures.

These remnants of establishment would eventually fail to preserve the town church as the model of covenanted community. The system ultimately crumbled for three confluent reasons. First, the language of religious liberty framed the church-state debate as a fight against tyranny and lent revolutionary fervor to the struggle for conscience. Second, spiritually and geographically scattered populations could not support town churches. And finally, as the last of the pre-1807 ministerial contracts expired (because ministers retired or died), the question of parish taxation became moot. Changes in church membership and styles of religious organization, along with continued migration and the religious diversity of northern New England's population, ultimately reshaped the state's religious culture. So, too, did the laity's insistence on creating religious communities of their own designs. But these shifts would take place in spite of—not because of—the law.

_____

NOTES

1. Aaron Cleveland to the Connecticut Missionary Society Committee of Missions, May 16, 1808, Connecticut Missionary Society Papers, reel 3, Connecticut Historical Society, Hartford.

2. Forms of establishment spanned a wide spectrum that included requirements of Sabbath worship, prohibitions against blasphemy, and Protestant or Trinitarian tests for voting or office holding. See Stephen Botein, "Religious Dimensions of the Early American State," in *Beyond Confederation: Origins of the Constitution and American National Identity*, ed. Richard Beeman, Stephen Botein, and Edward C. Carter II, 315–30 (Chapel Hill: University of North Carolina Press, 1987).

3. See, for example, Thomas J. Curry, *The First Freedoms: Church and State in America to the Passage of the First Amendment* (New York: Oxford University Press, 1986), chaps. 6–7; Nathan O. Hatch, *The Democratization of American Christianity* (New Haven, CT: Yale University Press, 1989) (quote on 7). On the other hand, some studies have pointed to a longer journey toward separating church and state. See the discussions of New Hampshire and Maine, in addition to Vermont, in Shelby M. Balik, *Rally the Scattered Believers: Northern New England's Religious Geography* (Bloomington: Indiana University Press, 2014), esp. chap. 3.

4. Vermont emerged from a territorial conflict between New Hampshire and New York, which began when New Hampshire governor Benning Wentworth issued land grants in the contested territory for settlers who wished to migrate to the western Connecticut River valley. After a series of border skirmishes, which preceded and overlapped with the American Revolution, Vermonters declared independence and petitioned for statehood in 1777. For more detailed discussions of this history, see William Doyle, *The Vermont Political Tradition and Those Who Helped Make It* (Montpelier, VT: Northlight Studio Press, 1984), chap. 1; David Jaffee, *People of the Wachusett: Greater New England in History and Memory, 1630–1860* (Ithaca, NY: Cornell University Press, 1999), 212–16; Peter S. Onuf, "State-Making in Revolutionary America: Independent Vermont as a Case Study," *Journal of American History* 67, no. 4 (1981): 797–815; and Michael Sherman, Gene Sessions, and P. Jeffrey Potash, *Freedom and Unity: A History of Vermont* (Barre: Vermont Historical Society, 2004), chaps. 2–3.

5. Stephen Foster, *The Long Argument: English Puritanism and the Shaping of New England Culture, 1570–1700* (Chapel Hill: University of North Carolina Press, 1991), 170–73; Edmund S. Morgan, *Visible Saints: The History of a Puritan Idea* (Ithaca, NY: Cornell University Press, 1965); Harry S. Stout, *The New England Soul: Preaching and Religious Culture in Colonial New England* (New York: Oxford University Press, 1986), 20–23.

6. T. D. Seymour Bassett, *Gods of the Hills: Piety and Society in Nineteenth-Century Vermont* (Montpelier: Vermont Historical Society, 2000), 12; John M. Comstock, *The Congregational Churches of Vermont and Their Ministry, 1762–1942* (St. Johnsbury, VT: Cowles Press, 1942), 8–9.

7. Isaac Backus to "My Dear Friend," June 3, 1796, Isaac Backus Papers, American Baptist Historical Society, Mercer University; William G. McLoughlin, *New England Dissent, 1630–1833: The Baptists and the Separation of Church and State* (Cambridge, MA: Harvard University Press, 1971), 2:791, 794.

8. Minutes, New England Conference of the Methodist Episcopal Church Records, vol. 1, Records of the New England Conference, 1797–1970, New England Methodist Historical Society, Boston University School of Theology Library, 75–76; Ann Lee Bressler, *The Universalist Movement in America, 1770–1880* (New York: Oxford University Press, 2001), 33–34; Paul Conkin, *American Originals: Homemade Varieties of American Christianity* (Chapel Hill: University of North Carolina Press, 1997), 100; Stephen A. Marini, *Radical Sects of Revolutionary New England* (Cambridge, MA: Harvard University Press, 1982), 125–27, 119–21; I. D. Stewart, *The History of the Freewill Baptists for Half a Century* (Dover, NH: Freewill Baptist Printing Establishment, 1862), 1:254, 61; New Durham Quarterly Meeting Records of the Elders' Conference, 1801–1813.

9. Sherman, Sessions, and Potash, *Freedom and Unity*, 120, 42.

10. Bassett, *Gods of the Hills*, 13.

11. Constitution of Vermont, 1777, in *Laws of Vermont, 1777–1780*, ed. Allen Soule, vol. 12, *State Papers of Vermont* (Montpelier, 1964), chap. 1, article 3; Constitution of Vermont, 1787, in *Laws of Vermont, 1785–1791*, ed. John A Williams, vol. 14, *State Papers of Vermont* (Montpelier, 1966), chap. 1, article 3; Constitution of Vermont, 1793, in *Laws of Vermont, 1791–1795*, ed. John A. Williams, vol. 15, *State Papers of Vermont* (Montpelier, 1967), chap. 1, article 3.

12. *Journals and Proceedings of the General Assembly of the State of Vermont, Part II*, vol. 3, *State Papers of Vermont* (Bellows Falls: P. H. Gobie Press, 1925), 189; An Act to Enable Towns and Parishes to Erect Proper Houses for Public Worship and Support Ministers of the Gospel, 1783, in *Laws of Vermont, 1781–1784*, ed. John A. Williams, vol. 13, *State Papers of Vermont* (Montpelier, 1965), 195; An Act for Supporting Ministers of the Gospel, 1787, in *Laws of Vermont, 1785–1791*, ed. John A. Williams, vol. 14, *State Papers of Vermont*, 348–50.

13. Vermont was distinctive for its many multidenominational religious societies and for the number of towns in which the first organized church was not Congregationalist. See McLoughlin, *New England Dissent*, 1:221–43, 2:863–71; Randolph A. Roth, *The Democratic Dilemma: Religion, Reform, and the Social Order in the Connecticut River Valley of Vermont, 1791–1850* (Cambridge: Cambridge University Press, 1987), 36; John C. DeBoer and Clara Merritt DeBoer, "The Formation of Town Churches: Church, Town, and State in Early Vermont," *Vermont History* 62 (Spring 1996): 69–88; and Charles Latham Jr., "Church and State in Thetford," *Vermont History News* 45 (September–October 1994): 61–64.

14. Petition of John Williams, William Deane, et al., February 3, 1787, Manuscripts of Vermont State Papers, Vermont State Archives, Montpelier, VT, 17:259.

15. Petition of the Baptist Society of Chester, August 31, 1787, Manuscripts of Vermont State Papers, 17:312; Petition for Postponement of Consideration of a Church Controversy, October 7, 1788, Edward A. Hoyt, ed., *General Petitions, 1788–1792*, vol. 9, *State Papers of Vermont* (Montpelier, 1955), 65–66.

16. Caleb Blood, *A Sermon Preached before the Honorable Legislature of the State of Vermont, Convened at Rutland, October 11th, 1792, Being the Day of General Election* (Rutland: Anthony Haswell, 1792), 34–36; McLoughlin, *New England Dissent*, 2:803.

17. McLoughlin, *New England Dissent*, 2:803–7.

18. Petitions for the Repeal of an Act Supporting Ministers of the Gospel, all October 1794, in *General Petitions, 1793–1796*, ed. Allen Soule, vol. 10, *State Papers of Vermont* (Montpelier, 1958), 90–96.

19. An Act for the Support of the Gospel, 1797, *Laws of the State of Vermont, 1797*, 474–79.

20. "An Address of the Council of Censors to the People of Vermont," October 21, 1799, Council of Censors Transcriptions, 1785–1820, Vermont Constitution Records, box 1, 72.

21. "An Address of the Council of Censors to the People of Vermont," 70–71.

22. An Act to Repeal a Certain Act, and Parts of an Act, Therein Mentioned, 1807, *Acts and Laws Passed by the Legislature of the State of Vermont, October 1807* (Randolph: Sereno Wright, 1807), 22.

23. McLoughlin, *New England Dissent*, 2:811; Aaron Cleveland to the Connecticut Missionary Society Committee of Missions, May 16, 1808, Connecticut Missionary Society Papers, reel 3; David Benedict, *A General History of the Baptist Denomination in America, and Other Parts of the World* (Boston: Lincoln and Edmands, 1813), 1:351–53.

24. Petition of the Selectmen of Ripton, October 15, 1831, Manuscripts of Vermont State Papers.

25. Petition of the Selectmen of Ripton, October 15, 1831, Manuscripts of Vermont State Papers, 62:21.

26. Petition of the Baptists for Use of the Town Meetinghouse, September 29, 1810, Crafts Family Papers, box 9, folder 34.

27. "The Town Meeting: A Comi-tragic Poem," n.d. (typed copy), Crafts Family Papers, box 8, folder 36.

28. An Act in Addition to an Act for the Support of the Gospel, 1814, *Laws Passed by the Legislature of the State of Vermont, 1814*, 112–13.

29. See, for example, Petition of Henry Smith and William Whitford, October 1, 1816, Manuscripts of Vermont State Papers, 51:240; Petition of Mary Baker, October 16, 1820, Manuscripts of Vermont State Papers, 54:2; Petition of the Baptist Church at Brandon, October 12, 1822, Manuscripts of Vermont State Papers, 56:157; *Journal of the General Assembly of the State of Vermont, 1824* (Bennington: Darius Clark, 1824), 154.

30. An Act to Enable Towns and Parishes to Erect Proper Houses for Public Worship and Support Ministers of the Gospel, 1783, *Laws of Vermont, 1781–1784*, 195; An Act for Supporting Ministers of the Gospel, 1787, *Laws of Vermont, 1785–1791*, 348–50.

31. An Act for the Support of the Gospel, 1797, *Laws of the State of Vermont, 1797*, 474–75; An Act to Repeal a Certain Act, and Parts of an Act Therein Mentioned, 1807, *Acts and Laws Passed by the Legislature of the State of Vermont, October 1807*, 22; An Act, in Addition to an Act for the Support of the Gospel, 1814, *Laws Passed by the Legislature of the State of Vermont, 1814*, 112–13.

32. Entries from May 23, 1815; November 20, 1818; and August 14, 1829, all in Middlebury, VT, Congregational Church Record Book, 1790–1853, Henry Sheldon Museum of Vermont History, Middlebury, VT.

CHAPTER SIXTEEN

CHURCH AND STATE IN MARYLAND
Religious Liberty, Religious Tests, and Church Disestablishment

Michael D. Breidenbach

MARYLAND HOLDS THE distinction of being the only one of the thirteen original American colonies in the British Empire to have been founded by a Catholic. George Calvert, the First Lord Baltimore, secured King Charles I's royal charter but died six weeks before the final seals were set in 1632. George Calvert's first son, Cecil Calvert, inherited the title and charter. As a Catholic convert and proprietor of a Crown charter, Cecil Calvert defied the anti-Catholic environment in England and its American colonies. English Catholics were second-class subjects of the Crown. Penal laws prevented Catholics from holding public office, bearing witness, worshiping publicly, and educating their children in the Catholic faith.

Calvert sought to create a colony where Catholics and Protestants could live in peace and equality under the rule of law. Despite this intention, for a century and a half this arrangement would be the target of criticism. During the proprietorships of Cecil Calvert and his son Charles, Protestants and Catholics alike agitated against this regime of toleration. Protestants complained that Catholics received special treatment under their Catholic lord, while Jesuits argued that a Catholic proprietor should proffer special treatment to Catholic clergy, such as they enjoyed in European Catholic countries.

The Maryland Charter of 1632 offered little guidance on what kind of church-state arrangements should govern.[1] Cecil Calvert governed Maryland as a broadly tolerant Christian colony without an established church. The final end of government, according to Calvert, was not to help his settlers get to heaven by a prescribed path of salvation, but to create the conditions for a "mutuall Love and amity amongst the Inhabitants." As long as settlers obeyed a "quiett and peaceable government," they were permitted to practice their religious faith.[2] Despite later Anglican attempts at various forms of church establishment, Maryland reverted eventually to Calvert's original commitment to religious toleration and nonestablishment.

I.

From the first settlers' journey to Maryland, Cecil Calvert practiced what he promised. Before their departing voyage in 1633, he instructed his brother, Governor Leonard Calvert, and his commissioners "to preserue unity & peace amongst all the passengers on Shipp-board" by ensuring, in particular, that Protestants "suffer no scandall nor offence" from Catholics. To that end, he required that Catholics be "silent upon all occasions of discourse concerning matters of Religion" and that the provincial officials should "treate the Protestants with as much mildness and favor as Justice will permitt."[3] Cecil Calvert made it easier for Catholics to settle in Maryland by redrafting the required Oath of Allegiance. A previous oath, originally issued by King James I, contained clauses damning the doctrine that popes can depose excommunicated kings. Since the pope threatened to excommunicate any Catholic who signed the oath, this presented a significant challenge to Calvert's efforts to recruit settlers. In 1638 the Maryland General Assembly removed the controversial clauses of the original Oath of Allegiance, so that any Catholic could swear it in good conscience.[4]

Despite these overtures, the Calverts' control over Maryland was continually threatened in the seventeenth century. The first major attempt to overturn Calvert's rule was in 1645. The English Civil War provided a pretext for proparliamentary forces in Virginia to settle long-standing territorial and religious disputes with its neighbor to its immediate north. In February 1645, professing to have Parliament's permission to seize property from Catholics and royal sympathizers, two Virginia ship captains, Anglican Richard Ingle and Calvinist William Claiborne, invaded the political center of Maryland, St. Mary's City, in the aptly named ship *Reformation*.[5] Governor Leonard Calvert eventually succeeded in suppressing the Ingle-Claiborne Rebellion in 1646. The attempted insurgence impressed upon Cecil Calvert the real possibility of religious insurrection and the need to secure toleration for his own settlers.

In 1649, four months after the formation of the English Commonwealth, the Maryland General Assembly passed the *Act Concerning Toleration*. The act became the first law in the British Empire to ensure a toleration that embraced all Trinitarian Christians.[6] In a reference to the new Cromwellian Republic, the act began: "Forasmuch as in a well governed and Christian Common Wealth matters concerning Religion and the honor of God ought in the first place to bee taken, into serious consideracion and endeavoured to bee settled." Calvert had settled the problem of religious difference not

theologically—that is, by catechizing or persuading those in disagreement—
but politically. Religious difference could remain, or even intensify, as long
as civil peace was maintained. According to the act, all people "professing to
believe in Jesus Christ" shall not be "troubled, Molested or discountenanced
for or in respect of his or her religion nor in the free exercise thereof . . . nor
any way compelled to the beleife or exercise of any other Religion against
his or her consent." Since the act protected Trinitarian Christians only, the
religious liberty of Jews and others remained vulnerable.[7]

The 1649 act allowed the proprietary government to punish blasphemers
and heretics of Christianity under pain of property confiscation or death,
as well as those who offended believers on account of their religion. The
act also mandated fines, imprisonment, or whipping for "frequent swearing,
drunkennes or by any uncivill or disorderly recreacion, or by working on
[the Sabbath] when absolute necessity doth not require it." To ensure Christian toleration, the act empowered civil magistrates to fine those who "use
or utter any reproachfull words or Speeches concerning the blessed Virgin
Mary the Mother of our Saviour or the holy Apostles or Evangelists" or those
who used certain terms pejoratively, including "heritick" and "Scismatick."[8]
The act therefore sacrificed some freedom of speech so that Catholics and
multiple Protestant denominations might all coexist.

The 1649 act was not a mere nod to religious toleration; its codification
was a culmination of previous practices by proprietary officials to avoid any
suspicion that Maryland was a "popish" colony. For instance, in 1638 William Lewis, the overseer of the Jesuit plantation of St. Inigoes, was accused of
proselytizing his Protestant servants, calling their clergy devils, and preventing them from reading Protestant books. The three Catholic officials who
adjudicated the case found Lewis guilty of "offensive & indiscreete speech"
that led "to the disturbance of the publique peace & quiett of the colony."
They imposed a hefty fine on Lewis. They failed, however, to prosecute Lewis's servants, who called the pope the Antichrist and Jesuits non-Christian.[9]
This seeming double standard was to prevent the charge that the Catholic
minority was persecuting Protestants. The policies—which did not result
in a single Protestant being charged with disturbing the peace in religious
affairs—allowed Catholics, who constituted most of the colony's adminis-
trators, to rule over a Protestant majority without giving the appearance that
Catholicism was the established religion. The result was an arena where religious inquiry and controversy were private matters and where the government neither encouraged nor discouraged any particular Christianity.[10]

Some Protestant settlers, whom Lord Baltimore's regime tolerated, did not themselves tolerate his rule or his religion. In 1654 William Claiborne again invaded Maryland, this time with a parliamentary order to seize control of Maryland's government. Claiborne's coup d'état installed a Protestant government that denied Catholics seating in the general assembly. The new government also amended the *1649 Act Concerning Toleration* to deny those "who profess and Exercise the popish religion" the "protect[ion] in this Province by the Laws of England." Calvert sought the help of Oliver Cromwell to repel Claiborne. In 1658 Cromwell reinstated the proprietary government and the original toleration act.[11]

A new Maryland proprietor, the Third Baron of Baltimore, Charles Calvert, upset the Protestant majority in 1676 by placing a disproportionately high number of Catholics in civil government and by refusing to establish the Church of England. Anti-Catholic Marylanders had already found the Calverts' Catholicism—especially their denial of the king's supremacy over religion—to be evidence of treason. So when Charles Calvert's instructions from England in support of the new Protestant monarchs, William and Mary, did not arrive (they were apparently lost en route), Protestants took up arms against what they considered to be a treasonous proprietary.[12] In 1689 seven hundred members of the Maryland Protestant Association took the Glorious Revolution as both an opportunity and a justification to change their own colonial government. Protestants stormed the proprietor's manor. They forced the civil government to deny the ability of Catholics to serve in public or military offices. Two years later, the English Lords of Trade rescinded Lord Baltimore's authority to appoint the Maryland governor. In 1692, with King William III's newly appointed governor, Lionel Copley, the Maryland General Assembly banned Catholics from practicing law and taxed all eligible persons forty pounds of tobacco yearly to construct Church of England buildings and to pay Anglican minister salaries. To those who backed these measures, the Church of England had already been the de jure established church—a law that previous Calverts had simply refused to enforce. In 1702, as a result of this forced takeover, the Church of England became the de facto established church.[13]

II.

The next seven decades witnessed continuous attempts by the Maryland Legislature to disenfranchise Catholics and buttress the Church of England. In 1704 the general assembly passed an *Act to Prevent the Growth of Popery in this Province*. It imposed a £50 fine or six-month prison sentence on priests who proselytized or celebrated Mass. A Catholic priest's second violation resulted in deportation to England, where the cleric would be subject to more onerous penal laws. The latter penalty also applied to Catholic schoolteachers. The 1704 act levied a £100 penalty for those sending one's children to European Catholic schools and revoked primogeniture for Catholic sons.[14] While these penal laws were not widely enforced and later repealed, the Protestant majority continued to remove Catholics from positions of power. Queen Anne's plea in 1707 to the Maryland General Assembly to amend the penal law of 1704 and allow priests to celebrate Mass privately in Catholic homes was no more than a brief respite. From 1715, subsequent Barons of Baltimore, in order to reinstate their proprietorship, renounced Catholicism and conformed to Anglicanism. In 1718 the general assembly enacted two laws that imposed stricter penal laws against Catholics and removed Catholics' right to vote.[15] And in 1756, despite the protests of Catholic gentry, the assembly passed legislation that taxed Catholics twice the standard amount to pay for the colony's militia.[16]

While Anglicans had successfully supplanted Catholic dominance in Maryland, their church establishment was neither stable nor complete. Protestant dissenters had a home in Maryland, where, according to the English Act of Toleration, they were not required to attend Anglican services. To be sure, the tobacco tax revenues supported the Church of England and sustained its ministerial presence. Maryland was second only to Virginia as the largest Church of England presence in North America based on the number of church buildings and ministers. The average salary for a Maryland rector in the 1760s was between £250 and £300—a sum ten times the salaries in other colonies.[17] Maryland official William Eddis noted that the revenues earmarked for Anglican ministers and church buildings were "amply sufficient to support an appearance perfectly consistent with the respectability of the clerical profession."[18] However, the tax assessments led to popular criticism and a perception of corruption.[19] Additionally, there was no Anglican bishop in North America. While there was a push for episcopacy in Maryland, it was only to curb some of the excessive lay-vestry claims to authority over ministers.[20] Maryland Anglicans preferred local vestry governance, including legislating ministerial salaries. The vestries opposed creating ecclesiastical courts to adjudicate cases of overlapping civil- and canon-law jurisdiction.[21]

Even these privileges were perceived as insufficient to what Anglicans feared was a growing Catholic influence in Maryland. Anglicans worried about French Catholic missionaries such as the Jesuits who appeared to be winning more converts than the Anglicans.[22] In 1709 Bishop William Dawes told Anglican missionaries, about to leave for English colonies in North America, that their duty was "to prevent Infidels from being made a Prey to the church of *Rome . . .* which, so industriously *compasseth Land and Sea to make Proselytes* to it."[23] In 1701 Thomas Bray founded the Anglican Society for the Propagation of the Gospel in Foreign Parts to counter the activities of the Catholic Church's own Sacred Congregation "de Propaganda Fide."[24] The need for the SPG indicates that Anglican establishments in colonial America, including Maryland, were decentralized and frail.

III.

The Anglican establishment fundamentally changed in 1776. Maryland-born John Carroll, the first Catholic bishop in the United States, later recalled that the revolution of disestablishment and religious liberty was "more extraordinary, than the political one."[25] His second cousin Charles Carroll, of Carrollton, was a principal drafter on a committee of seven delegates that composed both the Maryland Declaration of Rights and the state's first Constitution.[26] That Catholics supported and were influential in the formation of a state constitution was a significant step toward disestablishment. Although the 1776 Constitution eliminated the taxation that benefited the Anglican church, Maryland's church-state arrangement continued to prefer Christianity in its religious liberty protections, tax-assessment provision, and religious test for public office.

The privileged status of Christianity was evident in the Declaration of Rights. The drafting committee had initially put forward the following clause: "That the rights of conscience are sacred, and all persons professing the Christian religion ought for ever to enjoy equal rights and privileges in the state." The convention delegates, however, amended this proposal, designated Article XXXIII, into a curious construction: "[A]s it is the duty of every man to worship God in such manner as he thinks most acceptable to him; all persons, professing the Christian religion, are equally entitled to protection in their religious liberty."[27] While the second clause did not necessarily *exclude* the protection of religious liberty for non-Christians, it did not include them, either. Since the drafting committee did not keep a record of its proceedings, their voiced intentions are lost to history.

Although Charles Carroll's private letters provide little indication of his intentions concerning the article, John Carroll interpreted Article XXXIII as recognizing religious liberty as a natural right. Rev. Carroll later glossed that this protection was "fixed as a matter of natural justice" and that the article provided a "perfect equality of rights . . . secured to all Religions." By "all Religions," he did not mean those within Christianity only; for them, he used the word "denomination."[28] To him, it was an obvious corollary that, under Article XXXIII, no Maryland law could be "partial . . . to one [Christian] denomination to the prejudice of others." However, that did not necessarily exclude the religious freedom of non-Christians.[29]

The Maryland Constitution also included explicit caveats that signaled religious liberty was not an absolute. Article XXXIII stipulated that the state would not protect religious liberty if one used religion to "disturb the good order, peace, or safety of the state," "infringe the laws of morality," or "injure others in their natural, civil or religious rights."[30] Under such open-textured language subject to being read expansively, any prejudice might be smuggled in to curb someone's religious liberty.

The Declaration of Rights also featured a test oath. Like the religious liberty clause in Article XXXIII, the religious test preferred Christianity and was intended to maintain a broadly Christian state. The first draft of the Declaration of Rights, which remained unchanged in the final version as Article XXXV, stipulated: "That no other oath, affirmation, test or qualification ought to be required on admission to any office of trust or profit, than such oath or affirmation of support and fidelity to this state as shall be prescribed by this Convention, and such oath of office as shall be directed by law, and a declaration of a belief in the Christian religion."[31] As mandated by this provision, in 1777 the general assembly enacted an *Oath of Allegiance and Fidelity to the State of Maryland*. It required all free adult men, voters, and public officials to swear that they did not have "any allegiance or obedience to the King of Britain" and to pledge to "be true and faithful to the State of Maryland" and its independence. Unlike previous oaths, such as the English Oaths of Allegiance and Supremacy, which had presented problems for Catholics, this oath could be taken in good conscience by Catholics.[32]

Even as the 1776 Constitution required a belief in Christianity to hold public office, it barred clergy from certain offices.[33] Article XXXVII directed that no "minister, or preacher of the gospel, of any denomination . . . shall have a seat in the General Assembly or the Council of this State."[34] Later constitutional framers and judges assumed that the framers justified the clause on the principle of church-state separation. A delegate in the 1864 Maryland Constitutional Convention, for example, argued that the original prohibition was probably adopted to separate church and state, and the U.S. District Court in Maryland that eventually struck down the prohibition in 1974 registered "no doubt" that part of its justification was "to insure the separation

of Church and State."[35] More likely, however, the Maryland delegates in 1776
were simply following the practice of forbidding clergymen from the House
of Commons in England, a prohibition that parliamentarians thought was
sensible because the Church of England already held seats in the House of
Lords—an arrangement considered perfectly compatible with their established church.[36]

The Maryland Constitutional Convention in 1776 struck a similarly complicated compromise as it unraveled state support for the Anglican church.
The drafting committee for the Declaration of Rights recommended that the
state continue to pay Anglican ministers from tax revenue as long as they remained in America during the Revolutionary War (presumably as patriots)
and promised to remain in their parishes. That there were Anglicans who
had been British loyalists certainly did not help the cause for their church's
continued establishment. When the committee proposal came to the full
convention, the delegates allowed only that Anglican ministers be paid for
past wages and that certain Anglican churches be repaired with public funds.
These allowances were intended to secure the income of ministers who had
remained patriotic, not a sign of support for the established church. Indeed,
Article XXXIII of the Declaration of Rights ended all other taxation earmarked for the support of the Church of England—an act as yet without
parallel in the other states in 1776. Marylanders would no longer be forced
to pay for a church they did not attend.[37]

While Maryland had eliminated most of the state's financial support for
the Anglican church, it did not renounce all state control over religion. Article XXXIII stipulated that the Church of England would continue to hold
its glebes and other property in perpetuity and that all previous legislation
concerning the Church of England was still operable, except those provisions mandating that counties collect taxes for support of Anglican churches. These provisions were double-edged. Although the Anglican church's
revenue stream now slowed to a trickle, Maryland continued to control the
church in ways it had done in the colonial era. For instance, in 1779 the
Maryland Legislature passed a Vestry Act that imposed state control over the
selecting of vestrymen and ministers. Noncompliance carried fines.[38] Additionally, Article XXXIV required that "every gift, sale, or devise of lands,"
including private payments, to a "minister," "preacher of the gospel," or "to
any religious sect, order or denomination" had to be approved by the state
legislature.[39] Without the exclusive financial support for one church, the
1776 Declaration of Rights ensured that ending the remaining features of
establishment was not a matter of if, but when.[40]

Although Maryland constitutional framers had eliminated exclusive taxation for the Anglican church, it remained an open question at the convention whether the state should force citizens to pay a tax for the benefit of the Christian religion generally. Gustavus Scott proposed that the Declaration of Rights empower Maryland legislators to "lay a general and equal tax for support of the christian religion," to be directed by individual taxpayers to the beneficiary of their choice. The taxpayer could earmark the tax for "any particular place of worship or minister, or for the benefit of the poor of his own denomination, or the poor in general of any particular county."[41] The scope of this proposed general assessment was Christian churches—including the Catholic Church—yet the last provision allowed for the designation of a taxpayer's assessment to the poor. While eighteen of the forty-seven delegates voted against the general assessment, the majority believed that the health of civil society hinged on governmental support of religion. With the change from a tax for the exclusive benefit of the Anglican church to the general assessment, Maryland had shifted from an established church to the possibility of a tax-supported "plural establishment."[42]

A significant number of Anglican politicians wanted to ensure the state did not abandon their church altogether. After the Treaty of Paris in 1783, their strategy was to activate the general assessment that had been dormant for a decade. Maryland Anglicans first proposed an assessment to the legislature to counteract what they saw as moral malaise and impiety in their state.[43] Governor William Paca, an Anglican layman and one of the original drafters of the Maryland Constitution, was among the strongest proponents.[44] The legislature received many petitions in support of Paca's call.[45] Samuel Chase, also an Anglican lay politician, supported the measure. But it went nowhere.

In 1784 the assembly again proposed a general assessment, this time a four-shilling tax per person for the support of religion and the poor. It exempted Jews and Muslims from the tax—not on the ground that it would be unjust for them to be coerced, but because legislators did not want public funds supporting non-Christian religions. While Article XXXIII stipulated that the taxpayer could choose which church to support, the bill as introduced restricted beneficiaries to those stable congregations with a physical building, a minister who had served for more than one year, and a legal registration.[46] These stipulations were in place to deter new congregations from springing up to take advantage of the tax revenue, but its effect was discriminatory against those believers whose current congregations did not meet these criteria.

The proposal, known as the "Clergy Bill," met with fierce resistance in the legislature. To stall for time and convince others of their position, opponents of the assessment asked that the bill be sent to the people for their "consideration," an unusual procedure that solicited public opinion without authorizing a legally binding referendum.[47] A vigorous debate ensued in newspapers, the legislature, and private correspondence.

William Paca told justices of the peace that if they did not support the Clergy Bill, he would remove them from office.[48] For other Marylanders, coercion was unneeded. They understood the benefit of a tax for religious purposes as fitting within a broader notion that religion provided moral education as well as spiritual aid and thus was good for society. One anonymous newspaper writer wrote that religion should be supported through tax revenues, since it helped citizens "in co-operating for common good . . . civilizing the multitude, and forming them to union. It tames the fierceness of their passions."[49] He concluded that a general assessment would eliminate "the causes of public disunion" and promote "the good old times of our fathers": "families, neighborhoods, and communities, living in unbroken amity, and pursuing, with one heart and mind the common interest."[50] Thus, supporters of the Clergy Bill relied on the argument that republican government required a virtuous citizenry.

Opponents of the general assessment saw the bill as an attempt to reestablish the Anglican church. One Baltimore newspaper warned of the reestablishment of Anglicanism as the "camel's nose" poking under the tent.[51] John Carroll, the Catholic ecclesiastical superior in the United States, was unconvinced by the governor's assurance that the tax would benefit Christians equally. Carroll argued that the Clergy Bill was "calculated to create a predominant and irresistible influence in favour of the Protestant Episcopal Church." He saw legislation favoring one Christian church over another—in fact, if not in law—as dangerously close to an establishment and therefore contrary to the spirit of the Maryland Constitution. He wrote to English Jesuit Charles Plowden that the memory of having "smarted heretofore under the lash of an established church," and having been subjected to a "heavy tax" for Anglican clergy, kept him and other non-Anglicans "on our guard against every approach towards it."[52]

Charles Carroll of Carrollton, a framer of the Maryland Constitution, captured the popular opposition to the assessment bill when he wrote that "a great majority of the People in Washington, Frederick, & Baltimore counties are averse to a tax for the support of Ministers of the Gospel, and I suspect the other counties are not very hearty for the measure."[53] The Clergy Bill had the unintended consequence of unifying disparate Christians—namely, Catholics and non-Anglican Protestants—all but ensuring that the assessment would not pass.

Resistance to the Clergy Bill also stemmed from a broader opposition to the type of taxation proposed. Had the legislature attempted to enact a general assessment of four shillings per person right after the ratification of the Maryland Constitution in 1776, it would effectively have been a reduction of the mandatory tithe, not a new or increased tax.[54] Proposed a decade later, however, the Clergy Bill met opposition as a capitation tax, which levied the same amount per head (*caput*), regardless of income. "Simon Pure," writing in the *Maryland Journal*, called this regressive tax "unequal and oppressive," for "[i]t throws the burden chiefly on the poor, and lets the rich go free." Since the bill would levy a tax according to the number of people, not their wealth, "the rich Merchant in town whose capital in trade is of immense value, will not, perhaps, have so many taxables [people] to pay for, as the poor Farmer, not worth one hundredth part of his fortune." A capitation tax was reminiscent of colonial taxation, when it was used to favor the upper class. "Octavianus," writing in the same newspaper, argued that this form of taxation corrupted the republican polity by minting a class of wealthy merchants and landowners and, in his sarcastic rendering, "throw[ing] the burthen of taxation, where it ought to lie, on the sturdy shoulders of the rabble, on the lower class, or commonality."[55]

The Clergy Bill was just one of many tax programs proposed in the 1784–85 legislative session whose spending habits earned it the ignominious appellation "the Black Session." The assembly passed laws that offered grants to the new University of Maryland, capital improvements for navigation along the Potomac River, bond issuances to pay for these and other programs, and the allowance of counties to tax for infrastructure improvements.[56] George Lux, a Baltimore merchant and politician, noted that opponents of the Clergy Bill "blended the College Bill and the Clergy bill together" by arguing that the university would benefit churches in need of highly educated clergy. Both bills, they argued, would funnel funds to aid the Anglican church.[57]

When the legislature convened again in the fall of 1785, antiassessment politicians had won enough seats to gain the majority. The minority, meanwhile, divided on whether to use a capitation tax or a property tax. In a remarkable political maneuver, opponents to the Clergy Bill exploited this internal rift. They joined supporters of the property-tax clergy bill to table the bill with the capitation tax and then allied with supporters of the capitation-tax Clergy Bill to block the introduction of a bill with a property tax. Having exhausted the options to fund the Clergy Bill, the antiassessment legislators ensured that no bill came up for a vote. Their victory was not a complete triumph for disestablishment, however, since the provision permitting a general assessment still remained in Article XXXIII of the Constitution.[58]

Although the general assessment clause remained inactive, the Maryland state courts invested it with legal and symbolic importance. In 1796 the Maryland Court of Appeals heard the case of William Runkel, a German Reformed minister who was barred from his position by church elders for an allegedly improper ordination. In *Runkel v. Winemiller*, the court granted Runkel (whose counsel included U.S. constitutional framer Luther Martin) a writ of mandamus to reinstate Runkel in his church. The judicial reasoning echoed those constitutional framers who supported the general assessment clause: "Religion is of general and public concern, and on its support depend, in great measure, the peace and good order of government, the safety and happiness of the people." The court declared that under the Maryland Constitution, "the Christian religion is the established religion; and all sects and denominations of christians are placed upon the same equal footing, and are equally entitled to protection in their religious liberty." The propagation of Christianity, the court continued, required the "protect[ion of] the rights of ministers of the gospel."[59] *Runkel* was the earliest reported court case in the United States to affirm Christianity as part of the common law.[60] While that maxim enjoyed a long pedigree in the English common-law tradition, it was repurposed in American civil law, even in states without an established church.[61]

IV.

In 1810 the Maryland Assembly finally removed from the Constitution the allowance of a general assessment.[62] The November 1809–10 legislative session voted forty-eight to two to repeal the latent provision.[63] In the next session in November, the repeal was confirmed by a second passage of the act, as the Constitution required.[64] The large majority in favor of repeal, as well as its perfunctory confirmation a year later when new legislative elections to the assembly could have derailed its validity, indicated that repeal was mere housekeeping that confirmed the assembly's 1785 rejection of a general assessment. The period of "plural establishment" was nearing an end.

After 1810 the remaining constitutional elements of an establishment included religious liberty protections for Christians only and a religious test for public office. The first attempt to eliminate the Constitution's test oath had come in 1797, when Jewish businessman Solomon Etting submitted a petition to the legislature that called for the repeal of the Christian test for public office. The committee believed the appeal was "reasonable . . . but since it involved a constitutional question of considerable importance," it decided to act no further. Legislators obliged Etting's second petition by drafting what became known as the "Jew Bill," but it was defeated in 1802 and again in 1804. When the bill was reintroduced in 1817, Catholic priests, the Catholic archbishop, and Charles Carroll of Carrollton attempted to influence the Maryland Legislature to support the bill.[65] The legislator who introduced the original "Jew Bill," Thomas Kennedy, was Catholic, as was Roger Taney (later chief justice of the U.S. Supreme Court), a supporter of the bill. Despite Catholic support, the bill failed in 1818 and again in 1819.[66]

It would take until 1826 for the Maryland Assembly to annul the Christian test for public office. In its place, the act added a different test requiring a declaration of belief in a "future state of rewards and punishments," a stipulation that the 1851 Maryland Constitution later codified.[67] Yet a later Constitution allowed an alternative declaration in a "belief in the existence of God," rather than a Christian test oath.[68] The rationale for each of these religious tests was that good government requires recognition of Divine Providence in the affairs of state.

Marylanders still considered their state to be Christian. In 1834 the Maryland Court of Appeals reaffirmed the state as "a christian community," one that recognized "[t]he Sabbath" as "emphatically *the day* of rest, and the day of rest here is the 'Lord's day' or christian's Sunday."[69] The state's theistic test for office was not removed until 1961 by the U.S. Supreme Court in a decision captioned *Torcaso v. Watkins*.[70]

V.

The ambiguity of Maryland's church-state relations directly after the revolutionary period echoed the complexity of Maryland's 1632 founding, as Catholics and Protestants attempted to retain a common Christian legal structure despite their theological differences. The state's serpentine start to the disestablishment project was the result of compromises in 1776 by constitutional delegates who represented an array of different Christian denominations, many of which resented the disproportionate benefits accrued to the Anglican church. Yet they could all agree that the Constitution should prefer Christianity by guaranteeing religious liberty to Christians only, allowing the legislature to levy a tax to support Christian denominations nonpreferentially, and requiring a declaration of belief in Christianity for office holders. This "plural establishment" proved difficult to dismantle, even after the general assessment was struck from the Constitution in 1810. Christian preferentialism, especially concerning religious liberty protections and religious tests for public office, continued for almost two centuries.

What remains in the Maryland Constitution is a curious set of clauses that reflect its complicated history of church-state relations. Despite the U.S. Supreme Court's overturning of the theistic test oath in 1961, that clause remains in the current Constitution as a symbolic vestige of the state's checkered history of religious tests.[71] The religious liberty clause likewise retains language from the 1851 Constitution requiring a belief "in the existence of God, and that under His dispensation such person will be held morally accountable for his acts, and be rewarded or punished therefor either in this world or in the world to come." A statutory act ratified by the electorate in 1970 added the following addendum: "Nothing in this article shall constitute an establishment of religion."[72] This bald denial of any establishment is a fitting end to the long and circuitous process of disestablishment that was as complicated as the colony's beginning.

NOTES

1. "The Charter of Maryland," 1632, in *The Federal and State Constitutions, Colonial Charters, and Other Organic Laws of the State, Territories, and Colonies Now or Hertofore Forming the United States of America*, ed. Francis Newton Thorpe (Washington, DC: Government Printing Office, 1909), 3:1677–86.

2. "Maryland Toleration Act," September 21, 1649, in *The Avalon Project: Documents in Law, History and Diplomacy*, http://avalon.law.yale.edu/18th_century/maryland_toleration.asp.

3. Cecil Calvert to Leonard Calvert, November 13, 1633, in *The Calvert Papers*, ed. John Wesley Murray Lee (Baltimore: J. Murphy, 1888–99), 1:132.

4. "An Act for Swearing Allegeance," March 1638, in *Archives of Maryland*, ed. William Hand Browne et al. (Baltimore: Maryland Historical Society, 1883–1916), 1:40–41.

5. Maura Jane Farrelly, *Papist Patriots: The Making of an American Catholic Identity* (New York: Oxford University Press, 2012), 67, 91–92.

6. David Lynn Holmes, *The Faiths of the Founding Fathers* (New York: Oxford University Press, 2006), 20–22.

7. James Hennesey, *American Catholics: A History of the Roman Catholic Community in the United States* (New York: Oxford University Press, 1981), 42.

8. "Maryland Toleration Act."

9. "The Processe agst William Lewis, ffrancis Gray, Robt Sedgrave &c.," 1638, in *Archives of Maryland*, ed. Browne et al., 4:35–39.

10. John D. Krugler, *English and Catholic: The Lords Baltimore in the Seventeenth Century* (Baltimore: Johns Hopkins University Press, 2004), 166.

11. Farrelly, *Papist Patriots*, 103, 104, 108; Krugler, *English and Catholic*, 8.

12. Farrelly, *Papist Patriots*, 117–35.

13. John Frederick Woolverton, *Colonial Anglicanism in North America* (Detroit: Wayne State University Press, 1984), 140.

14. "An Act to prevent the Growth of Popery within this Province," 1704, in *Archives of Maryland*, ed. Browne et al., 26:340–41. See also "An Act for the Further Preventing the Growth of Popery," 1698, 11 Will. III, c. 4.

15. Farrelly, *Papist Patriots*, 132–34, 195–98, 201; Krugler, *English and Catholic*, 9; Ronald Hoffman with Sally D. Mason, *Princes of Ireland, Planters of Maryland: A Carroll Saga, 1500–1782* (Chapel Hill: University of North Carolina Press for the Omohundro Institute of Early American History and Culture, 2000), 91–95.

16. Farrelly, *Papist Patriots*, 206.

17. Frederick V. Mills Sr., *Bishops by Ballot: An Eighteenth-Century Ecclesiastical Revolution* (New York: Oxford University Press, 1978), 9.

18. William Eddis, *Letters from America*, ed. Aubrey C. Land (Cambridge, MA: Belknap Press of Harvard University Press, 1969), 26–28, quoted in John Corbin Rainbolt, "The Struggle to Define 'Religious Liberty' in Maryland, 1776–1785," *Journal of Church and State* 17, no. 3 (1975): 445.

19. Allen Bennett, *A Reply to the Church of England Planter's First Letter* (Annapolis, MD: Anne Catharine Green, 1770); Samuel Chase and William Paca to Jonathan Boucher, *Maryland Gazette*, January 14, March 18, and April 19, 1773.

20. Thomas Cradock, Sermon Preached at Annapolis, 1753, cited in Woolverton, *Colonial Anglicanism*, 232.

21. Thomas J. Curry, *The First Freedoms: Church and State in America to the Passage of the First Amendment* (New York: Oxford University Press, 1986), 153.

22. Woolverton, *Colonial Anglicanism*, 101–02, 155.

23. William Dawes, *A Sermon Preach'd before the Society for the Propagation of the Gospel in Foreign Parts, at the Parish-Church of St. Mary-le-Bow, on Friday February 18, 1708/9* (London: Three Crowns, 1709), 15.

24. [White Kennet], *An Account of the Society for Propagating the Gospel in Foreign Parts . . .* (London: Joseph Downing, 1706).

25. John Carroll to Vitaliano Borromeo, November 10, 1783, in *The John Carroll Papers*, ed. Thomas O'Brien Hanley (South Bend, IN: University of Notre Dame Press, 1976), 1:80.

26. Charles Carroll of Carrollton to Charles Carroll of Annapolis, August 17, 1776, in *Dear Papa, Dear Charley: The Peregrinations of a Revolutionary Aristocrat, as Told by Charles Carroll of Carrollton and His Father, Charles Carroll of Annapolis, with Sundry Observations on Bastardy, Child-Rearing, Romance, Matrimony, Commerce, Tobacco, Slavery, and the Politics of Revolutionary America*, ed. Ronald Hoffman, Sally D. Mason, and Eleanor S. Darcy (Chapel Hill: University of North Carolina Press for the Omohundro Institute of Early American History and Culture, 2001), 2:938.

27. "A Declaration of Rights," 1776, in *Federal and State Constitutions*, ed. Thorpe, 3:1689.

28. John Carroll to Charles Plowden, February 27, 1785, in *John Carroll Papers*, ed. Hanley, 1:168.

29. John Carroll to Charles Carroll of Carrollton, November 11, 1783, in *John Carroll Papers*, ed. Hanley, 1:82.

30. "A Declaration of Rights," 1776, in *Federal and State Constitutions*, ed. Thorpe, 3:1689.

31. "A Declaration of Rights," 1776, in *Federal and State Constitutions*, ed. Thorpe, 3:1690.

32. Charles, John, and Daniel Carroll were recorded as taking the oath. Bettie Stirling Carothers, *Maryland Oaths of Fidelity* (Lutherville, MD: printed by author, 1975–78), 1:15, 39, 2:4.

33. Marc Kruman missed Maryland from his list of states with clergy prohibition clauses, and Anson Phelps Stokes stated that the prohibition was from 1851 to 1864 only. Marc W. Kruman, *Between Authority and Liberty: State Constitution Making in Revolutionary America* (Chapel Hill: University of North Carolina, 1997), 47; Anson Phelps Stokes, *Church and State in the United States* (New York: Harper, 1950), 1:623.

34. "The Constitution, or Form of Government," 1776, in *Federal and State Constitutions*, ed. Thorpe, 3:1697.

35. Frederic S. Le Clercq, "Disqualification of Clergy for Civil Office," *Memphis State University Law Review* 7, no. 4 (1977): 572n94; *Kirkley v. State of Maryland*, 381 F. Supp. 327, 331 (D. Md. 1974).

36. William M. Hogue, "The Civil Disability of Ministers of Religion in State Constitutions," *Journal of Church and State* 36, no. 2 (1994): 332–33.

37. "A Declaration of Rights," 1776, in *Federal and State Constitutions*, ed. Thorpe, 3:1689; Rainbolt, "Struggle to Define 'Religious Liberty,'" 445; Curry, *First Freedoms*, 154.

38. "An Act for the Establishment of Select Vestries," 1779, in *Laws of Maryland . . .* , ed. Alexander Contee Hanson (Annapolis, MD: Frederick Green, 1787), chap. 9.

39. "A Declaration of Rights," 1776, in *Federal and State Constitutions*, ed. Thorpe, 3:1690. Maryland case law confirms that even private payments would be voided if the Maryland General Assembly did not approve of them. Later cases clarified that there were certain thresholds under which government approval would not be required. See *Trustees of the Zion Church v. Henry G. Hilken*, 84 Md. 170 (1896).

40. John C. Rainbolt, "A Note on the Maryland Declaration of Rights and Constitution of 1776," *Maryland Historical Magazine* 66 (1971): 420–25; Rainbolt, "Struggle to Define 'Religious Liberty,'" 445.

41. "A Declaration of Rights," 1776, in *Federal and State Constitutions*, ed. Thorpe, 3:1689.

42. Rainbolt, "Struggle to Define 'Religious Liberty,'" 447, 458.

43. Allan Nevins, *The American States during and after the Revolution, 1775–1789* (New York: Macmillan, 1927), 431.

44. *Votes and Proceedings of the House of Delegates of the State of Maryland*, April Session, 1783 (Annapolis, MD: Frederick Green, 1783), 6.

45. Rainbolt, "Struggle to Define 'Religious Liberty,'" 447.

46. *By the House of Delegates, January 20, 1785 . . . An Act to Lay a General Tax for the Support of Ministers of the Gospel of All Societies of Christians within this State* (Annapolis, MD: Frederick Green, 1785).

47. *Votes and Proceedings of the House of Delegates of the State of Maryland*, November Session, 1784 (Annapolis, MD: Frederick Green, 1785), 74–75, 88–89, 95, 102.

48. George Lux to Benjamin Rush, February 18, 1785, Rush Papers, Library Company of Philadelphia, cited in Rainbolt, "Struggle to Define 'Religious Liberty,'" 453.

49. *Maryland Journal*, March 22, 1785, quoted in Rainbolt, "Struggle to Define 'Religious Liberty,'" 452–54.

50. "Philander," *Maryland Journal*, March 22, 1785, quoted in Rainbolt, "Struggle to Define 'Religious Liberty,'" 454.

51. *Maryland Gazette*, 1785, cited in Leonard W. Levy, *The Establishment Clause: Religion and the First Amendment*, 2nd ed. (Chapel Hill: University of North Carolina Press, 1994), 54–55.

52. John Carroll to Charles Plowden, February 27, 1785, in *John Carroll Papers*, ed. Hanley, 1:168.

53. Charles Carroll of Carrollton to James McHenry, March 13, 1785, Huntington Library, San Marino, CA.

54. Rainbolt, "Struggle to Define 'Religious Liberty,'" 454–56.

55. "Simon Pure," *Maryland Journal*, March 1, 1785, and "Octavianus," *Maryland Journal*, February 25, 1785, quoted in Rainbolt, "Struggle to Define 'Religious Liberty,'" 456–57.

56. *Laws of Maryland* (Annapolis, MD: Frederick Green, 1785), chaps. 4, 7, 17, 33, 38, 55, 70, 74; *Votes and Proceedings of House of Delegates*, November Session, 1784, 59–60.

57. George Lux to Benjamin Rush, May 14, 1785, Rush Papers, Library Company of Philadelphia, quoted in Rainbolt, "Struggle to Define 'Religious Liberty,'" 458.

58. *Votes and Proceedings of the House of Delegates of the State of Maryland*, November Session, 1785 (Annapolis, MD: Frederick Green, 1786), 9; Rainbolt, "Struggle to Define 'Religious Liberty,'" 449–50.

59. *Runkel v. Winemiller*, 1799, in *Maryland Reports, Being a Series of the Most Important Law Cases*, ed. Thomas Harris and John McHenry (Annapolis, MD: Jonas Green, 1818), 4:450.

60. Steven Green, *The Second Disestablishment: Church and State in Nineteenth-Century America* (New York: Oxford University Press, 2010), 162.

61. Stuart Banner, "When Christianity Was Part of the Common Law," *Law and History Review* 16, no. 1 (1998): 27–62.

62. "An Act to Alter All Such Parts of the Declaration of Rights, Constitution and Form of Government, as Make it Lawful to Lay an Equal and a General Tax for the Support of the Christian Religion," 1810, in *Laws of Maryland . . .* (Annapolis, MD: Frederick Green, [1811]), chap. CLXVII.

63. *Votes and Proceedings of the House of Delegates of the State of Maryland*, November Session, 1809 (Annapolis, MD: Frederick Green, [1810]), 104.

64. *Votes and Proceedings of the House of Delegates of the State of Maryland*, November Session, 1810 (Annapolis, MD: Frederick Green, [1811], 38.

65. Charles Carroll of Carrollton to Ambrose Maréchal, January 31, 1817, in Archives of the Archdiocese of Baltimore and Associated Archives at St. Mary's Seminary & University; Charles Carroll of Carrollton to Ambrose Maréchal, December 19, 1818, in Baltimore Basilica Museum, Baltimore; Martin I. J. Griffin, "Did They Favor Repeal?," *American Catholic Historical Researches* 23, no. 2 (1909): 192.

66. Chief Justice John Roberts cited Maryland legislator H. M. Brackenridge, who argued in 1818 that the religious test amounted to persecution on account of religion that differed "only in degree" with persecutions "whose instruments are chains and torture." *Trinity Lutheran Church of Columbia, Inc. v. Comer*, 137 S. Ct. 2012, 2024 (2017) (Chief Justice John Roberts for the majority, citing speech by H. M. Brackenridge, December Session, 1818, in H. M. Brackenridge, William Worthington, and John Tyson, *Speeches on the Jew Bill* (Philadelphia: J. Dobson, 1829), 64).

67. "An Act for the Relief of the Jews in Maryland," 1826, in *Laws Made and Passed by the General Assembly of the State of Maryland* (Annapolis, MD: Jeremiah Hughes, 1825), chap. 33; Edward Eitches, "Maryland's 'Jew Bill,'" *American Jewish Historical Quarterly* 60, no. 3 (1971): 258, 265; Maryland Constitution, 1851, in *Federal and State Constitutions*, ed. Thorpe, 3:1722.

68. Maryland Constitution, 1864, in *Federal and State Constitutions*, ed. Thorpe, 3:1745.

69. *Kilgour v. Miles*, 6 Gill and Johns 268 (Maryland, 1834), quoted in Green, *Second Disestablishment*, 186.

70. *Torcaso v. Watkins*, 367 U.S. 488 (1961).

71. Maryland Constitution, 1867, Article XXXVII, as amended, 2015, http://mga-leg.maryland.gov/pubs-current/current-constitution-maryland-us.pdf.

72. Maryland Constitution, 1867, Article XXXVI, as amended, 2015, http://mga-lcg.maryland.gov/pubs-current/current-constitution-maryland-us.pdf.

CHAPTER SEVENTEEN

CONNECTICUT
A Land of Steady Habits

Robert J. Imholt

TRADITIONAL INTERPRETATIONS OF separation of church and state in Connecticut point to the 1818 Constitution as disestablishing the Congregational Church.[1] These accounts, however, both overemphasize the hold of Congregationalism prior to 1818 and oversimplify the evolution of church-state relations in Connecticut following the Constitution's ratification. At times, the Standing Order—the alliance of Congregational clergy and political leaders—dominated Connecticut public life; at other times, the Standing Order was in retreat and working to shore up churches, legally termed "ecclesiastical societies." Rather than ending at a specific time and with a specific law, disestablishment was the result of processes that stretched over decades and occurred for a multitude of reasons.

Seventeenth-century Puritans saw questions of religion and government as inextricably intertwined. Divine law as embodied in Scripture was the foundation of civil law. The role of governing institutions was, among other worldly concerns, to protect and sustain the ecclesiastical ones. Having already founded churches, in January 1639 the Connecticut River towns of Wethersfield, Hartford, and Windsor drafted the *Fundamental Orders of Connecticut* because "the word of God requires that to maintain the peace and union of such a people there be an orderly and decent government established according to God." Moreover, it was "to maintain and preserve the liberty and purity of the Gospel of Our Lord Jesus which we now profess, as also the discipline of the Churches, which according to the truth of the gospel is now practiced amongst us."[2] In the New Haven Colony, a 1656 compilation of its laws stated that the General Court "shall first with all care, and diligence from time to time provide for the maintenance of the purity of religion and suppress the contrary, according to their best light, and directions from the word of God."[3] The role and function of government were to assist the churches in fashioning a godly society and to preserve them from schism and doctrinal innovation. In seventeenth-century Connecticut, the boundaries of the town were the boundaries of the church, and when the church gathered every Sabbath, it was a public assembly that, in the words of historian Harry Stout, "represented the central ritual of social order and control."[4]

Even though the relationship between church and state evolved from the initial founding until well into the nineteenth century, one constant was the belief that religion was the bulwark of an orderly state, and thus the state had an interest in fostering religion. While often implicit, this understanding was regularly re-emphasized by the religious and civil elites. In the aftermath of the American Revolution, which disrupted and divided the state, the mutual dependence of religion and the state was highlighted in annual Election Day sermons before the governor, general assembly, and assembled clergy. In 1787 Durham minister Elizur Goodrich declared that "the immediate ends of the magistry and ministry are different, but not opposite. They mutually assist each other, and ultimately center in the same point. The one has for its object the promotion of religion and the cause of Christ; the other immediately aims at the peace and order of mankind in this world."[5] Three years later, Nathan Strong, pastor of Hartford's First Church, preached that as regards the civil and ecclesiastical departments, "neither of them is independent of the other. Civility and good order of political regulations are a great advantage to religion and its institutions are [the] best aid of government, by strengthening the ruler's hand, and making the subject faithful in his place and obedient to the general laws."[6] By the early nineteenth century, a growing number challenged this orthodoxy, but the belief that Protestant Christianity underlay Connecticut law, politics, and society remained strong.

Disestablishment in Connecticut, therefore, is as much a story of how the founders' vision, a utopian vision, confronted the realities of human frailty, unforeseen social and cultural developments, and the tensions inherent to Congregationalism itself. In the seventeenth century, these tensions were manageable. By the eighteenth century, dealing with the population growth and a more diverse society would require church-state adjustments.

I.

The founders of Connecticut were not in agreement concerning how to build the City of God in the wilderness. Reverend John Davenport and Governor Theophilus Eaton sought to construct a new Jerusalem on the shores of Long Island Sound. In New Haven, Scripture determined the layout of the town, the law code was drawn from Leviticus, and only full members of the church could become freemen. In the larger Connecticut colony, while freemen need not be full members of the church, the legal code (without the scriptural references) was similar to that of New Haven.[7] In New London, under the leadership of John Winthrop the Younger, a less idealistic polity developed, although no less committed to maintaining a Puritan communal ethos. Despite these differences, it was universally agreed that religious institutions were essential, as no community could succeed without divine favor.[8]

In less than a decade, problems emerged. The Congregational polity, in which each local church selected and ordained its minister, but made by both members and nonmember freemen, was a source of tension. The Hartford church was particularly troubled. Following the death of Thomas Hooker, the minister who had led the settlers to Connecticut, the church "became divided and inflamed" over the choice of a successor, and, according to historian Benjamin Trumbull, "the whole colony became affected."[9] In Middletown, when differences between the congregation and its minister became irreconcilable, the General Court allowed the church to find another minister, "able, orthodox, and pious."[10] In these cases and others, the civil government exercised its role, as the *Fundamental Orders* stated, "to maintain and preserve the liberty and purity of the gospel [and] the discipline of the Churches."

The Half-Way Covenant was another point of controversy. While most of the founding generation had provided evidence of conversion and were full members of the church and had their children baptized, by the 1650s some of these children, who had not become full members, were having children and presenting them for baptism. The General Court wrestled with the issue as early as 1656. In 1664 the court endorsed the baptism of offspring of these "half-way" members and conveyed this solution to the churches for comment.[11] The ensuing debate tore congregations apart. Those in the minority, whether for or against the Half-Way Covenant, petitioned the court. The dispute raged on until 1669, when the general assembly voted to allow congregations both with and without the Half-Way Covenant, "until better light in an orderly way doth appear," and declared that "no new churches could be gathered without the consent of both the Court and neighboring churches."[12] Connecticut was now a checkerboard of churches with differing policies on baptism. Most important, while the first settlers had formed ecclesiastical societies before the civil ones, now the assembly assumed the task of legally establishing churches.

The assembly's concern that no new churches be formed without its consent was also a response to a second problem, that of "outlivers." Connecticut's original settlers were a remarkably long-lived and procreative group. The settlers of the original towns lived close to the meetinghouse and school. As population grew, however, distributions of the common and undivided lands meant that more families moved farther from the town centers. Attendance at public worship became a burden for these "outlivers." They demanded churches and schools of their own. However, establishing a separate ecclesiastical society meant that the burden of supporting the original society and its minister fell on fewer rate payers. Given this dilemma, the assembly, reluctantly in most cases and over the objection of the original society, created new parishes, thus making the boundaries of the towns and the ecclesiastical society no longer identical.

Several developments early in the eighteenth century also altered church-government relations in Connecticut. The first was the *Saybrook Platform*, a document that set forth a framework to maintain the peace, harmony, and orthodoxy of the colony's congregations. In 1708 Gurdon Saltonstall was elected governor, the only minister to hold that office. As pastor of the First Church of New London, Saltonstall had personal experience with religious turmoil. New London was the home to John Rogers and his followers. Professing an amalgam of Seventh-Day Baptist and Quaker beliefs, the Rogerenes refused to pay taxes to support the established church or the wars against the French and Indians. One of Saltonstall's first acts was to secure during the May session of the assembly an act calling for a synod to "consider and agree upon those methods and rules for the management of ecclesiastical discipline, conformable to the word of God." Meeting in the town of Saybrook during the commencement at Yale College, the synod endorsed creedal beliefs and ministerial practices, but more important adopted a document organizing the Congregational churches of Connecticut into local associations, along with larger county-wide consociations and a colony-wide association providing final oversight. The local associations would oversee the orthodoxy of individual churches and serve as arbiter of parochial disputes, hopefully relieving the colonial assembly of this sensitive task. Also, under the *Saybrook Platform*, ministers would still be called by the individual church, but clergy would be licensed and ordained by the county-wide association. In October 1708, the assembly "declare[d] their great approbation of such a happy agreement and ordain that all churches within this government that are or shall be thus united in doctrine, worship, and discipline, and for the future shall be owned and acknowledged established by law."[13]

The *Saybrook Platform* replaced a congregational polity with a presbyterian one. Several congregations rejected the *Platform*, as it took away local autonomy and disputes between congregations and their ministers would now be handled by a group of ministers whose impartiality was open to question. This foreshadowed debates that would emerge in the democratic age following the American Revolution, when supporters of disestablishment found a useful target in the *Saybrook Platform* and its civil rule of church disputes.[14]

Another development was alteration in the manner in which ministers and parishes were supported. While initially ministers were to be supported by voluntary contributions, the *Cambridge Platform* of 1648, which Connecticut accepted, held that if funds were not forthcoming, coercion should be used.[15] Soon towns were annually setting the minister's rate and appointing collectors. While some clearly met their obligation, collecting from others was difficult. Recognizing the problem, the legislature in 1697 placed responsibility for collection on magistrates and allowed them to distrain property.[16] Even this did not help. In 1717 the assembly, recognizing that in many towns there were several ecclesiastical societies, placed responsibility for collecting the church tax on the societies themselves rather than the towns. At its December meeting, each parish was "to grant and levy such rates and taxes on the inhabitants for the support of ministry and schools" and to appoint collectors.[17] As historian Barbara Lacey notes, while scofflaws could be reported to civil authorities for collection, "the reluctance of parishioners to pay taxes for the minister's salary did not always come to court."[18]

Finally, the early eighteenth century saw the end of Connecticut's isolation from the larger British world. As Connecticut became enmeshed in the commercial and cultural networks of empire, Great Britain was no longer a place to escape from, as it was for Connecticut's first settlers, but a cultural and economic metropole to be cultivated and admired. In turn, Britain took a greater interest in its colonies. Even as the assembly approved the *Saybrook Platform*, Connecticut's desire for religious uniformity was under challenge. In 1705 the Crown nullified Connecticut's law against Quakers. At the same time, the general assembly, feeling pressure from London and wanting to safeguard its charter, adopted a *Toleration Act*, similar to that passed by Parliament in 1691, which granted certain rights to "sober dissenters," while retaining disabilities on heretics and Catholics.[19]

The early years of the century also saw the beginnings of denominational diversity. In 1705 a Baptist church was formed in Groton, and in 1718 an Anglican church gathered in Stratford. A few dissenting churches did not provide a challenge to the Standing Order. In 1722, however, the establishment was shaken when Yale rector Timothy Cutler and two tutors informed the trustees that they had converted to Anglicanism. Dismissed from his position and doubting the validity of his own ordination, Cutler traveled to England with a few others for Anglican ordination."[20] This drew the attention of the bishop of London, who in 1724 wrote Governor Talcott, inquiring why Anglicans were taxed to support Congregational churches. Talcott defended the tax. However, in 1727 the colonial legislature, ever fearful of having Connecticut's charter revoked, allowed taxes from Anglicans to be directed to their own churches. Two years later, a similar privilege was granted to Baptists and Quakers.[21]

II.

If allowing taxes to go to other denominations was a fault in Congregational dominance, the First Great Awakening was a veritable earthquake. With rumblings in the 1730s by Jonathan Edwards and magnified by the preaching of George Whitefield and his imitators, the revival shook Connecticut in the early 1740s. Itinerant preachers moved from town to town, afflicting the comfortable with fear that they were not saved and urging them to throw themselves on God's mercy. At times, suggesting that even some ministers were not among the saved, the Great Awakening tore congregations apart.

While ministers and even Governor Treadwell welcomed Whitefield to the colony in hope of overcoming religious torpor, by November 1741 the General Consocation complained to the assembly about "sundry persons . . . guilty of disorderly and irregular practices" and asked it to "prevent divisions and disorder among the churches and ecclesiastical societies." Connecticut, ever conscious of its role as the protector of religion, passed *An Act for Regulating Abuses and Correcting Disorders in Ecclesiastical Affairs*, reaffirming the *Saybrook Platform* rule that only clergy licensed by the county-wide association were allowed to preach and that no one should be permitted to preach in any town without an invitation from the settled pastor. Any clergyman violating the act would be barred from receiving a salary from the minister's rate.[22] The assembly also banished a few itinerant preachers from the colony.

The result was a splintering of the Congregational world. Some Connecticut towns went through years of acrimony, bitterness, and mutual recrimination. Even former Yale rector Elisha Williams protested the assembly's action in one of the first pleas for religious liberty in the colonies.[23] In the words of historian Douglas Winiarski, "Congregational ministers found themselves in a pitched battle to hold the center of a religious culture rapidly coming apart at the seams." Anglican churches attracted large numbers who found their stability and tradition a welcome refuge. Followers of the "New Light" separated from congregations under "Old Light" control and formed parishes of their own or aligned with the Baptist movement. In the end, the wrenching experience of the Great Awakening led to a new normalcy in New England, where "the ascendancy of individual experience over corporate discipline [and] church membership no longer related to parish boundaries, ecclesiastical order, or community expectations."[24]

After midcentury a religious calm returned to Connecticut. A spirit of toleration emerged, and town greens were now host to multiple houses of worship. The colonial government, faced with the choice of maintaining uniformity through ever-stricter controls on churches or accepting greater diversity, implicitly adopted the latter by its own actions when, in 1750, the state's new law code omitted the laws enacted in the early 1740s.[25] While the question of taxation to support religion occasionally raised its head, public attention turned to the war with the French and later the struggle with Great Britain. Exemplifying the new mood, in 1770 the assembly approved an addition to the law "for the due observation and keeping of the Sabbath," which repealed all penalties for Sabbath attendance by Protestants, "who soberly and conscientiously dissent" and meet "for the publick worship of God in a way agreeable to their consciences."[26] In 1777 all dissenting Protestant churches received the same recognition as Anglicans, Baptists, and Quakers had received earlier in the century.[27]

III.

The American Revolution brought fundamental change to Connecticut, especially in the relationship between church and state. The war impacted all aspects of Connecticut's religious life. Anglicans and their clergy, many of whom remained loyal to George III, were persecuted throughout the war. Large numbers fled to New York City or Long Island, both under British control.[28] Economic disruptions impacted both the clergy and civilians. Probably most important, however, the revolution imbued the populace with a spirit of republican activism that undermined both the political and the religious establishment.

When peace arrived, all aspects of civic life demanded reconstruction. The general assembly responded by establishing a committee to revise the laws. The new law code, approved by the legislature in 1784, made fundamental changes in matters of religion.[29] Most important was *An Act for Securing the Rights of Conscience in Matters of Religion to Christians of Every*

Denomination. Reasserting the position maintained by Connecticut's founders that "the happiness of a People, and the good order of Civil Society depend upon Piety, Religion, and Morality," and that it was the duty of the government to "provide Support and Encouragement" for churches, it declared that all "Protestant Churches . . . shall have Liberty and Authority . . . Powers and Privileges" as the Congregational churches. The act reaffirmed another principle that had been part of Connecticut law since the foundation: "Every Inhabitant in this State, shall . . . contribute to public charges, both civil and ecclesiastical, whereof he doth receive benefit; may, and shall be compelled thereunto, if need be, by Assessment and Distress." Ecclesiastical societies, like towns, had the authority to levy taxes on their members, the rate being determined by the society itself. Since implementation required clarity as to membership, all residents were counted as members of a religious society, and individuals could not change congregations "unless released by Act of the General Assembly or vote of such society, and joining another Society."[30] The unaffiliated were by law members of the Congregational church. By its absence from the code, the *Saybrook Platform* was no longer part of the laws of Connecticut, an action that jurist Zephaniah Swift later called "a complete renunciation of the doctrine, that an ecclesiastical establishment is necessary to the support of civil government."[31]

The *Saybrook Platform* excepted, the legislative action simply codified prewar law. Focus on legal codes, however, obscures the powerful currents buffeting Connecticut religious life. Baptist churches, fewer than a dozen before the war, numbered fifty-five by 1790. Others moved from the established churches to Episcopal and Methodist congregations.[32] Also, as historian David W. King notes, "[I]n the revolutionary and post-revolutionary period salary disputes" between clergy and congregations dramatically increased."[33] Because of inflation and decline in the number of households, many clergy resigned and the number of clerical dismissals greatly increased.[34] While clergy were esteemed before the revolution, in 1787 young lawyer David Daggett mourned "the loss of this happy influence of the clergy." Daggett ascribed the change "to two causes—knowledge has induced the laity to think for themselves, and an opposition to religion has curtailed the power of its supporters."[35]

In an attempt to stabilize churches, the assembly in May 1791 modified the law regarding church membership. Individuals wishing to change membership would need to appear before town officials, who would sign certificates only after inquiring whether those seeking to withdraw from a congregation were both attending and contributing to the support of another congregation.[36]

Popular opposition erupted almost immediately. With a long tradition of opposing state support of religion, much of the opposition came from the state's Baptists. "Pandor," writing in the *Connecticut Courant*, rejected the idea that religion would "not stand without the aid of civil law." The certificate law, Pandor concluded, "is as much worse than the act on tea, as religious fetters are worse than civil."[37] Supporters of the law were quick to respond to Pandor. In the next issue of the *Courant*, an anonymous writer defended the certificate law. "Instead of the least design to injure and oppress, . . . the law originated in a sense which the Presbyterians entertained of the justice of liberating Dissenters of taxes to support a religion disagreeable to them, and in a sincere desire, that they may be liberated!" Without the certificate law, dissenters might suffer the injustice of paying taxes for the support of the clergy of the established church as well as supporting their own ministers. The certificate law "enable[d] them to enjoy liberty of conscience without injuring their property." Pandor's argument suggested that he was "an enthusiast," "an infidel," "a Deist," or a "*Nothingarian*." In sum, the writer adamantly maintained that "the state have a right to regulate the temporal things necessary for the support of Ministers in the state."[38]

The debate roiled throughout the summer of 1791. Discussions continued among leaders of the dissenting sects, who organized to press their cause at the freemen's meetings in September that would select representatives for the October meeting of the assembly. To supporters of the certificate law, these "secret" gatherings seemed like conspiratorial cabals, and they urged "every Freeman, who wishes for order and regularity in the state" to attend the meetings or "we may see the Legislature . . . destroy every law made for the support of religion and the rights of conscience."[39] In the end, while dissenters were unable to change the composition of the legislature, the legislature heeded their message. The certificate law was repealed, and the state reverted to the practice of individuals signing their own certificates and filing them with the established church.[40]

This crisis was resolved only to have another rear its head. The colonial charter of 1662 set Connecticut's western boundary as extending to the Pacific Ocean. In 1786, when Connecticut ceded its claim to western land to the federal government, it retained a strip of land west of Pennsylvania known as the Western Reserve. In October 1793, the assembly voted that proceeds from the sale of these lands establish an endowment for the "Support of

Ministry and Schools of Education."[41] Having attempted to bolster church revenues through taxes with the certificate law and failed, supporters of the act hoped that the revenue from a fund generated from the sale would be sufficient to forego taxes to support the ministry. There were a number of concerns about the measure, foremost that the land had yet to be sold. Representative Charles Phelps likened it to a "person who sold the Bearskin before they caught the Bear."[42]

At the May 1794 session, there was a spirited debate whether to repeal the act. While there was almost unanimous support for funding education, division raged over the support of ministry. Opponents feared that an endowment fund would make the clergy independent, no longer relying on taxes, but also no longer dependent on their congregations. "To establish a separate order of men is contrary to the public good and to the real principles of republicanism." Representative William Judd argued that providing funds to the ecclesiastical societies would only result in higher clerical salaries, helping to "destroy that equality which is said to be the basis of republican government." Particularly strident was "Cato," who, in a letter to the *Connecticut Courant*, argued that the act was a result of "priestly pride and avarice." While repeal passed the assembly in May, it did not pass the council, the upper house of the legislature.[43] It was not until May 1795 that the issue was resolved. Support for the ministry was left out of the act, and a fund was established for the support of schools.[44] In placing authority in a separate school committee in each town, the act took power away from local clergy, who were previously responsible for local education.

The entire episode left a legacy that would carry into the nineteenth century. The actions of the Council in the appropriations controversy opened discussion over whether the frame of government set forth in the 1662 Charter, only slightly modified at the outset of the revolution, was suitable for a republican government.[45] The established church's failure to secure stable funding, combined with funding for schools outside ministerial purview, was a step in a long process in which public schools were seen as the primary agency through which the state molded a citizenry essential for republican government. Finally, the debate over the appropriation act contributed to a growing anticlericalism directed primarily at the Congregational clergy.

The most vocal critics of the Congregational establishment were dissenting clergy. John Cosens Ogden, an Anglican priest, who had already battled Congregationalism in New Hampshire, published a pamphlet in 1798 titled *An Appeal to the Candid on the Present State of Religion and Politics in Connecticut*. According to Ogden, while the laws provided for religious freedom, this right is "violated to the great disgrace of the State." His target was Yale president Timothy Dwight, who after assuming "control of Yale . . . is making great strides after universal controul in Connecticut, New-England, and the United States, over religious opinion and politics. . . . At this time, Connecticut is more completely under the administration of a Pope than Italy." The next year, Ogden took aim at the Standing Order as a whole. The regular meetings of the associations and consociations of the Congregational clergy "formed that union of *Church and State*—of laymen and ecclesiastics—which have created an order equally formidable with that body of men in any country of Europe. . . . Courting the rich and directing the politics of the country . . . they had united a formidable body with them among the laity, who received votes and preferments at the will of clergy."[46]

David Austin, a New Haven native and Presbyterian minister, took aim at the cozy relationship between the Congregational clergy and the government. Using biblical imagery, in 1799 he published a pamphlet titled *The Dance of Herodias, through the Streets of Hartford on Election Day*. Austin's target was the annual May meeting of the General assembly in Hartford, where legislators gathered to elect executive and judicial officers for the coming year and the Congregational clergy gathered to offer prayers and observe the proceedings. At the appointed time, the governor, assistants, and assembly rose and marched with the clergy, in full vestment, from the statehouse to First Church to listen to the election sermon. To Austin, the ceremony smacked of Romanism. The "Beast of Revelation," he argued, was the union of ecclesiastical and civil power at Rome. Citizens of Connecticut, however, should not rest content, for "the same guilt which is laid at the door of the *papal* household . . . must be disposed of by those who imitate her example in the *protestant* departments."[47]

Defenders of the Standing Order were not silent as critics engaged in heated rhetoric, but Ogden and Austin were more irritants than threats to the dominance of the Congregational establishment. More existential challenges were infidelity and the "cult of reason" associated with the French Revolution as well as the emergence of the Democratic-Republican Party. The national election of 1800 brought the issue of church-state relations fully to the fore. At the same time, Connecticut's Baptists began a petition campaign to bring an end to the state's role in religious matters. The first years of the nineteenth century, therefore, saw the strange coalition of Baptists with Democratic-Republicans who, while not infidels as claimed by some of the Federalist persuasion, were often critical of "religious superstition."[48]

A major spokesman for the Republican position was Abraham Bishop. In an address on the eve of the Yale commencement in September 1800, Bishop argued that citizens of Connecticut had been deluded by both Federalist orators and "some of the leading clergy [who] want to combine Church and State."[49] In another speech six months later, Bishop expanded on this theme. "An ecclesiastical and civil tyranny have formed a junction in New England," he argued, "for the express purpose of enslaving the minds of men on religion and political subjects." The American Revolution "will never be accomplished . . . till we separate church and state, till our clergy can be persuaded to address to the gospel and our statesmen to the true principles of our government." Bishop continued, "Church and State twine together. Moses and Aaron find it profitable to walk hand in hand. The clergyman preaches politics; the civilian prates of orthodoxy."[50] He followed with an even more determined effort in 1802, with a pamphlet titled *Proofs of a Conspiracy, Against Christianity, and the Government of the United States.* Connecticut's Congregational clergy, Bishop wrote, "so far from preaching and practicing Christianity . . . [they] preach a religion of this world, practice a life of pride, and equip these followers in the armour of earth to combat against the cause of heaven."[51]

An anonymous correspondent of the *American Mercury* (Hartford) wrote in June 1801 that "the strong prejudice in favor of the federal politics has impelled the clergy beyond the bound of moderation and candor." They have, claimed the correspondent, "forfeited that respect and esteem which had been attached to their character, and which were necessary for the support of their influence and usefulness among the people."[52] New London politician Christopher Manwaring went so far as to suggest, incorrectly, that Connecticut's laws on questions of religion violated the First Amendment to the U.S. Constitution.[53]

The Democratic-Republican rhetoric was pitched to reach the state's Baptists. In the first years of the century, Connecticut's Baptists petitioned the assembly for an end to the certificate law and the end of taxes for the support of religion. The 1802 petition, for example, argued "that all laws which oblige a man to worship in any particular mode, or which compel him to pay taxes . . . are tyrannical and unjust." In particular, Baptists took aim at the laws that "establish and invest the [Congregational] denomination . . . with many powers and claims over the other religious denominations," including laws on ministerial support and church formation. In response, while refusing to act on the Baptist petition, an assembly committee, chaired by former U.S. chief justice Oliver Ellsworth, reminded petitioners of the legislative responsibility "to countenance, aid, and protect religious institutions . . . wisely calculated to direct men to the performance of all the duties arising from their connection with each other, and to prevent those evils which flow from unrestrained passion." Comparing taxes for the ministry to those that support schools, Ellsworth pointed out that even an individual without children and who "believes [schools] useless" is compelled to pay. "On the same principle of general utility . . . the legislature may aid the maintenance of religion whose benign influence on morals is universally acknowledged. . . . [T]his principle has long been recognized and is too extremely connected to the peace, order, and happiness of the state, to be abandoned."[54]

The Republican and Baptist campaigns of the first five years of the century are most remembered for the involvement of Thomas Jefferson. In October 1801, the Danbury (Connecticut) Baptist Association wrote President Jefferson, expressing its "great satisfaction" at his election and summarizing the position set forth in the petitions. Jefferson's reply endorsed the Baptist campaign and wished them success and, in a phrase that would enter twentieth-century debates over church-state relations, argued for "building a wall of separation between Church & State." At the time, however, the letter did not generate any press coverage in Connecticut, and the Baptist Association itself refused to record the president's response in their proceedings.[55]

The tacit alliance between Connecticut's Baptists and Democratic-Republicans at the beginning of the century collapsed by 1805. Federalists still dominated state and most local elections, and the anticlerical and at times antireligious rhetoric of some Republicans alienated Baptists. The result was a decade in which interest in church-state questions in Connecticut waned. After the War of 1812, however, they were resurrected.

IV.

The years 1815 through 1818 witnessed a veritable revolution in Connecticut's political life. While few in Connecticut supported the War of 1812, the state's Federalists were divided between those who grudgingly cooperated with the war effort and those whose opposition led them to support the Hartford Convention of December 1814. Not only was the timing of the antiwar convention inauspicious, given the peace treaty with Great Britain and news of General Andrew Jackson's victory at New Orleans, but Federalists in the legislature revived the issue of religious establishment in a move reminiscent of the Appropriations Controversy of the 1790s.

In 1814 a group of wealthy Hartford Episcopalians petitioned the legislature to charter a bank. As an incentive to approve the charter, investors

offered the state a $50,000 bonus and recommended that it be divided be-
tween the medical school at Yale and an endowment fund for the Episcopal
bishop. The legislature approved $20,000 for the medical school, but refused
the "Bishop's Bonus." Episcopalians were outraged, especially as it came on
the heels of the rejection of Episcopal attempts to establish a college. For
some Episcopalians who had been supporters of the Federalist Standing
Order, the Bishop's Bonus controversy broke all remaining bonds with the
Federalists.[56]

In May 1816, the Connecticut Legislature, in another effort to financially
buttress churches, requested its U.S. senators to seek reimbursement for state
expenses incurred during the late war and in October passed an *Act for the
Support of Literature and Religion*.[57] As with the appropriations controversy
two decades earlier, the legislature approved plans for distribution of funds
it did not have. One-seventh would go to Yale College for new buildings
and other needs, one-third to the Congregational churches, one-seventh to
the Episcopal Bishop's Fund, and the rest to Methodist and Baptist churches in proportion to their relative membership. Since this benefaction had
been unsolicited by the dissenting churches, it seemed an attempt by the
Federalist-Congregationalist Standing Order to win back support. The effort
came too late. Three months earlier, a group of Episcopalians, disillusioned
Federalists, and Republicans had gathered in New Haven to endorse candidates for the April election as nominees of a new Toleration Party.[58] Oliver
Wolcott Jr., their nominee for governor, was the son and grandson of former
governors and had served as U.S. secretary of the treasury under Presidents
Washington and Adams.

In the April elections, Wolcott narrowly lost to incumbent governor John
Cotton Smith. However, the Toleration Party nominee for lieutenant governor, Jonathan Ingersoll, was victorious, and Toleration candidates won
eighty-five seats in the assembly, cutting into the Federalist majority. A year
later, the results were reversed, as Wolcott narrowly defeated Smith. The primary issue in electoral contests was Connecticut's need for a constitution.
Approved by King Charles II, the 1662 Charter remained the foundational
law of the state, only slightly revised at the beginning of the revolution to
remove references to the British Crown. Although supporters claimed that
the Charter drew its authority from the people, Republicans complained that
under it the legislature was all-powerful, even to the point of overturning
jury verdicts. As one Republican expressed it, Connecticut needed "*a written constitution of civil government*, with proper restrictions and limitations."
A new constitution drawing its authority from the people, he argued, would

take away power from the Congregational-Federalist Standing Order.[59] The Federalist position was unchanged since the time of the revolution. The Charter had provided "stability to the government. . . . No prudent people will . . . overturn a government successful in its operation" to experiment "in an effort to find a better one."[60]

Despite Wolcott's victory for governor in April 1817, the legislature did not call for a constitutional convention or alter church-state relations. While the Toleration Party won a majority in the assembly, Federalists still controlled the Council. Wolcott avoided controversy. As one of Wolcott's friends advised, the subject of religion was of a "delicate texture and should be approached with much caution and silence."[61] The most significant action occurred at the end of the October session. The "Stand-Up" law that gave advantage to Federalists in voting for members of the Council was replaced by paper ballots, virtually guaranteeing election of a Toleration Party majority in April 1818.[62]

The spring 1818 elections saw the Toleration Party take complete control of state government. The Rev. Harry Croswell, an Episcopal rector from New Haven, delivered the Election Day sermon. In his opening address, Governor Wolcott recognized the "desire that the form of civil government for this state should be revised."[63] The session was memorable for two measures. The first broadened the franchise by moving from a property-holding to a tax-paying qualification. The second was a call for a constitutional convention. The assembly scheduled elections for delegates to the convention on July 4, 1818, with the convention itself to convene at Hartford on August 26. Interestingly, the debates over calling a convention, either in the legislature or in the press, included few mentions of church-state relations.

The weeks between the end of the legislative session and Fourth of July election left little time for campaigning. Federalists, avoiding the religious question, argued that party affiliation should not be a factor in choice of delegates. "A Freeman," writing in the New Haven *Connecticut Journal*, argued that "the wall of partition between parties must be prostrated; the scales of prejudice, which have hitherto blinded the eyes of political opponents to each other's merits must be magnanimously removed [and voters] elect the wisest, and the best men."[64] As "Hampden" wrote to the *Courant*, delegates "*ought* to be wise, discreet, and honest men, without regard to sect, denomination or party."[65] The Toleration Party, having won control of state government, now seemed lukewarm on the question of a convention. When the results were tallied, the Toleration Party, which had a majority of more than sixty in the legislature, saw its majority in the convention cut by more than half. Since many of the Toleration delegates were recent Federalists, the convention would be dominated by conservatives and moderates.

During the summer of 1818, debates over the late August convention mostly concerned the structure of state government, but religious issues finally reappeared. At the end July, "John Davenport," using the name of the founder of the New Haven Colony, in a letter to the *Courant* wrote that "the religious institutions of the state must be held sacred."[66] A week later, "A Freeman" warned that during the convention, "a great effort is to be made to destroy the ecclesiastical laws and institutions of the State. . . . These laws cannot be dispensed with, without laying an axe to the root of the State's dignity, integrity, and highest social, moral, political and religious interests and character."[67] Such claims did not go unanswered. The Baptist Society of Hartford objected to what they saw as established religion, the preference for Congregationalism, and tax-supported churches. For them, "Religion [was] established by law . . . and the repeated application . . . for the repeal of laws so palpably unjust . . . have been rejected."[68]

V.

The convention convened in Hartford on August 26, 1818. Governor Wolcott was elected president and a drafting committee established under the chairmanship of Republican U.S. district judge Pierpont Edwards. Wolcott himself had prepared a draft constitution that served as the basis for the committee's deliberations. Religious questions were important in two of the eleven articles. The second and third sections of the drafting committee's "Article First—Declaration of Rights" affirmed "the exercise and enjoyment of religious profession and worship without discrimination, shall forever be free to all persons in this state," and that "no preference shall be given by law to any religious sect or mode of worship." When Article First was presented to the convention, considerable debate ensued over whether the wording would place Mohammedanism, paganism, and other forms of infidelity on an equal footing with Christianity. In the end, Section 3 was amended to "no preference shall be given by law to any christian sect or mode of worship."

Both Wolcott's and the committee's drafts of "Article Seventh—Of Religion" also sparked considerable discussion. The committee rejected much of Wolcott's proposal. In the governor's view, every town should be required to "provide public worship." Towns that "fail[ed] or omit[ted]" to do so would lose representation in the general assembly, and their votes for state offices would not "be received or counted." On the important question of financial support for religion, Wolcott's draft required all to pay taxes. The taxes of those who were not members of a religious community would be appropriated for the support of schools.[69] For those who wished for total disestablishment, Wolcott's draft was clearly disappointing.

The draft of Article Seventh, finally submitted by the drafting committee to the convention, did not include universal taxation for the support of churches or the political penalties on towns, but it did begin, like Wolcott's draft, by declaring that it was "the duty of all men to worship the Supreme Being, the great Creator and Preserver of the Universe." The submission elaborated on the religious sections of Article First, stating that "no person shall by law be compelled to join or support, nor be classed with, or associated to, any congregation, church or religious association." This statement was immediately followed by a clause that "every person now belonging to such congregation, church, or religious association, shall remain a member thereof, until he shall have separated himself therefrom." And every religious association had the power to tax its members for the support of its "ministers or teachers" and cover church expenses. Withdrawal required simply filing a written notice with the society clerk.

A spirited debate followed. Former governor John Treadwell wondered about the opening sentence that it was "the duty of all men to worship the Supreme Being," whether it opened the possibility that "man may think it his duty to worship . . . as the Romans and Grecians did." He also argued that the "wording of . . . Article Seventh might suggest the dissolution of all ecclesiastical societies in the State," as it "recognize[d] no ecclesiastical association, but leaves all . . . in a state of nature." Alexander Wolcott, a Republican leader, suggested leaving out the business of "duty" altogether. Another delegate, Nathaniel Terry, more in line with Governor Wolcott's draft, agreed with Treadwell that the provision might leave churches with insufficient funds and that "religion should be supported somewhere" because religious taxes interfered with the right of conscience no more than being "taxed to support a war, which I disapprove of . . . or laws for support of schools." Joshua Stow, a delegate from Middletown, responded by denying that "the Legislature have a right to compel a man to support public worship: if they have that right, they have a right to say what is public worship," even worship of the devil.[70] After debate the convention approved the first section of Article Seventh by a vote of 103 to 87. The second section of the article, outlining the process for withdrawing from an ecclesiastical society, a policy in place since the 1790s, was approved without debate by a vote of 97 to 69. On September

15, 1818, the convention approved the proposed constitution as a whole by a vote of 134 to 61.[71]

The draft constitution was now in the hands of the voters. The *Hartford Times*, which supported the Tolerationist Clause, was satisfied. "The rights of conscience have been settled upon principles more liberal and satisfactory than we expected." In the view of the *Times*, Article Seventh—Religion was "the most unexceptionable part of the Constitution."[72] "A Freeman," writing in the *Courant*, could not disagree more, "The proposed Constitution is de-signed to *unchristian* a large portion of the community."[73] Continuing his analysis the following week, Freeman warned that "if the proposed constitu-tion shall be ratified, Connecticut is in danger of being ruined—her realities as well as her visions, of political and social enjoyment, will be blasted, and the labors of her venerable statesmen, will be tumbled to the dust."[74] "An Episcopalian," writing in the *Connecticut Journal*, was equally pessimistic. If the constitution was approved and "no person shall be classed with, or associated to any congregation, church or religious association, I hesitate not to predict that it will brake up and destroy many well regulated religious societies in the State. . . . It is not freedom of conscience that this article proposes, but freedom to trample it in the earth; and escape from the most sacred obligation to both God and man."[75]

On the first Monday in October, the Constitution was approved, 13,918 to 12,364. Support was stronger in the counties along Connecticut's coast than inland. Opposition was strongest in the rural areas to the northwest, the same area where the fires of the Second Great Awakening had burned for almost two decades.[76] For supporters of the Constitution, there was a sense of relief, but for opponents, fear and dread. As "Alfred" wrote in the *Courant*, "The fatal die is cast—the freedom of Connecticut, reared at the expense of the blood and treasure of our venerable forefathers, is prostrated in the dust."[77]

VI.

The Constitution was ratified, but it was unclear what had changed. Con-necticut now had a Bill of Rights, a less cumbersome electoral system, and a clear separation of powers in state government. The equality of Christian denominations was now part of the fundamental law. But what did the Con-stitution mean for the status of religion and its relationship to the state? Some things did change quickly. In 1819, for example, as usual Congrega-tional clergy assembled in Hartford at the beginning of May for the annual

Election Day ceremonies, including dinner at the expense of the state, but they were now joined by six Baptist ministers. After 1820 the legislature no longer provided dinner at government expense, and ministerial attendance at the annual event began a steady decline.[78]

Just like their Puritan forebears, Connecticut's leaders saw religion and government as inextricably intertwined. In 1819 the legislature established a committee, chaired by Zephaniah Swift, to revise the statutes of the state. The result was approved by the legislature in May 1821. The laws regarding the Sabbath, as well as days of Fasting and Thanksgiving, still forbade commercial business, attendance at "public diversions," and "meeting in company or companies in the street, or elsewhere . . . except for the public worship of God, or some work of necessity or mercy." Towns were still required to "choose two or more tything-men in each society or congregation" whose job was to report all breaches.[79] In the section "Religious Societies and Congregations," while in a note declaring that "the people of this state have passed from religious establishment [to] perfect freedom," church officers were annually to set a tax on a congregation's members, with fines for dereliction of duty and local officials enjoined to ensure that the law was enforced.[80] In practice, however, since members could easily withdraw from a congregation, churches would be reluctant to use the threat of legal action to collect taxes. Extant records leave no evidence that they did.

Two cases that reached the Connecticut Supreme Court illustrate the still intertwined relationship between religion and state. In *Atwood v. Welton* (1828), a lawsuit arose over a loan. The issue before the appeals court, however, was whether a witness, who did not believe in the "imprecation of divine vengeance . . . if his testimony should be false," should be allowed to testify. Writing for the majority, Justice David Daggett held that he could not. Daggett explained:

> Christianity is part of the common law of the land. Our ancestors brought it with them to this state, and there is no statute abrogating it. Nay, our statute punishes, by fine, imprisonment and binding to good behavior persons guilty of blasphemy against God, either person of the Trinity, the Christian religion, or the holy scriptures; and profane swearing and violation of the Sabbath are punished by fine. Our constitution declares it to be the duty and obligation of all men to worship the Supreme Being according to the dictates of their conscience. These provisions do not look like annulling Christianity. The law does not, indeed, prescribe any rules of faith, no mode of worship, nor attempt to

enforce any practical piety. It simply recognizes the great doctrines of Christi- ·
anity, and preserves them from the open assault of their enemies.[81]

An effort in the legislature to overturn the decision failed.[82]

The second case, from 1854, was brought by the Second Ecclesiastical Society of Portland against the First Ecclesiastical Society of Portland and illustrates that the separation of church and state and Connecticut was changing,
however slowly. Members of the First Society divided over the placement of a
new meetinghouse. Those in the minority petitioned the legislature to establish a separate ecclesiastical society, which the general assembly approved.
Acting as the government had done since the seventeenth century, the assembly ordered that a share of the assets of the First Society be conveyed to
the Second Society. The First Society refused, and the Second sued. The issue
before the court was the authority of the assembly under the Constitution
of 1818 to establish religious societies and assigning it assets. The court was
divided. Three justices in the majority based their decision not on Article
Seventh—Religion but on Section 3 of Article Tenth, concerning corporations. While "from the earliest period of our government until the adoption
of our present constitution," they ruled, "the general assembly constantly exercised the power of establishing and dividing local ecclesiastical societies"
and made "provision for the support and maintenance of religious instruction and worship." But "the present constitution made a radical change in
our ecclesiastical polity." According to the court's interpretation of Section 3,
the assembly had no authority to divide and convey part of the assets of the
First Ecclesiastical Society, thus dismissing the claim by the Second Society.
Two justices dissented. Justice Henry Waite questioned why, "if so important
and radical a change was contemplated by the framers of that instrument,
[then] it is remarkable that no express provision to that effect should have
been inserted" in the document.[83]

VII.

To understand disestablishment in Connecticut, the desire for specific dates
and specific actions must be put aside. Disestablishment was a complex
process occurring over more than a century. The Congregational monopoly ended in the late 1720s, when Anglican, Quaker, and Baptist societies
retained the authority to collect their own rates. The First Great Awakening
and the explosion of sects compounded the difficulty of maintaining government control of religious life. For some, the exclusion of the *Saybrook*

Platform from the 1784 revision of the state's laws was disestablishment, but not to Baptists and other dissenters, so long as the state mandated taxes for the support of churches and Congregationalism still enjoyed privileged social and political status. The 1818 Constitution is important, as it embedded current practice in the state's fundamental law. Yet long after ratification of the new Constitution, Protestant Christianity pervaded the laws and civic life of the state.

NOTES

1. M. Louise Greene, *The Development of Religious Liberty in Connecticut* (Boston: Houghton Mifflin, 1905); Richard J. Purcell, *Connecticut in Transition, 1775-1818* (1928; reprint, Middletown, CT: Wesleyan University Press, 1963); Anson Phelps Stokes, *Church and State in the United States*, 3 vols. (New York: Harper & Brothers, 1950), 1:408; William G. McLoughlin, *New England Dissent: The Baptists and the Separation of Church and State*, 2 vols. (Cambridge, MA: Harvard University Press, 1971).

2. *The Public Records of the Colony of Connecticut*, ed. J. Hammond Trumbull et al., 15 vols. (Hartford, CT: Case, Lockwood, 1850), 1:20-21.

3. *Records of the Colony of Jurisdiction of New Haven, from May, 1653, to the Union*, ed. Charles J. Hoadley (Hartford, CT: Cass, Lockwood, 1858), 569.

4. Harry S. Stout, *The New England Soul: Preaching and Religious Culture in Colonial New England* (New York: Oxford University Press, 1986), 3.

5. Elizur Goodrich, *The Principles of Civil Union and Happiness Considered and Recommended* (Hartford, CT: Hudson and Godwin, 1787), in *Political Sermons of the American Founding Era, 1740-1805*, ed. Ellis Sandoz (Indianapolis: Liberty Press, 1991), 933-34.

6. Nathan Strong, *A Sermon, Delivered in the Presence of His Excellency Samuel Huntington, esq., LL.D., Governor and the Honorable General Assembly of the State of Connecticut . . .* (Hartford, CT: Hudson and Goodwin, 1790), 15.

7. *Colonial Records*, 1:77-78.

8. For these three settlements, see Francis J. Bremer, *Building a New Jerusalem: John Davenport, a Puritan in Three Worlds* (New Haven, CT: Yale University Press, 2012); Mary Jeanne Anderson Jones, *Congregational Commonwealth: Connecticut, 1636-1662* (Middletown, CT: Wesleyan University Press, 1968); and Walter W. Woodward, *Prospero's America: John Winthrop, Jr., Alchemy, and the Creation of New England Culture, 1606-1676* (Chapel Hill: University of North Carolina Press, 2010).

9. Benjamin Trumbull, *A Complete History of Connecticut, Civil and Ecclesiastical*, 2 vols. (New Haven, CT: Maltby, Goldsmith; and Samuel Wadsworth, 1818), 1:297.

10. *Colonial Records*, 1:318, 356.

11. *Colonial Records*, 1:438.

12. *Colonial Records*, 2:54–55.

13. *Colonial Records*, 5:51–53, 87.

14. Williston Walker, *Creeds and Platforms of Congregationalism* (New York: Charles Scribner's Sons, 1893), 502–6.

15. *Colonial Records*, 1:111–12.

16. *Colonial Records*, 4:198–200.

17. *Colonial Records*, 5:50–51, 6:33–35.

18. Barbara E. Lacey, "Gender, Piety, and Secularization in Connecticut Religion, 1720–1775," *Journal of Social History* 24, no. 4 (1991): 801.

19. *Colonial Records*, 4:546; 5:50.

20. Thomas S. Kidd, *The Protestant Interest: New England after Puritanism* (New Haven, CT: Yale University Press, 2004), 127–28.

21. McLoughlin, *New England Dissent*, 1:263; *Colonial Records*, 7:106, 237, 257.

22. *Colonial Records*, 8:454–57.

23. Elisha Williams, *The Essential Rights and Liberties of Protestants: A Seasonable Plea for Liberty of Conscience. Being a Letter from a Gentleman in Massachusetts-Bay to his Friend in Connecticut* (Boston: S. Kneeland and T. Green, 1744).

24. Douglas L. Winiarski, *Darkness Falls on the Land of Light: Experiencing Religious Awakenings in Eighteenth-Century New England* (Chapel Hill: University of North Carolina Press for the Omohundro Institute of Early American History and Culture, 2017), 372, 505.

25. *The Acts and Laws of His Majesty's English Colony of Connecticut in New-England in America* (New London, CT: Timothy Green, 1750).

26. *Colonial Records*, 13:360.

27. Charles J. Hoadly, *The Public Records of the State of Connecticut* (Hartford, CT: Case, Lockwood, Brainard, Long, 1894), 1:282–83.

28. Virginia DeJohn Anderson, *The Martyr and the Traitor: Nathan Hale, Moses Dunbar, and the American Revolution* (New York: Oxford University Press, 2017).

29. *Acts and Laws of the State of Connecticut in America* (New London, CT: Timothy Green, 1784).

30. *Acts and Laws*, 21–22.

31. Zephaniah Swift, *A System of the Laws of the State of Connecticut*, 2 vols. (Windham, 1795–96), 1:142.

32. Purcell, *Connecticut in Transition*, 47.

33. David W. Kling, "A View from Above: The Town Reports as Ecclesiastical History," in *Voices of the New Republic: Connecticut Towns, 1800–1832*, ed. Howard R. Lamar (New Haven, CT: Connecticut Academy of Arts and Sciences, 2003), 2:22.

34. James R. Rohrer, *Keepers of the Covenant: Frontier Missions and the Decline of Congregationalism, 1774–1818* (New York: Oxford University Press, 1995), 35.

35. David Daggett, *Oration, Pronounced in the Brick Meeting House, in the City of New-Haven, on the Fourth of July, A.D. 1787* . . . (New Haven, CT: T. and S. Green, 1787), 6.

36. McLoughlin, *New England Dissent*, 2:915–21, 949–61; *State Records*, 7:256.

37. *Connecticut Courant*, May 23, 1791.

38. *Connecticut Courant,* May 30, 1791. After the revolution, the Congregational churches were often referred to as Presbyterian.

39. *Connecticut Courant,* August 29, 1791.

40. *State Records,* 7:311–13.

41. *State Records,* 8:100–101.

42. *Connecticut Courant,* May 19, 1794.

43. *Connecticut Courant,* May 19, 1794.

44. *State Records,* 8:237–39.

45. James R. Beasley, "Emerging Republicanism and the Standing Order: The Appropriation Act Controversy in Connecticut, 1793–1795," *William and Mary Quarterly* 24, no. 4 (1972): 587–610.

46. John Cosens Ogden, *An Appeal to the Candid on the Present State of Religion and Politics in Connecticut* (New Haven, CT: T. S. Green, 1797) 3, 10; *A View of the New England Illuminati* (Philadelphia: James Carey, 1799), 3, 7.

47. David Austin, *Dance of Herodias . . .* (East Windsor, CT: [Luther Pratt], 1799), 7.

48. On the politics of infidelity, see Jonathan J. Den Hartog, *Patriotism and Piety: Federalist Politics and Religious Struggle in the New American Nation* (Charlottesville: University of Virginia Press, 2015), 45–69.

49. Abraham Bishop, *Connecticut Republicanism—An Oration on the Extent and Power of Political Delusion . . .* (New Haven, CT: n.p., 1800), iv, 39.

50. Bishop, *Oration Delivered at Wallingford on the 11th of March 1801, Before the Republicans of the State of Connecticut* (New Haven, CT: William W. Morse, 1801), iii–iv, 13.

51. Bishop, *Proofs of a Conspiracy, against Christianity and the Government of the United States Exhibited in Several Views of the Union of Church and State* (Hartford, CT: J. Babcock, 1802), 17.

52. *American Mercury,* June 4, 1801.

53. Christopher Manwearing, *Republicanism & Aristocracy Contrasted; or, The Steady Habits of Connecticut Inconsistent with or opposed to the American Revolution* (Norwich, CT: Sherry & Porter, [1804]).

54. *Connecticut Courant,* June 7, 1802.

55. Jefferson's letter to the Danbury Baptists has generated considerable historical interest. For an overview and interpretation, see Johann N. Neem, "Beyond the Wall: Reinterpreting Jefferson's Danbury Address," *Journal of the Early Republic* 27, no. 1 (2007): 149–54.

56. John H. Jacocks, *Bishop's Bonus, Seabury College, Divine Right of Presbyterianism and Divine Right of Episcopacy. A Series of Essays Appearing in Papers, 1815–1816* (New Haven, CT: Oliver Steele, 1816).

57. *State Records,* 18:37, 113–15.

58. Hartford *American Mercury,* February 27, 1816; McLoughlin, *New England Dissent,* 2:1025–33.

59. *Columbian Register* (New Haven, CT), February 10, 1818.

60. *Connecticut Courant,* March 4, 1817.

61. Elijah Boardman to Wolcott, April 21, 1817, Wolcott Papers, Connecticut Historical Society.

62. *State Records*, 18:264.

63. *State Records*, 19:107.

64. New Haven *Connecticut Journal*, June 16, 1818.

65. *Connecticut Courant*, June 23 1818.

66. *Connecticut Courant*, July 28, 1818.

67. *Connecticut Courant*, August 4, 1818.

68. *Connecticut Courant*, August 20, 1818.

69. Draft Constitution, Wolcott Papers, Connecticut Historical Society.

70. *State Records*, 19:279–90.

71. *State Records*, 19:276–77. Not until Connecticut's second Constitution in 1965 were the clause concerning "the duty of all men to worship the Supreme Being, the word "Christian," and the right of churches to tax removed from the state's fundamental law.

72. *Hartford Times*, September 22, 1818.

73. *Connecticut Courant*, September 22, 1818.

74. *Connecticut Courant*, September 29, 1818.

75. *Connecticut Courant*, September 28, 1818.

76. Purcell, *Connecticut in Transition*, 259–61.

77. *Connecticut Courant*, October 20, 1818.

78. James Means Morse, *The Neglected Period of Connecticut's History, 1818–1850* (New Haven, CT: Yale University Press, 1938), 49–51.

79. *The Public Statute Laws of the State of Connecticut as Revised and Enacted by the General Assembly, in May 1821* (Hartford, CT: H. Huntington Jr., 1824), 385–87.

80. *Public States Laws, 1821*, 430–36.

81. Atwood v. Weldon, 7 *Conn.* 66 (1828).

82. Morse, *Neglected Period of Connecticut History*, 102.

83. Second Ecclesiastical Society of Portland v. First Ecclesiastical Society of Portland, 23 Conn. 255 (1854).

CHAPTER EIGHTEEN

TOWNS AND TOLERATION
Disestablishment in New Hampshire
Brian Franklin

ON SEPTEMBER 11, 1780, members of the Congregational Church in Amherst, New Hampshire, petitioned their leaders, requesting they "join us in chusing a council to organize us" into a separate church in Amherst. These petitioning members had no quarrel with their congregation or with its newly installed pastor; they had a geographical problem. The petitioners thought the commute into town placed an undue burden on them for Sabbath service attendance, so they wanted to organize a separate congregation that met closer to their homes.[1]

Church leaders rejected their brethren's request as "unreasonable & premature." "Refresh your memories a little," the leaders jabbed. "[H]ave you not solemnly & explicitly covenanted . . . with us?" The petitioners still lived in the vicinity, and they had not received authorization "by an act of the Legislative Assembly" to incorporate as a separate parish. If they could find no "irregularity" in the church, then they had no grounds for their request. Over the next year, the leaders went further to assert their authority over the town's church. They accused some of the western Amherst members of "gross neglect" and denied the petitioners' request for certificates of membership necessary for an incorporation request. They even excommunicated some of the petitioning members.[2]

In denying the petition to form a new parish, the Congregational Church in Amherst acted well within its legal authority. As the first and only church in town, it had the right to receive a portion of the citizens' property taxes for supporting the parish's meetinghouse and minister. Without authorization by the state legislature, the petitioning group had no legal standing as a separate congregation or town. Through what one scholar called "a web of legislation, common law, and longstanding practice," the Amherst church maintained a religious establishment in its sphere of influence.[3]

351

What sets New Hampshire's story apart from many of its sister states concerning disestablishment is that the conflict revolved around one specific entity: the town. New Hampshire's towns functioned as the critical centers of power for religious establishment. Within the towns, the process of disestablishment from the seventeenth to the nineteenth century reflected long-standing tensions between two groups. On one side was the Standing Order, characterized by its attachment to historic Puritan New England and its commitment to protecting the authority of both the town and the Congregational town church. On the other side was a group composed of non-Congregational Protestants and their allies, committed to increasing religious toleration and willing to challenge the authority of towns and town churches. Throughout this contest, the Standing Order employed a rhetoric of religious toleration at the state level, while maintaining an underlying legal system that supported the establishment of Congregational churches in most towns.[4]

In 1819 dissenters won perhaps their greatest victory when the legislature of New Hampshire passed the *Act of Toleration*, removing the authority of towns to compel citizens to contribute tax dollars to a religious organization. Although a significant achievement, even the *Act of Toleration* had its limits. Left in place were the remains of a Protestant establishment for decades to come.[5]

I.

In 1623 Ferdinando Gorges and John Mason organized the Company of Laconia and sent a group of English subjects to establish two settlements along the Piscataqua River in what they called New Hampshire. By 1640 English colonists had four settlements, at Portsmouth, Dover, Exeter, and Hampton. Each of these towns attempted a form of religious establishment, which included a common town church and minister, both supported by public taxation—what Shelby Balik calls "the community of neighbors sustained by the community of believers." By the 1650s, New Hampshire towns had established a pattern of ministerial support via town taxation that remained essentially intact until 1819.[5]

What set New Hampshire apart from some of its neighboring colonies, even as early as the mid-seventeenth century, was its highly decentralized system. Even these first four towns took different paths toward public support for religion. Portsmouth established its affiliation with the Church of England. Hampton and Exeter established churches closer to the Puritan and Congregational model found in Massachusetts.[6]

Dover's winding road illustrates the dual status of New Hampshire church-state relations, as both decentralized at the colony level and centralized at the town level. From its settlement in the 1620s, Dover struggled to secure a permanent minister. Town squabbles erupted spectacularly in 1640 when factions formed in support of two ministers who had each been called to the town. The newer minister, Thomas Larkham, "laid violent hands" on the standing pastor, Hanserd Knollys. When John Underhill, the recently appointed local governor, arrived to "keep the peace," he found Larkham "carrying a Bible on a halberd for an ensign" and Knollys "armed with a pistol." Soon after, both Larkham and Knollys departed Dover.[7]

William Hubbard, a nineteenth-century historian, called these experiences in New Hampshire towns "an ordinary effect of loose and pragmatic spirits." In such a setting, towns often exercised more power than colonial authorities on either side of the Atlantic. Ironically, discussion about church-state matters in colonial New Hampshire did not revolve around the concept of a single "establishment." No one enforced a single establishment from above, even if every town attempted to do so within its own jurisdiction.[8]

One need only survey examples of religious groups *unwelcome* in colonial New Hampshire to understand the forces for establishment and against religious toleration at the local level. In October 1648, the Massachusetts General Court found Dover resident Edward Starbuck guilty of the "great misdemeanor . . . [of] profession of Anabaptism," a group that the court's records considered alongside "ruffians and barbarous Indians" who had "begun to invade New-England." Authorities also came down forcefully on Quakers in the mid-seventeenth century. They outlawed Quaker immigration into New Hampshire, revoked their right to vote, banned the import or verbal defense of Quaker writings, and placed severe penalties on convicted Quakers, including imprisonment, whipping, public shaming, and even execution.[9]

The provincial administrations of John Cutt and Edward Cranfield in the late seventeenth century illustrated an attempt by colonial leaders to balance the Church of England's privilege with the promotion of religious toleration. In 1679 Cutt's administration announced a series of proclamations that advocated for "liberty of conscience" for Protestants, "yet such especially as shall be conformable to ye rites of ye Church of Eng^d." In 1682 Lieutenant Governor Edward Cranfield pressed the issue of Anglican preeminence. Believing that dissenting pastors spread "pernicious and rebellious principles," he attempted to force non-Anglican ministers into conformity with Anglican worship. One Congregational pastor named Joshua Moodey refused to serve the sacraments in conformity to the Church of England and bore the brunt of this policy: imprisonment and self-exile from the province.[10]

The preeminent example of this balancing act came a few years later when in the wake of the Glorious Revolution, Parliament enacted the *Toleration Act of 1689*. The act presumed and emphasized the prominence of the Church of England. However, it also shored up the empire's broad Protestant identity for the next century by simultaneously promising freedom of worship to nonconformists while denying the same to Catholics.[11]

In response to the *1689 Toleration Act*, Lieutenant Governor John Usher approved a law that set a similar tone for New Hampshire: *An Act for Maintenance and Supply of the Ministry within this Province*. This 1693 act made New Hampshire one of the earliest colonies to have no colony-wide establishment. Any person in New Hampshire could be "excused from paying toward the support of the ministry of the Towne" by proving that they objected to the town church and regularly attended public worship elsewhere.[12]

But a stark reality endured: freedom depended entirely on a bureaucratic system of rules and requirements. Religious societies had to gain state recognition. Any citizen seeking to join a new religious society had to work with majority-elected town officials to obtain and file certificates of exemption from the town church. In short, the system appeared to offer local flexibility, but in fact buttressed majoritarian authority in towns and thus the continued establishment of the town-level church, which was usually Congregational.[13]

II.

From 1693 until the American Revolution, three parallel processes drove church-state relations in New Hampshire. First, the population of New Hampshire expanded both numerically and geographically. Second, these populations formed new towns and parishes at an unprecedented pace. Third, Protestants from dissenting or nonconformist persuasions grew at a disproportionate rate. These three processes sporadically collided, forcing authorities to contend with the web of establishment that blanketed the colony.

From the 1690s to 1713, the population of New England increased at a sustainable rate. With the conclusion of Queen Anne's War in 1713, New Hampshire's population began a half century of dramatic growth. Governor Benning Wentworth alone granted lands and settlements that produced more than one hundred new towns in present-day New Hampshire and Vermont. By the end of Wentworth's administration in 1767, New Hampshire's population had increased tenfold, primarily through immigration from southern New England, the British West Indies, and the British Isles, with dissenting Scotch-Irish Presbyterians from Ulster representing the single largest group.[14]

Any new town had to meet certain requirements, including a minimum number of settlers, proof of constructed and settled homes, and various religious requirements. For example, when Governor Samuel Shute granted tracts of land for settlement in 1722, his proclamation required that any application for town incorporation entail construction of a meetinghouse within four years and the reservation of land for the construction of a parsonage. Shute's proclamation presumed what the statements of others explicitly required, namely, the settlement of a permanent minister whose salary derived from the property taxes of townspeople.[15]

When citizens of an existing town attempted to form new towns, the process revealed the centrality of a religious ministry and taxes for that ministry. Whether colonists sought a new town for religious, population, or mere geographical reasons, town authorities tended to oppose new incorporations. The loss of residents resulted in the loss of tax dollars to support their ministry.[16]

Dissenting Protestants increased in number throughout New England as the population and number of towns exploded. By the 1730s, Quakers had reached positions of authority in towns and the provincial legislature. They had even found success petitioning for province-wide exemptions from swearing oaths and from collecting taxes if they occupied an elected office that required tax collection (such as selectman). Presbyterian influence grew as well, particularly as Scotch-Irish immigration continued. In Chester, for example, Presbyterians gained the authority to support a minister of their choosing in a town formerly dominated by Congregationalists.[17]

The First Great Awakening, a series of revivals in the American colonies during the mid-eighteenth century, also fueled dissenter gains. For example, in the early 1740s, Pastor Nicholas Gilman of Exeter visited Boston, where he experienced a personal conversion under the preaching and writings of transatlantic evangelist George Whitefield. In 1743 a group of "New Lights" in Exeter (those identifying with the theology and practice of the revivals) filed a written dissent with the town, announcing their withdrawal from the church and the parish and their intention of forming their own. The leaders of the town church refused the petition and opposed the New Lights in their midst. When Whitefield passed through the area in 1744, they met him at the border of the town and barred him from entering. Finally, in 1755 the society of New Lights successfully petitioned the legislature to allow all town residents to determine their own parish affiliations.[18]

Meanwhile, the two primary beneficiaries of religious establishment—the Church of England and Congregationalists—continued to press their own cases. Congregationalist ministers and missionaries resented the influx of dissenters. Successive provincial administrations from the 1740s through the 1760s dedicated themselves to the extension of the Church of England to counterbalance this growth of dissenters. As governor, Benning Wentworth gave the Church of England the upper hand by requiring that land grants in northern New Hampshire reserve not only shares for the town minister and parsonage, but also one share for the Church of England and "one whole share for the Incorporated Society for the Propagation of the Gospel," the missionary arm of the Church of England.[19]

Historian Charles Kinney assessed that by 1775, "it would be incorrect to say that New Hampshire by provincial law had a single established religion." Depending on the town, one might find any mix of Protestants and versions of tax support. Proclamations of religious toleration thus both empowered groups like Congregationalists to maintain majority power in their towns and simultaneously provided dissenters with the wedge they needed to challenge that power in the coming decades.[20]

III.

In May 1776, the Second Continental Congress called on the provincial governments of North America to adopt new governments inclined toward independence from Great Britain. This call set off a round of constitution making up and down the Atlantic Seaboard. New Hampshire, however, was ahead of the game. On January 5, 1776, a New Hampshire convention adopted the first written Constitution in the American colonies. Focused on political matters immediately at hand, the Constitution did not address religion.[21]

In 1784 the state convention wrote and received popular approval for a new state Constitution. This Constitution took significant inspiration from the Massachusetts Constitution of 1780 and included a thirty-eight-article Bill of Rights. Three of these articles dealt with religion and "Rights of Conscience." Articles IV and V defined rights of conscience as "unalienable" natural rights, which allowed every individual "to worship God according to the dictates of his own conscience, and reason," without interference by the state.[22]

Yet Article VI seemingly turned these rights on their head, and the article would remain at the center of the religious establishment debates over the next four decades in New Hampshire. Within Article VI, the delegates managed to create multiple paradoxes. They employed revolutionary-era rhetoric about toleration and religious liberty, but codified religious taxation and a Protestant requirement for governor and state representatives. They empowered "the people" to make decisions about establishment questions, but only by means of town authority, mediated through the state legislature. As a result, the 1784 Constitution paradoxically strengthened both the state's commitment to religious liberty as an ideal and its commitment to allowing towns to govern religion in practice.

IV.

In February 1791, the New Hampshire General Court (the state's house and senate together) met for its regular session. In the house, William Plumer, rising star of the Federalist Party and newly elected speaker, led the discussion. Amid its regular business, the General Court overwhelmingly approved *An act for regulating towns and the choice of town Officers*. Unbeknownst to them, this seemingly innocuous act would come to dominate statewide discussions about religious toleration.[23]

This 1791 act outlined the details of how towns would organize, regulate, and govern themselves. After codifying the various duties and powers of town officers and voting-eligible inhabitants, Section 10 described the appropriate process by which towns assessed estate taxes and collected money for the public good. There were three elements of this law that pertained to the issue of religious establishments. First, the law retained the authority of towns to tax citizens for the support of a minister and a meetinghouse. Second, this law retained the authority of towns to tax on behalf of a single ministry, chosen by the majority of voting-eligible citizens (male freeholders at least twenty-one years old). Third, this tax-based ministerial support occurred within a broader context of the "publick good." Alongside funding for churches and ministers, the 1791 act called for taxes to care for the poor, build and repair highways and bridges, and support education.[24]

In the common parlance, each of these—religion, infrastructure, and education—played intertwining roles in promoting the common good. Religion through town churches improved the moral fabric of society. In June 1790, newly elected governor Josiah Bartlett tied religion and education together in a letter to the president of Dartmouth College, insisting that the "happiness & prosperity of a people" depended on education in "true religion, virtue, morality and useful Literature." From the 1790s to the 1810s, the General Court approved the incorporation of dozens of new turnpike, road, and bridge companies to serve the state's expanding population and economy. Every act of incorporation barred companies from charging tolls in select cases, including for "any person who shall be passing . . . to or from public worship." Within this context of promoting the public good, critiques of nonsectarian public taxation for religion barely existed. If one considered this support of churches a "religious establishment," one may just as well have called the support of public roads "transportation establishment" or schools "education establishment."[25]

The first constitutionally required review of the 1784 Constitution occurred in September 1791. The people had expressed their dissatisfaction with issues such as the entanglement of the executive and legislative departments and the disproportionate power of Portsmouth and Exeter. William Plumer agreed, but he arrived with another cause: to expand toleration and eliminate the Constitution's Protestant religious tests for state office. Plumer had championed religious toleration all his adult life and called on his colleagues to answer why non-Christians lacked "an equal right to be protected by those laws, to whose support they contribute." The convention approved amendments to eliminate the Protestant test for gubernatorial office and to extend dissenter rights to withdraw from a town church, but the voters rejected both. New Hampshire would eventually embrace these ideas, but not for decades to come.[26]

In 1792 Jeremy Belknap, the renowned clergyman and historian, published the third of his three-volume history of New Hampshire. He concluded that at this moment, "There is therefore as entire religious liberty in New-Hampshire, as any people can rationally desire." In one sense, Belknap was right. Given the historic Puritan and Congregational town-church model, it was rational for him to believe that extensive religious liberty existed in New Hampshire. Given the combined forces of the Revolution, frontier expansion, and the flowering of evangelical denominations, this old rationality was fading away.[27]

V.

A two-decade controversy in the town of Durham illuminates the decline of religious establishment at the turn of the nineteenth century. In May 1780, Durham called Curtis Coe to serve as pastor of its Congregational church. In March 1805, after twenty-five years of relative peace, division arose suddenly.

A contingent of members called for Coe's removal and petitioned the legislature for permission to incorporate as a separate poll parish. This designation would allow the new church to collect taxes separately from the town church but remain with the town. The majority of the Durham church opposed the division, fearing it would create an unsustainable situation because neither congregation could pay a full-time settled minister. The fears proved prescient. The minority faction broke away, and the town could not come to an agreement with Coe, who left in May 1806. The original town church failed to attract a permanent minister for more than a decade.[28]

In 1814 uniquely named Federal Constitution Burt arrived in the town of Durham as a part-time domestic missionary with the Massachusetts Society for Promoting Christian Knowledge (MSPCK). His birth on March 4, 1789 (the first day the U.S. Constitution took effect), marked a new era, and Durham hoped his arrival would inaugurate the same for them. Two years later, in 1816, Durham's town congregation, dissident congregation, and the MSPCK agreed to draw on their collective resources to pay Burt $500 per year to minister to all in Durham. Supporters of the traditional town establishment decried such multilateral arrangements as an example of towns shirking their responsibilities to "throw themselves upon the charity of another state."[29]

The case of Durham exemplifies four trends in early-nineteenth-century New Hampshire that led steadily toward the dissolution of the town-church model. Rapid population increase and a disproportionate increase of dissenting groups continued trends from the prior century. A third trend was a growing dissatisfaction with a legal system that supported town establishments. Two court cases in particular energized opponents of establishment: *Muzzy v. Wilkins* (1803) and *Moore v. Poole* (1815). *Muzzy* reasserted the state's authority (and town authority) to determine which religious societies qualified for separate incorporation. The court in *Moore* affirmed the special rights of a particular set of ministers—those elected by town majorities and supported by town taxes, almost all of whom were Congregational. These decisions incensed dissenters and the rising Jeffersonian Democratic-Republican Party in the state congress.[30] In response to *Moore*, the state congress enacted a new statute in December 1816 that exempted from taxation "the real and personal estates of all ordained ministers of the gospel of every denomination," without regard to affiliation with a town.[31]

This victory points to the fourth current flowing through New Hampshire at the turn of the nineteenth century: the transfer of political power to the emerging Democratic-Republican Party. During the 1790s, Federalists maintained control of virtually every sector of New Hampshire government and monopolized the state's share of representatives to the U.S. Congress. Yet by 1800, after just ten years in power, New Hampshire Federalists had become a caricature of their party on a national scale. In that year, for the first time in a decade, Federalist governor John Gilman received less than 70 percent of the popular vote. By 1805 the Republicans turned their momentum into victory when Republican John Langdon defeated John Gilman for governor. From 1797 to 1806, New Hampshire sent four Federalist congressmen to the U.S. House; in 1807 they sent four Republicans. Republicans won these contests on platforms that lambasted Federalists for elitism and bank cronyism and, tellingly, continued support for the town-church power structure. Indeed, they referred disparagingly to their Federalist opponents as "Congregationalists."[32]

VI.

The gubernatorial election of 1816 provided a spark to the struggle for religious toleration in New Hampshire. William Plumer sought reelection as governor, having previously won in 1812 after declaring his switch from the Federalist to the Republican Party. Republicans, including Concord printer Isaac Hill, chose to make religious toleration the touchstone of the election. Hill's newspaper, the *New-Hampshire Patriot*, attacked opponents as a Federalist-Congregationalist cabal, "which sighs to unite Church and State." Days before the election, the front page depicted two majestic ships, emblazoned with "Peace, Glory, Honor, Prosperity," and attributing it all to "Republican Perseverance and Energy." The caption below the image reads: "Religious Freedom, the Rights of the *Baptist, Quaker, Methodist*, and of *all denominations*—in room of a *Law Religion*, imposed by an *intolerant sect*, who boast that they "will manage the Civil Government as they please."[33]

William Plumer won the election, and the Federalists would never hold the governorship again. In his inaugural address, Plumer addressed issues championed by Republicans, including wastefulness among political elites, improving the militia, redistricting, and court reform. One issue, though, threaded its way throughout the entire speech: religious liberty. He zeroed in on his opposition to the legislature's authority to decide whether a local religious society could incorporate. "If any religious associations request acts of incorporation," he argued, "it appears to be our duty to grant them." In opposition to the 1803 *Muzzy* case, Plumer declared, "The correctness of their tenets, is a subject that lies between God and their consciences."[34]

Great Election.....*Tuesday Next!*

PEACE, GLORY, HONOR, PROSPERITY,
Obtained by our Thundering Cannon on the Ocean, by invincible Heroism in the Field, by Republican Perseverance and Energy.

Religious Freedom, the Rights of the *Baptist, Quaker, Methodist,* and of *all denominations,*—in room of a *Law Religion,* imposed by an *intolerant sect,* who boast that they "will manage the Civil Government as they please."

Whig Ticket!

FOR GOVERNOR,
HON. WILLIAM PLUMER.

FOR COUNSELLORS,

Hon. ELIJAH HALL, *Rockingham.*
Hon. SAMUEL QUARLES, *Strafford.*
Hon. BENJAMIN PIERCE, *Hillsborough.*

Hon. ELISHA HUNTLEY, *Cheshire.*
THOMAS WHIPPLE, Jr. Esq. *Grafton &c.*

FOR SENATORS.

Hon. WILLIAM HAM,	District No.	1.
Hon. LEVI BARTLETT,	No.	2.
Hon. JOHN BELL. (&c of Chester)	No.	3.
JOHN HARVEY, Esq.	No.	4.
Hon. BEARD PLUMER,	No.	5.
Hon. WILLIAM BADGER,	No.	6.

Hon. JAMES WALLACE,	District No.	7.
JONATHAN HARVEY, Esq.	No.	8.
Hon. JOSEPH BUFFUM,	No.	9.
URIAH WILCOX, Esq.	No.	10.
JOHN DURKEE, Esq.	No.	11.
Elder DAN YOUNG,	No.	12.

The Republican-dominated General Court responded rapidly to Plumer's direction. It slashed government salaries, reorganized the militia, replaced judges, and approved funds for a new capitol building. Tellingly, the state congress made one more fateful decision. It set in motion a plan to take over Dartmouth College, the premier educational institution in the state.

For New Hampshire Republicans, Dartmouth College represented everything wrong with their state. They claimed Dartmouth functioned as an arm of the Congregational establishment, did not answer to the people or to the legislature, and thus existed as "hostile to the spirit and genius of free government." In his inaugural address, Plumer rehearsed the authority of the state regarding town incorporations, claiming that "whenever the legislature judged that the public good required a town be made into two, they have made the division, and in some instances against the remonstrance of a majority of its inhabitants." Plumer then connected these town and church incorporation laws to his proposed action toward Dartmouth College: "These facts show the authority of the legislature to interfere upon this subject."[35]

The legislature acted promptly. On June 27, 1816, it passed an act that gave them authority over the college and renamed it Dartmouth University. Led by influential Federalists, supporters of the original Dartmouth College responded in the courts. In March 1818, Daniel Webster and his legal team appealed the college's case to the Supreme Court of the United States. In *Trustees of Dartmouth College v. Woodward* (1819), the High Court handed down its decision, ruling in favor of Dartmouth College and against the attempt of the New Hampshire Republicans to convert the private religious college into a public institution.[36]

One irony throughout the Dartmouth College litigation was that Republicans, the champions of the rights of individuals and dissenters against the power of town majorities, based their argument for the takeover of Dartmouth on "the public good." The argument for the common good ran parallel to, and culminated in, the most important moment in New Hampshire church-state history: the *1819 Act of Toleration*.[37]

VII.

In the June 1819 session, the New Hampshire Legislature took up discussion of a bill offered by state senator and Methodist preacher Dan Young, called *An act in amendment of an act, entitled an act, for regulating towns and the choice of town officers, passed February 8, A.D. 1791*. Young had submitted a version of the bill for three years, but not until 1819 did it gain enough support for a full hearing. The bill aimed specifically to amend Section 10 of the 1791 act, which gave towns the power to allow a majority vote to determine the "necessary" taxes for supporting a town minister, meetinghouse, and potentially an affiliated school. The proposal called for three things: the authority of religious societies to incorporate and collect property taxes on equal footing, the protection from compulsion of any person to associate with or pay taxes toward a religious society, and the ability of any person who wished to separate from a religious society to merely notify the society's clerk, rather than obtaining a certificate of allowance. The state senate discussed the bill, approved it after three readings, and sent it to the house.[38]

From June 22 to 25, the house hotly debated the bill.[39] Its supporters lined up behind one central argument: that Section 10 of the 1791 act violated religious freedom because it allowed towns to tax citizens for religious purposes against their wills. Those who opposed the bill assembled a litany of arguments in favor of the 1791 act, and therefore against the 1819 bill. There were four basic arguments:

1. The "toleration bill" was unconstitutional and against the intent of the framers.
2. Allowing citizens to opt out of taxation for ministerial salaries would impair the fulfillment of already existing contracts.
3. The bill would allow people to claim a tax exemption for any professed religious reason, no matter how far-fetched.
4. The bill would limit general public support for religion and therefore allow for the spread of immorality.

The best argument that opponents of the Toleration Bill put forth centered on the constitutionality of the 1791 act. John Pitman of Portsmouth championed this claim. He argued that two major constitutional concepts worked seamlessly together. First, the government should not regulate conscience; second, the government should also tax for religious purposes. Article V of the Bill of Rights guaranteed "every individual" the right to worship "according to the dictates of his own conscience." Article VI guaranteed the rights of "religious societies" to contract for the support of religious teachers. The manner of interpreting Article V's individual right, Pitman argued, should not nullify the religious societies' rights in Article VI.[40]

Opponents of the bill went beyond the letter of the Constitution by appealing to the original intentions of those whom one contemporary dubbed "the wise and excellent men who framed our constitution." Tearing down the town-church system of taxation, Edmund Parker claimed, would be akin to tearing down "the edifice which our forefathers erected, because a tenant has done wrong." Edmund Toppan took the argument of the "framers" to its extreme when he invoked the framer above all framers, George Washington. From 1794 to 1795, Republicans in the U.S. Congress had attempted to block President Washington from enacting what became the Jay Treaty, by demanding documentation and withholding funding. "But Washington was President," Toppan asserted, and "the country was saved from anarchy, confusion, and war" by his rejection of the demands of the Republicans in Congress. Toppan and the New Hampshire Federalists laid claim to Washington's mantle by arguing that they, the true heirs of the first president, should also prevent the current Republican-led effort from succeeding.[41]

Some legislators in the state house also opposed the Toleration Bill for an eminently practical reason: contract law. For decades, towns had supported ministers by offering them employment contracts that guaranteed a salary. Edmund Parker argued that this new bill would significantly hinder or even prevent towns from coming to agreements with ministers in the future (a task already proving difficult in towns like Durham). Even more troublesome, the bill might create a legal morass in which churches and pastors throughout the state would sue towns for breach of contract.[42]

The deepest expressions of opposition focused on anxiety over unregulated religion and its negative effects on society. Henry Hubbard, a selectman from Charlestown, pointed to Section 3 of the bill as particularly pernicious in its allowing any legally incorporated "religious sect or denomination" to collect money from willing parishioners. Hubbard decried this authority as certain to produce "Societies for the pretended purpose of religious instruction and worship."[43]

Supporters of the bill saw no merit in this scenario of a New Hampshire teeming with "pretended" religions. They argued that no religious group could exercise any real power—in this case taxation power—until the group was "known and distinguished in law." In New Hampshire, this still required that a religious society record its existence with their own clerk, publish their information in a county newspaper, and petition for incorporation by the state. The Toleration Bill, supporters argued, would maintain the state's oversight while also providing equal liberty to emerging religious groups.[44]

The most common argument against the Toleration Bill was that it would produce disastrous results for public order and morality. This concern with what Henry Hubbard called the "intimate connexion" between religion and moral order went to the heart of New England society and to American society generally. In arguing against the bill's supposed immoral effects on society, legislators appealed to the masculinity of the members of the state congress: "Have our wives and our children no concern, no interest in the subject now under consideration?" Hubbard noted that "twelve sixteenths of the professing members" of New Hampshire churches were female, implying that a vote for the Toleration Bill was a vote against pious women, the backbone of religious society. In turn, Ichabod Bartlett mocked this fearmongering. He wondered aloud whether the bill had a clause that decreased the "proportion of pious women" or if Hubbard would be "more disposed . . . to restrain his wife or daughters from . . . publick worship" if the town did not pay the minister's taxes.[45]

The specter of irreligious women and children roaming the streets was a chimera, but opponents raised fear of two other scenarios that had a real presence in the New Hampshire mind: rogue religious groups and the terror of the French Revolution. At the same time the legislature debated the Toleration Bill, a notorious man named Jacob Cochran was roaming northern New England exhibiting "lascivious behavior," including adultery, promiscuous sexual intercourse, and polygamy. In May 1819, a grand jury in York County, Maine, had indicted Cochran, and a petit jury found him guilty of the crime of adultery. But before his bondsman could turn him over to the court, Cochran "hopped the twig" and disappeared for more than four months. Jacob Cochran disturbed New England society not because he violated sexual mores but because he did so under the guise of religion. A popular newspaper borrowed from the Gospel of Matthew to describe Cochran as "a Wolf in Sheep's Clothing." Cochran had come as a self-proclaimed Free Will Baptist, and with that mask he had "proved a common destroyer" to every place that had recognized him.[46]

Throughout 1819, even after Cochran's capture in October, New England newspapers connected his exploits directly with broader religious toleration laws and the people who advocated for them. No doubt, the *Portland (ME) Gazette* mocked, supporters of broader religious toleration would cry "*persecution*" in the case of Cochran, who along with other minority religious groups had claimed a "new and enlightened system of morals." But his claim for religious freedom actually represented "the greatest pretentions to religion" as a mask to cover "the grossest vices or the meanest villanies." The people should not be "surprized" then when other religious groups who sought legitimacy "wind up their drama" in the same way.[47]

In attacking the bill, Edmund Parker argued that societal morality could get much worse than Jacob Cochran; New Hampshire might become like France. "Look back on revolutionary France," Parker warned, "let loose from all the restraints of morality, piety, and religion." New Hampshire society with the 1791 act had remained "turbulent and ungovernable." Demanding proof of a negative, Parker claimed the bill's supporters could offer no convincing evidence that a repeal of the 1791 act would not result in the terror, violence, and atheism of the French Revolution.[48]

Parker's fearmongering fell flat because no such degeneration had occurred in the other states upon their disestablishments. By 1819, with the

sole exception of Massachusetts, every state in the Union had formally disestablished the church to which they had once given preference. Connecticut
disestablished just the year before, in 1818. Vermont had done so in 1807,
establishing a system very much like what the Toleration Bill aimed at. "Yet,"
Whipple quipped, "the State of Vermont is not ruined, as was then predicted; her mountains are as verdant, her yeomanry as happy and as virtuous as
while under the operation of these *State saving laws*."[49]

In the argument over public morals, both sides agreed on the principle
that government should encourage "the promotion of virtue, morality, and
true christian piety," but they differed sharply on "the *mode* of accomplish-
ing" that object. For opponents of the Toleration Bill, the argument came
back to Article III of the New Hampshire Bill of Rights, which stated that
citizens, as members of a society, must "surrender up some of their natural
rights to that society, in order to insure the protection of others." In this case,
individuals should be willing to sacrifice some of their particular religious
and economic practices in order to maintain a stable Christian society.[50]

Supporters of the Toleration Bill would not abide a constitutional interpretation that endlessly privileged the supposed needs of society over the
rights of individuals. The 1791 act was unconstitutional, they argued, because while it properly empowered towns to levy religious taxes (in line with
Article III), it did so at the expense of individual conscience (Article IV).
Dr. Whipple conceded that he would accept a state law that would both empower towns to collect taxes and "infringe no rights." But the writers of the
1791 act had done no such thing. Instead, in their "zeal for religion," they
had done something "repugnant to its precepts." The Toleration Bill would
undo that mistake.[51]

Opponents of the bill sought to postpone the vote or to jettison it altogether, but the majority of the General Court would not have it. On June 25,
1819, the house read the Toleration Bill a third time and narrowly passed it
by a vote of ninety-five to eighty-eight. The bill with its minor amendments
then went back to the senate, which approved it. On July 1, 1819, the Toleration Bill became law. New Hampshire towns and parishes could no longer
levy taxes on unwilling citizens for religious purposes, regardless of what the
majority desired.[52]

VIII.

Opponents of the Toleration Bill had predicted unintended consequences, some of which came to pass. Contract law, for example, became a briar
patch with which towns tangled for decades. Lawsuits developed as some

towns could no longer afford to pay ministerial salaries, because taxation had dropped off. Parties argued about who controlled the churches' collected tithes, taxes, and trust funds. Further, the *1819 Act of Toleration* left unaddressed which parties owned or maintained responsibility for managing church-related property.[53]

The 1819 act made it more challenging for some churches to survive financially. Without a guaranteed tax base, some churches implemented creative new ways to raise funds. As occurred earlier in Durham, some churches partnered with missionary societies or outside religious groups in order to support their pastors. In the town of Bedford, Presbyterians and Congregationalists decided that their only option was to join together in a new society, the United Presbyterian and Congregational Religious Society. In their founding documents, the group specifically cited the *1819 Act of Toleration* as the basis for their formation.[54]

These problems with implementation of the 1819 act, however, pale in comparison to the law's most significant limitation: it failed to disentangle the state from religious matters. Any incorporated religious society could continue to raise money by taxing the estates of its members. To be sure, religious groups could now only tax members who volunteered to pay, but this vestige of church-state entanglement remained nevertheless. Until 1868 new religious societies still had to receive official recognition and incorporation from the state, as confirmed in the 1803 *Muzzy* case. Moreover, "[t]o our discredit," Isaac Hill lamented, New Hampshire retained its Protestant religious test for office. In 1851 the people of New Hampshire reconsidered two constitutional requirements for holding statewide offices, such as representative and governor. They voted to end property holding as a requirement, but voted to keep the Protestant test. Not until 1876 would the people of New Hampshire narrowly obtain the two-thirds majority necessary for a constitutional amendment eliminating the Protestant test for office.[55]

The limits of the *1819 Toleration Act* must not detract from its achievements. Before the act, people like those in late-eighteenth-century western Amherst had limited recourse when their town-church leaders refused their request to break away and form their own parish. After passage of the Toleration Act, the situation changed. In 1822 it came to the attention of Amherst's Rev. Nathan Lord that a Unitarian-leaning portion of the congregation was meeting separately. They had even called a new pastor, Rev. Henry Ware, to preach for them periodically. Some leaders of the original church wrote to Ware, notifying him that the people inviting him "do avow the purpose of destroying the existing contract between the town and their minister." Ware responded, brimming with sarcasm: "I came to this place on an invitation to preach to some individuals, who had withdrawn from the established worship of the town. I supposed that they had a perfect right to procure such worship as they pleased." With confidence, Ware stood his ground. "I have not interfered . . . with the members of the parish, being only concerned with those who are not members of the parish."[56] That parish—now free to meet and free to withhold its taxes from the original parish—would separate and form its own congregation by the following year.

NOTES

1. Amherst Congregational Church Records, vol. 1, 1741–1816, New Hampshire Historical Society, Concord, NH (hereafter NHHS).

2. Amherst Congregational Church Records, vol. 1, 1741–1816, NHHS.

3. Michael W. McConnell, "Establishment and Disestablishment at the Founding, Part I: Establishment of Religion," *William and Mary Law Review* 44, no.5 (2003): 2010–11.

4. Shelby Balik, *Rally the Scattered Believers: Northern New England's Religious Geography* (Bloomington: Indiana University Press, 2014), 10.

5. Charles Kinney, *Church and State: The Struggle for Separation in New Hampshire, 1630–1900* (New York: Columbia University Press, 1955), 12–13; Balik, *Rally the Scattered Believers*, 15; Stephen Foster, *The Long Argument* (Chapel Hill: University of North Carolina Press, 1991), chap. 4.

6. Kinney, *Church and State*, 8–10; *Provincial Papers . . . Related to the Province of New Hampshire,* ed. Nathanael Bouton (Concord: George Jenks, 1867), 1:132. This volume is part of a forty-volume series known collectively as the *New Hampshire State Papers*, http://sos.nh.gov/Papers.aspx (hereafter cited as *NHSP*; Kinney, *Church and State*, 15. Exeter did not obtain a settled minister until 1650. See Charles Bell, *History of the Town of Exeter, New Hampshire* (Exeter, CT: Quarter-Millennial Year, 1888), 155–62.

7. *NHSP*, 1:119–24; Kinney, *Church and State*, 11; Jere R. Daniell, *Colonial New Hampshire: A History* (Millwood, NY: KTO Press, 1981), 34–38; William Hubbard, *A General History of New England* (Boston: Charles Little & James Brown, 1848), 353–64; Kenneth Newport, "Knollys, Hanserd," in the *Oxford Dictionary of National Biography Online*, https://goo.gl/FtFtU3.

8. Hubbard, *New England*, 222; Kinney, *Church and State*, 12–13; Thomas J. Curry, *The First Freedoms: Church and State in America to the Passage of the First Amendment* (New York: Oxford University Press, 1986), 82–83.

9. *NHSP*, 1:189–91, 226–35; 25:765.

10. *NHSP*, 1:373–408; Kinney, *Church and State*, 22–24, 80; Daniell, *Colonial New Hampshire*, 59–79; *NHSP*, 17:580–90. For Moodey's story, see *NHSP*, 1:482–87, 521–41.

11. Linda Colley, *Britons: Forging the Nation, 1707–1837* (New Haven, CT: Yale University Press, 1992), 18–22; Kinney, *Church and State*, 34–36.

12. Kinney, *Church and State*, 36; *NHSP*, 3:189–90; Gerard V. Bradley, *Church-State Relationships in America* (New York: Greenwood Press, 1987), 23–24.

13. *NHSP*, 3:189–90.

14. Daniell, *Colonial New Hampshire*, 133–215; Eric Morser, *The Fires of New England: A Story of Protest and Rebellion in Antebellum America* (Amherst: University of Massachusetts Press, 2017), 123–28; *NHSP*, 9:631; Kinney, *Church and State*, 50–67; Lynn Turner, *The Ninth State: New Hampshire's Formative Years* (Chapel Hill: University of North Carolina Press, 2011), 7–8.

15. *NHSP*, 9:630–31.

16. A survey of several of the eighteenth-century *NHSP* volumes reveals this petition process. See vols. 3, 7, and 9.

17. *Laws of New Hampshire* (Concord, NH: Rumford, 1913), 2:530, 584, 769; *NHSP*, 4:727–29. Another example can be found in the Presbyterian petitions in Londonderry, in *NHSP*, 9:495–506.

18. *NHSP*, 5:719–20; Charles Bell, *History of the Town of Exeter* (Exeter: Quarter-Millennial, 1888), 184–95; *NHSP*, 9:250–98. Similar examples include Baptists in South-Hampton, in *NHSP*, 13:62–69; and Presbyterians in Hampton Falls, in George B. Kirsch, "Clerical Dismissals in Colonial and Revolutionary New Hampshire," *Church History* 49, no. 2 (1980): 166–67. On social upheaval in the First Great Awakening, see George Marsden, *Jonathan Edwards: A Life* (New Haven, CT: Yale University Press, 2003), 201–90; Thomas S. Kidd, *The Great Awakening* (New Haven, CT: Yale University Press, 2007), 83–155; and Douglas L. Winiarski, *Darkness Falls on the Land of Light: Experiencing Religious Awakenings in Eighteenth-Century New England* (Chapel Hill: University of North Carolina Press for the Omohundro Institute of Early American History and Culture, 2017), 405–33.

19. *NHSP*, 25:25. On the Benning Wentworth administration, see Turner, *Ninth State*, 3–9; Kinney, *Church and State*, 63–83; and Daniell, *Colonial New Hampshire*, 204–15.

20. Kinney, *Church and State*, 78–79.

21. *Journals of the Continental Congress, 1774–1789* (Washington, DC: Government Printing Office, 1905), 313:9; "Constitution of New Hampshire," in *The Federal and State Constitutions*, ed. Francis Thorpe (Washington, DC: Government Printing Office, 1909), 4:2451–53; *NHSP*, 11:737–38.

22. New Hampshire Constitution of 1784, in *NHSP*, 20:9–31.

23. John Reid, *Legislating the Courts: Judicial Dependence in Early National New Hampshire* (DeKalb: Northern Illinois University Press, 2009), 41; *A Journal of . . . the Honorable House of Representatives . . . of New-Hampshire* (Portsmouth, NH: J. Melcher, 1791), 122.

24. *Laws of New Hampshire* (Concord, NH: Rumford, 1916), 5:587–96.

25. Josiah Bartlett to John Wheelock, Papers of Josiah Bartlett, MS-181, folder 30, Rauner Special Collections Library, Dartmouth College. Infrastructure incorporations appear throughout *Laws of New Hampshire*, vols. 6–8. A typical example may be found in *Laws of New Hampshire*, 7:68–71.

26. *Journal of the Convention . . . to Revise the Constitution of New Hampshire, 1791–1792*, in *NHSP*, 10:24; Lynn Turner, *William Plumer of New Hampshire, 1759–1850* (Chapel Hill: University of North Carolina Press, 1962), 6–12, 34–47; *Life of William Plumer*, ed. A. P. Peabody (Boston: Phillips, Sampson, 1857), 49–52, 185–88; Reid, *Legislating the Courts*, 42. Amendment votes in *NHSP*, 10:41–42, 113–42.

27. Jeremy Belknap, *The History of New-Hampshire* (Boston: Belknap & Young, 1792), 3:324–25.

28. Records of the Congregational Church, 1779–1909 (Durham, NH), vol. 1, NHHS. Documentation of this story in the Coe/Burt Papers, Series I, Subseries A, box 1, folder 11, NHHS, including Curtis Coe to Committee, March 25, 1805; Remonstrance of the Congregational Church in Durham to the General Court of New Hampshire, December 1805; Curtis Coe to the Selectmen of Durham, February 28 (or 25), 1806; Curtis Coe to the Committee Appointed by the Town . . . of Durham, March 27, 1806; and Committee . . . town of Durham to Curtis Coe, April 22, 1806. On the distinction between territorial and poll parishes, see Balik, *Rally the Scattered Believers*, 101–5.

29. Contract between the Town of Durham and Federal Burt, October 2, 1816; and Oliver Brown to Jonathan Steele, November 14, 1816, Coe/Burt Papers, Series II, Subseries A, box 2, folders 1–7, NHHS; Everett Stackpole and Lucien Thompson, *History of the Town of Durham, New Hampshire* (Durham, 1913), 204–6; William Smith, *Some Remarks on the "Toleration Act" of 1819* (Exeter, NH: Samuel Moses, 1823), 11.

30. Hereafter, I will refer to this as the "Republican Party," the most common designation in contemporary New Hampshire newspapers.

31. Turner, *Ninth State*, 190, table 11-1. Unitarianism represented the most significant threat from within Congregationalism. See Nathan Rives, "'Is Not This a Paradox?': Public Morality and the Unitarian Defense of State-Supported Religion in Massachusetts, 1806–1833," *New England Quarterly* 86, no. 2 (2013): 232–65. The decisions in *Muzzy v. Wilkins* (1803) and *Moore v. Poole* (1815) can be found in *Decisions of the Superior and Supreme Courts of New Hampshire* (Boston: Little, Brown, 1879), 1–38, 166–68. For context, see Steve Green, *The Second Disestablishment: Church and State in Nineteenth-Century America* (New York: Oxford University Press, 2010), 120–24.

32. Donald Cole, *Jacksonian Democracy in New Hampshire, 1800–1851* (Cambridge, MA: Harvard University Press, 1970), 16–21; Jonathan J. Den Hartog, *Patriotism and Piety: Federalist Politics and Religious Struggle in the New American Nation* (Charlottesville: University of Virginia Press, 2015), 201–6; Turner, *Ninth State*, 176–82. On the decline of the Federalist Party, see Stanley Elkins and Eric McKitrick, *The Age of Federalism: The Early American Republic, 1788–1800* (New York: Oxford University Press, 1995); and Ron Chernow, *Alexander Hamilton* (New York: Penguin Press, 2004), 619–29.

33. Turner, *William Plumer*, 57–58, 198–205; *New-Hampshire Patriot*, July 4, 1815, 2; March 5, 1816, 2; March 9, 1816, 1.

34. William Plumer, "Speech to the Senate and House of Representatives," June 6, 1819, in *Intelligencer* (Portsmouth: S. Whidden), June 13, 1816, 2–3.

35. Plumer, "Speech," *Intelligencer*, June 13, 1816, 3.

36. C. Edward Skeen, *1816: America Rising* (Lexington: University Press of Kentucky, 2003), 151–54. For contemporary coverage of the Dartmouth case, see *New Hampshire Patriot*, June 3, 1817; November 4 and 11, 1817; and December 30, 1817.

37. *New-Hampshire Patriot*, June 11, 1816, 1.

38. *Journal of the Honorable Senate of . . . New-Hampshire*, (Concord: Hill & Moore, 1819), 134–36; *Laws of New Hampshire*, 5:592. On Young's role, see Balik, *Rally the Scattered Believers*, 88–95; Cole, *Jacksonian Democracy*, 39–40; McLoughlin, *New England Dissent*, 2:796–811; and *Concord Observer*, June 28, 1819, 2.

39. The official journals of the House and Senate record only the most basic information related to the bill (dates, votes, and the like). However, the *Concord Observer* printed significant portions of the speeches and debates over the summer of 1819. Editor George Hough openly proclaimed his paper's opposition to the bill: "We have no wish to conceal our ideas upon the subject. We believe that the bill . . . was in its tendency decidedly mischievous . . . we see no good tendency in it." *Concord Observer*, June 28, 1819, 2–3. Conversely, Isaac Hill's *New Hampshire Patriot* openly proclaimed its support for the bill.

40. *Concord Observer*, July 12, 1819, 2. Edmund Parker echoed this argument in *Concord Observer*, July 26, 1819, 4.

41. Smith, *Some Remarks*, 14; *Concord Observer*, July 26, 1819, 4; August 23, 1819, 1. Edmund Toppan used the phrase "the framers" three times in one paragraph of his speech against the bill, in *Concord Observer*, August 23, 1819, 1. Henry Hubbard also used the phrase "framers of our constitution" in his opposition speech, in *Concord Observer*, June 28, 1819, 3. Thanks to Lindsay Chervinsky for helping me identify the Jay Treaty as the subject at hand, which Toppan neither named nor dated in his speech. The Jay Treaty debates of 1794 to 1795 concerned major trade and shipping disputes between the United States and Great Britain. President Washington appointed Supreme Court chief justice John Jay as special envoy to negotiate terms, which found widespread support among Federalists and vehement opposition among Republicans. On the Jay Treaty, see Todd Estes, *The Jay Treaty Debate, Public Opinion, and the Evolution of Early American Political Culture* (Amherst: University of Massachusetts Press, 2006).

42. *Concord Observer*, July 26, 1819, 4; July 19, 1819, 2.

43. Text of the bill in *Laws of New Hampshire*, 8:820–21. Hubbard's speech in *Concord Observer*, June 28, 1819, 3.

44. *Concord Observer*, June 28, 1819, 2. On the same day the New Hampshire House debated the Toleration Bill, they also approved the incorporation of "the First Freewill Anti-paedo Baptist Society in Pittsfield and its vicinity." See *Journal of the New Hampshire House of Representatives* (Concord, NH: Hill & Moore, 1819), 236.

45. *Concord Observer*, June 28, 1819, 3; July 12, 1819, 3; August 16, 1819, 4.

46. Periodicals throughout New England and beyond followed the Jacob Cochran story. See *Portland (ME) Gazette*, June 1, 1819, 3; *New-York Evening Post*, June 6–8, 1819, 2; *Concord Observer*, July 5, 1819, 4; and *Weekly Visitor* (Kennebunk, ME), May 29, 1819, 3.

47. For descriptions of Cochran's capture, trial, and sentencing, see *National Messenger* (Georgetown, DC), October 27, 1819, 2; *Salem (MA) Gazette*, October 12, 1819, 3; *Hampshire Gazette* (Northampton, MA), October 19, 1819, 3; *Portland (ME) Gazette*, November 9, 1819, 3; October 11, 1819; *Farmers' Cabinet* (Amherst, NH), November 20, 1819, 3; *Hallowell (ME) Gazette*, October 20, 1819, 3; and *New-England Galaxy & Masonic Magazine* (Boston), June 4, 1819, 135.

48. *Concord Observer*, July 19, 1819, 2.

49. *Concord Observer*, July 5, 1819, 2. The Constitution of Connecticut (1818), www.cga.ct.gov/asp/Content/constitutions/1818Constitution.htm; McLoughlin, *New England Dissent*, vol. 2, chaps. 52–53.

50. *Concord Observer*, August 2, 1819, 4; New Hampshire Bill of Rights, *NHSP*, 20:9.

51. *Concord Observer*, July 5, 1819, 2.

52. Hubbard called for the House to jettison the bill, because "justice can be obtained" under the current laws for aggrieved parties, with only "a few inconveniences." *Concord Observer*, June 28, 1819, 3; and August 23, 1819, 1. For the three readings, votes, and final approval, see *Journal of the . . . House of Representatives*, 224–28, 286–96; *Journal of the Honorable Senate* (1819), 269; and *Laws of New Hampshire*, 8:820–21.

53. See Balik, *Rally the Scattered Believers*, 89–100. Another example of similar contractual difficulties occurred in Salisbury from 1823 to the early 1830s. The records show evidence of a church split along Congregational-Unitarian lines, disputes about pastoral preaching rights and salaries, and failed negotiations for the two groups to support a common minister. See Records of the First Congregational Church, Salisbury, NH, vol. 1, NHHS.

54. "United Presbyterian & Congregational Society of Bedford," Broadside (1825), S 1996.523.079, NHHS.

55. *New Hampshire Patriot*, September 7, 1819, 3; James Colby, *Manual of the Constitution of the State of New Hampshire* (Concord: Evans, 1902), 205–16; Kinney, *Church and State*, 136–37; *Journal of the Constitutional Convention of the State of New Hampshire* (1877), 32–37, 264–70.

56. Amherst Congregational Church to Henry Ware Jr., 3 August 1822; and Henry Ware to the Church in Amherst, August 6, 1822, in Amherst Congregational Church Records, NHHS; John Ware, ed., *Memoir of the Life of Henry Ware, Jr.* (Boston: American Unitarian Association, 1880).

CHAPTER NINETEEN

MAINE

Marc M. Arkin

THE STORY OF disestablishment in Maine is, like much of Maine's history, overshadowed by events in the Commonwealth of Massachusetts, of which Maine was a district, or political subdivision, until 1820. The conventional account, rendered in a few sentences, is that Maine was first owned by Sir Ferdinando Gorges under a Crown patent and was purchased from Gorges's heirs by the Puritans of Massachusetts Bay in 1677, opening the district to Congregationalism and displacing both an earlier Catholic presence and a nominal Anglican establishment.[1] William and Mary's royal charter of 1691 formally incorporated Maine into Massachusetts, thereby subjecting it to the ecclesiastical laws of the Bay Colony that required every township to support an "able learned orthodox minister" by public taxation.[2] With the cessation of hostilities as a result of the American Revolution, Maine witnessed an influx of opportunity-hungry settlers, strengthening the existing Congregationalist presence in seacoast areas and opening the door to a wide range of religious dissenters primarily in the backcountry. After numerous vicissitudes—including occupation of much of Maine by the British during the War of 1812—Maine successfully established itself as a politically independent polity. Maine's dissenters and their objections to state entanglement with religion found vindication in Maine's 1820 Constitution, whose Article I, Section 3, established freedom of religion, forbade government preference for any religion, abolished religious tests for any state office, and gave each religious society the exclusive right to elect its public teachers and contract with them for their support. The Constitution became effective March 15, 1820, after Congress approved Maine's admission to the Union on March 3, 1820, as part of the Missouri Compromise.[3]

Although the received account is accurate as far as it goes, the story of Maine's disestablishment neither began nor ended with the Constitution of

1820. Rather, disestablishment in Maine was tied up with the growth and ultimate ascendancy of the district's Democratic-Republican Party and its two-decades-long effort to separate from Massachusetts. What is more, constitutional disestablishment was hardly the conclusion of the story. After 1820 Maine implemented its new voluntary religious order through legislation, leaving its state government deeply involved in church affairs. As the nineteenth century continued, Maine's legislators enacted and its courts maintained a regime of cultural Protestantism that echoed significant aspects of prior Massachusetts law.

I.

Even before the wave of new settlers, Maine's nominal Congregational establishment had been largely ineffectual. In 1790 only one-fifth of Maine's sixty communities had gathered a Congregational church and undertaken the obligation of paying the minister through parish taxes.[4] Significantly, most of Maine's frontier settlements could not afford a settled minister; of twenty-four backcountry communities, only one supported a Congregational church. Although population growth created opportunities for new Congregational clergy, the disruption of clerical education during the Revolutionary War—and the shift of many students to the legal profession—limited the number of ministerial graduates, especially those willing to choose the hardship of a frontier congregation over more comfortable pulpits to the south. Of the ministerial candidates who did elect to settle in the north country, anecdotes abound of their moral failings, hardly enhancing Congregationalism's reputation or appeal.[5]

The thinly populated and lightly churched backcountry proved hospitable ground for the itinerant evangelists of the Second Great Awakening, who provided settlers with a cultural identity and experiential religion that aligned with their agrarian politics and limited education. For example, in 1787 there were only 183 reported Baptists in the entire district of Maine, but by 1820 its 9,328 members made Baptists the state's largest denomination. Methodists enjoyed similar growth. In 1792 the district reported no Methodists; by 1820 Methodism had become Maine's second-largest denomination, with more than 6,000 members.[6]

Further adding to the religious mix was a population of freewheeling religious seekers and homegrown prophets, many of whom found even the radical evangelical denominations too constraining. Not only did the hill country on the Maine–New Hampshire border give birth to Benjamin Randel's Free Will Baptists, which by 1800 had become the region's largest indigenous denomination, but the Maine hinterland nurtured a distinctly rural Universalist movement led by local thinkers inspired by an expansive vision of "gospel liberty." Maine's frontier also provided a congenial home for the Christian Connexion, a loosely organized movement that advocated radical reform in religion, politics, and medicine. In addition, Maine sheltered a range of charismatic sects, ranging from Mother Ann Lee's celibate Shakers to Jacob Cochran's antinomian Society of Free Brethren.[7]

In political life, the Democratic-Republican takeover of the district was likewise rooted in Maine's exponential population growth in the decades after the revolution, an expansion fed largely by poor and uneducated migrants from elsewhere in New England who relocated to Maine's backcountry in search of cheap land. In 1770 Maine had a population of fewer than 10,000; by 1790, its population had grown to 96,540. By the time it attained statehood in 1820, that figure had roughly trebled again.[8] This expansion outstripped the reach of existing social and religious institutions. In the backcountry, primitive conditions, tenuous settler land titles—always under challenge by the Great Proprietors, who claimed legal ownership of vast swathes of Maine territory—and the itinerant evangelists of the Second Great Awakening together created an atmosphere of spiritual and social ferment deeply informed by the revolution's egalitarian rhetoric.

These conditions also provided fertile ground for the Democratic-Republican Party, whose seacoast opportunists, led by the Machiavellian hand of William King, resented Federalist control of the spoils of government from the distant reaches of Boston. These new men actively courted dissenters, playing upon their resentment of Federalist support for the Standing Order in religion and the Great Proprietors in land policy. Unlike Massachusetts Republicans, who remained lukewarm about creating a voluntary system of church support and whose class background led them to look down on dissenters both socially and theologically,[9] Maine's Jeffersonian Republicans united with dissenters in disaffection for the Standing Order and all its works.

Fortified by Maine's religious diversity and supported by their Democratic-Republican allies, the district's dissenters took the lead in legal challenges to the Massachusetts religious establishment. In 1799 Francis Matignan, a Roman Catholic priest who rode circuit from Boston to southern Maine, sued to recover the parish taxes paid by some of his communicants to the First Parish of Newcastle, Maine, which used the tax moneys to support the town's first settled Congregational minister. Matignan was represented by James Sullivan, a prominent lawyer and liberal Maine Republican involved in a number of religious freedom cases. Ultimately, the Massachusetts Supreme Judicial Court ruled that, although a dissenter had a statutory right to have his parish rates applied to "the public teacher of his own religious sect," the state's Constitution restricted these payments to "public protestant teachers,"[10] an obvious blow to Catholics and any group not deemed to be within the Protestant tradition. Almost simultaneously, Sullivan, as Massachusetts attorney general, prosecuted Father Jean Cheverus, for illegally marrying a couple in Maine, arguing that Cheverus had not been ordained to serve a particular parish and thus was not properly a minister under Massachusetts law. Apparently, Sullivan hoped to blunt the effect of the *Matignan* decision with a judgment favorable to Cheverus, and, indeed, Cheverus prevailed when a lower court held that because he had been properly ordained by the rites of his own church, he was legally authorized to perform marriages.[11]

Maine's Universalists were also active in mounting challenges to Massachusetts's treatment of dissenters.[12] Starting in the 1780s, some lower state courts had interpreted the Massachusetts Constitution to permit diversion of a dissenting resident's parish taxes only to incorporated religious societies, a position that favored the established Congregational Church.[13] The issue continued unsettled until 1810, when Universalist minister Thomas Barnes, who presided over an unincorporated congregation, sued to recover the religious taxes paid by two of his congregants to the support of the Congregational Church in the First Parish of Falmouth (now Portland), Maine. In his decision on behalf of Massachusetts's highest court, Chief Justice Theophilus Parsons, a conservative Federalist, resolved the matter in favor of the Standing Order, stating flatly, "We are all of opinion that the constitution has not authorized any teacher to recover, by action at law, any money assessed pursuant to the third article of the declaration of rights but a public Protestant teacher of some legally incorporated society."[14]

The *Barnes* decision was a serious defeat for sectarians, since many dissenters objected to incorporation as an improper extension of civil power into the internal affairs of their churches. Even dissenters who were willing to seek incorporation from the Massachusetts Legislature—the only body empowered to grant petitions for incorporation—faced obstacles ranging from cost and distance to politics. As the *Eastern Argus*, a Portland Republican newspaper, reported, "[E]very federal vote was repeatedly given against incorporating those societies" in order to favor the Federalists' supporters in the Congregational establishment.[15] Maine's Republicans were quick to capitalize on the situation.

The public uproar following *Barnes* contributed to a narrow Republican victory in the May 1811 elections, allowing dissenters to press their cause in the Massachusetts Legislature. The resulting passage of the *Religious Freedom Bill of 1811* afforded dissenting interests a qualified victory. Notably, the bill passed only because Maine's five representatives voted four to one in favor.[16] The act settled several controversies at once, requiring simply that to receive his share of the parish taxes a religious teacher of "a corporate or unincorporate religious society . . . be ordained and established according to the forms and usages of his own religious sect and denomination." Unincorporated societies were given the power to manage property and gifts through trustees selected by members. However, the law still required dissenters to file certificates for their religious teachers to receive their taxes, and, accordingly, disputes over church membership continued to be a staple of local life.[17]

II.

After a hiatus in challenges to the establishment due to the War of 1812, Maine's dissenters, especially its increasingly mainstream Baptists, turned their attention to educational equality. Bowdoin College, Maine's only institution of higher education, had long been a bastion of both Federalism and conservative Calvinistic Congregationalism. Baptists and other dissenters regularly complained that their sons were denied admission to the college and, even if admitted, were subjected to four years of distasteful theological instruction in order to graduate. William King, who had been appointed an overseer of the college in 1802 (before his conversion to Republicanism), had developed an intense antipathy toward Bowdoin, even suspecting its president, Jesse Appleton, of cooperating with the occupying British during the war. By 1816 the college's leadership was among the most vocal opponents of separation from Massachusetts, and King turned his personal animus to political advantage.[18]

From 1816 to 1819, against the backdrop of a referendum favoring separation and a subsequent district-wide convention that rejected it, King spearheaded an unsuccessful attempt in the Massachusetts Legislature to obtain state funds for the new Baptist-led Maine Literary and Theological Institute (now Colby College). Bowdoin, he pointed out, had received a number of townships of land as well as a yearly grant of $3,000 from the state. Baptists deserved equal treatment. For all King's efforts, however, the new school had received only a single township when it opened its doors in 1818.[19] King and fellow Republicans capitalized on the differential treatment as clear evidence of Massachusetts's contempt for Maine's people and its continuing discrimination against dissenters.

King timed the final confrontation over the Baptist college to heighten support for political separation. He introduced into the Massachusetts Legislature another bill calling for a grant of several townships and $3,000 a year to support the Baptist Institute, which risked closing its doors without further state aid. The bill failed. According to King, however, if two of Maine's senators, Samuel Fessenden and Lathrop Lewis—both Federalists and opponents of separation—had voted in favor, the bill would have passed. To extract maximum political advantage, King had an extract from Fessenden's speech published in the friendly pages of the *Eastern Argus*: "One college is all that is necessary in the District of Maine, and I have no idea of conveying or giving away any aid to any College whatever, that is to be in the way, or a rival to Brunswick [Bowdoin] College. If the Baptists want a College . . . I have no objection . . . provided they can afford it."[20] In reaction, Baptist leaders threw their support firmly behind Republicans and separation. Recognizing the shift in Maine's public opinion, the Massachusetts Legislature passed the *Separation Act of 1819*, which, if ratified by Maine voters, would lead to statehood.[21] In a special July election that year, Maine voters approved the act by a margin of more than two to one.

III.

On October 11, 1819, delegates representing nearly all of Maine's incorporated towns assembled in Portland to draft a state constitution. The delegates naturally chose William King to preside, and he, in turn, selected Republican allies for the drafting committee. Prominent Republican lawyer John Holmes of Alfred was elected chair. Groundwork for the constitution had been laid as early as 1816, when King began canvassing numerous sources for advice, and the committee soon presented a draft to the convention.[22]

For dissenters, the most significant provision was Article I, Section 3, which guaranteed freedom of conscience to all as long as they did "not disturb the public peace, nor obstruct others in their religious worship," and provided that "all persons demeaning themselves peaceably, as good members of the State, shall be equally under the protection of the laws, and no subordination, nor preference for any sect or denomination to another shall ever be established by law." In addition, the provision forbade any religious test as a condition for any state office or trust. Finally, Section 3 guaranteed that "all religious societies in this State, whether corporate or unincorporate, shall at all times have the exclusive right of electing their public teachers, and contracting with them for their support and maintenance."[23]

In the debate over Section 3, delegates unanimously voiced support for freedom of conscience and for no governmental preference among religious groups. The primary pushback came from conservatives, who believed that public religious observance was essential to preserving morality and civic order. These conservatives offered a series of amendments that would have empowered the legislature to require citizens to attend public worship and to pass laws mandating certain religious observances, particularly the Christian Sabbath.

Federalist George Thacher from Biddeford illustrated the fine line these conservative delegates threaded. His response to a memorial from Maine's Catholics asking for equality with Protestants is justly singled out for its commitment to freedom of conscience: "We are all children of the same God. . . . Whatever sects or denominations we may have divided ourselves into; and however through prejudice think ours is the favored of Heaven— nevertheless we are all equal in our rights, and equally dear to our Father, if we obey his laws. [In the new Maine,] no distinction or pre-eminence would ever be given to any religious sect . . . whether Catholic, Jews, or Mahometans. The liberal principals of our government ought to make no difference between them." Yet later in the same debate, Thacher offered a qualifying amendment to Article 3: "As it is the absolute duty of all men to worship God their creator, so it is their natural right to worship him in such a way and manner as their conscience dictates." In support, Thacher observed tartly that he "hoped none of the Convention wished to secure to themselves, or any body of people, *the right not to worship at all*, as well as the *right to worship* according to the dictates of conscience." After Thacher's proposal failed, a fellow conservative offered an amendment based on the Massachusetts Bill of Rights, affirming that "good order and preservation of the civil government especially depend on piety, religion, and morality" and granting the legislature power to encourage and support institutions of public worship on a nonpreferential basis.[24]

Republican John Holmes offered the dissenters' response: "To make it a *duty* to exercise a *right* is preposterous." Stressing the voluntary nature of worship, he warned that "[to] prescribe the duty would be to authorize the legislature to enforce it," and this would import "a whole body of ethics"— presumably reminiscent of Massachusetts law—into the constitution. Pointedly, he argued that the power to support religious observance would quickly turn into a power to persecute. As to the Sabbath, Holmes observed that it was within the "scope of [the legislature's] general powers" to prescribe a day of rest but proclaimed it had "no right to prescribe this as a day of *worship*." Without much further discussion, on October 19, 1819, Article 3 passed without amendment. The Republicans had made good on their promise to their dissenting allies.[25]

The convention's explanatory *Address to the People of Maine* that accompanied the draft constitution echoed Holmes in rejecting state-mandated worship: "The worship of Jehovah, to be acceptable must be a free will offering. The laws of man can reach no further than to external deportment. Our holy religion neither requires nor admits their aid." Yet the *Address* hinted that the "rights of conscience" and "the footing of most perfect equality" had their limits and that Maine was yet to be a freethinker's paradise. It reassured voters that although the constitution prohibited a religious test for public office, its requirement that all officials be under oath "necessarily presupposed that they believe in the existence of God."[26]

IV.

It remained for Maine's first legislature to provide the legal framework for the new settlement, and it did so in the *1821 Act Concerning Parishes*. The key provision, which effectively dismantled the existing parish system, enabled any person to "sign off" or exit from any religious society by writing his own certificate of resignation without requiring that she or he join any other society.[27] For those so disposed, freedom from religion was now a legal possibility. Most of the act, however, focused on forming and regulating religious organizations under the new dispensation. The act permitted any group to apply to a justice of the peace to call a meeting to organize themselves as a "body politic, to be known by such name and style as they may see fit to adopt . . . [with] all the powers and privileges incident by law to parishes and religious societies."[28] The act then laid out the structure and powers of these religious societies in a form that largely followed existing corporate governance rules. It provided for lay self-government, while establishing officer and trustee accountability to members through such devices as annual meetings, provision for member initiatives through petition to a justice of the peace if necessary, and the requirement of public records.

Religious societies were granted the right to assess charges on members for necessary expenses and to auction pews for unpaid charges. Perhaps foreseeing the complexities of the transition, the act also provided that when a pew owner regularly attended another church, upon written notice his charges were to be paid to the church he designated. Although the act gave religious societies the ability to hold property, concerned both with the potential for self-dealing and with undue accumulation of wealth, the legislature restricted the power of ministers and church officers to sell that property without members' consent and limited the annual income from church property to $3,000.[29]

This regime left Maine's government with considerable oversight of religious societies.[30] And, in Maine, the transition between regimes proved thornier than has generally been recognized. For many years, Maine's courts struggled with the relationship between territorial parishes created by the unrepealed *Massachusetts Act of 1786*, poll parishes recognized by the Massachusetts law of 1811, and the poll parishes organized under Maine's own 1821 act. Most cases involved disputes over voting rights in which the church or parish membership of a party to the lawsuit was in issue.[31] Other problems arose with regard to lands reserved to the use or support of the ministry or schools prior to statehood. Unassigned lands that had not yet vested in a minister or religious society usually reverted to the town in which the parish was located. The law concerning assigned lands remained unsettled, with significant variation among courts as to whether the fee vested in the minister or the town and whether the land could be sold without mutual assent.[32] Technical questions of who could exercise corporate powers abounded.[33] As late as 1849, the Maine Supreme Judicial Court invalidated a transfer of church property because only two of the three required signers of the deed signed in their proper office as trustees for the church and glebe lands; the third signed as treasurer of the town, although he was also a trustee and treasurer for the church properties.[34] By 1855 there was sufficient concern regarding self-dealing by those in control of church property that appraisal by "three discreet persons under oath, to be elected by ballot at any legal meeting of the owners or proprietors," was required before a religious corporation could sell any assets.[35]

V.

While Maine wrestled with the disestablishment of the parish system, it was also engaged in legislating state-supported cultural Protestantism.[36] In this the agendas of evangelicals and Federalist conservatives aligned surprisingly well.[37] For example, the same 1821 legislature that passed the *Act Concerning Parishes* enacted a blasphemy law based on the 1782 Massachusetts law. Maine criminalized not only "wilfully blasphem[ing] the holy name of God" and "contumeliously reproach[ing] the holy word of God" as contained in the Old and New Testaments but, for good measure, the lesser offense of cursing as well. To gauge the seriousness of the offense, the penalty for blasphemy was solitary imprisonment for up to three months and hard labor for a term not exceeding five years.[38]

Underscoring that Sabbath breakers acted to "their own great damage as members of a Christian Society," the 1821 legislature prohibited most forms of public entertainment and business on Sundays and protected Christian worship from disruption. Special "tythingmen," chosen by the towns, were empowered to enforce the law's provisions, particularly those involving inns and places of public resort.[39] Well into the 1850s, Maine courts reinforced Sabbatarianism with the doctrine of *dies non juridicus*, which held null and void all legal actions taken on Sunday.[40]

Even laws supporting freedom of conscience were enlisted in the service of cultural Protestantism. In 1833 the legislature passed a bill titled *An Act to secure to witnesses freedom of opinion in matters of religion*. Harking back to the *Address* of 1820, the act ensured that "no person who believes in the existence of a Supreme Being, shall be adjudged an incompetent or incredible witness" in judicial proceedings in the state. Eight years later, Maine's highest court interpreted the statute to require belief in a Supreme Being as a prerequisite to testifying and sustained a lower court's decision to hold a hearing regarding a potential witness's possible atheism and to exclude his testimony on that basis.[41]

In summary, Maine's story is one of individualistic "liberty men" who rejected the established church, whether for religious or political reasons. The voluntarist constitutional settlement they achieved embodied a vision of free religious choice and no denominational preferences on the part of state government. Yet the implementation of that settlement involved state support for cultural Protestantism and left Maine's government entangled with both religious polity and observance. Ultimately, Maine's settlement involved an uneasy tension between the vindication of individual rights of conscience and governmental regulation of their organized expression and institutional embodiment, a situation not without the potential for its own ironies.

NOTES

1. Ronald F. Banks, *Maine Becomes a State* (Portland: Maine Historical Society, 1973), 5 *passim*, pointing out that not only did the Bay Colony subordinate Maine's interests to its own, but the union was unnatural because the two were geographically separated by New Hampshire. Marshall J. Tinkle, *The Maine State Constitution*, 2nd ed. (New York: Oxford University Press, 2013), 4.

2. John D. Cushing, "Notes on Disestablishment in Massachusetts, 1780–1833," *William and Mary Quarterly* 26 (1969): 169–90, 169 (quoting the act of 1692).

3. "An Act for the Admission of the State of Maine into the Union," March 2, 1820, 16th Cong., 1st sess., chap. 19, p. 545. The act does not mention religion. Maine was admitted to the Union as part of the Missouri Compromise, which admitted Maine as a free state and Missouri as a slave state and excluded slavery in the remaining territory of the Louisiana Purchase north of latitude 36'30". Missouri was admitted in a separate bill, act of March 6, 1820, 16th Cong., 1st sess., chap 22, p. 545.

4. "Taxes" was the term commonly used to describe the moneys paid for support of the established church since the amount was within the purview of town government. See, for example, Mary Ellen Chase, *Jonathan Fisher: Maine Parson, 1768–1847* (New York: Macmillan, 1948), 99; Cushing, "Notes on Disestablishment," 171.

5. Alan Taylor, *Liberty Men and Great Proprietors: The Revolutionary Settlement on the Maine Frontier, 1760–1820* (Chapel Hill: University of North Carolina Press for the Omohundro Institute of Early American History and Culture, 1990), 132–34; Chase, *Jonathan Fisher.*

6. Banks, *Maine Becomes a State,* 140.

7. See Stephen A. Marini, *Radical Sects of Revolutionary New England* (Cambridge, MA: Harvard University Press, 1982), 66–67, 86–88, 76–77, 89–90, 7, 175; Taylor, *Liberty Men,* 123–53.

8. Marini, *Radical Sects,* 27–28.

9. William G. McLoughlin, *New England Dissent, 1630–1833: The Baptists and the Separation of Church and State,* 2 vols. (Cambridge, MA: Harvard University Press, 1971), 2:1067.

10. Jud. Ct. Rec, 1800–1803, f. 125 (Cushing, "Notes on Disestablishment," 182); *The American Catholic Historical Researches* 19 (1902): 122–25. In 1785, represented by Sullivan, Universalist John Murray led a similar protest to the parish tax system in Gloucester, Massachusetts, and was rewarded with a prosecution for illegally performing marriages. Cushing, "Notes on Disestablishment," 173–77; cf. McLoughlin, *New England Dissent,* 2:1065–84.

11. Letter of Rev. John Cheverus to Bishop John Carroll, Boston, March 10, 1801, in XIX *American Catholic,* 120–21; McLoughlin, *New England Dissent,* 1:658. Ultimately, Sullivan was elected governor of Massachusetts in 1807.

12. Massachusetts ostensibly permitted a dissenting resident's parish rates to be paid to the minister of his own religious society upon presentation of a certificate showing that he was a regular member of that church. Cushing, "Notes on Disestablishment," 173–75.

13. McLoughlin, *New England Dissent,* 2:1088–89.

14. *Barnes v. First Parish of Falmouth,* 6 Mass. 401, 5 Tyng 401, 420 (1810). See also McLoughlin, *New England Dissent,* 2:1086–88. Parsons had represented the Gloucester church in the Murray case.

15. *Eastern Argus,* May 2, 1811; McLoughlin, *New England Dissent,* 2:1089.

16. Paul Goodman, *The Democratic-Republicans of Massachusetts* (Cambridge, MA: Harvard University Press, 1964), 165; McLoughlin, *New England Dissent,* 2:1101; Cushing, "Notes on Disestablishment," 185–88.

17. McLoughlin, *New England Dissent*, 2:1098–1101; Mass. State AR, V, 387.

18. Banks, *Maine Becomes a State*, 140, 170.

19. Banks, *Maine Becomes a State*, 141.

20. *Eastern Argus*, March 16, 1819; Banks, *Maine Becomes a State*, 141–44.

21. Confirming Republican and Baptist concerns, Federalists inserted into the Act of Separation a provision ensuring state payments to Bowdoin for another five years. Maine's constitutional convention devoted substantial energy to drafting an article to circumvent the support provision and gain control over Bowdoin. Ultimately, Bowdoin's new president was someone acceptable to Republicans, and, encouraged by King's promise of a medical school, he persuaded Bowdoin's governing board to submit to state control. In 1821 Governor King enlarged the number of trustees and overseers, appointed Republicans to fill the new slots, and placed the college under Republican control. Banks, *Maine Becomes a State,* 177.

22. The relationship between the Maine Constitution and the Massachusetts Constitution of 1780 is the subject of some scholarly dispute. Cf. Tinkle, *The Maine State Constitution*, 6–7, arguing that specific provisions were drawn from other state constitutions adopted closer to 1819, with Banks, *Maine Becomes a State*, 153, arguing that Maine's Constitution was modeled on that of Massachusetts.

23. Maine State Constitution, Article I, Section 3; see Tinkle, *The Maine State Constitution*, 30–33, asserting that the provision was based on Article V of the New Hampshire Bill of Rights.

24. Jeremiah Perley, *The Debates, Resolutions and Other Proceedings of the Conventions of Delegates, Assembled at Portland on the Eleventh and Continued Until the Twenty-Ninth Day of October, 1819, for the Purposes of Forming a Constitution for the State of Maine*, 99, reprinted in *The Debates and Journal of the Constitutional Convention of the State of Maine, 1819–20* (Augusta, ME: Farmers Almanac Press, 1894), 105–10.

25. *Debates, Resolutions and Other Proceedings*, 96–97, 98. King personally harbored anticlerical—especially anti-Catholic—sentiments and therefore avoided taking the lead on religious matters in the convention. For example, John Fiske, *Reasons for Particular Consideration on the Death of Great Men; On Occasion of the Death of General William King* (Bath, ME: Haines & Freeman, 1852), 19; and Banks, *Maine Becomes a State*, 237. The Constitution was submitted to the people of Maine on December 6, 1819, and was approved by a vote of 9,040 to 797. It took effect with Maine's admission to the Union on March 15, 1820. See Tinkle, *The Maine State Constitution*, 9.

26. Perley, *Debates, Resolutions and Other Proceedings*, 106.

27. *Laws of the State of Maine; to Which are Prefixed the Constitution of the U. States and of Said State*, 2 vols. (Brunswick, ME, 1821), 2:592–66 ("Act Concerning Parishes"), chap. 85, section 8.

28. *1821 Laws*, 592, chap. 85, section 1.

29. *1821 Laws*, 595–96, chap. 85, section 10.

30. Sarah Barringer Gordon, "The First Disestablishment: Limits on Church Power and Property before the Civil War," *University of Pennsylvania Law Review* 162, no.

2 (2014): 307–72, 330 (describing the general development as a "new law of religion" tucked into state codes and interpreted by state judges).

31. See, for example, *Lord v. Bradley*, 2 Greenl. 67, 2 Me. 67 (Aug. 1, 1822); *Richardson v. Brown*, 6 Greenl. 355, 6 Me. 355 (May 1, 1830); and *Osgood v. Bradley*, 7 Greenl. 411, 7 Me. 411 (May 1, 1831). A poll parish was one organized by counting its members rather than by encompassing all those who lived within the territory of a town parish. See, for example, McLoughlin, *New England Dissent*, 1:367n13.

32. Act Concerning Parishes, PL 1821, chap. 85, sec. 10; PL 1824 chap. 254; cf., 13 M.R.S.A. 3161; *Stewart v. Cargill*, 15 Me. 414 (1839); *Flye v. First Congregational Parish of Newcastle*, 114 Me. 158 (1915); *Inhabitants of Bucksport v. Spofford*, 12 Me. 487 (1835); *contra State of Maine v. Cutler*, 16 Me. 351 (1839) (minister seized of the real property, but the town holds the fee).

33. For example, *Trustees of Ministerial and School Fund in Levant v. Parks et al.*, 1 Fairf. 441, 10 Me. 441 (June 1833) (whether a claim could be brought in the name of the officers or must be brought in the name of the corporation).

34. *Warren v. Inhabitants of Stetson*, 30 Me 231, 235 (1849).

35. Act of March 16, 1855, section 2, 1855 ME ACTS 196, 197.

36. See Steven K. Green, *The Second Disestablishment: Church and State in Nineteenth-Century America* (New York: Oxford University Press, 2010), 9, 81–119.

37. On this point, see Jonathan J. Den Hartog, *Patriotism and Piety: Federalist Politics and Religious Struggle in the New American Nation* (Charlottesville: University of Virginia Press, 2015), 201–6. The most salient example of Maine's legislative enactment of cultural Protestant norms was the 1851 Maine Liquor Law, which prohibited both manufacture and sale of alcohol within the state, a topic beyond the scope of this chapter. See, for example, Maine Statistical Society, *The Maine Liquor Law: Its Origin, History, and Results, Including a Life of the Hon. Neal Dow* (New York: Fowler and Wells, 1856); and Kelley Bouchard, "When Maine Went Dry," *Portland Press Herald*, October 2, 2011.

38. *Laws of the State of Maine*, vols. 1–2, *With the Constitution of the State of Maine*, ed. Francis Ormond and Jonathan Smith (T. Todd and Coleman, Holden, 1834), 1:72–73 (chap. 8, sections 1–3, February 5, 1821). The law was upheld in *State v. Mockus*, 120 Me. 84 (1921). It was not formally disavowed until 1980.

39. *Laws of New Hampshire*, 1:74–79 (chap. 9, sections 1–12, February 24, 1821). To this day, the Maine Department of Inland Fisheries and Wildlife prohibits hunting on Sundays and Maine lobstermen do not fish on Sundays.

40. *Towle v. Larrabee*, 26 Me. 464, 469 (1847) (refusing to enforce a promissory note executed on Sunday for the sale of a horse, leaving the defendant in possession even though he failed to pay for defendant's horse); *Bryant v. Inhabitants of Biddeford*, 39 Me. 193 (1855) (assuming without deciding that a contract renting a horse for Sunday travel was unenforceable), overruled by *PW & B Railroad Company v. Philadelphia & Havre de Grace Steam Towboat Co.*, 64 U.S. 433, 436 (1860).

41. Laws 12th February 1833, chap. 58; *Peter Smith v. Edmund Coffin*, 18 Me. 157 (1841).

CHAPTER TWENTY

FLORIDA

Nathan A. Adams IV

Ponce de león planted a cross for Spain near present-day St. Augustine in late March or early April 1513.[1] He called the land *La Florida*, in honor of *Pascua Florida*, the Spanish Feast of the Flowers at Easter.[2] It formed part of the Captaincy General of Cuba and the Viceroyalty of New Spain, and it extended into parts of present-day Georgia, Alabama, Mississippi, South Carolina, and southeastern Louisiana. From the start, Spain had a military and missionary purpose, but its control over *La Florida* was more official than fact.[3]

Ponce de León sailed around the "island of Florida," where he was wounded and repulsed by Indians near Charlotte Bay. He would return with several priests after King Ferdinand V commissioned and instructed him to "[t]reat the Indians as best you can . . . seeking in every possible way to convert them to our Holy Catholic faith." In 1521 León's second landing with about two hundred colonists, including priests, ended like the first.[4]

More Spanish explorers followed. Expeditions under Pánfilo de Narváez and Hernando de Soto landed near Tampa Bay in 1528 and 1539, respectively.[5] When Narváez "took possession of Florida," he entreated the unseen Indians to "recognize the Church as Mistress and Superior of the Universe, and the Supreme Pontiff, called Pope." Just four survivors of his expedition reached Mexico seven years later. De Soto's charter requiring priests to instruct "the natives of that province in our holy Catholic Faith" ended much the same.

The first settlement was pioneered by Tristán de Luna in 1559. The viceroy of Mexico instructed him "not to antagonize the Indians but 'to settle, and by good example, with good works and with presents, to bring them to a knowledge of Our Holy Faith and Catholic Truth.'" With a thousand settlers and five hundred soldiers, Luna established a settlement in Pensacola, but after a devastating hurricane and cultivation failures it was abandoned by 1561.[6] Huguenots fleeing the French Wars of Religion were the next to attempt colonization.[7] On May Day 1562, Jean Ribault arrived at the St. John River and prayed perhaps the first Protestant prayer in America. To the Natives who told him where to land, he pointed his finger upward to indicate that he worshipped God. The Natives pointed two fingers in the same way, signifying that they worshipped the sun and moon. Ribault raised a column claiming French ownership and sailed on, but his lieutenant René Goulaine de Laudonnière and roughly two hundred settlers returned two years later to build Fort Caroline, a short-lived colony associated with the Reformed Church.[8]

King Philip II learned in the spring of 1565 that Ribault was assembling a fleet to reinforce Fort Caroline. Then Huguenots were cooperating with the Dutch against Spain and would fight alongside them during the first years of the Dutch Revolt (1568–1609). Don Pedro Menéndez de Avilés answered the king's call to repel Ribault, destroy Fort Caroline, and establish a permanent Catholic settlement. The royal *asiento* charged him with a military and missionary responsibility, including "the salvation of those [Indian] souls" by conversion to "our Holy Catholic Faith."[9]

On the Feast of St. Augustine, August 28, 1565, Menéndez arrived on the heels of Ribault. Following an indecisive naval skirmish, Menéndez landed at St. Augustine on September 8, 1565. His entourage marched up to a cross planted by an advance party and knelt and kissed it with Indians watching and imitating them.[10] Mass was recorded here on September 8, 1565, the beginning of the parish of St. Augustine.[11]

Ribault pursued Menéndez before he could fortify but wound up shipwrecked to the south by a storm. Menéndez took advantage and struck Fort Caroline overland, killing most settlers.[12] Menéndez placarded them with a sign stating that he hanged them not as Frenchmen, but as Lutherans.[13] Menéndez turned south to find the remnant of Ribault's fleet and also massacred them as heretics.[14] The last chapter of Fort Caroline would be written by the French. In 1568, Dominique de Gourgues, a Catholic, took revenge on the fort, renamed San Mateo by the Spanish. Gourgues reportedly declared, "I do not this as unto Spaniards nor Mariners but as unto Thieves, Traitors and Murderers."[15]

Menéndez turned his attention to establishing a line of presidios in St. Lucie, Biscayne Bay, Charlotte Harbor, and Tampa, where Jesuits sought to convert the Natives. He also sent Jesuits north, but they abandoned the field after an Indian massacre in 1572. In 1587 Franciscans arrived to replace the Jesuits.[16] In 1597–98 several Franciscans were also killed during an Indian uprising, known as the Juanillo Revolt, begun when a friar had a warrior removed as heir to the chieftainship for polygamy. King Philip III thought seriously about terminating the Florida enterprise, but the Franciscans resisted, believing that the blood of the martyrs would secure their long-term success. Forty-plus Franciscans would report winning as many as twenty-six thousand Indians to Christianity by 1655.[17]

The mission system across the Panhandle to central Florida represented a strategic corridor that linked St. Augustine to the rich agricultural interior. It also became a part of a system of forced labor to move foodstuffs and later building materials to St. Augustine. In 1605 Governor Pedro Ibarra brokered a "Period of Friendship" with the Indians, but resentment over forced labor led to rebellions in 1638 and 1647.[18] During one uprising, chiefs specified that the rebellion was not against the Franciscans but against the forced labor system. However, the unity of church and Crown made it difficult to disentangle the two.

In the Spanish colonial system, the Catholic Church functioned as a branch of the royal government.[19] The Crown could appoint religious officials, but, in practice, the bishop of Cuba appointed clerics. King Philip II stipulated that each friar should receive maintenance from the local governor. Salaries were supposed to be paid from a tax on local produce, but due to meager yields tithes collected in Cuba or Mexico City supported the friars, together with the Indians' food offerings.[20] The Crown provided priests the same rations and pay as that of a common soldier. The Crown also provided for the friars' travel and needs of the missions. It is fair to say that "[t]he Crown . . . exercised direct jurisdiction over the entire mission process."

The English were just getting started in the Southeast when the "golden age" for Spanish Catholic Florida began (1607–74). An "undeclared" war broke out between Philip II and Elizabeth I between 1585 and 1604. Elizabeth ordered Sir Francis Drake to lead an expedition to the Spanish New World. Familiar with Menéndez's execution of fellow Protestants, and with the assistance of a French Huguenot taken prisoner six years earlier, Drake plundered and razed St. Augustine in 1586, including its forts and first cathedral.[21] English, French, and Dutch corsairs repeated these attacks on St. Augustine several more times as late as the 1680s, often in connection with their attacks on the Spanish treasure fleet, leading the Spanish to begin construction on the still standing Castillo de San Marcos in 1672.

In 1629 King Charles I formally asserted England's claim to the territory south of Virginia,[22] but nothing much came of it until 1663, when Charles II granted the Province of Carolina to eight Lords Proprietors.[23] The grant purported to extend south to Daytona Beach, Florida. The Charter of Carolina called for an increase in the Christian religion by building "churches, chappels and oratories," dedicated to the ecclesiastical laws of England.[24] Yet the Charter anticipated that some would not "in their private opinions, conform to the publick exercise of religion, according to the liturgy, form and ceremonies of the church of England." The Lords Proprietors had discretion to grant settlers "indulgencies and dispensations."[25]

In 1669 Governor William Sayle set sail for Carolina with one hundred settlers. They carried a constitution that declared the Church of England "the only true and orthodox and the national religion of . . . Carolina; and, therefore, it alone shall be allowed to receive public maintenance, by grant of parliament."[26] The constitution also allowed: "The natives who . . . are utterly strangers to Christianity, whose idolatry, ignorance, or mistake gives us no right to expel or use them ill . . . and also that Jews, heathens and other dissenters from the purity of Christian religion may not be scared and kept at a distance from it . . . therefore, any seven or more persons agreeing in any religion, shall constitute a church or profession."[27] The constitution was never fully implemented because there were too few settlers for the purpose.[28]

As a corollary to the War of the Spanish Succession, pitting Catholic France, Spain, Bavaria, Portugal, and Savoy against Protestant England, Holland, and German states, Queen Anne's War broke out in North America between 1701 and 1714. Carolina planters feared the entire Gulf region would be sealed off by a French-Spanish axis or, worse, that they would march on the Carolinas.[29] In 1702 Governor James Moore of Carolina led a flotilla of fourteen vessels and Colonel Robert Daniel led six hundred English militiamen and three to six hundred Indians against St. Augustine in retaliation for the Spanish capturing and plundering Port Royal back in 1686.[30] Although the fort held firm, Moore burned down the third Cathedral of St. Augustine.[31] Between 1702 and 1707, Moore's forces also razed the Franciscan missions, killed the friars, and killed, exported, or enslaved the Christianized Indians.[32]

In 1732, after seven of the Lords Proprietors sold their Carolina interests to the Crown, King George II granted James Oglethorpe a charter for the Province of Georgia. Oglethorpe also laid siege to St. Augustine, and the Spanish retaliated.[33] By 1748 an agreement was reached establishing the St. Mary's River as the border between Florida and Georgia.[34]

In 1763 Spain traded Florida to Great Britain for Havana, which the British had captured during the Seven Years' War. Although King George III agreed to allow "liberty of the Catholic religion," many of St. Augustine's colonists fled. Having defeated France, Britain also took over much of French Louisiana. Britain divided the area into East and West Florida, separated by the Apalachicola River. West Florida also consisted of the lower third of present-day Mississippi and Alabama.[35]

The Episcopal Church temporarily replaced the Catholic Church as the established church in East Florida.[36] The Society for the Propagation of the Gospel in Foreign Parts cooperated with the bishop of London to select clergymen for Florida posts. The British Parliament made provision for four ministers and four schoolmasters. The clergymen received a royal bounty to defray the cost of travel, and the government paid their salaries and that of the schoolmasters. St. Peter's Church replaced the house of the Roman Catholic bishop in St. Augustine.

The situation in West Florida was more primitive and Episcopal clergy harder to retain. No Episcopal clergy served there from 1765 to 1767, and no Episcopal church was erected during British rule. Instead, the Spanish Catholic priest at Mobile was allowed to hold services in Pensacola. In 1766 the provincial government also passed "an Act to encourage foreigners to come into and settle the province," permitting freedom of conscience and worship for Catholics.[37]

Thousands of British loyalists found refuge in Florida during the American Revolution.[38] Plantations sprouted along the St. Johns River from British land grants.[39] Skirmishes occurred between Georgia militia and loyalist East Florida Rangers, with each side raiding the other.[40] In a surprise attack, Spain recaptured Mobile in 1780 and Pensacola in 1781.[41] As a reward for helping the Americans during the revolution, the 1783 Treaty of Paris returned all of Florida to Spain.

Catholicism was again the established religion of Florida, but where once only Catholics lived, Protestants also resided.[42] The 1784 census listed 1,401 whites and 2,268 slaves in East Florida. More than 331 residents chose to depart with the British.[43] Episcopal services would not resume at St. Augustine for some forty years.[44] St. Peter's was demolished in 1792. In Pensacola, an estimated 292 whites and 141 blacks were Catholic and 161 were Protestants.[45] Spain continued to govern Florida as two separate territories but moved the boundary eastward to the Suwannee River.

To help secure the border, the Crown induced settlement by promising one hundred acres to each household plus fifty acres for each household member, free or slave, and an additional one thousand acres if he could cultivate them.[46] By a royal order of May 1786, Spain restricted immigration to Catholics. However, the Crown removed this largely disregarded requirement after 1790, provided that non-Catholics not openly practice their religion.[47] Protestants were officially constrained to be married by a Catholic priest, although many snuck across the border or to the Bahamas to do so.[48]

Most immigrants to East Florida were Protestants from Georgia and the Carolinas.[49] Instead of requiring American expatriates to become Catholics, King Charles III ordered special parishes for them that never materialized.[50] By 1793, when France declared war on Spain, the tax roll listed 262 Protestants in East Florida.[51] Bishop Cyril counted 1,078 whites, more than a quarter of whom had been British, and 651 blacks in St. Augustine.[52]

Spain was still too weak to govern Florida effectively.[53] Tied as it was to the Crown, the Catholic Church waxed and waned with Spanish fortunes.[54] When Napoleon placed his brother on the throne of Spain in 1810, "American agents succeeded at promoting a rebellion in Baton Rouge."[55] For seventy-four days, residents declared West Florida a republic with a constitution modeled after the United States. President James Madison directed its annexation into the Territory of Orleans.[56] In 1811 Congress approved the American occupation and authorized the president to take possession of the area west of the Perdido River on the spurious ground that the area was part of the Louisiana Purchase.[57]

In 1811 Congress also passed a secret joint resolution endorsing acquisition of Florida in certain circumstances. The "Patriot Revolution" followed in March 1812. Appointed as "commissioner" by Madison and Secretary of State James Monroe, former Georgia governor George Matthews led a military campaign including U.S. naval support and U.S. regulars to take Fernandina and declare a republic.[58] By April 1812, the Patriots had taken this second-largest town in East Florida and reached St. Augustine, but a military stalemate developed at the Castillo.

The Patriots adopted a manifesto inviting American annexation, complaining of several Spanish deprivations, including the "Worship of God."[59] As grounds for the revolution, they continued, "[T]rue a man might worship the supreme being in private, or in his family in his own house, but public worship unless according to the established order, was strictly forbidden." The day after the War of 1812 was declared, a bill failed by two votes in the Senate to empower President Madison to take possession of Florida. A like bill failed in 1813. Public opinion swung against what appeared to many a flimsy excuse for military action, leading Madison to withdraw federal troops and abandon the venture in 1814.

It was not long before U.S. troops returned. The First Seminole War broke out in March 1818. General Andrew Jackson amassed Tennessee and

Georgia militia, regulars, and friendly Creek Indians on the border at Fort Scott. Jackson chased Indians down the Apalachicola, swung east to take the Spanish fort at St. Marks, and captured and executed a Scotchman and two British Royal Marines. Jackson went on to the Suwannee in 1818, before turning west and taking Pensacola and Fort Carlos de Barancas.[60] Jackson's campaign desecrated the sacred sites of the Seminoles to demonstrate that the Great Spirit would not protect them.[61] U.S. troops also intervened in Fernandina in 1818 in response to disorder and did not leave.[62]

On February 22, 1819, Spain and the United States signed the Adams-Onis Treaty, whereby Spain ceded Florida.[63] The treaty guaranteed, "The inhabitants of the ceded territories shall be secured in the free exercise of their religion, without any restriction."[64] Jackson and Captain Richard Call accepted West Florida at Pensacola, and Colonel Robert Butler received East Florida at St. Augustine in 1821.[65]

The United States organized the Florida Territory on March 30, 1822, by combining East Florida with West Florida east of the Perdido River. The Territorial Act prohibited any law "which shall lay any person under restraint, burthen, or disability, on account of his religious opinions, professions, or worship; in all which he shall be free to maintain his own, and not burthened with those of another." It further restricted any law that "shall impair, or in any way restrain, the freedom of religious opinions, professions, or worship."[66]

Records indicate that the religious liberty clauses in the treaty and Territorial Act were never relied upon by claimants against the government. However, in 1821 a controversy developed over the ownership of church properties in St. Augustine. Alexander Hamilton, the U.S. commissioner, was under the belief that all religious properties had belonged to the king of Spain and were, therefore, with the transfer of power, the property of the United States. Through the intercession of Secretary of State John Quincy Adams and Attorney General William Wirt, in 1823 the parish church of St. Augustine and Tolomato Cemetery were secured to the Catholic Church. Titles would later be secured to the congregation by acts of Congress. Other properties, such as St. Francis Barracks and the old bishop's residence on the southwest corner of the plaza were not returned to church ownership.[67]

By 1822 the bishop of Havana turned over all matters relative to the Catholic residents of St. Augustine to the Diocese of Charleston. Both of the priests who remained in St. Augustine died shortly after, leaving East Florida without a single priest. In July 1823, Catholic laity formed a board of wardens to ensure that the church would remain. The lay trusteeship was believed justified by patterns in states to the north and that Congress had secured possession in the congregation.

Methodists, Baptists, Presbyterians, and Episcopalians sent missionaries to Florida beginning in the 1820s. The first Episcopal missionary arrived in St. Augustine in 1821. The same year, Methodists and Presbyterians arrived in Pensacola, where they discovered only one Catholic church.[68]

Pigeon Creek Baptist Church, founded in Nassau County on January 7, 1821, is the earliest known Baptist church plant. Several Baptist churches were entirely black. However, the Florida territorial legislature prohibited slaves from preaching on the plantations without their owners' permission. The unsupervised worship of even free blacks was prohibited by state law in 1832.[69]

Leading the Methodists, Rev. John Jerry arrived in St. Augustine in 1823–24. He was a circuit rider.[70] In 1823–24 the Methodists were the first to establish a congregation in Tallahassee at what had been the hub of Spanish western missions.[71] Episcopal ministrations began in Tallahassee shortly after in 1827.[72] Methodist missions were established in Gadsden and Quincy County for slaves.[73]

In 1838 delegates to the 1838–39 Constitutional Convention met at St. Joseph to discuss terms for Florida statehood and to draft Florida's first constitution, prohibiting any establishment of religion and guaranteeing free religious expression.[74] There is no record of the proceedings. Florida was admitted to the Union as the twenty-sixth state on March 3, 1845.[75]

By statehood several establishments had given way to Protestant religious pluralism. Methodists had 87 churches in Florida in 1850, the most of any denomination. Baptists were next with 56 and Presbyterians with 16. Episcopalians had 10 churches. Michael McNally observed, "As old as Catholicism was in Florida—311 years from 1565 to 1876—it did not have much to show for itself."[76] Compared to a total of 170 Protestant churches in the state, there were 5 Catholic churches, together with a few mission chapels, and no organized Vicariate Apostolic.[77] The reasons for the poor showing by Catholics are complex, from geopolitical conflict and Indian subjugation to poor ecclesial governance and damaging church-state entanglements.

NOTES

1. Rembert W. Patrick, *Florida under Five Flags* (Gainesville: University Press of Florida, 1945), 1–3.

2. T. Frederick Davis, *History of Jacksonville, Florida and Vicinity* (Jacksonville: Florida Historical Society, 1964), 1–2; Jonathan D. Steigman, *La Florida Del Inca and the Struggle for Social Equality in Colonial Spanish America* (Tuscaloosa: University of Alabama Press, 2005), 33; Michael V. Gannon, *The Cross in the Sand: The Early Catholic Church in Florida, 1513–1870* (Gainesville: University Press of Florida, 1965), 1.

3. Rodney Carlisle and J. Geoffrey Golson, *Colonial America from Settlement to the Revolution* (Santa Barbara: ABC-CLIO, 2007), 208.

4. Gannon, *Cross in the Sand*, 2, 3, 37.

5. Gannon, *Cross in the Sand*, 4; Patrick, *Five Flags*, 3.

6. Patrick, *Five Flags*, 5–6; Gannon, *Cross in the Sand*, 5, 6, 9, 14–16.

7. John T. McGrath, *The French in Early Florida: In the Eye of the Hurricane* (Gainesville: University Press of Florida, 2000).

8. Patrick, *Five Flags*, 7, 9; Davis, *Jacksonville*, 6–7; T. Frederick Davis, "Fort Carolina," *Florida Historical Quarterly* 2, no. 77 (1933): 77.

9. Gannon, *Cross in the Sand*, 20–21; Patrick, *Five Flags*, 9; Eugene Lyon, *The Enterprise of Florida: Pedro Menendez de Aviles and the Spanish Conquest of 1565–1568* (Gainesville: University Press of Florida, 1976); Charles E. Bennett, *Laudonniere & Fort Caroline: History and Documents* (Gainesville: University Press of Florida, 1964); Michael J. McNally, *Catholicism in South Florida, 1868–1968* (Gainesville: University Press of Florida, 1982), 1.

10. Patrick, *Five Flags*, 9; McNally, *Catholicism*, 1; Gannon, *Cross in the Sand*, 26.

11. Kenneth E. Lawson, *Religion and the U.S. Army Chaplaincy in the Florida Seminole Wars, 1818–1858* (Columbia, SC: Eastside, 2006), 46; Gannon, *Cross in the Sand*, 27.

12. Patrick, *Five Flags*, 10–11; Chuck Meide and John de Bry, "The Lost French Fleet of 1565: Collision of Empires," *Underwater Archaeology Proceedings* (2014): 79–92.

13. Davis, *Jacksonville*, 15.

14. Patrick, *Five Flags*, 11–12.

15. Davis, *Jacksonville*, 21.

16. McNally, *Catholicism*, 2; Gannon, *Cross in the Sand*, 29, 34; Patrick, *Five Flags*, 14–15; Kenneth Starr, *Continental Ambitions: Roman Catholics in North America* (San Francisco: Ignatius Press, 2016), 97.

17. Gannon, *Cross in the Sand*, 36, 57; Starr, *Continental Ambitions*, 98, 101.

18. Starr, *Continental Ambitions*, 99, 100, 104; Patrick, *Five Flags*, 15; Gannon, *Cross in the Sand*, 64–65.

19. R. Kapitzke, *Religion, Power and Politics in Colonial St. Augustine* (Gainesville: University Press of Florida, 1958), 19.

20. Gannon, *Cross in the Sand*, 36–37, 57, 60; Kapitzke, *Colonial St. Augustine*, 75, 85; Starr, *Continental Ambitions*, 103–4.

21. Gannon, *Cross in the Sand*, 37–38, 44, 45.

22. Starr, *Continental Ambitions*, 106.

23. Patrick, *Five Flags*, 17.

24. Charter of Carolina (March 24, 1663), cl. 3.

25. Charter of Carolina (March 24, 1663), cl. 18.

26. The Fundamental Constitutions of Carolina, cl. 96 (2nd version March 1, 1669; Mattie Erma E. Parker, "The First Fundamental Constitutions of Carolina," *South Carolina Historical Magazine* 71 (1970): 78–79.

27. The Fundamental Constitutions of Carolina, cl. 87 (July 21, 1669); The Fundamental Constitutions of Carolina, cl. 97 (March 1, 1669).

28. Vicki Hseuh, "Giving Orders: Theory and Practice in the Fundamental Constitutions of Carolina," *Journal of the History of Ideas* 63 (2002): 425, 431, 440.

29. Starr, *Continental Ambitions*, 107, 108.

30. Patrick, *Five Flags*, 18; Starr, *Continental Ambitions*, 108–9.

31. Kapitzke, *Colonial St. Augustine*, 34.

32. McNally, *Catholicism*, 5; Gannon, *Cross in the Sand*, 75–76; Starr, *Continental Ambitions*, 108–9. On the Spanish system of royal domination of Catholic ministries, see William George Torpey, *Judicial Doctrines of Religious Rights in America* (Chapel Hill: University of North Carolina Press, 1948), 5–8.

33. James G. Cusick, *The Other War of 1812: The Patriot War and the American Invasion of Spanish East Florida* (Athens: University of Georgia Press, 2003), 39.

34. Patrick, *Five Flags*, 22; Gannon, *Cross in the Sand*, 79; Carlisle and Golson, *Colonial America*, 210–11.

35. Davis, *Jacksonville*, 25; Patrick, *Five Flags*, 25–26; Gannon, *Cross in the Sand*, 83–84; McNally, *Catholicism*, 3.

36. Edgar L. Pennington, "The Episcopal Church in Florida, 1763–1892," *Historical Magazine of the Protestant Episcopal Church* 7, no. 1 (1938): 1, 4.

37. Pennington, "Episcopal Church in Florida," 5, 6, 8–9, 14.

38. Davis, *Jacksonville*, 28; Cormac A. O'Riordan, "The 1795 Rebellion on East Florida" (master's thesis, University of North Florida, 1995), 46.

39. Davis, *Jacksonville*, 26.

40. O'Riordan, "1795 Rebellion," 47.

41. Patrick, *Five Flags*, 30–31.

42. Parker, "First Fundamental Constitutions," 136; Cusick, *Other War of 1812*, 45.

43. O'Riordan, "1795 Rebellion," 25–26, 48.

44. Pennington, "Episcopal Church in Florida," 17.

45. Robert La Bret Hall, "'Do, Lord, Remember Me': Religion and Cultural Change among Blacks in Florida, 1565–1906" (PhD diss., Florida State University, 1984), 59.

46. Patrick, *Five Flags*, 32; O'Riordan, "1795 Rebellion," 37; Canter Brown Jr., *Ossian Bingley Hart: Florida's Loyalist Reconstruction Governor* (Baton Rouge: Louisiana State University, 1997), 7; Davis, *Jacksonville*, 39.

47. O'Riordan, "1795 Rebellion," 35–37.

48. Pennington, "Episcopal Church in Florida," 17; Cusick, *Other War of 1812*, 45.

49. O'Riordan, "1795 Rebellion," 22, 38–39, 41.

50. Gannon, *Cross in the Sand*, 95.

51. O'Riordan, "1795 Rebellion," 39.

52. Hall, "'Do, Lord, Remember Me,'" 60.

53. Carlisle and Golson, *Colonial America*, 213.

54. Gannon, *Cross in the Sand*, 99, 115.

55. Cusick, *Other War of 1812*, 4.

56. James Stafford, letter to U.S. Congress, January 25, 1814; Henry E. Sterkx and Brooks Thompson, "Philemon Thomas and the West Florida Revolution," *Florida Historical Quarterly* 39, no. 4 (1961): 385–86.

57. Patrick, *Five Flags*, 33; Cusick, *Other War of 1812*, 23, 26.

58. Lawson, *Religion and the U.S. Army Chaplaincy*, 29–30; Carlisle and Golson, *Colonial America*, 213; Cusick, *Other War of 1812*, 32.

59. Cusick, *Other War of 1812*, 5, 89–90, 125; James Stafford, letter to U.S. Congress, January 25, 1814.

60. Patrick, *Five Flags*, 36; Lawson, *Religion and the U.S. Army Chaplaincy*, 37, 76, 78–83.

61. Lawson, *Religion and the U.S. Army Chaplaincy*, 57.

62. Cusick, *Other War of 1812*, 304–5.

63. Patrick, *Five Flags*, 37; Isaac Joslin Cox, *The West Florida Controversy, 1798–1813* (Baltimore: Johns Hopkins University Press, 1918); David J. Weber, *The Spanish Frontier in North America* (New Haven, CT: Yale University Press, 1992).

64. Gannon, *Cross in the Sand*, 121.

65. Patrick, *Five Flags*, 39; Lawson, *Religion and the U.S. Army Chaplaincy*, 208.

66. Acts of the 17th Cong., 1st sess., chap. 13 (1822), cl. 5, 10.

67. Gannon, *Cross in the Sand*, 121–25.

68. Davis, *Jacksonville*, 393–407; Lawson, *Religion and the U.S. Army Chaplaincy*, 47; Pennington, "Episcopal Church in Florida," 18.

69. Hall, "'Do, Lord, Remember Me,'" 74–77, 88–90, 73–74, 89–105.

70. Davis, *Jacksonville*, 25, 393.

71. Canter Brown Jr. and Larry E. Rivers, *For a Great and Grand Purpose: The Beginnings of the AMEZ Church in Florida, 1864–1905* (Gainesville: University Press of Florida, 2004), 8; Lee L. Willis III, "The Road to Prohibition: Religion and Political Culture in Middle Florida, 1821–1920" (PhD diss., Florida State University, 2006), 18; Hall, "'Do, Lord, Remember Me,'" 107–34.

72. Pennington, "Episcopal Church in Florida," 20; Davis, *Jacksonville*, 395; Lawson, *Religion and the U.S. Army Chaplaincy*, 208.

73. Hall, "'Do, Lord, Remember Me,'" 108.

74. Willis, "Road to Prohibition," 5, 25, 26, 34.

75. Patrick, *Five Flags*, 46.

76. McNally, *Catholicism*, 5.

77. Hall, "'Do, Lord, Remember Me,'" 121, 139–40; Gannon, *Cross in the Sand*, 152, 163–64; McNally, *Catholicism*, 3; Lawson, *Religion and the U.S. Army Chaplaincy*, 400.

CHAPTER TWENTY-ONE

THE LAST AMERICAN ESTABLISHMENT
Massachusetts, 1780–1833

John Witte Jr. and Justin Latterell

THE 1780 CONSTITUTION of Massachusetts is the oldest continuously operating written constitution in the world.[1] Its principal drafter was John
Adams—the "atlas" and "colossus" of the revolution, America's future second president and already a formidable lawyer and legal historian.[2] In both
Massachusetts law and federal law, Adams sought to balance religious liberty with religious establishment while ensuring that "all men of all religions
consistent with morals and property . . . enjoy equal liberty [and] security of
property . . . and an equal chance for honors and power." The Constitution
reflected Adams's belief that, in order to improve society, "we should begin
by setting conscience free."[3] At the same time, the Constitution instituted
Adams's vision of a "most mild and equitable establishment of religion,"[4]
featuring Puritan covenant ceremonies, Protestant religious test oaths, and
special protections, privileges, and funding for preferred forms of Christian
worship, education, morality, and charity.

Adams's formulation sought to balance the demands of the Puritan Congregationalists who favored establishment with the demands of swelling
groups of Baptists, Methodists, Catholics, and freethinkers who wanted
the religious freedom guarantees available in other states. It mustered just
enough support to win ratification in 1780, but the balance fell apart in subsequent decades, as Congregationalists fractured into Unitarian and Trinitarian factions, and religious diversity grew. While the Constitution retained
ceremonial and moral features of the colonial establishment, amendments in
1821 and 1833 rejected religious test oaths and religious taxes.[5]

This chapter surveys the arguments for and against religious establishment and religious freedom that informed the Constitution of 1780 and
the amendments of 1821 and 1833. The coalitions of politicians, preachers,
and citizens making these arguments changed between 1778 (when the first

constitutional draft failed) and 1833 (when religious taxes were repealed). The logic of their arguments, however, remained relatively stable. Virtually everyone agreed that religion was an essential source of public and private morality and that the Constitution should safeguard diverse religious beliefs and practices, at least among Protestants. Nearly everyone also agreed that the laws should equally respect and reflect the religious sentiments of all citizens. What was controversial was how to achieve these goals. Did the integrity of governmental institutions require public officials to swear religious test oaths of office? Did religious liberty extend equally to all churches and creeds—including Catholics and non-Christians who remained deeply suspect? Did the moral functions and vitality of religion require tax-funded churches and clergy, or would religion flourish better if left on its own? Such questions divided Massachusetts lawmakers along political, regional, and religious lines and ultimately led to a new consensus about how best to order church-state relations.

I.

The Massachusetts Constitution of 1780 is a document of nearly twelve thousand words. It has a Preamble and two main parts. Part One is a Declaration of Rights in thirty articles. Part Two is a Frame of Government in six chapters. Religion figured in ten of these provisions—the Preamble; Articles I, II, III, VII, and XVIII of the Declaration of Rights; and Chapters I, II, V, and VI of the Frame of Government. These provisions reflect the long history of Congregational establishment going back to the Mayflower Compact of 1620 and the growing challenges by religious dissenters.

The 1780 Constitution replaced the 1691 Provincial Charter, issued by the British Crown to govern the Massachusetts colony. In 1778 a constitutional convention produced a draft constitution, but the people rejected it, in no small part because it lacked conventional civil and religious freedom provisions.[6] On February 20, 1779, the Massachusetts House of Representatives called for a new constitutional convention and "lawfully warned" the "Selectmen of the several Towns" to deliberate their concerns and instruct their delegates.[7]

Religion figured prominently in these deliberations and instructions, with some townships calling for complete religious freedom, others for continued religious establishment. The delegate of Pittsfield, for example, came armed with a provision guaranteeing wide religious freedom: "[E]very man has an unalienable right to enjoy his own opinion in matters of religion, and to worship God in that manner that is agreeable to his own sentiments without any control whatsoever, and that no particular mode or sect of religion ought to be established but that every one be protected in the peaceable enjoyment of his religious persuasion and way of worship."[8] By contrast, the township of Sandisfield instructed its delegate to seek protections for the local Protestant establishment, along with guarantees of toleration for other Christians:

> [Y]ou will Endeavour in the forming of the Constitution that the Free Exercise of religious principles or Profession, worship and Liberty of Conscience shall be for ever Secured to all Denominations of Protestants—and Protestant Dis[s] enters of all Denominations within the State, without any Compulsion whatever. Always allowing the Legislative Body of this State the Power of Toleration to other Denominations of Christians from time to time as they Shall see Cause, at the same time, Reserving to our Selves, the Right of Instructions to our Representatives Respecting Said Toleration as well as in other Cases.[9]

Delegates could also turn to scores of sermons and pamphlets that circulated in Massachusetts in the later 1770s.[10] The oft-printed pamphlet *Worcestriensis, Number IV*, for example, defended a generous toleration of all religions and a gentle establishment of the Protestant religion. The pamphlet demanded that "no part of the community shall be permitted to perplex and harass the other for any supposed heresy, but that each individual shall be allowed to have and enjoy, profess and maintain his own system of religion, provided it does not issue in overt acts of treason undermining the peace and good order of society. To allow one part of a society to lord it over the faith and consciences of the other, in religious matters, is the ready way to set the whole community together by the ears."[11] State officials should not, therefore, be able to command citizens to conform to their preferred religion or subject nonconformists "to pains, penalties, and disabilities" on account of their religious beliefs. But state officials could "give preference to that profession of religion which they take to be true." "The establishment contended for . . . must proceed only from the benign principles of the legislature from an encouragement of the General Principles of religion and morality, recommending free inquiry and examination of the doctrine said to be divine; using all possible and lawful means to enable its citizens to discover the truth, and to entertain good and rational sentiments, and taking mild and parental measures to bring about the design; these are the most probable means of bringing about the establishment of religion."[12] Under this view, the state could extract religious oaths from public officeholders, "for there is no stronger cement of society." The state could punish profanity, blasphemy, and debauchery, all of which "strike a fatal blow at the root of good regulation, and well-being of the state." Finally, the state could provide "able and learned teachers [ministers] to instruct the people in the knowledge of what they deem the truth, maintaining them by the public money, though at the same time they have no right in the least degree to endeavor the depression of professions of religious denomination."[13]

Phillips Payson, an influential Congregationalist minister, recommended a firm establishment and warned against the "dangerous innovations" pressed by dissenters. To be sure, Payson wrote, "religious or spiritual liberty must be accounted the greatest happiness of man, considered in a private capacity."[14] But, he insisted:

> [R]eligion, both in rulers and people [is] . . . of the highest importance to . . . civil society and government, . . . as it keeps alive the best sense of moral obligation, a matter of such extensive utility, especially in respect to an oath [of office], which is one of the principal instruments of government. The fear and reverence of God, and the terrors of eternity, are the most powerful restraints upon the minds of men; and hence it is of special importance in a free government, the spirit of which being always friendly to the sacred rights of conscience, it will hold up the gospel as the great rule of faith and practice. Established modes and usages in religion, more especially the stated public worship of God, so generally form the principles and manners of a people, that changes or alterations in these, especially when nearly conformed to the spirit and simplicity of the Gospel, may very well be esteemed very dangerous experiments in government. . . . Let the restraints of religion once be broken down, as they infallibly would be by leaving the subject of public worship to the humours of the multitude, and we might well defy all human wisdom and power to support and preserve order and government in the State.[15]

Religion, under this view, was too important to leave to chance and individual initiative. Supporting public worship—while also protecting the individual conscience—was an essential prerogative of the state.

By marked contrast, Isaac Backus, the most able Baptist advocate of the day, called for the end of all religious establishments. Backus charged that Massachusetts authorities were "assuming a power to govern religion, rather than being governed by it." "I am as sensible of the importance of religion and of the utility of it to human society, as Mr. Payson," Backus wrote. "And I concur with him that the fear and reverence of God and the terrors of eternity are the most powerful restraints upon the minds of men. But I am so far from thinking with him that these restraints would be broken down if equal religious liberty was established." Look at the long history of Christian establishment, Backus argued. It has led not to pure religion; instead, "tyranny, simony, and robbery came to be introduced and to be practiced under the Christian name." Look at Boston, which has had no religious establishment of late; there religion, state, and society all flourish without fail. Look at the principles of the revolution: "all America is up in arms against taxation without representation." Just as certainly as Americans were not represented in the British Parliament, so religious dissenters are not represented among the established civil authorities, yet they are still subject to their religious taxes and regulations. Look at the Bible: "God has expressly armed the magistrate with the sword to punish such as work ill to their neighbors, and his faithfulness in that work and our obedience to such authority, is enforced [by the Bible]. But it is evident that the sword is excluded from the kingdom of the Redeemer. . . . [I]t is impossible to blend church and state without violating our Lord's commands to both."[16] For all of these reasons, Backus and his fellow Baptists demanded that religion remain an entirely free and voluntary matter.

II.

Such were some of the discordant sentiments on religious establishment and religious freedom on the eve of the second constitutional convention. It was clear that the Congregationalists would insist on some form of religious establishment. As John Adams put it, "We might as soon expect a change in the solar system as to expect they would give up their establishment."[17] It was equally clear that religious dissenters would insist on disestablishment and the free exercise of religion—particularly since other states had granted such liberties. Some via media between these competing perspectives was needed.

On September 1, 1779, 293 delegates gathered in Boston.[18] In the convention were the leading lights of Massachusetts—39 merchants, 31 lawyers, 22 farmers, 21 clergy, 18 physicians, and 18 magistrates.[19] Most delegates were Congregationalists. Five delegates were Baptists. A few were suspected to be Quaker, Anglican, or Catholic.[20]

On September 4, the convention elected a committee of 27 members—later augmented by 4—to prepare a declaration of rights and frame of government. This committee, in turn, delegated the drafting to a 3-member subcommittee of James Bowdoin, Samuel Adams, and John Adams, with John Adams selected to push the pen for the subcommittee. He completed a draft by mid-October. First the three-member subcommittee and then the full drafting committee made modest alterations to Adams's draft. The committee submitted its draft to the Convention on October 28, 1779.[21] The convention debated the draft until November 12. Adams participated to this point, but set sail thereafter for France. The convention completed its deliberations between January 27 and March 1, 1780, now without Adams.

A Limited Freedom of Religion

The Constitution included several religious freedom provisions. Article I of the Declaration of Rights provided: "All men are born free and equal, and have certain natural, essential, and unalienable rights" of life, liberty, property, and pursuit of happiness.[22] Article II tendered more specific protections: "It is the right as well as the duty of all men in society, publickly, and at stated seasons to worship the SUPREME BEING, the great Creator and preserver of the Universe. No subject shall be hurt, molested, or restrained, in his person, Liberty, or Estate, for worshipping GOD in the manner and season most agreeable to the Dictates of his own conscience, or for his religious profession or sentiments; provided he doth not Disturb the public peace, or obstruct others in their religious Worship."

Article III tacitly acknowledged the right to form religious associations, to select one's own minister, and to pay tithes directly to one's own church. And Chapter VI on the Frame of Government exempted Quakers from the swearing of oaths because of their scruples of "conscience."

Yet the 1780 Constitution imposed several limits on religion as well. Religious worship was not just a right but also a duty in Article II. Indeed, Adams's original draft spoke only of "the duty" to worship. After other delegates objected, the article was amended to guarantee "the right as well as the duty of all men" to worship. Moreover, while a person could worship in "the manner and season most agreeable to the Dictates of his own conscience," such worship was to be directed to "the SUPREME BEING, the great Creator and preserver of the Universe," leaving nontheists unprotected. Moreover, worship, per Article III, was to include "conscientious and convenient" "attendance upon the instructions of ministers" "at stated times and seasons," as well as payment of tithes.

Religious freedom was more restricted for those in political office. In Chapter I of the Frame of Government, Adams stipulated that no person was eligible to serve in the House of Representatives "unless he be of the Christian religion." The convention struck this provision, but it left untouched Chapter II, where Adams imposed the same religious conditions upon the offices of governor and lieutenant governor.[23] In the same spirit,

Adams proposed in Chapter VI that all state officials and appointees swear the same religious test oath, "that I believe and profess the Christian religion and have a firm persuasion of its truth." The convention insisted on a slightly reworded oath for elected executive and legislative officers, requiring all other officers to declare their "true faith and allegiance to this Commonwealth." After several delegates argued for a specifically Protestant test oath, the convention added to both oaths a rather obvious anti-Catholic provision, which Adams and others later protested without success: "I do renounce and abjure all allegiance, subjection and obedience to . . . every . . . foreign Power whatsoever: And that no foreign . . . Prelate . . . hath, or ought to have, any jurisdiction, superiority, pre-eminence, authority, dispensing, or other power, in any matter, civil, ecclesiastical or spiritual within this Commonwealth."[24] Adams's draft oath had concluded "So help me God," but then made a specific provision, "that any person who has conscientious scruples relative to taking oaths, may be admitted to make solemn affirmation" by other means. After delegates protested that so generic an exemption might be abused, the convention restricted the exemption to Quakers.[25]

The Establishment of Religion

Not only was religious liberty narrowly drawn in the 1780 Constitution, but it was further limited by religious establishment norms. The establishment had ceremonial, moral, and institutional features. The *ceremonial* and *moral* features reflected a general consensus about the role of religion in both government and society, and these provisions passed with little controversy. The *institutional* features of establishment, especially the compulsory payment of religious taxes, were contested in the convention and ratification debates.

Ceremonial Establishment

The ceremonial elements of the establishment were most evident in the Preamble's declaration that "the whole people covenants with each Citizen, and each Citizen with the whole people, that all shall be governed by certain Laws for the Common good."

[T]he people of Massachusetts, acknowledging, with grateful hearts, the goodness of the Great Legislator of the Universe, in affording us, in the course of his Providence, an opportunity, deliberately and peaceably, without fraud, violence, or surprize, o[f] entering into an Original, explicit, and Solemn Compact with each other; and of forming a New Constitution of Civil Government for ourselves and Posterity; and devoutly imploring His direction in so interesting a Design, DO agree upon, ordain and establish the following Declaration of Rights and Frame of Government.

This was classic covenant liturgical language, rooted in New England tradition going back to the Mayflower Compact of 1620.[26] The nature of the Constitution was clear; it was a "solemn" covenant or compact with God invoked as witness, judge, and participant. The purposes of the covenant were clearly set forth: to create and confirm the identity of the "peoples" and "citizens of Massachusetts," and their devotion to the "common good," and to the rights of the people and the powers of the government. The ethic of the covenant was also defined—featuring "gratitude," "peacefulness," integrity ("without fraud, violence, or surprize"), and prayerful devotion ("devoutly imploring His direction in so interesting a Design").

Covenant rituals also informed the religious test oaths for public servants to be sworn before the people and their representatives in full assembly: "I, A.B., do declare, that I believe the christian religion, and have a firm persuasion of its truth . . . and I do swear, that I will bear true faith and allegiance to the said Commonwealth . . . so help me God." This language reflected the conventional view that oaths functioned as "a cement of society" and as "one of the principal instruments of government." Oaths were not merely symbolic, but a tangible confirmation of the covenant between God, the people, and the rulers, with solemn duties undergirded by "the fear and reverence of God, and the terrors of eternity."[27]

Beyond the Preamble and test oaths, the Constitution had other ceremonial elements of a religious establishment. God is invoked, by name or pseudonym (for example, "Great Legislator of the Universe" and "Supreme Being") a dozen times. References to the "common good" or "public good" appear four more times, as do two further references to divine "blessings" and "privileges." With the exception of the oath requirement, these provisions were passed without comment and still remain in place today.

Moral Establishment

The 1780 Constitution established not only covenant ceremonies but also Christian morals. Article II of the Declaration of Rights, we saw, rendered religious worship both a right and a duty. Article III followed with the reason for this duty: "the happiness of a people, and good order and preservation of civil government, essentially depend upon piety, religion, and morality;

and . . . these cannot be generally diffused through a Community, but by the institution of publick Worship of God, and of public instructions in piety, religion, and morality." Religion was closely bound to morality, the Constitution confirmed, and both were essential to happiness and social order.

Moral considerations also animated the constitutional provisions on education. Chapter V of the Frame of Government provided: "Wisdom, and knowledge, as well as virtue, diffused generally among the body of the people, [are] necessary for the preservation of their rights and liberties." Officials were thus called "to cherish the interests of literature and sciences, and all seminaries of them; . . . to encourage private societies and public institutions, rewards and immunities, for the promotion of [education] . . . ; to countenance and inculcate the principles of humanity and general benevolence, public and private charity, industry and frugality, honesty and punctuality in their dealings, sincerity, good humour, and all social affections, and generous sentiments among the people." The same Chapter V confirmed and commended the incorporation of Harvard College, since "the encouragement of arts and sciences, and all good literature, tends to the honor of God, the advantage of the christian religion, and the great benefit of this and other United States of America."[28] None of these provisions establishing a public religious morality triggered much debate during the Constitutional Convention, and most were not amended.

Institutional Establishment

The foregoing consensus on ceremonial and moral matters stood in marked contrast to the controversies over Article III's religious taxes "for the support and maintenance of public protestant teachers of piety, religion and morality." This provision continued colonial patterns. A Massachusetts colonial law of 1692 had effectively blended church and state for purposes of taxation.[29] The law designated each of the 290 odd territories within the colony as both a "parish" and a "township" under the authority of a single city council. In townships with more than one church, the multiple "parishes" were called "precincts," and each of these likewise was subject to the same council's authority. Each town or parish was required to have at least one Congregationalist "teacher of religion and morality." This minister would lead the local community in worship, and often in education and charity as well. The community was required to provide the minister with a salary, sanctuary, and parsonage. Funds to do so came from religious taxes usually called tithes, sometimes called church, parish, or religious rates. These were collected from all persons in the township, who were by definition also members of the parish, regardless of which church they attended.[30]

This system worked well enough when all persons within a township or parish were also active members of the established Congregational church. It did not work for persons who were religiously inactive or were members of a non-Congregationalist church, whether Baptist, Quaker, Anglican, Catholic, or other. As the number of dissenting churches grew, so did the protests to taxes to support Congregationalist ministers and churches. During the eighteenth century, colonial courts eventually carved out exceptions for some religious dissenters, allowing them to direct their tithes to support their own ministers and churches. Such dissenters, however, were required to register each church as a separate religious society and to prove their faithful attendance at the same. Not all dissenting churches were able or willing to meet the registration requirements, and not all townships cooperated in granting the registrations or tithe exemptions.[31] If the dissenting church was too small to have its own full-time minister, the township denied them registration. If the dissenting church was conscientiously opposed to incorporation or registration, as were Baptists after 1773, their members were not exempt from taxation. If a member of a registered dissenting church was lax in attending worship, he was denied exemption from tithe payments. And if a town treasurer was pressed for revenue, or prejudiced against a certain group, he could refuse to give dissenting ministers their share of the tithes. In many cases, the Massachusetts courts proved churlish in granting standing, let alone relief, to dissenters who protested such inequities.[32]

It was this century-long system of religious taxes that the 1780 Massachusetts Constitution aimed to perpetuate in Article III. The article proved so controversial that it took up more than a third of the convention's debates.[33] The initial draft of Article III, submitted to the convention on October 28, 1779, stated:

> Good morals, being necessary for the preservation of civil society; and the knowledge and belief of the being of GOD, His providential government of the world, and of a future state of rewards and punishment, being the only true foundation of morality, the legislature hath, therefore, a right, and ought to provide, at the expense of the subject, if necessary, a suitable support for the public worship of GOD, and of the teachers of religion and morals; and to enjoin upon all the subjects an attendance upon these instructions, at stated times and seasons; provided there be any such teacher, on whose ministry they can conscientiously attend.

All monies, paid by the subject of the public worship, and of the instructors in religion and morals, shall, if he requires it, be uniformly applied to the support of the teacher or teachers of his own religious denomination, provided there be any on whose instructions he attends; otherwise it may be paid towards the support of the teacher or teachers of the parish or precinct in which the said moneys are raised.[34]

The first paragraph of this draft, stipulating the necessity and utility of public worship and religious instruction, was not particularly controversial. The second paragraph, however, mandating the collection of religious tithes to support the same, was a matter of great controversy. The initial reaction to the draft was so heated that delegates voted to put off further debate for a three-day period starting November 1. They also voted to suspend the rule that no delegate could speak twice to the same issue without special privilege from the chair. Rancorous debate over the draft article broke out immediately when the floor was opened on November 1—some condemning the provision as "too pale an approximation of a proper establishment," others calling for abolition of the article altogether, and still others decrying the insufficient recognition of the concessions that dissenters had arduously won over the years.

With the convention deadlocked on November 3, the delegates appointed a seven-member ad hoc committee, chaired by a Baptist delegate, Rev. Noah Alden of Bellingham, to redraft Article III.[35] On November 6, this committee put a new draft before the convention that spelled out the religious tax system in more detail. This draft was debated intermittently for the next four days, and modest changes were approved.[36] On November 10, a motion to abolish the article altogether was defeated. A slightly amended committee draft was passed the following day. It stated in full:

As the happiness of a people, and good order and preservation of civil government, essentially depend upon piety, religion, and morality; and as these cannot be generally diffused through a Community, but by the institution of publick Worship of God, and of public instructions in piety, religion, and morality: Therefore, to promote the happiness and to secure the good order and preservation of their government, the people of this Commonwealth have a right to invest their legislature with power to authorize and require, and their Legislature shall, from time to time, authorize and require, the several Towns, Parishes precincts and other bodies politic, or religious societies, to make suitable provision, at their own Expence, for the institution of the Public worship of GOD, and for the support and maintenance of public protestant teachers of piety, religion and morality, in all causes which provision shall not be made Voluntarily.—And the people of this Commonwealth have also a right to, and do, invest their legislature with authority to enjoin upon all the Subjects an attendance upon the instructions of the public teachers aforesaid, at stated times and seasons, if there be any on whose instructions they can Conscientiously and conveniently attend.—PROVIDED, notwithstanding, that the several towns, parishes, precincts, and other bodies politic, or religious societies, shall, at times, have the exclusive right of electing their public Teachers, and of contracting with them for their support and maintenance.—And all monies, paid by the Subject of the support of the public teacher or teachers of his own religious sect or denomination, provided there be any on whose institution he attends; otherwise it may be paid towards the support of the teacher or teachers of the parish or precinct in which the said monies are raised—And every denomina[t]ion of christians, demeaning themselves peaceably, and as good Subjects of the Commonwealth, shall be equally under the protection of the Law: And no subordination of any one sect or denomination to another shall ever be established by law.[37]

This final text made some concessions to dissenters.[38] The tithe collection system was now to be "voluntary" and local rather than statewide—allowing Boston and, later, other townships to forgo mandatory tithing, with churches securing their own support from their members through voluntary tithes, tuition, or pew rents. Religious societies could contract individually with their own minister—allowing them to pay their tithes directly to their chosen minister rather than to a potentially capricious town treasurer. Local townships and religious societies could now participate in the selection of their parish minister, rather than be automatically saddled with a Congregationalist minister. In later years, this provision "had some unexpected results. Several of the towns and parishes, which thereby were given the exclusive right to elect their ministers . . . were converted to Unitarianism and settled Unitarian pastors over old Calvinist churches."[39]

Although it notably acknowledged the equality of diverse religious groups before the law, the final draft of Article III largely retained the traditional tithing system and jettisoned some of the hard-fought concessions that Baptists, Anglicans, and other dissenters had secured through litigation. As Samuel Eliot Morison wrote: "Article III was even less liberal than [the colonial] system, for instead of exempting members of dissenting sects from religious taxation, it merely gave them the privilege of paying their taxes to their own pastors. Unbelievers, non-church goers, and dissenting minorities too small to maintain a minister had to contribute to Congregational worship. The whole Article was so loosely worded as to defeat the purpose of the fifth paragraph [guaranteeing the equality of all sects and denominations]. Every new denomination that entered the Commonwealth after 1780, notably the Universalists and Methodists, had to wage a long and expensive lawsuit to obtain recognition as a religious sect. . . . [A] subordination of sects existed in fact."[40]

III.

On March 2, 1780, the convention put the draft constitution before the people for ratification. The convention also provided a committee report that explained the draft, including the provisions juxtaposing religious freedom and religious establishment:

> [W]e have, with as much Precision as we were capable of, provided for the free exercise of the Rights of Conscience: We are very sensible that our Constituents hold those Rights infinitely more valuable than all others; and we flatter ourselves, that while we have considered Morality and Public Worship of GOD, as important to the happiness of Society, we have sufficiently guarded the rights of Conscience from every possible infringement. This Article underwent long debates, and took Time in proportion to its importance; and we feel ourselves peculiarly happy in being able to inform you, that the debates were managed by persons of various denominations, it was finally agreed upon with much more unanimity than usually takes place in disquisitions of this Nature. We wish you to consider the Subject with Candor, and Attention. Surely it would be an affront to the People of Massachusetts-Bay to labour to convince them, that the Honor and Happiness of a People depend upon Morality; and that the Public Worship of GOD has a tendency to inculcate the Principles thereof, as well as to preserve a people from forsaking Civilization, and falling into a state of Savage barbarity.[41]

The people gave the draft their full "Candor and Attention" during the ratification process. Of the 290 eligible townships, 188 sent in returns that have survived, a number of them criticizing the religion provisions.[42] One group charged that Article III's establishment of religion contradicted the religious liberties set out in Article II.[43] The Return of the town of Dartmouth put it thus:

> It appears doubtful in said Articles whether the Rights of Conscience are suffi-
> ciently secured or not to those who are really desirous to, and do attend publick
> Worship, and who are not limited to any particular outward Teacher . . . we
> humbly conceive it intirely out of the power of the legislature to establish a
> way of Worship that shall be agreable to the Conceptions and Convictions of
> the minds of the individuals, as it is a matter that solely relates to and stands
> between God and the Soul before whose Tribunal all must account each one
> for himself.[44]

A second group of critics retorted that the happiness of a people and the good order and preservation of civil government did not, as a matter of historical fact, depend upon piety, religion, and morality.[45] The Return of the town of Natick put it well:

> When both antient History and modern authentik information concur to
> evince that flourishing civil Governments have existed and do still exist with-
> out the Civil Legislature's instituting the publick Christian worship of God, and
> publick Instruction in piety and the Christian,—but that rather wherever such
> institutions are fully [executed] by the civil authority have taken place among
> a people instead of essentially promoting their happiness and the good order
> and preservation of Civil Government, it has We believe invariably promoted
> impiety, irreligion, hypocrisy, and many other sore and oppressive evils.[46]

A third group of critics acknowledged the public utility of piety, morality, and religion, but thought that an establishment would jeopardize both religion and the state. The Return of the town of Petersham put it thus:

> We grant that the Happiness of a People and the good Order and preservation
> of Civil Government Greatly Depends upon Piety, Religion, and Morality. But
> we Can by no Means Suppose that to Invest the Legislature or any Body of
> men on Earth with a power absolutely to Determine For others What are the
> proper Institutions of Divine Worship and To appoint Days and seasons for
> such Worship With a power to impose and Indow Religious Teachers and by
> penalties and punishments to be able to Enforce an Attendance on such Pub-
> lick Worship or to Extort Property from any one for the Support of what they
> may Judge to be publick Worship Can have a Tendency to promote true piety

Religion or Morality But the Reverse and that such a Power when and where
Ever Exercised has more or Less Been an Engine in the Hands of Tyrants for
the Destruction of the Lives Liberties and Properties of the People and that Experience has abundantly Taught Mankind that these are Natural Rights which
ought Never to be Delegated and Can with the greatest propriety be Exercised
by Individuals and by every Religious Society of men.[47]

A fourth group of critics believed that to institute even a mild establishment
of religion would lead to more odious forms. A pamphleteer named "Philan-
thropos" puts this argument well:

> Perhaps it will be said that the civil magistrate has a right to oblige the people to
> support the ministers of the gospel, because the gospel ministry is beneficial to
> society. [But if so] it will follow, by the same law, that he may adopt any of the
> maxims of the religion of Christ into the civil constitution, which he may judge
> will be beneficial to civil society . . . if magistrates may adopt any the least part
> of the religion of Christ into their systems of civil government, that supposes
> magistrates to be judges what parts shall be taken, and what left; power, then
> which nothing can be more dangerous, to be lodged in the hands of weak and
> fallible men.[48]

A fifth group of critics repeated Isaac Backus's earlier charge that Article
III constituted a species of taxation without representation. As the Return
of Ashby put it: "Religeous Societys as such have no voice in Chusing the
Legeslature, the Legeslature therefore have no right to make law binding on
them as such; every religeous Society, as such, is intirely independent on any
body politick, the Legeslature having therefor no more right to make laws
Binding on them, as such, then the Court of Great Britton have to make
Laws binding on the Independent states of America." Indeed, the Ashby Return commented later, "[T]o invest their Legeslature with power [to] make
Laws that are binding on Religious Society . . . is as much to say we will
not have Christ to reign over us[,] that the Laws of this Kingdom are not
sufficient to govern us, that the prosperity of this Kingdom is not equally
important with the Kingdoms of this world."[49]

A sixth group of critics argued that Article III's guarantee of equality of
all denominations contradicted the provisions on tax support for only some
denominations. If "all religious sects or denominations peaceably demeaning themselves" are equal before the law, why are some supported by taxes
and others not? Why must religions be incorporated by the state in order to

receive taxes, when some religions do not accept religious incorporation by the state? True religious liberty would leave the "several religious societies of the Commonwealth, whether corporate or incorporate" to their own peaceable devices. It would grant them "the right to elect their pastors or religious teachers, to contract with them for their support, to raise money for erecting and repairing houses for public worship, for the maintenance of religious instruction, and for the payment of necessary expenses."[50]

Proponents of Article III responded harshly, accusing critics of religious bigotry and chastising them for inviting moral decay under the guise of religious liberty. The "ancient atrocities of the German Anabaptists were raked up" to discredit Backus and his fellow Baptists, who were portrayed as "Disguised tories, British emissaries, profane and licentious deists, avaricious worldlings, disaffected sectaries, and furious blind bigots."[51]

The Baptists, however, were not alone in opposing Article III. Indeed, the critics of Article III should have been numerically strong enough to block ratification. The clerks kept close tallies on the votes for Article III, and supporters "fell some 600 votes short of the necessary two-thirds majority for ratification"—with the popular vote in favor standing at 8,865 to 6,225, or a little more than 58 percent.[52] Though the individual township tallies were less closely kept for other provisions, it appears that Chapter II and VI, requiring the governor to be a Christian and profess his adherence to the same in an oath, did not garner two-thirds support.[53] Nevertheless, delegates to the convention—out of ignorance of the exact vote tally or perhaps indifference to the same given the political pressure to succeed—treated the Constitution as fully ratified. On June 16, 1780, James Bowdoin, the president of the convention, announced that the entire Constitution had garnered the requisite two-thirds vote.

On October 25, 1780, the Constitution went into effect, the first day that the General Court sat after ratification. Among the first acts of the General Court was a politically expedient pledge of support for religious liberty: "Deeply impressed with a sense of the importance of religion to the happiness of men in civil society to maintain its purity and promote this efficacy, we shall protect professors of all denominations, demeaning themselves peaceably and as good subjects of the Commonwealth, in the free exercise of the rights of conscience."[54]

IV.

Massachusetts's experiment with religious liberty and religious establishment encountered numerous challenges over the next half century. On the one hand, the 1780 Constitution—softened by a pair of *Religious Freedom Acts* passed in 1811 and 1824—was "mild and equitable" enough for dissenting churches to grow in number, membership, and influence. On the other hand, as some churches liberalized and split along theological lines, and as Congregational churches themselves splintered into Trinitarian and Unitarian factions, public support for the establishment eroded.[55] New political coalitions took up old arguments to challenge the 1780 Constitution.[56] Article III was the main target. But dissenters also challenged other aspects of the law—the laws and policies supporting traditional religious instruction at Harvard College, the hiring practices for clergy in parish churches, the tests used by courts and legislatures for dividing church property between schismatic factions, the imposition of religious oaths and tests for public office, the compulsory church attendance laws, and more. Between 1780 and 1833, citizens and legislators winnowed down the state's religious establishment, ultimately leading to final disestablishment in 1833.

Constitutional Convention of 1821

The Constitutional Convention of 1820–21 was a critical step in this disestablishment process.[57] Initiated by a popular referendum in 1820, the convention addressed a wide range of constitutional issues and initiatives—notably oaths and tests for public office, the leadership and religious affiliation of Harvard College, and the provision of public funds for religious worship under Article III.[58] A "capable and experienced body of legislators" debated these issues at length.[59] Baptists—now flanked by a growing number of Methodists, Universalists, Quakers, Episcopalians, and even a few Congregationalists[60]—again led the effort to reform the state's religious establishment laws. Support for the establishment was wobbly, with many legislators admitting they were of two minds.[61] The convention proposed fourteen amendments, four of which would have tweaked or transformed constitutional provisions on religion.[62] However, the only amendments that voters approved were those that repealed religious oaths and tests for public office.

The 1821 debates over religious oaths and tests echoed familiar themes. Virtually everyone continued to affirm the value of religion as a foundation of personal and political morality—something that was relevant for legislators tasked with promoting the common good. But critics challenged these provisions on practical, theological, and political grounds. James Prince of Boston, for example, emphasized that the rights of conscience were "unalienable" and that religion was solely "a matter between God and the individual."

In forming or revising the social compact, let us then take heed, that we do not insert or retain any principle which by *possible construction* may interfere with, or abridge such sacred, such inestimable rights by an inquiry into opinions for which man is only accountable to his God. Social duties are between man and man. Religious duties are between God and the individual. . . . Secondly—I hold that this act of injustice toward the individual is neither politic nor expedient; first, because . . . it may deprive society of talent and moral excellence, which should always be secured and cherished as one of the best means of preserving the prosperity of the Commonwealth; and secondly, while it may thus exclude men possessing such useful and amiable qualification, yet it is no effectual safeguard whereby to keep out ambitious, unprincipled men from office, or a seat in the public councils. And, I moreover hold, that the cause of christianity does not require such a qualification to support it. This religion is founded on a rock and supported by a power which humanity cannot affect—it does not want the secular arm to defend it—its divine origin, and its own intrinsic merit, ever have been, and ever will be, its firmest support.[63]

However, defenders of religious oaths and tests reminded the people of the importance of having rulers who could affirm and maintain Christian beliefs and practices in accordance with the founding covenant of the state. The Reverend Joseph Tuckerman of Chelsea, for example, asked, "If our religion be from God, and if it be our duty, by all means which are consistent with its spirit, to promote its progress, it is a question on which we ought to pause, whether we shall open the door of office indiscriminately to those who believe, and to those who reject, this revelation of God's will. . . . If men should be elevated to high and responsible stations, who are enemies of christianity, may we not look with some apprehension to the consequences?"[64]

Still others were ambivalent about religious tests and oaths for political office. The famed orator and statesman Daniel Webster saw no reason "the people" could not impose religious qualifications—or any other qualifications, for that matter—on public offices. "All bestowment of office remaining in the discretion of the people, they have, of course, a right to regulate it, by any rules which they may deem expedient." But Webster concluded that religious test oaths were not necessary, insofar "as there is another part of the constitution which recognizes in the fullest manner the benefits which civil society derives from those Christian institutions which cherish piety, morality, and religion." "I am desirous," he continued, "in so solemn a transaction as the establishment of a constitution, that we should keep in it an expression of our respect and attachment to christianity;—not, indeed, to any of its peculiar forms, but to its general principles."[65] For Webster, the general ceremonial and moral establishment provisions of the Constitution were enough to ensure adherence to Christian values.

Ultimately, the convention proposed to abolish the religious test requirement and to modify the oath to read, "I, A. B., do solemnly swear that I will bear true faith and allegiance to the Commonwealth of Massachusetts and will support the constitution thereof. *So help me God.*" The proposed amendment further allowed Quakers to "affirm" rather than "swear" the oath and to replace the words, "So help me God" with "This I do, under the pains and penalties of perjury." Isaac Parker, speaking on behalf of the convention in its official "Address to the People," reported these changes matter-of-factly: "We have agreed that the declaration of belief in the Christian religion ought not to be required in the future; because we do not think the assuming of civil office a suitable occasion for so declaring; and because it is implied, that every man who is selected for office, in this community, must have such sentiments of religious duty as relate to his fitness for the place to which he is called."[66] Massachusetts voters agreed and ratified these constitutional amendments in the spring of 1821.

Toward Disestablishment

The convention of 1821 proposed other amendments to Article III[67] that aimed to reform and clarify the patchwork of court rulings and political measures from 1780 forward, but these efforts were defeated.[68] One proposed amendment sought to raise to constitutional status the *Religious Freedom Act of 1811* that had standardized the application process for any group claiming exemption from tithes—a statute passed in response to the *Barnes v. Falmouth* result.[69] Another proposed amendment sought to regularize state procedures for the incorporation of religious groups.[70] Still another aimed to abolish mandatory church attendance. Another would have entitled citizens to transfer their religious taxes to any Christian church, rather than to Protestant churches alone.[71] The voters, however, rejected these amendments, leaving Article III in its original 1780 form.

Though Article III survived the convention of 1821, subsequent lawsuits and controversies continued to erode popular and political support for it. The *Dedham* case, for example, pitted liberal unitarian against traditional trinitarian Congregationalists in a contest over who controlled church property and clergy hiring decisions. The unitarian parish members (who were required to pay religious taxes in support of the local church) sought to appoint a liberal minister for that local church. The trinitarian members of the local church objected, claiming to be the true owners of the church and entitled to elect their own clergy. As the controversy unfolded, the local trinitarian congregants left the church, taking the communion silver and other valuable church property with them. The Massachusetts courts held for the liberals—arguing that the parish, not the local church, controlled the church property and had the authority to decide on clerical appointments.[72] Unitarians won legal victories in several other intrachurch disputes in the 1820s and 1830s and gradually consolidated their control of other parishes, as well as the Harvard Divinity School.

In response, Trinitarians formed political alliances with opponents of the traditional establishment, making legislative concessions that ultimately undermined the religious tax system created by Article III. For example, a new *Religious Liberties Act of 1824* made it even easier for nonchurch members and religious dissenters to claim exemptions from religious taxes, weakening the ability of parishes to collect tithes from dissenters and to support traditional Congregationalist ministries.[73] In other quarters, Article III proved to be increasingly "fruitful in lawsuits, bad feeling, and petty prosecution."[74] By 1831 Samuel Lathrop, a leading member of the Senate, observed that Article III had grown decrepit. Serious disjunctions had developed between the law on the books and the law in practice:

> Whenever any provision of the Constitution ceases to have any obligatory effect—when public opinion clearly and unequivocally demands of the legislature a disregard of its injunctions—when we are obliged to frame our laws in such a manner as to evade it, or directly to contravene it, and when our judicial tribunals give the sanction of constitutionality to such enactments, the continuance of the article remains not merely useless—it also tends to diminish our veneration for the whole instrument, and necessarily leads to a practice of immoral tendency. Will not these observations apply to the third article in our Bill of Rights?[75]

One year later, a widely circulated set of petitions decried the Constitution's religion provisions as anachronistic, un-American, and even tyrannical—and quite in contrast with other New England states that had recently rejected religious taxes and other supports for religion. "Massachusetts stands alone among the States in the Union in making *legal* provision for the support of Religion; and notwithstanding the reverence which has by some been paid to the Third Article, it has become settled that it is a subject of vexation to many, a means of petty tyranny in the hands of a few, and altogether injurious to the cause of pure and undefiled religion."[76]

In 1833 those who sought to foster such "pure and undefiled religion" by way of church-state separation finally prevailed by passing the Eleventh Amendment to the Massachusetts Constitution. This amendment replaced Article III with a system of religious voluntarism:

> As the public worship of God and instructions in piety, religion and morality, promote the happiness and prosperity of a people and the security of a republican government;—therefore, the several religious societies of this commonwealth, whether corporate or unincorporate, at any meeting legally warned and holden for that purpose, shall ever have the right to elect their pastors or religious teachers, to contract with them for their support, to raise money for erecting and repairing houses for public worship, for the maintenance of religious instruction, and for the payment of necessary expenses: and all persons belonging to any religious society shall be taken and held to be members, until they shall file with the clerk of such society, a written notice, declaring the dissolution of their membership, and thenceforth shall not be liable for any grant or contract which may be thereafter made, or entered into by such society:— and all religious sects and denominations, demeaning themselves peaceably, and as good citizens of the commonwealth, shall be equally under the protection of the law; and no subordination of any one sect or denomination to another shall ever be established by law.[77]

The Eleventh Amendment thus made church membership and funding entirely voluntary. It granted all religious societies—Christian or not, incorporated or not—the right to hire their own clergy, to build their own churches, and to manage their own membership rolls. It promised equal protection of the law to believers of all sects and non-believers, alike, and it ensured that individual members of those sects could exit without incurring liability for contracts subsequently made by the other members of that sect.

V.

Additional amendments to the Constitution in 1855, 1917, and 1974 closed the door tightly against any form of state fiscal and material aid to religious institutions and endeavors—provisions that the Massachusetts courts have enforced with alacrity.[78]

For all of these changes, however, religion remains a feature of Massachusetts's Constitution, and the ceremonial and moral establishment policies remained in place after 1833. To this day, Article II protects the "right as well as the duty of all men in society, publicly, and at stated seasons to worship the Supreme Being, the great Creator and Preserver of the universe." The Eleventh Amendment still justifies the principle of religious voluntarism on the ground that "the public worship of God and instructions in piety, religion and morality, promote the happiness and prosperity of a people and the security of a republican government." The Preamble still acknowledges, "with grateful hearts, the goodness of the great Legislator of the universe, in affording us, in the course of His providence, an opportunity, deliberately and peaceably, without fraud, violence or surprise, of entering into an original, explicit, and solemn compact with each other; . . . [while] devoutly imploring His direction" in this constitutional covenant. In some ways, the chastened remnants of Massachusetts's religious establishment, combined with the strengthened protections for religious freedom, more fully reflect John Adams's original vision of a truly "mild and equitable establishment of religion."

NOTES

1. Robert J. Taylor, *Construction of the Massachusetts Constitution* (Worcester, MA: American Antiquarian Society, 1980), 317. Among countless overviews, see esp. the classic of Samuel Eliot Morison, *A History of the Constitution of Massachusetts* (Boston: Wright & Potter, 1917). For principal primary texts, see Oscar Handlin and Mary Handlin, eds., *The Popular Sources of Political Authority: Documents on The Massachusetts Constitution of 1780* (Cambridge, MA: Harvard University Press, 1966); Robert J. Taylor, ed., *Massachusetts, Colony to Commonwealth: Documents on the Formation of Its Constitution* (Chapel Hill: University of North Carolina Press, 1961); and Ronald M. Peters Jr., *The Massachusetts Constitution of 1780: A Social Compact* (Amherst: University of Massachusetts Press, 1978).

2. See John Adams, *A Defense of the Constitutions of Government in the United States of America* (1787), in *The Works of John Adams*, ed. C. F. Adams, 10 vols. (Boston: Little, Brown, 1850–56), vols. 4–6.

3. Adams to Dr. Price, April 8, 1785, in Adams, *Works*, 8:232, and quotations in *The John Adams Papers*, ed. Frank Donovan (New York: Dodd, Mead, 1965), 181. Also see Adams, *Works*, 4:290–97; and John Adams, *A Dissertation on the Canon and Feudal Law* (1774), in *Works*, 3:451.

4. Adams, *Works*, 2:399 (referring to the Congregational establishment of colonial Massachusetts, largely preserved in the 1780 Constitution).

5. See overviews in Jacob C. Meyer, *Church and State in Massachusetts from 1740–1833: A Chapter in the History of the Development of Individual Freedom* (1930; reprint, New York: Russell & Russell, 1968); William C. McLoughlin, *New England*

Dissent, 1630–1833: The Baptists and the Separation of Church and State, 2 vols. (Cambridge, MA: Harvard University Press, 1971); Johann N. Neem, "The Elusive Common Good: Religion and Civil Society in Massachusetts, 1780–1833," *Journal of the Early Republic* 24, no. 3 (2004): 381–417; and John D. Cushing, "Notes on Disestablishment in Massachusetts, 1780–1833," *William and Mary Quarterly* 26, no. 2 (1969): 169–90.

6. Handlin and Handlin, *Popular Sources*, 190–201.

7. "Resolve on the Question of a Constitution" (February 20, 1779), in Handlin and Handlin, *Popular Sources*, 383–84.

8. In Taylor, *Construction of Massachusetts Constitution*, 118.

9. In Handlin and Handlin, *Popular Sources*, 419.

10. Peters, *Massachusetts Constitution of 1780*, 24–30.

11. *Worcestriensis, Number IV* (1776), in Charles S. Hyneman and Donald S. Lutz, *American Political Writing During the Founding Era, 1760–1805*, Liberty Fund Library of the American Republic (Indianapolis: Liberty Press, 1983), 449–54, esp. 450.

12. *Worcestriensis*, in Hyneman and Lutz, *American Political Writing*, 452.

13. *Worcestriensis*, in Hyneman and Lutz, *American Political Writing*, 452–53. See also Samuel West, *A Sermon Preached Before the Honorable Council . . . of the Massachusetts-Bay in New England* (Boston: John Gill, 1776), in J. W. Thornton, *The Pulpit of the American Revolution* (Boston: Gould and Lincoln, 1860), 259–322, esp. 297–99.

14. Phillips Payson, "Election Sermon of 1778," in Hyneman and Lutz, *American Political Writing*, 523–38.

15. Payson, "Election Sermon of 1778," 528–30.

16. William G. McLoughlin, ed., *Isaac Backus on Church, State, and Calvinism: Pamphlets, 1754–1789* (Cambridge, MA: Harvard University Press, 1968), 351, 357–58, 361, 373–75.

17. As reported by Isaac Backus in McLoughlin, *Backus*, 12. See also Adams, *Works*, 2:399.

18. The delegates did not attend all sessions; the highest recorded vote on any issue was 247. Samuel Eliot Morison, "The Struggle over the Adoption of the Constitution of Massachusetts, 1780," *Proceedings of the Massachusetts Historical Society* 50 (1916–17): 356.

19. Peters, *Massachusetts Constitution of 1780*, 24.

20. Peters, *Massachusetts Constitution of 1780*, 23–31; McLoughlin, *Backus*, 386.

21. The draft is in Adams, *Works*, 4:213–67.

22. In 1976 Article I was amended by Massachusetts Constitution Article CVI, which rendered "all men" as "all people" and added, "Equality under the law shall not be denied or abridged because of . . . creed . . ."

23. Chapter I, Section III. See Chapter II, Section II (requiring that the governor "shall be of the Christian religion") and Section III (requiring that the lieutenant governor "shall be qualified, in point of religion"). Adams, *Works*, 4:241, 242, 245, 251.

24. See Chapter VI, Article I. See also *Journal of the Convention for Framing a Constitution of Government for the State of Massachusetts Bay, from the Commencement of Their First Session, September 1, 1779, to the Close of Their Last Session, June 16,*

1780 (Boston: Dutton and Wentworth, printers to the state, 1832), 97, 109–10 (summarizing debates on February 10, 14, and 15, 1780 about the same).

25. Chapter VI, Article I, in Adams, *Works,* 4:260–66.

26. See esp. Donald S. Lutz, *The Origins of American Constitutionalism* (Baton Rouge: Louisiana State University Press, 1988). See also John Witte Jr., *The Reformation of Rights: Law, Religion, and Human Rights in Early Modern Calvinism* (Cambridge: Cambridge University Press, 2007), 277–320.

27. See Payson, "Election Sermon," 529. This was also one reason that Adams wrote into his draft of Chapters I and II that every official must be "of the Christian religion."

28. For an overview of the subsequent controversies concerning the leadership and religious affiliation of Harvard College, see Meyer, *Church and State,* 87–91; and Yan Li, "The Transformation of the Constitution of Massachusetts, 1780–1860" (PhD diss., University of Connecticut, 1991), 82–84. See also debates in Nathan Hale and Charles Hale, eds., *Journal of Debates and Proceedings in the Convention of Delegates, Chosen to Revise the Constitution of Massachusetts, Begun and Holden at Boston, November 15, 1820, and Continued by Adjournment to January 9, 1821, Reported for the Boston Daily Advertis.,* rev. ed., Making of Modern Law: Primary Sources, 1620–1926 (Boston: Boston Daily Advertiser, 1853), 15–16, 491–93, 527–32, 556–57, 619, 630–31.

29. Ellis Ames, Abner Cheney Goodell, John H. Clifford, Alexander S. Wheeler, Wm. C. Williamson, Melville Madison Bigelow, Massachusetts, and Massachusetts General Court, *The Acts and Resolves, Public and Private, of the Province of the Massachusetts Bay: To Which Are Prefixed the Charters of the Province: With Historical and Explanatory Notes, and an Appendix,* 21 vols., Making of Modern Law: Primary Sources, 1620–1926 (Boston: Wright and Potter, printers to the state, 1869–1922), 1:62–63.

30. See sources and discussion in John Witte Jr., "Tax Exemption of Church Property: Historical Anomaly or Valid Constitutional Practice?," *Southern California Law Review* 64, no. 2 (1991): 368–80.

31. Morison, "Struggle over the Adoption," 353–412, esp. 370.

32. See details in Cushing, "Notes on Disestablishment," 169–90; McLoughlin, *New England Dissent,* 547–65; and Meyer, *Church and State,* 32–89.

33. Taylor, *Construction of Massachusetts Constitution,* 331.

34. In Adams, *Works,* 4:221–22; a slightly reworded version appears in the *Journal of the Convention,* appx. 2,, 193.

35. *Journal of the Convention,* 38–40.

36. *Journal of the Convention,* 43.

37. *Journal of the Convention,* 46–47.

38. See Yan Li, "Transformation of the Constitution," 68, arguing that members of dissenting churches were not uniformly opposed to Article III.

39. Morison, "Struggle over the Adoption," 375.

40. Morison, "Struggle over the Adoption," 371.

41. *Journal of the Convention,* appx. 3, 218.

42. Morison, "Struggle over the Adoption," 364–65.

43. See, for example, "The Returns of New Salem," in *Popular Sources*, ed. Handlin and Handlin, 482; "Town of Shutesbury," 597; "Town of Ashby," 633; "Town of Sherborn," 674; "Town of Westford," 682–83; "Return of Buxton," 731; "Town of Petersham," 855 and "Return of Ashby," in Taylor, *Documents*, 151–52.

44. "Return of Dartmouth," in *Popular Sources*, ed. Handlin and Handlin, 509–10.

45. Peters, *Massachusetts Constitution of 1780*, 33–35.

46. "Return of Westford," in *Popular Sources*, ed. Handlin and Handlin, 681, 682.

47. "Return of Petersham," in *Popular Sources*, ed. Handlin and Handlin, 855.

48. *Continental Journal*, April 6, 1780, quoted in Peters, *Massachusetts Constitution of 1780*, 82. See also "Return of the Town of Westford," in *Popular Sources*, ed. Handlin and Handlin, 682–83.

49. Quoted in Taylor, *Documents*, 151–52.

50. Taylor, *Documents*, 151–52.

51. Meyer, *Church and State*, 111. See also original quote in Morison, "Struggle over the Adoption," 368: "Baptist Advocates of religious liberty . . . retorted by comparing religious taxation to a certain practice of the sons of Eli" (likely referring to 1 Sam. 2:12–36). Even John Adams allegedly tried to inflame the convention against Backus in order to secure passage of the controversial Article III. See Taylor, *Construction*, 333, as cited in Wood, *Friends Divided*, 175.

52. Meyer, *Church and State*, 113. The township Returns are included in Handlin and Handlin, *Popular Sources*, 475–932.

53. Taylor, *Documents*, 113.

54. In Taylor, *Documents*, 162–65, esp. 164. See also Meyer, *Church and State*, 110–11, noting that the convention "seems to have counted as in favor of an article all those who did not definitely and specifically vote in the negative on it, if the votes were needed to pass the article. This is the procedure which Professor Samuel Eliot Morison has called 'political jugglery.'"

55. See also Jonathan J. Den Hartog, *Patriotism and Piety: Federalist Politics and Religious Struggle in the New American Nation* (Charlottesville: University of Virginia Press, 2015).

56. See the careful sifting of this case law in McLoughlin, *New England Dissent*, 636–59, 1084–1106, 1189–1284, with summaries in William G. McLoughlin, "The Balkcom Case (1782) and the Pietistic Theory of Separation of Church and State," *William and Mary Quarterly* 24, no. 2 (1967): 267–83; and Cushing, "Notes on Disestablishment."

57. See McLoughlin, *New England Dissent*, 1145–85.

58. McLoughlin, *New England Dissent*, 1156.

59. McLoughlin, *New England Dissent*, 1157.

60. Meyer, *Church and State*, 187.

61. McLoughlin, *New England Dissent*, 1159.

62. See *Journal of Debates and Proceedings*, 612–39.

63. *Journal of Debates and Proceedings*, 163–65.

64. *Journal of Debates and Proceedings*, 170.

65. *Journal of Debates and Proceedings*, 161.

66. *Journal of Debates and Proceedings*, 620, 630.

67. *Journal of Debates and Proceedings*, 613–14, 623–24, 634.

68. See, for example, the "exemption laws" of 1790–91, in McLoughlin, *New England Dissent*, 925–28, 935–38.

69. See McLoughlin's discussion of "The Barnes Case and the Religious Liberty Act, 1810–1817," in *New England Dissent*, by McLoughlin, 1084–1106.

70. Debates about the legal status of church corporations played a notable role in the emergence of nonprofit corporations in the United States. See Johann N. Neem, "Politics and the Origins of the Nonprofit Corporation in Massachusetts and New Hampshire, 1780–1820," *Nonprofit and Voluntary Sector Quarterly* 32, no. 3 (2003): 344–65.

71. McLoughlin, *New England Dissent*, 1183.

72. See McLoughlin, "The Dedham Case and the Amendment of the Religious Liberty Act, 1821–1824," in *New England Dissent*, by McLoughlin, 1189–1206.

73. McLoughlin, *New England Dissent*, 1205.

74. Morison, *History of the Constitution*, 24–25.

75. "Domestic Intelligence: Massachusetts Legislature," *Christian Register*, March 19, 1831, 47.

76. McLoughlin, *New England Dissent*, 1246.

77. Massachusetts Constitution amend., Article XI (1833).

78. Massachusetts Constitution amend., Article XVIII (1855), provides that tax "moneys shall never be appropriated to any religious sect for the maintenance exclusively of its own schools." This was superseded by Article XLVI (1917) that provides, in pertinent part, that "no law shall be passed prohibiting the free exercise of religion" and that no tax money was to be paid to religious groups or activities. Article XLVI, in turn, was further amended by Article CIII (1974): "No grant, appropriation, use of public money or property or loan of credit shall be made by the Commonwealth or any political subdivision thereof for the purpose of founding, maintaining, or aiding any . . . charitable or religious undertaking which is not publicly owned and under the exclusive control of [the Commonwealth]." For summary of the cases, see Herbert P. Wilkins, "Judicial Treatment of the Massachusetts Declaration of Rights in Relation to Cognate Provisions of the United States Constitution," *Suffolk University Law Review* 14 (1980): 892–94.

SELECT BIBLIOGRAPHY

Published monographs and articles that address in any comprehensive manner the process of disestablishment in the original American states are very few. A select compilation appears below. We are omitting from this list publications devoted to a single colony or state. For the latter, see the chapter endnotes for each individual state.

Ariens, Michael S., and Robert A. Destro. *Religious Liberty in a Pluralistic Society.* 2nd ed. Durham, NC: Carolina Academic Press, 2002. See esp. 48–75.

Bradley, Gerald V. *Church-State Relationships in America.* New York: Greenwood Press, 1987. See esp. 19–68.

Cobb, Sanford H. *The Rise of Religious Liberty in America: A History.* New York: Macmillan, 1902.

Curry, Thomas J. *The First Freedoms: Church and State in America to the Passage of the First Amendment.* New York: Oxford University Press, 1986.

Esbeck, Carl H. "Dissent and Disestablishment: The Church-State Settlement in the Early American Republic." *Brigham Young University Law Review* 2004, no. 4 (2004): 1385–1592.

Gill, Anthony. *The Political Origins of Religious Liberty.* New York: Cambridge University Press, 2008.

Hutson, James H. *Religion and the Founding of the American Republic.* Washington, DC: Library of Congress, 1998. See esp. 59–74.

Laycock, Douglas. "Regulatory Exemptions of Religious Behavior and the Original Understanding of the Establishment Clause." *Notre Dame Law Review* 81, no. 5 (2006): 1793–1842.

Levy, Leonard W. *The Establishment Clause: Religion and the First Amendment.* Rev. ed. Chapel Hill: University of North Carolina Press, 1994.

McConnell, Michael W. "Establishment and Disestablishment at the Founding, Part I: Establishment of Religion." *William and Mary Law Review* 44, no. 5 (2003): 2105–2208.

McLoughlin, William G. *New England Dissent, 1630–1833: The Baptists and the Separation of Church and State.* 2 vols. Cambridge, MA: Harvard University Press, 1971.

Muñoz, Vincent Phillip. "Church and State in the Founding-Era State Constitutions." *American Political Thought* 4, no. 1 (2015): 1–38.

Stokes, Anson Phelps. *Church and State in the United States.* 3 vols. New York: Harper & Brothers, 1950.

Wilson, John K. "Religion under the State Constitutions, 1776–1800." *Journal of Church & State* 32, no. 4 (1990): 753–73.

INDEX